Complete
Economics
for Cambridge IGCSE® & O Level

Third Edition

Brian Titley
Sir Dan Moynihan

Oxford excellence for Cambridge IGCSE® & O Level

OXFORD
UNIVERSITY PRESS

OXFORD
UNIVERSITY PRESS

Great Clarendon Street, Oxford, OX2 6DP, United Kingdom

Oxford University Press is a department of the University of Oxford. It furthers the University's objective of excellence in research, scholarship, and education by publishing worldwide. Oxford is a registered trade mark of Oxford University Press in the UK and in certain other countries

British Library Cataloguing in Publication Data

Data available

978-0-19-840970-0

10 9 8 7 6 5 4 3

Paper used in the production of this book is a natural, recyclable product made from wood grown in sustainable forests. The manufacturing process conforms to the environmental regulations of the country of origin.

Printed in India by Multivista

Acknowledgements

The publishers would like to thank the following for permissions to use copyright material:

Extracts and statistical data from publications produced by the Office of National Statistics (ONS), are Crown copyright material and are reproduced under the terms of the Open Government Licence.

Anglesey Sea Salt Company for 'Anglesey Sea Salt goes Global', from an exports case study published by the Food & Drink Federation in 2015.

Bangkok Post Plc for 'Government policies fail the poor', *Bangkok Post*, 12.7.2009.

Guardian News and Media Ltd for 'Supermarket suppliers "helping destroy Amazon rainforest"' by David Adam, *The Guardian*, 21.6.2009, copyright © Guardian News and Media Ltd 2009; 'UK plans skills academies to close productivity gap' by Polly Curtis, *The Guardian* 22.3.05, copyright © Guardian News and Media Ltd 2005; 'World faces "perfect storm" of problems by 2030' by Ian Sample, *The Guardian*, 18.3.2009, copyright © Guardian News and Media Ltd 2009; 'The food rush: rising demand on China and West sparks African land grab' by David Smith, *The Guardian*, 3.7.2009, copyright © Guardian News and Media Ltd 2009; 'China's worst oil-spill threatens wildlife as volunteers assist in clean-up' by Jonathan Watts, *The Guardian*, 21.7.2010, copyright © Guardian News and Media Ltd 2010; and Economics Leader: 'The UK jobs engine isn't working any more', *The Guardian*, Business, 17.12.2017, copyright © Guardian News and Media Ltd 2017.

The Independent for 'Beijing's billions buy up reserves' by Sarah Arnott, *The Independent*, 2.10.2010, copyright © The Independent 2010; 'Turks and Caicos PM quits after corruption inquiry' by Kunal Dutta, *The Independent*, 24.3.2009, copyright © The Independent 2009; and 'Finland suffers double-dip' by Brett Young, *The Independent*, 10.6.2010, copyright © The Independent 2010.

The Irish Times for 'Overseas aid is funding human rights abuses' by Paul Cullen, *The Irish Times* 20.1.2011, copyright © The Irish Times 2011.

Nine Network Australia for 'Romania tackles obesity with fatty foods tax', 19.2.2010.

Solo Syndication/ Associated Newspapers Ltd for 'Vets accused of overcharging by up to 500% for some pet medicines!', *The Daily Mail*, 27.9.2010; 'Nike Workers 'kicked, slapped and verbally abused' at factories making Converse', *MailOnline*, 13.7.2011; 'Is the real of unemployment £61 billion per year?' by James Chapman, *The Daily Mail*,

3.1.2007; and 'Household debt binge hits pre-crisis levels as Britons go mad for new cars and cheap loans, Bank of England warns', including chart 'Consumer credit' by Rachel Rickard-Straus, *This is Money*, 15.4.2016.

Transparency International for extract on 'Poverty and Development' and statement by Jose Ugaz, T I Chairman, www.transparency.org, licensed under Creative Commons CC-BY-ND 4.0

Cover images: Shutterstock; **p3:** Leo Francini/Shutterstock; **p4 (TR):** Jie Zhao/Corbis/Getty Images; **p4 (TL):** Xtrekx/Shutterstock; **p4 (BL):** Richard Jones/REX/Shutterstock; **p4 (BR):** Makspogonii/Shutterstock; **p5 (T):** Monkey Business Images/Shutterstock; **p5 (B):** Jorge Fernandez / Alamy Stock Photo; **p7:** JHershPhoto/Shutterstock; **p8 (BL):** Sabina Pensek/Dreamstime; **p8 (BM):** Okea/iStockphoto; **p8 (BR):** Drozdowski/ Shutterstock; **p12 (T):** Vasiliy Ganzha/Dreamstime; **p12 (B):** Maksim Toome/123RF; **p15 (TL):** Peter Jordan_NE/Alamy Stock Photo; **p15 (TR):** Olaf Doering/Alamy Stock Photo; **p16:** Oorka/Shutterstock; **p20 (L):** Jeff Dalton/Dreamstime; **p20 (M):** Yangchao/Dreamstime; **p20 (R):** PaulVinten/ iStockphoto; **p22 (T):** Stockbyte/Getty Images; **p22 (B):** Janine Wiedel Photolibrary / Alamy Stock Photo; **p46:** Nigel Cattlin / Alamy Stock Photo; **p89 (L):** Vchal/Shutterstock; **p89 (R):** Kot2626/iStockphoto; **p91 (T):** AP Images; **p91 (B):** Ulet Ifansasti/Getty Images; **p92 (ML):** Monkey Business Images/Shutterstock; **p92 (BL):** Monkey Business Images/Shutterstock; **p96:** SkyTruth/NASA; **p100 (T):** Michael Kemp / Alamy Stock Photo; **p100 (B):** Ian Bracegirdle/Shutterstock; **p105:** Barry Iverson/Alamy Stock Photo; **p94:** PhotoStockFile / Alamy; **p95:** Keith Morris / Alamy Stock Photo; **p93 (T):** Steve estvanik/Shutterstock; **p93 (B):** Christopher Waters/Shutterstock; **p134:** Ruth Peterkin/Shutterstock; **p135:** Sputnik/ Science Photo Library; **p139:** Bazuki Muhammad/Reuters; **p141 (TL):** Kevpix / Alamy Stock Photo; **p141 (TM):** Justin Kase zsixz / Alamy Stock Photo; **p141 (TR):** ANDREW WALTERS / Alamy Stock Photo; **p141 (TRB):** Crack Palinggi / Reuters; **p182:** Rodger Whitney/Shutterstock; **p184 (TL):** Photodisc/Getty Images; **p184 (TR):** Martin D/ Science Source/Getty Images; **p186:** Bela Szandelszky/AP Images; **p191 (T):** Keith morris/ Alamy Stock Photo; **p191 (B):** To come; **p198 (TL):** Patrick Landmann/ Science Photo Library; **p198 (TR):** Jeanma85/Fotolia; **p198 (BL):** Nick Stubbs/Shutterstock; **p198 (BR):** David Parker/Science Photo Library; **p199 (T):** David Pearson/REX/Shutterstock; **p199 (B):** Monkey Business Images/Shutterstock; **p201 (TL):** David Pearson/REX/Shutterstock; **p201 (TR):** TED ALJIBE/AFP/Getty Images; **p206 (T):** Chris Whitehead/ Photographer's Choice/Getty Images; **p206 (B):** Glow Images, Inc/Glow/ Getty Images; **p208 (BR):** TIM SLOAN/AFP/Getty Images; **p221 (TL):** STAN HONDA/AFP/Getty Images; **p221 (TR):** Alex Segre/REX/Shutterstock; **p227 (TL):** Natasha Owen/Fotolia; **p227 (TR):** Rainer Plendl/Shutterstock; **p243 (BL):** INTERFOTO/Alamy Stock Photo; **p243 (BR):** Peter Probst/ Alamy Stock Photo; **p250 (L):** Sutton-Hibbert/REX/Shutterstock; **p250 (R):** Kevpix/Alamy Stock Photo; **p258 (L):** Chris Parypa Photography/ Shutterstock; **p258 (R):** Wakila/iStockphoto; **p269 (L):** Rob Marmion/ Shutterstock; **p269 (M):** Pedro Monteiro/Shutterstock; **p269 (R):** Sturti/ Getty Images; **p282:** Luke MacGregor/Reuters; **p288 (L):** Dewayne Flowers/Shutterstock; **p288 (M):** XM Collection/Alamy Stock Photo; **p288 (R):** 2happy/Shutterstock; **p290 (L):** Andersen Ross/Blend Images/Getty Images; **p290 (R):** Wrangler/Shutterstock; **p297 (L):** Hung Chung Chih/ Shutterstock; **p297 (M):** Andre Joubert/Alamy Stock Photo; **p297 (R):** JTB Photo Communications, Inc. / Alamy Stock Photo; **p302 (TL):** Macana/ Alamy Stock Photo; **p302 (TR):** Xavier Lhospice/Reuters; **p302 (BL):** DR JUERG ALEAN/SCIENCE PHOTO LIBRARY; **p302 (BR):** Loop Images Ltd/Alamy Stock Photo; **p313 (T):** COLIN CUTHBERT/SCIENCE PHOTO LIBRARY; **p313 (B):** Zick Svift/Shutterstock; **p315:** © Crown copyright; **p202 (L):** AlenaPaulus/iStockphoto; **p202 (R):** Jane Williams/Alamy Stock Photo; **p248 (TL):** Aluxum/iStockphoto; **p248 (ML):** KREUS/Shutterstock; **p248 (MBL):** Piotr Malczyk/Alamy Stock Photo; **p248 (BL):** Panther Media GmbH/Alamy Stock Photo; **p325 (T):** Maksim Dubinsky/Shutterstock; **p325 (M):** FRED GUERDIN/REPORTERS/SCIENCE PHOTO LIBRARY; **p325 (B):** Digital Vision/Photodisc/Getty Images; **p331 (T):** Tim Graham/Alamy Stock Photo; **p331 (B):** Paper Girl/Fotolia; **p354:** Library of Congress; **p382 (TL):** Joanna Zielinska/Fotolia; **p382 (TR):** Bruder/Fotolia; **p382 (BL):** Akhter Soomro/Reuters; **p382 (BR):** Jitendra Prakash/Reuters; **p397:** on Jones/Sygma/Getty Images; **p408 (L):** Kyodo News via Getty Images; **p408 (R):** Mohammed Zaatari/AP Images; **p411 (T):** Inga Spence/Photolibrary/ Getty Images; **p411 (B):** Universal Images Group/Getty Images; **p413 (T):** Paulaphoto/Shutterstock; **p413 (B):** Gilles Lougassi/Shutterstock; **p431:** Jo Yong-Hak/Reuters; **p434 (L):** Paul Weatherman/U.S. Air Force; **p434 (M):** JIL Photo/Shutterstock; **p434 (R):** Turumtaev Ildar/Shutterstock; **p439 (L):** Geoffrey Robinson/REX/Shutterstock; **p447:** Aksaran/Gamma-Rapho/Getty Images; **p459:** Wiklander/Shutterstock; **p473 (TL):** S_oleg/Shutterstock; **p473 (TR):** Justin Kase zninez/Alamy Stock Photo.

Artwork by Aptara Corp. and OUP.

Introduction

Learning about economics will provide you with the knowledge, understanding and skills you will need to succeed

Whether you want to one day start your own business, work for a major international company or a government, become a teacher or doctor, or run a charity, the study of economics will provide you with the knowledge, understanding, critical thinking and skills you will need to succeed.

The newspapers often describe complicated economic problems such as inflation, unemployment, balance of trade deficits, anti-competitive behaviour, changes in exchange rates, economic recessions and supply shortages. It is sometimes difficult to understand these and what impact they could have on our daily lives without an understanding of economics.

People who have studied economics are good at problem solving because they learn to identify problems, to suggest alternative solutions, to determine what information is relevant, and to weigh up different costs and benefits in decision making.

Knowledge of economics also helps us understand what determines the prices of different products, why people earn different amounts in different jobs and why these can change over time, why some countries are poor and others are rich and how and why governments influence the behaviours of different groups of consumers and producers. But above all, the study of economics makes us realize that we are all dependent upon one another and that the decisions we make will affect others.

By studying for the Cambridge Assessment International Education IGCSE or O Level in Economics you will therefore develop valuable lifelong skills including:

- an understanding of economic theory, terminology and principles

- the ability to apply the tools of economic analysis to real-world situations

- the ability to distinguish between facts and personal judgements in real economic issues

- an understanding of, and an ability to use and interpret, basic economic data, numeracy and literacy

- the ability to take a greater part in decision-making processes in everyday life

- an understanding of the economies of developed and developing nations

- an excellent foundation for more advanced study in economics.

Complete Economics will help you to build these skills quickly. It contains everything you need to master the content of the Cambridge IGCSE and O Level Economics courses in an enjoyable and exciting way by providing real insight into how different markets and entire economies work.

Final examinations will assess your skills and knowledge of economics

At the end of your Cambridge IGCSE or O Level course in Economics you will take two papers:

Paper 1 Multiple choice	45 minutes
Candidates answer 30 multiple choice questions.	
30% of total marks.	

Paper 2 Structured questions	2 hours 15 minutes
Candidates answer one compulsory question that requires them to interpret and analyse previously unseen data relevant to a real economic situation, and three questions from a choice of four.	
70% of total marks.	

The following key skills will be assessed in the examination papers.

Knowledge and understanding
Show your knowledge and understanding of economic definitions, formulas concepts, principles and theories
Use economic vocabulary and terminology.

Analysis
Select, organize and interpret data
Use economic information and statistics to recognize patterns in data and to deduce economic relationships
Apply your economic knowledge and understanding to written, numerical, diagrammatic and graphical data
Analyse economic issues and situations, identifying causes and links

The requirement to demonstrate evidence of the key skills in the different examination papers varies. The importance placed on each skill in each examination paper is as follows:

Assessment objective	Paper 1 (%)	Paper 2 (%)
A: Knowledge with understanding	50	35
B: Analysis	50	35
C: Evaluation		30

Complete Economics contains a wealth of exam preparation questions for you to practise to help you develop these key skills. Model answers to help you attain top marks for all the questions in this book are provided on the support website.

Best of luck with your studies and examinations!

Contents

What's on the website?

- Guidance and answers to all the activities and exam preparation exercises in this book
- Answers to all the end of chapter assessment exercises in this book
- Printable versions of all the crosswords in this book along with their solutions
- An economics dictionary containing definitions for all the essential terms used in the course

www.oxfordsecondary.com/9780198409700

Matching chart

Syllabus overview	Unit in Student Book
PART 1 The basic economic problem	**PART 1 The basic economic problem**
1.1 The nature of the economic problem	1.1 The nature of the economic problem
1.2 The factors of production	1.2 The factors of production
1.3 Opportunity cost	1.3 Opportunity cost
1.4 Production possibility curves (PPC)	1.4 Production possibility curves (PPC)
PART 2 The allocation of resources	**PART 2 The allocation of resources**
2.1 Microeconomics and macroeconomics	2.1 Microeconomics and macroeconomics
2.2 The role of markets in allocating resources	2.2 The role of markets in allocating resources
2.3 Demand	2.3 Demand
2.4 Supply	2.4 Supply
2.5 Price determination	2.5 Price determination
2.6 Price changes	2.6 Price changes
2.7 Price elasticity of demand (PED)	2.7 Price elasticity of demand (PED)
2.8 Price elasticity of supply (PES)	2.8 Price elasticity of supply (PES)
2.9 Market economic system	2.9 Market economic system
2.10 Market failure	2.10 Market failure
2.11 Mixed economic system	2.11 Mixed economic system
PART 3 Microeconomic decision makers	**PART 3 Microeconomic decision makers**
3.1 Money and banking	3.1 Money and banking
3.2 Households	3.2 Households
3.3 Workers	3.3 Workers
3.4 Trade unions	3.4 Trade unions
3.5 Firms	3.5 Firms
3.6 Firms and production	3.6 Firms and production
3.7 Firms' costs, revenues and objectives	3.7 Firms' costs, revenues and objectives
3.8 Market structure	3.8 Market structure
PART 4 Government and the macroeconomy	**PART 4 Government and the macroeconomy**
4.1 The role of government	4.1 The role of government
4.2 The macroeconomic aims of government	4.2 The macroeconomic aims of government
4.3 Fiscal policy	4.3 Fiscal policy
4.4 Monetary policy	4.4 Monetary policy
4.5 Supply-side policy	4.5 Supply-side policy
4.6 Economic growth	4.6 Economic growth
4.7 Employment and unemployment	4.7 Employment and unemployment
4.8 Inflation and deflation	4.8 Inflation and deflation
PART 5 Economic development	**PART 5 Economic development**
5.1 Living standards	5.2 Living standards
5.2 Poverty	5.3 Poverty
5.3 Population	5.4 Population
5.4 Differences in economic development between countries	5.1 Differences in economic development between countries
PART 6 International trade and specialization	**PART 6 International trade and specialization**
6.1 International specialization	6.1 International specialization
6.2 Globalization, free trade and protection	6.2 Globalization, free trade and protection
6.3 Foreign exchange rates	6.3 Foreign exchange rates
6.4 Current account of balance of payments	6.4 Current account of balance of payments

The basic economic problem

The resources available to produce goods and services are scarce compared with our limitless wants. Land (natural resources), labour (human effort), capital (human-made resources) and enterprise (the knowledge and skills people need to organize production) are all scarce resources. They are factors of production because they are organized into firms by entrepreneurs to produce goods and services to satisfy our needs and wants.

Resources are inputs to productive activity and products (goods and services) are outputs from productive activity. However, because there are not enough resources to produce everything we need and want, we must make choices. For example, if we choose to use up scarce resources in the production of cars, those same resources cannot be used to produce food. This opportunity is foregone.

Making a choice between alternative uses of scarce resources therefore always involves a cost in terms of what we have to give up in return. The benefit of the next best alternative foregone is the opportunity cost of that decision.

Scarcity of resources relative to human wants is the basic or central economic problem. The study of economics therefore involves examining and informing decisions about how best to use scarce resources in an attempt to satisfy as many of our needs and wants as possible to maximize economic welfare.

Unit 1.1   The nature of the economic problem
Unit 1.2   The factors of production

1.1.1	Finite resources and unlimited wants	▶ Define the economic problem and provide examples of how it affects consumers, workers, producers and governments.
1.1.2	Economic and free goods	▶ Explain the difference between economic goods and free goods.
1.2.1	Definitions of the factors of production and their rewards	▶ Using examples, define the factor inputs used in production - land, labour, capital and enterprise.
		▶ Describe the different factor payments or rewards received by factors of production.
		▶ Use examples to explain the nature of each factor of production.
1.2.2	Mobility of the factors of production	▶ Identify the influences on the mobility of the various factors of production.
1.2.3	Quantity and quality of the factors of production	▶ Describe the causes of changes in the quantity and quality of the various factors of production.

World News

Tuesday 24th May 2127

Oil runs out

Today the world's oil supply has dried up. A crisis meeting of world leaders took place in Washington last night.

Yesterday the top oil-producing companies of the world declared that the world's supply of oil was now exhausted. The last barrel of oil has been filled and the oil rigs will drill no more. The world now faces an energy crisis. No more oil will mean no more petrol for transport or machinery. There can be no more plastic for components in many household products like televisions, microwave ovens, cars and telephones.

Energy ministers from around the world are meeting today in Switzerland to discuss the crisis and try to find a solution. Coal deposits are low and nuclear power stations are already overworked to meet the demand for electricity.

Resources are finite

PROBLEM

The newspaper article above paints a gloomy picture of what could happen in the future. It is hard to imagine a world without oil but even now there is only a limited amount of oil left in the ground. In other words, it is **finite** or limited in supply. As more and more is used up there will come a time when no oil remains. The world's oil took many millions of years to form but we may use it all up in a few hundred years.

However, it is not just oil that is finite. Some forecasters suggest if we continue to consume goods and services in the future at the same rate as we do today many natural resources, such as aluminium, copper, lead, tin, zinc, and timber from the last remaining rainforests, will all be used up within the next 50 years. Even the land we farm or build on, and the clean air and drinking water we need are all finite or limited in supply.

If you imagine the world as a round ball then it is possible to see that only a limited amount of these **resources** can be squeezed from it.

Resources are used up in the production of goods and services

PROBLEM

Resources are important because they are used to make **goods** such as bread, televisions, cars, fruit and vegetables, and to provide **services**, including banking, insurance, transport, healthcare, policing and cleaning.

Production therefore involves using resources to make and sell different goods and services. Resources such as natural materials, land, machinery and workers, are the **inputs** to productive activities and goods and services are their products or **outputs**. ➤ 3.6.3

Any activity that fails to satisfy a human need or want is not a productive activity according to economists. So, for example, if resources are used to make clothes nobody wants to wear, televisions that fail to display moving images, clocks that cannot keep time or any other good or service that fails to satisfy a human need or want, then those resources have not been used productively.

The people and organizations which make and sell goods and services are known as **producers**.

▼ Resources used to produce other goods and services include natural materials, people, machinery and land

Definitions of the factors of production and their rewards

But human wants are without limit

PROBLEM

So what if the resources we use to produce goods and services are limited in supply? The world is a big place and it may take many years for **non-renewable resources** like oil, coal, gas, copper and iron to run out.

We can also renew or replace other resources such as trees for timber, corn to eat and people to work in shops, offices and factories. In fact, the population of the world is growing rapidly. A larger global workforce will be able to produce more machines, build more factories and invent new materials and better ways of producing food and other goods and services.

Does this mean limited resources is not such a big problem? Before you agree or disagree, look at Activity 1.1 below.

ACTIVITY 1.1

Needs and wants

A

B

Look at the two photos A and B. Photo A represents modern city life; photo B shows a group of people living in a poor African village.

1 What needs have the two families in common?

2 Which family will not be able to satisfy all its needs?

3 What do you think are the wants of the family in picture A?

4 What do you think are the wants of the family in picture B?

5 Why can't the wants of either family be satisfied?

6 What do you think are the main differences between **needs** and **wants**?

7 If the world population continues to grow, what do you think will happen to the total of human needs and wants over time?

Human needs and wants

All people have the same basic **human needs**. Whether rich or poor, we all need food, clean water and some shelter from the extremes of weather in order to live safely and to survive. However, people usually want far more than they need. We want fashionable clothes, big televisions, smartphones, cars, holidays, insurance and banking services, and much more. However, unlike our human needs we do not need to satisfy our **human wants** to survive.

Just imagine if we could list all the goods and services that everyone in the world wanted. The list would go on forever and would grow longer as the world population expands. Our human wants are therefore without limit and it is not possible to satisfy them all. This is because there will never be enough resources in the world to do so. Resources are scarce compared to our unlimited wants for goods and services. Some people cannot even satisfy all of their basic needs because of the scarcity of resources.

ACTIVITY 1.2

What do we need and what do we want?

Below is a jumbled collection of different goods and services. Draw a table like the one below and sort them into needs and wants, giving reasons for your choice.

You should now understand the difference between needs and wants. Write a sentence to explain what these two words mean.

Needs	Wants	Reason
Bread	Television	Bread is food
		Televisions provide entertainment but are not essential for survival

We must choose what to produce and consume

PROBLEM

Free goods are items we may need or want that are without limit. For example, air is so abundant in supply that you can breathe it without reducing the amount available to other people. Similarly, there is enough natural light during every day for everyone to enjoy as much as they want without it running out. As such, there is no point paying for air or natural light if they are freely available and without limit.

Many ideas and inventions are also free goods. For example, new dance moves or yoga exercises can be copied freely by one or more people without reducing the ability of others to do the same. Similarly, when you view a web page it does not prevent other people from viewing it, although if everyone in the world did so at the same time it might crash the internet.

However, there are very few truly free goods. Most of the goods and services we need and want are limited in supply compared to our demand for them. This is because our wants are without limit and there are just not enough resources available to produce everything we want. We must therefore choose what goods and services to produce with our scarce resources. For example, producing more cars will leave fewer resources available to produce computers. ➤ **1.3.2**

Unlike free goods, cars and computers along with most other goods and services are **economic goods**. This is because they are limited in supply. If you drive a car, use a computer or even wear a coat or eat a cake, these goods will no longer be available to others to use. Because they are limited in supply people are therefore willing to pay to obtain these and other economic goods in order to satisfy some of their wants.

▲ A free good is without limit

▲ An economic good is limited in supply

▲ This good may be given away for 'free' but it is still limited in supply because scarce resources are needed to produce it

▲ Consumption

What is consumption?

We consume goods and services when we use them to satisfy our human needs and wants.

When we eat we are consuming food. When we watch television we are consuming electricity, the television set and the services of a television company. When we go to schools and colleges, we are consuming the services of teachers. We are consuming when we read books, sit on chairs, sleep on beds, put money into a bank account, ask a policeman the time, listen to the radio and use up any other goods and services in order to satisfy our wants.

Consumption therefore involves the using up of goods and services to satisfy human needs and wants.

However, because these goods and services are finite we will be unable to satisfy all of our wants. We must all therefore choose which goods and services we will consume. The choices we each make will also affect other people. This is because our consumption of economic goods will result in fewer economic goods being available to other people. This is because economic goods are limited in supply.

The people and organizations which buy economic goods and services to satisfy their wants are known as **consumers** and the total amount they spend each period on economic goods is called **consumption expenditure**. ➤ **3.2.1**

What is exchange?

Some people may be able to satisfy some of their wants by producing a number of goods and services for their own consumption. For example, keen gardeners may grow vegetables to eat to satisfy part of their need or want for food. Others may make furniture from wood for their families to use.

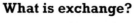

However, very few people can make all the things they want. Consumers must therefore engage in trade or **exchange** with producers to obtain those economic goods they cannot produce themselves. In modern economies most people are able to do this by going to work to earn money. They then exchange this money for the goods and services they want that are produced by other workers. ➤ **3.1.1**

Different goods and services satisfy different needs and wants. Economists group together different products into four main categories.

Consumer goods or capital goods?

We can choose to use scarce resources to produce many different types of consumer goods and services. However, scarce resources can also be used to produce capital goods. Allocating more resources to the production of capital goods will therefore reduce the amount of resources available to produce consumer goods and services.

A **consumer good** is an economic good that satisfies an immediate consumer need or want. Some consumer goods are called **consumer durables** because they last a long time, for example cars, washing machines, televisions, furniture and computers. They can be used repeatedly over many months or years to satisfy a want before they eventually wear out. In contrast, **non-durable goods** are perishable or used up quickly, for example food, drink, matches, petrol and washing powder.

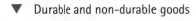
▼ Durable and non-durable goods

However, not all of our wants can be satisfied with physical products. We also want firms to provide us with services. For example, we may want the services of doctors, bankers, insurance agents, window cleaners and teachers. They provide **consumer services**.

Capital goods such as screwdrivers, drills, tractors, lorries, power stations and factory buildings do not satisfy any immediate human needs or wants. They are human-made resources used in the production of other goods and services.

The purchase of capital goods is known as investment. Investments in capital goods, like factories and machines, will increase the capacity of organization to produce goods and services. ➤ **1.4.4**

How the economic problem affects us all

So, we now know what the central problem in economics is.

The economic problem

Resources are finite – or limited in supply.

They are used up in the production of goods and services.

But human wants for goods and services are without limit.

We must therefore choose what to produce and consume.

Because we cannot satisfy all of our wants!

The scarcity of resources relative to human wants is the central problem in economics. Scarcity means we must all make choices about how we use our limited resources. That is, we must decide what goods and services we will produce and consume. ➤ **2.2.2**

HUMAN WANTS
UNLIMITED!

RESOURCES
SCARCE!

▲ The economic problem

What's the big problem?

The economic problem affects every person and every organization in the world. Explain how the following situations illustrate the basic economic problem.

Local anger as an area of ancient woodland is sold to a property developer to build new homes.

China closes mines and warns its rare-earth minerals are running out

China has cut exports of rare-earth minerals to Japan, Europe and the United States, undermining high-tech manufacturers that rely on the minerals for the production of wind turbines, smartphones, missile-guidance systems and many other electronic goods.

China controls the production of more than 90 percent of the world's rare-earth minerals and claims its reserves may be exhausted in the next 20 years.

BMW halts car production

German car producer BMW has been unable to complete the production of thousands of cars this week due to a shortage of steering systems from its supplier Bosch.

'One meal a day': Consumers on low incomes are being forced to choose between food and paying power bills

Welfare organisations are warning that many consumers on low incomes are struggling to pay their electricity bills as prices continue to rise.

For some people, things have become so desperate that they are going without essentials like food and medicine to try and meet their bill payments.

Building new schools 'must be top priority' for government

Hundreds of extra schools could have to be built in England to cope with the school population bulge, say public sector buildings specialists.

Official figures suggest there will be almost 730,000 more school age children by 2020 than there were last year.

What are factors of production?

The scarce resources we use up in the production of goods and services to satisfy human needs and wants are also known as **factors of production**. In addition to natural resources, such as timber, coal and many crops, they include the people who go to work or run business organizations and the buildings, machinery and equipment they use.

All these resources or factors of production are scarce because the time people have to spend working, the different skills they have and the land on which factories, shops and homes are built are all limited in supply and scarce relative to our unlimited wants. Still not convinced? Just take a look at some of the real newspaper headlines on the next page.

Economists group together different factors of production under four main headings.

Land

The fertile soil vital to the growth of plants, minerals such as coal and oil, and animals for their meat and skins, are known as **natural resources**, but to simplify economists call all of these **land**. Land therefore includes the seas and rivers of the world, trees and plants, all manner of minerals from the ground, chemicals and gases from the air and what we usually think of land (those surfaces on our planet which we use for farming or to build houses, factories and roads upon).

Labour

Nothing can be produced without people. They provide the physical and mental effort required to design, make and sell goods and services. People who work with their hands and use their brains to produce economic goods and services provide **human resources**, or **labour**.

The size and ability of a country's labour force are very important in determining the quantity and quality of the goods and services that can be produced. The greater the number of workers, and the better educated and skilled they are, the more a country can produce.

Enterprise

While most people are able to contribute to the production of goods and services as workers and employees, not everyone can successfully combine different resources and organize production in a **firm**. A firm is an organization that employs resources to produce and supply goods and services. ➤ **3.5.1**

The ability to organize production in a firm is known as **enterprise**. The people who have enterprise and 'business know-how' and are able to control and manage firms are called **entrepreneurs**. They are the people who take the risks and decisions necessary to make firms run successfully.

Capital

To make the task of production easier, we have invented many tools: pens to write with, computers to calculate, screwdrivers, spanners, hammers, rulers, and many more. On a grander scale, turbines drive engines, tractors plough the land, railways and ships transport goods, lathes shape and refine metals and wood, and factories, offices and airports have been built. All the **human-made resources** used to produce other goods and services, are known as **capital**.

Economists tend to talk of **units** of factors of production. For example, an economist might say that 'a firm has employed 30 more units of capital'. This could simply mean that it has bought 30 new identical machines. Similarly, if an economist refers to units of land, it could mean tonnes of coal, barrels of crude oil, or hectares of land. Likewise, employees or the individual hours they work are units of labour for an economist.

ACTIVITY 1.4

Classifying resources

1   Below is a list of many of the scarce resources that are used to produce cartons of orange juice. Draw three columns and label them **natural resources**, **human resources** and **human-made resources**, and then in pairs decide in which column each item should go.

Telephones	Oil	Shops
Advertising people	Lorries	Ship's crew
Cotton for clothing	Printing machines	Factory buildings
Fertile soil	Orange trees	Insecticide sprays
Squeezing machines	Bank clerks	Oranges
Orange pickers	Power stations	Roads
Package designers	Coal	Accountants
Calculators	Warehouse workers	Shop assistants
Water	Lorry drivers	Wood

2   Now try to produce a list of resources you think are used to produce cars. Compare your list with the rest of the class, and again sort them out into natural, human and human-made resources.

What are factor rewards?

Since productive resources are scarce, firms are willing to pay money to obtain them. Few people provide their labour for free. Similarly, few owners or producers of natural and human-made resources will provide them to other producers without payment. Even entrepreneurs are unlikely to set up and start firms without reward for their efforts.

Factor rewards are therefore the payments different factors of production require and receive in order to participate in productive activity.

Rent

Owners of land require the payment of **rent** to supply these resources to firms, for example, for the purpose of farming, producing timber or extracting fossil fuels, metal ores and minerals. Rent is also required by owners of buildings, such as office blocks, to lease them to organizations.

▲ Owners of land receive rent to bring it into productive use

▲ People supply their labour in return for wages

▲ Suppliers of capital receive interest

▲ Profit is a reward for enterprise

Wages

People will supply their labour to firms in return for payments c[...]
Some people may be paid a wage for every hour they work whil[...]
receive a wage for every task they complete. Different workers n[...]
very different wages depending on where they work, what job they do and
the skills they have. ➤ **3.3.2**

Interest

Investments in capital goods such as factory buildings and machinery are
expensive and must be financed. The money invested or 'employed' in
capital goods by firms is therefore also called capital. **Interest** is paid to
people and organizations that supply or invest capital in firms. The
interest is what the people and organizations charge for supplying the
money. ➤ **3.1.2**

Profit

To organize production in a firm an entrepreneur must pay out rents, wages
and interest to the suppliers of the factors of production it needs. These are its
costs of production. ➤ **3.7.1**

A firm must be able to generate enough income or revenue to cover its costs
of production if it is to continue making and selling its products. A firm that
earns more revenue from the sale of its products than it costs to produce them
will therefore have a surplus left over after all its costs have been paid. This
surplus is a **profit**. It is the reward entrepreneurs receive for successfully
organizing production in a firm.

However, not all entrepreneurs will earn a profit. Some may even make a loss
if their costs exceed their revenues. ➤ **3.7.5**

SECTION 1.2.2

Mobility of the factors of production

SECTION 1.2.3

Quantity and quality of the factors of production

The economic problem can never be solved: resources will always be scarce
relative to limitless human wants. However, changing the way in which
resources are used or increasing the amount and quality of resources available
can allow more goods and services to be produced and, therefore, more wants
to be satisfied.

But how easy is it to change how scarce resources are used? And what affects
the quantity and quality of resources available for production?

What is factor mobility?

Factor mobility refers to the ease with which resources or factors of
production can be moved from one productive activity to another without
incurring significant costs or a loss of output. For example, factors of
production may be moved:

- **Occupational mobility** or task mobility refers to the ability to move factors between different productive tasks.
- **Geographic mobility** is the ability to move factors of production to different locations.

- Within a firm, for example, when an office assistant is moved from the human resources department to the finance department;

- Between firms in the same industry, for example, when one paint manufacturer closes but sells its machinery and equipment to another paint manufacturer;

- Between industries, as when a worker leaves employment at a clothing firm and begins work at a car factory;

- Between different countries, for example, when a doctor migrates to another country or when the head office of a bank is relocated overseas. The migration of workers to a country will increase its supply of labour but will reduce the supply of labour in the countries they leave.

The ability to move or reallocate factors of production between different productive uses in different locations is important for a number of reasons:

✔ Moving factors of production to more productive activities from less productive activities will increase their total output of goods and services.

✔ It allows different factors of production to be moved into their best possible uses. For example, it is a waste of resources to use a trained engineer to clean floors in a shop, or to use rich agricultural land that could be used to grow food to store old vehicles for scrap metal.

✔ It enables firms to improve the way they produce different goods and services as the quantity and quality of factors of production changes. For example, modern technology has meant that some tasks previously undertaken by labour can now be carried out quicker and cheaper by computerized machinery and robots.

✔ It allows firms to change the type of goods and services they produce as human needs and wants change. For example, concern for the environment has increased consumer demand for renewable energy. In response, resources have been moved into the production of wind turbines and solar panels.

Why are some factors more mobile than others?

Moving factors of production from one use to another is not always easy or without cost. For example, some workers have very specific skills, such as doctors. They may be good at providing healthcare but may be far less productive if they became farmers or construction workers. They would first need to be retrained and this can be expensive.

In fact, many workers are **occupationally immobile**. This means they cannot change jobs very easily because they have specific skills. For example, train drivers could not become lawyers overnight without years of training and shop assistants would not be able to apply for jobs as skilled engineers.

In addition, many workers are **geographically immobile** because they are reluctant to move to jobs in different locations because of family ties or because moving home can be expensive.

Many natural and human-made resources also have specific characteristics or functions that may limit the range of productive activities they can be used for. For example, specialized asphalt-laying vehicles are designed to lay asphalt surfaces on roads and snow ploughs are used to move snow. They have no other use, but they can be used in different locations so they are not geographically immobile.

▲ Road surfacing equipment is geographically mobile but cannot be used for other productive tasks

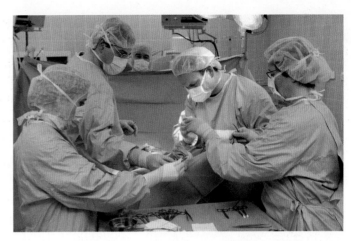

▲ Many workers can change job relatively easily but some have specialized skills that make them occupationally immobile, such as surgeons

Land is also geographically immobile and, in some areas, may have few alternative uses. For example, it is difficult to build on farm wetlands, on the slopes of mountains or in very cold regions of the world. However, it may be possible to use land in other areas to produce different crops each year or for dairy farming, to grow trees to provide wood or as parkland. It could also be built on to provide new houses or business premises but this may be costly and time consuming to achieve, especially if permission to do so is required from government.

However, many factors of production can move relatively easily between alternative productive uses. People often have many skills they can use in many different jobs in factories, offices and shops. Lorries can transport different goods for different firms to different locations and computers and other tools and equipment can be used in many different ways.

ACTIVITY 1.5

Getting mobile

Reproduce and complete the table below. For each of the productive resources listed: identify what type of factor of production they are; how their use in production is rewarded; how mobile you think they are and why (for example, how many alternative productive uses do you think they each have and how easy do you think it is to change their use?).

Resource	Factor of production?	Factor reward?	Factor mobility?	Reasons for factor mobility?
Computer programmers	*Labour*	*Wages*	*Quite mobile*	*Although they have very specific skills and cannot change occupation easily, general computer skills are used in so many different ways in different firms and industries*
A combine harvester				
Cotton				
An oil platform				
A woodland				

What affects the quantity and quality of factors of production?

Some natural resources such as fossil fuels, metal ores and minerals are non-renewable, because they have taken many thousands or millions of years to form. We may be able to find and extract some further deposits over time but once they have all been used up they cannot be replaced. ➤ **1.1.1**

However, other scarce resources are renewable. It may also be possible to increase both their quantity and quality over time so that more goods and services can be produced with them.

For example, more trees can be planted to increase the supply of wood. Woods and metals from old unwanted goods can also be recycled and re-used.

More machines and other capital equipment can be produced instead of consumer goods. New technology is also increasing the quality of capital equipment. The power and capabilities of computers has increased significantly in the last few decades and they are now used extensively to design products and control machinery in many modern production processes. Industrial robots are also replacing the jobs of some manufacturing workers who are then able to move into other productive uses.

Population growth is increasing the global workforce and training can teach workers new skills including how to run successful firms, how to improve production and how to reduce the amount of natural resources wasted during production. ➤ **3.6.3**

▲ New technologies can produce energy from renewable sources and reduce the use of oil, gas and coal in electricity production

Discovering new sources of natural resources and increasing both the quantity and quality of other factors of production available for productive use enables firms to:

- produce more goods and services;
- produce a wider range of goods and services;
- improve the quality of goods and services;
- invent new products and ways of producing them.

As a result, more human needs can be met and more human wants can be satisfied.

We can show the impact of changes in the quantity and quality of factor resources on production using **production possibility curve diagrams**. ➤ **1.4.4**

▼ How the quantity or quality of a factor of production can be increased

Factor of production	How can factor quantity be increased?	How can factor quality be increased?
Land	• An increase in rents may persuade more landowners to release their land into productive uses • New discoveries of fossil fuels, minerals and other natural resources – and new equipment and techniques – can improve the amount it is possible to extract • Making use of other previously unused natural resources. For example, modern technologies have enabled us to use the sun, wind and other renewable resources to produce energy. This is reducing the amount of oil, gas and coal we need to burn to produce electricity. • Planting and growing more trees and plants • Recycling and re-using used vegetable oils and engine oils, and metal and wooden parts in durable consumer and capital goods that we no longer use or want	• Fertilizers and better land management can improve soil conditions allowing more crops to be grown • New technologies can improve the resilience of plants to drought and insect infestations • Reducing the use of chemicals in farming which can pollute water courses • Using organic and more humane animal farming methods can improve the quality of crops, meat and milk produced
Labour	• An increase in wages may persuade more people to supply their labour to firms • An increase in the population of working age • Improvements in healthcare reduces the number of days people are absent from work due to sickness and will help people to live and work for longer	• Training and education can improve workforce skills and the amount, range and quality of goods and services people can produce
Capital	• A decision by producers to produce more capital goods • An increase in interest payments will increase the amount of capital investors are willing to supply to firms	• Advances in technology have improved, and continue to improve, the speed and accuracy of modern equipment
Enterprise	• An increase in the prices consumers are willing to pay for goods and services may increase profits and encourage more people to start firms • A fall in the number of paid jobs available and a rise in unemployment may result in more people starting up their own businesses instead	• More and better training courses for people wanting to become entrepreneurs • More and better business advice and support for new entrepreneurs

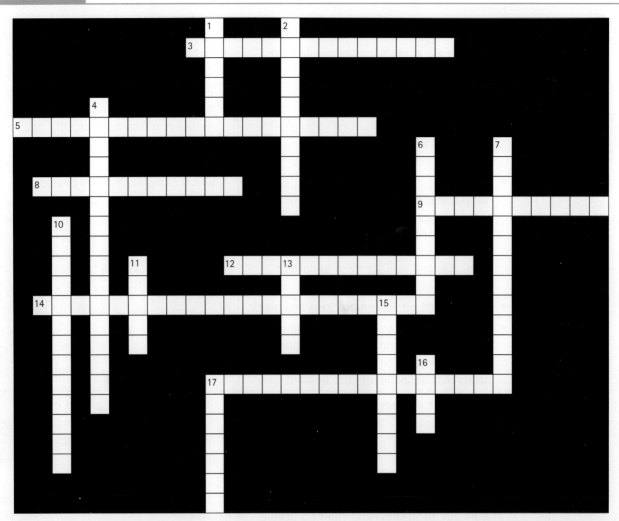

Clues across

3. The ability to move factors of production from one productive use or location to others (6, 8)
5. Scarce resources used to produce other goods and services – they are the inputs to productive activities (7, 2, 10)
8. The using up of goods and services by consumers to satisfy their human needs and wants (11)
9. Skills possessed by successful entrepreneurs including the ability to organize resources into firms for the purpose of production (10)
12. Any resources of products that are limited in supply and scarce relative to human wants (8, 5)
14. Finite resources which cannot be replaced or replenished once they have been used up (3-9, 9)
17. Physical products with long useful lives, including cars and computers, that can be used repeatedly to satisfy a human need or want over many months or even years (9, 8)

Clues down

1. Human effort used up in productive activities (6)
2. The act or process of using resources to make and supply goods and services to satisfy human needs and wants (10)
4. The outputs or 'products' of productive activities (5, 3, 8)
6. Any resources or products that are unlimited in supply (4, 5)
7. People with enterprise skills who are willing to take the risks and decisions necessary to organize resources into firms for production (13)
10. Payments made to the owners of factors of production in return for supplying them to firms for productive use (6, 7)
11. Human desires for different goods and services – these desires are without limit and are increasing (5)
13. Basic human requirements for life and survival (5)
15. People and organizations who buy and use goods and services to satisfy their needs and wants (9)
16. All natural resources used in the production of other goods and services (4)
17. Human-made resources including machinery, tools and factory buildings, used in the production of other goods and services (7)

Unit 1.3
Unit 1.4

Opportunity cost
Production possibility curves

IN THIS UNIT

1.3.1	Definition of opportunity cost	▸ Define opportunity cost
		▸ Use examples to demonstrate the opportunity cost of different economic decisions
1.3.2	The influence of opportunity cost on decision making	▸ Analyse how opportunity cost can affect decisions made by consumers, workers, producers and governments to allocate their resources to different productive uses or activities
1.4.1	Definition of a production possibility curve (PPC)	▸ Define and draw a production possibility curve (PPC)
		▸ Use appropriate diagrams to demonstrate how PPCs can be used to illustrate the concepts of resource allocation and opportunity cost in firms and in an economy
1.4.2	Points under, on and beyond a PPC	▸ Explain the significance of different production points on or off a PPC
1.4.3	Movements along a PPC	▸ Evaluate movements along a PPC and their opportunity cost
1.4.4	Shifts in a PPC	▸ Identify and explain the causes and consequences of shifts in a PPC in terms of an economy's growth

Definition of opportunity cost

The influence of opportunity cost on decision making

What is opportunity cost?

The central economic problem is that the resources we need to produce goods and services to satisfy our wants are scarce compared to our unlimited wants. As a result we cannot produce everything we want so we must choose what goods and services to produce and consume.

Choice is necessary not only because resources are scarce but because many can be used in different ways to produce different goods and services.

For example, many football clubs have spare land next to their grounds. The problem facing these clubs is to choose what to do with this land. They could build a sports complex or leisure centre to serve the local community, or a supermarket, or an apartment block or even an office complex. Whatever they do, they can only choose one of these options because land is a scarce resource.

▼ For example, a piece of land can be used for agriculture or to build a motorway on

People and nations all over the world must therefore choose how scarce resources are to be used. That is, we must all choose which goods and services we will produce and consume because we cannot make everything we want.

The true cost of something is what we have to give up to get it. This cost is known as the **opportunity cost**. It is the benefit we could have enjoyed from the next best alternative we choose to go without.

For example, in Activity 1.6 below you were asked to state what you would go without to purchase the items in the first column. The goods or services you listed in column two are therefore your second-best choices or next best alternatives. You would forego their benefit in order to enjoy the items in column one. For example, you may have chosen to go without the benefit of a holiday in order to buy a large flat-screen television. The benefit of the holiday you have given up is the real cost of choosing to buy a large flat-screen television instead.

The next best thing

Look at the items listed in the first column. What goods or services would you also like to have and what would you go without in order to be to able to buy them?

Products I want to buy	Products I could go without
Large flat-screen television	
Four-bedroom house	
Cakes and sweets	
A ticket to the World Cup Final	

Opportunity cost is the cost of choice

Every decision we make either as consumers or producers involves an opportunity cost because the resources we need to produce goods and services are limited in supply and scarce relative to our wants. Choosing one use of resources always means going without another. For example:

- Consumers must choose how much of their limited incomes to save and how much to spend. For example, if a consumer chooses to save $500 they have given up the opportunity to enjoy $500 of consumer goods and services instead. ➤ **3.2.1**

- A family can choose to cover the floors of their home with carpets or tiles. If the family chooses to buy and fit carpets then it has decided to go without the benefit of tiled floors.

- Workers also face many choices. For example, Rafa chose to train as engineer in a local factory for which he is paid $600 per week. To do so he gave up his next best option to work as a gym instructor earning $500 per week in a local sports centre. His supervisor in the factory has now asked him if he wants to work an extra 10 hours each week. If he agrees, he will earn $200 more each week but will have to give up 10 hours of his leisure time. ➤ **3.3.1**

- Producers must decide what goods or services they will produce, how much they will produce, how much money they will invest in their firms, where to locate them and how best to obtain and organize the resources they need for production. ➤ **3.6.1**

For example, a group of entrepreneurs have purchased an area of land and raised $5 million to pay for the resources they need to build 20 new homes for sale or a new hotel. After considering the two proposals they decide the construction of a new hotel is their preferred option and the construction of new homes, the next best alternative use of $5 million of resources. This is because they estimate the hotel will be more profitable than the construction and sale of new homes. They are therefore willing to give up the profits they would earn from this next best alternative use of resources.

- Governments must determine how best to spend public money and how they will finance it. For example, should they spend more on providing schools and education or on the construction of new motorways? The opportunity cost of building more motorways will be the foregoing of additional schools and educational services. Alternatively, a government may decide to increase taxes on the wages of workers and profits of entrepreneurs so that is able to finance the building of more schools and roads at the same time so that neither is foregone. However, the opportunity cost of doing so for taxpayers will be the amount of money they must give up from their incomes to pay higher taxes. ➤ **4.3.2**

All of the above decisions involve making choices because the goods and services we consume and the resources we use to produce them are limited in supply and scarce relative to our wants.

However, scarce resources are unevenly distributed within and between countries. Some countries have more resources than others. Therefore some consumers, workers, producers and governments have more choices available to them than others.

ACTIVITY 1.7

Free to choose?

1   Look at the photographs and copy the table below. Put a tick in the first column if you think the children in the first photograph are free to choose. Tick the second column if the boys in the second picture are free to choose.

Free to choose? ✗ or ✓	First picture	Second picture
Can go to a soccer match.		
Can eat in a restaurant.		
Can catch their own food.		
Can drive a car.		
Can visit foreign countries.		
Can own their own house.		
Can obtain medical help when needed.		
Can receive an Economics education.		
Can receive a daily paper.		
Can be independent.		
Can receive radio and television.		

2   Which group of children do you think has more choice and why?

Based on the photographs, we assume that the boys in the second picture in Activity 1.7 have a greater choice of goods and services to enjoy than the children in the first picture. This is because the boys in the second picture live in a country which has far more resources to produce more of the goods and services people want.

The children in the first photograph have far less choice. There are fewer resources in their country that can be used to produce goods and services to satisfy their wants.

In some countries, many people may have very little choice. For example, in the poorest countries of Africa, not even basic needs for food can be satisfied with the available resources. This great difference in choice is caused by the relative lack of resources in the poorer countries. Yet in both rich and poor nations people want more resources than are available. ➤ **4.3.2**

The purpose of economics involves advising how best to use scarce resources in order to make as many goods and services to satisfy as many wants as possible. In other words, economics attempts to increase choice and maximize their economic welfare. When people have more goods and services to choose from, opportunity costs are reduced and they are better off. For example, the Western boys are better off than the children in Bangladesh simply because they have the ability to choose between and consume more goods and services.

ECONOMICS IN ACTION

Discuss how the two newspaper articles below illustrate the concepts of scarcity of resources and opportunity cost.

Fears over the development of new homes

Developers have submitted plans to build a total of 3,500 new homes in Northumberland.

There is currently a shortage of homes in the area. The project will create 500 affordable houses on the outskirts of Ponteland and enhance the town's infrastructure.

However, local campaigners fear the development will destroy large areas of nearby agricultural land and woodland, and increase pressure on local schools and healthcare services.

"We are not against development", said one local resident, "We know new homes need to be built but they should not be built upon open land. Once it has been developed it is lost forever".

People must choose between higher taxes or spending cuts

PEOPLE IN Northern Ireland should be given an opportunity to vote on whether to accept spending cuts or pay higher taxes to save public services, according to a leading Northern Ireland economist.

Mike Smyth, president of an influential European Union economic think tank, believes the scale of the public expenditure cuts proposed by the UK government will result in a 'severe decline in living standards' in Northern Ireland.

However, government officials have argued the tax rises needed to continue paying for current levels of public service provision would also cause hardship for many people and businesses across the region.

Definition of a production possibility curve (PPC)

Points under, on and beyond a PPC

Movements along a PPC

ACTIVITY 1.8

The cost of making choices

A factory employs 10 people and has 2 machines able to produce and pack 300 glass bottles each day. The same employees and machines could instead be used in the same factory to make and pack 400 glass jars each day.

The same 10 employees used to work on a farm and were very skilled at growing and harvesting corn until the farm was sold and the factory was built on the farmland. Compared to the farm the factory is noisy and pollutes the air with smoke.

1 What is the opportunity cost to the factory owners of using the 10 employees and 2 machines to make 300 bottles each day?

2 What is the opportunity cost to the employees of working in the factory?

3 What is the opportunity cost to society of the factory?

What is a production possibility curve (PPC)?

The firm in the activity above can use all its factors of production to produce a maximum of 300 glass bottles or a maximum of 400 glass jars each day. Using all its resources to produce 300 bottles each day will however mean that the opportunity to use them to produce 400 jars instead is given up.

Additionally the firm could also choose to allocate some of its factor resources to the production of bottles and the remainder to the production of jars. We can plot all the different combinations of bottles and jars the firm can produce with its resources on a production possibility frontier or **production possibility curve diagram (PPC).**

▼ Production possibility curve for a firm producing glass bottles and jars

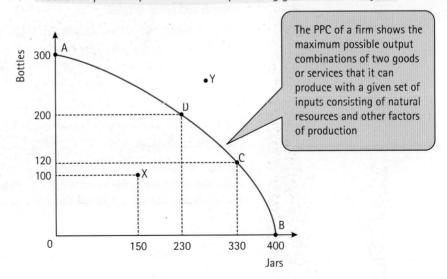

The PPC of a firm shows the maximum possible output combinations of two goods or services that it can produce with a given set of inputs consisting of natural resources and other factors of production

The production possibility curve in the diagram shows all the production choices available to the firm assuming it uses all of its labour and other resource inputs as fully and as efficiently as possible to maximize their output.

Moving along a PPC involves the reallocation of resources from one productive use to another

At point A on the vertical axis the firm will be using all of its resources to produce 300 glass bottles each week. At point B it will be using all its resources to produce 400 glass jars each week. The opportunity cost of producing 400 jars each day is therefore 300 bottles foregone.

At any point on the PPC between A and B the firm will be using its resources to produce some combination of bottles and jars each week.

For example, if the firm chooses to produce at point C it will be producing 330 jars and 120 bottles each week.

Moving from point C to D will require the firm move some of its resources out of the production of jars and into the production of bottles. Doing so will allow the firm to produce an additional 80 bottles each week but at the loss of 100 jars. That is, the opportunity cost of producing an extra 80 glass bottles each week is the 100 glass jars foregone.

Moving even further along its PPC from point D towards point A will mean the firm moving even more of its resources into the production of bottles and giving up even more jar production. Its PPC therefore shows the opportunity costs faced by the firm when choosing between different allocations of its resources.

Inefficient and unattainable allocations of resources

Now imagine that the firm is actually producing at point X below its production possibility curve. At point X it is producing just 150 jars and 100 bottles each week. However, we know from its PPC that it could produce 330 jars and 120 bottles each week at point C or 230 jars and 200 bottles each week at point D.

This is because at point X it is not using all of its resources and/or not used them as efficiently as possible. The same will be true of any other point of production below the PPC. For example, at point X some of its machines may be broken or they are only being used for 12 hours each day instead of being run continuously for 24 hours each day. Correcting these problems would therefore allow the firm to increase its total output of both bottles and jars.

However, it could not increase output to as far as point Y above its PPC. This is because its PPC shows the maximum possible output combinations of bottles and jars the firm can achieve when all its resources are fully and efficiently employed. Production at point Y or any other point above its PPC will therefore be unattainable unless the firm is able to either:

- improve the quality of its existing resources so they can produce more, for example, by training its workers to use more advanced production techniques and machinery; and/or

- increase the quantity of resources it employs, for example, by hiring more workers and investing in additional machinery. ➤ **1.2.3**

EXAM PREPARATION 1.1

All countries face the economic problem and so choices have to be made.

a Explain what is meant by the *economic problem.* [2]

b Explain **two** characteristics of the factor of production referred to as 'enterprise'. [4]

c Using a production possibility curve diagram, analyse how the curve can be used to show the effects of a change in the allocation of resources between the production of two goods. [6]

d Discuss whether a decision by a government to increase public expenditure on education is likely to be a sensible economic decision. [8]

SECTION 1.4.4

Production possibility curves for an economy

Shifts in a PPC

Imagine we could add together all the different production possibility curves for all the different firms in different industries in a country. Doing so would derive the production possibility curve for that country or national economy.

What is an economy?

People and firms produce, exchange and consume goods and services in an **economy**. An economy is therefore any area in which the economic activities of production, exchange and consumption take place. ➤ **1.1.1**

A village or small town will have a small local economy, but may be part of a much larger regional or even national economy. For example, Nairobi is the capital city within the national economy of Kenya. In turn, the Kenyan economy is part of the African economy in which all other African countries are included, such as Algeria, Cameroon, Egypt, Mauritius, Swaziland and South Africa. Similarly, all African national economies form part of the global economy along with the economies of all other countries in the world.

The size of a national economy is measured by the amount or value of all the goods and services it produces each week, month or year. An economy will therefore grow in size as it produces more goods and services. ➤ **4.6.2**

The efficient reallocation of resources in an economy

The production possibility curve (PPC) in the diagram shows the total amount of consumer goods and capital goods a national economy can produce using its scarce resources. It shows the economy has enough resources to produce 1,000 tonnes of consumer goods or 800 tonnes of capital goods. ➤ **1.1.1**

Or the economy can produce a combination of consumer goods and capital goods. The maximum combined amount of the two types of goods the economy can produce with its resources is shown by its PPC.

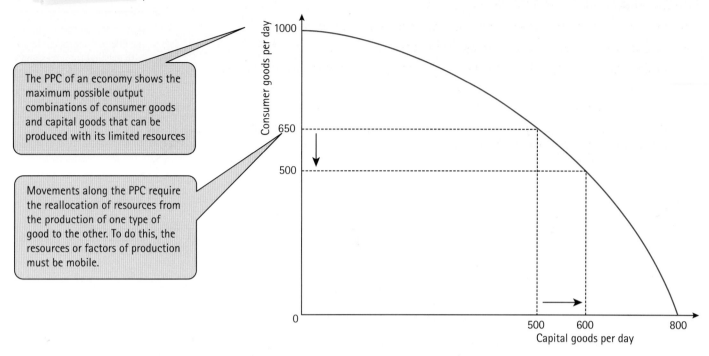

The PPC of an economy shows the maximum possible output combinations of consumer goods and capital goods that can be produced with its limited resources

Movements along the PPC require the reallocation of resources from the production of one type of good to the other. To do this, the resources or factors of production must be mobile.

For example, let us assume that the economy is currently producing 650 tonnes of consumer goods and 500 tonnes of capital goods each day. This combination of outputs is marked on the PPC diagram.

To increase its output of capital goods by another 100 tonnes each day (to 600 tonnes) will require a reallocation of resources within the economy. Mobile factors of production will be moved out of firms producing consumer goods and into other firms producing capital goods. From the PPC for the economy we can see that this will result in a reduction in the amount of consumer goods produced each day by 150 tonnes (from 650 tonnes to 500 tonnes).

The opportunity cost to the economy of an additional 100 tonnes of capital goods is therefore the loss of 150 tonnes of consumer goods. ➤ **1.3.2**

Inefficient allocations of resources

The diagram below is the PPC of another national economy. Its PPC shows all the maximum possible output combinations of consumer goods and capital goods it is capable of producing when all its scarce resources are fully and efficiently employed.

However, the economy is currently producing consumer and capital goods at point A, well below what it is capable of producing shown by its production possibility curve. This means it is not using all of its scarce resources or it is not using them in the best or most efficient ways possible. For example, many workers may be unemployed while others may be in jobs they are not trained for or skilled enough to do. Farmland, factory buildings, offices, machinery and other productive resources may be unused or idle.

If the economy made better use of its scarce resources it could increase its total output of both consumer goods and capital goods each year. For example, if it used all its resources efficiently the economy could produce the output combination at point B or C or at any other points along its PPC.

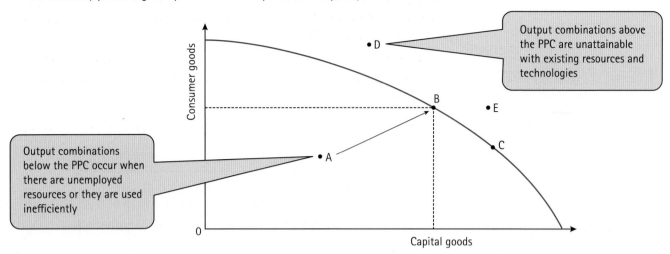

However, the economy is unable to produce output combinations D or E. These points lie outside of its PPC and therefore above the maximum possible output combinations of consumer and capital goods it can produce with its existing resources, production processes and technologies.

An increase in the quantity or quality of resources available to an economy

Firms in the economy will only be capable of producing more consumer goods and capital goods each period at points such as D and E if they have more resources to use or if the quality of their existing resources improves so that they become more productive.

An increase in the quantity and/or quality of factors of production available to the economy will move its PPC outwards (from PPC1 to PPC2) as shown below. ➤ **1.2.3**

▼ An increase in productive capacity

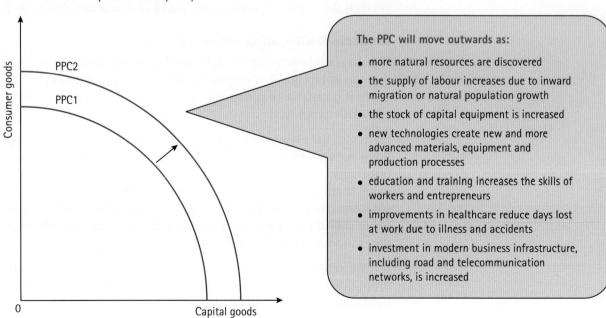

An outward shift in the PPC shows that the economy has the capacity to produce more goods each period than it did before there was an increase in the quantity or quality of its resources.

If the economy uses this capacity to produce more goods than it did previously, the size of the economy will increase. This is called **economic growth**. ➤ **4.6.1**

A reduction in the quantity or quality of resources available to an economy

In contrast, if the economy suffers a decrease in the quantity or quality of its resources, its capacity to produce goods will shrink. This will cause its PPC to shift inwards (from PPC1 to PPC3 in the diagram below). Its total output of goods will fall and there will be **negative economic growth**.

▼ A decrease in productive capacity

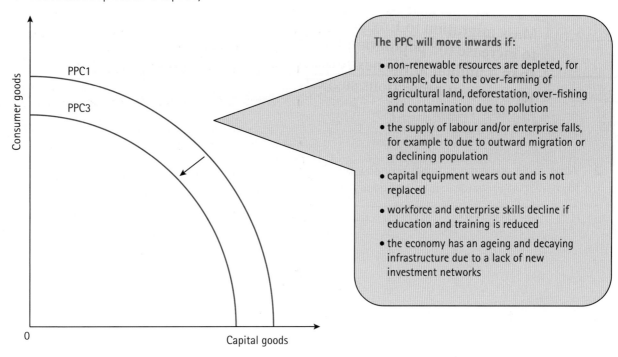

The PPC will move inwards if:

- non-renewable resources are depleted, for example, due to the over-farming of agricultural land, deforestation, over-fishing and contamination due to pollution

- the supply of labour and/or enterprise falls, for example to due to outward migration or a declining population

- capital equipment wears out and is not replaced

- workforce and enterprise skills decline if education and training is reduced

- the economy has an ageing and decaying infrastructure due to a lack of new investment networks

Shift it!

1   According to the news articles below, which countries are most likely to have experienced (a) an increase in their resources and productive capacity, and (b) a decrease in their resources and productive capacity?

Many developing countries are losing their better-educated nationals to richer countries including young healthcare workers and entrepreneurs

Approximately 75 percent of land in Uganda could be used for agriculture according to a new study. However, only around 30 percent of arable land is currently being cultivated. It is also estimated that up to 12 percent of output has been lost due to environmental degradation through soil erosion and nutrient loss.

Mass migration to England is expected to increase the population by more than 4 million in the next decade, new government projections suggest.

New oil reserves have recently been discovered in Canada, Norway, Cuba, Brazil, Russia and Israel.

2   What could prevent a national economy that has experienced an increase in its resources and productive capacity from increasing its total output of goods and services?

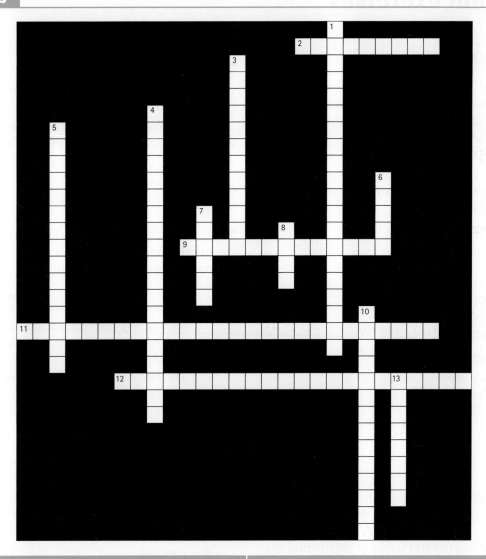

Clues across

2. An area such as a town, region or country in which the economic activities of production, consumption and exchange take place – its size can be measured by the total amount or value of goods and services produced within it each period (2, 7)

9. Physical products produced and supplied by firms in an economy to satisfy immediate consumer needs or wants (8, 5)

11. A graphical representation of the maximum output combinations of two goods that could be produced by a firm or an entire economy using its existing factor resources as fully and as efficiently as possible (10, 11, 5)

12. Factor mobility is required in an economy to move along its production possibility curve because it requires a reallocation of resources from one productive use to another. However, some workers have very specific skills which means they cannot easily be moved to different jobs requiring different skills. What is this problem called? (12, 10)

Clues down

1. Factors of production will have this characteristic if they are easy to relocate (12, 8)

3. These products do not satisfy an immediate consumer need or want – instead they are produced and supplied by firms in an economy to use in the production of other goods and services (7, 5)

4. The basic economic problem (8, 2, 9)

5. The real cost of choosing one use of scarce resources over another – it is the benefit from the next best alternative given up or foregone (11, 4)

6. These are paid to people to supply their labour to firms (5)

7. The reward for enterprise (5)

8. This type of factor reward is received by the owner of land in return for its use in production (4)

10. This will have occurred in an economy that is able to produce more goods and services each period than it did in previous periods – it refers to an increase in the size of an economy (8, 5)

13. Factor rewards received by the owners of capital that has been invested in firms (8)

Assessment exercises

Multiple choice

1 What is the basic economic problem?

   A Finite resources and limited wants

   B Finite resources and unlimited wants

   C Infinite resources and limited wants

   D Infinite resources and unlimited wants

2 Which statement best explains why drought is an economic problem?

   A Rainfall cannot be predicted easily

   B The effects of drought require government action

   C Droughts cannot be prevented

   D Water is a scarce good

3 New oil reserves are discovered. What has increased in supply?

   A Capital

   B Enterprise

   C Labour

   D Land

4 Which statement about the factors of production is correct?

   A Capital includes human-made machines that lose value over time to wear and advances in technology

   B Enterprise is a natural factor of production that cannot be taught

   C Labour is an immobile factor that does not change its skill level

   D Land refers only to farmland that cannot be improved by human effort

5 The following are four ways factors of production are used. What is likely to require the greatest use of the factor enterprise?

   A A carpenter making wooden articles in his leisure time for sale at a monthly market

   B A corn farmer negotiating with other farmers to hire expensive machinery

   C A food shop owner sometimes selling flowers in the shop

   D A householder harvesting vegetables grown at home

6 Hala makes cakes she bakes in her kitchen at home. She sells them at a local market. To produce more cakes she decides to invest in a larger oven and to employ someone to help.

   Which factors of production have changed?

   A Labour

   B Capital

   C Labour and capital

   D Enterprise and capital

7 A new dam is built in Turkey to provide hydroelectric power and a water supply. What is the opportunity cost to the country of building the dam?

   A The cost to households and businesses of consuming the water supply

   B The benefits foregone from other uses of the money used to pay for the dam

   C The cost to consumers of using hydroelectric power

   D The money used to pay for the construction and running of the dam

8 A social club has sold raffle tickets at US$10 each. The owner of the winning ticket received a prize of US$250. A student bought a ticket, but did not win. What is the opportunity cost to the student?

   A US$10

   B US$250

   C What could have been bought with the US$10

   D What could have been bought with the US$250

9 A firm can produce a number of possible combinations of two goods. It can either produce 500 of good x and 300 of good y, or 600 x and 250 y. What is the opportunity cost of producing an extra 100 of good x?

   A 100 y

   B 250 y

   C 50 y

   D The extra wages paid to the workers

10 In the diagram below what is the opportunity cost of increasing the output of wheat from 300 tonnes to 400 tonnes per month?

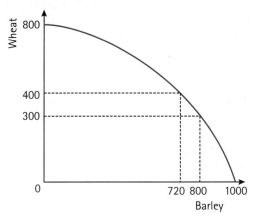

- **A** 800 tonnes of barley
- **B** 80 tonnes of barley
- **C** 120 tonnes of barley
- **D** 720 tonnes of barley

11 The diagram below shows the production possibility curve for an economy.

Which point in the diagram represents the most efficient allocation of resources to the production of both consumer goods and capital goods in the economy?

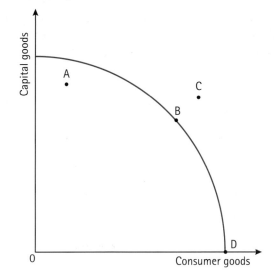

12 The movement in the production possibility curve from PPC1 to PPC2 in the diagram indicates there has been growth in the productive potential of an economy.

What is most likely to have caused this?

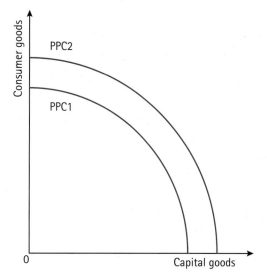

- **A** An increase in wages
- **B** A better educated workforce
- **C** A decrease in the availability of natural resources
- **D** An increase in factor mobility

Structured questions

1 In 2017, a series of powerful hurricanes destroyed many homes and factories in the British Virgin Islands. Rebuilding will take time and involve an opportunity cost as resources will need to be diverted from other uses. As a result, many people may decide to emigrate.

   A Define *opportunity cost*. [2]

   B Explain why it is impossible to solve the economic problem. [4]

   C Using a production possibility curve diagram, analyse the effect of a reduction in the resources available to an economy. [6]

   D Discuss whether a country will benefit from emigration. [8]

2 In 2012, the US Government approved spending of US$1.5 billion to send a third robotic exploration vehicle to Mars in 2020. Some economists argued that it would be better to use the same scarce resources including labour and enterprise, to improve education or to build more roads instead.

   A Define *enterprise*. [2]

   B Explain why scarcity of resources creates an opportunity cost. [4]

   C Using a production possibility curve diagram, analyse the impact an increase in education could have on an economy. [6]

   D Discuss whether the construction and use of more roads will benefit an economy. [8]

The allocation of resources

Choosing what goods and services to produce, how to produce them and who to produce them for, involves making decisions about the allocation of scarce resources. How these decisions are made is called an economic system.

Every country has an economic system or economy involving decisions about the production, consumption and exchange of goods and services. In a market economic system, the spending decisions of consumers determine what, how and for whom to produce: private sector firms seeking to earn profits will allocate scarce resources to the production of goods and services for consumers with the greatest willingness and ability to pay for them.

In a free market the price of a good or service will be determined by the decisions of consumers to buy that product and the production decisions of firms. Effective demand is the willingness and ability of consumers to buy goods and services. In general, as the price of a product rises demand will tend to contract. Supply refers to the willingness and ability of producers to provide goods and services. In general, as the price of a product rises and it becomes more profitable to make, producers will expand its supply.

The market for a good or service will be in equilibrium when consumer demand for that product is exactly equal to the amount producers are willing and able to supply. At equilibrium the market price for the product will be stable.

However, if consumer demand increases, for example if incomes rise or if the product becomes fashionable, then the market price will tend to rise. Or supply of the good or service may increase and reduce market price, for example, if the cost of producing it is reduced due to technological advance.

However, some producers and consumers in a market economic system may allocate scarce resources to activities that are wasteful, inefficient or even harmful to other people, the economy and the environment. This is because private sector firms and consumers will usually only be concerned with their own private costs and benefits. They may fail to take account of the external costs of their decisions and actions on others, including pollution and the rapid depletion of natural resources and habitats. In a mixed economic system a government can also organize resources and productive activities to help correct market failures that may otherwise reduce economic welfare. In a mixed economic system, resource allocation decisions are therefore taken by the government or public sector as well as by the private sector.

IN THIS UNIT			
	2.1.1	Microeconomics	▶ Understand the difference between microeconomics and macroeconomics and the decision makers involved in each
	2.1.2	Macroeconomics	
	2.2.1	Resource allocation decisions	▶ Establish how the economic problem creates three key questions about the allocation of resources – what to produce, how, and for whom
	2.2.2	The market system	▶ Understand how a market system works including the interactions of buyers and sellers, and how it determines the allocation of scarce resources
			▶ Distinguish between a market equilibrium and market disequilibrium
	2.2.3	Introduction to the price mechanism	▶ Explain how the price mechanism provides answers to the key resource allocation questions

SECTION 2.1.1

Microeconomics

SECTION 2.1.2

Macroeconomics

Economics involves the study of how humans work together to convert limited resources into goods and services to satisfy as many of their unlimited wants as they can. Economics can be divided into microeconomics and macroeconomics.

What is microeconomics?

Microeconomics studies the economic decisions and actions of individual consumers, producers and households and how these economic decision makers interact. For example, microeconomics will consider:

- How individual firms organize production and why;
- What determines the wages paid to different groups of workers;
- What affects the purchasing decisions of individual consumers;
- What determines the prices of different goods and services;
- What determines the amounts individual households spend or save from their incomes;
- How the decisions and actions of different consumers, firms or households affect others;
- How government policies and actions can affect the decisions and behaviours of individual consumers, producers and households.

These and other microeconomic issues are considered in Parts 2 and 3.

What is macroeconomics?

In contrast to the study of microeconomics, which divides up a national economy into many smaller parts or sectors, **macroeconomics** considers economics issues and actions that affect the whole economy.

Macro means 'big' and the term **macroeconomy** is often used to refer to a national economy. The study of macroeconomics therefore considers 'big' issues such as:

- What determines the total output of all firms in an economy?
- What is the total or national income of the economy and what causes it to change over time?
- What determines the overall level of employment and unemployment?
- What causes inflation in the general level of prices and what impact does it have?
- How can governments influence total consumer spending, the rate of price inflation, the level of employment and the total output of all firms in the economy?
- What impacts can changes in taxes and government spending have on an economy?
- What are the reasons for differences in living standards between countries?
- What affects population growth and how is it affecting different economies?
- Why do different countries engage in international trade with each other and what impact can it have on their macro economies?

These and other macro-issues are examined in Parts 4, 5 and 6.

SECTION 2.2.1

Key resources allocation decisions

The resource allocation problem

Scarcity of resources relative to human wants is the basic economic problem. Every economy must therefore choose what goods and services to produce with their limited resources. ➤ **1.1.1**

Some national economies have access to more resources than others but all have far fewer resources than they need to produce all the goods and services their populations want. All economies must therefore choose which wants will be satisfied and how. For example, an economy may choose to allocate some of its scarce resources to the production of electricity to satisfy a want for energy, but will it produce electricity from coal-fired power stations, nuclear power plants or from renewable sources such as solar panels or wind turbines?

Deciding how to best to allocate limited resources to different productive uses is the problem of **resource allocation**.

ACTIVITY 2.1

Tropical trouble

Divide into groups of three or four people. Now read on . . . you are part of the crew of a cargo vessel. After weeks at sea a violent storm lashes against your ship. It is forced on to rocks and a group of you are shipwrecked on a deserted island. You salvage what little you can from the ship but most of your supplies are lost in the storm.

In the bright tropical sunlight of the next day you take stock of your available resources. You realize that the wreck of the ship provides metal and wood, and the natural vegetation of the uninhabited island provides a valuable source of food.

In your group discuss and provide answers to the following questions.

1   What is the central economic problem facing your group of survivors?

2   What is the best way of organizing and using the resources available to you?

Write down how your group has decided to overcome the problems facing it.

The basic economic problem therefore creates three questions or puzzles every economy has to solve: what goods and services to produce, how to produce them and whom to produce for.

What to produce?

One problem facing people when there is scarcity is deciding exactly **what** goods and services to produce. This involves choosing which wants to satisfy. Every society, no matter what its size, is faced with the same choice. In the case of the deserted tropical island in Activity 2.1 the choice may be between using its scarce resources to produce food, clothing and shelter. In a more advanced national economy, its people and organizations may have to decide between producing more weapons or more hospitals.

How to produce?

Once the question of what goods and services to produce has been addressed, the next problem is deciding **how** to make them. What tools are required? How many workers and what skills will they need? How much land is essential? In addition, there are many different ways of making goods and services. For example, when producing corn a lot of machinery could be used to plough the land, plant seeds and eventually harvest the crop with relatively few workers. Alternatively, a lot of workers could be used to physically plough, plant and harvest, using very little machinery.

For whom to produce?

When the questions of what to produce and how to produce have been answered, a final issue remains. Scarcity means it is impossible to satisfy the wants of every person. Each economy must therefore determine **who** gets the goods and services that have been produced. Some people are stronger than others, while some people may work harder than others – perhaps they should obtain more goods and services? Others may be weak and be unable to work – should they get any goods and services? Or should everybody receive an equal share of all the goods and services produced, even if some people are in greater need than others? Or should goods and services simply be distributed according to how many each person can afford to buy?

How did your group decide whom to produce for on the tropical island? There is no right answer. Each society may decide to distribute goods and services in a different way depending on people's beliefs or their value judgements.

ACTIVITY 2.2

Problem solving

Remember your solutions to the problems you faced as a group of survivors on a desert island.

1   Copy out the table below and write down your solutions to the problems posed in each column.

2   If you can think of any other ways to solve these problems include these in your table.

3   Compare your answers with those of another group in your class and make a note of any other ways they have thought of to answer the three questions.

How to decide what to produce?	How to decide how to produce?	How to decide for whom to produce?
Build shelter	Everyone helps using large palm leaves	Everyone shares a shelter

---

'Solving' the resource problem requires an economic system

There are many different solutions to the problem of resource allocation. How a national economy answers the questions of what to produce, how to produce and whom to produce for is called its **economic system**.

How the macroeconomics system of a national economy 'solves' the resource allocation problem will depend on the many decisions and actions of different people in that economy, just as you did in the imaginary island economy in Activity 2.1. Some people may be very caring and want everyone to have an equal share of scarce resources, while others may want to be rich and powerful by keeping most of the available resources for themselves.

Economic systems therefore develop from the way people think and behave, and may also change over time. However, without economic systems few decisions will be made about the allocation of resources, fewer goods and services will be produced and more human needs and wants will be unmet.

Economists describe three main types of economic system. They differ according to how much government involvement there is in making decisions about how resources are used, what goods and services are produced, how they are produced and who they are produced for.

Market economic system

In a **free market economic system**, the actions of individual consumers, firms and households in the private sector will determine the allocation of resources. There is no role for a government or a public sector and therefore no taxes or public spending. ➤ **2.9.1**

Planned economic system

A planned economic system is the extreme opposite of a market economic system. In a **planned economy** almost all decisions about how resources are used, what is produced, and how goods and services are priced and allocated, are taken by organizations owned, controlled and accountable to the government. Individual consumers, firms and households have little control over the allocation of resources.

Mixed economic system

In reality there are no completely free market economies or planned economies. All economies are mixed to some degree. In a **mixed economic system**, ownership of scarce resources and decisions about how to use them are split between the **private sector** and a **public sector** consisting of government authorities and organizations.

A mixed economy therefore combines the market system with a system of government planning and control over some resources. In some mixed economies like Iceland, Slovakia and Romania, the public sector is large and controls significant resources. In others, including the USA, Hong Kong, the Philippines and Brazil, the private sector dominates and the role for government in resource allocation decisions is relatively small.

0% ◀ less government involvement   more government involvement ▶ 100%

MARKET ECONOMY	MIXED ECONOMY	PLANNED ECONOMY

SECTION 2.2.2

The market system

SECTION 2.2.3

Introduction to the price mechanism

What is a market?

A market economy is made up of different markets for different goods and services. In these markets the owners of factors of production will exchange them with producers and consumers to obtain the goods and services they want from producers. Their market interactions will ultimately determine what goods and services are produced, how they are produced and who they are produced for. Markets are therefore a very important concept in microeconomics.

Very simply a **market** is any set of arrangements that brings together all the producers and consumers of a good or service so they may engage in trade or exchange. The market for a good or service is therefore made up of all those producers or *sellers* willing and able to supply that product and all those consumers or *buyers* willing and able to buy it.

For example, the market for computers consists of all buyers and sellers of computers. Similarly, there is a market for every different type of food, for clothes, televisions, cars, holidays, insurance and all other goods and services.

In economics, therefore, a market does not refer to a particular location where goods and services might be traded, such as Billingsgate fish market in London, the famous Khan el-Khalili market in Cairo in Egypt, or the local market in the town or village where you live. For an economist, any organization or any person who wants to buy or sell a particular good or service, wherever they are in the world, is part of the market for that good or service. Markets can therefore be spread over a small area or a very large area. For example, the market for a local newspaper or the services of a particular hairdresser at a beauty salon will both tend to be very localized. The markets for national daily newspapers such as *El País* in Spain, *The Times* in the UK, or *L'Express* in Mauritius will be national domestic markets. Some goods and services, however, are exchanged all over the world. For example, the markets for crude oil, aircraft and computers are **international** or **global markets**.

Market outcomes

Most privately owned firms in a market economy aim to make as much profit as possible. Firms will earn a profit if they sell their goods or services to consumers at prices that exceed the cost of their production. The higher the prices, the more profit firms are likely to make. ➤ **3.7.4**

Firms will therefore allocate their factor resources to the production of those goods and services that will earn them the most profit. This will depend on what goods and services consumers want and what they are willing to pay for them. The more consumers are willing to pay for a product, the more profit firms are likely to earn from their production and the more they will be willing to supply.

Firms will supply a certain quantity of their goods or services to consumers in return for an agreed price that will earn them a profit. The outcomes of exchange between producers and consumers in a market, for any good or service, are therefore a quantity traded and a market price. ➤ **2.5.1**

For example, producers of ballpoint pens may agree to supply consumers with 1,000 pens each week at a price of $1 each. At this price, the quantity producers are willing and able to supply using their factors of production is exactly equal to the quantity consumers are willing and able to buy. This means there is a **market equilibrium**. Unless something changes the market price per pen and the quantity traded will remain the same from week to week. That is, price and quantity will be stable in any market in a state of equilibrium.

However, now imagine that there is an increase in the number of consumers who want to buy pens but producers are unable to immediately increase their supply. This will result in a **market disequilibrium**. The quantity producers are willing and able to supply each week is less than the quantity consumers are willing and able to buy. Some consumers may therefore be willing and able to pay more to obtain the pens they want. If so, producers of pens will be able to increase the prices they charge consumers for their pens.

If the cost of producing pens is unchanged, higher pen prices will mean higher profits so producers may be encouraged to employ more resources to increase the number of pens they can produce and supply each week.

In contrast, suppose consumers are buying more pens instead of pencils. Consumer demand for pencils is falling. As a result, producers of pencils will be left with a surplus they will be unable to sell unless they can encourage consumers to buy their pencils by reducing their price or by cutting the number of pencils they produce each week.

Changes in prices and quantities are therefore features of markets that are in a state of disequilibrium. ➤ **2.5.2**

➤ **2.5.2**

ACTIVITY 2.3

An introduction to the workings of a market system

Savita Shah has employed 30 people to work in her firm or business organization. She owns a patch of land, a factory building and hires 15 machines. Savita wants to make as much money or profit as possible for herself. This is the aim of her firm. At present she uses her scarce resources to make pairs of bright multicoloured boots.

The latest fashion among young people is pastel-coloured shoes and Savita notices that sales of her boots are falling. That is, the market for boots is shrinking. Younger people are no longer willing to use their money to buy brightly coloured boots, but will instead pay a high price for pastel-coloured shoes. In other words, the market for shoes is expanding.

As her profits begin to fall, Savita realizes there is more money to be made from the production of shoes and so switches her scarce resources away from making boots into the production of pairs of pastel shoes to satisfy the wants of fashion-conscious young people.

Savita now faces a problem. There are two ways of making the shoes. The first method only requires 20 of her 30 workers and 10 of her machines, and each pair of shoes will cost $6 to produce. The second method requires all 30 workers with only 7 machines, and each pair of shoes will cost $10 to produce. Savita decides to use the first and cheapest method because she wishes to make as much profit from the sale of her shoes as possible.

After only a short time, Savita's profits have increased dramatically and are far greater than her profits when she made boots. Eager young people who can afford to pay for the pastel-coloured shoes can now satisfy their wants.

Questions

In a market economy there are often many thousands of firms all behaving like Savita's.

1   What is the main aim of a firm producing goods and services in a market economy?

2   How do firms in this type of economy decide **what** to produce? *Hint* Why did Savita decide to produce shoes instead of boots?

3   In a market system how do firms decide **how** to produce goods and services?

4   Once the goods and services have been produced who are they for? *Hint* Which teenagers could not satisfy their wants for shoes?

5   In deciding to produce shoes Savita chose the cheapest method which meant she needed only 20 of her 30 workers. What will happen to the 10 workers who are not needed?

How the price mechanism works

Changes in market prices play a very important role in a market economy.

If consumers begin to spend more on a product than they did in previous periods, firms producing that product may be able to increase their prices and earn more profit without reducing their sales of the product.

For example, sales of Savita's shoes are rising rapidly. She therefore decides to increase the prices of all her shoes by 10%. This will help cover the costs of buying more materials and using more electricity, but will also increase her profit on each pair of shoes sold. The rise in consumer demand for Savita's shoes and the increase in their prices will be noticed by other firms. For example, sales and profits of the Charvi Clothing Company have been falling and so its owners and managers decide the business will make more profit in future by making and selling shoes to satisfy the increasing consumer demand for them. As a result, the clothing company stops producing clothes and moves its resources into the production of shoes. Many other firms may also decide to enter the market to supply shoes if they are more profitable than other products.

High or rising **market prices** therefore provide private firms with important signals about what products consumers want and what they are willing to pay. That is, price signals help private firms identify products that will be profitable to make and sell.

In the same way, if the market price and profitability of a product falls because consumer demand for it is falling, it will act as a signal to firms to move their resources to the production of more profitable products.

What has just been described is called the **price mechanism**. In a market economic system, changes in market prices provide the means by which decisions taken by private firms and consumers interact to determine how scarce resources are allocated between competing uses. The price mechanism therefore determines what goods and services are produced, how they are produced and who they are produced for in a market economy.

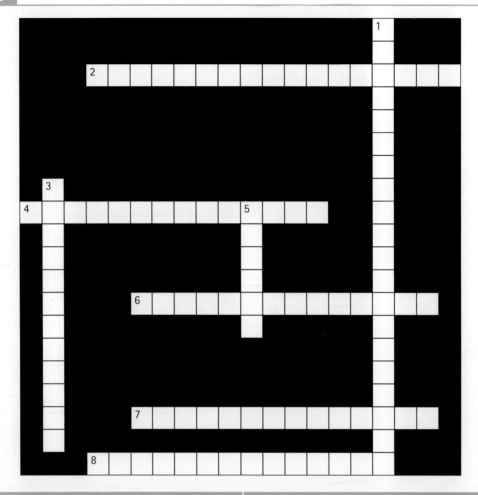

Clues across

2. This will occur in the market for a particular product when the quantity producers are willing and able to supply each period matches the quantity consumers are willing and able to buy. As a result the product price and quantity traded will be stable over time (6, 11)

4. The study of 'big' economic issues that affect a whole economy such as changes in national income, price inflation and unemployment (14)

6. The study of the economic decisions and actions of individual consumers, producers and households and how they interact (14)

7. The system or 'mechanism' within a market economy that involves changes in prices being used by producers to make decisions about what goods and services to produce with scarce resources, how to produce them and who to produce them for (5, 9)

8. Every national or macro-economy has one. It refers to the ways in which all people and organizations within a national economy resolve the resource allocation problem and decide what goods and services to produce, how to produce them and who to produce them for (8, 6)

Clues down

1. This will occur in the market for a particular product when the quantity producers are willing and able to supply each period exceeds or falls short of the quantity consumers are willing and able to buy. There will be changes in the product price and quantity traded as a result (6, 14)

3. Another term used to describe a 'big' or national economy (12)

5. Every good or service has one. Each one consists of all the producers and all the consumers of a particular good or service and involves exchange between them. The outcomes of their exchange will be an agreed price and quantity traded (6)

Unit 2.3	Demand
Unit 2.4	Supply
Unit 2.5	Price determination
Unit 2.6	Price changes

IN THIS UNIT

2.3.1	Definition of demand	▶ Define, draw and interpret diagrams showing individual and market demand curves
2.3.2	Price and demand	▶ Illustrate and describe movements along a demand curve using the following economic terms – extensions in demand and contractions in demand
2.3.3	Individual and market demand	▶ Understand the link between individual and market demand
2.3.4	Conditions of demand	▶ Explain the causes of shifts in a demand curve using the following economic terms – an increase in demand and a decrease in demand
2.4.1	Definition of supply	▶ Define, draw and interpret of individual and market supply curves
2.4.2	Price and supply	▶ Illustrate and describe movements along a demand curve using the following economic terms – extensions in supply and contractions in supply
2.4.3	Individual and market supply	▶ Understand the link between individual and market supply
2.4.4	Conditions of supply	▶ Explain the causes of shifts in a supply curve using the following economic terms - an increase in supply and a decrease in supply
2.5.1	Market equilibrium	▶ Define, draw and interpret demand and supply schedules and curves and use them to establish the equilibrium price and sales in a market
2.5.2	Market disequilibrium	▶ Define, draw and interpret of demand and supply schedules and curves and use them to identify disequilibrium prices and shortages (when demand exceeds supply) and surpluses (when supply exceeds demand)
2.6.1	Causes of price changes	▶ Understand and explain how changing market conditions cause price changes
2.6.2	Consequences of price changes	▶ Use demand and supply diagrams to illustrate changes in market conditions and their consequences for equilibrium price and sales

Definition of demand

What is demand?

Consumers' demand for goods and services has a key role in determining the allocation of resources in a market or mixed economy. **Demand** is the want or willingness of consumers to buy goods and services. However, to be an **effective demand** consumers must have enough money to buy the goods and services they need and want. Producers in the private sector will only supply those goods and services consumers are willing and able to pay for, and at prices that exceed their costs of production.

From the previous unit we know that changes in prices provide firms with important signals about what consumers want and are willing to pay for, and therefore which products will be profitable to make and sell. A rising market price for a product may signal that consumer demand for that product is rising and becoming more profitable to make and sell. As a result, firms may allocate more resources to the production of that product. In contrast, if the market price and profitability of a product is falling, firms may decide not to produce it anymore. This unit looks at how this **price mechanism** works. ➤ **2.2.3**

ACTIVITY 2.4

Food for thought

HEALTHY FOODS MEAN HEALTHY PROFITS AT SAINSBURY'S

A growing range of premium and healthy food has boosted profits at Sainsbury's by 42 per cent.

Rising consumer demand for healthier foods has led the supermarket chain to expand its range of organic food products to more than 1,000 lines. Sales of organic foods rocketed by 450 per cent last year.

Wal-Mart goes for organic growth

Wal-Mart, the world's biggest retailer, has announced its stores will sell more organic food products and has asked its suppliers to increase their range of products to meet rising consumer demand.

Although organic foods still only make up around 2.5% of total Wal-Mart sales, the prices of organic foods are around 20 to 30% more than non-organic varieties and demand is forecast to grow strongly by over 15% a year.

1 Who makes up the market for food products?

2 How are consumers' wants changing in the market for food products?

3 Why do you think more consumers now want and are able to buy healthier food products?

4 What has happened to the prices and profits of healthy foodstuffs as a result of the change in consumer demand for them?

5 What has happened to the allocation of resources in the food industry as a result of changes in the pattern of consumer demand?

Price and demand

Individual and market demand

The amount of a good or service consumers are willing and able to buy is known as the **quantity demanded** of that product. Economists measure the quantity demanded of a particular good or service at a particular price over certain periods of time, say the number of oranges bought per week, litres of petrol per month, or the amount of electricity consumed per year.

Individual demand is the demand of just one consumer, while the **market demand** for a product is the total demand for that product from all its consumers willing and able to buy it.

ACTIVITY 2.5

What is your individual demand?

1   Imagine your favourite chocolate bar was on offer at a number of possible prices. How many bars of chocolate would you be prepared to buy each month at each possible price?

Price of a chocolate bar (cents)	Your demand per week
200	?
150	
100	
50	
25	

2   Copy and complete the table. You have now completed your **demand schedule** for the chocolate bar, that is, a table of figures relating quantity demanded to price.

Use this information to plot a line graph below to show your individual **demand curve** for the chocolate bar.

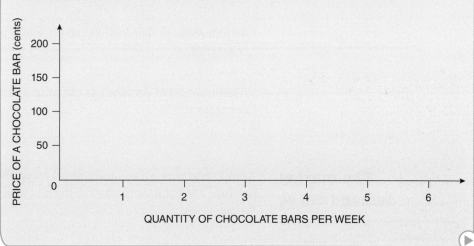

Don't be surprised if all three statements in question 3 in Activity 2.5 apply to your demand curve. For the vast majority of goods and services, the quantity demanded each period will rise as the product price falls. In general, demand curves will normally be downward sloping when plotted against price.

▼ An individual consumers' demand curve for a product

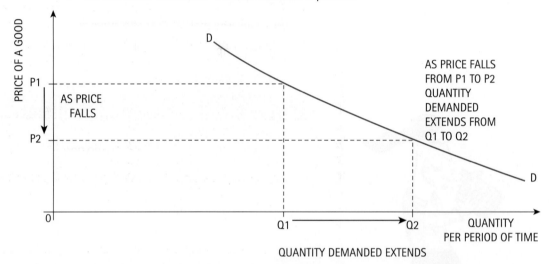

QUANTITY DEMANDED EXTENDS

Consumers will *move along* their individual demand curves for a product as the price of that product changes. That is, the quantity they demand each period rises or *extends* as the price falls and their demand *contracts* as the price rises.

An extension in demand: as the price of a product falls, quantity demanded rises or extends.

A contraction in demand: as the price of a product rises, quantity demanded falls or contracts.

The market demand curve

Adding together all the individual consumer demand curves for a product will produce the total or market demand curve for that product.

Market demand curve

Producers of orange light bulbs have the following information about the amount of orange light bulbs consumers *will* buy each *month* given a number of possible prices. The market demand schedule is as follows.

Price of an orange light bulb (cents)	Market demand per month
50	100,000
40	150,000
30	200,000
20	260,000
10	370,000
5	450,000

1 With price on the vertical axis, and quantity per month along the bottom axis, plot the market demand curve for orange light bulbs and label it DD.

2 Use the graph to work out how many orange light bulbs would be demanded at a price of:

    a 35 cents   **b** 15 cents

3 If orange light bulb producers together wished to sell the following amount of bulbs each year, approximately what price should they charge?

    a 225,000   **b** 400,000

4 Explain why the market demand curve for orange light bulbs slopes downwards.

5 Explain the difference between individual demand and market demand.

In general the **market demand curve** for any given good or service shows the relationship between the total quantity demanded by consumers each period and the price of that product.

▶ A market demand curve for a product

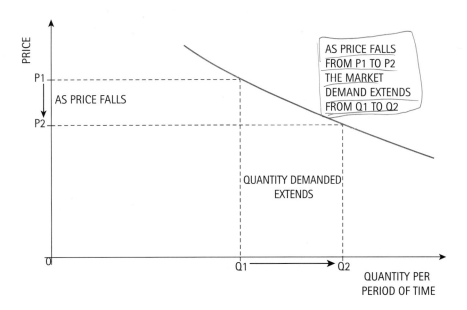

In exactly the same way as an individual demand curve, the market demand curve for a product shows how quantity demanded extends as the price falls and contracts as the price rises. Only changes in the product price can cause these movements along the demand curve. Anything else that could affect consumer demand for the product, regardless of its price, such as a change in incomes or tastes, is assumed to be constant. This is called the **ceteris paribus** assumption in economics, meaning 'all other things remain unchanged'.

Conditions of demand

What happens to consumer demand for goods and services when factors other than their prices change? For example, will a fall in people's income cause them to demand less of a product whatever its price? What effect will an advertising campaign for a product have on demand, regardless of the price of the product? And what if fashions and consumer's wants change? Changes in these, and other conditions that affect consumer demand, will cause market demand curves to shift.

An increase in demand

For example, let's take the market demand for chocolate bars:

Price (cents) of a chocolate bar	Original demand per month	Increased demand per month
50	100,000	200,000
40	150,000	250,000
30	200,000	300,000
20	260,000	360,000
10	330,000	430,000
5	400,000	500,000

▼ An increase in market demand

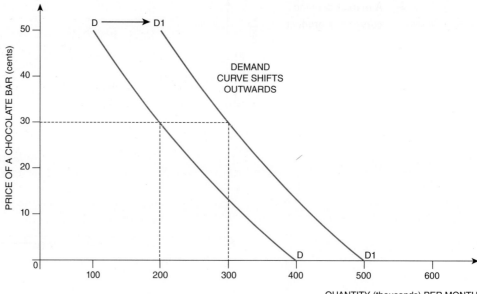

The diagram above shows an increase in demand for chocolate bars, but it could be any other good or service because the same rules apply. At each price consumers are now willing to buy more chocolate bars than they did before. The whole demand curve has shifted outwards from DD to D1D1.

> **An increase in demand** means that consumers now demand more of a product at every price than they did before. The market demand curve will shift out to the right.

A fall in demand

For example, let's look at the market demand for rechargeable AAA batteries.

Price of a battery (cents)	Original demand per week	Decreased demand per week
100	10,000	5,000
80	15,000	10,000
60	20,000	15,000
40	25,000	20,000
20	30,000	25,000

▼ A fall in market demand

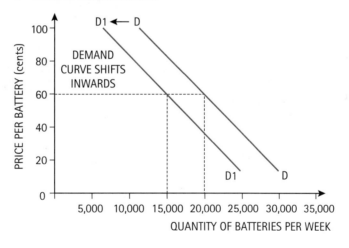

A fall in demand at all prices will cause the demand curve to shift to the left, or inwards, from DD to D1D1.

> **A fall in demand** means that consumers now demand less of a product at every price than they did before. The market demand curve moves in towards the left.

An increase in market demand

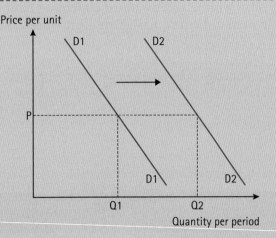

A rise in the market demand for a product may be caused by:

- an increase in consumers' incomes, for example due to rising employment
- a reduction in taxes on incomes
- a rise in the price of substitutes
- a fall in the price of complements
- consumers' tastes or fashions changing in favour of the product
- increased advertising of the product
- a rise in the population
- other factors, for example, a hot summer can boost demand for cold drinks and summer clothes.

A fall in market demand

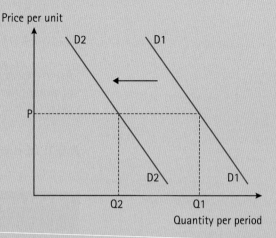

A fall in the market demand for a product may be caused by:

- a fall in consumers' incomes, for example due to rising unemployment
- an increase in taxes on incomes
- a fall in the price of substitutes
- a rise in the price of complements
- consumers' tastes or fashions changing in favour of other products
- product advertising being cut back or banned
- a fall in the population
- other factors, for example, a ban on smoking in public places may reduce demand for cigarettes.

ACTIVITY 2.7

What causes a shift in demand?

Income tax cut in Malaysian Budget

The Prime Minister of Malaysia yesterday announced a series of new tax measures and incentives. Among these was a cut in income tax rate charged on the highest individual annual incomes above MYR100,000 from 27% to 26%. The amount of income an individual is able to earn each year before paying tax was also raised from MYR8,000 to MYR9,000.

'These tax cuts will increase the disposable income of Malaysian taxpayers, make working more attractive and improve the international competitiveness of Malaysia's tax system', said a spokesperson for the Government.

Demand for online music services soars

The falling price of personal music players, such as the Apple iPod and Sony Walkman, able to download music, video and other files from the internet has boosted demand for such online content while sales of CDs and DVDs continue to fall.

According to new projections released by the United Nations, the World population is forecast to grow from 6.9 billion in 2010 to 8.9 billion in 2050.

India tries to keep its cool

Soaring temperatures across India are boosting the sales and prices of ice-cream and beverages, including Coca-Cola and Pepsi. As a result demand for sugar from food and drink manufacturers has also been rising rapidly.

The hot weather is also likely to benefit makers of lassi, a sweetened yogurt served on street corners in Northern India in the summers.

1 Look at the articles above and for each one suggest:
   a What factors have changed that could affect consumer demand for different goods and services?
   b Will consumer demand increase, fall or remain unchanged given the changing factor?

2 Now draw a diagram to show the market demand curve for soft drinks such as Pepsi and Coca-Cola, before and during the hot weather in India described in the article above and to the right.

Australia Raises Interest Rate to 4.75%

Concerns over accelerating price inflation have forced the Central Bank of Australia to raise the interest rate by 0.25% to 4.75%. The move will increase the cost of borrowing money for many consumers and businesses.

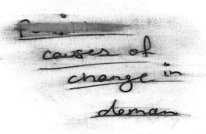

The following factors are likely to result in changes in demand conditions and shifts in market demand curves.

1 Changes in consumers' incomes

Consumers must not only want a product but must also be able to purchase it for their demand to be effective. A rise in consumer incomes will increase their ability to pay and is therefore likely to increase their demand for many goods and services. It follows that a fall in consumer incomes will reduce their demand for many products. However, the precise nature of the relationship between income and demand will depend on the type of product considered and the level of consumers' income. For example, a rise in income is unlikely to make most consumers want to buy more salt or newspapers each day or week, but it might allow them to travel less by bus and take a taxi more often, or even buy a bigger car.

In general, if the demand for a product tends to rise as incomes rise the product is said to be a **normal good**. On the other hand, if demand tends to fall as incomes rise the product is said to be an **inferior good**. For example, as incomes rise people can afford to travel longer distances by plane rather than by train. Long-distance train journeys might therefore appear to be an inferior good in consumer preferences as incomes rise.

2 Changes in taxes on incomes

Disposable income refers to the amount of income people have left to spend or save after any taxes on their incomes have been deducted. Any change in the level of income tax rates and allowances are therefore likely to result in a change in the quantity of goods and services demanded.

3 The prices and availability of other goods and services

Some of the goods and services we buy need other things, or accessories, to go with them. For example, cars need petrol, Blu-ray discs need disc players, bread is often consumed with butter or margarine. These **complementary goods** are said to be in **joint demand**.

If the prices of new cars rise, consumer demand for them may contract and in turn reduce the demand for petrol. A fall in the price of Blu-ray disc players is likely to result in a rise in the demand for Blu-ray discs. As the quantity of disc players demanded by consumers extends following the fall in their price, the market demand curve for discs will shift out to the right.

On the other hand, some goods and services are **substitutes**. A product is a substitute when its purchase can replace the want for another good or service. For example, margarine is considered a close substitute for butter. A rise in the price of butter may therefore result in some consumers switching their demand to margarine. Different makes of car are also close substitutes for each other. A fall in the price of Toyota cars may cause a fall in the demand for cars made by Ford.

A firm will find it useful to gather information on changes in the prices and quality of competing and complementary products from rival producers because any changes in them can affect consumer demand for their own products.

4 Changes in tastes, habits and fashion

The demand for goods and services can change dramatically because of changing fashions and the tastes of consumers. For example, many consumers all over the world are now demanding goods that are kinder to the environment and animals, and foods that are healthier.

Carefully planned advertising campaigns based on market research information about consumers can also help to influence tastes and shift demand curves for the advertised products out to the right. ➤ **4.4**

5 Population change

An increase in population will tend to increase the demand for many goods and services in a country. For example, the population of India has expanded rapidly over time and is forecast to grow to around 1.7 billion people by 2050. In contrast, population growth in many Western countries is now negligible. Birth and death rates have fallen and this has resulted in a rise in the average age of their populations. The growing number of middle-aged and elderly people has resulted in a changing pattern of demand. ➤ **5.3.1**

6 Other factors

There are a great many other factors that can affect consumer demand for different products. The weather is one example. A hot summer can boost sales

▼ Complementary goods

▼ Substitute goods

▼ Change in fashion can cause a shift in demand

of cold drinks and ices. A cold winter will increase the demand for warm clothing and fuel for heating. Higher interest rates can increase demand for savings schemes but reduce the amount of money people want to borrow from banks, including mortgages for house purchases. ➤ **3.2.1**

Changes in laws may also affect demand for some products. For example, it is illegal in many countries to ride a motorbike without a crash helmet, and a large number of countries have outlawed smoking in public places.

ACTIVITY 2.8

Competing or complementary?
Below is a list of goods and services. Think of some possible complements and substitutes for each of them.

Goods and services	Possible substitutes	Goods and services	Possible complements
Electric oven	?	Flat-screen televisions	?
Woollen jumpers		Fountain pens	
Gas supplies		Guitars	
iPods		Toothbrushes	
Passenger rail journeys		Computers	

SECTION 2.4.1

Definition of supply

SECTION 2.4.2

Price and supply

SECTION 2.4.3

Individual and market supply

What is supply?

Supply refers to the amount of a good or service firms or producers are willing to make and sell at different prices. The amount of a good or service producers are willing and able to make and sell to consumers in a market is known as the **quantity supplied** of that product, measured per period of time, say each week, month or year.

However, a private sector firm interested in profit will only make and sell a product if it can do so at a price over and above what it cost the firm to make. The higher the price of the product, the more the firm will supply because the more profit it will expect to make. This can be applied generally to the supply of all goods and services. As price rises, quantity supplied will usually extend.

The **market supply** of a product will be the sum of all the individual supply curves of producers competing to supply that product.

In general, the supply curve for any product will slope upwards, showing that as price rises, quantity supplied extends.

As price of a product falls, quantity supplied contracts. This is because the difference or margin for profit between the revenue from the sale of each item and the cost of producing each item will be reduced as price falls.

▼ A market supply curve for a product

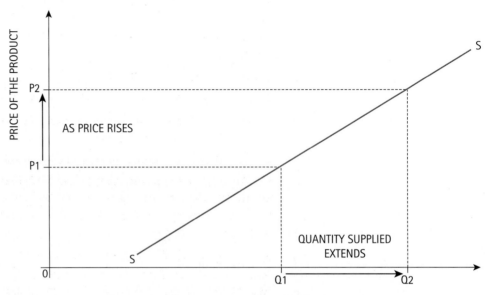

As price rises from P1 to P2 the market supply extends from Q1 to Q2. That is, a change in the price of the product causes a **movement along** the supply curve.

An extension in supply: as the price of a product rises, quantity supplied rises or extends.

A contraction in supply: as the price of a product falls, quantity supplied contracts.

ACTIVITY 2.9

The market supply curve
The following table represents the market supply schedule for silver-plated tankards. Copy the graph axis below, plot this information on the graph axis and label your curve the market supply curve (SS).

Price of tankards $	Market supply per month
20	1,600
16	1,100
12	700
8	300
6	100

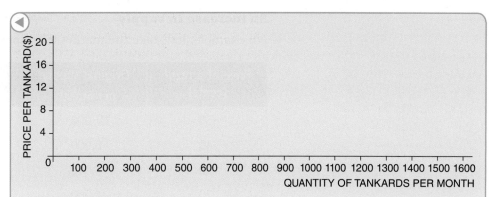

1 How does the quantity supplied change as price changes if all other factors that could affect supply do not change?

2 What will cause an extension in supply?

3 What will cause a contraction of supply?

4 Use your graph to work out how many tankards will be supplied at a price of:

  a $14   b $10

5 a If consumers wished to be able to buy 700 tankards each month how much must they be prepared to pay for them?

  b What will be the tankard producers' total revenue?

6 The following table displays the costs and revenues involved in the production and sale of tankards by all the producers in the market. Using the market supply schedule complete the table and explain why the market supply curve for tankards slopes upwards from left to right.

Output of tankards per month	Total cost ($)	Total revenue ($)*	Profit ($)
100	600	600	500
300	1,800		
700	4,000		
1,100	6,200		
1,600	9,000		

* at lowest price

Shifts in supply curves

Conditions of supply

The market supply curve for a product shows how the quantity or amount firms are willing and able to supply of that product will change as the price of the product varies. The relationship between quantity supplied and price will remain unchanged unless something other than price changes that affects supply. For example, changes in the weather or changes in technology can affect the supply of many different products regardless of the prices producers can sell them for. Changes in factors other than price will therefore result in shifts in market supply curves.

An increase in supply

For example, let's take the market for disposable razors.

Price of a razor (cents)	Original supply per month	Increased supply per month
50	10,000	12,000
40	8,000	10,000
30	6,000	8,000
20	4,000	6,000
10	2,000	4,000

▼ An increase in market supply

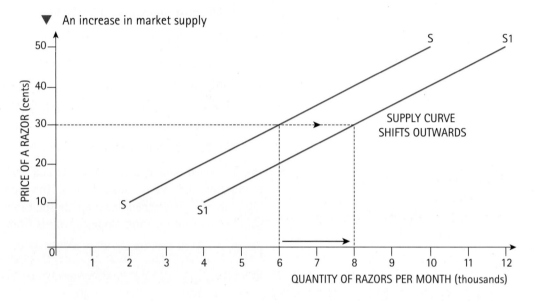

The diagram above shows an increase in the supply of disposable razors, but it could be any other good or service. At each and every price, razor producers are now willing to make and sell more razors than they did before. The whole supply curve has shifted outwards from SS to S1S1.

> **An increase in supply** means that producers are now more willing and able to supply a product than they were before at all possible prices. The market supply curve shifts out to the right.

A fall in supply

For example, let's take the market supply of potatoes.

Price per kg of potatoes (cents)	Original supply per month (kg)	Supply per month (kg)
100	50,000	40,000
80	40,000	30,000
60	30,000	20,000
40	20,000	10,000
20	10,000	0

▼ A fall in market supply

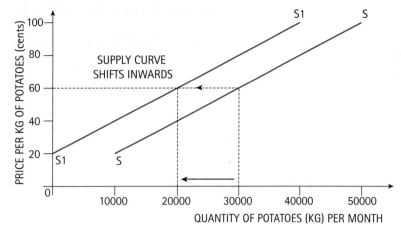

A fall in supply at all prices will cause the supply curve of a commodity to shift inwards from SS to S1S1.

> A **fall in supply** means that producers are now less willing and able to supply a product at each and every price than they were before at all possible prices. The market supply curve shifts in to the left.

ACTIVITY 2.10

What causes a shift in supply?

Read the following passage and try to pick out all the factors that have caused a change in the supply of potatoes and cabbages.

Farmer Bumpkin plans to plant five fields of potatoes and three fields of cabbages each year. The price he can usually get for a kilogram of potatoes is 30 cents, while the price of a kilogram of cabbages is 50 cents. Farmer Bumpkin has estimated that his time, effort, machinery and fertilizer costs add up to an average 12 cents per kg of potatoes and 20 cents per kg of cabbages.

- Which crop is the more profitable one to grow?

However, in the following season the price of potatoes rises to 45 cents per kg.

- What would you advise Farmer Bumpkin and farmers like him to do? Given your advice what will happen to the supply of cabbages?

In the very next growing season, Farmer Bumpkin discovers a new 'Speedo' cabbage harvester is available, and at a very reasonable price. He used to pay some boys and girls from the nearby village to help pick his crops each year, but now he can pick them all by himself using the machine. He estimates that this saving has reduced the average cost per cabbage grown to only 10 cents per kg.

- If the price of potatoes and cabbages have remained unchanged what would you now advise Farmer Bumpkin and farmers like him to do? How will this affect the supply of potatoes and cabbages?

- In the very next season the landowner who rents her land to Farmer Bumpkin decides to cut the rent of land from $500 per year to $300. That is, from $100 per field to $60 per field. Farmer Bumpkin wonders if he should rent an additional field now that it costs much less to produce potatoes and cabbages. If he decides to do this what will be the likely effect on the supply of his potatoes and cabbages?

- A farmer's year is not without its problems. Towards the end of the season an early but very hard frost damages Farmer Bumpkin's entire cabbage crop.

- What will happen to the supply of cabbages now?

- What factors have caused changes in the supply of potatoes and cabbages?

Changes in the following factors will cause changes in market supply conditions and shifts in the market supply curves of different product.

1 Changes in the cost of factors of production

By far the largest determinant of supply is the cost of resources used in production, including the cost of buying raw materials and power supplies, wages for labour, and rents or leasing costs for buildings and machinery.

A rise in the costs of production, for example due to workers gaining an increase in wages or an increase in the market prices of raw materials, will tend to reduce profits. Producers affected by these rising costs will tend to cut back their demand for labour and raw materials in an attempt to save money and will therefore be less willing and able to supply as much of their particular goods or services as they did before. An increase in the costs of other factors of production will also tend to have the same effect.

In contrast, a fall in the costs of land, labour and capital will tend to increase profits and market supply. This was the case in Activity 2.10 as Farmer Bumpkin enjoyed a cut in the rent he paid for the land he uses to grow cabbages, encouraging him to increase production.

Governments may also try to influence the willingness of private sector firms to supply some products using taxes and subsidies. Taxes can be regarded as an additional cost of production while subsidies help to offset costs. ➤ **2.11.2**

2 Changes in the price and profitability of other goods and services

Price changes act as the signals to private sector firms to move their resources to and from the production of different goods and services. In a free market, resources are allocated to those goods and services that will yield the most profit.

For example, in Activity 2.10 a rise in the price of potatoes will cause Farmer Bumpkin to move his resources from the production of cabbages into the production of potatoes. As a result, the supply curve for cabbages will shift inwards at every possible price as farmers are now less willing to grow them.

The same will apply to almost all other goods and services. A fall in the price of one may cause producers to cut production of that product and instead supply more of another, more profitable product.

3 Technological advance

Technical progress can improve the performance of machines, employees, production methods, management control, product quality and many other aspects of production. These changes can reduce production costs and increase the quantity of goods and services firms are able to produce with their factor resources. For example, advances in deep water mining technology and rig design have helped a number of countries to drill for oil in deep oceans once thought too costly to exploit. ➤ **3.6.1**

In the case of Farmer Bumpkin his new 'Speedo' cabbage harvester will allow him to shift the supply curve of his cabbages outwards.

4 Business optimism and expectations

In a market economic system, firms will allocate resources to the production of those goods and services they expect will earn them the most profit. As expectations change so too will the amount of different goods and services they are willing and able to supply. For example, fears of an economic downturn may cause some firms to move resources into the production of goods and services they feel will be less affected by a fall in consumer incomes and demand. For example, consumer demand for high-cost, luxury items such as cars and overseas holidays will often fall the most during economic recessions. Conversely, expectations of an economic recovery may result in a reallocation of scarce resources into new products and markets, thereby shifting their supply curves out towards the right. ➤ **4.6.3**

5 Global factors

The supply of goods and services can be affected by many factors that cannot be controlled by producers. For example, sudden changes in weather, international trade sanctions, wars, natural disasters and political factors may all have a material impact on the supply of many goods and services.

On the Bumpkin farm the weather will be a major factor affecting the supply of the farmer's crops. A good summer growing season will help increase the quantity he is able to supply.

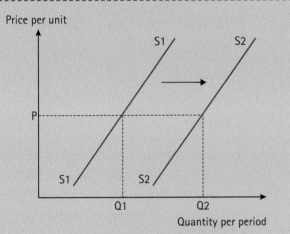

An increase in market supply

A rise in the market supply of a product may be caused by:

- other products becoming less profitable
- a fall in the cost of employing factors of production, for example due to falling wage costs or lower prices for materials
- an increase in resources, for example from new sources of raw materials
- technical progress and improvements in production processes and machinery
- an increase in business optimism and optimistic expectations of profit
- the government paying subsidies to producers and/or cutting taxes on profits
- other factors, such as a good summer to boost crops of fruit and vegetables.

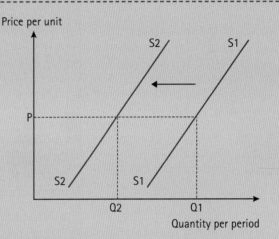

A fall in market supply

A fall in the market supply of a product may be caused by:

- other products becoming more profitable
- a rise in the cost of employing factors of production, for example due to increased hire charges for machinery
- a fall in the availability of resources, for example a shortage of skilled labour
- technical failures, such as a cut in power supplies or mechanical breakdowns
- a fall in business optimism and profit expectations becoming more pessimistic
- the government withdrawing subsidies and/or increasing taxes on profits
- other factors, such as wars and natural disasters.

Market equilibrium

Market disequilibrium

Reaching a market equilibrium

We have now looked at the two market forces that determine the price of a product. For each good and service there is a market supply schedule and a market demand schedule. If the two are combined we can find the price at which quantity demanded and quantity supplied will be equal. This is the market price at which the product will be exchanged. The market price of a particular product can also be found using its market demand and supply curves.

ACTIVITY 2.11

Finding the market price

Consider the market demand and supply schedules for chocolate bars.

Price of a chocolate bar (cents)	Quantity demanded per month	Quantity supplied per month
50	100,000	420,000
40	150,000	300,000
30	200,000	200,000
20	260,000	120,000
10	330,000	60,000
5	400,000	40,000

On graph paper plot the demand and supply curves for chocolate bars on one graph with 'Price of a chocolate bar' on the vertical axis and 'Quantity per month' along the bottom axis.

1   Using the above table state at which price demand equals supply.

   This will be the **market price** for chocolate bars because at that price producers are willing to make and sell just as many bars as consumers are willing to buy.

2   a   Find the market price of chocolate bars using your demand and supply curves.

   b   What is the quantity of chocolate bars traded at this price in the market?

3   a   When the quantity demanded is greater than the quantity supplied economists say there is an **excess demand**. At which prices in the table is there an excess demand for chocolate bars?

   b   Similarly, when the quantity supplied exceeds the quantity demanded there is said to be an **excess supply**. At which prices in the table is there an excess supply of chocolate bars?

4   a   If there is excess demand what do you think will happen to the price of chocolate bars?

   b   If there is excess supply what do you think will happen to their price?

   c   At which price will there be no excess demand or supply?

▼ Equilibrium in the market for chocolate bars

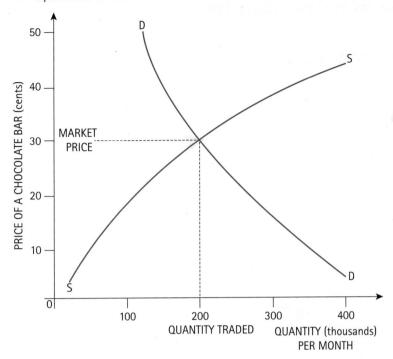

In the above exercise it should be clear that a market price will be determined at 30 cents per chocolate bar. Only here will market demand equal market supply. Another name for market price is **equilibrium price** because it is the price at which the amount supplied equals or satisfies the amount demanded.

In a demand and supply diagram, equilibrium occurs where the market demand and supply curves cross each other. In the diagram to the left, the equilibrium quantity of chocolate bars traded each week is 20,000 at the equilbrium or market price of 30 cents per bar.

At prices higher than the market price (for example 40c) firms will supply more than consumers demand and so there will be an **excess supply**. In order to persuade consumers to buy up this excess supply, the price will have to fall.

At prices lower than the market price (for example 20 cents) the quantity demanded by consumers exceeds what firms will supply. There will be an **excess demand**. As a result, the price will rise.

When demand does not equal supply this is known as a **disequilibrium**.

▼ Disequilibrium in the market for chocolate bars

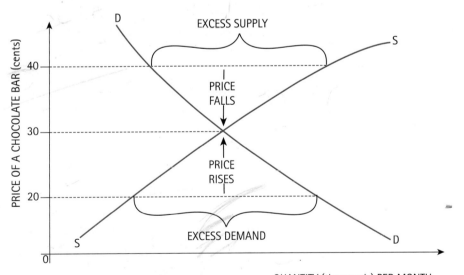

Only when a market is in equilibrium, where the market supply matches the market demand, will there be no pressures to change the market price. That is, there will be no excess demand or excess supply. As a result the equilibrium or market price will be stable. Only a change in the market demand or supply conditions will cause the equilibrium price and quantity traded of the product to change.

Causes of price changes

Consequences of price changes

Changes in market prices

Changes in market prices will occur as a result of changes in demand and/or supply conditions.

▼ An increase in demand and market price

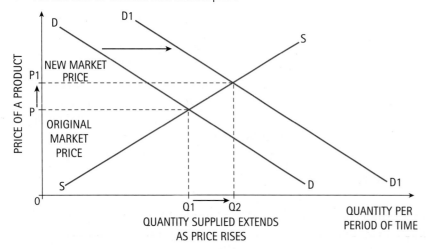

1 A shift in the market demand curve

An increase in demand for a product, because people's incomes have risen or because the price of a substitute good has gone up, will cause its market demand curve to shift outwards.

In the diagram to the left it shifts from DD to D1D1. As a result, the market price rises from P to P1. The increase in price is a signal to producers to expand or extend their supply of the product from Q1 to Q2 to satisfy the increased quantity consumers want to buy.

A fall in consumer demand will therefore have the opposite effect. Market price will fall and producers will cut the amount they are willing to supply as their sales and profits fall.

ACTIVITY 2.12

A fall in demand and market price

Below is a market demand and supply schedule for ballpoint pens.

Price per pen (cents)	Original demand per week	Original supply per week
300	100	500
250	200	400
200	300	300
150	400	200
100	500	100

1   Plot and label the demand curve (DD) and supply curve (SS) for ballpoint pens.

2   Mark in the market price (P) and the quantity traded (Q) at this price.

3   Imagine now that demand falls by 200 units at each and every price. Draw and label the new demand curve (D1D1).

4   What is the new market price (P1) and the new quantity traded (Q1)? Show these on your graph.

5   What has happened to supply and why?

6   Suggest four reasons why demand for ballpoint pens might fall.

2 A shift in the market supply curve

An increase in the amount producers are willing and able to supply of a particular product will cause its market supply curve to shift outwards, from SS to S1S1 in the diagram below. This may occur if there is a fall in the costs of production, for example, due to falling wages or improvements in the speed and accuracy of equipment due to technical progress. As a result of the increase in supply the equilibrium or market price will fall from P to P1. As the market price falls consumers will extend their demand for the product from Q to Q1.

▼ An increase in supply and market price

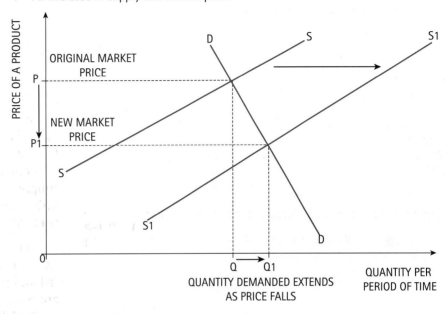

ACTIVITY 2.13

A fall in supply and market price

Below is the market demand and supply schedule for wheat (tonnes per year).

Price per tonne (dollars)	Original demand per year	Original supply per year
500	100,000	500,000
400	200,000	400,000
300	300,000	300,000
200	400,000	200,000
100	500,000	100,000

1   Plot and label the demand curve (DD) for wheat and its supply curve (SS).

2   Mark in the market price (P) and the quantity traded (Q) at this price.

3   Imagine now that supply falls by 200,000 tonnes at each and every price. Draw and label the new supply curve (S1S1).

4   What is the new market price (P1) and the new quantity traded (Q1)? Show these on your graph.

5   What has happened to demand and why?

6   Suggest four reasons why the supply of wheat may fall.

A fall in the supply of a product will cause its market supply curve to shift inwards and market price will rise. Consumer demand for the product will contract along the market demand curve as the market price increases until demand equals supply once again.

We have now looked in detail at how the **price mechanism** works in a free market. The forces of demand and supply establish the market price of a product and the quantity producers will exchange with consumers at this price.

Changes in demand and supply conditions will result in changes in market price and the allocation of resources to the production of different goods and services. For example, an increase in consumer demand for a product will raise its market price making its production more profitable. As a result, firms will allocate more resources to the production of that product to satisfy the increased consumer demand for it. Because resources are limited, they will be moved from the production of less profitable products.

ACTIVITY 2.14

Families count cost of rush for a flat-screen TV

FAMILIES who paid out for the latest in large flat-screen TVs might be wishing now that they had waited a little longer.

Manufacturers have produced so many that there is a worldwide glut. Retailers are admitting that prices for state-of-the-art LCD and plasma sets, which originally cost in the thousands, are now 'dropping every day'.

Manufacturers and retailers launched a big push on the sets over the last six months, tied to the World Cup and the launch of high definition services promising much sharper pictures and sound.

During the build-up to the football World Cup, major retailers were selling a high value flat-screen television every 15 seconds. But even during the busiest periods retailers warned that there would be a lull in sales immediately after the tournament, which has now led to rival stores having to slash prices to clear stocks.

In the meantime, so many large flat-screen TVs have been produced that the glut has forced manufacturers to slash their premium prices.

A flat-out market

1   What happened to the demand for large flat-screen televisions in the run-up to the World Cup?

2   What impact do you think the increase in demand for large flat-screen televisions (larger than 32 inches) has had on the market for TV models with screen sizes less than 32 inches?

3   What happened to the supply of large flat-screen televisions? What affect did this have on the prices of these products?

4   What is likely to happen to the quantity traded of flat-screen televisions following the increase in their supply?

5   Draw a diagram to illustrate the movements in demand and supply curves in the market for large flat-screen televisions.

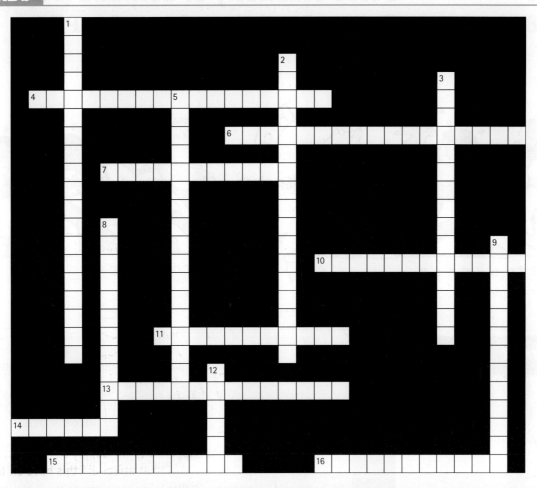

Clues across

4. A line drawn on a diagram to show the relationship between market prices and the quantity demanded of a given product. The line is the sum of the individual demand curves of all the consumers of that product. (6, 6, 5)
6. Term used describe the movement along a market demand curve for a product as its market price falls (9, 2, 6)
7. The price in a market that balances market demand and market supply. Also known as the equilibrium price. (6, 5)
10. This will occur in a market when market demand is greater than the market supply because the price of the product is below what it should be to balance demand and supply (6, 6)
11. Products that compete to satisfy the same or a very similar consumer demand, for example, margarine and butter (11)
13. The system present in a market economy in which changes in consumer demand and market prices determine what goods and services will be produced with scarce resources (5, 9)
14. The willingness and ability of producers to make and sell a given product (6)
15. A collective term for products for which demand will rise as consumer's incomes rise (6, 5)
16. Products that are in joint demand because they are consumed together, for example, razors and razor blades (5 6)

Clues down

1. Term used describe the movement along a market supply curve of a product as its market price falls (11, 2, 6)
2. An economic situation in which the market demand for a product is exactly equal to the quantity producers are willing and able to supply to the market. At this point, the market price of this product will be stable. (6, 11)
3. The willingness and ability of one or more consumers to purchase a product (9, 6)
5. A line drawn on a diagram to show the relationship between market prices and the quantity supplied of a given product. The line is the sum of the individual supply curves of all the producers of that product. (6, 6, 5)
8. This will occur in a market when the market supply is greater than the market demand because the price of the product is above what it should be to balance demand and supply (6, 6)
9. Demand for these type of products will tend to fall as consumer's incomes rise because consumer's will be able to afford to buy better or more superior products instead (8, 5)
12. The desire of one or more consumers to buy and use a product to satisfy their needs or wants (6)

Unit 2.7 Price elasticity of demand (PED)
Unit 2.8 Price elasticity of supply (PES)

Definition of PED

Calculation of PED

What is price elasticity of demand (PED)?

Consumer demand for most goods and services will contract if their price is raised, but by how much? Producers will want to know the answer to this important question.

For example, a train company will want to know what is likely to happen to consumer demand for its services, and therefore the revenue it earns from tickets, if it increases its fares. Increasing fares in peak periods when many people have to travel by train to and from work in busy cities may have very little impact on demand because many people have few or no alternative means of travel. Journeys by road by car or bus may take too long, the traveller may not own a car, or car parking in the city is too expensive. However, raising train fares for journeys off-peak and at weekends may cause demand, and therefore revenue, to fall significantly because people may decide against travelling and spend their leisure time doing something else or travelling by car or bus instead because the roads are not so busy.

Consider the two diagrams below.

The demand curve is quite steep. As price rises by 25% from $2.00 to $2.50 demand contracts very little from 1,000 to 900 units per period, a fall of just 10%. This might be very similar to the demand for train journeys during busy peak periods.

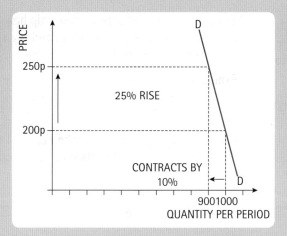

The demand curve is quite flat. As price rises by 25% from $2.00 to $2.50 demand contracts significantly, from 1,000 to 500 units, a fall of 50%. This could be what the demand curve for off-peak travel by train looks like.

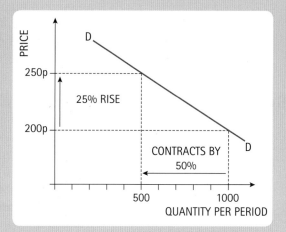

In this case **demand** is said to be **price inelastic** as the percentage change in price is much larger than the percentage change in demand.

In this case **demand** is said to be **price elastic** as the percentage change in price is less than the percentage change in demand.

The responsiveness of consumer demand to changes in the price of a good or service is known as the **price elasticity of demand (PED)** of that product.

If a small change in the price of a product causes a big change in the quantity demanded by consumers, their demand for that product is said to be **price elastic**. That is, the quantity demanded 'stretches' (extends or contracts) significantly when the price of the product is changed.

Price elasticity of demand (PED) 69

On the other hand, if a small change in the price of a product causes only a very minor change in quantity demanded, consumer demand for that product is said to be **price inelastic**. That is, the quantity demanded only extends or contracts by a relatively small amount as the product price changes.

ACTIVITY 2.15

A problem to 'stretch' you

Assume there is a rise of about 10% in the prices of the following goods. State whether there is likely to be large, small or no change in the quantity demanded. Then state whether you think demand is price elastic or inelastic, and why.

Product	Small or large change in quantity demanded	Price elastic or price inelastic	Why?
Electricity			
Luxury holiday			
Bread			
A Toyota car			
A newspaper			

Products such as electricity and bread are essential items for many consumers. An increase in price may only have a very small impact on the quantity demanded. Demand for these goods therefore tends to be relatively price inelastic. Similarly, purchases of newspapers only account for a relatively small amount of many people's incomes and this tends to make demand for them price inelastic. In contrast, demand for more luxurious, high-value products such as holidays and cars may contract significantly if their prices rise. Demand for these types of products tends to be price elastic.

How to calculate PED

PED compares the percentage change in quantity demanded with the percentage change in price that caused it. For example, imagine producers of cricket bats raise the price of each bat from $20 to $25, that is, by 25%. If the quantity demanded contracts from 1,000 per week to 500 per week then this represents a 50% reduction in quantity demanded, which is double the percentage change in price. As demand has changed by a greater percentage than price, demand is price elastic. That is, each 1% change in price will cause a 2% change in the quantity of cricket bats demanded.

If, on the other hand, the percentage change in price caused a much smaller percentage change in quantity demanded, demand would be price inelastic.

The PED for a product is calculated as follows:

$$PED = \frac{\% \text{ change in quantity demanded}}{\% \text{ change in price}}$$

Percentage changes are worked out as follows:

$$\% \text{ change in quantity demanded} = \frac{\text{change in quantity}}{\text{original quantity}} \times \frac{100}{1}$$

$$\% \text{ change in price} = \frac{\text{change in price}}{\text{original price}} \times \frac{100}{1}$$

For example, look at the following demand schedule.

Price of the good	Quantity demanded per week
$5	100
$4	110

Taking $5 as the original price and 100 as the original quantity, the change in price is $1 and the change in quantity 10.

1 % change in quantity demanded $= \dfrac{10}{100} \times \dfrac{100}{1} = \dfrac{1,000}{100} = 10\%$

2 % change in price $\dfrac{\$1}{\$5} \times \dfrac{100}{1} = \dfrac{100}{5} = 20\%$

3 PED $= \dfrac{\% \text{ change in quantity demanded}}{\% \text{ change in price}} = \dfrac{10\%}{20\%} = \dfrac{1}{2} = 0.5$

Demand is price inelastic because the percentage change in price of 20% is greater than the percentage change in quantity demanded of 10%. The PED is 0.5.

ACTIVITY 2.16

Using the formula

Below is the demand schedule for tins of beans.

Price of beans per tin (cents)	Market demand per week
40	1,000
30	1,500

1 Calculate the PED. (*Hint:* Use 40 cents as your original price.)

2 Comment on its value.

3 What will the demand curve for beans look like? Draw a simple diagram to show this.

The demand for baked beans in the above example is price elastic because the percentage increase in quantity demanded of 50% is greater than the 25% fall in price that caused it (PED = 2). The demand curve for beans will therefore be quite flat.

In general when PED is **greater than 1**, demand is price **elastic**. If PED is **less than 1**, demand is price **inelastic**.

Determinants of PED

Why is consumer demand for some products insensitive to changes in prices and yet highly price elastic for others? A number of factors can explain whether demand for a product will be price elastic or inelastic.

1 If the product a necessity

Demand for products that are necessities is usually more price inelastic than the demand for products that satisfy consumer wants. This is because it is difficult to go without necessary items such as basic foods and medicines if their price is increased. We are also unlikely to buy significantly more bread and other basic foodstuffs or medicines if their prices fall.

2 The number of close substitutes a product has

When consumers can choose between a large number of substitutes for a particular product, demand for any one of them is likely to be price elastic. For example, there are many different brands of washing liquids, soups and crisps. If the price of one brand increases, consumers can easily switch their demand to less expensive ones. In contrast, demand for a product will be price inelastic when it has few substitutes. For example, there are few alternative sources of electricity.

3 The amount of time consumers have to search for substitutes

If the price of a product rises consumers will search for cheaper substitutes.

The longer they have, the more likely they are to find one. For example, large screen televisions are expensive items and not a necessity. Consumers can afford to spend some time looking around for the best products at the best prices. Demand will therefore be more price elastic in the long run.

4 The cost of switching to a different supplier

Switching demand to an alternative supplier can be expensive even if their products are cheaper if it means breaking a contract with your existing supplier. This is because some products such as telephone and broadband services, electricity, car insurance and satellite television services, are usually only supplied to consumers who have agreed to long supply contracts. These contracts will 'lock' consumers into an agreement with a particular suppliers for periods of 12 or 18 months or possibly longer, and usually at a fixed price per month or per unit supplied. Consumers may have to pay a fee to be released early from these contracts. They may also need to purchase different equipment, for example, a new wireless router or new satellite receiver, to use the services of another supplier.

5 The proportion of a consumer's income spent on the product

Goods such as matches or newspapers may be price inelastic in demand as they do not cost very much and any rise in their price will only require a tiny bit more of a person's income. If the price of cars was to rise by 10% this could mean paying an extra $1,000 or more for a car. This is a considerable proportion of a person's income. Demand for cars and other expensive items is therefore more likely to be price elastic.

Modest rise in sales of *Daily Star* after price cut

The decision to slash the price of the *Daily Star* newspaper by 50% helped to boost month on month sales of the tabloid newspaper by 0.27% to 864,315 copies.

A study by health economists in Japan found that the price elasticity of demand for influenza vaccinations was very low at just 0.0441 to 0.0187 nationally.

In contrast, a study of Australian livestock grazing industries found price elasticities of demand for beef, lamb and pork were between 1.4 and 1.6. There was also evidence that the meats were strong substitutes for each other in consumer demand.

Toyota sales surge after slashing prices

The world's biggest carmaker saw US sales of its vehicles rise by 41% in March from a year earlier, having fallen 16% year on year in January and 9% in February.

Toyota attributed this increase in sales to providing buyers with discounts of up to $2,250 a vehicle last month. The price incentives, including interest-free loans and discount leases, were worth an average of 10% on each new vehicle.

1 Why do you think the PED for flu vaccinations was much lower than the PEDs for different meats?

2 What is meant by beef, lamb and pork being strong substitutes in consumer demand?

3 Calculate the PEDs for Toyota cars and the *Daily Star* newspaper suggested by the data in the articles. For which product is consumer demand more price elastic and why?

SECTION 2.7.4

SECTION 2.7.5

The relationship between PED and total consumer spending on a product

PED and total spending on a product, and revenue

Significance of PED

What will happen to the amount consumers spend on a product when its price rises or falls? What effect will it have on the revenue its suppliers earn from its sale? The answers to these questions will depend on the price elasticity of consumer demand for that product.

If demand for a product is price elastic, consumers will spend less on the product as its price is increased because they will switch their demand to cheaper alternatives. Firms selling the product will therefore lose revenue following an increase in its price.

For example, the producer of Whizzo chocolate bars has increased their price by 10% from $1.00 to $1.10. As a result, weekly sales of its chocolate bar have fallen by 20%, from 2,000 to 1,600. This means total weekly spending by consumers on the chocolate bar has fallen from $2,000 to $1,760 per week. The producer of Whizzo bars is therefore losing $240 in revenue each week as a result of having increased its price by 10%.

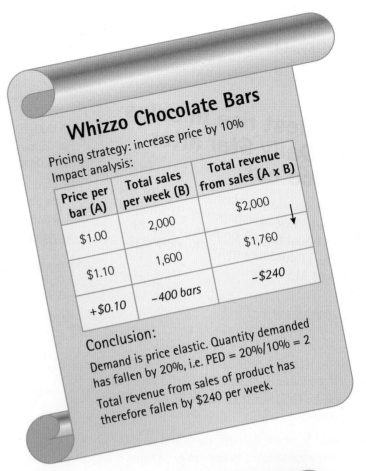

Whizzo Chocolate Bars

Pricing strategy: increase price by 10%
Impact analysis:

Price per bar (A)	Total sales per week (B)	Total revenue from sales (A x B)
$1.00	2,000	$2,000
$1.10	1,600	$1,760
+$0.10	−400 bars	−$240

Conclusion:
Demand is price elastic. Quantity demanded has fallen by 20%, i.e. PED = 20%/10% = 2

Total revenue from sales of product has therefore fallen by $240 per week.

If the producer of Whizzo chocolate bars wanted to increase its revenue then it should reduce the price of the bars instead to encourage consumers to switch their demand to its product from more expensive alternatives.

If the price elasticity of demand for its chocolate bars is 2 then a 10% reduction in their price from $1.00 to 90 cents would increase the weekly quantity sold by 20% from 2,000 to 2,400. Total revenue from sales of the bars would increase by $160 per week.

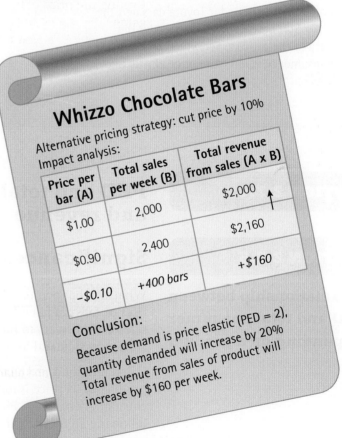

Whizzo Chocolate Bars

Alternative pricing strategy: cut price by 10%
Impact analysis:

Price per bar (A)	Total sales per week (B)	Total revenue from sales (A x B)
$1.00	2,000	$2,000
$0.90	2,400	$2,160
−$0.10	+400 bars	+$160

Conclusion:
Because demand is price elastic (PED = 2), quantity demanded will increase by 20% Total revenue from sales of product will increase by $160 per week.

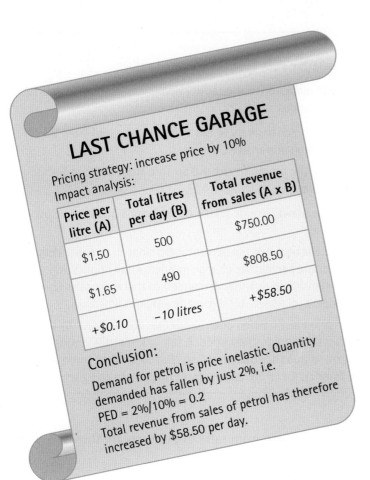

LAST CHANCE GARAGE

Pricing strategy: increase price by 10%

Impact analysis:

Price per litre (A)	Total litres per day (B)	Total revenue from sales (A x B)
$1.50	500	$750.00
$1.65	490	$808.50
+$0.10	–10 litres	+$58.50

Conclusion:

Demand for petrol is price inelastic. Quantity demanded has fallen by just 2%, i.e. PED = 2%/10% = 0.2

Total revenue from sales of petrol has therefore increased by $58.50 per day.

Now consider a garage selling petrol near the junction with a major motorway. The next nearest petrol station is 20 miles away. Drivers needing to fill up their cars or trucks with petrol before joining the motorway therefore have no alternative but to buy petrol from the garage. Demand for its petrol is therefore likely to be price inelastic. Due to this the garage owners decide to increase the price of each litre of petrol by 10% from $1.50 to $1.65. The impact on demand and revenue from the sale of its petrol are shown in the diagram and table.

As there is only a 2% fall in the quantity of petrol demanded from the garage following the 10% increase in price, consumers end up spending more in total each day on their purchases of petrol. The increase in price therefore increases the total revenue of the garage because demand for its petrol is price inelastic.

Cutting the price of its petrol would therefore not be a sensible strategy for the garage. Demand, and therefore total sales of petrol, are unlikely to increase very much. As a result, total revenue is likely to fall.

ACTIVITY 2.18

What happens to total revenue?

Below are two demand schedules, one for bread and one for passenger flights between two US cities.

Price per loaf	Quantity demanded per month
*25 cents	10,000
20 cents	10,500

Price per airline ticket	Quantity demanded per month
*$500	1,000
$400	1,800

* original price and quantity

◀

1   In each case calculate the PED. Comment on their values.

2   Calculate the total revenue (price × quantity demanded) for bread and for airline tickets at each price.

3   a   Would you advise bread-makers to cut the price of a loaf from 25 cents to 20 cents? Explain your answer.

    b   Would you advise the airline to cut the air fare from $500 to $400? Explain your answer.

4   Using the information above, decide which of the words in italics below does not apply in each case.

    a   Demand is price elastic when the percentage change in quantity demanded is *more/less* than the percentage change in price. A fall in price will cause a *large/small* extension in quantity demanded so that total sales revenue *falls/rises*. If price is increased, total revenue would *fall/rise*.

    b   Demand is price inelastic when quantity demanded changes by a *greater/smaller* percentage than price. A fall in price will cause a *small/large* extension in quantity demanded so that total sales revenue *falls/rises*. A rise in price therefore causes total revenue to *fall/rise*.

PED and revenues producers earn from sales of products are therefore very closely linked.

In the activity above, because the demand for bread is price inelastic (PED = 0.25) a small reduction in its price will result in a loss of revenue. This is because as its price falls the extension in demand for bread is relatively minor. It follows that increasing the price of bread will increases the amount consumers spend in total on bread and therefore increase the revenues of bakers because the contraction in demand for bread will be small.

In contrast, in the case of airline tickets it is advisable for the airline operators to lower the fare from $500 to $400. This is because demand for air travel is price elastic (PED = 4). Ticket sales will expand proportionately more than the cut in price and revenue will rise. An increase in fares will therefore reduce revenue if demand for air travel is price elastic because demand will contract by more than the percentage increase in price.

Why knowledge of PED is useful

Knowledge of the price elasticity of demand therefore allows firms to optimise the pricing and promotional strategies for their products to best achieve their sales, revenue or profit targets.

For example, it would not be sensible for a firm to significantly increase the price of its product if demand for it is price elastic because it has many close substitutes. Consumers would simply switch their demand to cheaper alternatives.

However, the firm may be able to persuade consumers to continue buying its product despite the increase in its price through advertising and other promotional strategies, for example, by offering customers free gifts or entries into competitions to win prizes if they make repeated purchases. Advertising may also be used to persuade consumers that the product supplied by the firm is of better quality than rival products and therefore worth paying extra for. In these ways a firm may be able to make consumer demand for its product less elastic so it is able to increase its price without losing sales.

In contrast, a firm that supplies a product which has few competitors and for which consumer demand is price inelastic will be able to increase its revenues by raising its price.

Similarly, knowledge of the price elasticity of demand for different products will be useful to a government seeking to use taxes to raise public revenue or to dissuade consumers from buying harmful products.

For example, many governments levy excise taxes on top of the prices of cigarettes to discourage people from smoking. However, despite taxes on cigarettes many people continue to smoke because demand for them is relatively price inelastic. ➤ 4.3.3

In contrast, using a tax to increase the price of a product for which demand is price elastic will reduce the quantity consumed. For example, many governments have introduced taxes or charges on plastic carrier bags to reduce the number we use and throw away because of the harm they cause to wildlife and the natural environment.

How can knowledge of the PED of different consumer groups help firms to plan their pricing strategies? Why do you think advertising may reduce the price sensitivity of consumers?

FLAT PACKED AND PRICED

IKEA, the Swedish home products company that designs and sells ready-to-assemble furniture, appliances and home accessories, is the world's largest furniture retailer with more than 300 stores in over 35 countries. It opened its first store in China in 1998 and now has a number of outlets across the country including in Shenyang, IKEA's second largest store in the world with 47,000m² of floorspace.

Whereas in most areas of the world IKEA products are considered 'good value' by most consumers, in China its products were thought to be aimed at consumers with high incomes. However, this also meant that many Chinese consumers were very sensitive to price and a small reduction could persuade many more to buy IKEA products because they also wanted to be associated with a high income 'lifestyle' created by the IKEA brand. After cutting all its prices by 10% IKEA's China sales rose by 35% that year and 50% the following year.

It all Ads up!

Market research carried out by the Neilson Company and Arbitron in the USA using a panel of 11,000 people across 5,000 households found that it is possible to identify consumer groups whose sensitivity to price depends on their exposure to advertising.

Their analysis found that increased exposure to advertising appeared to reduce the sensitivity of consumers' demand to price changes: there was a negative relationship between price elasticity of demand and advertising exposure. Audiences with the highest exposures showed the least sensitivity to price changes.

EXAM PREPARATION 2.1

a   Define *price elasticity of demand*. [2]

b   Using examples, explain why different products have different price elasticities of demand. [4]

c   Many more people travel by aeroplane today than 10 years ago. With the help of a demand and supply diagram, analyse what might have happened in the market for travel to cause this increase. [6]

d   Discuss whether knowledge of price elasticity of demand is of use to a company selling holiday tours. [8]

Definition of PES

Calculation of PES

Assuming other factors remain unchanged, an increase in consumer demand for a product will cause an increase in its market price. As a result of this price mechanism there will be an extension in the market supply of the product. However, as economists we will want to know by how much quantity supplied will change in response to a price change. **Price elasticity of supply (PES)** measures the responsiveness of quantity supplied to a change in price.

▼ Price elasticity of supply (PES)

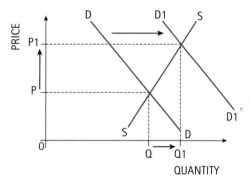 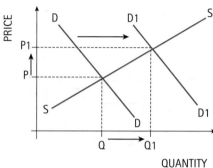

In the above diagram the increase in demand from DD to D1D1 has caused market price to rise from P to P1. However, despite this large rise in price the extension in supply is only small from Q to Q1. Supply is price inelastic.

In this diagram the increase in demand from DD to D1D1 has caused only a small increase in price from P to P1 but a large extension in supply from Q to Q1. Supply is price elastic.

To measure PES we use the following formula:

$$PES = \frac{\% \text{ change in quantity supplied}}{\% \text{ change in price}}$$

If the percentage change in price is greater than the percentage change in quantity supplied, supply is price inelastic and the value of PES will be less than 1.

If the percentage change in price causes a much larger percentage change in quantity supplied, supply is price elastic. PES will therefore be greater than 1.

Below is the supply schedule for carnations, a popular cut-flower, in the springtime.

Price per bunch of five carnations	Quantity supplied per month
100 cents	10,000
200 cents	12,000

$$\text{\% change in quantity supplied} = \frac{\text{change in quantity}}{\text{original quantity}} \times \frac{100}{1} = \frac{2{,}000}{10{,}000} \times \frac{100}{1} = 20\%$$

$$\text{\% change in price} = \frac{\text{change in price}}{\text{original price}} \times \frac{100}{1} = \frac{100c}{100c} \times \frac{100}{1} = 100\%$$

$$\text{PES} = \frac{\text{\% change in quantity supplied}}{\text{\% change in price}} = \frac{20}{100} = 0.2$$

The PES of carnations is less than 1, that is, supply is price inelastic. This is because it will take some time to plant and grow more carnations following an increase in their market price.

SECTION 2.8.3

SECTION 2.8.4

Determinants of PES

Significance of PES

How much and how quickly the supply of a product by a supplier is able to respond to an increase in consumer demand and price, will depend on a number of factors.

What affects PES?

1 The availability of stock of finished goods and components

Firms with plenty of stock can increase the supply of their products relatively quickly and easily. For example, many shops hold a stock of goods in reserve they can draw from to sell in case there is an unexpected increase in demand. Similarly, many manufacturers keep a stock of both finished goods and component parts in case of a sudden increase in demand for their products.

2 Degree of unused or 'spare' production capacity

Some firms may be able to increase output of their goods or services relatively quickly if they have spare or unused machinery and other equipment. For example, a firm could stay open and remain productive for longer periods each day or by working at weekends. Employees could be paid overtime to work more than their normal hours.

3 Time period required to adjust the scale of production

The supply of a product will be less elastic the longer the time period its producers require to increase their output.

At any given point in time, the momentary supply of goods and services is fixed. No matter how much their prices rise, their supply will be unable to respond immediately. For example, a shop will only have a fixed quantity of newspapers, cakes or flowers to sell each morning. It will take time to obtain more of these items unless the shop holds some in stock. In all these cases their market supply curves will be a vertical line showing that whatever their price, the quantity supplied is **perfectly price inelastic**.

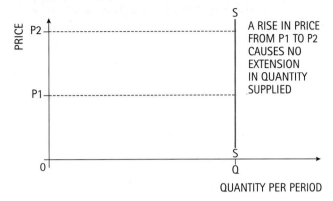

▼ Supply at any given moment is fixed

A RISE IN PRICE FROM P1 TO P2 CAUSES NO EXTENSION IN QUANTITY SUPPLIED

In the short run, a firm will only be able to increase the quantity it produces and supplies of its product by using up any spare productive capacity is has, for example, by working longer hours. For example, more flowers could be picked to meet an increase in consumer demand for them. However, once all the flowers available have been picked it will take time to plant more seeds and on more land to further increase their supply.

Similarly, existing machinery in manufacturing plants can only be run 24 hours each day. It will take time to install additional machines and to recruit more skilled workers to operate them.

The supply of many goods and services is therefore relatively price inelastic in the short run.

▼ Supply is price inelastic in the short run

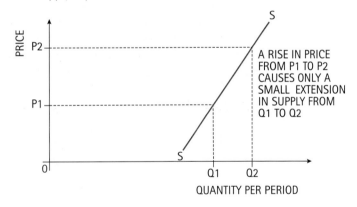

A RISE IN PRICE FROM P1 TO P2 CAUSES ONLY A SMALL EXTENSION IN SUPPLY FROM Q1 TO Q2

In the long run, firms can obtain more labour, land and capital to expand their scale of production, so in the long run the supply of most products becomes more price elastic. ➤ **3.5.5**

▼ Supply in the long run is price elastic

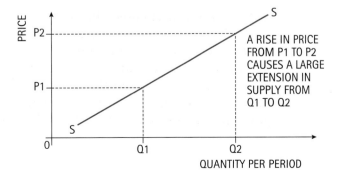

A RISE IN PRICE FROM P1 TO P2 CAUSES A LARGE EXTENSION IN SUPPLY FROM Q1 TO Q2

Price elasticity of demand (PED)

However, while it may take a car and van rental business only a few months to buy more vehicles, rent more premises and recruit some more workers it may take several years for a shipbuilder to build and supply more ships. Similarly, it will take several years for an electricity supplier to build more power stations to increase the supply of electricity.

4 The mobility and availability of factors of production

Ultimately the ability of firms to expand production and supply in response to an increase in consumer demand and prices will depend on the availability of resources. If it is easy to employ more factors of production then the more price elastic supply will be.

However, if the economy is already using most of its scarce resources then firms will find it difficult and expensive to buy or hire additional factors of production. The supply of many goods and services will therefore be relatively price inelastic when an economy is at or near full employment.

The more mobile resources are the easier it will be to reallocate resources from the production of products for which demand and prices are falling to the production of more popular and profitable products. Therefore, the greater the mobility of labour and other factors of production, the more responsive supply will be to changes in consumer demand and prices. However, workers do not always have the right skills and may be in the wrong locations. Many machines will have been purpose built for particular production processes.
➤ **1.2.2**

ACTIVITY 2.19

Stretching supply

Below are imaginary supply schedules for natural rubber and man-made rubber.

Price per kg (cents)	Quantity supplied of natural rubber per month
80	1,000
100	1,100

Price per kg (cents)	Quantity supplied of man-made rubber per month
80	2,000
100	2,800

1   Calculate the PES for natural rubber and man-made rubber.

2   Comment on their values and suggest reasons why they differ.

Why is PES important?
It is important for firms and for their customers to know how quickly and effectively suppliers can respond to changing market conditions.

Most firms will want to expand their supply as quickly as possible to take full advantage of any increase in demand and the prices of their products. Increased demand means more customers and more sales and higher prices means more profit. A high price elasticity of supply is therefore desirable for many firms.

A firm may take a number of actions to improve its speed of response to changing market conditions over that of its competitors. These actions may include:

- increasing storage to keep stocks of its products

- investing in additional and spare productive capacity

- employing the latest production equipment and processes

- training its workers in new skills so they become more mobile and are able to undertake a wider variety of tasks.

However, the more difficult it is to increase the supply of a product in response to an increase in demand and the longer it takes, the lower the impact will be on sales and the greater the impact will be on its market price.

▼ The lower the price elasticity of supply the greater the impact of a shift in demand on the market price of a product

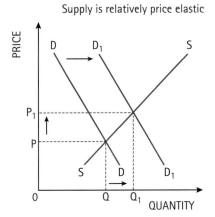

The supply of many necessary items is inelastic, including medicines, many food items, houses and electricity. This is because it takes time to develop and test new medicines and it takes both time and additional land to grow more fruit and vegetables and to build new homes and power stations.

Rising populations are increasing the demand for food, medicines, housing and power and the prices for these things are increasing as a result. This is causing hardship for many people especially those on low incomes who cannot afford these higher prices. In turn, many governments are having to increase support to poor families and to subsidize the expansion of farming, house building, drug development and renewable energy in their economies.

But what if there is a fall in demand for a product instead? How quickly can and should supply respond? In some cases it may not be sensible for firms to cut production to reduce supply too quickly especially if the fall in demand is only temporary, for example, if an unusually warm spell of weather during the winter reduces the demand for coats for a short while.

Some firms are also unable to reduce supply quickly in response to falling demand. For example, farmers cannot easily reduce their supply of corn and other crops once they have been planted, grown and harvested. If there is a fall in demand then there will be an excess supply and the prices of their crops and their profits will fall sharply.

The low price elasticity of many agricultural products means that prices and, therefore, farm incomes are very volatile. Because supply is slow to respond, any sudden increase in demand will result in a shortage and rapidly rising prices while a sudden fall in demand will result in an excess supply and falling prices. Knowing this allows both farmers and governments to prepare for this volatility. For example, farmers can draw from savings to support their businesses when revenues and profits are falling. Governments may also provide farmers with income support and import crops when there are shortages to stabilize prices.

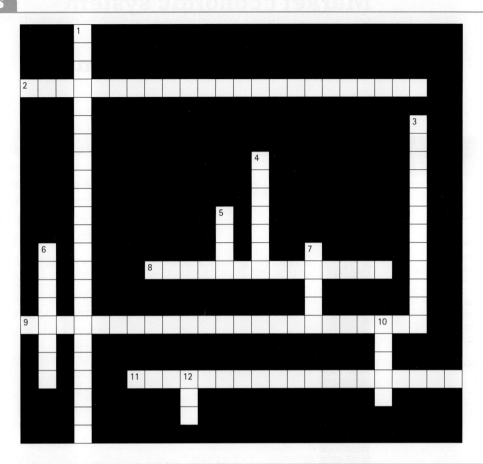

Clues across

2. The responsiveness of supply to a small change in product price (5, 10, 2, 6)
8. Term used to describe a product demand or supply that is relatively unresponsive to changes in its price (5, 9)
9. The term used to describe the price elasticity of supply of any good or service at any given moment in time because their supply will be fixed and cannot vary with price (9, 5, 9)
11. Term used to refer to a reduction in the quantity demanded of product in response to an increase in its price as shown as a movement along its market demand curve (11, 2, 6)

Clues down

1. The responsiveness of demand to a change in product price (5, 10, 2, 6)
3. Term used to describe a product demand or supply that has a price elasticity greater than one because a small change in its price will result in a proportionately greater change in quantity (5, 7)
4. In which time period in economics is the supply of any given product most price elastic? (4, 3)
5. A product has a large number of close substitutes. Is the value of the price elasticity of demand for the product likely to more than one or less than one? Answer: 'more than' or 'less than' (4, 4)
6. A product has a price elasticity of demand of 3. What will happen to the revenue its suppliers earn from the sale of the product to consumers following an increase in its price? Answer: 'increase' or 'decrease' (8)
7. Demand for a product is price inelastic. Its producer wants to increase revenue from its sale. Should the producer raise or lower its price? Answer: 'raise' or 'lower' (5)
10. If a 2% increase in the price of a product results in a 6% increase in its quantity supplied, what is the value (in letters) of the price elasticity of supply of the product? (5)
12. What is the value (in letters) of the price elasticity of demand for a product if a 1% increase in its price results in a 2% reduction in quantity demanded? (3)

Unit 2.9   Market economic system
Unit 2.10   Market failure
Unit 2.11   Mixed economic system

IN THIS UNIT

Recipe card

Step 1: Add free markets

Step 2: Introduce public spending and taxes

Step 3: Sprinkle liberally with regulations

Step 4: Mix thoroughly

MARKETS

GOVERNMENT

MIXED ECONOMY

2.9.1	Definition of market economic system	▶ Including the roles of the private sector (firms and consumers) and the public sector (government) in a market economy; plus examples of how it works in a variety of different countries.
2.9.2	Advantages and disadvantages of the market economic system	
2.10.1	Definition of market failure	▶ Key terms associated with market failure: public good, merit good, demerit good, social benefits, external benefits, private benefits, social costs, external costs, private costs.
2.10.2	Causes of market failure	▶ Including examples, with respect to public goods, merit and demerit goods, external costs and external benefits, abuse of monopoly power and factor immobility.
2.10.3	Consequences of market failure	▶ The implications of a misallocation of resources: over consumption of demerit goods and goods with external costs, and the under consumption of merit goods and goods with external benefits.
2.11.1	Definition of the mixed economic system	▶ Definitions, drawing and interpretation of appropriate diagrams showing the effects of three government microeconomic policy measures: maximum and minimum prices in product and labour markets, indirect taxation and subsidies.
2.11.2	Government intervention to address market failure	
		▶ Definitions of government microeconomic policy measures: regulation; privatization and nationalization; and direct provision of goods.
		▶ The effectiveness of government intervention in overcoming the drawbacks of a market economic system.

Definition of market economic system

Advantages and disadvantages of the market economic system

What is the market economic system?

In the previous unit we looked at how the prices and quantities produced of different goods and services are determined, in markets by the decisions of producers and consumers. Their decisions therefore determine what goods and services are produced, how they are produced and who they are produced for in a **market economic system**. ➤ **2.1.1**

The **price mechanism** is the key to how the market economic system works and how resource allocation decisions are made. Firms compete with each other to sell their goods and services to consumers at the highest prices they are willing and able to pay. Changes in market conditions, that is changes in the quantities of different products consumers and willing and able to buy and the quantities producers are willing and able to supply to them, will affect the prices firms can charge for their products and the profits they can make from their production.

Firms will therefore move or reallocate resources between products as their prices and profitability change. Factors of production will be moved from the production of products that are falling in price and profitability into the production of those products that are rising in price and profitability, because consumer demand for them is increasing.

Advantages of the market economic system

Allowing private firms and consumers to determine what goods and services are produced and who they are produced for, has a number of benefits.

1 A wide variety of goods and services will be produced

This is because private firms compete to earn as much profit as they can from producing as many different goods and services as they can with their resources to satisfy the wants of consumers.

2 Firms will respond quickly to changes in consumer wants and spending patterns

Private firms will quickly move resources into the production of goods and services that become more profitable to make and sell because consumer demand for them is rising. On the other hand, if a product is no longer wanted it becomes unprofitable to produce and supply then resources will be reallocated to more profitable uses instead.

3 The profit motive of firms encourages them to develop new products and more efficient production methods

Most firms in a market economy will aim to make as much profit as they can. Firms therefore have an incentive to develop new products and product designs to increase their sales at the expense of rival producers. The research, development and use of new materials, production equipment and methods can also help to reduce the cost of making and selling goods and services, and therefore boost profits.

4 There are very few, if any, taxes and regulations

In a totally free market economy there is no role for a government or public sector. There is, therefore, no reason to collect taxes from incomes or wealth of private firms and individuals to pay for a public sector. Similarly, there will be no laws or regulations to control the behaviour of private firms and individuals.

Disadvantages of the market economic system

The decisions of private firms and consumers in a market economic system may also result in some wasteful or harmful market outcomes that have a negative impact on social and economic welfare or well-being.

1 Some worthwhile goods and services will not be produced because they are not profitable enough

Some services, such as street lighting, flood barriers and national parks, are unlikely to be provided by private firms because they will be unable to charge individual consumers a price according to how much they use them or benefit from them. Similarly, postal services or roads to rural areas may not be provided. They will be expensive to supply and too few people may benefit from them to cover the cost of their creation. ➤ 2.10.2

2 Firms will only supply products to consumers who are most able to pay for them

People with the most money have the most freedom to choose and buy what they want. In a market economy, people who have very little money have much less freedom and spending power. For example, private sector firms in a market economy will not provide education or healthcare for people who cannot afford to pay for these services. Similarly, private firms may only produce houses that people who are wealthy or earn high incomes can afford.

3 Resources will only be employed if it is profitable to do so

Private firms will not employ factors of production if a profitable use cannot be found for them. Meaning that more people may remain unemployed and unproductive.

4 Harmful goods may be produced if it is profitable to do so

If it is profitable, private firms will develop, for example, dangerous drugs and weapons and these may be freely available to consumers who are willing and able to buy them.

5 Firms may disregard the welfare of people, animals and the environment

Most private firms aim to make as much profit from their activities as possible. Protecting the environment, minimizing waste and pollution, and ensuring animals are treated humanely will increase costs and reduce profits. As a result, some firms purposefully ignore the harm and negative impacts their production decisions may cause.

▼ Some market outcomes are undesirable and reduce economic welfare

What is the role of a government or public sector in a market economy?

There is little or no government intervention or central planning in a free market economic system. However, in reality there are no totally free market economies because governments do exist and do intervene in markets. Government actions can affect the decisions of private firms and consumers and alter market outcomes.

A government may intervene in one or more markets in a number of ways:

- As a **regulator**: This can include setting maximum prices for products that firms are not allowed to exceed in some markets or setting the minimum standards of a service they must provide or, in some cases, banning the production and sale of some specific items altogether, such as guns and harmful drugs;

- As a **consumer**: Using its significant buying power to force some firms to increase the supply of certain goods and services at reduced prices. For example, the government funded National Health Service (NHS) in the UK is a major buyer of medicines from private pharmaceutical companies and is able to uvase its purchasing power to negotiate heavily discounted prices for the supply of medicines;

- As a **producer**: By directly employing factors of production to produce goods and services private sector firms will not provide or will only provide at high prices few people can afford. For example, even in the most free market economies, governments supply police forces to maintain law and order and many other essential public services such as refuse collection and national security. In many countries, government owned organizations also supply passenger rail and postal services, healthcare and school education and may even run farms and manufacture cars and aircraft.

The more ways a government intervenes in an economy and the more markets it controls the smaller the role there is for private firms and consumers to freely determine what goods and services are produced, how they are produced and who they are produced for.

According to the Heritage Foundation, a US research organization, Singapore, Australia, New Zealand and Switzerland are among the most free market economies in the world.

In contrast, those countries with little to no free market economies are North Korea, Venezuela, Cuba, Republic of Congo and Eritrea. In these countries, the governments control most markets and the allocation of resources to different productive uses.

SECTION 2.10.1

SECTION 2.10.2-3

Definition of market failure

Causes and consequences of market failure

What are market failures?

The disadvantages of a market economic system are the result of **market failures**. These occur when free markets fail to produce outcomes in terms of prices and quantities that are socially or economically desirable.

For example, products that increase social and economic welfare such as education and healthcare, may be over priced and under-produced. In contrast, products that reduce social and economic welfare, because they create pollution or destroy the natural environment, may be underpriced and over produced.

Market failures therefore result in a **misallocation of resources** or an **inefficient allocation of resources** and a reduction in social and economic welfare. This means that other uses of resources and market outcomes will be more efficient and worthwhile but a market economic system will not achieve them.

How markets fail and the consequences

The interaction of consumer demand and producer supply decisions in markets can result in an inefficient and undesirable allocation of resources in an economy, in the following ways.

1 Public goods will not be provided

Street lighting, policing and flood defences are examples of **public goods** because they have the following characteristics in common:

- They are socially and economically desirable to have. For example, street lights help to reduce road accidents and crime at night;

- Once they have been provided it is impossible to exclude individual consumers from benefiting from them just because they haven't paid for them. For example, street lamps will not automatically switch on and off according to who is passing by them and whether they have paid for them or not;

- People who consume them will not reduce the amount available to others. For example, a person who eats a cake will have reduced the number of cakes available to other people by one. The same applies to many other goods and services. However, in contrast, a person who is protected from crime by a police force or walks down a lit street at night does not reduce the amount of protection or street lighting available to others;

Free failings

What market failures and other disadvantages of the market economic system are identified in the following news articles and headlines?

Tortured for Greed and Profit

In many countries dogs are much loved family pets or work companions. They are intelligent, able to learn and respond to many commands, faithful and fun loving. This allows them to contribute to a society in many ways including assisting people who are blind, deaf or disabled; guarding other animals and property; and locating people trapped under collapsed buildings, or harmful drugs and explosives. Some dogs are even able to detect the presence of some cancers in people and the onset of epileptic fits before they occur.

However, in some countries including South Korea, China, Vietnam and the Philippines, dogs are farmed for their meat and fur. The dogs spend their short lives in cramped cages with little food or water, their sores and injuries often left untreated, until they are considered big enough to be taken to market to satisfy a demand for dog meat and skins. They will often have their legs broken so they are unable to escape before they are brutally hung or beaten to death or torched, thrown into boiling water or skinned while they are still alive.

The pain and suffering inflicted on the animals is horrific, cruel and unnecessary. They are not bred, farmed or killed humanely simply because it would a cost a little more to do so. Providing more food, open space and veterinary care will increase the costs and reduce the profits of those people and organisations that supply dog meat and furs.

By 2050, There Will Be More Waste Plastic in the World's Oceans Than Fish

Ready meals and designer shoes fuelling destruction of the rainforest

Supermarkets are helping to destroy rainforests by selling beef and leather goods from farms responsible for chopping down large areas of trees, according to a report by Greenpeace.

Canadian drugs firm accused of overcharging Health Service by hiking price of life-changing medicines by 6,000%

Car manufacturing ends in Australia leaving thousands unemployed

Australia's near 100-year automotive industry ended last week as GM Holden Ltd, a unit of U.S. carmaker General Motors Co (GM.N), closed its factory in South Australia to move manufacturing to cheaper locations overseas.

Lack of affordable housing sparks protests

Toxic pollutants from oil and gas companies are poisoning communities and increasing risks of cancer and respiratory disease, finds new report

Customers warned energy bills are to stay high despite skyrocketing profits at power companies

For the above reasons, it is impossible to charge individual consumers a price according to how much they have used and benefited from public goods such as street lighting, policing and flood defences. Private firms will therefore be unable to cover the costs of supplying them. This means that private sector firms will not supply public goods because they will not be able to do so profitably

Paying for public goods

Oi! Are you going to pay fot that!

Imagine that someone knocked at your door and asked you to pay $20 towards the cost of providing street lighting outside your home. The collector argues that the street lamp provides you with light to help you see at night, when you are driving or walking home. It also benefits your neighbours and other people who use the street on which you live. You know that if they all gave $20 to the collector this will be enough to keep the street lamp on at night, whether you pay or not. That is, you can still enjoy the benefit of street lighting even if you pay nothing towards it. This means you will be a 'free rider' able to enjoy the benefit of the street light without paying for it.

However, if all of your neighbours thought in the same way as you, the collector would be unable to get anyone to pay $20 for the street lighting and it could not be kept running. The only way that street lighting can be provided therefore is if the government provides it and by collects taxes from everyone to pay for its provision. The same is true for other public goods. ➤ **2.11.2**

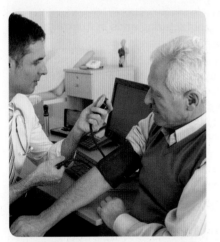

▲ Healthcare and education are merit goods. They will be under-provided and under consumed in a free market economy

2 Too few merit goods will be supplied and consumed

It is good for a country to have a healthy and educated population and workforce. The healthier people are the more knowledge and skills they have, the more productive they will be and the more output and incomes they will generate. Therefore the provision and widespread consumption of healthcare and education by many people in a country benefits everyone in that country.

Healthcare and education are examples of **merit goods** because their provision and consumption is socially and economically beneficial. The more people who consume merit goods the better it is for them and everyone else.

However, supplying good healthcare and education to large numbers of people is expensive. Private firms will only provide them if they are able to charge high prices that cover their costs and earn them a good profit. But few people will be able to pay such high prices. Private firms are therefore only likely to provide healthcare and education to those few people who can afford to pay high prices because they are wealthy or earn high incomes. Avs a result, only relatively few people will benefit directly from the consumption of these services, far below what is best for the population as a whole and the economy. That is, there will be under provision and **under consumption** of these merit goods below what is socially and economically optimal.

3 Demerit goods will be over-supplied and consumed

Firms in a market economy will be willing to supply goods and services to consumers who are willing and able to pay for them even if their use or consumption may be harmful to them and others.

For example, the smoking of cigarettes can cause lung disease and cancers. People who buy and smoke cigarettes may not only be unaware of the damage they are causing to their own health but also the damage to the health of family members and other people who may breathe in their smoke.

Similarly, drinking too much alcohol can cause health problems and also result in anti-social behaviours. People who consume a lot of alcohol may not realise the costs to their own health or the costs they impose on others who may have to pay more taxes to the government to provide additional healthcare and policing.

Cigarettes and alcohol are examples of **demerit goods** because their consumption is unhealthy and has negative impacts on others. However, if the production and sale of demerit goods is profitable then private firms will supply them in a free market economy to consumers who are willing and able to buy them. That is, more demerit goods will be provided and consumed in a free market economy than is socially or economically desirable.

4   Some firms may exploit their consumers and employees

Some large powerful firms in a free market economy may reduce the supply of a product to a market to force up the market price consumers must pay for it. If these firms have few or no competitors and the product has few or no close substitutes, such as fresh water supplies or peak period rail journeys into a city, then consumers will find it difficult to switch their demand to alternatives.

Because consumers have no choice but to pay more for the product it will leave them with less income to spend on other goods and services. As a result, fewer resources will be allocated to the production of other goods and services.

A firm that is able to control the market supply and price of a product is said to have a **monopoly** market position. It may use its commanding position to restrict the supply of its product so that it is able to raise prices and earn excessive profits. ➤ **3.8.2**

Similarly, some firms may seek to increase their profits by paying their workers very low wages and by providing poor and possibly unhealthy or dangerous working conditions.

5   Factor immobility obstructs the ability of firms to allocate resources efficiently

Factor immobility occurs when it is difficult to move factors of production, notably labour and capital, to different productive uses and locations as patterns of consumer demand and methods of production change. ➤ **1.2.2**

Factor immobility is therefore a cause of market failure because it stops the market economic system from allocating resources to their most efficient uses.

For example, people located in the wrong places and with the wrong skills are likely to end up in jobs they are not very good at, or be unemployed. Both such outcomes will result in less output being produced.

▲ Destruction of the environment and smog created by the decisions of some firms and consumers impose significant external costs on others

6 Goods and services with significant external costs may be over-provided

Smoke from another person's cigarette can be harmful to other people. It can make their clothes smell and it may also cause them to suffer lung disease and breathing difficulties. This is despite the fact these people did not make the decision to smoke cigarettes. Smoking by some consumers therefore imposes **external costs** on others. They will better off if fewer people consumed cigarettes.

In the same way, the production of some goods and services causes air, water and noise pollution that can badly affect other firms and consumers. Pollution is therefore another example of an external cost that society may be better off without. However, private firms will continue to make goods and services that cause pollution if it is profitable for them to do so.

7 Goods and services with significant external benefits may be under-provided

If you are vaccinated against flu or small pox your vaccination not only protects you from catching these diseases but it also stops you from passing them on to other people. However, your decision to consume vaccinations may not take any account of the **external benefits** it has for other people.

In many economies, vaccinations are therefore provided for free to make sure as many people as possible have them in order to reduce the spread of diseases and therefore to reduce future healthcare costs.

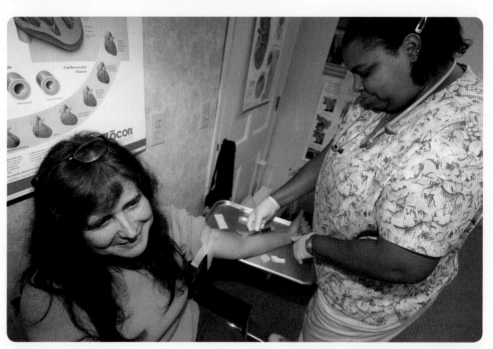

▲ Decisions to produce and consume vaccinations have external benefits

However, developing and supplying vaccinations can be expensive. In a free market economy private firms will want to charge high prices for vaccinations, which cover the cost of their provision and earn the firms a profit. Fewer consumers will therefore demand and consume vaccinations and the population as a whole will be less well-protected from the spread of diseases.

More days will be lost from work due to the spread of sickness, total output will be lower and healthcare costs will be higher as a result.

Goods and services that have significant external benefits like vaccinations are therefore likely to be under-provided and under-consumed in a free market economy.

ACTIVITY 2.21

Smoking

Look at the picture of a man smoking in a café.

1 Give three private costs that a cigarette manufacturer will have to pay.

2 How will the manufacturer calculate the total revenue from the sale of cigarettes?

3 How are other people in the café affected by the man's decision to consume a cigarette?

4 Many countries have introduced laws to ban smoking in public places. What sort of things will a government have to pay for in order to make sure the ban is observed?

5 Research has shown that smoking can damage your health.

    a What is the opportunity cost of increased health spending on treating smokers?

    b Who will bear the cost of increased health spending?

6 Imagine that the government decides to increase the tax payable on a packet of cigarettes. What affect may this have on:

    a The number of cigarettes consumed?

    b The revenue of cigarette-makers?

    c The workers in cigarette factories?

We will now examine the concepts of external costs and benefits and their implications in more detail.

Positive and negative externalities

When many hundreds of thousands of gallons of thick, toxic oil gushed from ruptured pipelines in China in July 2010, it had a devastating impact on marine and wildlife, and many communities and businesses located around the Dalian coastline of the country.

A man was killed during the clean-up operation while many businesses in the fishing and tourism industries were unable to continue operating and significant revenue was lost. The loss of life, the damage to the natural environment and wildlife and the losses suffered by other organizations represent the **external costs** of the oil spill.

China's worst-ever oil spill threatens wildlife and local industries as volunteers assist in clean-up

Chinese officials have warned of a severe threat to wildlife from one of the country's worst reported oil spills as an army of volunteers was dispatched to beaches to try to head off the black tides.

Five days after two pipelines exploded at the north-east port of Dalian, oil had reportedly spread over an area of 430 square kilometres, prompting a dispersal mission along the coast.

Hundreds of local volunteers are spreading absorbent matting along the Yellow Sea shoreline in an attempt to stop the slick from damaging beaches enjoyed by an increasing number of tourists each year on which many local hotels, restaurants and tour companies rely heavily for revenue.

Out at sea, authorities have started to use oil-consuming bacteria to try to disperse the slick, along with chemical agents and lengthy floating barrages.

The fishing industry has also suffered a major blow as fishing in the waters around Dalian has been banned for at least a month but local fisherman are worried that fish stocks may take many years to recover.

'The oil spill will pose a severe threat to marine animals and water quality, and sea birds for some time,' the deputy bureau chief for the city's Maritime Safety Administration told a regional TV station.

In contrast, Chinese oil companies, like many other oil companies all over the world, spend many millions of dollars each year using resources to explore and drill for new sources of oil, and on pipelines and petrochemical factories. These are their private costs. The revenues they earn from the sale of oil and petroleum products to consumers are their **private benefits**.

However, despite the precautions taken by oil companies and many other firms, a society can be left worse off as a result of their activities if they create serious negative externalities, including pollution and destruction of the natural environment.

A **negative externality** imposes external costs on other people and organizations that did not agree to the action that caused it. An **external cost** is a cost incurred by another party but not by those responsible for the harmful activity. A negative externality is therefore something bad and will therefore reduce satisfaction and lower economic welfare.

Because most private sector firms are motivated to make a profit they may overlook any negative externalities their resource allocation decisions may cause.

However, many uses of resources are clearly beneficial. They create goods and services to satisfy our needs and wants, provide employment and incomes, and therefore increase our living standards and economic welfare.

For example, many firms invest in technological advances and the training of their employees. These investments represent additional financial costs to those firms but they can in turn create **positive externalities**.

For example, Swiss multinational Roche Pharmaceuticals recently invested around $182 million in two European production facilities to manufacture a patient-friendly device that will allow people to administer their own cancer-fighting drugs at home and therefore reduce the time they need to spend in hospital.

Roche is a profit-making company but its investments in the advance of medicine and healthcare can help improve the health and life expectancy of many people, reduce the costs of sick leave and lost production due to staff illness in many other firms and reduce the cost to governments of providing public healthcare.

In the same way, private sector investments in early laser technologies many years ago, initially by AT&T (American Telegraph and Telephone), now benefit many millions of other firms and consumers worldwide because different types of lasers are now used in DVD players, for laser light shows, to measure distances accurately, in the cutting and welding of metals, for fingerprint detection, in surgical procedures, and for much more. These are all examples of positive externalities or spillovers from the investment in early laser development to other uses and organizations.

A **positive externality** therefore produces external benefits for other people and organizations that were not involved in the decision or action that created it. An **external benefit** is a benefit enjoyed by another party without that party having paid for it. Positive externalities are therefore good things to have and encourage. They increase satisfaction and improve economic welfare.

▼ The production of new drugs can produce positive externalities

▼ But the production of drugs may also produce negative externalities

Now let's apply what we know about externalities and private and external costs and benefits to a particular use of resources to examine whether or not that use is economically worthwhile.

River life dead!

The river Eden today is a dead river. Over the last year nearly all the fish and plant life in the river have been destroyed. In the past month cattle grazing along the banks of the river have been poisoned. Fears are growing that local children will be next.

A report has found that the river has been highly polluted by the nearby Chemix plastics plant. Chemix has, for the past two years, been dumping chemical waste into the river. The waste is pumped into the river along an underground pipeline from the Chemix plant.

Scientists estimate that it will cost $2 million to clean up the damage caused to the river each year unless the dumping of chemical waste is stopped.

Social costs and benefits

In the news article above, the estimated $2 million cost to clean up pollution in the River Eden each year is not the only cost of the decisions by Chemix about how to use resources to produce plastics and how to discharge its waste chemicals. All the costs and benefits arising from its activities have been estimated in the tables below.

Plastics production	$m per year
Private costs	$10 m
- wages	
- purchases of chemicals and materials	
- equipment charges	
- factory and office rent	
- costs of electricity, insurance, transport, etc.	
Private benefits	$15 m
- sales revenue	
Profit	$5 m

External costs and benefits	$m per year
Lost revenues to farming and costs of restocking	$5 m
Lost revenue from fishing and tourism	$2 m
Cost of cleaning up the polluted river	$2 m
Total external costs	$9 m
Benefits to other people and firms who use plastics	$2 m
Value to other firms of employees trained by Chemix	$1 m
Total external benefits	$3 m

Local farmers use water from the River Eden to irrigate their land and for their animals. They have suffered a loss of cattle and crops as a result of pollution from Chemix. As news spreads of the poisoning, all farmers in the area, regardless of whether their produce has been affected or not, may be unable to sell their output to fearful consumers. Local fishermen have also lost their livelihood because the waste has killed all the fish in the River Eden. In addition, tourists no longer visit the area to stay in waterside inns and hotels that have developed along the riverbanks.

The lost revenue to the farming, fishing and tourist industries are estimated to be worth $7 million each year Chemix continues to pollute the river, meaning the total external cost incurred by others as a result of the activities of Chemix are $9 million per year. Chemix does not pay for the external costs it creates, nor does it compensate the other people or firms affected by them.

The costs to the people, farms and other organizations near to the Chemix plant are significant, yet Chemix as a private sector firm may be uninterested in these costs. Chemix is likely only to be concerned with its own **private costs** of plastics production, including the hire of equipment and machinery, factory and office rent, the purchase of chemicals, the payment of wages, insurance and electricity charges, etc. ➤ **4.2**

The private costs of Chemix plus the external costs to the rest of society is the total **social cost** ($19 million) of the firm's decision to use resources to produce plastics, that is,

private costs + external costs = total social cost

The price Chemix charges consumers for its plastic is greater than the private costs of producing them. Chemix is therefore able to earn a profit from using resources to produce plastics. However, the market price of the plastic does not cover the external costs of the firm's production. If it did, price would be much higher and consumers may buy less plastic as a result. Sales and therefore the profits of Chemix would be much lower.

Chemix earns revenue of $15 million each year from the sale of its plastics to consumers compared to its private costs of production of $10 million each year. Producing plastics is therefore a profitable use of resources for Chemix. The difference between its private benefits and private costs is an annual profit of $5 million. If this amount of profit is more than Chemix could earn from using the same resources in their next best use then Chemix would conclude it is using its resources in the best possible way. The problem is, however, that many other people and firms think it is not the best use of these resources because of the widespread pollution Chemix has caused. Despite a profit of $5 million from the production of plastics, Chemix has imposed external costs on the rest of society of $9 million.

However, the management of Chemix argues that the company also creates many external benefits worth an estimated $3 million each year. Plastics are used in many modern, labour-saving products such as microwave ovens and cars and many other firms would be unable to make these products if Chemix did not supply them with plastic. The firm also trains its workers in specialist moulding techniques, computer assisted design and production and in management and financial skills. These skills may benefit other firms in the future when workers leave Chemix and take jobs elsewhere.

These external benefits should also be taken into account when deciding whether or not using resources to produce plastics is worthwhile for society and the economy as a whole.

Taken together, therefore, the private benefits of Chemix and the external benefits it creates for the rest of society gives the total **social benefit** ($18 million) of the firm's decision to use resources to produce plastics, that is,

private benefits + external benefits = total social benefit

So, we now know that the total social cost of the decision by Chemix to use resources to produce plastics is $19 million each year and exceeds the total social benefit of that same decision of $18 million each year. This means society could be better off if those resources were used in the production of other goods and services, despite the profit made by Chemix. That is, economic welfare could be higher if the resources employed by Chemix are used in productive activities that are less harmful to other people, firms and the natural environment and/or create more external benefits.

An economic or uneconomic use of resources

▼ An economic use of resources?

▼ An uneconomic use of resources?

Whenever the social costs of an activity exceed its social benefits, as in the case of Chemix, society as a whole is made worse off even if some people and firms enjoy profits and external benefits.

A use of resources is **uneconomic** if its total social cost exceeds its total social benefit. Society will be better off – and economic welfare higher – if the same resources are allocated to another use.

Only an **economic use of resources** will raise economic welfare because the social benefit created by that use will be greater than its social cost. It follows that if a productive activity creates significant social benefits then a society will be better off allocating more resources to it. For example, society may benefit from having access to more parks and open spaces, more healthcare and investments in medical advances, but private firms will not allocate resources to these uses if it is not profitable for them to do so.

ACTIVITY 2.22

Not painting a pretty picture

The Non-drip paint company is considering whether or not to locate a new factory near the town of Greensville. The company estimates that the new plant will cost $5 million a year to run, but should add $6 million to revenue from the sale of the paint it produces.

The people of Greensville are worried that the new factory will release smoke, containing harmful chemicals, into the air. These chemicals will pollute the air and even get into the soil and water supplies as rain will bring the chemicals back down from the air.

The local health authority estimates that over many years this smoke will damage people's health and increase the need for medical care at an estimated cost of $4 million a year.

The local authority believes that the smoke will blacken the walls of historic buildings in the area and cause their eventual erosion. Regular cleaning will therefore be needed at an estimated cost of $2 million each year.

On a more positive note, it estimates that the paint factory will encourage other firms to locate in the area as suppliers of materials, providers of transport, etc., and that this will reduce local unemployment and help other local businesses. These external benefits are valued at $3 million.

1   What does the Non-drip paint company take into account when deciding whether or not to produce paint with its resources?

2   From society's point of view, should the firm take other factors into consideration?

3   Which of the following statements do you think are correct?

   a   From the point of view of the paint company, resources are being used in the best way if:
   i   Private benefits are greater than private costs.
   ii   Private benefits equal private costs.

◀

    iii Private benefits are less than private costs.

    iv External benefits are greater than external costs.

  b From the point of view of society, scarce resources are in their best use when:

    i   Social benefits exceed social costs.

    ii Social benefits equal social costs.

    iii Social benefits are less than social costs.

    iv Private benefits are greater than private costs.

4 Using the figures presented in the case study calculate:

  a The paint company's estimated yearly profit.

  b Whether or not paint production at the factory is worthwhile for society.

5 A conflict of interest between the paint company and the local community has arisen. How does this illustrate the central economic problem?

Group exercise

Divide into groups of eight or nine. One half of each group will play the role of the directors of the Non-drip paint company, while the other half are local community representatives.

1 The directors of the company prepare a report stating why they feel they are right to go ahead with the paint factory even if it does mean producing smoke. For example, the aim of the company is to make a profit because it has a duty to its shareholders.

2 The local community group prepares a report stating why they feel the paint factory should not locate in their area.

3 The company directors and local community representatives in each group now meet to read and discuss their reports. They must attempt to reach a solution to the conflict. If no solution is reached, the teacher may act as an arbitrator.

4 Each group's recommendations and findings are then reported back to the teacher.

In the above exercise, the location and production decisions of the Non-drip paint company ignore any external costs and benefits. The company is only interested in making a profit, or **commercial return**, from producing paint. The result is that because social costs are greater than the social benefits of paint production, society will be worse off. In fact, private and external costs ($5 million + $6 million) exceed private and external benefits ($6 million + $3 million) by $2 million each year.

SECTION 2.11.1

What is a mixed economic system?

Definition of the mixed economic system

Almost all national economies in the world have a mixed economic system because of the problems of the free market economic system.

A **mixed economic system** combines government planning and ownership of resources with the use of the free market economic system to determine the allocation of resources in the economy, that is what it produces, how and for whom. ➤ **2.2.2**

Ownership and control of resources in a mixed economy is therefore divided between a **private sector** consisting of private sector firms and households and a government run **public sector**.

A system of government can help to overcome many of the disadvantages of the market system in an economy. For example, a government can:

- employ factors of production to produce and supply worthwhile goods and services that private firms will not provide because they are not profitable enough;

- provide welfare benefits to people who are poor so they can afford to buy the goods and services they need from private firms who will only supply these products at high prices;

- support people who are unemployed because private firms cannot find a profitable use for them – this can include providing them with financial support and retraining them so they can gain new skills and find employment;

- ban the production and sale of harmful goods such as weapons and drugs;

- introduce laws to protect animal welfare and the environment;

- intervene in markets to address market failures using indirect taxes, subsidies and regulations. ➤ **2.11.2**

Some economies are more 'mixed' than others

Most national economies combine a market economic system with government planning to determine their resource allocations.

In many mixed economies the size of the public sector is relatively small compared to the private sector. The market economic system dominates resource allocation decisions in these economies.

In contrast, some national economies have very large public sectors measured by the amount they produce, earn or spend each year. For example, in 2015 the public sectors in France and Finland accounted for almost 57% of the total value of output in their economies.

▼ Public sector expenditure as a percentage of total output, selected countries 2015

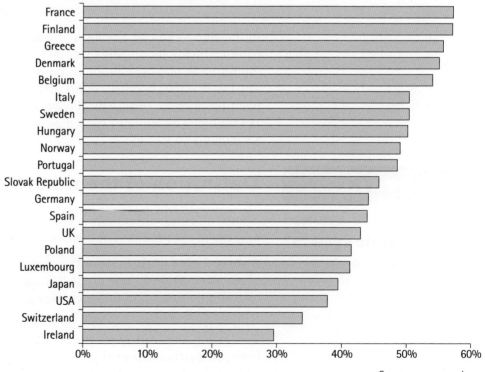

Source: *www.oecd.org*

Government intervention to address market failure

The great advantage of a mixed economic system is that it can correct some of the worst failures of the free market economic system that reduce social and economic welfare.

If government planning is able to correct market outcomes (i.e. prices and quantities) that are undesirable it can increase output, increase incomes and living standards, and improve social and economic welfare in an economy.

A government may intervene in different markets to correct their failures using the following **microeconomic policy measures**:

- the **direct provision of goods and services**, for example, by investing in new schools and hospitals and employing nurses, doctors and teachers to provide public healthcare and education;

- **regulations** including **price controls**, such as capping the prices some large firms are able to charge for their products;

- **indirect taxes** to raise the prices and reduce the consumption of some undesirable products such as cigarettes;

- **subsidies** to reduce the costs of producing some desirable products, such as medicines and renewable energy, so that private firms supply more of them.

We will now look at how each of these policies works in more detail.

Market failure	What can a government do to correct it?
Public goods will not be supplied	It can pay for the provision of public goods including street lighting, policing and flood defences, using money collected from taxes.
Too few merit goods will be supplied and consumed	It can directly employ factors of production to increase the supply of healthcare and education available to people. Their provision can be paid from taxes so that they can be provided for free so that everyone is able to consume them.
Demerit goods will be over-supplied and consumed	It can ban the production and sale of demerit goods or raise their prices using indirect taxes so that fewer people consume them. Alternatively it may set high minimum prices in the markets for demerit goods and other goods that create significant external costs.
Some firms may exploit their consumers and employees	It can regulate the behaviour of large powerful firms that may abuse their market power. For example, if can set maximum prices they are not allowed to exceed in order to protect consumers. It may also take over the ownership and running of large powerful firms from the private sector using a process called nationalization. The introduction of employment laws and minimum wage laws to protect the working conditions and wages of low-paid workers.
Factor immobility obstructs the ability of firms to allocate resources efficiently	It can provide education and retraining for workers who are occupationally immobile because they do not have relevant skills. It can also encourage private firms to move to areas of high unemployment by subsidizing their costs.
Goods and services with significant external costs may be over-provided	Indirect taxes can be used to raise the market prices of goods and services with significant external costs so that demand for them contracts.
Goods and services with significant external benefits may be over-provided	Subsidies can be paid to private firms to reduce the costs of producing goods and services with significant external benefits. This will encourage them to increase the supply of these goods and services.

Direct provision of goods and services

Government-run organizations in the public sector of an economy can employ labour and other factors of production to supply public goods such as street lighting and flood defences, and supply merit goods including healthcare and education that the private sector will under-provide.

Many goods and services provided by a government can be supplied 'free of charge' to consumers so that people are encouraged to use them, including those with low incomes who would not be able to afford them if they were provided for profit by private firms. Instead, a government will raise taxes to pay for the public provision of these goods and services.

Similarly, many governments run or fund scientific research organizations to research and develop new products, processes and technologies that will have significant external benefits. Examples of this include medical research to improve surgical procedures and equipment, research to develop new and clean renewable energy technologies and measurement facilities to map land masses, oceans and even space.

Scientific research is expensive, can take a long time and may not always result in useful outcomes. Private firms are therefore unlikely to fund scientific research unless they can profit directly from it.

In addition, many governments operate **state-owned enterprises** to supply goods and services directly to consumers that are considered essential or too important to be provided solely for profit by private sector firms. For example, state-owned enterprises might supply electricity, postal and rail services or run airports, airlines and television stations. ➤ **3.5.1**

Many state-owned enterprizes have been created through a process called **nationalization**. This occurs when a government takes over the ownership of private sector companies or even entire industries. It allows a government to have direct control over the market supply and prices of the products they provide.

For example, bus and train services are nationalized in many countries. A government may keep fares low to encourage more people to use these services for their travel instead of using private cars. This will help to reduce the external costs of traffic congestion and harmful exhaust fumes and air pollutants.

Why are some industries nationalized?

- Nationalization is carried out to control large powerful private sector monopolies, especially those providing essential services to consumers such as electricity, gas and water supplies. In private hands these firms may restrict the market supply of these goods in order to increase the prices they can charge consumers.

- Some industries are nationalized to protect employment in large firms which may otherwise be forced to close down by their private sector owners if they fail to make a profit.

- Nationalization can be carried out for national security. For example, some industries such as nuclear energy are thought to be too dangerous to be controlled by private entrepreneurs.

- Some industries are nationalized because they are considered too important to the economy in terms of national output and income to be under private sector control.

- Some industries are nationalized to protect public services. Nationalized industries can continue to provide essential services even if they make a loss, such as many postal and rail services in rural areas.

- Nationalization may be carried out for political reasons. The governments of some countries believe they should control the vast majority of resources and industries rather than the private sector.

▲ The Saudi Arabian Oil Company is an example of a nationalized and state-owned enterprise

There are many examples of nationalized industries around the world. For example, the US government owns Amtrak, the national passenger train operator, and the United States Postal Service.

The oil and gas industries in many countries including Libya, Kuwait, Mexico, Nigeria, Saudi Arabia and Venezuela are also nationalized.

Many banks across many different countries were also taken into public ownership during the banking crisis and global economic recession in 2008 to prevent them from running out of money and being closed down by their private sector owners.

Regulations including price controls

Regulations are legal rules made by a government to control the way something is done or the way people or firms behave. People and firms that fail to comply with regulations could have to pay significant fines.

Regulations are therefore used to control the forces of demand and supply in regulated markets to produce outcomes that are considered more socially or economically desirable than those that would otherwise occur.

For example, regulations may be used to control markets in the following ways:

- To ban or restrict the production or consumption of demerit goods and products which create significant external costs. For example, the French government has announced it will ban the production and sale of petrol and diesel cars from 2040 in order to stop harmful exhaust emissions that contribute to health problems and climate change. Only clean electric vehicles will be permitted.

- To protect animal welfare and the natural environment. Examples include a ban on the testing of cosmetics on animals and limits on the types and amount of pollutants different firms can release into the environment or the times at which they can carry out productive activities that create significant noise.

- To set minimum acceptable service standards including product safety and quality, delivery times and consumer complaint procedures.

- To control market prices.

Price controls are legal minimum or maximum prices set by a government in the markets for certain goods or services. For example, high minimum prices can be used to reduce the consumption of undesirable products while low maximum prices can stop private firms from overcharging for goods that are beneficially or essential for people to consume.

Setting maximum prices

Some private sector firms seeking to maximize their profits may attempt to exploit consumers by charging them very high prices for their products. To prevent this a government may use regulations to cap the prices they can charge by setting maximum prices they cannot exceed.

For example, the diagram below represents the market for electricity in an economy. The market has the following characteristics:

- Market demand is relatively price inelastic. This is because electricity is an essential good for many people and firms, and it has few close substitutes.

▼ A maximum price is introduced below the equilibrium market price

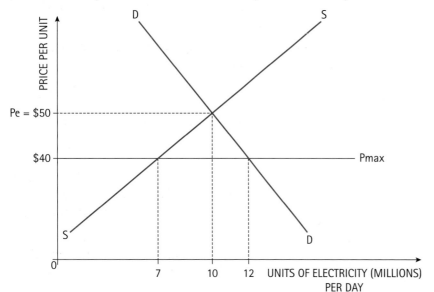

- Market supply is monopolized by a small number of large private firms. Because demand is price inelastic they could raise the price of electricity significantly and earn more revenue and profits. ➤ **2.7.4**

- The equilibrium market price (Pe) is $50 per unit of electricity. However, the government considers this price too high and introduces a **maximum price** (Pmax) of $40 per unit. As a result the quantity demanded expands from 10 million to 12 million units per day.

- However, electricity suppliers will only be willing to supply 7 million units at the maximum price of $40 per unit. There will be a shortage of electricity unless the government also regulates that suppliers must expand supply to 12 million units per day at this price and accept lower profits.

Imagine now that the government introduced a maximum price of $60 per unit instead. This maximum price will be above the equilibrium market price of $50 per unit and will therefore have no effect.

▼ A maximum price is introduced above the equilibrium market price

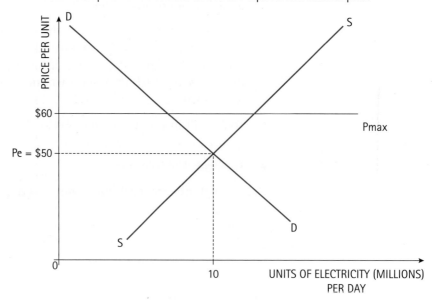

Maximum prices are often used by governments in markets, for essential products such as rented accommodation, water supplies and food and energy products, to stop suppliers from overcharging consumers and to make these items more affordable to people with low incomes.

Setting minimum prices

A government may regulate to raise the prices of demerit goods in an attempt to reduce their consumption. Similarly, governments may force private firms to charge higher prices for products that cause excessive pollution, waste or increase other external costs. People and the economy will be better off if fewer such products were produced and consumed.

For example, the diagram below represents the market for cigarettes in an economy. The market has the following characteristics:

▼ A minimum price is introduced above the equilibrium market price

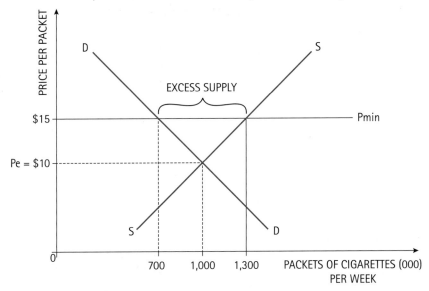

- Cigarettes are a demerit good. Their consumption is harmful and creates negative externalities. People who smoke can damage their health and that of others who inhale their smoke. As a result, the government has to raise more taxes from households and firms to pay for additional public healthcare.

- The equilibrium market price (Pe) is $10 per packet of 20 cigarettes and the equilibrium quantity supplied and consumed at this price is 1 million packets per week.

- However, the government considers the market price to be too low and the consumption of 1 million packets each week at this price to be too high. It therefore introduces a **minimum price** (Pmin) of $15 per packet. As a result the quantity demanded contracts from 1 million to 700,000 packets per week.

- Because the price has increased, cigarette suppliers are willing to expand the quantity they supply to 1.3 million packets per week. If they did there would be an excess supply of 600,000 packets they would be unable to sell off at a lower price. It would therefore be sensible for producers of cigarettes to cut production and supply just 700,000 packets each week to match the amount consumers are now willing and able to buy.

▼ A minimum price is introduced below the equilibrium market price

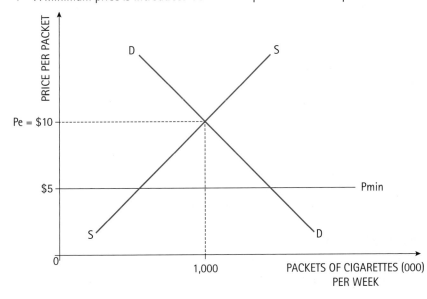

Imagine now that the government introduced a minimum price of $5 per packet instead.

This minimum price will be below the equilibrium market price of $10 and will therefore have no effect on the quantity demanded or supplied.

To reduce the quantity supplied and consumed of a product a minimum price must therefore be set above the market equilibrium price. However, if consumer demand of the product is relatively price inelastic, the policy measure may be ineffective because quantity consumed in unlikely to contract significantly.

Minimum price controls are often used by governments in markets for demerit goods such as cigarettes, alcohol, gambling and fatty foods, to reduce the amount people consume.

Minimum prices can help to cut the demand for products that result in significant external costs when they are produced or consumed, such as pollution and litter or harm to animals and the environment. For example, compulsory charges have also been introduced for plastic carrier bags in a number of countries to reduce their use and cut harmful waste.

Many governments have also introduced a legal **minimum wage** to prevent employers from paying some groups of workers very low wages. ➤ **3.3.2**

Indirect taxes

Indirect taxes are imposed on the producers or suppliers of specific goods and services. They are an additional cost of production that private firms must pay to their government. Private firms will therefore attempt to pass on the additional costs of these taxes to consumers by raising the prices of their products. However, this should contract demand for their products making their production and sale less profitable. The aim of indirect taxes is therefore to reduce both the consumption and production of the products they are applied to. ➤ **4.3.4**

For example, the diagram below represents the market for bottled beers in an economy. It has the following characteristics:

▼ The effect on an indirect tax on equilibrium market price and quantity

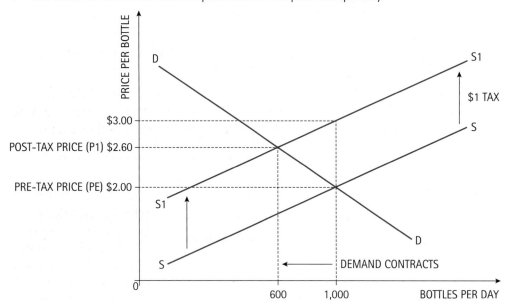

- The current market price per bottle is $2. The government considers this price to be too low. As a result, there is over-consumption of beer in the economy. Excessive consumption of alcohol is considered to be undesirable. It can cause health problems in heavy drinkers and drunkenness can result in anti-social behaviours. As a result a government will have to raise more in taxes from people and firms to pay for additional healthcare and policing.

- The government therefore imposes an indirect tax called an **excise duty** on bottled beers (and also on cans of beers). The excise duty is set at $1 per bottle. The tax has to be paid for by producers of beer. It is an additional cost of beer production that will reduce the profitability of supplying bottled beers. As a result, they reduce market supply of their bottled beers in an attempt to raise their market price and pass on the cost of the tax to beer consumers.

- At the pre-tax market price (Pe) of $2 beer producers were willing to supply 1,000 bottled beers each day. However, as a result of the additional cost of a $1 tax per bottle they are only willing to supply this quantity if they can sell their beers for $3 per bottle.

- The excise duty therefore has the effect of moving the market supply vertically upwards by the amount of the tax. The vertical distance between the old pre-tax supply curve (SS) and the new post-tax supply curve (S1S1) is $1, the value of the excise duty on each bottle produced.

- The new post-tax equilibrium market price is $2.60 (P1). This shows that producers of beer have been unable to pass on the full cost of the excise duty to consumers. This is because the market demand for bottled beers has contracted from 1,000 bottles per day to 600 bottles per day. It would contract even more if producers were able to charge $3 per bottle.

- Consumers will therefore pay an extra $0.60 for each bottle they buy. Beer producers will have to pay this extra amount plus an additional $0.40 per bottle to the government to cover the cost of the $1 excise duty per bottle. The revenue and profit they earn from the sale of each bottle has therefore been reduced by $0.40.

Many governments use excise taxes to increase the market prices of demerit goods and other products that are considered undesirable. For example, excise duties are commonly applied to tobacco products, alcoholic drinks, petrol and gasoline products, aircraft fares and vehicles. Although they help to raise revenue for a government, the primary aim of these taxes is to reduce the harmful external costs of these and other specified products by reducing their consumption and the quantities producers are willing to supply. However, the effect on sales and consumption of these products may be small if demand for them products is price inelastic. ➤ **2.7.4**

Subsidies

A **subsidy** is a financial support or payment provided by a government to private firms to encourage desirable activities.

Subsidies are usually paid as non-repayable grants but may also include tax reductions and low cost loans. All subsidies have the effect of reducing costs and, therefore, increasing the profitability of the activities or products they support.

For example, the diagram below represents the market for solar energy. It has the following characteristics:

▼ The effect on a subsidy on equilibrium market price and quantity

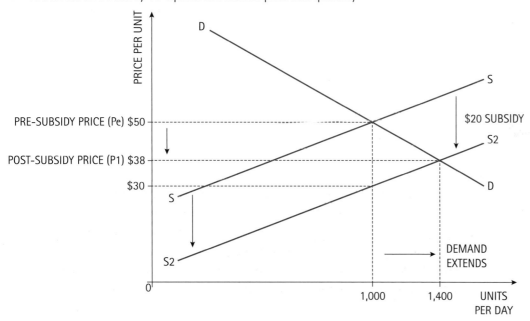

- The current market price for electricity generated from solar panels is $50 per unit (Pe). The total quantity of solar-generated electricity produced and consumed at this price is 1,000 units per day.

- However, the government consider this price too high. It wants more solar energy to be supplied and consumed to reduce the amount of electricity generated and consumed from oil, gas and coal fired power stations. Solar energy provides a clean, renewable source of energy whereas the burning of oil, gas or coal in power stations uses up finite resources and creates harmful air pollutants and emissions that contribute to health problems and climate change.

- The government therefore decides to pay producers of solar energy a subsidy of $20 per unit. At the pre-subsidy market price of $50 per unit, producers were willing to supply 1,000 units of solar energy per hour. But now they are willing to supply the same quantity at a price of $30 per unit because, in addition to this price, they will be paid a subsidy of $20 per unit from the government.

- The subsidy therefore has the effect of moving the market supply curve vertically downwards by the amount of the subsidy. The vertical distance between the original supply curve (SS) and the new, post-subsidy supply curve (S1S1) is $20, which is the subsidy paid per unit of solar energy.

- The new equilibrium market price per unit is $38 per unit (P1). Producers of solar energy do not have to pass on the full amount of the subsidy to consumers. This is because as supply increases and price falls, consumer demand for solar energy expands from 1,000 units per day to 1,400 units per day.

- Consumers will therefore pay $12 less for each unit of solar energy they consume than they did before it became subsidized. Producers of solar energy therefore lose $12 per unit in revenue from sales but gain $20 per unit in subsidies from the government.

- However, because solar energy producers are able to sell an additional 400 units of solar power each day, at the lower market price they earn an extra $3,200 in revenue. In addition, they receive a total subsidy per day from the government of $28,000 (i.e. $20 per unit × 1,400 unit supplied).

Solar energy pre-subsidy:	Solar energy post-subsidy:
Price per unit (A): $50	Price per unit (A): $38
Total units sold (B): 1,000	Total units sold (B): 1,400
Total revenue (A × B): $50,000	Total revenue (A × B): $53,200
Total subsidy: 0	Total subsidy: $28,000 ($20 × 1,400 units)

Subsidies are usually targeted at firms that provide products that have significant external benefits or products that are considered socially and economically important. For example, subsidies are often used to encourage firms to research and develop new products and technologies, to invest more in training their workers in new skills, to move production to areas of high unemployment and to encourage farmers to increase food production.

All subsidies have the effect of reducing costs and therefore increasing the market supply of the products they target. This is depicted by a downward shift in their market supply curves. As a result, market prices will fall and consumer demand for the subsidized products will extend.

Ringing the price changes

1. Draw a demand and supply diagram to illustrate the impact of a minimum price of 50 pence per unit in the market for alcoholic drinks in Scotland.

   In your diagram, assume the current market price per unit is 40 pence.

Scotland introduces minimum price for alcoholic drinks

The Scottish government estimates that a minimum price of 50 pence per unit, aimed at stopping the sale of cut price alcoholic drinks, will reduce the number of alcohol-related deaths in Scotland by 392 over the next five years and reduce hospital admissions by more than 8,000 cases.

Diesel fuel tax in Australia set at A$0.40 per litre

2. Draw a demand and supply diagram to illustrate the impact of an indirect tax of A$0.40 in the market for diesel petroleum in Australia.

   In your diagram assume the current market price is A$1 per litre free of tax.

   Give two reasons why many governments impose indirect taxes on diesel and other petroleum products.

a   Define the term *economic system*.   [2]

b   Explain how resources are allocated in a mixed economic system.   [4]

c   Analyse the reasons why it might be desirable for a government to act as a producer of goods or services.   [6]

d   Sometimes the government does not act as a producer of goods and services but still influences private producers. Discuss how it might do this.   [8]

ECONOMICS IN ACTION

How and why have the governments of Romania and India, like many others, used taxes and subsidies to alter the market prices of the products in the articles?

India sails into the wind

At the end of 2009 the Indian government announced it was to invest 3.8 billion rupees (Rs) in a new programme to encourage greater use of cleaner, renewable energy.

Producers of electricity from wind turbines are expected to receive a subsidy of Rs 0.5 per unit of electricity they produce against an average cost of Rs 3.0 per unit. The subsidy is intended to promote increased investment in wind turbines and use of renewable energy by lowering the costs of production and final energy prices for consumers.

Romania introduces a fat tax

Romanian people love their food, so much so that more than half of the population of 22 million people is overweight. Poor diets among both adults and children are blamed, with instances of obesity having doubled among 10-year-olds.

Growing concerns about the rising cost of health care and to the economy of the obesity epidemic has prompted the Romanian government to introduce a tax on fatty foods in an attempt to reduce the problem. The new tax means it will cost far more to buy burgers, chips, fizzy drinks and other fast foods with high fat and sugar content.

Romania joins a long list of other countries also trying to tackle rising obesity in their populations.

Problems created by government interventions

The mixed economic system can therefore overcome many of the problems of the free market economic system through government ownership and control of some scarce resources and government interventions to control or regulate the decisions of private sector firms and consumers in some markets.

However, the mixed economic system can also combine many of the problems and failings of both market and centrally planned economic systems. Some government interventions in markets may also worsen the market failures they were designed to correct, and may even create additional ones. This may happen for the one or more of the following reasons.

1 Government interventions often take a long time to agree and may take even longer to have an impact

Governments will need a lot of information on how different markets works, how firms and consumers behave and the price elasticity of supply and demand, before they will be able identify which markets outcomes are the most undesirable and how it may be best be able to correct them. Designing and then agreeing regulations, price controls, taxes or subsidies and which markets to apply them to, takes time to plan and then to agree within a government. Once they are implemented such policy measures may then take a long time to have their desired effect or may have no impact at all if, for example, consumer spending patterns, firm's supply decisions and technologies have all changed.

2 Price controls may encourage smuggling and black markets

Setting high minimum prices for demerit goods such as cigarettes and alcohol can create an illegal **black market** for these products. For example, some people may smuggle them into the country illegally from other countries where their prices are much lower. They may then sell them on to other people at prices that are lower than their regulated minimum price.

3 Taxes, subsidies and other policy measures can distort price signals and incentives

Indirect taxes, price controls and subsidies will all change the final market prices of the goods or services they are targeted at. They may over or under correct for market failures if they are set too high or too low. For example, private firms may be less concerned about controlling their costs if they are paid generous subsidies that boost their profits. It may also cause them to divert resources to the production of the subsidized product from other desirable uses because they can earn more profit.

4 Regulations can increase production costs and prices

Complying with health and safety, employment, environmental, consumer protection and other regulations used to control the activities of firms can increase the costs of producing goods and services. As a result, fewer goods and services may be produced and market prices will be higher.

5 Public sector organizations may be inefficient and produce poor quality goods and services

Many public sector organizations are not required to make a profit from their activities. As a result, managers of these organizations may place less importance on controlling their costs than private firms would. As a result, resources may not be used efficiently in the public sector and the quality of publicly provided goods and services may be poor.

6 Government interventions can cause conflicts of interest

For example, paying subsidies to some firms will need to be paid for from taxes collected from other firms and from individuals. Similarly, increasing the direct provision of merit goods to people on low incomes will require people and firms to pay more in taxes to pay for them. Introducing taxes or price controls on alcohol will affect all consumers who enjoy alcohol and not just those who drink heavily. In turn, supermarkets, restaurants and bars that sell alcohol will lose some revenue. Owners of these firms will experience a loss of profits. There are always 'winners' and 'losers' from government policy measures.

7 Some government interventions may be based on political and personal choices and not the best interests of society and the economy

Many governments and government officials in mixed economies want to be popular and to be voted back into power when there are elections. They may therefore choose policy measures that are popular with voters rather than measures that are necessary and will be most effective.

For example, a government may avoid increasing taxes on alcohol if they are likely to be unpopular with many voters. Similarly, important businesses in the economy that donate funds to the ruling party in government may put pressure on the government to amend regulations or taxes that affect them.

Some government officials may even accept bribes from some companies to stop or amend government decisions that would affect them. Similarly, some officials may introduce or remove measures that affect firms they own or have a close personal relationship with.

Mixing it up

All the newspaper headlines and articles below are real. What problems do they describe about government interventions in a mixed economy?

New research from the British Chambers of Commerce (BCC) reveals that new employment regulations and taxes will cost UK businesses a staggering £25.6 billion over the next four years, which could reduce future job creation.

French consumers can expect a three-fold increase in taxes on electricity to pay for government subsidies for solar energy, according to the energy watchdog.

Government policies failing the poor

Despite all the public spending initiatives, the very poor in Bangkok are still trapped in poverty.

A 25 per cent corporate tax on the profits of local businesses is too high, local business representatives have argued. Fewer small businesses are starting up as a result.

Inefficient public hospitals 'wasting billions of pounds every year'

A review of public spending on the National Health Service has discovered a damning catalogue of waste. For example, one hospital was found to be spending £10,000 a month unnecessarily by allowing staff to take too many holidays. In another hospital, managers were wasting over £40,000 each year buying soluble tablets for liver failure costing £1.50 each when non-soluble tablets were available at just 2p each.

The report also suggests the NHS is wasting billions of pounds a year by admitting too many patients unnecessarily, persisting with treatments that bring little benefit, and not carrying out more operations at weekends.

Turks and Caicos PM quits after corruption inquiry

The premier of the Turks and Caicos Islands has resigned after an investigation found 'clear signs of corruption'.

Michael Misick, who denies selling Crown land for personal gain, quit a week earlier than expected. His departure follows allegations that his government misused public funds and profited from the sale of government-owned land in controversial deals, including one to build a Dubai-style luxury resort off the coast of the islands in the West Indies.

Microsoft, the world's largest software company, threatens to move some jobs overseas if US taxes on profits are increased

'It makes US jobs more expensive' said a company spokesperson.

Increasing the role of markets in mixed economies

Many national governments have been reducing the size of their public sectors and increasing the role of the market economic system in their economies, because of the problems associated with government planning and market interventions in a mixed economy. They have done this by:

- selling off or transferring state-owned enterprises and public sector activities to private sector firms. This is called **privatization**. For example, many governments have transferred the provision of electricity, mail delivery, refuse collection and rail and bus services from the public sector to private sector firms;

- encouraging the private sector to produce more and create more jobs, for example, by removing regulations and cutting taxes on businesses. ➤ **4.5.2**

For example, the government of Cuba has been changing the balance between its public sector and private sector. In 1991 the public sector of Cuba employed 91% of the Cuban workforce and public sector spending accounted for almost 90% of its total economy. Today, the private sector of Cuba employs around 28% of the Cuban workforce and public sector spending has fallen to around 66% of the Cuban economy.

The same is true in many other economies, even those with much smaller public sectors than Cuba.

▼ Many countries have been reducing the size of their public sectors to reduce costs and increase efficiency

Pakistan plans privatisation of state-owned Pakistan International Airlines Corporation to reduce losses

Italy's new government targets ambitious public spending cuts

Brazil to cut $18.5bn in public spending

UK prime minister argues cuts to public spending will pay for lower taxes

Reducing the size of the public sector in an economy and encouraging growth in the private sector is argued to have the following advantages for an economy by increasing the role of free markets in resource allocation decisions:

- Running public sector organizations is expensive. They employ many people and consume many goods and services. Their costs are financed from taxes paid to the government from the incomes and wealth of private individuals and businesses. Reducing the size of the public sector may therefore allow a government to reduce taxes. ➤ **4.3.6**

- As many public sector organizations are not required to make a profit they can be inefficient and wasteful. Private sector firms will make better use of resources in order to reduce their costs and increase their output and revenues because they aim to make profits. However, some people argue the profit motive of private sector firm's results in cuts to product quality and service levels, and higher prices.

- State-owned enterprises are usually not in competition with other firms. However, private sector firms do compete with each other for customers and sales. To do so, each firm will try to offer better quality products and lower prices than rival businesses.

- Growth in the public sector will require more government spending to be funded from taxes. In contrast, private sector firms are funded privately and can be more entrepreneurial. They can respond to new business opportunities and will create more jobs, incomes and output to benefit the economy. ➤ **4.6.4**

ACTIVITY 2.25

Public or private provision?

Lee plans meeting on water-sewer privatization

There is to be a special informational meeting on the potential privatization of the town's sewer and water systems. Privatization means that the local government would hire a private company to take over the operation of its sewer and water systems.

The company would be under contract to the town of Lee, and would run the two systems under one company umbrella. The principal reason for such a move would be to save money and improve service levels. At this point, most town officials concede that it is unclear whether privatizing the sewer and water operation would be a money-saver. A consulting engineer would, in theory, be able to make that assessment.

However, many residents fear the principal task of the private sector firm would be making money for itself and have asked town officials how they would be able to ensure consistent quality service from a profit-making entity.

But perhaps the most controversial aspect of the plan is that the present workforce would all have to reapply for their jobs. Many workers have argued that there was no way to ensure they would get the same health and retirement benefits they currently do as public employees of Lee. In addition, the for-profit entity would not be bound to retain the workforce presently under contract to the town.

1 What is privatization?

2 How is the town of Lee planning to privatize its water and sewer systems?

3 What economic arguments does the article highlight for and against the privatization of Lee's water and sewer systems?

4 What are the likely implications and conflicts arising from the privatization for the employees, local residents and local taxpayers?

5 Investigate examples of privatization in your own country. What arguments have different groups of people used for and against these privatizations? What impact, if any, has privatization had on you and your family?

Why and how have these governments intervened in their economies?
What problems have these interventions caused?

Cyprus, Latvia and Macedonia joined a growing list of countries to ban smoking in public places such as restaurants and bars to protect the health of customers and employees. However, many owners of restaurants and bars have complained to their governments that the introduction of the smoking ban has led to a sharp drop in consumer demand and put jobs at risk.

Environmentalists have argued that financial help given to firms by the US government to boost the production of biofuels is damaging the environment and increasing food prices globally.

The US government claims the production of fuel from arable crops such as corn and soybeans will cut environmental damage because it reduces the need to drill for crude oil and because emissions from biofuels used in vehicles and energy production are less harmful than those from fossil fuels.

In contrast, environmentalists point to food prices worldwide having risen dramatically in the past few years due in part to more corn and soybean crops being diverted from use in animal feed and foodstuffs to the production of biofuels. More and more forests and woodlands are also being cleared to grow crops for the biofuels industry in the USA.

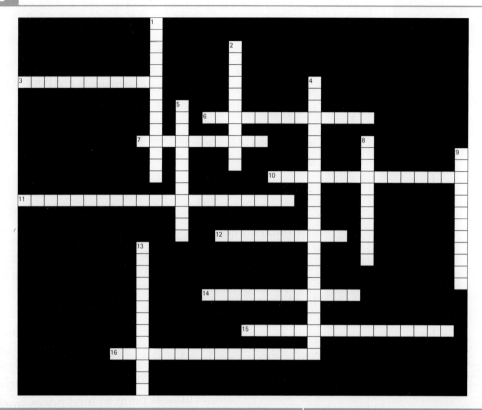

Clues across

3. A financial cost of production for a firm, such as wages, or a reduction in a consumer's utility resulting from his or her consumption decisions (7, 4)
6. Costs resulting from negative externalities created by an economic activity. They are imposed on other people and firms not directly involved in the activity. For example, a firm's decision to burn or dump waste materials that creates harmful air pollution and smog (8, 5)
7. Goods and services that benefit a society and economy, such as education and healthcare, that people will under consume if they had to pay for their provision in full (5, 5)
10. This process involves a government taking over the ownership of private firms or entire industries in its economy. It allows the government to have direct control over the market supply and prices of the products they provide (15)
11. These occur when a production or consumption decision imposes external costs on others (8, 13)
12. The total cost to society of an economic activity or use of resources including both its private costs and external costs (6, 4)
14. Consumption of these type of goods is unhealthy for those consumers who use them and socially undesirable because of the negative impacts it has on others (7, 5)
15. Term used to describe a situation when the purchase or use of a product by consumers is far less than what is socially and economically desirable, for example, because of the wider external benefits of the product (5, 11)
16. Benefits resulting from any positive externalities created by an economic activity. They are enjoyed by other people and firms not directly involved in the activity. For example, a decision by one person to be vaccinated against a transmittable disease will also protect other people and firms from the impact and spread of the disease (8, 8)

Clues down

1. A financial benefit enjoyed a firm, such as sales revenue, or an increase in the utility of a consumer resulting from his or her consumption decisions (7, 7)
2. Legal rules made by a government to control the way something is done or the way people or firms behave in different markets in order to produce more desirable outcomes (11)
4. Term used to describe an activity or use of resources that reduces social and economic welfare because its social cost exceeds its social benefit. Society and the economy will be better off if the activity was reduced or stopped and its resources reallocated (10, 3, 2, 9)
5. A cap or ceiling on the price firms are allowed to charge consumers for their products in a market regulated by a government (7, 5)
8. Socially or economically beneficial goods provided by a government because no private firm will provide them. This is because it is impossible to exclude anyone from consuming them whether they pay for them or not (6, 5)
9. A price floor set by a government in a regulated market, for example, to reduce over consumption of an undesirable product by raising its market price (7, 5)
13. The transfer of public sector organizations and activities to private firms (13)

Assessment exercises

Multiple choice

1 The market demand curve for a product shows the relationship between the quantity demanded of that product and...

A A change in income

B Consumer tastes

C The supply of the product

D The price of the product

2 Other factors unchanged, an increase in the market demand for a product will cause...

A The market price to rise and supply to contract

B The market price to fall and supply to extend

C The market price to rise and quantity supplied to extend

D The market price to rise and an increase in supply

3 Which of the following pairs of products is an example of goods in complementary demand?

A Beef and lamb

B Coffee and tea

C Butter and margarine

D Quilts and quilt covers

4 What is meant by the equilibrium quantity in the market for a product?

A The quantity produced each period

B The quantity at which demand matches supply

C The quantity at which maximum profit occurs

D The quantity which maximizes revenue

5 The diagram shows the market for corn.

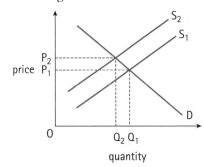

What would have caused the equilibrium price to rise from P1 to P2?

A A government subsidy to corn farmers

B Poor weather conditions

C A successful advertising campaign for corn

D Improved farming methods

6 There is excess demand in the market for a product. What change would cause the market to reach equilibrium?

A A decrease in market supply

B A fall in price

C An increase in market supply

D A rise in price

7 The diagram shows the market for halogen light-bulbs with an initial equilibrium point X.

The introduction of new technology reduces costs and increases production. Which point represents the new market equilibrium?

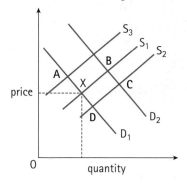

8 Demand for a product is likely to be price inelastic the...

A Fewer substitutes it has

B Fewer complements it has

C Higher its market price

D Greater the proportion of income spent on it

9 Demand for a product is price elastic. What will happen to total revenue from sales of the product following a 10% increase in its price?

A It will fall by less than 10%

B It will fall by more than 10%

C It will rise by less than 10%

D It will rise by more than 10%

10 Why is knowledge of price elasticity of demand useful?

A To monitor the rate of price inflation

B To calculate changes in disposable incomes

C To estimate the effects of changes in production costs

D To forecast the impact on revenues of different pricing strategies

11 Which pair of economic institutions would exist in a pure market economy?

A Charities and nationalized industries

B Multinationals and commercial banks

C State-owned enterprises and private limited companies

D Private schools and government hospitals

12 A government decides that an economy should make more use of the market economic system. Which policy measure might help to achieve this?

A A decrease in controls on imported goods

B An increase in government ownership of land

C An increase in subsidies to industry

D The fixing of minimum wage levels for workers

13 A mixed economy is one that has…

A Farms and factories

B A public and a private sector

C Capital and consumer goods

D Goods and services

14 In a market economic system the price mechanism…

A Helps the government to provide services

B Measures the total value of wealth

C Makes profits for firms

D Determines the allocation of resources

15 During the 1990s the economies of Eastern Europe changed from planned economies to market economic systems. Which of the following best describes the change that took place?

A More centralized government planning to allocate resources

B Fewer price controls

C Increased dependence on the price mechanism to allocate resources

D Increased resource unemployment

16 What is an advantage claimed for the market economic system?

A It responds quickly to consumer wants

B It provides public goods

C Unemployment can rise rapidly

D It relies on traditional methods of production

17 Which of the following is a market failure?

A Some workers receive higher wages than others

B Private firms aim to maximize their profits

C Natural resources are used up in production

D The market prices of products will not take account of their external costs and benefits

18 What is an external cost of building a new airport?

A The price paid for the land

B The cost of materials

C The noise caused by construction

D Wages paid to workers

19 A large supermarket has applied to build on protected woodland. Despite the loss of the woodland and its recreational value, the proposal is likely to be profitable and create many new jobs.

What economic concepts are directly involved in this statement?

A External costs and private benefits

B Income distribution and inelastic demand

C Private investment and a decrease in supply

D Social costs and monopoly

20 If the production of a good or service results in high external benefits, but low private benefits, then…

A Private firms will produce more than the society wants

B Private firms will produce just enough to satisfy the wants of the society

C Private firms will produce less than the society wants

D Private firms will use resources to produce something else

21 A government intervenes in the market for rented accommodation. It sets the maximum weekly rent a landlord can charge per square metre of accommodation below the current market equilibrium rent. What is most likely to be observed at the new rental charge?

A Demand for rented accommodation will contract

B The supply of accommodation for rent will extend

C There will be an excess demand for rented accommodation

D There will be an excess supply of rented accommodation

22 A government subsidizes the production of electric cars. This is likely to…

   A Increase the market price of electric cars

   B Raise the costs of supplying electric cars

   C Raise revenue for the government

   D Increase the supply of electric cars at every possible price

23 The diagram below shows the market for alcoholic drinks. The government has set a minimum price of $0.60 per unit of alcohol. What will be the impact of this policy measure?

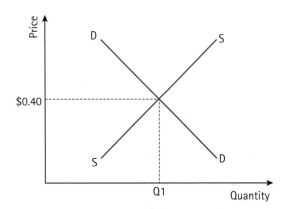

   A It will cause supply to exceed demand

   B It will reduce the market price

   C It will cause demand to exceed supply

   D It will have no effect on the market

24 The diagram below shows the market for fizzy drinks with a high sugar content. The initial market equilibrium is at point X.

Which point will represent the new market equilibrium following the introduction of an indirect tax on these drinks?

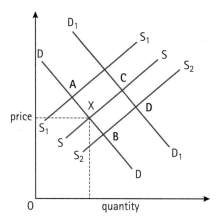

25 Governments may intervene in their economies when free markets fail to produce desirable outcomes. Why may an intervention make these problems worse?

   A A government may introduce new taxes to reduce negative externalities

   B Government subsidies can make firms less efficient

   C A government will have to use scarce resources to enforce regulations

   D A government may set the legal minimum price for a demerit good above its market equilibrium

Structured questions

1 The following headline appeared in UK newspapers in 2017: 'More resources must be devoted to the National Health Service'. This would involve making some difficult choices because of the basic economic problem.

   A Define the basic *economic problem.* [2]

   B Explain and contrast how resources are allocated to different uses in market and mixed economic systems. [4]

   C Using a production possibility curve diagram, analyse why choices have to be made to allocate resources. [6]

   D Discuss whether an economy would benefit from an increase in resources allocated to healthcare. [8]

2   Global food prices have increased significantly in recent years. Food poverty has also increased as result. In an attempt to reduce the prices of basic foodstuffs, some governments have introduced policy measures to encourage farmers to increase their output and shift market supply curves to the right.

   A   Identify what determines an *equilibrium price* in a market. [2]
   B   Explain **two** factors that may cause the supply curve of a product to shift out to the right. [4]
   C   Analyse what effect a fall in food prices may have on the profit of farm owners. [6]
   D   Discuss whether food prices are likely to continue rising in the future. [8]

3   Global demand for bicycles has been rising rapidly and sales are expected to reach US$60 billion a year by 2021 according to a report published in 2016. The highest growth in demand is expected in countries in the Asia Pacific region. Here, the price elasticity of demand for bicycles is estimated to be around −0.2, much lower than in many Western countries. Cigarette consumption also continues to rise in many countries in the Asia Pacific region.

   A   Define *demand*. [2]
   B   Explain **two** probable causes of an increase in consumer demand for bicycles. [4]
   C   Analyse why consumer demand for a product may be more price elastic in one country than in another. [6]
   D   Discuss whether a government should increase indirect tax on cigarettes. [8]

4   To combat rising levels of obesity, many governments have introduced measures to discourage people from eating processed foods with high fat and high sugar content whilst encouraging more people to eat fruit, including apples and pears. The success of these measures will depend in large part on the price elasticity of supply of these products and the responsiveness of consumer demand.

   A   Define *price elasticity of supply*. [2]
   B   Explain **two** reasons why the supply of apples may decrease. [6]
   C   Apples are a close substitute for pears. Use diagrams to analyse the effect a rise in the price of apples will have on the market for pears. [6]
   D   Discuss whether governments should only impose indirect taxes on products for which consumer demand is price inelastic. [8]

5   About half the land in Nigeria used to be covered in trees. Today all but about 10% of those trees have been cut down. The deforestation rate in Nigeria has been among the highest in the world along with Honduras, The Phillipines and Benin. It is seen as evidence of market failure by some economists who want the sector to be regulated by governments.

   A   Define *regulation*. [2]
   B   Explain how resources are allocated in a market economic system. [4]
   C   Analyse the causes of market failure. [6]
   D   Using examples, discuss whether or not an economy will benefit from cutting down its forests. [8]

3 Microeconomic decision makers

Households, workers and firms including banks, are key decision makers in most economies. Their decisions and actions as consumers and producers will help to determine how resources are used, what goods and services are produced and their prices. It is therefore important to understand what motivates the decisions and actions of households, workers and firms.

Households are both owners of factors of production and consumers of goods and services. Households will exchange their labour and other factors of production with firms in return for money so they are able to buy the goods and services they need and want. Money is a good that is generally accepted in exchange for other goods and services and the role of the banking system in a modern economy is to ensure there is enough money in circulation to allow production, consumption and exchange to take place.

The wages received by workers in different occupations are determined by labour market conditions and are a key determinant in how much they are able to spend, save and borrow. People earning low wages and those without work tend to spend all or most of their incomes satisfying their basic needs for food and shelter.

Most private sector firms aim to maximize their profits by combining labour and other factor inputs in the most productive way possible. Firms will therefore tend to employ more factor inputs the more productive and profitable they become. An increase in productivity means more output can be produced with the same factor inputs. As a result, firms will be able reduce their costs and increase their profits.

Profit is the difference between the total cost of producing goods and services and the total revenue from their sale.

Large firms often enjoy cost advantages over smaller ones. Some large firms may also have sufficient market power to restrict competition from smaller firms and the supply of its product in order to boost its profits. As a result, the market price and profit may be higher and product quality lower than what they may have been in a more competitive market. The abuse of market power by large, dominant firms, known as monopolies, is a form of market failure. Governments will often intervene to control the prices monopolies are able to charge.

SECTION 3.1.1

Money

Why do we need money?

To support specialization and exchange

Just imagine how different life would be today if there was no money. How could we buy all the different goods and services we need or want? How would people be paid for the work they do?

For example, when you have finished your studies and go out to work would you want to be paid in oranges or tea for your labour? Or perhaps you'd prefer to start your own business in the future. If so, would you be happy to exchange the good or service of your firm with consumers in return for olives or shoes or meat?

Your answer to both these questions will probably be no, but many years ago before the widespread use of money you would have had no choice. You would either have had to accept other goods or services as payment or be **self-sufficient** by producing everything you needed or wanted for yourself.

Many of our ancestors had to be self-sufficient. All individuals or small communities would produce all the things they needed or wanted for themselves, for example by growing and hunting their own food supplies, building their own shelters, making clothes from wool and animal skins, producing cooking pots from clay and so on.

However, it is difficult to produce everything you need or want for yourself. People have different skills. Long ago some people were better at making spears and pottery while others were more skilled at hunting and fishing. Similarly, some villages were located on good farmland while others were in woodland areas able to supply timber for building materials and spear rods. People and also entire communities therefore began to specialize in those productive activities they were best able to do.

ACTIVITY 3.1

How specialization began

The cartoon tells a simple story of how a caveman named Og discovered the benefits of **specialization** over self-sufficiency by growing and exchanging tomatoes for other products.

Write a story to go with the pictures and include as many advantages and disadvantages of self-sufficiency and specialization as you can think of.

Specialization was the first step towards a wealthier society. A community that practised specialization was able to produce more than enough food, clothes, pots and other things that it needed. The increased production achieved by specialization is the result of the **division of labour**, whereby each worker specializes in doing a particular task rather than being a 'Jack of all trades'. ➤ **3.2**

However, with specialization people need to exchange or trade. If people specialized in producing one particular good or service, like Og and his tomatoes, then they must swap or exchange any surplus they do not require themselves for goods or services produced by other people, in order to obtain a greater variety of products to satisfy more of their needs and wants.

To overcome the problems of barter

Exchanging one good or service for another is called **barter** but it has many problems. For example, if a farmer had some spare corn and needed an axe he or she would travel to a local market to find someone who was willing and able to exchange an axe for the corn. But how much corn would need to be exchanged for an axe? And what if the axe maker wanted apples in return rather than corn? Perhaps the farmer could travel to other markets to find an axe maker who wanted corn in exchange, but the farmer would have to be quick because eventually the corn would turn bad and rot.

You may have discovered from the activity that **bartering** is a very inconvenient way to conduct economic activity. In fact three main problems arise.

1   Fixing a rate of exchange

Look at the diagrams on the next page. How many pencils are worth one ruler? How many pencils are worth one apple? How many oranges are equivalent in value to one ruler? Indeed, how many rulers could Farmer Giles get for a cow? And so it goes on.

In a barter system the value of each and every good must be expressed in terms of every other good.

But I've already got fourteen.

2 Finding someone to swap with

Miss Swap may want some apples from Mr Trade and in return may be prepared to offer him some cheese. If by chance Mr Trade would like some cheese they can barter. But if Mr Trade does not like cheese no deal can take place. In this case an economist would say no **double coincidence of wants** exists. In other words, before two people can barter they must both want the good that the other person has.

3 Trying to save

A final problem is how to save under a barter system. A carpenter could store tables and chairs but would need a large room, but imagine trying to save some meat or cheese for a long period of time without the help of a refrigerator.

Barter is therefore a very inefficient method of exchange. No wonder many years ago people had to produce most of the basic goods and services they needed for themselves and go without many others. Clearly it would be much easier if there was a single commodity or good that everyone was willing to accept in exchange for their labour and all other goods and services. This commodity is called **money** and it overcomes the problems of barter.

The functions of money

Having money enables people, communities and firms in modern economies to specialize in the production of those goods or services they are best able to, and then to use the money they earn to buy all the other goods and services they may need or want from other producers. Without money, specialization and exchange will be difficult and therefore far fewer goods and services will be produced and far fewer wants are satisfied.

Money overcomes the problems of barter by performing the following functions.

1 Money is a medium of exchange

Because money is a good that is generally acceptable in exchange for all other goods we do not have to search for a person who is willing to barter. That is, money overcomes the problem of needing a double coincidence of wants. Now, Miss Swap can sell her cheese to anyone who is prepared to buy it with money. In turn Miss Swap can use this money to buy the apples she wants from Mr Trade, or anyone who is willing to sell her some apples. Therefore, trade is brought about by two transactions with money being used in each.

2 Money is a unit of account

Just as a thermometer measures temperature and a ruler measures length, so money provides a measure of value. Using money helps those producers and consumers engaged in trade to avoid the problems of fixing prices of goods and services in terms of all other goods and services.

Instead of arguing and attempting to remember how many pencils you can get for one ruler, all goods have a price expressed in terms of one single product called money. That is, money is a unit of account used to measure and compare the value of different goods and services, and used to express their prices.

3 Money is a store of value

One of the problems with barter is that many goods are difficult to save either because they take up too much space or they lose their value over time because they perish.

Money is usually a good store of value. Unless prices are rising rapidly, money tends to hold its value over time. In other words, it allows people to save in order to make purchases at a later date.

Some people save by storing valuable antiques and works of art, things that we do not regard as money but which can be exchanged for money in the future. People may save in this way because as the prices of goods rise over time, the purchasing power of money, or what it will buy, is reduced. When prices rise rapidly due to **inflation**, money will fail to be such a good store of value. ➤ **4.8.4**

4 Money is a means of deferred payment

When a person buys goods on credit the consumer has the use of the goods but does not have to pay for them immediately. The consumer can pay some time after he or she receives the goods. In the case of hire purchase, payment is made by instalments spread over a number of months or years.

Credit in a barter system would be very confusing and open to cheating. For example, imagine a person who trades a box of nails for a dozen apples to be paid one month later. Would the apples be fresh? Would they be large or small apples? Using money to pay later overcomes these problems and therefore encourages people to engage in trade, reducing the worry of giving credit. ➤ **3.2.1**

What makes a good money?

A vast range of objects have been used as a medium of exchange at one time or another in the past in different countries. These have ranged from beads used by the American Indians to large stone discs used by the inhabitants of Yap, a small island in the Pacific Ocean.

Money, as we know it today, has been the product of a long period of development. Man has slowly discovered, by a process of trial and error, that some objects fulfil the functions of money better than others.

dog's teeth   Stone Money (Yap)   Manillas (Africa)   knife money (China)

Funny money

How fake money saved Brazil

IN 1994 BRAZIL replaced its currency, the Cruzeiro, with a new money called the Real. This was part of an economic stabilization plan designed to rid the economy of crippling hyperinflation, restore confidence in the economy and reduce poverty. For many decades Brazil had one of the most unequal income distributions in the world and the lack of economic growth coupled with rampant price inflation in prices was causing widespread hardship.

During the 1980s and early 1990s, Brazil's runaway inflation rate peaked at an annual rate of 2,439 per cent, or just under 92 per cent per month. This meant products such as eggs that cost just $1 at the start of a year, would cost almost $2 just one month later and a staggering $2,439 by the end of the year. Shops would have to raise their prices almost every hour of every day just to keep up. In turn consumers would need to go to the shops with more and more cash each day simply to buy the same amount of products they did the previous day. Many would try to run ahead of shopkeepers just to avoid the latest mark-ups in prices. More and more people were forced into poverty as a result. Eventually confidence was lost in the currency, in the economy as place to

invest and do business, and in the government's ability to control inflation.

So in 1992 the new finance minister invited Edmar Bacha, an economist, to advise the Brazilian government. Bacha started by telling it to slow down the rate at which it was creating new money. Without growth in Brazil's output of goods and services to match, the additional money simply forced up prices.

Bacha also knew it was vital to restore people's confidence in the currency. The Cruzeiro had become worthless. Nobody held on to it or wanted it because in fell in value every minute of every day as prices continued to soar. People would trade in US dollars or other stable currencies. A new currency was therefore needed that people could trust to hold its value. Bacha therefore advised playing a trick on people by introducing a fake money called the URV or Unit of Real Value. The URV didn't actually exist but every product would be priced in URVs. Similarly all wages and taxes were expressed in URVs.

Prices, wages and all other monetary values listed in URVs were kept stable over time. The only thing that changed was the exchange rate between Cruzeiros and URVs. So, for example, eggs now priced at say 100 URVs one month would be the

same price the next month and the month after that and so on, but 100 URVs might be worth 100 Cruzieros one month and 200 the next.

Bacha argued that eventually people would get used to prices in URVs being stable and stop expecting prices to rise so rapidly. In turn they would become used to paying for goods and services in URVs and stop thinking about the Cruzeiro and how much it was worth. This was despite the URV or what had become known as the 'real' not being a real currency. However, once this had happened it did in fact become real. New notes and coins were printed and the Real became the new currency of Brazil in 1994.

And the magic trick worked! By 1996 the monthly inflation rate had fallen to less than 1 per cent from over 45 per cent in 1994. Economic activity had increased strongly during the second half of 1994 and thereafter, led by a boom in domestic demand that was fuelled by lower inflation and higher real wages including for many of the country's poorest workers. Since then Brazil has emerged as a rapidly developing economy and major exporter, and some 20 million people have been lifted out of poverty.

1 Why did the Brazilian government replace the national currency, the Cruzeiro, with a new currency called the Real as a measure of value in 1994?

2 Which of the following functions of money was the Cruzeiro failing to perform before it was replaced by the Real? Give reasons for your answer.

a a medium of exchange

b a measure of value

c a store of value?

What is a 'good' money?

In groups discuss which of the items shown below would make a good money. Appoint a spokesperson for your group to record your views and to present your arguments to the class.

Your discussion may have led you to the conclusion that characteristics such as the following are important for a good money to possess.

1 Acceptability

Anything can be used as money as long as it is generally acceptable. This is why a worthless piece of paper can be used as money, for example, a 10 dollar or a 50 euro note. It is only worth this amount in spending power because everyone accepts it as such. Thus our present money is a **token money** – as a piece of paper or metal coin it is worth much less than the face value printed upon it.

2 Durability

Any good used as money must be hard-wearing. Money would be useless if it just melted away in your pocket. Coins and notes must be strong and durable so that they may act as a store of value.

3 Portability

Money should be easy to carry around. A house would clearly be far too heavy to move. A cow would be reluctant to go shopping with you, and even more reluctant if you tried to squeeze it into your wallet or purse. Paper notes are lightweight and can be folded into a wallet or purse, while a handful of small metal coins can be carried easily in your pockets.

4 Divisibility

If cars were used as money a problem would arise if you tried to buy something priced at half your car. Sawing the vehicle into half would reduce its value. One whole working car is worth much more than two halves.

Therefore it must be possible to divide money of a large value into smaller values to make small purchases or to give change, without it losing value. This is why we have notes and coins with different face values to buy goods and services with different prices and to give change.

5 Scarcity

A good money must be limited in supply or scarce if people and firms are to value it. For example, small stones or pebbles would not be a good money because people could simply pick up as many as they liked from the ground whenever they wanted to. A shopkeeper would not exchange her goods for pebbles that were freely available. Only if money is scarce will people value it as a good that can be used in exchange.

So why is money so important?

In Section 1 we learnt how people living in a self-sufficient society began to specialize in the jobs they were most able to do. Specialization was the first step towards a wealthier society and people in a community that practised specialization were for the first time able to produce more than enough food, clothes, pots and other things that they needed. They had some left over – a surplus.

If people specialize they must trade. A man concentrating on making pins could not satisfy his need for food by eating pins or his need for clothes by wearing pins. Therefore trade is a necessity for individuals to obtain those things they cannot make on their own.

But in a barter system trade is difficult. There is no guarantee that an expert pin-maker will be able to find people willing to swap their goods for his or her pins at a fair rate of exchange. The result is the pin-maker and others will be unable to specialize to their full potential. They would have to spend their time and effort producing a range of goods and services in order to increase their chances of trading successfully for the other products they needed.

This would mean that much less would be produced by whole economies than if they had specialized in the production of those goods and services they were best able to produce.

Money therefore encourages specialization by making trade easier. This enables an economy to increase its national output and income and allows people to enjoy a much higher standard of living. In turn, the more an economy specializes the more money it needs to finance an increasing amount of production and trade. ➤ **4.6.4**

Money is needed by consumers, firms and governments to make payments to hire labour and buy other resources, and goods and services. The banking system can provide this money and make it easier to make payments. Therefore, as the output of an economy grows and more trade takes place, so the banking system must develop and create more money.

The history of money

It is interesting to understand how modern money developed, although you will not be assessed on this knowledge in your exams. There have been five main stages in the development of money, with each stage being the result of mankind's attempt to find objects that display the characteristics of a good money.

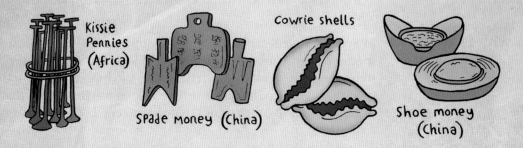

Kissie Pennies (Africa)

Spade money (China)

Cowrie shells

Shoe money (China)

Stage 1

The earliest form of money was goods. Knives, beads and shoes among other objects were used as money because many people were willing to accept these in exchange for their produce. However, such commodity money was quickly abandoned because many of the goods did not possess the essential characteristics of a good money: acceptability, divisibility, portability, durability, scarcity.

1 Ring money, Gold, 100-50 BC

2 Sceat, Silver AD 734-766, Anglo-Saxon

3 Silver AD 802-839, King Egberht Anglo-Saxon

4 Halfcrown, Silver, AD 1644, Charles I

▲ Early coins of the UK

Stage 2

Precious metals, such as gold and silver, have always been scarce enough to make them a possible money. However, trading with metals involved carrying around a weighing scale and tools to cut the metals.

Stage 3

The problem of portability that cursed metals led to the natural development of **coinage**. Precious metals in predetermined weights were often stamped with the face of the king or queen, and with another stamp to show their value.

But one problem remained. Throughout history the temptation to 'clip' coins, trimming a fine filing of the precious metal from the edges, has been greater than the fear of being caught.

The invention of the ribbed edge on coins overcame the problem of 'clipping'. Another problem with early precious coins was that the rulers of countries often debased them. Coins would be called in for re-minting on a special occasion. The rulers would then mix cheap metals with gold or silver, producing perhaps six coins for every four received, cleverly keeping two for themselves. The result of this

today is that the metal content of coins is virtually worthless, yet people still accept such coins in exchange for goods because they know they are generally acceptable.

Stage 4

The first paper money was issued by early goldsmiths who accepted deposits of precious metals for keeping in their safes. In return they issued a paper receipt to the owner. It was quickly realized that these paper claims to gold were far easier to exchange for goods than spending time and effort withdrawing the gold only for it to be given to someone who would then re-deposit it with a goldsmith for safe keeping.

Stage 5

Goldsmiths' receipts for deposits of precious metals were to become the first paper money, and goldsmiths the first banks. In most countries today only the central bank has the right to issue notes and coins, but this money can no longer be converted into gold.

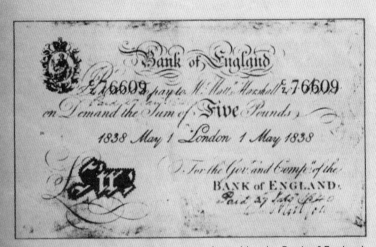

▲ An example of an early paper note issued by the Bank of England in the UK.

What is money? We now know that money is a generally acceptable medium of exchange. However, we also know that to be money a commodity must also act as store of value. Given this, our savings in banks and other financial institutions can be classified as money because we can withdraw these deposits so that they may be exchanged for the goods and services we want.

Notes and coins (cash), and deposits with banks and other financial institutions therefore make up the **money supply** in an economy.

Mrs Mint's money

Mrs Mint is tempted by a luxury cruise advertised in the local travel agency. The only problem is the cost of $3,000. At home she tries to figure out just how much money she has.

Emptying the contents of her purse she finds that she has $50 in notes and coins. The jar on her sideboard contains $100 in crisp notes. But not nearly enough for that cruise!

Remembering that she has a savings account at the bank which allows her to withdraw any cash immediately, Mrs Mint calculates that another $300 can be added to her list. But still not enough to pay for that cruise!

After waiting seven days Mrs Mint can withdraw her savings from another account she also keeps at the bank. This account contains $400. It appears that she will have to withdraw her long-term savings. In 90 days she can obtain $600 from a government savings scheme. In 120 days $700 can be withdrawn from a credit union that she saves with each month. Mrs Mint also has $800 tied up for two years in a government bond. Finally, she considers selling some of the jewellery she has kept for several years to enable her to sail away on the luxury cruise liner for the holiday of a lifetime.

In the above passage Mrs Mint has a variety of ways by which she can raise the necessary money to pay for the luxury cruise.

1   If money is purely a medium of exchange, list those items included in the passage that you consider would be money and give reasons for your choice.

2   If instead we focus upon money being a store of value, which other commodities would you also class as money, giving reasons for your choice?

It is not an easy task to decide exactly what is money. **Cash** or notes and coins with different face values are generally accepted and recognized as money in all economies. However, cash can lose its value over time as prices rise.

In contrast, many **financial assets** can provide a good store of value and may therefore be a good form of money, especially if they can be converted easily and quickly into cash in order to make payments. If they can they are **liquid assets** and may be thought of as **near money**.

For example, personal savings can be withdrawn quickly from an instant access savings account held at a bank. However, savings tied up in a bond for two years will not become a medium of exchange until the bond has matured at the end of the two-year period. So although different savings accounts and other **financial assets** can perform all of the functions of money, some do so better than others and at different times.

Jewellery, valuable antiques and other **physical assets** may also provide a good store of value but are not generally acceptable in exchange for other goods and may be difficult to sell quickly to raise cash. That is, they are not near money. Physical assets may also go down in value over time if they become less collectable or damaged.

In summary therefore, some assets are nearer money than others because:

1 Some assets fulfil the functions of money better than others. For example, cash is a good medium of exchange, but antiques are not.

2 Some assets can be converted to cash more quickly than others. For example, financial assets held in a bank deposit account can usually be withdrawn instantly or within a few days, whereas assets in some other saving schemes cannot be converted into cash for many months or longer.

3 Some assets retain their value on conversion to cash better than others. For example, those in savings accounts hold their value because banks reward people who save with them with periodic payments or interest, whereas cars lose their value over time.

▼ Two ways of creating money are printing notes and coins, and bank loans

Many savings accounts and other **bank deposits** held at banks and other financial institutions can be easily converted to cash, usually for little or no cost. Bank deposits have therefore become the most important form of money in most modern economies. For example, look at the table below for the US economy at the end of March 2017. Banks are able to create deposit money by constantly re-lending any cash that returns to them in the form of bank deposits. An increase in bank lending will therefore increase the supply of money in an economy. ➤ **4.8.3**

▼ The supply of money in the USA, March 2017

	Amount ($ billion)	Percentage share of total
Notes and coins	1,530	11
Bank deposits	11,850	89
Total	13,380	100

Source: *US Federal Reserve*

The difference between the money supply and national income of an economy

The national income of an economy is not the same as its supply of money. This is because each unit of money can be exchanged many times each year. For example, imagine you have just received one dollar in payment for some work you have completed. You use the dollar to buy a magazine. The shopkeeper then uses the dollar to buy some petrol and the owner of the petrol station uses it to pay his electricity charges. Already this one dollar has been exchanged four times and has created $4 of income.

The number of times money is exchanged or passes from one holder to another in any given period is called the **velocity of circulation** of money. It can vary over time. For example, if the velocity of money is increasing it means money is changing hands more frequently or faster than before. This is often a sign that total spending and economic activity in the economy is rising. ➤ **4.6.4**

What is the market for money?

In a modern economy people, firms and government need somewhere they can keep their money safely and need easy ways to make payments to others. They may also want to borrow money, make investments and exchange the money used in their country for the currency used in another so they can make payments overseas. Business organizations that specialize in providing these services are called **financial institutions**. Without financial institutions, specialized production and trade on the scale enjoyed today would not be possible, costs of production would be much higher, economies would be less developed and economic growth would be much slower. ➤ **4.8.1**

The **money market** is really no different from any other market. It is made up of all those people and organizations that want money, and all the people and organizations willing and able to supply money, namely a banking system that creates deposit money, and a central bank that issues notes and coins.

What is a bank?

The main types of financial institutions in the market for money are **banks**. They are just like any other business except the product they supply is money, in the form of loans and other financial products.

A bank is a **financial intermediary** because it brings together customers who want to save money and customers who want to borrow it.

▶ Banks are financial intermediaries between customers who want to deposit money and customers who want to borrow money

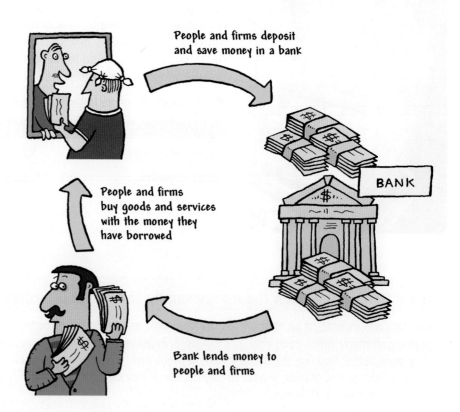

People and firms deposit and save money in a bank

People and firms buy goods and services with the money they have borrowed

BANK

Bank lends money to people and firms

Most but not all banks are large, profit-making companies. Banks are among some of the world's largest corporations in terms of their revenue, profit or number of employees. They earn revenue in a number of ways.

Charging interest on loans

Banks accept deposits of money and savings from their customers and make loans from this money. They attract deposits and savings by paying customers interest on their money or a share of banking profits.

A bank will not keep all their customers' deposits and savings in its vaults. It will lend most of this money to other customers, including individuals and firms, for example to buy cars, overseas holidays, machinery and property. In turn, these people and firms will use the borrowed money to pay others for goods and services. People and firms receiving payments will then deposit or save money they receive, with a bank. In this way, banks create money in an economy in the form of additional bank deposits.

A customer who borrows money from a bank must repay the loan with interest over an agreed period of time. The interest charge is calculated as a percentage of the amount of a loan. So, for example, a customer who is loaned $1,000 repayable over one year in 12 monthly instalments and is charged interest at 5% of the loan value will repay the bank $1,050 in total.

The percentage of interest charged on a loan, or **interest rate**, represents the cost of borrowing money. Interest rates can vary over time and by different types of loan and customer. For example, a large loan over 10 years to a new, small business may be charged a higher rate of interest than a smaller loan to be repaid over 2 years to a person in regular, paid employment. This is because banks may consider there to be a greater risk of non-repayment of loans made to small businesses. Many small businesses fail and may be unable to repay their debts.

Making loans is inherently risky, so the greater the risk the higher the interest rate a bank will charge. Also, over time, price inflation may rise and reduce the value of the loan in terms of what the money will be able to buy after it has been repaid. Interest charges will help to compensate a bank for any reduction in value of the money it has tied up in loans due to rising price inflation.

As long as loans are repaid and interest charges on loans exceed interest payments on savings, a bank will make a profit from making loans.

Charging fees for the provision of other financial services

For example, a bank may charge its customers fees for the following services:

- withdrawals from automated cash machines
- exchanging and transferring foreign currencies
- buying and selling shares in public limited companies
- providing life, property and travel insurance
- issuing debit and credit cards
- storing valuables
- organizing customer payments in the form of cheques or electronic transfers to the bank accounts of other people, businesses or government authorities
- telephone and internet banking services.

Making investments

A bank can use money deposited by its customers to invest in the shares of other public limited companies. If the shares it holds increase in value the bank will make a gain from selling them. It will also receive a share of any profits made by these other companies. ➤ **3.5.1**

The 10 biggest banks in the world by market value, 2017

Banking group	Country	Market value US$ billion
JP Morgan Chase & Co	US	299.4
Wells Fargo & Co	US	276.6
Industrial & Commercial Bank of China (ICBC)	China	229.7
Bank of America	US	228.8
China Construction Bank	China	186.8
HSBC Holdings	UK	165.8
Citigroup Inc	US	159.9
Agricultural Bank of China	China	148.1
Bank of China	China	145.7
Commonwealth Bank of Australia	Australia	106.4

ACTIVITY 3.6

Why do we need banks?

Digital Dreams is a small but rapidly expanding company manufacturing digital video equipment. It has recently received a $200,000 loan repayable over 20 years to buy new business premises.

Digital Dreams sells much of its equipment online to customers who use credit and debit cards and so it accepts all these forms of payment. It also accepts cheques from customers.

The company keeps most of its sales revenue in a savings account. The balance is kept in a deposit account to pay wages to employees and other costs, including electricity, gas and local taxes, by direct debit.

If there were no banks:

1 How would Digital Dreams make and receive payments?

2 Where could it store its sales revenue safely?

3 How could it finance its new business premises?

4 What would be the likely impact on the costs of running Digital Dreams?

Types of bank

There are several different types of bank in a modern economy. They all offer very similar services, but each type tends to specialize in particular financial products and groups of consumers.

1 Commercial banks

Commercial banks are often called 'high-street banks' because they have retail branches located in most cities and towns. However, many banks provide telephone and online banking facilities for their customers so there is no need to visit a branch.

▼ Maybank is the largest commercial bank in Malaysia with over 380 branches

Commercial banks are also known as **clearing banks**. This is because they transfer funds between each other on behalf of their customers through a process known as clearing. For example, when the customer of one bank wants to make a payment to another person or business, that customer must instruct their bank to move money from their bank account to the bank account of that other person or business. The instruction can be made in writing using a cheque or by using a debit card or through online banking. Once a bank has received the instruction and agreed the payment it is cleared for transfer to the other bank account. Helping customers make and receive payments in these ways is a key function of commercial banks. However, they also provide other financial services:

- accepting deposits of money and savings
- making personal and commercial loans
- buying and selling shares for customers
- providing insurance
- operating pension funds
- providing financial and tax planning advice
- exchanging foreign currencies.

Types of account

A **deposit account** is a current account, savings account or another type of bank account which allows money to be deposited and withdrawn by the account holder.

A **current account** or **checking account** is used by the account holder for everyday transactions. Most people will have their weekly or monthly wages or salaries paid directly into their current account.

A **savings account** is a safe place to store your savings. Interest will usually be added to your savings by a bank depending on how much you have saved and how often you can make withdrawals.

Types of loan

An **overdraft** allows bank customers to overdraw their account by an agreed amount. It provides a convenient short-term loan, for example to pay unexpected bills.

A **personal loan** is repaid with interest over a fixed period, usually for more than 6 months and up to 10 years.

A **commercial loan** is a loan to a business to pay for operating costs and the purchase of materials and machinery. The loan is repayable with interest over a fixed period of time.

A **mortgage** is a long-term loan, often up to 25 years, used by people or firms to buy property.

Methods of payment

Using **cash**, or notes and coins, is the easiest way of paying for goods and services in person. Many banks allow account holders to withdraw cash from their accounts at any time of the day, from many different locations, using cash machines or ATMs.

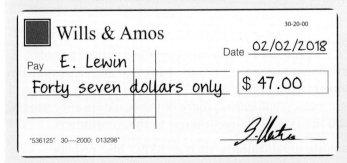

A **direct debit** is an easy way to make regular payments of varying amounts to the same organization from your account, for example to pay monthly bills from an electricity or telephone supplier. Once set up, the supplier will simply provide your bank with its account details, the amount to be paid each month, and your bank will make these payments on your behalf.

A **cheque** (or check) is a written promise to pay cash to, or transfer money into the account of, another person or organization. If you write a cheque it must show your name, your account number, the amount you are promising to pay, and to whom it is to be paid. The person or organization receiving your cheque will pay it into their bank account. Once received the amount written on the cheque will be transferred into their bank account from your bank account.

A **debit card** is an electronic method of making a payment to another business organization. It means you do not have to use cash or write a cheque. Once your card is 'swiped' through or tapped on a payment machine, your bank details and the amount to be withdrawn from your account, and the details of the account to receive your payment, are transmitted electronically to your bank headquarters and the transfer is made instantaneously.

A **credit card** can be used to make payments in much the same way as a debit card except it allows the card holder up to a month or longer to pay for purchases made using the card. A credit card therefore provides a short-term loan. Interest is payable if the amount on the credit card is not repaid in full in the specified period.

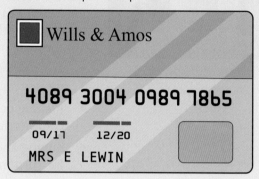

2 Credit unions

A credit union is a cooperative, not-for-profit organization, owned by and for its members. Credit unions were started by people who worked or lived together to provide low-cost loans to members who were on low incomes and unable to borrow money from other banks, for example to help with home repairs, school fees and medical expenses. Credit unions are popular in the USA. Many now offer their customers a full range of financial services.

3 Mutual societies

These are also known as savings and loans associations or building societies in some countries. They are owned by and run on behalf of their members or customers. Traditionally they specialized in providing mortgages to buy property but now offer many commercial banking services.

3 Investment banks

These banks specialize in helping large business organizations raise finance to fund their operations and expansion, usually through helping them to issue and sell stocks and shares on the stock market. They can also provide advice on company mergers and takeovers. Today, most large commercial banks also provide investment banking services.

4 Islamic banks

Islamic banking is based on principles of Islamic Sharia law, which forbids interest charges and payments. Instead, an Islamic bank can earn a profit from the fees it charges customers for banking services including making loans, and people who deposit their money will earn a share of the bank's profits. This is because Islamic Banks do not pay or charge interest to their customers.

Many multinational banking organizations, such as HSBC, also provide Sharia-compliant banking services in many countries.

The role of a central bank

The central bank is the centre of the banking system in most economies. The main function of a central bank is to maintain the stability of the national currency and the money supply.

In many countries the central bank is owned by the government and run by a public corporation. The oldest central bank in the world is the Bank of Sweden, which was opened in 1668. This was followed in 1694 by the Bank of England in the UK.

A central bank usually performs the following functions:

- **It issues notes and coins for the nation's currency**

The central bank in a country will normally have the exclusive right to print and issue new notes and coins and to replace old worn out ones in that country.

- **It manages payments to and from the government**

The tax and other revenues of the government of a country will be held in an account at the central bank. Government payments, including for contracts to build roads and the wages of government employees, will also be made from the government's account.

- **It manages the national debt**

A central bank can issue and repay public sector debt on behalf of the government. ➤ **4.3.1**

- **It supervises the banking system, regulating the conduct of banks, holding their deposits and transferring funds between them**

A central bank can set rules to make sure banks conduct their business properly and to determine which organizations can become banks. It will also hold the deposits of commercial and other banks, and transfer funds between their accounts to settle the many millions of cheque, debit card and other payments made by their customers to the accounts of other people and firms or even to the government.

- **It is the 'lender of the last resort' to the banking system**

A central bank will lend money to the banking system if one or more banks run into difficulties meeting payments. It does this to prevent banks from running out of money and going bankrupt.

- **It manages the nation's gold and foreign currency reserves**

These reserves are used to make payments to other countries and to stabilize the value of the national currency. For example, if the value of the national currency is falling against other world currencies the central bank can use these reserves to buy up the national currency on the global foreign exchange market. As a result of this increase in demand for the national currency, its foreign exchange value will tend to rise. ➤ **6.3.3**

- **It operates the government's monetary policy**

Governments will use monetary policy in an attempt to influence price inflation, employment and growth in their economies. Monetary policy involves changing the interest rate to influence the level of borrowing, saving and spending by individual and business consumers. For example, price inflation can be caused by people and firms spending too much money on goods and services. Raising the interest rate in the economy will make borrowing money more expensive and reduce demand for loans. It will also make saving more attractive and increase demand for savings. The central bank can increase the interest rate in the economy by raising the interest rate it charges the banking system in the economy when it loans it money. ➤ **4.4.2**

It is usually the job of the government finance minister to decide what the interest rate should be, but some central banks are able to set interest rates without political interference from government ministers. For example, a government may lower interest rates for political reasons before an election simply to boost its popularity rather than for economic reasons to control inflation. Lowering interest rates too much may increase borrowing and, as a result, increase the problem of inflation in an economy. In contrast, a central bank can decide what the interest rate should be to control inflation over time by observing wage increases, raw material costs, house prices and other economic variables that provide an early warning of inflationary pressures in the economy. ➤ **4.8.3**

Examples of 'independent central banks' include the US Federal Reserve, the Bank of England (since 1997), the Reserve Bank of India (1935), the Bank of Mexico (1993), the Bank of Japan, the Bank of Canada, the Reserve Bank of Australia and the European Central Bank.

EXAM PREPARATION 3.1

The euro replaced the national currencies of many European countries in the European Union in 2002 to become the sole legal tender in the eurozone.

a Define *money*. [2]

b Explain **two** characteristics of the euro currency that make it a good money. [4]

c Analyse the impact price inflation in Europe might have on the functions of the euro. [6]

d Discuss the role of a central bank in an economy. [8]

You can bank on it!

Compare and contrast the functions and activities of a commercial bank with the central bank in your country.

1 What are the main functions of the two banks?

2 What services do they provide and to whom?

3 How are they organized, controlled and financed?

4 What are their relationships with other banks in your country and globally?

5 What role do they play in your economy?

ECONOMICS IN ACTION

How and why did the Central Bank of Nigeria intervene to save its banking sector from collapse? Why did the Central Bank of Chile buy US dollars?

Central Bank acts boldly to stabilize banking sector

In 2009 the Central Bank of Nigeria announced a N400 billion (US$2.5 billion) bailout for five of the country's banks – Oceanic Bank, Intercontinental Bank, AfriBank, FinBank and Union Bank. The CEOs and executive directors of the five banks were also suspended and immediately replaced.

The Central Bank said the injection of money was necessary because the banks were running out of cash and other liquid assets that could be converted easily and quickly into cash. The decision to inject N400 billion into the troubled banks would be sufficient to enable them to continue their normal business and would protect the savings of their depositors.

According to the Central Bank the banks had loaned too much money to organizations in financial difficulties and had too many bad loans with repayment arrears. This was due it said to poor governance and credit control in the banks.

Chilean Central Bank to intervene to stop slide in value of US dollar

According to a media statement, the central bank said it expects to buy US$12 billion from national reserves.

The fall in the value of the US dollar has caused problems for Chile's fruit growers and exporters who have suffered a fall in their export earnings from the USA. Over the last six months the US dollar has fallen in value from 520 Chilean pesos to just 465 pesos, its lowest exchange rate in 32 months.

After the announcement, the dollar shot up to become worth 490 pesos.

Clues across

5. A long-term loan for the purchase of property (8)
6. The term used to describe financial assets that can be converted into cash easily and quickly (6, 6)
9. The main bank in an economy responsible for managing the stability of the national currency and the money supply (6, 4)
10. Also known as clearing banks, these banks provide financial services to many individuals and businesses via the internet and through retail branches located in many towns and cities (10, 5)
11. Trading or swapping goods and services without money. This form of exchange requires a double coincidence of wants (6)
12. A good money must be acceptable to fulfil this function (6, 2, 8)

Clues down

1. A measure of the average number of times each unit of the money supply in an economy changes hands in a given period of time (8, 2, 11)
2. A charge applied to a loan as a percentage of the amount borrowed. It is the cost of borrowing money (8, 4)
3. Term used to describe an organization, such as a bank or credit union, that brings together customers who want to save money and others who wish to borrow it (9, 12)
4. The total of bank deposits and notes and coins in an economy (5, 6)
7. A function of money that is eroded when there is high or rapidly rising inflation in an economy (5, 2, 5)
8. Another term used to describe the exchange of goods and services between producers and consumers, usually for money (5)

SECTION 3.2.1(i)

The influences on spending

Household spending decisions

Householders are owners of factors of production and also consumers of goods and services. They earn money from factor rewards to buy the goods and services they want and need but cannot or choose not to produce themselves. ➤ **1.2.1**

For example, many people in households sell or hire out their services as labour in return for wages and other earnings. Others may earn rents from firms that use their land and other natural resources or interest from money they have saved or invested in firms. Some householders even become successful entrepreneurs and earn profits from the firms they organize and run.

But what do householders do with the income they earn? How much of it do they spend? What do they spend it on and why? And, how much do they save?

People hire out their services as labour in return for wages and other earnings. Some people also invest in companies and earn dividends from profits, while others invest in savings and other investment schemes and earn interest on their money. Other people may rent out land and buildings they own to other people and firms. But what do people do with all the income they earn?

People are the owners of factors of production and also consumers of goods and services. They earn money to buy the goods and services they want and need but do not produce themselves in their work. Any income they do not spend, and which is not taken in tax, can be saved.

What is disposable income?

Wages and salaries, dividends from company profits, rents and interest payments are all forms of taxable income in many countries. The income a person has left after income-related taxes and charges have been deducted is called **disposable income**, because that person is able to choose how to dispose of it, i.e. how much of it to spend and what to spend it on, and how much of it to save to spend at a later date. A rise in income taxes will therefore reduce disposable income and the amount people have to spend or save. Some people may, however, simply choose to save less if taxes rise rather than to cut their spending. ➤ **4.3.6**

The more disposable income a person has, the greater their potential **consumer expenditure** on goods and services, and the more they will be able to save. But how much people can buy with their disposable income will also depend on prices. Increasing prices will reduce the real purchasing power of income. ➤ **4.8.4**

The amount individuals can choose to spend on goods and services therefore depends on their **real disposable income**. Some people with very low real disposable incomes may only be able to afford to satisfy their basic needs for food and shelter, while others with high disposable incomes may choose to consume a vast array of different goods and services mainly for pleasure.

Global economic growth has increased real incomes and, with it, consumer expenditure over time. For example, the charts below demonstrate how closely income and consumer expenditure are related in Australia and Mexico. The same is true in all countries.

▼ Real income and consumer expenditure are closely related in all countries

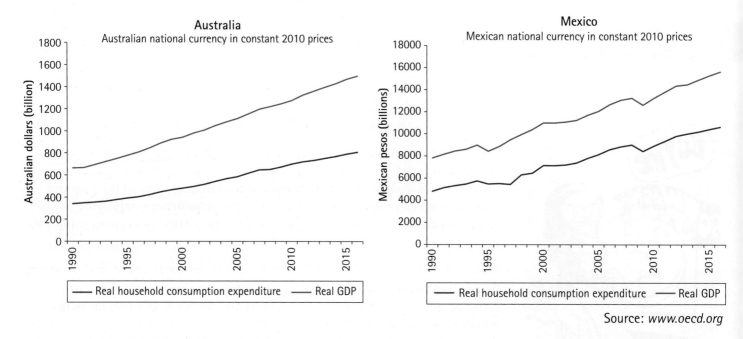

Source: *www.oecd.org*

Why do people consume goods and services?

People buy goods and services to satisfy their wants and needs. **Consumption** therefore involves the using up of goods and services to satisfy our needs and wants. ➤ **1.1.2**

In general, people will choose to spend their disposable incomes on consuming those goods and services that provide them with the most satisfaction or **utility**. That is, a person with a given disposable income, and faced with a set of prices and places to buy different goods and services, will consume those goods and services that maximize his or her total utility.

Consider a simple example of a boy eating cakes. He likes cakes but if he buys too few to eat he will not maximize his utility. However, if he buys and eats too many at once he may start to feel sick and his utility will start to fall. Let's say he does buy too many cakes. He should have bought fewer and instead spent his money on things that would have given him more pleasure than those extra cakes, such as a visit to the cinema to watch a film. The same will apply to the consumption of shoes, holidays, cars and all other goods and services. The more we consume of a particular product the less satisfaction we will get from each additional dollar we spend on that product. Hence there is a saying that 'you can have too much of a good thing!'

Patterns of consumer expenditure can vary greatly even between people with similar incomes, simply because people have different tastes. Tastes may vary between different groups of consumers according to their age, sex and family circumstances, for example whether they are married and have children. ➤ **2.3.4**

People's tastes can also change over time and may be influenced by the views of other consumers. For example, we might change our mind about going to the cinema to watch a particular film or visiting a local restaurant, because we have heard bad reports from other people who have seen the film or eaten at the restaurant. Similarly, we might use a car mechanic or hairdresser and really like their services, in which case we will tend to use them again and again. All of these types of products are called **experience goods and services**, because it is difficult to judge how much we might like them until we have consumed them, and because we can also tell other people about our experience of them.

After income, the following are the three most important factors that affect the level of consumer expenditure in an economy:

Wealth

The wealthier people feel, the greater their spending on goods and services is likely to be. Private **wealth** consists of the stock of goods people own that have a money value. It includes financial assets such as cash, savings accounts and holdings of company shares, and physical assets such as houses, jewellery and other valuable items.

Consumer confidence

If consumers are confident about their jobs and their future incomes then this might encourage them to spend more now, perhaps even to borrow money to buy a house, a new car or other expensive items. However, income and employment can change over time as economic conditions change. If consumers think they may become unemployed or suffer falling income during an economic recession then this may persuade them to save more of their incomes just in case they need to draw on them in the future. ➤ **4.6.3**

Interest rates

If interest rates are high people may save more of their disposable income because it pays them to do so. However, if interest rates are low people may spend more, and may even borrow more because loan repayments will be less.

Spending patterns

▼ Household expenditure as a % of total household expenditure, by lowest and highest gross income households, UK 2016

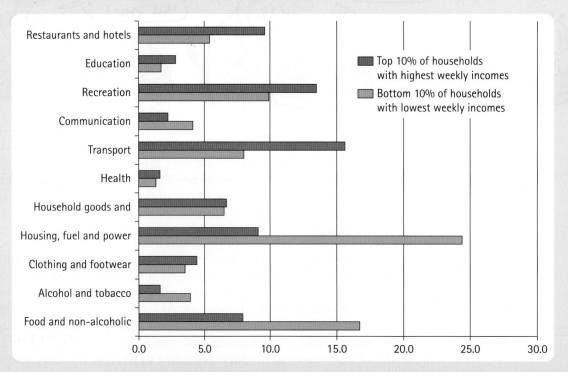

Source: *Family Spending in the UK, UK Office for National Statistics*

Look at the chart comparing how the average low-income household and average high-income household in the UK divide up their weekly spending between different goods and services.

1 Which type of household spent the highest proportion of their total spending on the following categories?
- ▶ Food and non-alcoholic drinks
- ▶ Housing, fuel and power
- ▶ Recreation and culture
- ▶ Alcohol and tobacco
- ▶ Transport
- ▶ Restaurants and hotels

2 What do you think explains these different expenditure patterns?

Analysing consumer spending patterns

Why do some people spend more of their disposable incomes than others? Why do some people spend more on clothes and cars than others? How do our spending patterns change as we age?

What we buy and how much we spend varies greatly across populations according to our incomes, age, sex and tastes. It is therefore useful to examine the consumption patterns of different income groups, age and gender groups and the factors that influence their spending decisions.

Firms find this information useful because it allows them to target the goods and services they produce and advertise at particular groups of consumers they want to attract to buy their products.

Consumer spending varies with income

The proportion of disposable income a person spends on goods and services is measured by their **propensity to consume**. For example, people with very low incomes may have to spend all their incomes meeting their basic needs for food, clothing, housing and heating. Their propensity to consume their disposable incomes is high and they are likely to spend any additional income they receive.

In contrast, people with very high incomes may be able afford to buy luxury holidays and cars to satisfy many more of their wants. They can spend much more in total than people on low incomes but they will also be able to save a proportion of their incomes.

For example, a person earning $100,000 may choose to spend $80,000 and save $20,000 of their income. If their income rises to $110,000 they may increase their spending to $85,000 and their savings to $25,000. That is, their propensity to spend additional income is lower than people on much lower incomes because they are already spending so much.

Our incomes therefore determine how much we can spend in total and what we can buy. However, two people who receive exactly the same level of disposable income may nevertheless have very different spending habits due to differences in their age, gender, family circumstances and tastes.

▼ Spending patterns vary and change with income, age and gender

Young male

Middle-aged female with young children

Retired couple

- Low income.
- Spends nearly all his weekly income on food including fast-food; rented accommodation; travelling to work and to meet friends.
- Cannot afford to save very much but instead prefers to spend money on nights out with friends, fashionable clothes, music and rock concerts.

- Relatively high income.
- High propensity to spend on children's clothes and toys; household items; travel including petrol; clothes and cosmetics; housing costs including electricity bills.
- Saving a proportion of income each month to pay for her children to attend university and to fund a pension.

- A good income from a pension but less than they were earning from paid employment.
- High propensity to spend on holidays; eating out at restaurants; healthcare… but they also still like to attend rock concerts.
- Dissaving (withdrawing their savings to help fund their consumer spending).

Consumer spending varies with age

What we buy tends to change as we get older. For example, young people may spend more on fashionable clothes, going out to clubs and bars, and on music than older people, who will tend to spend more on furniture and other household goods for their homes and on clothes, toys and education for their children.

As we age further, and any children we have grow up and leave home, we may be able to spend more on holidays and leisure activities. We may also need to spend more on health care.

Our incomes also tend to rise as we get older before falling again as we retire from work and draw from pensions or other savings to fund our spending.

Spending patterns and gender

Men and women will also have different spending patterns.

Spending patterns and tastes

Finally, regardless of our incomes, age, family circumstances or gender, a key reason why our spending patterns differ is because we all have different tastes.

For example, some people choose to be vegetarians. They will not eat meat or fish because it is healthier to do so or because they object to way the many animals and fish are treated and killed.

Similarly, some people like loud rock music and will spend some of their incomes buying music CDs or downloads and attending rock concerts. Other people may prefer dance music and attending dance clubs and discos, while others may prefer to spend more of their incomes and leisure time eating at restaurants or attending sporting events.

Recent trends in consumer spending

The chart below shows how household spending patterns have changed over time in the USA.

Spending by US households on clothing and footwear, transportation, furnishings and alcohol as a proportion of their total spending has fallen and they are now devoting a greater proportion of their total expenditure to recreation, financial services and healthcare.

The same trends have been observed in many developed countries, and also now in some developing countries. They are the result of a number of factors:

- **Real incomes have risen**

More people are now better off. Higher incomes enable people to spend more on satisfying their wants. The increased use of credit cards to boost spending also reflects a change in attitudes over time towards borrowing and debt.

- **People work fewer hours than many years ago**

This has given people more leisure time, and increased spending on holidays, sporting activities, garden plants and equipment, and eating out in restaurants.

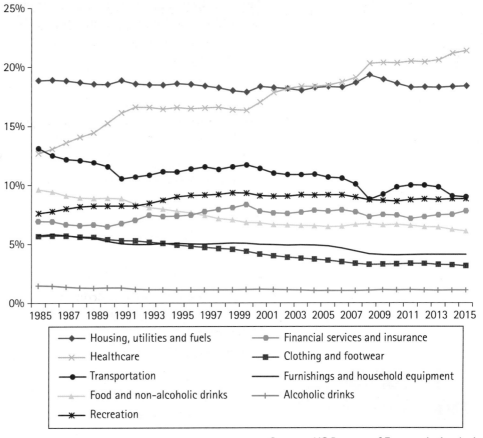

▼ Trends in US household expenditure, 1985–2016

Legend:
- Housing, utilities and fuels
- Healthcare
- Transportation
- Food and non-alcoholic drinks
- Recreation
- Financial services and insurance
- Clothing and footwear
- Furnishings and household equipment
- Alcoholic drinks

Source: *US Bureau of Economic Analysis*

● **Social attitudes have changed**

More females are going out to work in many countries. This means they have less time to look after their families and has increased the demand for time-saving appliances such as microwave ovens and dishwashers.

● **Population trends**

Consumption patterns for different goods and services, and also savings patterns, are changing over time as the average age of populations rises in many developed and rapidly developing countries, due to falling birth and death rates. This has helped to increase spending on recreational activities and healthcare in many economies.

In many societies, people are also choosing to marry and start families later in life. This has resulted in an increase in the number of single people and an increase in the number of households, but a fall in their average size. In turn, this has increased spending on housing and household goods and furnishings over time. Unmarried people also tend to spend more on going out and travel.

● **People have become more health conscious**

Spending on sports activities, exercise equipment and gym membership has increased. Demand for healthier foods has also risen.

- **Concern for the environment is growing**

This has increased the demand for products which release fewer harmful pollutants into the atmosphere when they are produced or consumed, can be recycled, and are not tested on animals.

- **Technology has advanced rapidly**

New products have become available and have created new consumer wants. For example, spending on new high-tech consumer products such as smartphones, flat-screen televisions, game consoles and electric vehicles has increased over time.

EXAM PREPARATION 3.2

a   Define *disposable income*.   [2]

b   Neil and Natalia work for the same company. It is Neil's first job after leaving school. Natalia has been in the company 12 years and is now a senior manager. Explain how the expenditure pattern of these two people might be different.   [4]

c   Analyse the motives that might cause a person to save rather than to spend.   [6]

d   Discuss the impact an increase in consumer spending may have in an economy.   [8]

ACTIVITY 3.9

Shop 'til they drop

1   What patterns and trends in consumer spending can you identify from the charts below?

2   Suggest possible reasons for the patterns and trends you have identified.

3   Do you think these trends will continue in future? Give reasons for your views.

4   How might private sector firms and government organizations use this information and why?

5   How do these trends compare to consumption patterns and trends in your own country? Suggest and explain reasons for any similarities or differences.

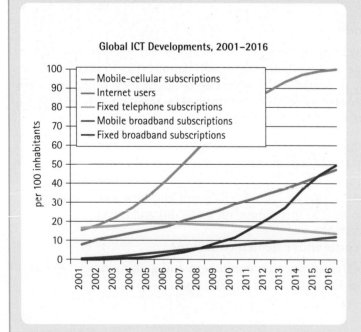

Global ICT Developments, 2001–2016

- Mobile-cellular subscriptions
- Internet users
- Fixed telephone subscriptions
- Mobile broadband subscriptions
- Fixed broadband subscriptions

per 100 inhabitants

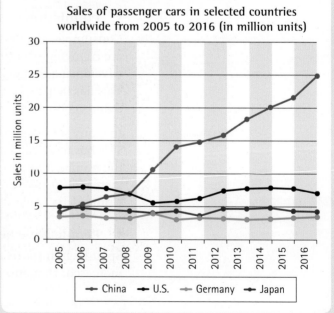

Sales of passenger cars in selected countries worldwide from 2005 to 2016 (in million units)

Sales in million units

China   U.S.   Germany   Japan

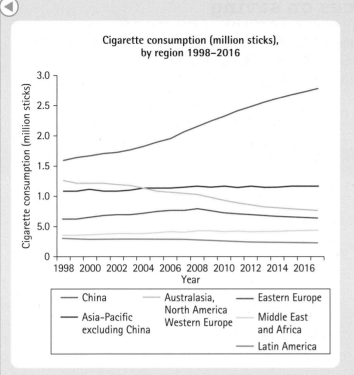

Cigarette consumption (million sticks), by region 1998–2016

Cigarette consumption (million sticks)

Year

- China
- Asia-Pacific excluding China
- Australasia, North America Western Europe
- Middle East and Africa
- Eastern Europe
- Latin America

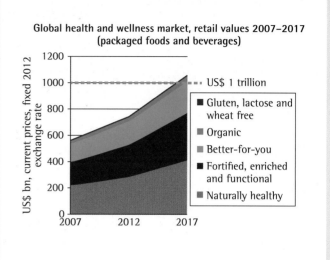

Global health and wellness market, retail values 2007–2017 (packaged foods and beverages)

US$ bn, current prices, fixed 2012 exchange rate

US$ 1 trillion

- Gluten, lactose and wheat free
- Organic
- Better-for-you
- Fortified, enriched and functional
- Naturally healthy

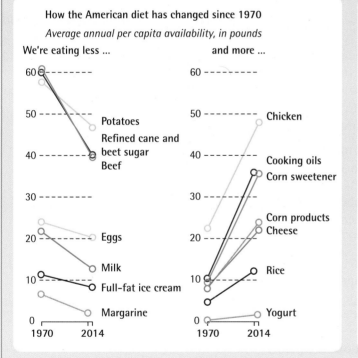

How the American diet has changed since 1970

Average annual per capita availability, in pounds

We're eating less ...

- Potatoes
- Refined cane and beet sugar
- Beef
- Eggs
- Milk
- Full-fat ice cream
- Margarine

and more ...

- Chicken
- Cooking oils
- Corn sweetener
- Corn products
- Cheese
- Rice
- Yogurt

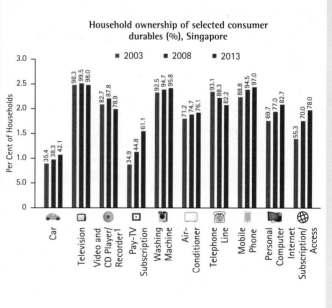

Household ownership of selected consumer durables (%), Singapore

■ 2003 ■ 2008 ■ 2013

Per Cent of Households

Car: 35.4, 38.3, 42.1
Television: 98.3, 99.5, 98.0
Video and CD Player/Recorder1: 82.7, 87.8, 78.9
Pay-TV Subscription: 34.9, 44.8, 61.1
Washing Machine: 92.5, 94.7, 95.8
Air-Conditioner: 71.2, 74.7, 76.1
Telephone Line: 93.1, 88.3, 82.2
Mobile Phone: 88.8, 94.5, 97.0
Personal Computer: 69.7, 77.0, 82.7
Internet Subscription/Access: 55.3, 70.0, 78.0

What determines savings?

The influences on saving

Saving involves people delaying consumption until some later time when they will withdraw and spend their savings plus any interest. Just as with consumer spending, the more disposable income individuals have the more they will be able to save. So, as income rises, total savings tend to rise. But the relationship is not so straightforward.

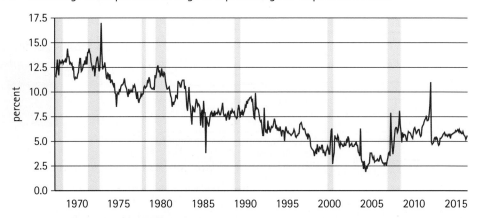

▼ US savings ratio: personal savings as a percentage of disposable income

Note: Shaded areas show US economic recessions

Source: *US Bureau of Economic Analysis*

The **savings ratio** measures the proportion of the total disposable income saved in an economy. The chart above shows the savings ratio for the US economy between 1970 and 2017. It has varied a lot, from a peak of 17% in May 1975 to a low point of 1.9% in July 2005. However, the trend over time has been very clearly downwards despite rising real incomes.

The savings ratios in many other countries also tend to vary widely as a proportion of their incomes over time. This suggests the amount of savings in an economy depends on many other factors. For example, increases in the US savings ratio in the above chart have been closely associated with economic recessions in the US economy, notably in 1975, the early 1980s and most recently between 2007 and 2009.

Why do people save?

Just like the consumption of goods and services, saving money and feeling wealthier also gives people utility. But the amount people choose to spend will depend on a number of factors.

Saving for future consumption

People will often save money in order to make bigger purchases later on, for example, the purchase of a new car, or for a deposit on an apartment or house. They may also save money to spend on goods and services when they get older and only have a pension to live on. Many people save money in pension schemes. Recall from 3.1 how a good money will be a store of value and means of making deferred payments.

Interest rates

The higher the rate of interest the more return on money people save in bank savings accounts. As a result, people may choose to save a greater proportion of their disposable incomes when interest rates are high. In contrast, when interest rates are low, and especially if the rate of price inflation is higher, people may choose to save less and consume more. This is because the value of any savings in terms of their purchasing power, or real value, will be eroded by price inflation faster than interest can add to the value of savings. ➤ **4.8.4**

Consumer confidence

How confident people feel about their financial situation now and in the future can affect consumption and savings behaviour. Many people save as a precaution in case their circumstances change. If people think they could be made unemployed in the future then they may start saving more so they can draw on their savings if and when they lose their jobs and have little or no income. Similarly, if people think inflation will rise in future they may save more now so that they can afford to pay the higher prices of goods and services later on. They may also increase their savings during periods of rising price inflation in order to protect the overall value of their wealth.

Availability of saving schemes

The more ways people can save, the more they might be tempted to do so. Banks and other financial institutions now offer a wide variety of savings schemes with different terms and conditions to suit different people. ➤ **3.1.2**

The more people are willing to save, and the longer they are willing to save without withdrawing their money, the higher the rate of interest they can normally get. Similarly, there are schemes that offer returns that are tax-free, linked to stock market performance, or a mark-up over the rate of price inflation. Some governments even offer national savings schemes that do not pay interest but enter people's savings certificates into a draw each month to win prize money. A national savings scheme is one way a government can borrow money from savers to help finance public sector expenditures.

Savings patterns

Not everyone wants to save money, even if they could. Our desire and ability to save tends to vary according to our income, age and family circumstances.

In general, the higher a person's income the more the individual tends to save in total and as a proportion of their income. Young people also tend to save less of their incomes than middle-aged people, and people with children tend to save more to help pay for their children's education later in life. However, people on low incomes with children, especially single-parent families, often find it very difficult to save. Similarly, older people also tend to save less in general because they face greater financial hardships and lower incomes from pensions in their old age. They may also withdraw or spend savings they have accumulated over time to help pay their living expenses. This is known as **dissaving**.

What impact did deflation have on consumer spending and borrowing decisions in Japan? Why did these decisions simply cause further deflation?

Deflation in Japan

Deflation refers to a general decline in prices in an economy. This happened in Japan in the early 1990s and prices continued to fall for many years. It began following a collapse in Japanese stock market and house prices after they had risen dramatically in the late 1980s. Many banks had loaned money to companies and individuals to buy real estate but when house values dropped, these loans could not be repaid or recovered in full from the sale of the property. These factors triggered a fall in spending by consumers and, as a result, firms cut their prices. As prices fell, consumers delayed their spending, expecting prices to fall further so they could buy for cheaper later on.

As Japanese consumers delayed spending, firms reduced their prices further in an attempt to encourage greater demand. Revenues fell and Japanese firms were forced to cut wages and lay off workers. The fear of unemployment caused many Japanese workers to save more and the downward deflationary spiral continued.

In an attempt to boost borrowing and spending the Japanese government cut interest rates to zero. However, this policy did not work because consumers still expected prices to fall and as they did the real value of debts increased so borrowing was not worthwhile.

Savings behaviour can also vary due to differences in culture. For example, people in China tend to save a far higher proportion of their incomes than people in many other countries. According to recent data, households in China save almost 40% of their total disposable income each year. This compares to savings of less than 5% of total household disposable income in countries such as Canada, Italy, Japan and the UK.

If savings as a proportion of total household disposable income are less than zero it means there is dissaving the economy. For example, there has been dissaving in Greece since 2005. In 2015 Greek households withdrew savings equal to almost 20% of their total disposable income.

The influences on borrowing

Consumers may borrow money to increase their expenditure on goods and services, usually for a particular good or service they want, such as a new car or overseas holiday, that is expensive relative to their weekly or monthly earnings. They can then pay off their loans gradually over time from their future earnings. However, some people on very low incomes may borrow simply to help pay living expenses such as charges for electricity.

One of the biggest purchases a person or family can make is to buy a house or apartment to live in. Loans to buy property are called **mortgages** and may take many years to pay off. However, property is an asset and will add to the stock of wealth a person has. It can therefore be considered to be a form of saving. For most people their home is their biggest asset. Some people may also borrow money to buy other assets, such as shares in companies, hoping that any dividend payments from company profits and any and appreciation in the value of shares will be more than enough to repay their loans and leave them with a nice profit.

Small business owners may also borrow money to help set up their businesses and will repay their loans from future revenues. Similarly, self-employed workers may borrow money to buy tools that will help them do their job. For example, a builder may need to buy a van and power tools.

A person may also borrow money to finance a training or education course that will help improve his or her skills and qualifications so that they can get a better-paid job in the future. For example, low-interest government loans to students are common in many countries to help them finance studies at university. They are able to repay their loans from their future earnings, with the amount repaid per month often depending on how much they earn.

Personal debt

The total stock of accumulated borrowing by a person or a household is called their **personal debt**. For example, if a person borrows $100,000 to buy a house, another $15,000 to buy a car, and $5,000 to go on a luxury holiday their personal debt will be $120,000. If the interest rate is 10% per year on all these loans then that person will have to pay $1,200 in interest in the first year even before he or she is able to pay off some of their debt. Even if that person could repay $20,000 of their debt in the following year interest charges would still add up to $1,000.

What determines the level of borrowing?

You will not be surprised to learn that the main reasons are very much the same as those that determine household spending and savings, but by far the most important is the interest rate.

Interest rates

People who borrow money from banks and other financial intermediaries will have to repay their loans with interest. Interest is therefore the cost of borrowing money, and the higher the rate of interest charged the more costly it becomes to repay a loan. The demand for loans will therefore tend to contract as interest rates rise and expand as interest rates fall.

In general, the more money a person borrows and the longer the period of time over which they will repay the loan, the higher the rate of interest a bank will charge.

The base rate of interest in an economy is normally determined by its central bank. This is the rate at which it will lend money to the entire banking system. To cover the cost of borrowing money from the central bank and to earn a profit, commercial banks and other financial institutions will therefore set their own interest rates, on loans they give to individuals and businesses, above the base rate. A rise in the base rate of interest in an economy will therefore push up the interest rates charged by banks and make borrowing more expensive. ➤ **4.3.3**

Wealth

The more wealth a person owns, the more he or she will be able to borrow from a bank or another lender. Banks are often willing to lend more money to wealthy people than to people who have little or no valuable assets, and also at lower rates of interest. This is because lending money to wealthy people involves less risk. They will be able to sell off some of their assets to repay their loans if they run out of cash to make repayments. That is, wealthy people may be less likely **default** on their loan repayments than poorer people. To default means to fail to repay a loan.

Banks and other lenders will often secure large loans to people against physical assets they own, for example houses, valuable artworks and luxury cars. These assets provide lenders with **collateral** or security against their loans. Banks can take possession of secured assets or force their owners to sell them off if their loans are not repaid. People who have little or no wealth have very little of value they can offer banks and other lenders as security against loans.

Consumer confidence

How confident people feel about their current and future financial situation may affect their decision to borrow money. For example, people on a low income or who believe they could soon lose their job are less likely to borrow large amounts of money over long periods of time.

In contrast, if people think the prices of many goods will rise more rapidly in future due to increasing inflation they may borrow now to buy the goods they want before prices rise.

Ways of borrowing and the availability of credit

The easier it is to borrow money – that is the greater the availability of credit – the more inclined people may be to borrow. These days it is possible for many more people to arrange credit and in so many more and different ways than ever before. People can arrange overdrafts, loans and mortgages with banks, quickly and easily over the Internet. They can use credit cards issued by banks, credit card companies and even retailers.

However, using credit cards and Internet banking can involve risks. Card and Internet fraud is on the increase. It involves criminals hacking into personal bank accounts and stealing credit card details. These criminals can then use this information to make fraudulent purchases and applications for loans.

Problems with borrowing

Borrowing money is not a problem as long as you can afford to repay your credit card or bank loan in full including interest charges. If your income rises each year then meeting loan and interest repayments becomes easier.

US household debt approaching record levels

South Korean household debt climbs to 90% of GDP

Australia's sky high household debt is a ticking time bomb

Asian Nations Swimming in Debt at Risk From Interest Rate Hikes

However, personal debt may become a problem for many people, but especially for those on low or fixed incomes, if

- they continue borrowing more money so that their monthly loan repayments increase significantly;

- if they have variable rate loans and there is an increase in interest rates. This will increase the interest charges they must pay on their existing loans as well as any new loans they might take out. For example, if a person owes a bank $100,000 even a relatively small increase in interest rates from 5% to 6% will increase the annual interest charge payable on this amount from $5,000 to $6,000.

- if their incomes fall, for example if they are made unemployed or if poor health prevents them from working or running a business.

People who are unable to repay their personal debts will be declared bankrupt or **insolvent** by a court of law. Any property and other goods they have bought with bank loans or on credit cards may be repossessed. Or they may be forced to sell their assets to repay their personal debts.

Personal borrowing and debt levels have increased significantly in a number of developed and other economies during the last decade. This has raised concerns that money to fund consumer spending has become too cheap and easy to borrow. If interest rates rise people will have to devote a greater proportion of their disposable incomes to paying off their debts. As a result they will have less to spend on goods and services. If consumer spending falls, some firms may be forced to cut production and lay off some of their workers. As unemployment rises, more people will suffer financial hardship and may be unable to repay their debts. Consumer spending will fall further and could result in many economies experiencing an economic recession or negative economic growth. ➤ **4.6.3**

'If I owe you a pound, I have a problem; but if I owe you a million, the problem is yours'
John Maynard Keynes (1883–1946), English economist

Household debt binge hits pre-crisis levels as Britons go mad for new cars and cheap loans, Bank of England warns

British households are taking on new debt at a frenzied pace not seen for more than a decade, new figures reveal.

Loans for new cars made up the bulk of new borrowing, but a growing appetite for cheap cash through personal loans also drove up debt.

The annual growth rate in consumer borrowing or credit hit 9.3% in February, the highest pace since December 2005, the Bank of England survey revealed.

Borrowing has been boosted by low interest rates, which has brought the cost of personal loans to record lows.

Borrowing is expected to continue to rise. At present, total household debt is around 140% of total household income. By 2020 it is expected to reach 170%. The big question therefore is how sustainable it is for households to continue borrowing?

Millions have been able to gorge themselves on cheap money thanks to low interest rates. However as interest rates start to rise or if a turn in the state of the economy leaves higher numbers out of work, high levels of debt could become more of a concern not just for indebted households but for the entire economy.

Government figures show that increasing consumer spending has been a strong contributor to economic growth in the UK.

If consumer spending subsequently falls because UK households are spending more of their disposable incomes paying off their debts this may hurt economic activity.

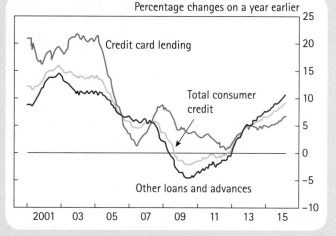

Source: *This is Money.co.uk*, April 2016

1 Identify two factors from the article that increased consumer debt in the UK.

2 What problems are highlighted in the article concerning high levels of personal or household debt?

3 Suggest two ways a government could reduce consumer demand for borrowing.

4 Describe how and why consumer spending, savings and borrowing patterns may differ between the following types of household in a developed economy such as the UK: young, unmarried university graduate; married couple with young children; retired couple receiving a pension.

5 According to the article, what is the relationship between consumer spending, household debt and economic growth in an economy. Explain your answer.

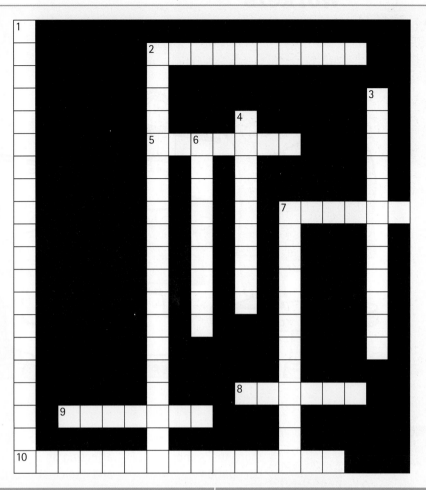

Clues across

2. Security against a loan, such a valuable asset that a bank can sell if the loan is not repaid (10)
5. The satisfaction a person gains from consuming a good or service (7)
7. Delayed consumption to accumulate wealth (6)
8. The stock of assets a person or a household owns that have monetary value (5)
9. A term used to describe a situation when a person fails to meet loan repayments on time (7)
10. Products for which it is difficult to judge how much we will enjoy them until we consume them (10, 5)

Clues down

1. Personal income remaining after income- related taxes have been deducted and after allowing for the effect of inflation reducing its purchasing power, that a person can choose to spend or save (4, 10, 6)
2. The amount spent on goods and services for final consumption (8, 11)
3. The stock of total borrowing accumulated by a person (8, 4)
4. Withdrawing or spending from savings, for example to meet living expenses when income is insufficient (9)
6. A person or organization will be this if they are unable to raise enough cash to pay off their debts (9)
7. Savings as a percentage of total disposable income (7, 5)

Unit 3.3 Workers

Factors affecting an individual's choice of occupation

Why do people work?

Labourer Wanted

General labouring and odd jobs. Hours 8am – 5pm. Monday to Friday. Must be willing to travel.

Restaurant and Bar Manager

To lead, manage and operate a restaurant and bar with cutting edge cocktails and global cuisine. 50 hours per week. Late evenings and shift-working required.

Hair stylist

To wash and cut hair. Part-time. Mornings only.

Warehouse staff

You could be earning instead of looking!

WAREHOUSE STAFF – We've found the way to make temporary assignments more interesting for YOU.

You'll have the opportunity to select from a variety of assignments locally or in city locations offering excellent rates of pay, holiday pay and other benefits.

If you're available for a week or more we can put you to work.

Economist

An international oil company is looking for an Economist to join their Business Environment Division, initially on a 2-year contract.

The successful candidate for this unusual opportunity to experience the oil industry at first hand is likely to have a degree and postgraduate degree in economics, a strong quantitative background including familiarity with PCs and a high level of analytical, written and oral communication skills.

The post can be filled at various levels of previous experience, with a remuneration package to match, but preference will be given to those whose understanding of the economy within a global environment can be readily acknowledged.

The planning team is responsible for analysing and identifying economic trends and developments, in particular those relating to energy demand and supply.

Fruit picker wanted

for busy farm for three months during summer. Must be prepared to work long hours and outdoors in all weathers.

Security guard required

We require a security person for the reception area at our Group Head Office.

The hours of work involved are Monday to Friday 10pm to 7am and duties include dealing with all overnight visitors and deliveries to the building, whilst maintaining an effective security presence.

Applications are invited from mature persons who are confident and alert, and of a smart appearance.

We offer a good rate of pay for this responsible position.

Book Shop Assistant

A great opportunity for a bright, enthusiastic person interested in literature, art, music and foreign languages to gain valuable experience in bookselling and publishing. 5 days per week. 10 am till 7 pm

In groups, look at the job advertisements above.

1. For each job, discuss with your group what you think the monthly wage or annual salary for the job is likely to be.

2. Which job do you think offers the highest wage or salary, and which one offers the lowest? Why do you think this is the case?

3. Which job do you think is likely to get the most applicants and why? Try to think of reasons other than just the wage or salary.

4. Which of the jobs above would you most like to do and least like to do, and why? Again, try to think of reasons other than the wage or salary the job may offer.

5. Which job would you most like to do when you leave school or college, and why? Try to find out what the job currently offers in terms of pay and other monetary and non-monetary benefits. Are you still attracted to this job?

The decision to supply labour

Most people will supply their labour to firms to earn an income. Firms pay **wages** to workers to supply their labour to produce goods and services. Paid employment therefore provides people with money to buy the goods and services they need and want but are unable to produce themselves.

However, some people may supply their labour for free, for example by undertaking voluntary work to assist charities. So money may not be the only reason people go to work.

In addition to a desire for money, working satisfies many more of our different wants and needs. For example, working makes us feel useful, it provides the opportunity to meet new people and make new friends, and it teaches us new skills and ideas. Combinations of all these different reasons, both financial and non-financial, therefore motivate people to supply their labour to different organizations.

Payments for labour

Firms will advertise a **wage rate** for each job to attract people to supply their labour. The wage rate for a job can be paid in many ways:

- **A time rate** is a rate of pay per hour worked, so the more hours an employee works the more he or she will earn. For example, if an employee is paid $20 per hour and works 35 hours each week the employee's **gross weekly wage** will be $700. Workers who work additional hours during evenings or weekends, may receive an **overtime rate** at 1.5 times or even twice the normal time rate.

- **A piece rate** is paid to an employee of a firm per unit of output produced, for example for each article of clothing made or kilogram of apples picked, so the more output produced by an employee the more he or she will earn. Piece rates are often paid in addition to time rates to workers in manufacturing firms to encourage them to increase their productivity.

- **A fixed annual salary** for a job will be divided into 12 equal monthly payments regardless of the number of hours actually worked by the jobholder each week over and above an agreed amount of time, often between 35 to 40 hours per week. Salaries are often paid to managers, office staff and other employees in non-manual occupations.

- **Performance-related payments** may be offered to individual employees or teams of workers who are highly productive. For example, commission may be paid to retail employees and others involved in sales, such as financial advisers and travel agents. The more sales they make or revenue they earn for the organization they work for the more they will earn, usually as a percentage of their sales. Some firms may also pay their employees a share of an increase in their profits.

The total or **gross earnings** of an employee each week or month may therefore vary and be made up of many different payments, including a basic wage or salary, overtime payments, commission and a performance-related bonus.

All of these forms of payment are referred to as **wage factors** and are clearly very important in the decision of a person whether to supply his or her labour.

In addition to wage payments, firms may attract a supply of labour by offering workers other benefits that have a monetary value such as free medical insurance, use of a company car, price discounts, pension contributions and free membership and use of a gym. These are often referred to as perks or **fringe benefits**.

Choosing an occupation

Most people specialize in a particular activity or occupation for all or most of their working lives. So how do people choose an occupation to supply their labour to?

Clearly differences in wage factors between occupations will be important. However, as already mentioned, in addition to a desire for money, working satisfies many more of our different wants and needs. For example, working makes us feel useful, it provides the opportunity to meet new people and make new friends, and it teaches us new skills and ideas.

For example, a job that offers few promotion prospects, involves repetitive and uninteresting tasks and working long unsociable hours may be unattractive to many people even if that job offers a high wage rate.

In contrast, some people may be attracted to occupations that pay relatively low wages because they offer interesting careers, generous holiday entitlements or are considered to more worthwhile and satisfying, such as nursing or charity work. These are all **non-wage factors** that can attract people to different occupations.

A person seeking employment may therefore accept a lower wage if a job offers attractive non-wage benefits. However, a person may only accept a job that has unattractive non-wage features, for example, dangerous work or working late nights and weekends, if the wage rate is high enough to compensate for them (see Section 4 below).

People will therefore choose between different occupations and employers by comparing their wage factors and non-wage factors.

Non-wage factors include:

- hours of work
- holiday entitlement
- promotion prospects
- flexible working arrangements
- qualifications required

- quality of working environment
- how secure the job is
- how satisfying the work is
- fringe benefits
- training opportunities

- pension entitlement
- opportunities for promotion
- interesting and varied tasks
- distance or time it takes to travel to and from work.

All the wage and non-wage factors that affect the attractiveness of a particular job or occupation are called its **net advantages**. A person will compare and select jobs or occupations by comparing their advantages and disadvantages. Choosing between different occupations will therefore involve trade-offs. For example, the opportunity cost of choosing a job with high wages may be a loss of leisure time because of the need to work longer hours or to travel further to and from the place of work.

For example, a person hoping to become a medical surgeon will have to complete up to eight years of study at university and medical school before training can begin in a hospital. It may take a further three to seven years before that person can eventually become qualified as a surgeon. During this time medical students may have to borrow money to pay their fees, while subsequent training at a hospital will often involve further study and long hours of work, including during evenings and weekends, often for relatively low pay. However, qualified surgeons are among the highest paid workers in the world and have rewarding careers saving the lives of many people. Those thinking of becoming a surgeon will have to weigh up all these factors before they decide to specialize in this occupation.

In contrast, very little training is required to become an office cleaner. The job does not require long periods of study to gain qualifications so a person can start earning an income immediately they leave school. However, the wage rate for cleaners is often very low, the work can be uninteresting and dirty, and the job offers little chance of promotion or advancement.

SECTION 3.3.2

Labour markets

Wage determination

Wage rates for different occupations are determined in labour markets. There is a **labour market** for every type of occupation just as there are markets for every type of good or service. Firms will demand labour with the skills they need to carry out different productive activities. People who are willing and able to carry out these activities will supply their labour to those firms. We can therefore use demand and supply analysis to examine the economics of labour markets, including what causes changes in the demand for labour and the supply of labour to different occupations, what determines the amount people earn, and why wage rates differ. ➤ **2.5.1**

Markets for labour can be local, national or even international if people are willing and able to migrate overseas to work. There will also be labour markets for different skills and occupations. For example, there are labour markets for bricklayers, doctors, train drivers, accountants, soldiers, shop assistants, nurses and even economists. We can also distinguish between labour markets for young workers who may have little work experience and older workers with more experience, and between labour markets for temporary, part-time and full-time employees.

The demand for labour

The demand for labour is a derived demand because firms want labour to produce goods and services that consumers want and are willing to pay for. It follows that the greater the demand for goods and services, the more labour firms will demand. This is because an increase in demand for goods and services will increase their market prices and make their production more profitable.

However, private and public sector organizations are only likely to employ additional workers if they add more value than they cost to employ. In a private profit-making firm this value is measured by how much extra revenue and profit each worker creates. So, for example, a worker will be worth employing if he or she generates an additional $5,000 in revenue each month but only costs $3,000 per month to employ. If, however, this employee would only generate extra output worth $2,000 each month he or she would not be worth employing. The demand for labour is therefore closely related to the wage rate workers receive for their employment and how productive they are. ➤ **4.2**

In general, therefore, the higher the wage rate in a particular labour market the more expensive it is to employ workers and the fewer will tend to be demanded. This is shown in the diagram below. Economists use the symbol n to denote labour and w to represent the wage rate. The demand curve for labour (DnDn) is downward sloping so that as the wage rate rises from w to w1 the demand for labour contracts from n to n1.

▼ The demand for labour with specific occupational skills

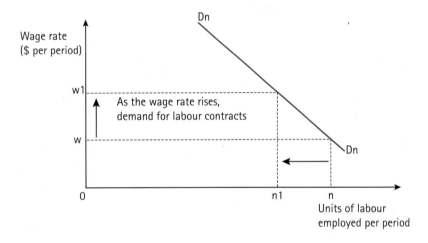

The supply of labour

The total supply of labour in an economy is its working population or labour force. ➤ **5.3.3**

However, the supply of labour to a particular occupation will depend on how many people are willing and able to do the jobs on offer. So, for example, the market supply of train drivers will consist of people currently employed as train drivers, people employed in other occupations who want to become train drivers, and people who are unemployed but are also willing and able to be train drivers.

It is likely that as the wage rate for train drivers increases, so more and more people will want to be train drivers. The market supply curve for train drivers will therefore slope upwards. Indeed, this is generally the case. The higher the wage rate in a particular labour market the more labour will be supplied. This is shown in the next diagram. The supply curve for labour (SnSn) is upward sloping so that as the wage rate rises from w to w1 the supply of labour extends from n to n1.

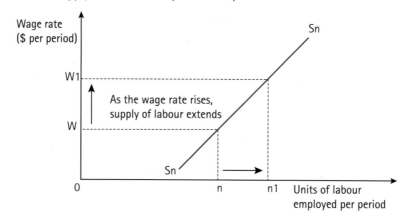

▼ The supply of labour with specific occupational skills

However, while the positive relationship between labour supply and wages holds in general, it may not always be the case that an individual will be willing to work more and more hours as the wage rate rises. At some point individuals might decide they earn enough and would like to take more leisure time. For

▼ A backward bending supply curve for our builder

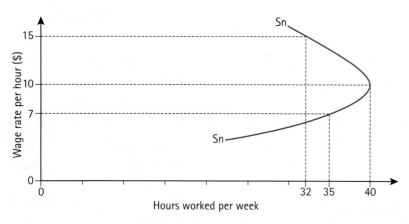

example, consider a builder currently earning $7 per hour. At this wage rate he might choose to work 35 hours each week and earn $245. If the wage rate rises to $10 per hour he may work 40 hours and earn $400. But at $15 per hour he may only work 32 hours and choose to spend more time relaxing because he is still better off with earnings of $480 each week. As a result, the supply curve of our individual builder, and many other workers like him, will be backward bending. At very high wage rates it is possible to have both more wage income and more leisure.

Although most people do work a fixed number of hours each week, there is still evidence to suggest that the total supply curve of labour is backward bending. This is evidenced by trade unions' attempts to reduce working hours as living standards have improved, and in the reduction of the working week in many developed countries from 60 hours at the start of the century to an average today of around 41 hours or less per week.

Wage determination

Just as in a market for any good or service, the market price of labour, or **equilibrium wage rate**, for an occupation will be determined where the demand for labour is matched by a supply of labour.

The equilibrium wage rate for a particular job can be illustrated graphically. At this wage we find how much labour will actually be employed by firms.

▼ Equilibrium in an occupational labour market

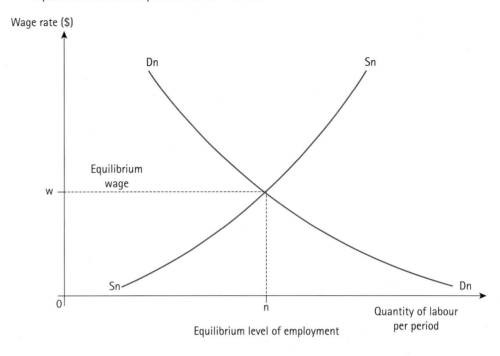

The equilibrium wage rate and the amount of labour employed by firms will change if there are changes in labour demand and supply conditions.

If the demand for labour changes

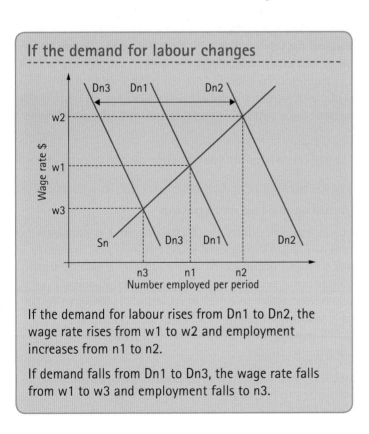

Number employed per period

If the demand for labour rises from Dn1 to Dn2, the wage rate rises from w1 to w2 and employment increases from n1 to n2.

If demand falls from Dn1 to Dn3, the wage rate falls from w1 to w3 and employment falls to n3.

If the supply of labour changes

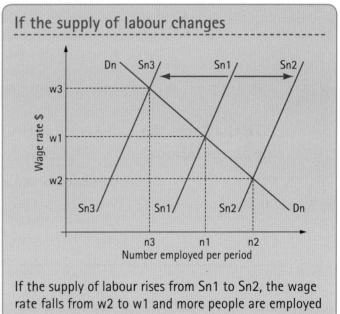

Number employed per period

If the supply of labour rises from Sn1 to Sn2, the wage rate falls from w2 to w1 and more people are employed at n2.

If supply falls from Sn1 to Sn3, the wage rate rises from w1 to w3 and employment falls.

What affects the demand for labour?

The following factors may affect the demand for labour.

Changes in consumer demand for goods and services

If consumer demand rises, firms may expand output in response. To do so they will tend to increase their demand for labour. This may initially mean asking their existing workers to work additional hours, but may also involve hiring more workers if the increase in consumer demand is permanent. Changes in the pattern of consumer demand over time, due to population changes and changing tastes, can therefore mean demand for some types of labour will be increasing while demand for others is falling. ➤ **2.2**

Changes in the productivity of labour

If labour becomes more productive and increases the value of output it can produce over and above the cost of wages, then firms may demand more labour. New technologies and working methods, and training programmes, can help increase the productivity of labour. ➤ **4.2**

Changes in the price and productivity of capital

If machinery and equipment becomes cheaper or more productive than labour, then a firm may replace labour with more capital-intensive production methods.

Changes in non-wage employment costs

Wages are not the only cost to an organization of employing people. For example, employers in many countries have to pay employment taxes and welfare insurance for each worker they employ. If these are increased by the government then the demand for labour may fall. Employment laws and regulations may also change over time and affect the cost of employing labour, for example by requiring employers to spend more on health and safety equipment in their workplaces in order to protect their workers. In contrast, a fall in non-wage employment costs can boost the demand for labour by firms.

What affects the supply of labour?

The supply of labour at any given wage rate may change due to a number of factors.

Changes in the net advantages of an occupation

We know that people are attracted to different jobs by their net advantages. Changes in the advantages and disadvantages of different jobs will therefore affect the supply of labour to those occupations. For example, a decline in the promotion prospects or holiday entitlement of school teachers relative to other occupations is likely to result in a fall in the supply of school teachers at every possible wage rate, from SnSn to Sn1Sn1 in the diagram to the left.

In contrast, a cut in required hours of work and the introduction of free medical insurance for airline pilots will tend to increase the supply of labour to airline operators.

▼ A fall in the supply of teachers

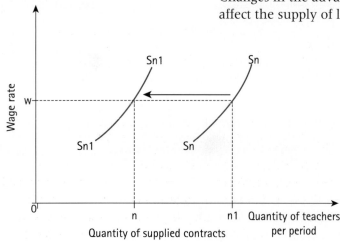

Changes in the provision and quality of education and training

Changes in the level and type of education and training courses offered can increase the supply of workers with different skills. For example, the introduction of courses in computer programming and cellular engineering has increased the number of people able to supply these skills to occupations that require them.

Demographic changes

Changes in the size and age distribution of the population in an economy will also cause changes in the supply of labour to different occupations. ➤ 7.2

For example, inward migration to many developed economies has helped boost the supply of labour to many occupations. In contrast, the increasing average age of their populations because birth rates are low means that more people are leaving the labour market due to old age. Others are moving from full-time employment in industry to part-time jobs in services as they get older and want to enjoy more leisure time.

ACTIVITY 3.12

The rise and fall of labour

Look at the factors listed below that could affect labour market outcomes. In each case indicate whether you think there will be an increase or decrease in the demand for labour, an increase or decrease in the supply of labour and whether the equilibrium market wage rate for each occupation will tend to rise or fall as a result.

What has changed?	Impact on labour demand	Impact on labour supply	Impact on market wage rate
• Nurses are offered new contracts with shorter working weeks			
• Consumer spending on flat-screen televisions increases significantly			
• The government raises the retirement age of public sector workers			
• Overtime payments for airline employees are to be scrapped			
• Computerized assembly lines boost labour productivity in car plants			
• A major retail chain announces it will remain open 24 hours each day			
• Assaults on police increase			
• The government announces it will tax tips received by restaurant and hotel staff from next April			
• A survey finds more people are working part-time and flexible hours			
• Statutory maternity leave and pay are to be increased			
• New technology allows more office workers to work from home			

SECTION 3.3.3

Why do the earnings of employees differ?

Reasons for differences in earnings

Differences in wages between different occupations and employees in the same occupations are called **wage differentials**. For example, an experienced doctor may earn over $200,000 per year while a farm labourer in the same country may earn less than $10,000 each year. Differences in the wages and earnings of workers are common in all countries. For example, the average weekly earnings of full-time female employees in the USA were $657 in 2009, or about 80% of the average weekly earnings of $819 of full-time male employees. Wages can also vary significantly between countries.

What explains occupational wage differentials?

Clearly two people with similar skills and experience doing the same job for the same hourly wage but working different hours each week will have different earnings at the end of each week. However, in economics we are interested in explaining differences in wage rates between different occupations and groups of employees using demand and supply analysis.

We know the demand for labour is derived from consumer demand for goods and services and depends on how productive labour is. We also know that labour supply decisions are related to the net advantages of different occupations. We can therefore use our knowledge of these factors to explain wage differentials.

1 Different abilities and qualifications

Workers do not all have the same education, training and ability. For example, an accountant is a more skilled worker than a cashier. If both workers were paid the same amount, very few people would be willing to undertake the many years of study necessary to become an accountant.

Because the training period is so long for some jobs the supply of these particular workers may be very low and, as a result, their wages may be very high. For example, it takes doctors over six years to qualify to do their job and up to 15 years, perhaps more, to become a skilled surgeon.

People with skills that are in very short supply relative to the demand for those skills will have significant bargaining power in negotiations with employers and will be able to command very high market wages. This explains why such highly skilled footballers as Neymar, Carlos Tevez and Lionel Messi, and talented actresses such as Jennifer Lawrence and Deepika Padukone, receive huge salaries for their skills.

2 'Dirty' jobs and unsociable hours

Some jobs are dirty or dangerous and so workers must be paid more in order to attract a supply of labour. Some people have to work nights or other unsociable hours and may be paid more to compensate for this. These are called **compensating differentials**.

3 Job satisfaction

The satisfaction provided by undertaking a job can compensate for relatively low wages for some people. Some occupations, such as nursing, are considered worthier than others by some people and this makes these occupations more attractive. Market wage rates will be relatively low in those occupations that attract a large supply of labour.

4 Lack of information about jobs and wages

Sometimes people will work for less than they could earn in other roles simply because they do not know about the availability of better-paid jobs elsewhere. Lack of information about job availability can restrict the supply of labour to those jobs and can therefore help explain some differences in earnings between different jobs in different areas.

5 Labour immobility

The ease with which workers can move between different occupations and different areas of a country is known as **labour mobility**. If workers are very mobile, they can move easily to those jobs that offer them the most pay, and they will also move from places with high unemployment to areas with more job vacancies. High labour mobility or willingness to move can help to increase the supply of labour to different occupations in different areas and reduce regional differences in unemployment and wage rates in a country.

ACTIVITY 3.13

How's your differential?

1   Look at the chart of average weekly earnings by gender and broad occupational category in the UK. What economic factors could explain the differences in earnings?

2   Find examples of jobs in each occupational group in your own country and compare their earnings. Do they follow the same pattern as in the UK? Explain any wage or earnings differentials using your knowledge of factors that can affect labour demand and supply for different occupations.

▼ UK average weekly earnings before tax, April 2016, full-time employees by occupational group

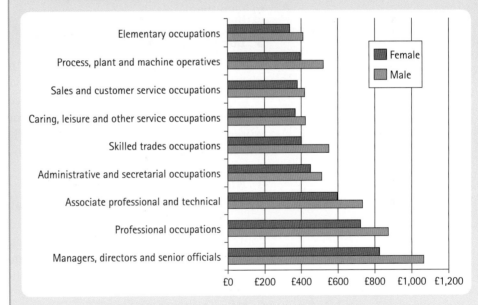

Source: *Annual Survey of Hours and Earnings, UK Office for National Statistics*

However, because many people are not very mobile large differences in wage rates for different occupations and even for the same jobs but in different areas can persist. For example, some workers may not wish to leave their families and friends in order to move to better-paid jobs elsewhere. Even if they wanted to move to a better-paid job elsewhere they may not be able to afford housing in the new area or the cost of retraining in new occupational skills. For example, the length of time and costs involved in training to be a surgeon restricts the **occupational mobility of labour** and therefore the supply of labour to that profession. ➤ **1.2.2**

6 Fringe benefits

Some jobs may offer lower wages than others because they offer more perks instead, such as company cars, free life insurance or cheap travel. However, it is usually the higher-paid jobs that also tend to offer the most perks in order to attract the most skilled workers.

Why do earnings differ between people doing the same job?

People in different occupations can earn different amounts of money, but even people in the same jobs can earn very different amounts. This can happen for the following reasons.

1 Regional differences in labour demand and supply conditions

For example, there may be shortages of workers with particular types of skills in some parts of the country. Firms in such areas needing these workers may offer higher wages to attract workers from rival firms or from elsewhere in the country.

2 Length of service

Many firms have pay scales that offer pay increases linked to the number of years a worker stays with the firm. This extra pay is both a bonus for loyalty and also a payment for having more experience and skill. Firms reward their more experienced and productive workers with higher pay because they want to keep them.

3 Local pay agreements

Some national trade unions may agree a national wage rate for all their members through collective bargaining with employers. All workers belonging to the union with similar work experience and levels of skill will therefore receive the same wage wherever they work in a country. However, many workers and employers can often agree their pay locally, so regional differences in pay in the same occupation can occur.

4 Non-monetary rewards differ

Some firms may offer their workers more fringe and other benefits than rival firms, such as longer holidays, free medical care and enhanced pension contributions, instead of higher rates of pay. In some countries non-pay rewards are not taxable so they may offer a worker better value than paying higher wages from which income and other payroll taxes will be deducted.

5 Discrimination

Workers doing the same job may be treated differently by different employers simply because of their sex, age, race or religion. Personal discrimination unrelated to the skills and productivity of different workers is a non-economic reason why wage differentials may exist between different workers doing the same jobs. Such personal discrimination is outlawed in many countries.

Government interventions in labour markets

The government and public sector is a major employer in many countries, often employing the labour of many thousands of teachers, doctors, civil servants, military personnel and other public sector workers. Since it is such a major source of demand for labour it is able to influence the market wage rates for many different occupations.

The minimum wage debate

Minimum wages do create some jobs – for economists. In the USA and the UK economists have been studying whether setting a floor under pay destroys jobs or reduces poverty.

A study by the OECD suggests the policy is ill suited to dealing with the problem of poverty. In most countries, many low earners have well-paid partners or affluent parents. Since most low-paid workers are not in poor households, most of the income gains that might come from a minimum wage would benefit families which are not poor.

Critics of minimum wages frequently argue that a government-mandated pay level reduces total employment because firms will scale back hiring rather than adding employees who must be paid more than they are worth. Those in favour argue an imposed wage minimum could have an opposite effect where the employer is large and powerful in relation to the pool of suitable workers. A powerful employer may be able to hold down wages by restricting its demand for labour. If a government sets a higher minimum wage, the employer no longer has this incentive. Because the employer must pay the higher wage there is no point any longer in restricting its demand for labour.

The OECD study – which considered data from nine countries, including the USA, Japan, France and Spain –

found that a 10 per cent rise in the minimum wage reduced teenage employment by around 3 per cent in both high and low minimum wage countries.

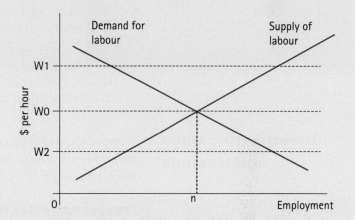

1. From the article, what are the arguments for and against a minimum wage? Does it matter what level the minimum wage is set at? Explain your answer using diagrams where possible.

2. How could you try to monitor the impact of a minimum wage over time?

3. In the diagram, what will be the impact of a minimum wage set at (a) W1 and (b) W2?

4. Calculate the wage elasticity of demand for teenage labour suggested by the findings of the study.

Governments will also intervene in other labour markets to improve the wages, working conditions and legal rights of different groups of workers. For example:

- **Minimum wage laws** have been adopted in many countries to protect vulnerable and low-paid workers from exploitation by powerful employers. The first national minimum wage law was introduced in New Zealand in 1896, followed by Australia in 1899 and the UK in 1902, and again in 1999. Apart from raising the pay of low-paid workers, it is argued that favourable minimum wages will make them work harder and achieve higher levels of productivity. However, some employers argue that minimum wages set above free market wage levels will simply raise production costs and reduce the demand for labour. ➤ **2.11.2**

- It is unlawful in many countries to discriminate against people because of their gender, race, religion or disability, and also their age in some countries. For example, the Equal Pay Act in the UK makes it unlawful for employers to discriminate between men and women in terms of their pay and conditions where they are doing the same or similar work of equal value. Many other countries have similar laws and regulations.

- Laws have been introduced in a number of countries to limit the powers of trade unions to take strike action and to restrict the supply of labour in order to force up the wages of their members. For example, closed shop agreements that require firms to employ union members only are illegal in the UK. Further, trade unions no longer have the right to strike without first conducting a full ballot of their members. ➤ **3.4.2**

Investigating wage differentials

Economists, social researchers, trade unions, employers' groups and governments often compare and monitor differences in earnings between different groups of workers.

Younger and older workers

The earnings of individuals will tend to increase over time as they become more experienced and skilled in their jobs and therefore more productive and valuable to their employers. Workers will often receive an annual pay rise from their employers for each year they work to reward them for their increased experience and productivity. Older workers therefore tend to earn more than younger workers doing the same or very similar jobs simply because they have been in work longer.

Young workers, entering work for the first time, may have very few relevant skills. To develop their skills and productivity they will need training and this can be expensive for their employers. As a result they will tend to receive relatively low wages compared to older employees in the same occupation.

Older, more skilled workers may also be able to achieve promotions to more senior and responsible positions that pay more than their younger colleagues.

However, some younger workers may earn more than older workers doing different jobs in different locations due to occupational and regional wage differentials. For example, a young skilled city lawyer will tend to earn far more than an older, unskilled agricultural worker.

Similarly, some workers towards the end of their working lives may also choose to retire early and take lower paid jobs with less responsibility in different occupations nearer to their homes. For example, a skilled and well-paid 55-year-old senior manager in a factory may decide to leave and take a low-paid part-time job as an unskilled sales assistant in a shop so he or she can enjoy more leisure time.

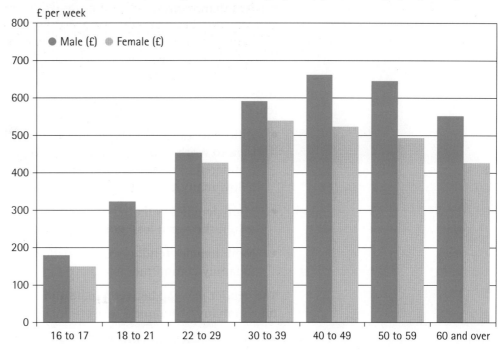

▼ Average gross weekly earnings of full-time employees by gender and age group, UK April 2016

£ per week

● Male (£) ● Female (£)

Source: *Annual Survey of Hours and Earnings (ASHE) - UK Office for National Statistics*

▼ The earnings of an employee will vary over his or her lifetime

Aaleyah aged 20	Aaleyah aged 45	Aaleyah aged 60

• Few skills • Less work experience • Less productive • Training can be expensive	• More skills and knowledge • Years of work experience • More productive • Promoted to more senior positions	• Semi-retired • Working part-time • Less productive

Male and female workers

The average earnings of male employees exceed those of female employees in every country. In some countries the **gender pay gap** is wider than others. For example, in South Korea in 2015 female earnings were on average 37%

lower than male earnings but in New Zealand females earned on average just 5% less than males.

Females may earn less than males doing the same or similar jobs due to discrimination. For example, some employers may favour male employees over female employee in job interviews and for promotions to more senior levels.

However, much of these differences in the average earnings of male and female workers can be explained by the following factors:

- Differences in the occupational choices of men and women. More females tend to work in occupations such as teaching, nursing and retailing compared to males. Market wage rates for these occupations are often below many those of many other occupations;

- Many females will often take career breaks to raise children and, as a result, they gain less work experience and career progression than males;

- More females tend to work part-time compared to males, again often due to family commitments.

The gender pay gap between male and female workers has been declining over time in many economies. Reasons include:

- More females are entering the workforce and taking jobs in occupations once dominated by males;

- An increase in the number of females choosing to stay on in higher education and study for academic qualifications including university degrees;

- Falling birth rates because females are choosing to have fewer children and take fewer career breaks;

- A reduction in the number of males in full-time employment;

- The introduction of equal pay laws to prevent pay discrimination by employers.

Skilled and unskilled workers

The supply of skilled workers such as surgeons, engineers and computer software developers is limited compared to the supply of unskilled labour. This is because specialist skills and knowledge take time to develop and not everyone has the time or ability to develop them.

The demand for skilled labour from firms also tends to be greater than the demand for unskilled labour. Competition between firms to attract the brightest and the best skilled workers is usually therefore more intense.

The combination of these factors means that skilled workers will often earn far higher wages than unskilled workers.

Increasing global competition between firms has increased the demand for skills in many economies and this has in turn increased wage inequality between skilled and unskilled workers.

Public sector and private sector workers

Governments are major employers in many countries. The public sector therefore competes with private sector firms to attract many of the same types of workers with the same skills and so governments need to be aware of what private sector firms are paying their workers.

Yet some people argue that because the government is such a big employer it has the power to hold down the wages of public sector workers relative to those paid in the private sector. However, lower public sector pay might be explained by many of its employees having more secure jobs and, in some cases, more secure and better pensions than private sector workers. For example, civil servants, police and teachers are not at risk of losing their jobs due to falling consumer demand.

But data is mixed. While there are many relatively low-paid workers in public sector jobs, others appear to earn as much if not more than private sector workers in very similar jobs.

For example, a study in Pakistan suggested its public sector workers earned on average 49% more. This was explained by public sector workers generally having higher levels of education and productivity.

A similar study in the UK also concluded there was very little difference in the pay of public sector and private sector workers once differences in their levels of education and qualifications were taken into account. On average the pay of public sector workers was between 3.3% and 4.3% lower than private sector workers, in April 2014.

Industrial wage differentials

Differences in wage rates between industries will reflect differences in the labour market demand and supply conditions for those industries and also local or regional labour market conditions in areas where firms in those industries are concentrated. For example, wages will tend to be lower in areas where there is high unemployment and therefore a large supply of labour seeking work.

▼ Average gross hourly wage by industrial sector, 2016

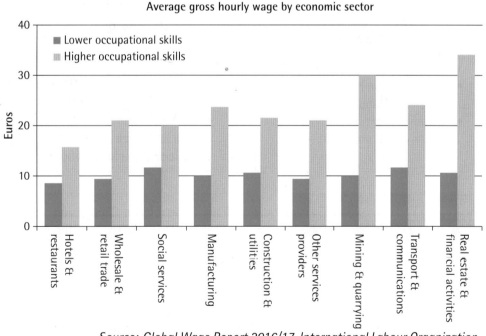

Source: *Global Wage Report 2016/17, International Labour Organization*

Industries that require a lot of unskilled or low-skilled labour tend to pay lower wages than industries that require skilled labour. This explains why the average earnings of agricultural workers and workers in many service industries such as catering, retailing and cleaning, are usually lower than skilled engineers and other manufacturing workers.

However, the average earnings of other service providers such as accountants, computer software designers, lawyers, doctors and airline pilots will all tend to exceed those of skilled manufacturing workers. This is because their skills are in short supply relative to the demand for them.

Expanding industries, such as aviation, the computer games industry and electric vehicles, will also tend to offer higher wages in order to attract an increasing supply of workers with the skills they need. In contrast, the demand for labour in old, declining industries will be falling and this will tend to reduce the market wage rates in these industries.

▼ Industrial wage differentials reflect differences in their labour market conditions

Agricultural worker	Skilled manufacturing worker	Computer games designer

• Low-skilled • Mechanization has reduced demand for labour • Unemployment is relatively high in many rural areas	• Many skilled engineering jobs • Many older manufacturing industries have declined • Mechanization of production in new, high-tech industries has reduced demand for labour	• Highly skilled • Expanding industry – has increased demand for these skills • Skills are in short supply

ECONOMICS IN ACTION

Why are wage rates in China rising rapidly? Why might this cause some firms to relocate overseas? What are the possible implications of rising wages on inflation in China and countries that import Chinese goods and services?

China's labour pains

In the early 2010s, labour shortages combined with a series of strikes over low pay in Guangdong helped to significantly boost wages in the province known as China's 'factory to the world'. In perhaps the best-known strike of 2010 at Nanhai Honda in Foshan, workers won a 35 per cent (500 yuan per month) pay increase plus the promise of a more effective union representation.

Regional governments across China have also been forced to increase their minimum wages in a bid to retain workers. For example, in the financial capital of Shanghai, which has the highest minimum wage in China, the monthly rate increased from 1,120 yuan in 2010 to 2,190 yuan in 2016.

As early as 2012, many commentators were announcing the end of cheap labour in China and the country's status as a powerful magnet for inward investment from Western economies.

Many manufacturers, especially those in the garment, shoe and toy industries, have already relocated from China to smaller Asian countries such as Bangladesh, Cambodia and Vietnam, in many cases replicating the pay and working conditions seen in China a decade ago. However, it is unclear how many more firms will move overseas in search of cheaper labour. There are already signs that wages are beginning to rise in these countries.

Regional differences in wages between China's provinces may instead encourage firms to relocate internally. Average salaries in many of China's relatively poor and overpopulated inland provinces are currently some 20 to 30 per cent less than those in the southern coastal province of Guangdong.

SECTION 3.3.4

The division of labour in production processes

Division of labour and specialization

People usually make their future career choices while they are still at school or college according to their interests and abilities and some view of the net advantages of different jobs. They may choose subjects to study that will help them develop the skills and obtain the qualifications they will need for the occupations they want to pursue.

However, many hundreds of years ago, workers were usually identified according to the type of good or service they produced. For example, a boat builder would build boats as units, completing all the tasks necessary to make each boat before starting another. Similarly, a blacksmith would heat, beat and shape raw metal ores to produce metal objects such as spearheads, swords and horseshoes, carrying out all the tasks necessary to complete each one before making something else.

Workers skilled in making the same goods or providing the same services began to form guilds to protect their trades and provide training for new apprentices. There were guilds for bakers, blacksmiths, butchers, boat builders, carpenters, goldsmiths, rope makers, stonemasons, tailors, weavers and many more.

However, since then many guilds have been replaced by trade unions and professional organizations while production processes have been broken down into a series of sequential operations or tasks, each one performed by a different employee or group of employees. This became known as the **division of labour**.

By focusing their efforts on completing a single task in a production process over and over again, workers became more skilled at doing so. For example, in the early days of the motor car industry one employee would put together an entire engine before starting another one. Then Henry Ford decided to divide up the work involved into 84 separate and varied operations, so that 84 employees were needed to build a whole engine instead of just one person. Each engine would be assembled piece by piece as it was passed from worker to worker along an assembly line. As a result, many more completed engines 'rolled off' the end of the assembly line each day.

How did the division of labour benefit the Ford Motor Car Company and Ford assembly line workers?

The Ford Model T

Work on the famous Model T began in 1907, and the production began two years later in 1910 at the company's new plant in Highland Park, Michigan.

As simple as the Model T was, there remained the problem of volume production. Each car was practically hand-built. To boost production Mr Ford and his associates began sub-dividing jobs, bringing parts to workers and scheduling parts to arrive at the right spot at the right time in the production process.

Finally, they devised the moving assembly line, which, with later refinements, pointed the way to mass production. In the beginning it took 12 hours and 28 minutes to assemble a Model T. The time was cut to 5 hours and 28 minutes, then to 93 minutes. Mr Ford set a goal of a car a minute, but eventually Model Ts were rolling off the assembly line at the rate of one every ten seconds during each working day. With increased production, the price of cars came down and the pay of workers went up.

The division of labour in production has brought many advantages for firms and has been a key driver of economic growth in the last 200 years in many economies. ➤ **4.6.4**

Advantages of the division of labour

1 More goods and services can be produced

When workers specialize in particular tasks, repetition of the same operation increases their skill and speed and, as a result, more is produced in the same time.

2 Full use is made of employees' abilities

Firms will be able to choose workers to perform those tasks they are best suited to. Through repetition of individual tasks, employees are also able to increase their skills and also their earnings as they become more productive.

3 Time is saved

If a person had to do many different tasks or operations then too much time is wasted switching from one task to another. It also means less training is needed. For example, it would take many years to train someone to build an entire car, but a person can be trained quickly to install a bonnet, seats or headlamps.

4 It allows the use of machinery

As labour is divided up into specialist tasks it becomes worthwhile to use machinery. This allows further savings in time and effort. For example, cars are now painted by computer-controlled industrial robots whereas previously they were painted by workers using hand-held spray paint guns.

The disadvantages of the division of labour

Despite the clear benefits of dividing up production processes and labour into separate tasks, it also has a number of potential disadvantages for firms, their workers and consumers.

1 Work may become boring

A worker who performs the same operation each and every day is likely to become very bored. As a result, the quality of their work may suffer.

2 Workers may feel alienated

Workers may feel undervalued and lose pride in their work because they can no longer see the final result of their efforts. Boredom and alienation among workers may also cause industrial disputes. ➤ **3.4.3**

3 Products become too standardized

Whether this is a disadvantage is a matter of people's own opinion. For example, there is probably enough variation in the colour and design of cars and clothes to please most people. However, it is not possible to please everyone because in most factories it would be difficult and expensive to change the production process to suit individual tastes. This is because many large, modern manufacturers employ **mass production** processes that use the fewest number of workers to produce the greatest number of goods at the lowest possible cost. ➤ **3.6.2**

4 Firms are unable to use labour flexibly

Production may be held up in a firm if one or more employees in a production line are off work because no other workers in that firm will be able to complete their tasks. For example, imagine the impact on production if the engine fitters on a car assembly line were off work due to sickness and no other workers in the factory were trained to fit engines. Similarly, imagine the problem a shop would experience if the only staff member that could operate the cash register was away on holiday. These problems could be overcome if workers within these organizations were multi-skilled and able to complete a range of different tasks because then they can be used more flexibly, for example, to cover for staff absences.

Occupational specialization of labour

Today, most people choose to specialize not in the completion of one relatively simple task in a production process but in a range of skills relevant to one or more occupations. The growth of services, the development of modern technologies and the problems associated with the division of labour, have all created a demand for workers with multiple and more specialized skills in many economies.

Specializing in particular occupational skill sets, such as electrical engineering, marketing, computer programming, web design, tourism and hospitality, accounting, construction or medicine, has both advantages and disadvantages. For example, people with skills that are in demand will tend to attract much

▼ Some specialist skills may become outdated and unwanted due to modern technology

higher rates of pay than unskilled labour. However, people who have occupational skills that are no longer in demand may find it difficult to find other jobs they can do.

For example, the introduction of modern technology, especially in agriculture and many manufacturing industries, has had and continues to have a major impact on many employees. Many people have lost their jobs because their skills have become out of date and are no longer required. For example, welders in car manufacturing have been replaced with new advanced machines and industrial robots able to carry out their tasks faster and more efficiently.

Replacing labour with capital equipment in production is known as **factor substitution**. ➤ **3.6.2**

The benefits of occupational specialization

✔ Specialization allows individuals to make the best use of their skills and abilities.

✔ Skilled employees will often earn more than unskilled employees because their supply is limited, they tend to be more productive and there is greater demand for skilled labour.

As a result, firms and the economy should benefit from a more efficient allocation of resources, lower production costs and higher levels of output.

The disadvantages of occupational specialization

However, over-specialization in too few skills or too narrow a skill set can cause problems for many workers, firms and an economy. For example, a bricklayer may find it difficult to find alternative employment if there a downturn in the construction sector and demand for bricklayers falls. Similarly, taxi drivers may find their jobs replaced in the future by driverless cars.

Over-specialization by workers therefore increases occupational immobility and stops people moving between available jobs either within the same firm, in different firms and in different locations. For example, a good accountant will be unable to become an engineer, dentist or mechanic without significant retraining. Being a good accountant also doesn't necessarily mean that person will be a good manager or supervisor of other accountants, or good at marketing accountancy services to customers. ➤ **1.2.2**

Occupational immobility resulting from over-specialization can therefore cause the following problems:

● higher wages as there is less competition between workers for jobs;

● higher levels and longer periods of unemployment;

● higher levels of government spending on unemployment benefits or welfare payments.

To avoid these problems, firms are increasingly demanding workers with multiple skills so they can be used more flexibly within their organizations. Similarly, workers too are seeking out education and training courses and jobs that can provide them with a wide range of skills to improve their chances of future employment, higher wages, promotion and a more varied and satisfying career.

KEYWORDS

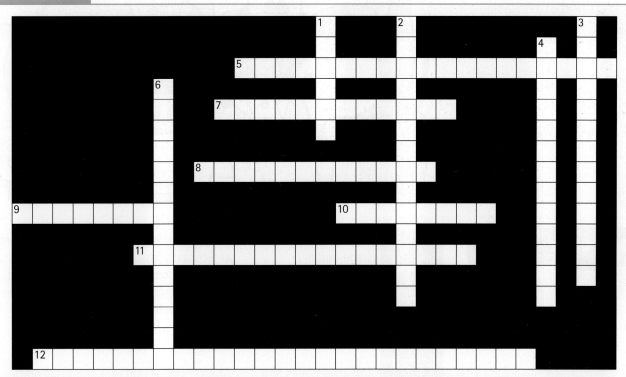

Clues across

5. The market clearing rate of pay at which the amount of labour demanded by firms will match the amount supplied (11, 4, 4)
7. The term used to describe the differential in average earnings between male and female employees (6, 3, 3)
8. Any set of arrangements that brings together all those people willing and able to supply their labour with organizations that want to hire labour (6, 6)
9. A wage rate for additional hours worked, usually during evenings or weekends, over and above agreed hours (8)
10. The amount paid to an employee per period of time worked or per unit of output produced (4, 4)
11. Differences in rates of pay between different occupations, industries, locations and group of workers (4, 13)
12. Higher rates of pay offered to workers to attract their labour to unpleasant, unsociable or dangerous jobs (12, 13)

Clues down

1. An annual rate of pay, often paid to employees in professional and other non-manual occupations (7)
2. Perks or rewards for employees, such as free medical insurance or use of a company car, that have monetary value (6, 8)
3. The balance of all the advantages and disadvantages of a particular job or occupation that people will consider when deciding whether or not to supply their labour (3, 10)
4. The total pay received by an employee for his or her labour per week or month. This may consist of wages or a salary, a piece-rate payment and other performance-related payments (5, 8)
6. Features of a job other than wage factors, such as hours of work and holiday entitlement, that make it attractive (3–4, 7)

SECTION 3.4.1

Definition of a trade union

SECTION 3.4.2

The role of trade unions in an economy

Many workers belong to labour unions or **trade unions** all over the world. Trade unions promote and protect the interests of their members with the purpose of improving their wages and working conditions. In return, members will usually pay a union membership fee to help fund the union organization.

Trade unions first developed in European countries during the Industrial Revolution in the 18th and 19th centuries following the development of factories and mass production. During this time the structure of the UK and other Western economies changed rapidly from ones based on farming and craft industries, to industrialized economies in which manufacturing industries produced most of the total output and provided most of the jobs. Work in factories was often poorly paid and undertaken in appalling conditions. Workers therefore began to organize themselves into unions to challenge the owners of factories to improve their conditions.

Why I'm part of the union!

Training Courses

Through the union stewards, health and safety (H&S) representatives, branch officials and active members can benefit from an extensive range of training courses to improve their skills. These include:

- Bargaining issues and negotiating skills
- Company information and accounts
- Human resource management
- New technology and change at work
- The law at work
- Communication and tutoring skills
- Trade unionists and the environment
- Organization and recruitment

Union movement asks government for tougher regulations of health and safety to reduce industrial injuries and accidents in the workplace

The union centre at the coast offers premium holiday accommodation to members looking for reduced rate holidays and short breaks. Convalescent patients can enjoy up to two weeks' free accommodation, subject to conditions. In addition, the centre boasts professional, state-of-the-art conferencing and seminar facilities.

South African Truck Drivers to Strike Over Wages

South African truckers plan to go on strike next week in a dispute over wages.

The South African Transport and Allied Workers' Union is demanding a 20 per cent increase for 2011 and 2012, while the Road Freight Employers' Association is offering 15 percent. The strike will be joined by the Transport and Allied Workers' Union of South Africa and the Professional Transport Workers' Union.

Public sector unions reacted angrily at the government announcement of 'significant' job cuts across public sector organizations over the next 3 years. They are demanding the government abandons its plans and improves pay and pensions for millions of low-paid workers.

1 From the above articles what do you think are the aims of trade unions?

2 What do you think are the possible benefits or problems for a business that has a high level of trade union membership among its workforce?

3 Would you join a trade union? What would be the possible costs and benefits of your membership?

The trade union movement worldwide has helped fight and bring to an end child labour in many countries; it has improved workers' safety, increased wages for both union and non-unionized workers, reduced hours of work and improved education and other benefits for many poor and working families.

The functions of trade unions

Trade unions have a number of aims regarding the welfare of their members. These include:

- negotiating improvements in and other non-wage benefits with employers

- defending employees' rights and jobs

- improving working conditions, such as securing better hours of work and better health and safety policies

- improving pay and other benefits, including holiday entitlement, sick pay and pensions

- encouraging firms to increase workers' participation in business decision making

- supporting members who have been dismissed or who are taking industrial action

- developing the skills of union members, by providing training and education courses

- providing social and recreational amenities for their members

- influencing government policy and employment legislation to protect jobs, the rights of workers and their wages and working conditions.

Before trade unions existed, a worker had to negotiate on his or her own for increased pay and better working conditions with his or her employer. With few rights, a worker could face being sacked for asking. Trade unions, however, can negotiate with and put pressure on employers on behalf of all their members to secure these aims. Trade unions therefore helped to reduce the power employers had over their workforces.

However, trade unions do not have the legal right to represent workers in some countries, or this right may not be recognized by employers and politicians. Unions are even outlawed in some countries and union officials can be jailed.

In contrast, in some countries unions work closely with, and even help to fund political parties. They can also use their power to influence government policies and employment laws to be more favourable to their members or to workers in general. In addition, many trade unions offer their members education and training to improve their skills and provide their members with recreational amenities including social clubs.

Types of trade unions

Trade unions are often grouped into four main types.

1 **General unions** represent workers from many different occupations and industries. For example, Unite in the UK represents all sorts of clerical, manufacturing, transport and commercial workers in both the public and private sector.

2 **Industrial unions** represent workers in the same industry, for example, the Turkish Union of Defence Workers (TÜRK HARB-İS¸), the National Union of Mineworkers in South Africa (NUM) and the Overseas Telecommunications Services Employees Association of Mauritius (OTSEA).

3 **Craft unions** are often small and relatively few in number today. They usually represent workers with the same skills across several industries, such as the Union of Operators and Technicians in Cinema and Video Projection in Spain and the United Brotherhood of Carpenters and Joiners of America.

4 **Non-manual unions** and **professional associations**, sometimes called white-collar unions, represent workers in non-industrial and professional occupations, such as the Association of Iranian Journalists (AOIJ), All India Bank Officer Association (AIBOC), German Police Union (GDL) and the National Union of Teachers (NUT) in the UK.

EXAM PREPARATION 3.4

a	Define *trade union*.	[2]
b	Explain **two** reasons why people join trade unions.	[4]
c	Analyse **three** factors that might determine an individual's choice of occupation.	[6]
d	Discuss why some occupations receive higher wages than other occupations.	[8]

What is collective bargaining?

The process of negotiating over pay and working conditions between trade unions and employers is known as **collective bargaining**.

Trade unions will often argue for improved wages and other working conditions if:

- price inflation is high and rising
- other groups of workers have received pay rises
- new machinery or working practices have been introduced in the workplace
- the labour productivity of their members has increased
- the profits of the employing organization have increased.

Depending on how collective bargaining is organized, negotiations between a union and employers can determine the pay and conditions for all workers in all firms in a particular industry in the economy, or they will reach local area agreements between individual firms and their workforces.

How collective bargaining is organized depends on the relationship between a union and the firms that employ the union's members. One or more trade unions can represent employees in a firm or a workplace. For example, there may be several trade unions present in one organization representing workers with different occupational skills, such as engineers or clerical workers. Alternatively, a single trade union may represent all the workers in a particular business or even an entire industry regardless of their occupations and skills.

Union representation in the workplace	
Closed shop	Trade union membership is made a compulsory condition of a taking a job in an organization. The closed shop is outlawed in many countries because it gives a union too much power to dictate who a firm should employ and to call all the workers in that firm out on strike
Open shop	A firm can employ both unionized and non-unionized labour
Single union agreement	An employer agrees to a single union representing all its employees

Single union agreements are increasingly popular because they offer an employer a number of advantages:

- Time is saved by negotiating with only one union.
- It avoids disagreements arising between different unions.
- It is easier to implement changes in working practices through one union.
- A closer working relationship with the union should develop and help to reduce industrial disputes.

The main problem with a single union agreement in a workplace is that it gives the trade union significant bargaining power. Because of this most firms will only agree to single union representation for their employees if the trade union agrees to commitments on improved levels of productivity, maintaining skill levels in the workforce and not to take strike action.

What determines the bargaining strength of different trade unions?

> **Public sector electricity workers in Nigeria launch an indefinite strike over wages**

> **Nigeria's National Union of Electricity Employees (NUEE) called off its nationwide strike today after reaching an agreement with the federal government**

Look at the two headlines below to your left. How long do you think it took for the second headline to be published in a Nigerian newspaper after the first one appeared announcing a strike by electricity workers? The answer is just one day!

An indefinite strike by all 40,000 employees of the government-owned Power Holding Company in Nigeria would have left many people and businesses in the country without power, causing hardship and halting production. As a result, the government of Nigeria held urgent talks overnight with union representatives and together an agreement on wages was reached.

In contrast, when 1,500 cleaners at Dutch Railways went on strike to highlight the poor wages and working conditions of all 150,000 cleaners employed in the Netherlands, it took nine weeks to resolve with employers. So why did reaching an agreement take so long in this case? Much depends on the bargaining strength of the workers' trade union.

The National Union of Electricity Employees in Nigeria was in a strong bargaining position to negotiate higher wages because its members strike was supported by all of Nigeria's electricity workers and because they were responsible for providing an essential service to a great many people and businesses. In contrast, only 1% of cleaners in the Netherlands went on strike over improved pay and conditions. Most cleaners continued providing useful but non-essential cleaning services to different firms in the Dutch economy. Other Dutch railway employees were also able to help keep railway stations and trains clean when the cleaners took strike action.

The bargaining power of a trade union to secure improved pay and other working conditions from employers is therefore stronger when:

- the union represents most or all of the workers in that firm or industry

- union members provide products and public services consumers need and for which there are few close substitutes, such as electricity, public transport, healthcare and education

- the union is able to support its members financially during strike action to compensate them for their loss of earnings.

Unions and employers will also negotiate over employment levels and other benefits such as pension rights, holiday entitlement, training and the introduction of new technology and working practices.

Why do industrial disputes occur?

Collective bargaining between trade unions and employers can sometimes fail to reach an agreement. For example, if a union demands a wage increase for its members not matched by higher productivity, then production costs will rise. Firms will either face trying to pass on higher wage costs to consumers in higher prices, or the profits of the owners of the firm will be reduced. Demand for more holidays, better pensions and sick pay, and resistance to new working practices, will also tend to raise costs and could mean that a firm becomes uncompetitive. As a result, a firm may try to reduce its costs by reducing its demand for labour and making some workers unemployed. ➤ **3.3.3**

Disputes over demarcation can also arise. These occur when a union insists that its members can only carry out certain jobs and will not take on new tasks, or when a firm employs non-union members to carry out the same or similar tasks instead.

Industrial actions

When negotiations between employers and unions fail to end in agreement, workers may take disruptive **industrial action** to put pressure on their employers to address their demands or grievances. **Official action** has the backing of their trade union, and other unions may also take action in support. **Unofficial action** means that workers taking the industrial action do not have the support of their union.

▼ Workers on strike over equal pay

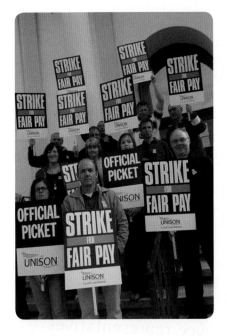

Forms of industrial action	
Overtime ban	Workers refuse to work more than their normal hours
Work to rule	Workers deliberately slow down production by complying rigidly with every rule and regulation
Go-slow	Workers carry out tasks deliberately slowly to reduce production
Strike	Workers refuse to work and may also protest, or picket, outside their workplace to stop deliveries and prevent non-unionized workers from entering

Industrial action can increase the bargaining strength of workers to force employers to agree to their wage and other demands. However, union action also has major implications:

- **Businesses** suffer higher costs and lose output, revenues and profits during industrial action. If the action goes on for a long time a business may also lose important customers to rival firms.

- **Union members** will not be paid their wages or salaries during a strike although some may receive income support from their union's strike fund. Some workers may also lose their jobs if employers cut back their demand for labour because the industrial action has lost them customers and profits.

- **Consumers** may be unable to obtain the goods and services they need and may also have to pay higher prices if firms pass on their increased costs.

- The reputation of **an economy** as a good place for business may be damaged by frequent and widespread industrial action. Firms may decide to invest and set up businesses elsewhere. This will increase unemployment and lower incomes.

Arbitration may be necessary to settle industrial disputes. This involves employers and unions agreeing to let an independent referee, often a senior government official or lawyer, help them reach agreement. This normally means both sides in the dispute accepting a compromise – something that is satisfactory to both parties but rather less than they had initially wanted.

Because industrial action can be so damaging some employers and unions have reached 'no strike' agreements. In return, employers may agree to more generous wages and improved working conditions. Alternatively, both sides agree to accept the judgement of an independent arbitrator who will determine what a fair wage increase or change in working conditions should be, based on evidence and recommendations presented by the union's and employer's representatives.

Laws have also been introduced in many countries relating to the power of trade unions to take industrial action. For example, an employer in the UK can seek legal damages from a union for lost profits if industrial action is taken without first balloting its members. Mass picketing is also unlawful. Only a handful of strikers are allowed to picket outside their workplace.

ACTIVITY 3.16

A tough negotiation

In groups of four, act out the following roles in an industrial dispute between an employer and a trade union. Your job is to try to find a settlement that both sides in the dispute are willing to accept. The roles in the dispute are shown opposite.

Union representatives

the shop steward

a machine operator

Employee representatives

the managing director

the work study engineer

Union threatens action over new machinery

The Association of Metalworkers is today threatening to take industrial action if the decision to install new computer-assisted metal shaping and grinding machinery in PK Metals plc is taken without assurances on pay and redundancies. The local branch of the union has asked for a 5% wage increase for members to operate the new machinery.

'Any strike action could damage the company considerably,' said Mr Graham Stone, managing director of PK Metals. 'A major new order from an overseas customer has recently boosted the company's prospects and we must deliver on time and to quality.'

Any disruption could threaten the international reputation of the company. The management are also keen to avoid any increase in wage costs that may make the firm uncompetitive.

Workers are claiming that the new technology requires a higher level of skill and concentration, and compensation is sought. They are also seeking management assurances that there will be no redundancies as a result of the new machines.

The two sides in the dispute have agreed to meet and negotiate today.

The machine operators want a pay rise for operating more complex and demanding machinery. You also want to set an example for the future. You do not want your employer to think that every time it introduces new ways of working it can overlook its workforce. What you want is a share in the increased profits that can come from the increased output of the new machines.

You also fear that redundancies may follow as machines replace workers, and you want to limit the number of jobs lost.

You both know that the firm has recently received a large order from overseas, so you need to be careful that you do not cause the firm to lose the order. This could mean losing jobs.

Your task before negotiations

Before you enter negotiations write a brief report for all your union members to read, pointing out your demands and the management's position. This should include answers to questions such as:

- ▶ What is your pay claim?
- ▶ Why have you made this pay claim?
- ▶ What has been the management response?
- ▶ What forms of action could the union take if necessary?
- ▶ Why are both you and the management keen to avoid a strike?

Your tasks after negotiations

Write a report highlighting the results of negotiations, that is, what agreements, if any, were reached.

If no firm agreement was reached, do you advise your members to accept or reject the management's offer? If no agreement was reached, what will the union do next?

The work study engineer has concluded that the machines require no more effort to operate than the old ones. In fact, you feel that they ease pressure on the skilled operator. No pay rise is necessary to compensate.

As the managing director you fear that any cost reductions from the increased output from specialist machinery may be lost if workers push for higher wages. It may even allow lower-cost competitors to undercut your prices. If you are also unable to cut the number of jobs your plant will be over-staffed and wage costs will be much higher than they need to be.

However, you do not want to lose the goodwill of the workforce at a critical time for the company with an overseas order to fulfil.

Your task before negotiations

Write an information sheet for the management team including answers to such questions as:

- ▶ What wage claim has the union made?
- ▶ What are the implications of accepting or rejecting this claim?
- ▶ Why you are keen to avoid a strike?
- ▶ What will be discussed with the union?

Task after negotiations

Prepare another management document to report on agreements reached and their effects on the company and the action that will be taken if negotiations break down and no firm agreement is reached.

The negotiations

The four people in the role-play should try to negotiate an agreement acceptable to both sides. If you cannot reach an agreement perhaps your tutor can join in to act as an independent commentator, or ask for the meeting to take a short break while you work out what to do next.

SECTION 3.4.3

The advantages and disadvantages of trade union activity

The benefits of trade union representation

From reading the previous sections in this unit we can identify many of the advantages to workers, firms and a government and economy of organized trade unions. These advantages are summarized below.

For workers:

- ✔ trade unions represent their views and fight to maintain their jobs and working conditions;
- ✔ they protect their wages and other benefits;

✔ they prevent discrimination and exploitation at work;

✔ they can provide training and educational courses.

For firms including public sector organizations:

✔ trade unions protect and maintain the skill levels of their members;

✔ they provide a single point of contact. Having a single body for negotiating terms and conditions for workers is simpler than dealing with workers individually;

✔ they can help to improve labour productivity. Improvements in working conditions and wages can create an incentive for workers to be more productive. Unions may also agree to pay or profit sharing deals linked to higher levels of productivity.

For government:

✔ the trade union movement in an economy provides a single point of contact and source of information to inform and discuss economic issues and government policy measures including employment laws;

✔ they can help to reduce inequality in society by raising the wages of low paid workers;

✔ to the extent they can raise productivity within firms, they will help to boost output and economic growth in the economy;

✔ improving and maintaining workforce skills increases the mobility of labour in the economy.

The disadvantages of trade union representation

The actions of trade unions may also have a number of disadvantages for workers, firms and government. These advantages are outlined below.

For workers:

✘ belonging to a trade union requires the payment of weekly or monthly membership fees;

✘ individual workers who are more productive and have more experience and skills than their workplace colleagues will be unable to negotiate higher wages separately with their employers;

✘ in some workplaces with closed shops or single union agreements, employees have no other choice but to join a union and to follow union rules.

For firms:

✘ wages and other working conditions may be better, more productive and working hours lower than they might otherwise be if there was no union representation in workplaces;

✘ they will have less control over who they can hire and dismiss, and may face more challenges and legal actions from trade unions if they do not agree with the reasons for certain dismissals and the procedures used;

✘ they are normally required to collect trade union membership fees from the pay of their workers and then pay over these fees to their unions. This increases administrative and accounting costs;

trade unions may organize workers to participate in disruptive industrial actions including strikes, to increase their bargaining strength in negotiations over jobs, workers' rights, pay and working conditions.

For government:

the demand for labour in the economy may be lower and unemployment higher if trade unions push up wages. In turn, a government may have to spend more of unemployment benefits or welfare payments and raise taxes to pay for them;

trade unions may contribute to rising wage inflation if they are successful at raising the wages of their members without improving their productivity at the same time;

industrial disputes and actions can result in lost production and may reduce economic growth.

KEYWORDS

Clues across

2. The process of negotiating pay and working conditions between trade union representatives and employers (10, 10)
5. An industrial action that involves workers refusing to work more than their normal hours (8, 3)
6. A disruptive action taken by a group of workers who refuse to work (5)
7. A type of trade union with members drawn from many different industries and occupations (7, 5)
8. This exists when trade union membership is made a compulsory condition of a taking a job in a particular workplace or organization (6, 4)

Clues down

1. An agreement between an employer and a single trade union to represent all workers at a particular workplace. The arrangement saves time by negotiating with only one union and avoids disagreements arising between different unions (5, 5, 9)
3. The term used to describe all disruptive activities, such as a strike or work to rule, that workers may carry out to support their wage or other demands (10, 6)
4. An association representing employees in a particular workplace or industry with the aim of improving their pay and working conditions (5, 5)

Unit 3.5 Firms

SECTION 3.5.1

Classification of firms

What is a firm?

Human effort and natural and human-made resources are needed to produce goods and services. However, these resources alone will not produce goods and services that satisfy human needs and wants. For example, simply buying some wood and other materials and hiring a group of people to work together in a factory will not result in the production of tables and chairs. Production will only take place if resources are properly organized, financed and important decisions are taken to manage and control what they produce from day to day. These decisions are taken within **firms**. ➤ **1.2.1**

Resources are combined and organized into firms to carry out productive activities. Firms are therefore important decision makers within any economy. Decisions taken within firms by the entrepreneurs and managers who own, finance or run them will determine how scarce resources are allocated and used, and therefore what goods and services are produced, how they are produced and who they are produced for. ➤ **2.2.1**

Different types of firm

There are many different types of firms in a modern, mixed economy. Therefore, in order to identify and compare different types of firms and how they behave, economists classify or group them together according to common characteristics. For example, economists will distinguish between different firms according to:

- the **industrial sector** in which they operate;
- whether they are privately owned, financed and controlled in the **private sector, or state-owned enterprises** in the **public sector**;
- their **size** or scale of production.

Classifying firms into different industrial sectors

Decisions taken by firms in an economy about what and how to produce will result in scarce resources being allocated to different productive activities, often located in different areas or regions of that economy. Economists therefore group or classify similar productive activities together into different **economic sectors**.

An economic sector may also be referred to as an **industrial sector**. An **industry** or industrial sector contains firms that use similar production processes and specialize in the production of a similar range of products. An industry will include both small, local firms employing very few workers and large, national or even huge multinational firms employing many thousands of workers and selling products all over the world. ➤ **6.2.2**

For example, the automotive manufacturing industry consists of all firms making and supplying vehicles and engines, tyres, body parts and components. Similarly, the air transport industry includes all firms providing air passenger and airfreight transport services and facilities, including airports and airlines.

Most national economies will have a variety of different industries or industrial sectors. In turn, each industry can be classified into one of three broad economic sectors: the **primary sector**, **secondary sector** or **tertiary sector**.

The primary sector

Firms in industries within the primary sector of an economy specialize in the production or extraction of natural resources by growing crops, managing forests, mining coal and other minerals, and extracting oils and gases.

The production or extraction of natural resources is often the first stage of production for most goods and services. ➤ **3.4.5**

- Crop and animal production
- Forestry and logging
- Fishing
- Mining
- Quarrying
- Oil and gas extraction

The secondary sector

Firms within industries in the secondary sector of an economy will use unprocessed natural resources and other unfinished products to make other goods. This process is called **manufacturing**. For example, oil is used in plastics, glass is made from sand, and paper is made from pulped wood. Many electrical products are made from metals and plastics.

Construction firms using materials to build homes, offices, roads and other infrastructure, and firms processing oil, gas and other fuels to supply electricity are also part of the secondary sector of an economy.

Some secondary sector industries

- Food processing
- Textiles
- Paper, pulp and paperboard
- Chemicals
- Oil and gas refining
- Pharmaceuticals
- Rubber and plastic products
- Fabricated metals
- Computer, electronic and optical products
- Water collection, treatment and supply
- Electric power generation, transmission and distribution
- Construction

The tertiary sector

Firms within industries that provide services are part of the tertiary sector or **services sector** an economy. The distribution and sale of manufactured goods and the provision of services to consumers is the final stage in their production. Firms in the wholesale and retailing industries specialize in these activities.

However, there are many other firms providing services that are used at every stage of production, such as banking, insurance and transport. Some firms also provide personal services such as hairdressing, decorating, healthcare and personal training.

Some tertiary sector industries

- Wholesaling, retailing and repairs
- Transportation and storage
- Accommodation and food services
- Publishing and broadcasting
- Telecommunications
- Banking and insurance
- Real estate
- Public administration
- Defence services
- Education
- Arts and entertainment
- Healthcare
- Legal services

Every economy can be divided up into primary, secondary and tertiary sectors. However, in some economies more firms and more resources are engaged in primary sector activities than other productive activities. In contrast, other usually more advanced or developed economies allocate far more resources to secondary and tertiary sector activities than to primary sector activities.

The relative size of the primary, secondary and tertiary sectors in an economy, measured by the number and size of firms in each sector, the amount of resources they employ and the amount they produce, therefore provides a useful indicator of how developed an economy is. ➤ **5.4.1**

ACTIVITY 3.17

Which stage of production?

Under three column headings sort the following list of industries into primary, secondary and tertiary industries.

Television broadcasting	Health service	Advertising
Film-making	Farming	Shipbuilding
Shipping	Banking	Universities
Decorating	Hotels	Motor cars
Construction	Furniture	Mining
Fishing	Retailing	Chemicals
Forestry	Engineering	Restaurants

Private sector firms

Most firms are owned and financed by private individuals. Most aim to generate more revenue from their productive activities than their costs so that they earn a surplus or profit. ➤ **3.7.5**

Privately owned firms are part of the private sector in an economy and can take many different legal or organizational forms according to how they are owned, controlled and financed. ➤ **2.11.1**

For example, a **sole trader** or sole proprietorship is a business organization owned, controlled and financed by one person. The owner receives any profits but is also personally liable for any debts left by the business in the event it fails. Most sole traders are small firms but they are also the most popular type of firm in the world because they are easy to set up.

In contrast, **public limited companies** are some of the biggest firms in the world. They can finance their operations from the sale of shares to investors through a stock exchange. A public limited company is therefore owned by its shareholders and any profits made by the company will belong to them. They will also appoint a board of directors to manage their company.

While it is useful to know some of the main differences between these and other types of firm in the private sector of an economy, you will not need to learn about them in any detail.

▼ Types of firm or business organizations in the private sector

Legal form	Ownership	Control	Main sources of finance	Distribution of profits (or surplus)
Sole trader	Owned by one person	The owner is the main decision maker	The owner's personal savings	The owner receives any profits but is also personally responsible for any business debts
Joint-stock or limited company	A company is owned by one or more shareholders	A company will be managed by one or more directors appointed by its shareholders	A company is financed by the sale of shares to shareholders. A private limited company can only sell shares to private individuals. A public limited company can sell shares publicly through a stock exchange.	Any profit made by a company belongs to its shareholders. Shareholders are not personally liable to repay any company debts.
Cooperative	A cooperative is owned by its members	A cooperative is managed by a board of directors appointed by its members	From membership fees and drawing on reserves	Members receive any surplus revenue that is not added to reserves
Charity	A charity can be set up and registered by a private individual or another organization to provide beneficial services for public benefit but it cannot be owned	A charity is run by a board of trustees	Gifts and donations from people and organizations	Charities do not aim to make a profit. Any surplus income left over after costs have been deducted will be reinvested in the charity to fund the services it provides

State-owned enterprises

Indian Railways is the state-owned railway company of India, which owns and operates most of the country's rail transport.

Each year the government allocates Indian Railways a budget to operate rail services and to invest in the new and replacement tracks and rolling stock it needs.

Pradesh Verma, a regional manager, explained that all the railway managers are accountable to the Indian Parliament. 'We are entrusted by government to spend public money efficiently' he said, 'and to meet performance targets for punctuality, safety, passenger and freight traffic and more.'

'Ticket prices are kept low to enable people on low incomes to use the rail service and to carry freight to rural areas where there may be no other way of getting goods to people who need them. However, the company is still expected to generate an operating surplus or profit each year for the government.'

XIAN-LI IS THE CHIEF EXECUTIVE of one of Hong Kong's public hospitals funded by the government. Her job is to ensure that the objectives of the hospital and the government's health care policy are met.

'The hospital is not required to make a profit from the provision of health care' she explained, 'but it does have to meet targets including for patient care and satisfaction, treatment waiting times, hospital cleanliness, and surgical and running costs.'

Unlike private sector firms owned and run by private individuals, the two organizations above are owned and controlled by their governments. They are state-owned enterprises and therefore part of the public sectors in the economies of Hong Kong and India.

A **state-owned enterprise (SOE)** is a firm or trading organization that is wholly or partially owned and operated by a government primarily to carry out commercial activities in order to earn revenues and, in many cases, to make profits such as a state-owned railway, postal service, power company or airline. Any profits made by SOEs will be re-invested in improving the goods or services they provide or used by government to fund other public sector spending. However, any losses made by these enterprises will have to be funded from taxes and other government revenues. ➤ **4.3.2**

Some SOEs also have public policy objectives including running the central bank, delivering essential public services such as electricity and sanitation or the provision of merit goods such as national parks and affordable healthcare. Governments will often pay subsidies to their state-owned enterprises to reduce the cost of providing essential services and merit goods to people on low incomes who may not otherwise be able to afford them. ➤ **2.11.2**

Australia	India	United Kingdom
Australian Broadcasting Corporation	Air India	British Broadcasting Corporation
Australian postal service	Cotton Corporation of India	Channel 4 television
Australian Rail Track Corporation	Indian Oil Corporation	National Air Traffic Services
Reserve Bank of Australia	Indian Telephone Industries	National Nuclear Laboratory
	State Bank of India	Network Rail
	State Road Transport Corporation	Scottish Water
France	**Thailand**	**US**
La Poste	Airports of Thailand	Amtrak (national rail corporation)
France Télévisions	Electricity Generating Authority	Corporation for Public Broadcasting
Radio France	Metropolitan Waterworks Authority	Federal Crop Insurance Corporation
Électricité de France	Port Authority of Thailand	Federal Prison Industries
Aéroports de Paris	Provincial Waterworks Authority	Legal Services Corporation
	Thai Airways International	National Park Foundation

Many state-owned enterprises have been created through a process called **nationalization**. This occurs when a government takes over the ownership of private sector organizations, for example, through the compulsory purchase of all the shares in a private or public limited company. ➤ **2.11.1**

Local government authorities may also own and control trading enterprises

In addition to the national or central government in a country, local government authorities may also operate public sector enterprises selling services to direct consumers. These may include local theatres, libraries, children's nurseries and swimming pools. Many of these services may be run at a loss or will at least be expected to cover their costs with their revenues. However, some may be able to set their prices or charges at a level that will earn a profit.

▲ Some examples of local government enterprises

Walmart Stores is one of the world's largest business organizations employing some 2.3 million people worldwide and with almost $200 billion invested in buildings, computers, vehicles, forklift trucks and other capital assets.

The Toyota Motor Group also ranks as one of the world's largest firms. It employs 348,877 people worldwide but has assets worth over $400 billion. So does this make Toyota a smaller or larger firm than Walmart?

Of course both these giant organizations are huge compared to the many millions of other firms worldwide that serve small local markets, employ very few workers and have few capital assets.

It is useful to group firms together according to whether they are large, **small and medium-sized enterprises (SMEs)** or **micro-enterprises**. The size of firms can be measured in a number of ways and these also provide useful clues about the reasons why some firms grow into very large organizations while others remain small.

There are a number of ways to measure and compare the size of firms:

- how many workers they employ
- how they are organized
- how much capital they employ
- their market share.

Measure 1: number of employees

This is a straightforward measure of firm size. Firms employing up to 50 people are usually considered small while a micro-enterprise is generally defined as a small firm employing nine or fewer people.

However, just counting the number of employees a firm employs can be misleading. This is because some large firms are capital-intensive and employ relatively few workers. Instead they use a lot of machinery and computer-controlled equipment to automate their production processes in order to mass-produce large quantities of output. ➤ **3.6.3**

Measure 2: organization

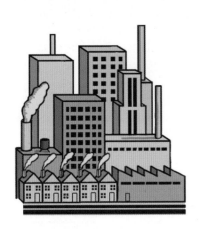

Larger firms are often divided up into different departments specializing in particular functions, such as purchasing, sales and marketing, finance and production. In smaller firms the owners and employees tend to carry out all the various functions between them. Larger firms may also have many different layers of management and different offices, factories and/or retail outlets spread across different locations, and in different countries if the firm is a multinational. The size of an organization can therefore be judged by how it is organized internally.

Measure 3: capital employed

Capital employed is money invested in those productive assets in a firm that help it to generate revenue. They are assets used to produce and sell goods and services. ➤ **3.7.3**

Assets used in production include machinery, factory and office buildings, stocks of materials and components and money held by a firm to pay wages and other costs.

The more capital employed in a firm the more it can produce and therefore the greater its size or scale of production. However, some large firms may be labour-intensive. This means their production process requires the employment of a lot of workers but relatively little capital.

Measure 4: market share

The market for any good or service consists of all those consumers willing and able to buy it no matter where they might be located. ➤ 2.2.1

The size of the market for a good or service is measured by the total amount spent by consumers on that product per week, month or year. The bigger the market demand for a particular good or service, the more scope there is for firms supplying that market to increase their scale of production. The share of the total market sales any one firm is able to capture is its market share.

The **market share** of a firm measures the proportion of total sales revenue or turnover that is attributable to that firm. For example, the global market for carbonated soft drinks was worth an estimated $342 billion in 2015. The market is dominated by the Coca-Cola Company. Its share of the global market was 48.6%. In comparison, its major rival PepsiCo captured only 20.5% of the total market.

But not all markets are so large. For example, a local hairdressing salon may be a very small business in terms of the number of people and amount of capital equipment it employs but it may have a very large share of the local market it serves because it is the only salon in a town where most local people can have their hair cut and styled.

ACTIVITY 3.18

Size matters

The table below contains information on four different business organizations.

▶ Which firm is the largest?

▶ Is it sensible to use only one measure of a firm's size?

▶ What are the problems with the individual measures used to determine a firm's size?

Name	Industrial sector	Total employees	Capital employed ($ million)	Total output ($ million)	Global market share (% of revenues)
Google	Software and computers	20,222	21,795	31,768	67%
ExxonMobil	Oil and gas production	79,900	228,052	459,579	10%
GlaxoSmithKline	Pharmaceuticals	35,637	57,647	101,133	6%
Toyota Motors	Automobiles and parts	358,304	112,196	261,837	13%

Because the size of markets for different goods and services varies considerably from huge global markets to small, localized markets, it is not sensible to compare the volume of output or sales of firms in different industries. For example, a major ship building company may produce only one large warship or cruise liner each year while a small local bakery may produce and sell many thousands of bread and cake products each year.

Small firms

Most firms in any national economy are small sole traders or private limited companies owned by one or a small number of shareholders. Some may grow over time into much larger organizations but the vast majority of firms in any economy will remain small.

ACTIVITY 3.19

Staying small

Most firms are small and remain small. Make a list of all the reasons given in the quotes below from owners of small businesses against expanding their businesses

'I can't be bothered to run a larger business. It would be too stressful and take up too much of my time. I am happy being small. I make enough profit and I get to keep it all! My business taxes are also low because I run a small business.'

'I own and run a small restaurant serving a small, local market. There is no point growing larger. I know all my customers and can offer them a good personalized service. Large restaurant chains can't provide this.'

'I work from my home designing and building websites for major business customers all over the world. I don't need to be big. I only need a computer and access to high-speed Internet.'

'We make exclusive and luxury designer knitwear. All our garments are hand-made and sell for between $500 and $1,000 each. Our market is therefore quite limited. Most of our customers are high net-worth individuals, including film, TV and music industry celebrities.'

'My bank wouldn't lend me enough money to finance the purchase of the new premises and equipment I need.'

So what explains why so many firms are small and remain small?

1 The size of their market is small

The most efficient size for a firm is closely related to the size of its market. If there are only a relatively small number of consumers willing and able to buy a product there is no point in a firm supplying that market expanding in scale significantly.

There are many examples of sectors in which small firms thrive because the markets they serve tend to be localized. For example, hairdressers, restaurants and cafés, window cleaners, decorators and many hotels, taxi services and shops only supply the villages and towns they are located in. They are also able to offer their customers more innovative and personalized services than large firms that mass produce goods or provide standardized services across all their business locations. For example, tailors can make made-to-measure suits and carpenters can make furniture to order.

Similarly, firms that produce luxury items may have relatively small or niche markets. Only consumers with very high incomes may be willing and able to pay high prices for 'exclusive' products such as designer clothing and jewellery, sports cars and luxury holidays.

2 Access to capital is limited

Sole traders often have to use their personal savings to set up their firms. Banks are not normally willing to lend money to small, untested business propositions. This is because small firms usually lack assets they can offer as collateral against loans, face fierce competition from larger rivals and may not be able to make enough revenue each month to repay a loan.

Recognizing that lack of capital is a problem for small firms, many governments encourage new start-ups by providing grants to cover the costs of premises and equipment, or by subsidizing wages and other costs.

They may also benefit from lower rates of tax on their profits, and can often seek help and advice on business issues from specialist advisers employed by government agencies. Governments do this because small firms are often very innovative: they invent new products that help to boost trade and new processes that other firms can eventually use to increase their productivity. Some small firms will also eventually grow into much larger firms that help to create wealth in an economy through additional employment and profits.

3 New technology has reduced the scale of production needed

The size and cost of new technology has reduced significantly over time. Most small firms now have access to computers and other modern equipment. Many years ago they would not have been able to afford such equipment. Also, through the internet many small businesses can easily communicate with suppliers and consumers all over the world.

4 Some business owners may simply choose to stay small

Some entrepreneurs may simply decide they do not want to increase the size of their firm as long as they continue to make a reasonable profit after tax. Running a larger enterprise can also be very time-consuming and stressful. Some entrepreneurs may lack the skills they need to manage and run larger firms employing many more people and much more capital.

The vast number of small firms that exist across many industrial sectors in almost every economy can therefore be explained by their advantages and also the barriers and disadvantages that ultimately prevent their growth.

▲ Smaller firms usually supply small, local markets and can offer a more personalized goods and services than larger firms

▼ Advantages and disadvantages of small firms

Advantages of small firms	Disadvantages of small firms
1 Small firms can usually be set up very easily: ✔ there are normally few legal requirements involved in setting up a sole trader or small, private limited company; ✔ many can be run from home or rented premises with little capital; ✔ some small firms may receive grants from their local or central government to help them set up. 2 Paid managers rather than business owners often run large firms. In contrast, the owners of small firms tend to run them from day-to-day and are their main decision makers. This can be an advantage because:	1 Because owners of small firms usually have full responsibility for running them day-to-day: ✘ they will need to keep accounts, advertise, recruit and manage staff, deal directly with customers and suppliers, and carry out many other tasks. However, few owners have all the skills necessary to run their firms successfully; ✘ they will often have to work very long hours; ✘ they may have to close their firms and lose revenue when they are sick or on holiday unless they are able to employ someone else to manage and run their businesses in their absence.

- ✔ they are motivated to run them well because they receive all the profits;
- ✔ decisions can be made and communicated to their employees quickly;
- ✔ they are in closer contact with customers than the owners of larger firms. This can help small firms build up customer trust and personalize their products to better meet their customer's requirements;
- ✔ they are in closer contact with their employees and this can build up trust and loyalty. Employees of small firms may be more motivated as a result even if their wages may be lower than in larger firms.

3 In addition, small firms may be able to react to changes in economic and market conditions more quickly than larger firms because:

- ✔ their owners are their main decision makers and because they are in closer contact with customers they will learn of and understand changes in customer preferences and buying behaviour better and more quickly than in much larger firms;
- ✔ unlike many larger firms, smaller firms usually do not have a significant amount of capital invested in machinery and premises. This means they may be able to change their production processes and products more easily as conditions change.

2 Small firms are usually more vulnerable than larger firms. Many do not survive because:

- ✘ they lack financial resources;
- ✘ they are in competition with many other firms;
- ✘ in the event of failure, sole traders face the additional risk they will have to pay off any business debts from their own personal savings.

3 Small firms find it difficult to raise capital to pay their running costs or to finance their growth:

- ✘ banks and other financial institutions are not as willing to give loans to small firms because they are riskier and have few assets they could sell to pay off their loans in the event of business failure;
- ✘ suppliers may be unwilling to sell their products to small firms on credit terms because of the risk they will be unable to repay them;
- ✘ unlike limited companies, sole traders cannot sell shares.

4 The average cost of delivering a service or producing or selling each product is often much higher for a small firm than for a larger firm because:

- ✘ small firms may be unable to buy in bulk and receive bulk purchase price discounts from their suppliers;
- ✘ they cannot afford to employ specialist equipment and staff that can help them to improve their efficiency and lower their average costs.

SECTION 3.5.3–4

Mergers and the causes and forms of the growth of firms

Why do some firms grow in size?

In economics, firms can only grow in size in a time period known as the **long run**. In the long run a firm can expand its scale of production by buying or hiring larger premises and more machinery and equipment. This is because all factors of production can be varied in the long run.

In contrast, in the **short run** capital is a fixed factor of production and cannot be varied. Firms can hire more workers and buy more materials but will only be able to produce more output if they can make more and better use of their existing premises, machinery and equipment.

The difference between the short run and long run can be a matter of days or weeks in some firms. For example, a small firm making and selling greetings cards may be able to buy and install an additional printer relatively quickly. In contrast, it may take a large supermarket chain a year or more to build and fit out a new store.

Not all firms can or should remain small if they are to survive and generate profits. Growing in size can help a firm to reduce its market and financial risks. It may be able to raise more money to finance new, more efficient equipment and to employ more specialist workers. This can help the firm to improve the quality and appeal of its products, reduce the cost of producing them and increase its sales and profit margins.

However, producing more output means increasing the scale of production in a firm. This can be expensive to achieve. Cost may rise initially and this will reduce profits. However, in the long run a larger firm may enjoy significant cost advantages over smaller firms and capture a much larger market share, both of which should help to it to increase its total profits. ➤ **3.5.5**

There are two main ways a firm can grow in size and expand its scale of production in the long run.

Internal growth

Internal growth or **organic growth** involves a firm expanding its own scale of production through investments in new and additional equipment and technology, and increasing the size of its premises. This will increase its fixed costs of production. ➤ **3.7.1**

To finance this growth the owners will need to use the profits of the firm, borrow money from banks and other lenders or sell shares in the ownership of their business to other investors. To sell shares a firm must become a joint-stock company. The new investors will become the owners or shareholders of the company and be entitled to a share of any profits.

External growth

External growth in the size of firms is more common. It involves one or more firms combining their factors of production to form a larger enterprise. This is known as **integration** through **merger**.

A **merger** occurs when the owners of one or more firms, usually of a similar size, agree to combine their operations to form a new, larger enterprise.

However, a merger can also result from the **takeover** or **acquisition** of a smaller public limited company by a larger one. This involves the larger company buying up all the shares of the smaller company with or without the agreement of its managers.

▶ ExxonMobil was formed in 1999 following an agreement by US companies Exxon and Mobil to merge their operations. The combined company is now one of the largest in the world and benefits from a large market share and significant economies of scale in oil and gas exploration, production and sales.

Types of merger

▼ Horizontal merger

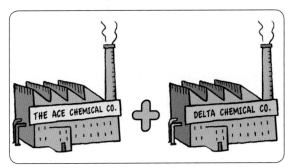

Integration or mergers between firms can take a number of forms.

Horizontal merger occurs between firms engaged in the production of the same type of good or service. Most integration between firms is horizontal.

Horizontal mergers can benefit firms in the following ways:

✔ The combined business will have a larger market share;

✔ It will reduce the number of competing firms in the industry. This is called **consolidation**;

✔ Integrated firms may gain a number of cost advantages due to their combined size. These are called **economies of scale**. For example, by merging their finance, purchasing and other administrative functions the new firm can reduce staff and other costs. It may also benefit from price discounts offered by suppliers for the bulk-buying of goods from them;

✔ Similarly, if common ownership results in the firms moving closer together geographically then it will reduce their transportation costs.

However, combining horizontally to form a much larger firm can create problems:

✘ for the owners and managers because it may become more difficult to coordinate and manage the productive activities of a larger number of workers, especially if they are spread across many different locations. As a result production costs may rise; ➤ **3.5.5**

✘ for consumers, because horizontal mergers can create large firms able to restrict market supply and competition in order to raise their prices and increase their profits. ➤ **3.8.2**

Vertical merger occurs when firms at different stages in the supply chain for a product merge together. For example, a car manufacturer may combine with a car retailer in order to control the sale of its cars. This involves **forward vertical merger**. The car manufacturer may benefit in the following ways:

✔ It can be certain it has a retailer through which it can promote and sell its cars and accessories;

✔ It can instruct the retailer not to stock vehicles produced by rival manufacturers;

✔ It can absorb the profit made by the retailer on each sale.

Backward vertical merger can also occur between firms when one firm combines with another at an earlier stage in its supply chain. For example, a cheese producer may combine with a dairy farm so that it is guaranteed supplies of milk, and may benefit in the following ways;

✔ It can be assured regular and exclusive supplies from the farm. This greatly reduces the risk of production being held up by late deliveries;

▲ Vertical merger

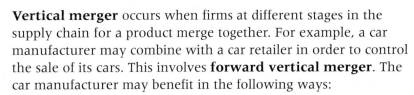

Firms 209

✔ It can control the costs and quality of supplies from the farm;

✔ It can absorb the profits of the farm.

Vertical mergers with other firms in its supply chain therefore enable a firm to have greater control over the cost, quality and delivery of items it needs to either make or sell its products.

However, vertical integration can be expensive and problematic:

✘ The takeover of other firms in a supply chain can require significant amount of capital;

✘ If the firms differ significantly in size there will be an excess capacity in one part of the supply chain. For example, if the car manufacturer above produces more cars than the retailer can sell or if the cheese maker requires more milk than the farm can produce to keep its existing equipment and workforce fully employed;

✘ Once a firm has control over its supply chain in one region or country it cannot easily relocate parts of its supply chain to cheaper locations overseas, for example, where wages or taxes on businesses may be lower. To do so will greatly increase transport costs and reduce supply chain coordination;

✘ Running a successful manufacturing firm requires a different set of skills to running a profitable retailer or producer of component parts or natural resources;

✘ The different firms may have very different ways of working and interacting with employees and customers. A clash of cultures can lead to misunderstandings, conflict and lost productivity in the merged organization.

Lateral integration or **conglomerate merger** occurs between firms that are involved in unrelated activities and industries. Conglomerate mergers between one or more firms therefore creates firms called **conglomerates** that produce a wide range of different products. For example, Samsung is a major global business group well known for its televisions, mobile phones and other electronic products, but it also has business interests in shipbuilding, construction, chemicals, financial services and entertainment. This benefits the Samsung Corporation in the following ways:

✔ It has been able to expand its customer base, thereby increasing its sales and profits;

✔ It has allowed the company to diversify its produce range and reduce market risks. Producing and selling a wide range of different products reduces the impact a fall in consumer demand for any one of them will have on its total sales and profits;

✔ It can exploit synergies between different parts of its business. They can share ideas and innovations. For example, the development of touch-sensitive screens and voice-operated controls have been used in many different applications within Samsung including televisions, cameras, computers and smartphones.

✔ It has enabled the company to achieve significant economies of scale, for example, by spreading the costs of research and development, advertising and workforce recruitment across its different business units. It helps in reducing the production cost per unit and helps in achieving economies of scale.

▲ Conglomerate merger between unrelated firms

However, conglomerate diversification can sometimes create significant problems in a company:

✘ Managers may find it difficult to govern and control a much larger firm made up of very different businesses producing and selling different products to different groups of customers. This can result in mismanagement and misunderstandings between the various parts of the business;

✘ When merging unrelated firms, managers will require a lot of effort to understand the products and operations of each business. This can result in a loss of focus leading to poor performance in all the businesses;

✘ Workforce issues can arise when workers who are used to working for different firms in different industries and who have different skills, attitudes and wages, are brought together into a single organization. As a result, disputes can occur and their motivation and quality of work can suffer.

ACTIVITY 3.20

What type of integration?

Which of the following mergers involve horizontal, vertical or lateral integrations?

Merger or takeover	Horizontal?	Vertical?	Lateral?
A chocolate maker takes over a cocoa plantation		✔	
A travel insurer merges with an online holiday company			
A clothing retailer takes over a clothes manufacturer			
A bus manufacturer merges with a car maker			
An investment bank takes over an electronics producer			
An aircraft maker merges with an aero-engine company			

SECTION 3.5.5

What are economies of scale?

Economies and diseconomies of scale

Reliance Industries Limited (RIL) is a conglomerate and India's largest private sector firm. It began as a small textile maker in the 1960s using imported polyester to make a range of garments under the brand name 'Vimal' which is now a household name in India. It soon began to manufacture its own polyester yarn and fibres and is now the world's largest producer of these synthetic materials. It went on to develop and merge with businesses involved in oil and gas exploration, petroleum refining, petrochemicals and also retail stores. In this way the business successfully controls its supply chain from the production of natural oils and gases which are used in the manufacture of petrochemicals needed to make polyester fibres for textile production, and retail outlets that sell its brand of clothing. The business has a saying: 'Growth is life'.

Through growth RIL, like many other large firms, is able to enjoy a number of cost advantages over much smaller firms. When a firm expands its scale of production it has the chance to become more efficient and to lower its average costs of production.

Average cost measures the cost of producing or selling a single unit of output. Average or unit costs can be reduced as a firm grows in scale because it gives the owners or managers an opportunity to reorganize the way their firm is run and financed. Such decisions are taken within the firm and so the advantages or economies they bring are known as **internal economies of scale.** These are cost savings that result from large-scale production.

Big is beautiful

Case 1: Cleaning up their act

A global detergent manufacturer has recently decided to invest in new equipment to expand its production. The new machines are very expensive but can produce twice as many soaps each hour as their existing machines.

A bank loan will be used to finance the expansion. Banks are willing to lend to the firm on very reasonable terms because it owns many valuable assets it is able to use as security or collateral against loans. Banks also recognize that because the firm produces a wide range of detergents for many different overseas markets, any demand fluctuations are unlikely to seriously affect the firm's ability to repay its debts. Smaller competitors, however, will find it difficult to raise money for their modernization. Even if loans are made available, interest charges tend to be higher because smaller firms are often less financially secure than larger ones and therefore their risk of business failure is higher.

The large manufacturer has a new soap coming on to the market next week and it is planning a big advertising campaign to launch it. The cost of the campaign is around $1 million, but with an output of 10 million bars of soap per month, this only adds 10 cents to the cost of producing each unit of soap. If it was producing, say only 2 million soap bars a month, like many of its smaller rivals, the campaign would add 50 cents to the unit cost of each bar.

Case 2: Blasting off!

The large iron smelting company in Northern Ecoland has recently announced how pleased it is at having won a big overseas order as a result of it being able to offer a lower price than its main overseas rivals in Nomicia.

'Our specialist sales staff were a great help in winning the order,' enthused Mr Justin Time, the Company Director. 'Our Nomician competitors could not afford to employ such specialists.'

He went on to say how his company had managed to offer a lower price than Nomician producers. He explained that unit costs were much lower in Ecoland because its plant had managed to invest in a large blast furnace, while the smaller Nomician plants had to band together in certain areas to be able to afford such furnaces. Mr Time also added that some Nomician firms incurred higher transport costs as a result of their scale of operations being smaller. They have to use external road haulage services and therefore will be paying a profit margin in transport costs to these providers. The Ecoland Company, however, has its own fleet of juggernauts able to carry far more tons of iron than smaller trucks. Petrol costs per mile are lower and fewer drivers are also required.

Time also explained how his firm's average costs were lower because it is able to buy bulk quantities of iron ore. 'Because we buy 40 million tons of the stuff every year, our suppliers are willing to sell it for just $50 per ton,' he said, 'whereas the average Nomician firm only buys 10 million tons a year, but pays $60 per ton.'

Internal economies of scale

Internal economies of scale reduce the average cost of producing each unit of output as the scale of production expands within a firm. There are five main types of internal economies of scale.

1 Marketing economies

Advertising in newspapers, on television or through social media can be expensive. A firm would therefore have to make and sell a large number of items to justify spending a large amount of money on advertising its products. The more units of output a firm produces and sells the lower the advertising cost per unit will be. For example, if the cost of designing and placing an advert is $10,000 then the advertising cost per unit will be just $1 for a large firm that produces and sells 10,000 items. For a smaller firm producing and selling just 2,000 units in the same period, the advertising cost per unit will be $5.

Large firms may also buy or hire their own vehicles to distribute their products rather than hiring other firms to deliver them. In this way a large firm can reduce its costs because it does not have to pay the profit margins of other firms providing transportation services. A large firm may also be able to increase the reliability and efficiency of its distribution system.

2 Purchasing economies

Large firms are often able to buy the materials, components and other supplies they need in bulk because of the large scale of their production. Suppliers will usually offer price discounts for bulk purchases because it is cheaper for them to make one large delivery to a single customer than several smaller deliveries to numerous small firms.

3 Financial economies

Large firms are often able to borrow more money from banks than small firms and at a lower rate of interest rate. This is because large firms are usually more financially secure and can offer more assets including property and other investments, to use as collateral against loans. Banks can sell these assets in the event a firm fails and cannot repay its debts. Unlike small sole traders and private limited companies, large public limited companies are also able to sell shares through the global stock market to raise large amounts of money that never has to be repaid.

4 Technical economies

Larger firms often have the financial resources available to invest in specialized machinery and equipment, to train and recruit highly skilled workers, and to research and develop new products and processes to increase the efficiency of their production. Smaller firms lack financial resources and their scale of production is often too small to justify such investments.

5 Risk-bearing economies

A large firm may have more customers, sell into more markets at home and overseas and offer a wider range of products than a smaller firm. In this way a large firm is able to reduce the risk to its business of losing one or more major customers or a fall in consumer demand on one of its product markets.

Producing a varied range of products and expanding into different consumer markets to reduce market risks is called **diversification**. For example, Unilever is a firm famous for its soap and detergent brands but it also has interests in the production of food, paper, plastics, animal feeds, transport and tropical plantations.

External economies of scale

Firms within an industry may also share additional cost advantages known as **external economies of scale** as the size of their industry increases. For example, average costs of production may be further reduced within firms in a particular industry because:

- **They have access to skilled workers**. The recruitment of skilled workers becomes easier as many other firms in the industry have already trained workers with the skills needed by the industry. Similarly, universities and colleges may develop courses to train workers with specialized skills required by large, advanced industries such as aerospace, automotive, computer software and pharmaceutical industries. This will reduced their training costs.

- **They can benefit from shared infrastructure**. For example, suppliers in other industries may find it becomes profitable to invest in infrastructure improvements to meet the needs of a growing industry, including new power stations, high-speed digital communication networks and airports. Similarly, a government may invest in new road and railway links to encourage and benefit growing industries.

- **Their suppliers can also benefit from economies of scale** because they too are able to expand as the industry they supply grows. Suppliers can therefore lower the prices of the goods and services they supply to the industry without cutting their profit margins.

- **They can benefit from specialist service providers** who develop to supply the specific requirements of a large industry for specialist equipment, transport, recruitment or marketing services. Universities may also invest in **research and development facilities** that firms within a large industry can use. It would not be profitable to provide specialist equipment or services for a much smaller industry.

Many of the above external economies of scale are examples of **agglomeration economies**. These arise when similar firms within one or more industries co-locate or cluster together in the same geographical location. By locating together they can also encourage major business customers and suppliers to relocate close by, skilled labour to move to these areas and investments in modern infrastructure. For example, London and New York are important banking and financial centres. 'Silicon Valley' in California in the USA is home to many internet and high-technology companies including Apple, Google and Facebook. Wine producers also tend to cluster together, unsurprisingly where good weather and soil conditions produce good quality grapes in large quantities.

What evidence is there in these articles that large firms enjoy lower average costs than smaller firms producing the same or similar products?

Larger businesses fare better than smaller ones during recession

According to a new report, larger businesses continue to enjoy many cost advantages over smaller businesses that has allowed them to discount their prices more heavily in the economic recession to maintain customer demand. Larger businesses also benefit from serving more than one market, many overseas, which has reduced their risk of falling demand at home.

Tech Group signs major contract to supply Hinshu

Tech Group, a leading supplier of engine cooling systems, has signed a $1.5 billion contract to supply Hinshu Motors over the next 3 years.

Hinshu Motors is scaling up production of its successful range of automobiles. Delton Williams, Marketing Director at Hinshu, said the deal was a good one for both companies because 'Tech Group offers high-quality components, fast delivery times and substantial discounts for bulk orders to its largest business customers. It is cheaper for them to make one large delivery each week than several smaller deliveries over the same period.'

Can some firms grow too much?

The answer to this question is yes. For example, this is exactly what happened when Mozambique's Mozal aluminium smelter wanted to expand its operations and increase output but was unable to do so because of a shortage of electricity in the country.

Similarly, the global US coffee shop chain Starbucks had to sell off 600 stores in the USA in 2008 because of falling coffee sales and a fall in the value of properties owned by the firm. Starbucks had expanded significantly in the 1990s and invested a lot of money in business properties. A steep fall in property prices and consumer spending during 2008 therefore had a big impact on the business. Starbucks also had to close 61 of its 85 shops in Australia due to weak sales. The business had failed to attract consumers away from established cafés and coffee bars in Australia's main cities.

Many firms can experience costly problems if they grow too large. These **diseconomies of scale** occur when a business grows so large that its average costs rise. They include:

1 Management diseconomies

Controlling and coordinating production in a large firm can be difficult especially if it produces and sells a wide variety of products in many different locations. A large firm can have thousands of employees and many different layers of management. This can cause communication problems and disagreements between managers at different levels in different parts of a firm.

2 Labour diseconomies

It is harder for senior managers to stay in day-to-day contact with employees in large firms that employ many hundreds or thousands of workers. Production is also automated in many large firms using computer-controlled equipment and machines. As a result, workers in large firms may feel their ideas and skills are not valued by their managers. This can reduce their motivation with damaging consequences for output and quality. Labour disputes including strikes may occur if workers feel they are not being consulted or treated fairly.

3 Supply constraints

Some very large firms may need vast quantities of materials, components or power for production. They may have to pay much more to obtain the supplies they need and they may also experience shortages that can hold up production.

4 Skill shortages

Some large firms may be unable to attract enough workers with the right skills. They may have to spend more money on training their workers and increasing their wages to ensure that they do not leave to take jobs in other firms.

5 Regulatory risks

Some firms grow so large that smaller firms are unable to compete with them. As a result they can dominate the market supply of a product and control its market price. Large firms with dominant market positions in an economy may attract the attention of the government. It may introduce laws and regulations that control the prices charged by large firms and the quality of the services they provide. The need to understand and comply with regulations will increase running costs in the affected firms. ➤ **3.8.2**

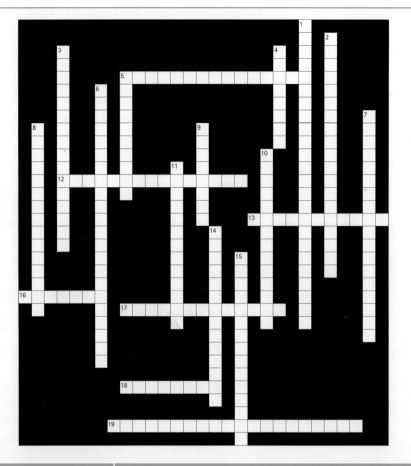

Clues across

5. Firms in this sector of an economy process natural and human-made materials and components to manufacture or construct other goods (9, 6)
12. The smallest type of firm with 9 or fewer employees (5, 10)
13. The percentage of the total market sales of a product that is earned by a particular firm in a given period of time (6, 5)
16. The time period in economics in which all factors of production can be varied within firms in order to change their scale of production (4, 3)
17. The merger of many smaller firms into much larger ones. It reduces the number of firms competing within an industry (13)
18. Firms are unable to grow their scale of production in this time period in economics because capital is a fixed factor of production and cannot be varied (5, 3)
19. A firm or organization that is wholly or partially owned and operated by a government to carry out commercial activities (5, 5, 10)

Clues down

1. Cost advantages gained from increasing the scale of production within a firm. They reduce the average cost of producing or selling each item (8, 9, 2, 5)
2. These occur when a firm grows too large and as a result its average costs rise (12, 2, 5)
3. This occurs when two or more firms producing the same or similar products in the same industry combine to from a larger enterprise with an increased market share (10, 6)
4. The type of long run growth in the size of firms occurs as they combine or merge their operations (8)
5. A private sector firm owned and controlled by one person (4, 6)
6. Cost advantages enjoyed by firms in an industry that co-locate or cluster together in the same geographical location so they can jointly attract skilled labour, new suppliers and investments in shared infrastructure (13, 9)
7. This occurs when two or more firms with unrelated activities combine their operations to form a larger, more diversified enterprise (12, 6)
8. A strategy that involves a firm expanding its range of products and the markets it supplies to expand its customer base, reduce market risks and increase sales (15)
9. This type of long run growth in firm size occurs without merger as a firm expands its own scale of production through investments in new capital and technology (8)
10. Firms in this sector of an economy provide services (8, 6)
11. Firms in this sector of an economy produce natural resources (7, 6)
14. A firm or organization owned by its shareholders (7,7)
15. The value of all the productive assets or capital goods employed within a firm (7, 8)

Unit 3.6
Unit 3.7

Firms and production
Firm's costs, revenue and objectives

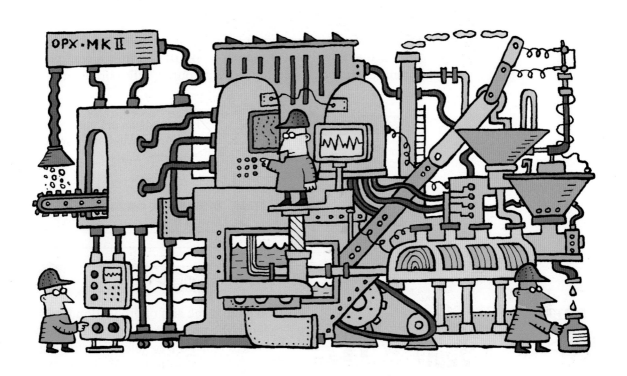

Production and productivity

Goods and services are produced to satisfy consumer wants. The **production** of goods and services is organized by entrepreneurs in firms. A firm combines the factors of production land, labour and capital (**inputs**) to make goods and services (**outputs**). Goods and services are produced to satisfy consumer wants. ➤ **1.1**

A firm may own one or more plants where resources are employed and productive activity is carried out. A **plant** is simply a workplace and includes premises such as a warehouse, retail outlet, office or factory.

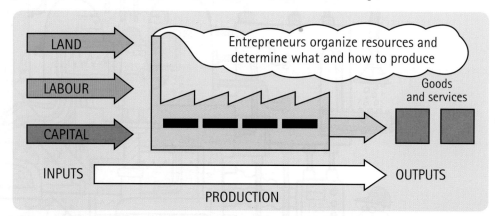

BEFORE

AFTER

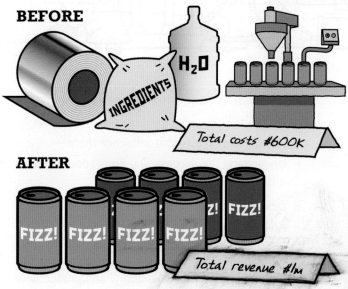

▲ How production adds value to resources

Given that the aim of production is to satisfy consumer wants, the process is not complete until the goods and services reach the people and other organizations who want them. Warehouses and shops that sell goods and services to consumers, as well as all those people and machines involved in transportation, insurance and many other tasks, are all part of the production process.

By combining resource inputs to produce outputs consumers want and are willing and able to buy, productive activity adds value to those resources. For example, a firm that produces 1 million cans of fizzy drink which are sold for $1 each but cost only $600,000 to produce has added $400,000 to the value of the resources used in their production, including labour, water, aluminium, machinery, vehicles and electricity.

Value added in production is the difference between the market price paid for a product by a consumer and the cost of the natural and man-made materials, components, tools and equipment used to make it. Value added is therefore equal to the wages paid to workers who have been employed to produce the product and the profit received by the owners of the firm that organized its production.

Specialization in production by firms

Imagine you set up a firm and try to produce lots of different products to sell, from light bulbs and garden tools, to designer clothes and bus services. You are unlikely to be successful at all these activities. This is because you and the people you employ would be trying to do too many things at the same time.

It would be far more sensible for you and your employees to concentrate on producing what they are best at. This is called **specialization**. ➤ **3.1**

▲ The Toyota Motor Corporation specializes in making cars, buses and commercial vehicles and HSBC specializes in providing financial services

Specialization means a firm can make the best possible use of all the skills and resources it has and therefore add much more value to them. However, a firm that specializes in the production of just one product could fail if there is a fall in demand for its product. Some firms therefore produce a range of different products in case consumer demand for any one of them falls. This is called **diversification**.

Because firms specialize in particular activities, production will normally involve a **chain of productive activity**.

ACTIVITY 3.22

Dough!

1 The jumble of cartoons and numbered descriptions that follow on the next page together describe how bread is produced. Match each picture to a description. Write down the descriptions to form a chain of the productive activities involved in bread production, right through to final sale to consumers. Some descriptions may be used more than once.

1   Wheat, water, yeast and other ingredients are mixed together to produce dough

2   Coal and oil are used to power electricity stations for use by firms and households

3   Farms plant seeds to grow wheat

4   Supermarkets and other shops sell bread to consumers

5   Road haulage service providers transport harvested wheat and finished breads

6   Consumers buy bread

7   Wheat is harvested

8   Insurance firms provide insurance to protect firms from risk of damage or theft

9   Dough is poured into baking pans and placed in ovens to cook

10 Sealed packets for the bread are produced and labelled in printing machines

11 Consumers make sandwiches or toast to consume

12 Finished loaves of bread are sealed in plastic packaging

13 Commercial banks provide loans and payment services to firms

14 Food inspectors check the quality and hygiene of the breads and the bakery

2 Investigate and list the chain of productive activities involved in the production and sale of the following products:

▸ a new computer game   ▸ sweets   ▸ hairdressing

▸ fresh orange juice   ▸ washing powders   ▸ a good or service of your choice

Each chain of productive activity will link together many different firms, industries and industrial sectors – from firms in the primary sector producing natural resources such as coal, corn and oil, to manufacturing firms that use raw materials to make component parts and finished goods and services for consumers, and finally to those tertiary sector businesses that operate warehouses, transport services and shops to distribute and sell products to customers. ➤ **2.1**

What is factor productivity?

Productivity measures the amount of output (goods and services) that can be produced from a given amount of input (land, labour and capital resources).

For example, a business that uses 10 units of resources to produce 40 units of output per week is twice as productive as a business that uses 10 units of the same resources to produce just 20 units of output per week.

The aim of any business will be to combine its resources in the most efficient way. That is, it will aim to produce as much output as it can with the least amount of resources it can, and therefore at the lowest cost possible.

For example, farms in Pakistan obtain 33 million tonnes of milk from 20 million milking animals, compared with over 37 million tonnes obtained by Chinese farms from 15 million animals and 84 million tonnes of milk produced in the USA by 9.1 million cows.

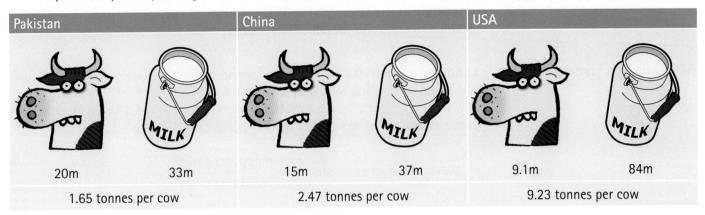

Pakistan		China		USA	
20m	33m	15m	37m	9.1m	84m
1.65 tonnes per cow		2.47 tonnes per cow		9.23 tonnes per cow	

Although the combined farms in Pakistan are the fourth largest producer of milk in the world after farms in India, the USA and China, the productivity of milking animals in Pakistan is clearly much lower than that of US or Chinese cows.

Low milk yields increase the cost of production of milk. For example, US farmers feed one cow to obtain the same quantity of milk that a Pakistani farmer obtains by feeding 4.5 cows.

According to livestock experts, milk yields of dairy herds in Pakistan could be increased by around 600 litres per animal by providing them with adequate clean drinking water. Feeding them a balanced diet and improving hygiene could lead to an increase of another 600 litres of milk per animal.

Productivity therefore measures how efficiently resources are being used in production.

In general, productivity in a firm or entire economy will have increased if:

- more output or revenue is produced from the same amount of resources
- the same output or revenue can be produced using fewer resources.

Resources cost money to buy or hire. For example, materials must be purchased from suppliers, wages must be paid to hire labour, machinery and equipment must be purchased outright or leased, and premises must be rented. Therefore, if the same amount of labour, land and capital can produce more output for the same total cost, then the cost of producing each unit of output (or average cost) will have fallen. Increasing the productivity of resources can therefore reduce production costs, make a firm more competitive, and increase profits.

TOTAL COST OF LABOUR MATERIALS & CAPITAL... $200·00
TOTAL OUTPUT... 4000 UNITS
AVERAGE COST PER UNIT $0·05

▲ Productive

TOTAL COST OF LABOUR MATERIALS & CAPITAL... $200·00
TOTAL OUTPUT... 5000 UNITS
AVERAGE COST PER UNIT $0·04

▲ More productive

A firm that fails to increase the productivity of its resources or factors of production at the same pace or at a faster rate than rival firms will have higher production costs and therefore lower profits than its competitors.

Measuring productivity

Labour productivity is the most common measure of factor productivity. It is calculated by dividing total output over a given period of time, for example a day, week or month, by the number of workers employed. This gives a measure of the average productivity per worker per period.

$$\text{Average product of labour} = \frac{\text{total output per period}}{\text{number of employees}}$$

The average productivity of labour is a useful measure of how efficient workers are and how efficiently they use other resources. For example, if a company employs 10 workers who produce 200 plant pots each day, the average product per employee per day is 20 pots. If daily output is able to rise to 220 pots per day without employing additional workers then productivity will have increased to 22 pots per worker per day.

Productivity in business organizations producing services can be more difficult to measure. For example, a hair salon could measure the number of customers or hair treatments per day per employee, but not all employees in the salon will be hairdressers. Some may be office staff and cleaners. So how can we measure their productivity?

A better measure of overall productivity is the average revenue per worker per period.

$$\text{Average revenue product of labour} = \frac{\text{total revenue per period}}{\text{number of employees}}$$

Productivity is also difficult to measure in organizations that do not produce a physical output or earn revenue, for example government-funded hospitals or schools, government departments or a police force. Other performance measures, such as time spent waiting for an operation, meeting deadlines, numbers of students passing qualifications and numbers of arrests, will often be used instead.

Another problem with productivity measures is that they take no account of the quality of work. Increasing productivity should also include improvements in product quality. A firm that reduces the quality of its products to cut its costs risks losing customers to rival firms offering better quality products. Consumers may also be willing to pay a higher price for better quality. Improving quality in production can therefore boost sales, revenues and profits.

Passport to success

Manteau Designs Ltd is a small private limited company that manufactures luxury passport holders. The company started four years ago with just five production workers. Since then it has successfully expanded its sales, output and workforce.

Productivity at the factory has also increased over time as workers have become more experienced in the production of passport holders. The increase in workforce to 20 full-time production workers has also meant that the machinery and equipment installed at the factory is now fully employed throughout each working day.

With sales continuing to grow, the company's owners are thinking of expanding output further over the next year. They are considering two options.

Option 1: Employ five more workers, costing the business an additional $100,000 in wages each year to be funded from revenues.

Option 2: Use retained profits to finance the purchase and installation of new, more advanced machinery costing $300,000. The new machinery should remain productive for 10 years.

Year	Total output achieved (* forecast)	No. of workers	Average annual labour productivity
1	100,000	5	
2	210,000	10	
3	330,000	15	
4	460,000	20	
5	570,000*	25 (*Option 1*)	
5	540,000*	20 (*Option 2 using new machinery*)	

1. Calculate the average output of each worker each year to complete the table.

2. Do you think the company is right to consider increasing the workforce by employing five more workers?

3. Should the company install new machinery instead of employing five more workers? Justify your answer.

4. Suggest other ways the company may be able to improve the productivity of its workforce.

How can firms increase factor productivity?

A firm that is able to increase the productivity of its resources will produce more output from the same or fewer resource inputs, reduce its costs of production and therefore can potentially earn more profit from each item it sells. However, improving productivity can be difficult and slow to achieve. It can require multiple actions and investments, including:

- training workers to improve their existing skills and learn new skills
- rewarding increased productivity with performance-related pay and bonus payments

- encouraging employees to buy shares in their organization – improved productivity will help to raise profits and pay higher dividends on shares

- increasing job satisfaction, for example by improving the working environment, making jobs more varied, introducing more team working, involving workers in business decision making and giving regular feedback on performance

- replacing old plant and machinery with new, more efficient machines and tools for workers to use

- introducing new production processes and working practices designed to continually reduce waste, increase speed, improve quality and raise output in all areas of a firm. This is known as **lean production.**

Many of the above initiatives will tend to raise the cost of employing labour in the short run. However, if productivity improves, the average cost of producing each unit of output will fall and profits will tend to rise. Lower costs can be passed on to consumers as lower prices in an attempt to increase consumer demand and generate more sales revenues. If consumer demand expands, then the demand for labour may also increase.

SECTION 3.6.2

Labour-intensive and capital-intensive production

SECTION 3.6.3

Demand for factors of production

Different production methods require different factor combinations

Production requires factor inputs to produce goods and services. Firms will therefore attempt to combine land, labour and capital in the most productive and efficient way possible to maximize their outputs and minimize their costs.

For example, many modern firms employ **capital-intensive production** methods that require far more capital input than labour. Capital-intensive production processes are often partially or fully automated. They aim to mass-produce similar or identical products faster and cheaper than workers could by hand. However, total costs may initially be high because specialized machinery and other capital equipment can be expensive to hire or purchase.

In contrast, **labour-intensive production** is common in many service industries and also in the agricultural sector where capital-intensive methods are not feasible. For example, many hospitals, hotels, restaurants, supermarkets and other retailers employ large workforces because they provide personalized services. Similarly, many delicate fruits and vegetables are carefully hand-picked on farms to avoid bruising or damaging the crops. Some goods may also be handmade by workers using handheld tools to produce more personalized or customized items.

For products that can be produced using either capital or labour-intensive methods, firms will therefore choose the production method that offers them the greatest overall advantage in terms of efficiency and profitability.

▲ Labour-intensive production

▲ Capital-intensive production

Advantages of capital-intensive production	Advantages of labour-intensive production
✔ Products can be mass-produced if the market size is large;	✔ Consumers may pay a premium price for handmade and more personalized products;
✔ Mass production will reduce the average cost of producing each unit compared to slower, more labour-intensive production methods;	✔ Labour costs can be kept low if workers are unskilled or hired on temporary contracts, for example, to pick crops during summer months;
✔ Wages and other labour employment costs are far lower;	✔ There is a lower risk of losses due to machinery breakdowns or power cuts halting production;
✔ There is less risk of disruption to production from shortages of labour or from industrial disputes;	✔ Workers may take more pride in their work and produce better quality products than they would if they were simply operating machinery or carrying out repetitive tasks in an automated production process;
✔ Automated production can be continuous, 24 hours a day and every day;	✔ Labour can be used more flexibly than installed and therefore immobile machinery;
✔ Programmed equipment cannot lose skill or concentration. As a result there is less risk of human error and product quality may be more uniform than with hand-produced products.	✔ Product quality is easier to observe, monitor and change at each stage of the production process.
Disadvantages of capital-intensive production	**Disadvantages of labour-intensive production**
✘ Machinery and other capital equipment can be very expensive to buy or hire;	✘ Wages and other employment costs can be high;
✘ Maintenance costs can also be high and may increase over time as equipment wears out;	✘ Firms may find it difficult to find and hire workers with the skills they need and may have to pay higher wages to attract skilled labour;
✘ Training costs may be high if workers need to be trained to operate complex equipment;	✘ Disputes with trade unions and workers can result in industrial actions which can disrupt production;
✘ It may be difficult to change production, for example if consumer demand or technology changes, once a firm has installed a significant amount of machinery and other equipment;	✘ Workers may need to be retrained in new skills and production methods as consumer demand changes;
✘ Technological advance is increasing the rate at which machines and other equipment need to be replaced to remain competitive with new firms installing the latest equipment;	✘ The average cost of producing each item will be much higher than in firms using more capital-intensive methods to mass-produce the same or similar products;
✘ Breakdowns and power cuts will hold up production;	✘ Labour-intensive methods are best suited to small-scale production or the production of individual or personalized products.
✘ It is not suitable for many service industries or in markets where consumers want more personalised or custom-made products.	

What determines the demand for factors of production?

Firms that choose to employ capital-intensive production methods will demand more capital inputs than labour compared to labour-intensive firms. But how much capital and how much labour will each type of firm demand? How much land and other natural resources will they require? What affects their demand for these different factors of production?

1 Consumer demand for their products

The more goods and services consumers want and are willing and able to buy, the more factors of production firms will need to produce them. That is, their demand for factors of production is a **derived demand**. The demand for land, labour and capital by firms depends on there being sufficient demand from consumers for the goods and services they produce. It follows that an increase in demand for their products will result in an increase in factor demand while a fall in demand will reduce factor demand.

2 Factor prices

As consumer demand for their products increases, will firms hire more capital or more labour to increase production? This will depend on their relative factor prices.

Just like the demand for all other goods and services, the demand for factors of production by firms will depend on their market prices. The higher their prices the more costly it will be to produce goods and services and, therefore, the less profitable production becomes. For example, as wage rates increase, the demand for labour will tend to contract. Similarly, if the cost of buying or hiring capital equipment increases then demand for capital will also tend to contract. However, if capital is relatively cheap, then firms may cut their workforces and employ more machinery and other capital equipment instead.

3 Factor availability

Factor availability will affect both the price and quantity supplied of different factors of production. For example, the supply of workers with highly specialized skills is low relative to demand for them. As a result, the wages they can command tend to be very high. ➤ **3.3.2**

Shortages of skilled labour can disrupt production. Firms will therefore compete with each other to attract skilled labour with offers of higher wages and better working conditions. Alternatively, firms may have to hire less experienced workers and provide them with training in the skills they require but this can take time and be expensive especially if those workers leave to take higher paid jobs elsewhere once they have been trained. As a result, some firms may be forced to adopt more capital-intensive production methods instead to reduce their labour requirements.

In much the same way, firms will often have to compete with each other to buy or rent a limited supply of premises in the most advantageous locations. Many firms are also having to modify their products and production methods as many of the natural resources they use run out and become more difficult and more expensive to obtain. ➤ **1.1.1**

4 Factor productivity

A profit-maximizing firm will only employ additional land, labour or capital if it is profitable to do so. For example, a worker that costs $100 each day in

▼ Table lamp production

Number of workers	Total output per week	Extra output per worker per week	Value of extra output (quantity × price)
4	300	–	–
5	350	50	$500
6	390	40	$400
7	420	30	$300
8	440	20	$200
9	450	10	$100

wages to employ who only adds $90 to the value of output each day will not be worth employing. However, it will be profitable to employ a worker costing $100 who adds $120 to output. The demand for labour as well as all other factors of production therefore depends on how productive they are.

Imagine a firm producing table lamps. Each lamp sells for $10. At present, four units of labour (that is, four employees) are employed producing a total output of 300 lamps each week. The firm wants to increase output but doesn't know how many extra workers it should employ. To help the firm decide, it estimates the amount of output each additional worker is likely to produce.

The firm has estimated that adding a fifth worker would raise total output by 50 lamps each week. When these extra lamps are sold, the firm's revenue will increase by $500. The revenue productivity of the fifth worker is therefore $500 per week.

If the wage rate is $300 per week, it is worth employing the fifth worker as well as a sixth worker. A seventh worker will add $300 to the value of total output each week, and costs $300 in wages to employ. In a profit-maximizing firm this worker is worth employing because each one of the extra lamps produced will be adding to profit. However, if the firm attempted to employ an eighth worker it would gain only $200 in extra output but lose $300 in extra wage costs. Profits would fall by $100. The only way the firm would extend its demand for labour to eight workers would be if wages fell to $200 each week. The firm's demand curve for labour therefore slopes downwards. ➤ **3.2**

Alternatively, our table lamp manufacturer could attempt to increase the productivity of all its workers. It estimates that if it trains new and existing employees in more productive techniques each worker could produce a further 10 lamps worth an additional $100 each week.

▼ Demand for table lamp makers

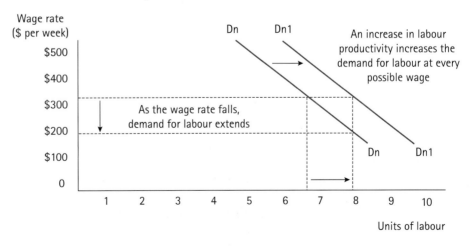

So now, a fifth worker would increase output by 60 lamps each week, worth $600 in extra revenue. A sixth worker would increase output by another 50 lamps, worth $500 in revenue, and so on. This has the impact of shifting the demand curve for labour to the right at every possible wage rate (from DnDn to Dn1Dn1 in the diagram above). If the weekly wage rate remains at $300 per employee, then clearly it is now worth employing up to eight workers, since the eighth worker will now add as much to revenue as he or she will cost to employ.

Exactly the same will apply to a decision to increase the amount of capital employed in the table lamp firm if it could employ computerized machinery to make the lamps instead of extra workers. If the productivity of capital rises, and/or the cost of capital falls, firms will tend to expand their demand for capital.

A firm will want to combine its resources in the most efficient way to maximize overall productivity for the minimum of costs. It will therefore compare the costs and productivity of labour with capital and will tend to employ more of the most productive factor. It follows that if wages rise or the productivity of capital rises, a firm will tend to replace labour with more capital. This is known as **factor substitution.**

Factor substitution

Factor substitution involves replacing labour in a production process with new capital equipment and machinery. The substitution of labour with capital has occurred in many modern industries in many countries. Technological advance has greatly lowered the cost of new equipment and machinery and has increased their productivity relative to labour. For example, the work of once skilled typesetters and compositors in the printing industry has now been replaced by desktop publishing software on computers operated by writers and journalists. Intelligent robots controlled by computer have taken over human tasks in manufacturing processes such as car assembly and food packaging. This is known as **computer aided manufacture (CAM).**

However, labour and capital are not perfect substitutes. The ability of a firm to substitute capital for labour will very much depend on the type of product and the production process used. For example, automated mass production processes are used to produce many thousands or millions of very similar products, such as newspapers, cars, paints and computer disks. However, machines cannot replicate the work of a doctor, solicitor, hairdresser or other workers providing personalized care and services. Similarly, some consumers want personalized jewellery or furniture made for them. This production is usually by hand, and involves many hours of labour.

Just remember, no-one is irreplaceable №259B.

PERSONNEL

The costs of installing and maintaining new machinery and other equipment can also be very expensive and will affect the decision by a firm to employ more capital at the expense of labour, even if the new capital is more productive. Short-term production costs may also rise, as workers may need to be retrained to use new machinery and equipment.

Substituting capital for labour may also cause bitter labour disputes between trade unions and their employers over possible job losses. Strikes by workers and redundancy payments for those forced to leave can be very expensive for a firm. ➤ **3.4.3**

March of the robots

India Steps Up to Robotics

With the Indian manufacturing sector booming, the robotics industry is gearing up for sharp growth. At India's biggest auto manufacturer, Tata Motors, the workforce has been reduced by 20 per cent, while the company's turnover has increased 2.5 times. Its Pune plant alone has invested in 100 robots.

At the same time the country's top government scientists are at work on robot and artificial intelligence (AI) technologies for use in everything from border patrols to the deployment of 'robot armies' to replace human soldiers.

'The use of robots is growing extremely fast in India' say industry analysts. 'Robots can be expensive to buy and implement but they save labour and help companies raise their productivity and quality, to meet the demands of international competition. Customers in India are also beginning to understand how useful robots are in production: they not only save costs, but are a safer and a healthier option.'

1   What do you think are some of the advantages of employing robots in business?

2   Why do you think industrial robots are described as labour-saving technology?

3   How can the use of robots in business affect workers and consumers?

4   What do you think may be some of the main obstacles to employing more robots in firms in your economy and other national economies?

Definition and calculation of costs of production

Bear Necessities

Sue Brennan used to make toys when she was a young girl at school. Her friends and relatives thought that they were so good that they asked her to make some for them to give as presents to others. This gave Sue an idea for the future.

When she left school she went to work in a local furniture-making factory for two years where she gained experience of using cloth to make seat covers. She saved some money and asked her bank to lend her some more so that she could start up her own firm under the name of 'Bear Necessities'.

Sue rented a small factory unit on a new industrial estate. The cost of the building including fittings is $100 per week. She also hired some machinery at a cost of $45 per week. Sue employs her two brothers to help her to make toy bears. Sue pays herself and her brothers a piece rate of $1 for each bear they complete.

Since she started, Sue's toy bears have become very popular and she has many orders for them. She must, however, rely on regular custom from other firms and shops for her bears and so she must try and keep quality high and prices low. The average price she charges for her bears is $10 each.

The costs of Bear Necessities

In running her toy-making business Sue has a number of things she has to pay for. These are her costs. Some things have to be paid for each and every week no matter how many bears Sue makes and sells. These are her **fixed costs** that do not vary with the number of bears she produces. On the other hand, **variable costs** change with the number of bears produced. The more Sue produces the more fabric and foam she needs. Wages paid to herself and her brothers also rise.

Fixed costs per week ($)		Variable costs per bear ($)	
Factory rent	100.00	Fabric	6.00
Machinery hire charges	45.00	Foam	1.00
Electricity supply	5.00	Wages	1.00
Bank loan repayments	50.00		8.00
	200.00		

Sue keeps any **profit** that is left after she has taken away her costs from the money or **revenue** she earns from selling bears.

Answer the following questions.

1 Write a definition of fixed costs and give two examples.

2 If Sue produced 100 bears in a week, how much would her fixed costs be that week?

3 If Sue produced 1,000 bears in a week, how much would her fixed costs be that week?

4 Write a definition of variable costs and give two examples.

5 If Sue produced 100 bears, how much would her variable costs be?

6 If Sue produced 1,000 bears, how much would her variable costs be?

7 The **total cost** of producing a given number of bears each week is found by adding together all the fixed costs (total fixed costs) and all the variable costs (total variable costs).

Total cost (TC) = total fixed costs + total variable costs

   a If Sue produced 100 bears in a week, what would her total cost be?

b If Sue produced 1,000 bears in a week, what would her total cost be?

8 Copy the table below and work out the fixed, variable and total costs of producing different numbers of toy bears in a week. The costs of producing 400 bears and 500 bears have already been done for you. We will then plot all this information on a graph. (Do not complete the final column in the table for now.)

Bears produced per week	Total fixed costs $	Total variable costs $	Total cost $	Average cost per bear $
0				
50				
100				
200				
300				
400	200	3,200	3,400	8.5
500	200	4,000	4,200	8.4
600				
700				
800				
900				
1,000				

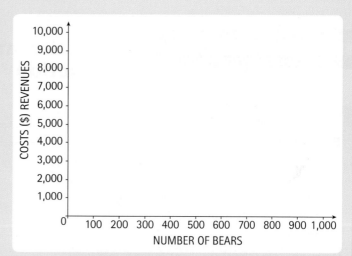

9 Now draw a pair of axes for a graph like the one above on a large piece of graph paper. Use your calculations to plot the total fixed cost curve, total variable cost curve and total cost curve to show how costs change with the number of bears produced. Do not forget to label each line you plot with its correct name.

10 What is the price charged for each bear?

11 How much money or revenue does Sue receive from the sale of each bear?

You will notice that your answers to questions 10 and 11 are the same.

Clearly if Sue sold five bears for $10 each, the revenue per bear is $10, while her **total revenue** is $50. Total sales revenue is also known as **turnover**.

Total revenue (TR) = price per bear × number of bears sold

If the total revenue from the sale of five bears is $50, then the average revenue for each of those bears is $10, which is the same as the price of each bear.

$$\text{Average revenue (AR)} = \frac{\text{total revenue}}{\text{number of bears sold}}$$

12 If Sue sold 100 bears what would her total revenue be?

13 If Sue sold 1,000 bears what would her total revenue be?

14 Draw the table below and calculate the total revenue from the number of bears sold. Again, this has already been done for 400 and 500 bears sold.

15 Now look back at the graph you drew earlier and on it plot your figures for total revenue in a different colour and label this line total revenue.

Bears produced and sold per week	Total revenue $	Total cost $	Profit or loss $
0			
50			
100			
200			
300			
400	4,000	3,400	600
500	5,000	4,200	800
600			
700			
800			
900			
1,000			

16 To calculate ⬛⬛⬛⬛ producing a⬛⬛⬛⬛ costs (TC) fr⬛⬛⬛ are greater t⬛⬛⬛ loss. If she is⬛⬛⬛ her total cost⬛⬛⬛

Profit (or loss⬛⬛⬛

On the table you c⬛⬛⬛ costs of producing⬛⬛⬛ calculate the profit⬛⬛⬛ bears she makes.

On your graph the a⬛⬛⬛tal revenue and the total cost curves represents the profit or loss. Where the total cost curve is above the total revenue curve the area in between them represents loss. Label this area and shade in one colour. Where the total cost curve lies below the total revenue curve the area in between represents profit. Label this area and shade in another colour.

Where the two curves cross, no profit or loss is made. This level of output and sales is known as the **break-even level of output**. This means that if Sue manages to sell all the bears she makes at this point, she will just cover her costs and be able to remain in business. You should find from your tables and graphs that to do this Sue must make and sell at least 100 toy bears each week.

Break-even level of output occurs where TR = TC, i.e. profit or loss is zero.

17 Now look again at the total costs of producing a different amount of bears each week. We now wish to calculate for Sue just how much it costs on average to make one bear. This is known as the **average cost** or **unit cost** of production.

We found in question 8 that when Sue produced 400 bears per week her total costs were $3,400. Clearly then if 400 bears cost $3,400 to make then one bear costs $8.50 to make (i.e. $3,400/400).

$$\text{Average cost (AC)} = \frac{\text{total cost}}{\text{number of bears produced}}$$

Go back to the table you drew in question 8 and, in the final column, calculate the average cost of producing each bear if 50, 100, 200 and so on bears were made.

18 We will now plot the a⬛⬛ graph with the numb⬛⬛ horizontal axis a⬛⬛ will need you⬛⬛ you have⬛⬛ the sl⬛⬛ ave⬛⬛

...erage cost curve on another ...er of bears produced along the ...d cost ($) on the vertical axis. You ...cost axis to go up to at least $12. When ...done this write down what you notice about ...pe of the curve; that is, what happens to the ...rage costs of production as more and more bears ...re produced? Can you suggest reasons for this? (Hint: Even if no bears or 1,000 bears are produced, what costs does Sue have to pay?)

Well done! By completing the activity about Bear Necessities you have learnt all about costs and revenues associated with production in a firm, how to calculate them and what they mean for profit. The rest of this unit will now help you to understand these important business and economic concepts fully, and to apply your knowledge to other examples.

Just like the Bear Necessities toy-making firm in Activity 3.25, most private sector firms aim to make as much profit as possible. Profit is calculated as the difference between what it costs a firm to produce its goods or services and the revenue it earns from their sale. That is:

profit = total revenue – total cost

To maximize profit a firm will aim to raise as much revenue as it can, for example by using advertising to boost demand and pricing strategies to attract consumers from rival firms, and it will also aim to minimize costs. Controlling costs is also very important in non-profit making organizations such as charities. However, to control costs a firm must be able to identify and measure the costs of all the factors of production it employs and uses up in production. These are the cost of wages for labour, payments for capital goods, components and materials, and the costs of many other goods and services supplied by other producers, including banking and insurance services, telecommunications, energy, legal services, transportation and much more.

Fixed costs

Before a firm can begin production and make goods and services for sale it will need to buy or hire many items. It may need premises, vehicles, computers and other equipment, stationery and it may need to undertake market research. These are start-up costs. Starting a business or developing a new product can be expensive and there will be no revenue to cover these start-up costs until production begins and products are sold.

Fixed costs, such as mortgage payments or rents for premises, interest charges on bank loans, leasing charges for machinery, telephone bills, cleaning costs and insurance premiums, will continue to be paid once production has started, no matter how much a firm produces and sells. That is, fixed costs do not vary with the level of output.

We can plot the total of fixed costs for a firm on a graph just like the one you drew for Bear Necessities in Activity 3.25. You will have noticed from your graph that the total fixed cost curve is flat because fixed costs do not vary with the level of output. However, this is only true up to the point at which a firm is operating at full capacity. This is because when a firm has no more space or equipment to raise output further it will need to hire or buy more equipment and possibly invest in larger premises to expand its scale of production.

The graph below plots total fixed costs for an imaginary firm producing motor vehicles. It is a large manufacturing organization that can produce up to 10,000 cars each month and has fixed costs of $10 million each month whether it produces 10,000 cars or not. If it wants to increase its scale of production up to, say, 20,000 cars each month it will need to hire or buy a new, bigger factory and more equipment.

▼ Total fixed costs for car production

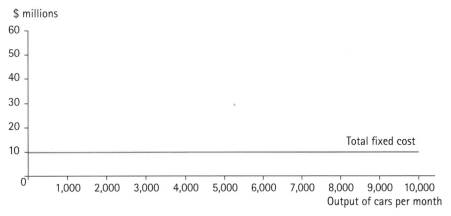

Output of cars per month

Variable costs

To increase output a firm will need more materials or component parts. Similarly, more electricity may be needed to power machines and computers, and to heat and light premises, over longer periods of time. The firm may also need to employ more workers or pay its existing workers overtime to work more hours.

If we plot the total variable costs for a firm on a graph the variable cost curve will slope upwards. This is because **variable costs** vary directly with the level of output. For example, our car manufacturing firm can produce up to 10,000 cars per month with its existing factory and equipment. The total cost of materials and other variable items per car is $2,000. So, if the variable cost of producing one car is $2,000, then the total variable cost of producing 10,000 cars will be $20 million.

▼ Total variable costs for car production

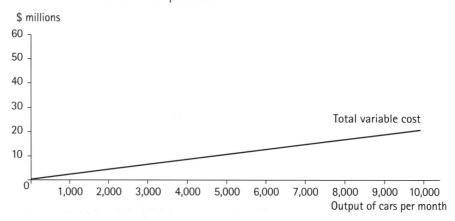

In general, therefore, the total variable cost of a given level of output is calculated as follows.

Total variable cost = variable cost per unit × quantity produced

If we add together all the fixed and variable costs of production of a firm we can calculate the total cost of producing each level of output.

Total cost = total fixed cost + total variable cost

If a firm produces no goods or services its total costs will be equal to its total fixed costs. Adding total variable costs to fixed costs means total costs will also increase as output rises, so the total cost curve will be upward sloping.

In our car firm the total cost of producing no cars will therefore be the fixed costs it will have to continue paying for at $10 million per month, while the total cost of producing 10,000 cars each month will be $30 million of fixed costs plus variable costs.

▼ Total cost for car production

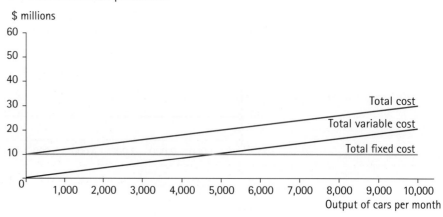

Average costs

If the total cost of producing 10,000 cars each month is $30 million, average cost of producing each car, or cost per unit of output, is $3,00⟨ . can calculate the average cost per unit of output using the following equatio⟨⟩

$$\text{Average cost per unit} = \frac{\text{total cost}}{\text{total output}}$$

To make a profit the car company must therefore sell each car for more than $3,000 to make enough revenue to cover its costs and leave a surplus. But the car company must be careful not to charge too high a price for each car, otherwise consumers may not buy them, especially if demand for cars is highly price elastic. ➤ **2.7.2**

A firm can calculate the average cost per unit of providing a service in exactly the same way. For example, the average cost of one hour of labour from a car mechanic, the average cost of one mile of journey on a train, or the average cost of treating one patient at a hospital. All a firm needs to know are the fixed and variable costs of providing its service. So, if it costs a passenger rail company a total of $20,000 each day to run a train service over 1,000 kilometres then the average cost per kilometre travelled is $20.

From Activity 3.25 you will have discovered how the average cost of producing a toy bear fell as the number of bears produced by Bear Necessities increased.

At a production rate of 400 bears per week each bear cost $8.50 to produce. The unit cost per bear fell to $8.20 as output was raised to 1,000 bears each week. Similarly, if our car firm produces only 500 cars each month the average cost would be a massive $22,000 per car, which is unlikely to be a profitable level of production.

In general, therefore, the average cost of each unit of a good or service will tend to fall with the volume produced, simply because fixed costs remain the same but their burden is spread over a much larger output. However, after a point, average costs may start to rise again because it can become more difficult and expensive to increase output further.

▼ Average cost curve

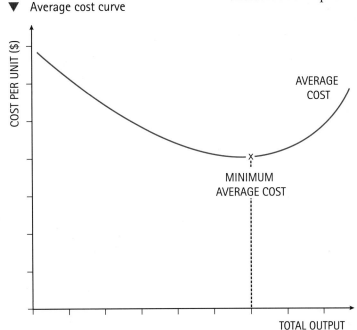

For example, imagine the Bear Necessities business in Activity 3.25 attempts to increase output to 1,100 bears each week. However, the producer supplying synthetic fur fabric and foam to Bear Necessities is unable to increase the amount it supplies. The owner of Bear Necessities, Sue Brennan, may then have to buy the extra fabric and foam she needs from another supplier where prices are higher. In addition, Sue may have to employ more people to work in the firm and may have to increase wages to attract a supply of labour. ➤ **3.3.2**

Sue pays herself and her two brothers $100 each week regardless of how many bears they produce. Her total wage bill per week is $300. If she employs another three workers to produce more bears, wage costs will double to $600 or may more than double if she has to increase wages. However, as more labour is added, output will rise but may only do so at a diminishing rate as the average productivity of labour falls. So, while wage costs double, the output of bears may not double. Therefore, the average cost of producing each bear will begin to increase.

If we plot the average cost of production on a graph it will appear as a U-shaped curve for many firms, showing that as output rises, average costs fall up to a point and may then begin to increase slowly as output is raised yet further.

Similarly, our car manufacturer may find that there is a shortage of the skilled manufacturing workers it needs to increase output from, say, 8,000 cars per month up to full capacity of 10,000 cars per month. It may have to hire unskilled workers and spend more money training them, or it will have to increase wages to attract skilled workers away from other manufacturing firms. It too will find, therefore, that its average cost curve is U-shaped, with the average cost of producing each car falling at first but then rising after output increases beyond 8,000 cars per month.

SECTION 3.7.3–4

Definition and calculation of revenue

What is revenue?

Firms earn revenue from the sale of their goods and services to consumers. **Total revenue** is therefore the total amount sold multiplied by the price per unit sold.

Total revenue = price per unit × quantity sold

Revenue from sales is also known as **turnover**.

What happens if a firm sells its goods or services to different consumers at different prices? For example, in Activity 3.25 Bear Necessities charged a price of $10 per bear. Now imagine that the firm wants to expand into overseas markets, but to do so the bears will have to be sold at a lower price than $10 each in order to attract overseas consumers to buy them. For example, if the firm sells 1,000 bears at $10 each and another 500 overseas at $7 each then total revenue will be $13,500, and the average revenue per bear sold will be $9 as follows:

Total revenue = ($10 × 1,000 bears) + ($7 × 500 bears) = $13,500

$$\text{Average revenue per bear sold} = \frac{\$13,500}{1,500} = \$9$$

A firm can calculate the average revenue or average price per unit of output sold using the following equation:

$$\text{Average revenue per unit} = \frac{\text{total revenue}}{\text{total units sold}}$$

Average revenue will often fall as output and sales rise. This is because demand tends to expand as price falls and to sell more output firms will

therefore need to lower their prices. We also know that as the market s[...]
of a product increases so market price will tend to fall. ➤ **2.6.1**

A firm entering a new market may also price low to attract demand. This
pricing strategy is known as penetration pricing. ➤ **4.4**

Profit and loss

Every firm will monitor its costs of production and revenues over time so that it
is possible to calculate whether it is making a profit or a loss. Profit or loss is
calculated as the difference between total revenue and total cost at each level of
output. That is:

Profit (or loss) = total revenue – total cost

If total revenue exceeds total cost a firm will make a profit. Profit is therefore
maximized when the difference between total revenue and total cost is at its
greatest.

However, if total revenue does not cover total costs, a firm will make a loss. If
this continues the firm will go out of business and its resources will be moved
to more profitable uses.

We can identify profit and loss in a firm from a graph of its total revenues and
total costs at different levels of output.

Returning to the example of the car manufacturer, let us assume each car sells
for $6,000. Total revenue therefore appears as an upward sloping curve, from
zero when no cars are sold to $60 million when 10,000 are sold. The car firm
makes a loss on all sales up to 2,500 cars per month, and a profit on all sales
over and above this level of output.

▶ Total revenue, total
cost, profit and loss for
car production

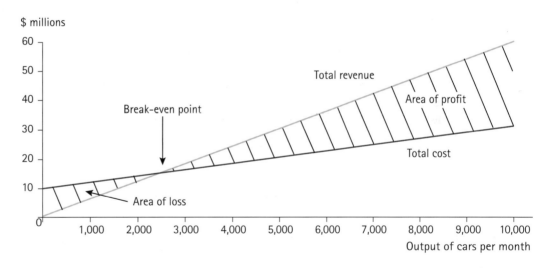

It is also useful to know how much profit or loss is made from every unit
of output sold by calculating the difference between average revenue and
average cost.

Profit (or loss) per unit = average revenue – average cost

This is particularly informative for a firm planning to expand production. We already know that average cost per unit may start to rise after a certain level of output is reached because extra wages may have to be paid to attract more workers or there may be supply problems with component parts and other materials. We also know that average revenue may start to fall after a certain level of sales is reached, as prices may need to be cut to attract additional demand or when entering new markets. It follows, therefore, that a firm may find it unprofitable to expand output too much if its average revenue falls below its average cost.

Breaking-even

The **break-even level of output** is that level of output, which if sold, will generate a total revenue that will exactly equal total cost. At the break-even level of output a firm will neither make a profit or a loss. That is, break-even occurs where:

total revenue = total cost

or where:

total revenue – total cost = 0

For example, Bear Necessities broke even when output and sales reached 100 bears per month. Sales below this level of output made a loss, while sales above it earned a profit. Similarly, the car manufacturer has a break-even level of output of 2,500 cars per month.

The break-even level of output can be found graphically where the total revenue line crosses the total cost curve. At break-even a firm is able to cover all its costs and so can remain in business, although clearly if it wants to make a profit it must either increase revenue and/or lower costs otherwise it might as well stop production and move its resources to more profitable uses.

How to calculate the break-even level of output for a firm without using a graph

If you want to it is easy to calculate the level of output a firm needs to sell to break even using the equation below. All you need to know is the price at which the good or service is to be sold and its fixed and variable costs:

$$\text{Break–even level of output} = \frac{\text{total fixed cost}}{\text{price per unit} - \text{variable cost per unit}}$$

Let's quickly calculate break-even this way for Bear Necessities and our car firm example.

From Activity 3.25 we know the fixed costs of bear production were $200 per month, variable costs were $8 per bear and the final price per bear sold was $10. So, the break-even point is:

$200/($10 – $8) = $200 / $2 = 100 bears per month.

Our car firm has fixed costs of $10 million per month, variable costs of $2,000 per car, and sells its cars for $6,000 each. So, the level of output and sales needed to break even is:

$10,000,000/($6,000 – $2,000) = $10,000,000/$4,000 = 2,500 cars per month.

A calculated issue

1 Below are different levels of output of a new rock and pop magazine. The producer of the magazine intends to price each copy for sale at $5 each. The cost of hiring printing machinery is $2,400 per month and the print factory costs $1,600 per month to rent. The cost of materials and wages per magazine is $3. There are no other costs in this simple example. Use a calculator or a spreadsheet to complete the table with costs, revenue and profit or loss.

Magazines per month	Total fixed costs	Total variable costs	Total cost	Average cost	Total	
0	$4,000	0	$4,000	–		–$4,000
1,000						
2,000						
3,000						
4,000						
5,000	$4,000	$15,000	$19,000	$3.80	$25,000	$6,000
6,000						
7,000						
8,000						

2 At what level of output will the magazine publisher break even?

3 Plot and label the following curves on a graph with 'magazines per month' along the bottom axis and costs and revenues ($) in $1,000 intervals along the side axis. This needs to extend up to $40,000.

   a Total cost

   b Total revenue

4 Label those areas that represent profit and loss on your graph.

5 Investigate productive activities in a local small business. How is production organized?

Identify different costs incurred running the business as fixed and variable costs. How do costs vary with the scale of production or level of service provided (for example, if a shop opened longer hours or a hairdresser booked more appointments)? At what level of output per period does the business break even at current prices and costs? Suggest potential advantages and disadvantages to the business from expanding its current level of output or service.

EXAM PREPARATION 3.6

During 2017 and 2018, Irish airline Ryanair had to cancel thousands of flights to and from many European destinations. Ryanair blamed the cancellations on a combination of air traffic control delays and strikes, bad weather and shortages of pilots and cabin crew due to increase annual leave allocations.

a Define *profit*. [2]

b Explain the difference between a fixed cost and a variable cost of production. [4]

c Analyse what might have happened to the level of profits for Ryanair as a result of the problems stated. [6]

d Discuss whether the cancellation of a flight would have affected the fixed and variable costs of Ryanair. [8]

tivates firms to
produce goods and
services?

Objectives of firms

Different firms have different aims or objectives at different times. However, the ultimate goal of most private sector firms is to maximize their profits.

1 Profit maximization

To earn a profit a firm must generate more revenue from its productive activities than they cost to carry out. The ability to make a profit from production motivates entrepreneurs to set up and run firms. ➤ **1.2.1**

Profit maximization therefore involves choosing factor inputs, production methods, outputs and prices that will earn a firm the greatest amount of profit possible. It means maximizing the difference between its total costs and total revenues. However, profit maximization can be difficult and take time to achieve. For example, designing, making and testing a new aircraft takes many years and may cost many billions of dollars before the manufacturer is ready to start making the aircraft for sale to airlines.

Before a firm can increase its profits it may first need to increase its total sales and capture a sizeable share of the market for the product it supplies. It may only be able to do this by spending a large amount of money on developing and advertising its product. It may also have to sell its product at low prices initially to attract customers. All of these actions will initially reduce profits. A new firm may even have to operate at a loss for a time. Many private sector firms therefore aim to achieve **long run profit maximization**: after a period of growth, to earn a significant and sustained profit each year thereafter from its resources.

In contrast, some entrepreneurs may simply aim for a satisfactory level of profit that provides them with enough income to buy and enjoy the goods and services they want, without having to work long hours or pay too much in tax.

Why is profit important?

✔ Profit is a necessary reward for risk-taking: without it people would not invest their time or money in firms to produce the goods and services consumers need and want.

✔ Profits provide a source of finance for a firm: profits can be reinvested in a firm to expand its scale of production and/or to develop new products and technologies. Using profits to fund productive activities will be cheaper than borrowing money from a bank.

✔ Profit is a measure of success and financial stability: a firm can use its record of profitability to secure low-cost bank loans or to attract new investors or shareholders to supply capital.

▼ Revenue – Costs =

---

2 Growth

Internal growth, or external growth through merger, is a key objective for many private sector firms. It will normally involve increasing sales and market share and, thereafter, the scale of production. Growth can therefore be

> ## The benefits of growth
> - ✔ Lower average costs due to economies of scale
> - ✔ Increased sales and market share
> - ✔ The ability to diversify into different products and markets to reduce market risks
> - ✔ Improved chances of survival

expensive to achieve but should help to boost profits in the long run. This is because larger firms enjoy many cost advantages over smaller ones. These advantages are called **economies of scale**. ➤ **3.5.5**

Growth will be easier if demand for the goods or services of a business is rising. If consumer demand isn't growing then a business may only be able to expand if it attracts customers away from rival firms.

3 Survival

Starting and running a new firm can be difficult. Set-up costs can be high, consumer tastes and spending patterns can change quickly and competition from larger businesses can be fierce. Many new firms close within their first year of operation. **Survival** is therefore often the most important objective for newly created firms.

However, survival will also be an important objective even for large and established firms during an economic recession when unemployment rises and consumer spending falls for many goods and services. Many firms are forced to close during economic recessions. ➤ **4.6.3**

New technology can also change many production processes and product designs. Production, sales and profit targets may need to change as a result.

Similarly, new sources of competition from new start-ups or from firms located overseas can cause an established firm to rethink its objectives. For example, it may have to cut its prices and earn less profit in order to compete for sales and maintain its market share.

4 Social welfare and environmental objectives

Social entrepreneurs are people who organize resources and activities to help address social and environmental issues rather than to maximize profit. They will usually reinvest any profit or surplus revenue their activities make into their firms to help attain their social and environmental goals.

Firms created by social entrepreneurs are known as social enterprises. Examples can be found in many countries and industrial sectors, including health and social care, retailing, renewable energy, recycling, sport, housing and education.

Unlike many other private sector firms a social enterprise uses business strategies to maximize improvements in social and environmental well-being, rather than maximizing profits for its owners. A social enterprise can therefore be organized and financed as a sole trader, partnership or limited company, or even a charitable organization.

Social enterprise objectives

√ **social objectives:** to support the most disadvantaged people in society, including the poor, the sick and disabled;

√ **environmental objectives:** to protect the natural environment, oceans and wildlife;

√ **financial objectives:** to earn a surplus of revenue over costs that can be reinvested back into the firm to improve or expand its social or environmental work.

ACTIVITY 3.27

What's the objective?

What is likely to be the main objective of each of the private sector firms described below?

A large car manufacturer suffering a significant downturn in sales during an economic recession

A new small business offering window cleaning services to local homeowners

An established low-cost airline wanting to introduce flights to new overseas destinations

A leading supermarket chain based in the north of a country seeking to develop superstores in the south

A small manufacturing firm employing people with disabilities who may otherwise find it difficult to obtain paid employment, to make and sell craft items to raise money to help people living in poverty in developing economies and to rescue and care for sick and abused animals.

ECONOMICS IN ACTION

The CEO of the fashion firm SuperGroup, owner of the clothing retailer Superdry, reports that it has broken even in the US due to increased sales both online and in its stores. Explain this statement.

Suggest ways in which SuperGroup could boost its profits further by reducing the level of sales it requires to cover its costs of production and break even.

Fashion firm SuperGroup gets a boost from plunging pound

SuperGroup has reported a bumper rise in revenues after enjoying a boost from the plunging pound. The company behind fashion retailer Superdry which has operations in Europe, the US and China, said that full-year sales rose 27.2% to £750.6m.

Chief executive Euan Sutherland said: "2017 has seen another good year of sales and profit growth". This he said had been achieved by improving product ranges and investing in new markets.

SuperGroup, which has 555 stores globally added that a strong online performance and improving store sales has seen it break even in the US.

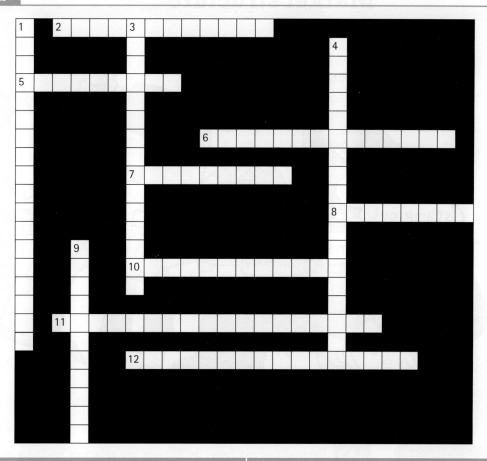

Clues across

2. Average price or revenue per unit sold multiplied by the total number of units sold in a given period of time (5, 7)

5. Any cost of production, such as the cost of insurance or factor rent, that does not vary with the level of output in a firm (5, 4)

6. The revenue per unit of output sold. It is found by dividing the total amount of money raised from the sale of a given number of items at one or more different prices by that exact same number of items sold (7, 7)

7. The sum of all the private costs of production in a firm for a given level of output per period of time. It is the sum of total fixed costs plus the average variable cost per unit multiplied by the number of units produced (5, 4)

8. The primary objective of most new firms especially those entering very competitive markets (8)

10. A cost of production that is directly related to the volume of output in a firm, such as the purchase of components or electricity used to power production machinery (8, 4)

11. A measure of the average output or revenue per worker per period of time (6, 12)

12. A production method that requires or uses significantly more capital input than labour (7, 9)

Clues down

1. The main long run objective of most private sector firms, measured by the greatest possible difference they can individually achieve between their total revenues and total costs of production (6, 12)

3. Term used to describe a production method process that requires or use proportionately more labour input than capital (6, 9)

4. Replacing one factor of production with another in a production process, for example, to make production more capital intensive (6, 12)

9. The cost per unit of output, calculated by dividing the total cost of a given level of output by the total volume of that output (7, 4)

SECTION 3.8.1

Competitive markets

What is market structure?

From Unit 2.5.1 we know that the market for a product consists of a set of buyers and sellers who, through their interactions, will determine the price of that product.

Market structure therefore refers to the characteristics of a market that influence the behaviour of buyers and sellers and the market outcomes they achieve in terms of product quantity, quality and price. These characteristics include:

- the number of firms competing to supply the market;

- how much competition there is between those firms;

- the ability of each firm or group of firms acting together, to determine the market price; and

- the ease with which new firms can enter the market to compete with existing firms.

The degree of competition in a market is therefore a key focus in the study of market structure. This is because competition between private sector firms is, in most cases, good for the consumer. Competition encourages private sector firms to make the best use of their scarce resources in order to maximize their profits. Firms will only be able to do this if they produce items that consumers want at prices they are willing and able to pay that exceed their costs of producing. Firms producing the same or similar products will therefore compete for consumers by offering them the most attractive product features at the lowest possible price. This in turn means firms must keep their costs of production as low as possible. Any restriction on competition may therefore result in a misallocation of scarce resources with costs and prices higher than they would otherwise be and with fewer wants being satisfied.

Firms can compete with each other in a number of ways:

- **Price competition** involves competing to offer consumers the lowest or best possible prices for rival products. Cutting price below that of rival products is one way a firm can try to boost its sales and market shares at the expense of competing firms. However, the ability of a firm to undercut rivals will be constrained by market conditions and its production costs. If demand is price inelastic, cutting price may not boost sales and it will also reduce the profit margin between price and average cost.

- **Non-price competition** involves competing on all other product features other than price. It can involve new product development, product placements in different retail outlets and at trade fairs, providing after-sales care and promotional campaigns including advertising, attractive in-store displays, running competitions and issuing consumer loyalty cards. Non-price competition is important because consumers do not just compare product prices. They are also looking for the best value for money in terms of the quality of the good or service, ease of purchase, levels of customer service and whether or not there is good after-sales care should anything go wrong and they want to exchange their product.

Perfect competition

Economists have identified a number of different types of market structure. Two particularly important ones are perfectly competitive markets and monopoly.

Perfect competition

A perfectly competitive market or **perfect competition** has the following features.

Features of perfect competition	Impact on market outcomes
• A large number of firms compete to supply the market • All firms supplying the market have **perfect knowledge**	• Each firm produces a small share of the total market supply • All firms have access to the same materials, technical knowledge, equipment and skills and will therefore face the same costs and be able to supply products of equal quality
• Each firm supplies the same identical product	• There is no product differentiation. All of the products supplied to the market by all the different firms all look, smell, taste, etc. the same and have the same quality. That is, they all supply a **homogenous product**
• All firms are **price takers** and can only maximize their profits by selling as much as they can at the market price	• Because there are so many firms competing to supply identical products, no one firm is able to raise its price. If a firm does increase its price its sales will fall to zero as consumers will buy the product from other firms
• Profits will attract new firms into the market. New firms can enter and the market freely	• Competition will lower the market price and reduce profits until firms remaining in the market earn only **normal profits** (the minimum amount of profit they need to stay in the market)

▲ Fresh fruits and vegetables, unrefined sugar and crude oil are examples of 'homogenous products'

In a perfectly competitive market the market price is therefore completely determined by the market forces of supply and demand. No one firm has any power to influence the market price. The same applies to consumers. ➤ **2.5.1**

That is, all firms and consumers in a perfectly competitive market have to be price takers: they will only be able to exchange goods and services at the equilibrium market price.

If a firm did try to raise its price its sales would fall to zero because consumers will be able to buy the same identical product from other firms supplying the market at the lower market price.

Similarly, a firm would be unable to lower its price below the market price without losing money unless it was able to produce it at a lower cost than others. Even if it could lower its costs rival firms would soon find out how and purchase the same resources or use the same methods of production to lower their own costs and prices. This is because all firms share the same knowledge of production techniques and costs.

Monopoly

Pure monopoly is the opposite extreme to perfect competition. A **pure monopoly** has the following market features.

Features of pure monopoly	Impact on market outcomes
• Only one firm supplies the market	• A pure monopoly controls the total market supply. Consumers must either buy the product of the monopoly or go without
• The firm is a **price maker**	• The monopoly can determine the quantity it will supply to the market and therefore determine the market price. For example, by restricting market supply a monopoly can raise the market price
• New firms will be prevented from entering the market	• New, smaller firms will find it difficult to compete with a large monopoly. The monopoly may also use pricing and other strategies to protect its market position from competition
• The firm will be able to earn **abnormal profits**	• A monopoly can set a market price that will earn it a very high or excessive profit. By preventing new firms from entering it market it can also ensue its excess profits are not competed away

A pure monopoly therefore controls the total supply of a product to a market and has significant market power. It allows the firm to set the market price.

In addition, a monopoly can restrict competition so that it can set a price that will earn it profits far in excess of what it would earn if had to compete with other firms. This is because consumers will be unable to switch their purchases to other suppliers if the monopoly raises the market price.

Features of competitive markets

Despite the term *perfect competition*, there is no price or non-price competition in a perfectly competitive market. This is because all firms are price takers and supply identical products. So, for example, there is no point in a firm in a perfect competitive market advertising its product because its product is identical to those of all other suppliers. Advertising would simply increase its costs above its competitors without increasing its sales.

Similarly, there is no need for price or non-price competition for the market in a pure monopoly. A pure monopoly has no competitors and is able to set the market price. Consumers must either purchase the product of the pure monopoly or have to go without.

In reality there are very few perfectly competitive markets or pure private sector monopolies, but there are many markets with similar features to one or other of these two extremes. This is why the concepts of perfect competition and pure monopoly are still very useful. Economists will compare their features with those of other, intermediate market structures to assess how much competition there is and how much influence any one firm or group of firms acting together has over the total market supply and market price. The more control one or more firms acting together have over the quantity supplied and price in a market the less 'perfect' the market is.

Firms in competitive markets will compete for sales and profits using different competitive pricing, product and promotional strategies.

Competitive pricing strategies

Competitive pricing strategies will usually involve setting prices at the same level or below the prices of rival products.

- **Destruction pricing** (or **predatory pricing**) will often be used by a large firm when its market position is threatened by a smaller rival or a new firm entering the market for the first time. It involves the firm lowering its price significantly to below the costs of the competitor in order to 'destroy' its sales, causing it to lose money. If the large firm is successful at forcing its competitor to exit the market it can then raise its prices again and recover any losses it may have made.

- However, destruction pricing can result in a **price war** if competitors respond by cutting their own prices. In a price war each firm will try to undercut the prices of its rivals. Deeper and deeper price cuts therefore occur and all firms supplying the market can end up losing money. Price wars will often occur in markets dominated by a small number of large firms.

- **Follow-the-leader pricing** is a price matching strategy that helps to avoid damaging price wars in competitive markets. It involves each firm in a market setting its price or prices equal to those of its closest rivals. The firm with the largest market share will usually be the price leader. If the price leader raises its prices, all other firms in the market will do the same. Similarly, if the price leader cuts its prices, all other firms will reduce theirs.

Product differentiation

Firms supplying the same or very similar products usually attempt to differentiate their products in some way from those of their competitors in order to attract and retain customers. **Product differentiation** can include changing product features such as brand name, image shape, taste, smell, colour and durability or other aspects such as warranty periods and after-sales care.

For example, consider just how many different laundry detergents there are on sale in your local supermarket. Each one has different brand name, perfume and packaging. Significant advertising is used to reinforce brand names and images and will often make different claims about the superiority and cleaning power of each detergent to attract the attention of consumers.

All this is despite the fact that all laundry detergents, either in powder form or a liquid, are basically the same. However, through product differentiation firms may be able to exert some control over price. If a firm is able to persuade consumers that its product is superior to the products of close competitors then it may be able to charge a higher price without losing significant sales.

There are many real-world examples of highly differentiated product markets in which large numbers of firms compete on price and product features to sell very similar products.

'Small numbers' competition

Not all competitive markets have large numbers of firms competing with each other to supply consumers. There are many national and international markets in which the market supply is dominated by a small number of large firms. For example, Apple and Google dominate the global supply of operating systems for smartphones while the market for computer operating systems is dominated by Apple and Windows. Similarly, Boeing and Airbus dominate the global market supply of passenger aircraft and Coca-Cola and PepsiCo are the leading global suppliers of carbonated soft drinks.

Despite the fact that each firm has considerable market power, competition between them for sales and market shares can still be very fierce. Price wars can develop as each firm tries to undercut the prices and sales of its close rivals. This can be very damaging to their profits so the firms may instead agree to act together to control market supply and set common prices, much the same as a pure monopoly. This is called **collusion**. Instead firms in these markets will agree to compete on product features other than price.

In general, therefore, a market will be considered competitive in the real world if it displays the following features:

- There is vigorous price competition and non-price competition between firms supplying the market;

- Firms pursue different pricing, output and advertising strategies depending on the type and amount of competition they face from new and existing competitors;

- Product features and brand images will be highly differentiated and the range of product features and designs available, the quality of after-sales services and product prices will tend to change frequently as firms develop new ones they hope will attract consumer demand away from rival suppliers;

- The market shares and profits of competing businesses will vary over time through competition and as new businesses enter the market and inefficient firms are forced to exit the market (i.e. close down or cease trading).

ACTIVITY 3.28

All washed up

1 What is a price war?

2 What motives do you think P&G had for cutting its prices?

3 What impact has the price war had on the profits of the two companies?

4 Explain why Hindustan Unilever's 'much larger size, market share and product portfolio should enable it to continue aggressive pricing strategies more than the smaller P&G'.

5 Do you think demand for detergents is price elastic or inelastic? Explain.

6 What other pricing strategies could the two companies have used to avoid a price war?

Will Hindustan Unilever tide over price war?

Shares in Hindustan Unilever have fallen in price amid concerns about a renewed price war emerging in the detergents category.

The previous such turf war in 2004 had led to profit margins for both main players taking a substantial hit, though Hindustan Unilever (HUL) did manage to hold on to its market share by matching Procter & Gamble's moves.

The renewed concerns about a price war with HUL's arch rival (P&G) have been triggered by a series of events. Selling prices of detergents in the mass-market category have been heading down for several months now but the battle for market share entered a fresh chapter recently with aggressive television advertisements pitting HUL's Rin brand against P&G's Tide Naturals.

Reports now suggest that P&G has increased volumes for its Tide Naturals by 25 per cent, without changing prices. This translates into a 20 per cent reduction in effective prices for the brand.

HUL's much larger size, market share and product portfolio should enable it to continue aggressive pricing strategies more than the smaller P&G. This suggests that the company may be able eventually to ward off this new threat to its market share. However, for investors in HUL this could mean a loss of pricing power and profits in one of HUL's key product categories for some time to come.

ECONOMICS IN ACTION

Why do you think markets for modern telecommunications are prone to price wars? (Hint: what is happening to the cost of the technologies; growth in market size and productive scale; the number of new market entrants?)

India's Bharti offers free data, deepening price war with rivals

Bharti Airtel Ltd, India's top wireless carrier, will offer free data to woo new and existing 4G customers, intensifying a price war in the sector and sending profits and share prices tumbling.

The package is Bharti's latest response to the entry last year of new operator Reliance Jio, which shook India's telecom sector by offering new customers free data services.

Price war heats up in New Zealand telecoms

2degrees launched an aggressive calling plan yesterday that will challenge the prices of Vodafone and Telecom.

The mobile carrier has dropped the cost of calls between networks by nearly a third, in a bid to increase its market share.

Monopoly markets

The disadvantages of monopoly

The absence of competition in a pure monopoly market structure can be a major problem for consumers and an economy. This is because a pure monopoly can use its market power to restrict output and therefore the market supply in order to increase the market price so that it is able to earn excessive or abnormal profits. A monopoly that behaves in this way is said to be behaving 'opportunistically' and against the public interest.

We can show the impact of this strategy in a simple demand and supply diagram. In a highly competitive market the market price will be set at P where market demand and supply are equal. At P the total quantity exchanged or traded each period with consumers by the many firms competing to supply them is Q. ➤ **2.5.1**

In contrast, if the market was a pure monopoly and there was no competition from new entrants, the monopoly could restrict the quantity it was willing to supply each period to Q1, forcing the market price to rise to P1. It may also reduce product quality to reduce its costs and boost its profits further.

In addition, the monopoly could reduce product quality to save costs and boost its profits further. If there is no competition there will be no close substitutes for consumers to buy instead.

Monopoly therefore represents a market failure because it can have the following disadvantages compared to more competitive market structures.

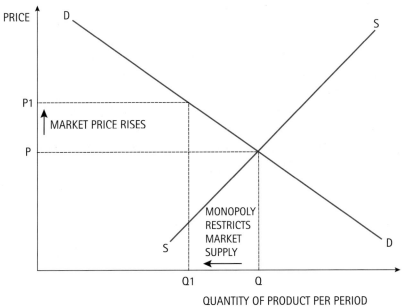

▲ The potential impact of monopoly on market supply and price

1 Less consumer choice

By restricting competition from rival producers and products, a monopoly will offer the consumer less choice than they would have in a competitive market.

2 Lower output and higher prices

If a monopoly can restrict market supply it can force the higher market price to rise over and above the price that would occur in a competitive market. Total output and employment in an economy will be lower. Consumers faced with few alternative choices may simply have to continue buying the product of the monopoly or go without. If consumer demand is relatively price inelastic, particularly if the product is an essential product, then demand will not contract by much and the monopoly will increase its revenue and profit.

3 Lower product quality

Faced with little or no competition, a monopoly has no great incentive to improve the quality of the good or service it supplies. On the contrary, a monopoly may reduce quality in order to cut its production costs to increase its profit margins.

4 X-inefficiency

Because a pure monopoly has no competitors and is able to earn abnormal profits, it may make less effort than a competitive firm to ensure that its resources are used in the most efficient way. This means a monopoly may be managed inefficiently and its production costs may be higher than they would otherwise be in a competitive firm. In economics this is called **x-inefficiency** but is more commonly known as organizational slack.

5 Governments may need to devote scarce resources to the control of monopolies that act against the public interest

Many governments around the world have introduced laws and regulations to control private sector monopolies that act against the public interest. To monitor and regulate the behaviours of monopolies, governments will have to employ scarce resources paid for from tax revenues. In the absence of monopolies these scarce resources could have been put to other, more productive uses instead.

Competition policy (also antitrust policy) refers to laws or measures that are used by a government to control the behaviour of firms that restrict competition and act against the public interest. Measures may include:

- imposing fines on firms that abuse their market power to exploit consumers or suppliers to earn excessive profits;
- forcing monopolies to 'break up' into smaller competing firms;
- regulating the profits, prices, outputs and/or service levels of monopolies. This can involve setting maximum prices, capping price rises and setting minimum standards or service.

Many governments have set up regulatory bodies or 'regulators' to monitor and enforce competition laws in different industries. For example, the Office for Gas and Electricity Markets (Ofgem) regulates the prices and service levels of suppliers in the UK gas and electricity markets. Similarly, Ofwat regulates prices and service levels in the water industry in England and Wales while Ofcom is the regulator and competition authority for the UK communications industries. There are many more and similar examples of regulatory bodies around the world.

Additionally, a government may impose higher taxes on the excess profits of monopolies.

A government may even nationalize (take into public ownership) private sector monopolies so that it is has direct control over their prices, output and customer service levels. ➤ **2.11.2**

United Utilities profits slip after Ofwat brings in price cuts

United Utilities, the UK's largest listed water company, has suffered a 9% slide in pre-tax profits after the regulator ordered water companies to slash prices for consumers.

The profit hit was a result of new rules from Ofwat, the regulator, which will force all water companies to cap customer bills below inflation until 2020, boost customer service and make significant investments to drive innovation and competition in the sector over a five-year period.

How monopolies may restrict competition

If a private sector monopoly wishes to protect its market position and abnormal profits it must prevent new firms from entering its market to compete. This is because any increase in market supply from new firms will force the market prices and its profits down.

Barriers to entry are obstacles that prevent or make it difficult for new firms to introduce their products into existing markets. There are broadly two main types:

- **Natural barriers to entry** occur when new firms find it difficult to compete with larger established and often more efficient firms due to differences in their size, costs and scale of production.

- **Artificial barriers to entry** are those created by larger, more powerful firms purposefully to restrict competition.

Natural barriers to entry

Natural barriers to entry are not necessarily bad for consumers or an economy. They occur because large-scale production in one or a small number of large firms is often more efficient than small-scale production spread across many competing firms.

1 Economies of scale

If a single firm is able to produce the entire market supply of a product at a lower average cost than a number of smaller competing firms together then it has a **natural monopoly**. Networks of pipelines and grids are all examples of natural monopolies. Because of the significant fixed costs involved in providing network infrastructure it would be far more costly and wasteful to have more than one firm competing to connect each house, office or factory in a country to a different set of gas or water pipes or electricity cables.

It therefore makes economic sense for a natural monopoly to be a pure monopoly and to supply 100% of the market in which it operates. As a result, many natural monopolies are either state-owned enterprises or are closely regulated by governments.

2 Capital size

The supply of a product may involve the input of such a vast amount of capital equipment that new, smaller competing firms will find it difficult to raise enough finance to buy or hire their own. For example, consider the amount of capital a firm would need to produce electricity from a new nuclear power station or offshore wind farm. Only large companies able to raise and manage a significant amount of low-cost finance will be in a position to fund such large-scale investments.

3 Historical reasons

A business may have a monopoly because it was the first to enter the market for a product and has built up an established and loyal customer base. For example, Lloyds of London dominates the world shipping insurance market primarily because of its established expertise dating back to the eighteenth century.

4 Legal considerations

The development of new production methods and products can be expensive but can be encouraged by granting innovative producers patents or copyright to protect them from other firms copying their ideas and quickly reducing their potential sales and profits. In this way a government can create a **legal monopoly** with the sole right to supply a new and innovative good or service.

Artificial barriers to entry

Some large, dominant firms may introduce pricing, output and marketing strategies purposefully to restrict new competition from eroding their market power and profits. Monopolies and oligopolies are often accused, and found guilty of, using artificial barriers to entry to restrict competition.

Activity 3.29 below contains some examples of artificial barriers and how they might be used to restrict competition.

1 Destruction or predatory pricing

In the Flyhigh Airlines example below, the company has routes all over the world and makes many millions of dollars in profits each year. A smaller competitor could not afford to operate so many routes. In fact, Cut Price Airlines can only afford to operate two flights per week on just one route.

The new company has offered fares $40 cheaper than Flyhigh Airlines. However, Flyhigh can afford to cut its fares on the Atlantic route by more than $40. This will capture the market and should force Cut Price out of business. Flyhigh will lose money on the route by offering such low fares but it can afford to cover these losses from profits on other routes. Once Cut Price has been forced to close, Flyhigh can raise its fares again.

This is an example of predatory or destruction pricing. It occurs when a large firm cuts its prices, even if it means losing money in the short run, in order to force new and smaller competing firms out of business. Once the new competitor has been removed, the dominant firm can raise its prices again.

2 Restricting supplies to rival firms

New firms will only be able to enter a market if they can obtain supplies of the materials, components and business services they need to begin production. Existing firms in the same market with a dominant share can threaten to take their custom away from their suppliers if they supply their products to any new firms. Suppliers are likely to agree to this if they rely on the dominant firms for the majority of their sales. For example, in the case of the Big Sell Supermarket in Activity 3.29, the store could threaten to stop purchasing goods from its wholesaler if it supplies other retailers.

3 Exclusive dealing

This occurs when a monopoly prevents retailers from stocking the products of competing firms. That is, they are forced by contract to purchase and sell only the products supplied by the monopoly. This method of restricting competition is particularly effective if the products supplied by the dominant firm are popular with consumers and generate significant sales and profits for the wholesalers and retailers who sell them.

In the example of Spreadwell Limited, the firm was the main supplier of popular margarines to supermarkets and other retailers who were able to attract consumers into their shops as a result of offering Spreadwell products. Spreadwell can use this brand power to threaten to stop supplying retailers if they stock competing margarines. Spreadwell's significant advertising effort will also be an entry barrier to many smaller firms.

Google may face $7 billion fine for forcing phone manufacturers to pre-load its apps onto Android handsets which cannot be deleted

The European Commission's antitrust lawsuits against Google threaten to impose a $7 billion fine on the tech giant for forcing Android phone manufacturers to use Google Search.

Google Play is an extremely desirable, almost indispensable, application for phone manufacturers because it facilitates downloading and updating Android applications. Phone manufacturers must therefore use Google Play. However, to use Google Play on their phones, manufacturers have been forced to install Google Search.

The European Commission has argued this tied arrangement is illegal and anti-competitive because it prevents phone manufacturers from installing competing internet search engines.

Additionally, Google demands uniformity from its customers. For example, if Samsung installs Google Play in one particular type of its phones, Google requires it to install Google Search in all its phones or it will not allow it to use Google Play in any phones.

Creating barriers

Divide into groups. Each group should consider one of the following cases based on imaginary firms. You play the role of company directors of different monopolies and your task is to find barriers to entry to stop competition from other firms. You will report your findings to your shareholders (the rest of the class) who will then vote on whether or not to allow the directors to continue to manage the company depending on how well you have protected profits.

Big Sell Supermarket plc

You are the board of directors of the large Big Sell Supermarket in a town. There are very few other food shops in the town apart from some very small stores. The supermarket is supplied by a nearby wholesaler and your supermarket is its single most important customer.

Your monopoly position ensures that the supermarket continues to earn high profits. However, other firms know this and want to set up large shops in the same area to compete. The owners of Big Sell are worried about losing trade and profits to these new stores. They have asked you to find barriers to prevent new shops from setting up nearby.

You must report on what you plan to do before the next AGM, at which the shareholders will decide whether or not to re-elect you as directors.

Flyhigh Airlines

You are the directors of a large airline flying to countries all over the world.

A new airline company, Cut Price Atlantic, is about to enter the market with two scheduled flights per week on your most profitable route between the USA and Spain. Cut Price Atlantic intends to undercut your $150 fare by $40 for a one-way flight between the two countries.

Your shareholders in Flyhigh Airlines are very anxious. Because demand is price elastic they fear that the new low-cost airline will make large sales on the route across the Atlantic and will be able to use its profits to buy more planes in order to start up cut-price flights on other routes as well.

Your task as directors is to stop the new airline from taking away custom from your company by devising barriers to entry. (Hint: Flyhigh operates many profitable routes throughout the world, so what can you afford to do to try and force Cut Price Airlines out of business? Remember, your failure to do so could mean your rejection as directors by shareholders at their next meeting.)

Spreadwell Limited

You are the board of directors of Spreadwell Limited. You have a dominant share of the market for margarine, producing nearly all of the well-known brands on sale.

Spreadwell Limited relies heavily on television advertising to sell its products and will often help chains of supermarkets to publicize the sale of their margarines. Supermarkets benefit from the additional customers they attract as a result.

Because of your monopoly position, Spreadwell earns high profits and shareholders are keen to protect them from new firms who wish to produce margarine.

As the board of directors you need to limit any new competition. Try to decide how you can set up barriers to entry. Your report must prove favourable to your shareholders.

4 'Tying' or 'bundling'

'Tying' or 'bundling' arrangements are similar to exclusive deals. A tying arrangement involves a firm agreeing to sell one product to a customer but only on the condition that the customer also purchases one or more different (or tied) products from the same firm even if the customer does not want the other products. The main product usually has few or no substitutes and is therefore essential for customers to have. Tying its sale to the purchase of other products therefore prevents customers from buying possible alternatives from competing firms. In this way, tied arrangements restrict competition.

Are all monopolies bad?

It would be wrong to think every pure or near pure monopoly will try to restrict competition and exploit consumers to earn excessive profits. For example, Boeing in the USA and Airbus in Europe dominate the global market supply of large passenger aircraft but nevertheless compete vigorously against each other for market share.

Some monopolies, because of their size and ability to earn high profits, can benefit consumers. Here are some examples:

- A monopoly may be more efficient than smaller firms supplying the same market because of its scale of production. Because of their cost advantages they will be able to charge customers lower prices without losing profits.

- A monopoly may still face competition from firms overseas or from firms selling products that can satisfy similar wants. For example, a monopoly provider of air or railway services could still face competition on some routes from providers of bus, coach or boat services.

- A monopoly may offer competitive prices and continue to offer high-quality products to protect its dominant market position if its market is contestable. In a **contestable market** barriers to entry are low. This means that new firms would be easily able to enter the market of the monopoly if it was to charge high prices to earn abnormal profits. The best way to restrict competition in a contestable market is therefore to charge competitive prices.

▲ Some revolutionary products, like the jumbo jet and photocopier, may never have been developed if the business organizations that invented them were unable to enjoy monopoly profits. Abnormal profits were a reward for their significant investment risks

- Without abnormal profits many monopolies would not have the incentive or the money they need to fund large, risky investments in new inventions and the development of better products. In a competitive market, any profits from new products would be quickly competed away. Due to its market power, large scale of production and low average costs, a national monopoly will be able to withstand fierce competition from large overseas firms far better than smaller firms could. This in turn will help to protect jobs and incomes in the economy.

EXAM PREPARATION 3.8

Horizontal mergers between two or more competing firms will create a bigger enterprise with a larger market share. In some cases it can create monopolies.

a   Define *horizontal merger*.   [2]

b   Explain **two** characteristics of a competitive market.   [4]

c   Analyse how some large firms can experience economies of scale,
    while others suffer diseconomies of scale.   [6]

d   Discuss whether the disadvantages of a monopoly always outweigh
    the advantages.   [8]

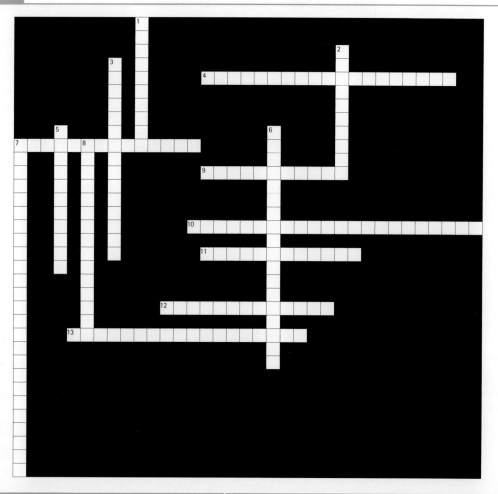

Clues across

4. Rivalry between firms supplying the same market involving advertising, promotional and product differentiation strategies (3-5, 11)

7. The surplus of revenue over costs enjoyed by a monopoly that is in excess of the surplus it might expect to earn in a more competitive market (8, 5)

9. Term used to describe firms in a highly competitive market who must accept the market price because they are unable to individually influence market outcomes (5, 6)

10. A price matching strategy often used by large dominant firms in a competitive market to avoid damaging price wars between them (6-3-6, 7)

11. A market structure in which a single firm controls 100% of the supply of a product to a market and is therefore able to determine the market price (4, 8)

12. Higher costs resulting from organizational slack in a monopoly because it is protected from competition (1-12)

13. A market structure characterized by a large number of firms supplying an identical product such that no individual firm has any influence over the market price (7, 11)

Clues down

1. Term used to describe the ability of a monopoly to determine the market price through its control over market supply (5, 5)

2. Term used to describe identical products supplied by firms in a perfectly competitive market (10)

3. A market structure in which a single firm is able to control the entire market supply because it has an overwhelming cost advantage over more competitive market structures involving more than one firm (7, 8)

5. Term used to describe a market in which a monopoly set price at a competitive level because it would otherwise attract new entrants because there are no or only very low barriers to competition (11)

6. A pricing strategy used by a dominant firm or firms in a market that involves slashing prices below costs to deter or destroy new competition (11, 7)

7. Obstacles created by a monopoly to purposefully restrict competition from other firms (10, 8, 2, 5)

8. Collectively, the characteristics of markets that influence the behaviour of buyers and sellers and market outcomes in terms of product quantity, quality and price. They include the number of firms competing to supply the market, the degree of competition or collusion between them and the ease with which new firms can enter the market (6, 9)

Assessment exercises

Multiple choice

1 What is the usual reason why people trust notes and coins issued by the government or central bank in their country?

   A They are generally acceptable for trade and exchange

   B They are easy to carry and are in infinite supply

   C They are backed by gold at the central bank

   D They are convertible into the US dollar or Euro

2 The use of a mobile phone app to make payments from a bank account is an example of which function of money?

   A A store of value or wealth

   B A unit of account

   C A means of deferred payment

   D A medium of exchange

3 A key function of a money is to be a measure of value. What does this mean?

   A It is used for future savings

   B It is used to enable monthly payments for expensive goods

   C It is used to pay the price of a good

   D It is used to compare the worth of different goods

4 Which of the following statements about different banks in economy is correct?

   A The central bank determines the tax and spending policies of the government

   B The central bank loans money to small businesses and members of the public

   C Commercial banks hold the gold and foreign currency reserves of the government

   D Commercial banks settle debts by clearing customers' cheques and debit card payments

5 Which one of the following types of household is most likely to spend the highest proportion of its disposable income?

   A High income, middle-aged with no children

   B Low income, young single parent with young children

   C Middle income, young single person with no children

   D High income, middle-aged couple with two grown-up children

6 Why might a period of rapid inflation combined with low interest rates be of concern for a consumer?

   A Because the consumer lives on a pension linked to the consumer price index

   B Because the consumer needs to draw from savings to pay monthly bills

   C Because the consumer pays a fixed rent for their accommodation

   D Because the consumer has a large bank loan to repay

7 What may cause an individual to increase their savings as a proportion of their current income?

   A A belief that the prices of goods will rise in the future

   B A fall in the rate of interest paid by banks

   C A fear that the individual may be made unemployed in the future

   D A desire to increase current consumption

8 Karimah works part-time in a local supermarket. She lives with her parents in a small house.

Akram runs a successful business and owns a large apartment.

Which of the following statements is most likely to be correct?

   A Karimah spends a smaller proportion of her disposable income than Akram

   B Karimah has a lower disposable income than Akram

   C Karimah saves most of her disposable income

   D Karimah will find it easier than Akram to borrow money

9 What shows the correct examples of income and wealth?

	Income	Wealth
A	Annual salary	Dividends from shares
B	Wages	Overtime payments
C	Dividends from shares	Rent from letting a house
D	Rent from letting a house	Shares

10 In the diagram, D1D1 and S1S1 represent the demand for and the supply of labour to the hotels and restaurants sector. W indicates the legal minimum wage.

An increase in migrant labour causes the labour supply curve to shift from S1S1 to S2S2.

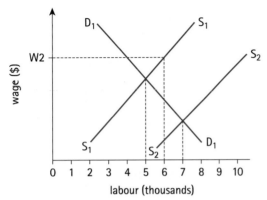

How many people would be employed in the sector if the minimum wage is abolished?

A 4,000   **B** 5,000   **C** 6,000   **D** 7,000

11 In which occupations do wages tend to be lowest?

A In those where there is an excess supply of labour

B In those where the work is dangerous

C In those where employees are paid an annual salary

D In those where employees need advanced educational qualifications

12 Why might manufacturing workers have higher wage rates than agricultural workers?

A Manufacturing workers are in greater supply

B Manufacturing workers face fewer health and safety risks

C Manufacturing workers have better working conditions

D Manufacturing workers use more productive equipment

13 Which of the following is most likely to limit increases in wages in an industry?

A An increase in profits in the industry

B An increase in consumer demand for the industry's products

C An increase in the wages of workers with similar jobs

D An increase in the substitution of labour in production processes by robots

14 The table shows how the average weekly earnings of four workers (A to D) changed between ages 16 and 64.

Which row is most likely to represent the change in the weekly earnings of an unskilled, manual labourer over time?

	Age 16	Age 35	Age 49	Age 64
A	$600	$600	$600	$600
B	$900	$800	$700	$600
C	$600	$700	$800	$700
D	$600	$700	$800	$900

15 What might be a disadvantage to a trade union in discussions with the owners of a firm to increase the pay of its members?

A An increase in imports of a cheaper, similar product

B The closure of a training centre resulting in fewer skilled workers

C Increasing consumer demand for the firms' product

D The development of new techniques that increase productivity

16 A manufacturer of sports equipment expands by merging with a sports retail chain. What type of merger does this describe?

A Backward vertical

B Conglomerate

C Forward vertical

D Horizontal

17 Which type of economy of scale will benefit a firm producing a range of different products?

A Buying

B Financial

C Technical

D Risk-bearing

18 India is experiencing rapid growth in air travel. The number and size of airlines is increasing every year. Which effect arising from this growth is an external economy of scale?

A Banks offer low-cost credit facilities to large airlines

B Fuel suppliers charge lower prices to airlines that buy in bulk

C Colleges are established to train flight crew

D Larger airlines operate aircraft which can carry more passengers

19 Which change must occur when a firm starts to experience diseconomies of scale?

   A   Average costs begin to rise
   B   Average revenue falls
   C   Total fixed costs increase
   D   Total variable costs rise

20 How can a firm guarantee that it earns a maximum profit?

   A   By maximizing its prices
   B   By minimizing the difference between average revenue and average cost
   C   By maximizing the number of items it sells
   D   By maximizing the difference between its total revenue and total cost

21 A firm produced 4,000 cars each month and employed 100 workers. A fall in demand caused the firm to cuts output to 3,200 cars a week and its workforce to 64. What was the percentage change in the firm's labour productivity?

   A   It fell by 20%
   B   It increased by 25%
   C   It increased by 20%
   D   It fell by 25%

22 Some worker co-operatives in the agricultural sector have changed from using labour-intensive methods of production to capital-intensive methods. What might be the cause of this change?

   A   Some agricultural land has been sold for housing.
   B   Farming equipment has become more efficient.
   C   People are eating less food for health reasons.
   D   Average productivity of agricultural workers has increased.

23 A firm's total variable cost is $3,000 when it produces 1,000 units each week and its total fixed cost is $27,000. What is the average cost of producing each unit of output?

   A $3
   B $27
   C $30
   D $300

24 Thc table shows a firm's average revenue and average cost. What level of output, A, B, C or D will maximize its profit?

	Output (units)	Average revenue ($)	Average cost ($)
A	10	40	50
B	25	52	45
C	30	55	32
D	35	62	43

25 The diagram shows the costs of a firm.

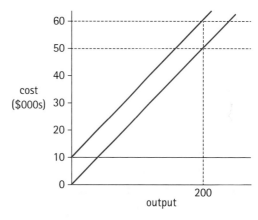

The firm is currently producing 200 units per day. What are the firm's total fixed costs at this level of output?

   A   0   **B** $10,000   **C** $50,000   **D** $60,000

26 A firm intends to expand its scale of production by investing in additional factory space and machinery. What immediate impact will this decision have on its costs?

   A   Total variable costs will rise
   B   Total fixed costs will rise
   C   Total cost will be unchanged
   D   Average costs will rise

27 Why are firms in perfect competition price takers?

   A   They have no information about market price
   B   They are unable to influence market equilibrium
   C   They are no natural barriers to entry
   D   There are only a few firms in the industry

28 What exists in highly competitive market but not in monopoly?

   A   Barriers to entry
   B   Economies of scale
   C   Many sellers
   D   Product differentiation

29 Prices tend to be lower in a competitive industry than in a monopoly. Why is this?

  A Profits are lower in a monopoly
  B A monopoly is a price taker
  C Competitive industry has more economies of scale
  D New firms are free to enter the competitive industry

30 What is a possible advantage to the consumer of a monopoly supplier in a market?

  A It's average production costs will be lower than if there were many suppliers.
  B It's profits will be higher than if there were many suppliers.
  C It is able to restrict competition.
  D It can determine the market price.

Structured questions

1 Driving the changes in the car manufacturing industry

Around 72 million cars were produced in 2017, over 50% of which were produced by just 10 companies. The global car market is dominated by Japanese giant Toyota. It produces over 10 million cars each year and captures over 9% of global sales.

Toyota has production plants all over the world including two in the UK. Other major car producers including Nissan and Honda also have factories in the UK.

The UK automotive industry is the 10th largest in the world. According to the Society of Motor Manufacturers and Traders (SMMT), 1.67 million cars left UK factories in 2017, a decline of 3% compared with the year before. The SMMT said the fall was primarily the result of lower demand from UK consumers worried about future economic conditions and further rises in interest rates. Buyers of cars often withdraw savings and borrow money from commercial banks to make their purchases.

However, despite this decline, car manufacturing in the UK remained high by historical standards. UK factories saw production of motor vehicles increase by 45% between 2012 and 2016. The number of cars produced per worker also increased significantly, partly because the industry replaced the jobs of some less skilled employees with new capital equipment.

Over the same period, the wages of the lowest paid car workers fell by 7.5%, according to data from the UK Office of National Statistics. Manufacturers say that reduced wages and hours were among deals struck with trade unions during the economic recession in 2008/9 to protect UK jobs and factories from closures as demand fell. In comparison, declining car sales in Europe forced the closure of a number of car plants in Germany, France, Belgium and Italy.

The global car industry is now undergoing significant change. The development of electric, connected and potentially driverless cars is having a powerful impact on the way established, volume car makers organize their operations. It is forcing them to work with software and battery producers and is creating opportunities for many smaller automobile and parts manufacturers.

  A Identify three ways of measuring whether an industry in a country is large or small. [3]
  B Explain, using information from the extract, why wages in the UK car industry fell. [2]

    C Using information from the extract, explain how trade union membership may benefit workers. [4]

    D Analyse two reasons, referred to in the extract, why a decrease in employment may increase labour productivity. [4]

    E Using information from the extract, explain two functions of commercial banks. [4]

    F Discuss whether a government should protect a declining car industry. [5]

    G Discuss whether small car manufacturers can compete successfully with large car manufacturers. [8]

2 A modern economy cannot function without money.

    A Define *money*. [2]

    B Explain how money functions as a unit of account and a means of deferred payment. [4]

    C Analyse the possible effects of an increase in bank lending on the supply of money and economic growth. [6]

    D Discuss whether the interest rate is the only influence on a person's decision to borrow money from a bank. [8]

3 Over the last 50 years, rapid growth in the use of electronic payment cards has changed how consumers pay for goods and services. Electronic payment cards have reduced the use of cash and cheques making payments more secure and reducing costs to business of cash management and handling.

They have also increased financial inclusion. The number of people with bank deposit and savings accounts and bank loans has increased.

    A Identify **two** influences on the amount people save. [2]

    B Explain why notes and coins are money. [4]

    C Analyse the role that commercial banks can perform in an economy. [6]

    D Discuss whether poor people are more likely to borrow than rich people. [8]

4 Canadian manufacturer Bombardier began making and selling regional passenger jets in 1991. It employs a high value of capital goods and was the monopoly supplier of regional jets until Embraer of Brazil entered the global market with a rival aircraft in 2002. Bombardier also specializes in the production of trains.

    A Define *specialization*. [2]

    B Explain why fixed costs are high in the aircraft-making industry. [4]

    C Analyse what determines a firm's demand for capital goods. [6]

    D Discuss whether the quality of products is likely to be higher in a monopoly or in a perfectly competitive market. [8]

5 Capital is a fixed factor of production in economics in the short run. This means that firms are only able to increase production in the short run if they have spare capacity or if they employ more variable factors of production. However, in the long run firms will also be able to employ more capital to increase their scale of production. As a result, many firms should be able to reduce their average costs of production.

    A Identify the **two** human factors of production. [2]

    B Explain **two** influences on demand for factors of production. [4]

C Analyse why some people are prepared to work in low-paid occupations. [6]

D Discuss whether or not the average cost of production will always fall as a firm increases its scale of production. [8]

6 The factor resources available to an economy will determine its output of economic goods. The relationship between resources and output can be shown on a production possibility curve diagram. For example, growing demand for meat free, vegetarian and vegan diets is changing the way resources are being used in food production and processing in many countries. Many existing suppliers of vegan foods are new and relatively small, but the expanding market is creating opportunities for growth. The price elasticity of demand for different types of foods has also been changing over time.

A Define *economic good*. [2]

B Explain **two** economic concepts shown by a production possibility curve diagram. [4]

C Analyse why demand for a product may become more price elastic over time. [6]

D Discuss whether the growth of a firm is advantageous for both the firm and consumers. [8]

4 Government and the macroeconomy

In many mixed economies the government is a major consumer as well as producer of goods and services, consequently providing employment and incomes for many people. Government spending, or public expenditure, therefore accounts for a large share of total spending in many economies.

To pay for their spending, governments receive revenues from direct taxes taken from the incomes of individuals and firms, and from indirect taxes added to the prices of many goods and services. Governments will use their public expenditures and taxes as well as a number of other demand-side and supply-side policy instruments to achieve their macroeconomic aims of economic growth, full employment, low and stable price inflation and a stable balance of international trade and payments.

Governments may also have additional aims to improve social and economic welfare through a redistribution of income to poor and low-income households. However, achieving and maintaining their aims both individually and all at the same time can be difficult as economic conditions change.

For example, rates of inflation and unemployment tend to vary with the economic cycle in activity in an economy. During an economic recession, falling demand results in slower or negative economic growth, rising cyclical unemployment and disinflation as the rate at which prices are rising slows down. If a recession is particularly deep and prolonged, economic activity may continue to shrink and result in falling prices or deflation.

In contrast, rising total demand can boost employment and growth but if it increases faster than output is able to expand, demand-pull price inflation is likely to accelerate. Wages are also likely to increase rapidly at or near full employment in the economy, creating additional cost-push inflationary pressures.

Fiscal and monetary policy instruments can be used by governments to moderate the demand-side of their macroeconomies. For example, expansionary fiscal policy may be used to boost total demand during an economic recession to help create jobs and boost economic growth. It involves increasing public expenditures and /or cutting taxes. Similarly, a government may 'loosen' its monetary policy to boost total demand by cutting interest rates to encourage more borrowing and to discourage saving. A government may also expand the money supply if other measures fail to work.

Cutting public spending, raising taxes and increasing interest rates can therefore reduce total demand in an economy or reduce its rate of growth if it is causing price inflation to accelerate. Supply-side policy measures may also be deployed at the same time to boost factor productivity and total output in the economy. Prices are less likely to rise or rise rapidly if the total supply of goods and services is able to expand at the same rate as total demand is increasing.

Unit 4.1 The role of government
Unit 4.2 The macroeconomic aims of government

The role of government

Governments perform many roles or functions in modern mixed economies. A primary function of any government is to correct failures of free markets to produce socially and economically desirable outcomes. However, how governments do this and how much they intervene in their economies varies significantly between different countries. Different governments can have very different priorities and these will often depend on the economic, political and sometimes personal beliefs of those in power. ➤ **2.11.2**

The government as an employer

To perform its functions, a government will need to be an employer, producer, consumer and regulator in the economy. For example, government or public sector organizations in France employ around 22% of the French workforce and are responsible for around 57% of total expenditure in the French economy.

Public sector employees will work in the following public sector organizations:

- national, regional and local government authorities and their administrative departments and offices;

- government agencies responsible for the delivery of public services such as a food standards agency, a health authority or law enforcement agency;

- state-owned enterprises. ➤ **3.5.1**

Together these organizations make up the general government or public sector of an economy.

▲ Government is a major employer in many countries. Public sector employees include civil servants employed in government departments, members of the armed forces, the police and judiciary, teachers, doctors and nurses

The government as a producer

A government may own factors of production such as land and capital and will combine them with labour to produce and supply certain goods and services that private sector firms may undersupply. These may include merit goods such as education, healthcare and public goods including national defence and security, national parks and street lighting. ➤ **2.10.2**

State-owned enterprises in some countries may also run airports, banks and television stations and provide public transport, postal services and essential items such as power and water supplies. ➤ **3.5.1**

The government as a provider

Governments will often provide or pay for the provision of goods and services direct to certain groups of people in their economies. For example, people on low incomes may be provided with free or low-cost housing and travel. Children may also receive free or subsidized travel and dental care from their governments. Old people and people with severe disabilities may be cared for in government-run homes. Older people who have retired from work may also receive a state pension from the governments of some countries.

Similarly, a government may pay for or provide research facilities to support private sector firms developing new products and support the incomes of farmers to protect domestic food supplies.

The government as a consumer

The government is a major consumer of different goods and services in many countries. That is, government spending or **public expenditure** accounts for a large share of total spending in many economies. ➤ **2.11.1**

Recurrent government spending on goods and services that are consumed within each financial year is called **current expenditure**. It includes the wages and salaries of public sector workers, state pensions and welfare payments as well as payments for many consumable items such as pens and paper, and the day to day running costs of government offices.

In contrast, **capital expenditures** are government investments in long-lived productive assets such as roads, dams, schools, hospitals and other public infrastructure. Capital expenditure can therefore have a lasting impact on an economy and can help to expand its productive capacity. ➤ **4.3.2**

The government as a law maker and regulator

Governments will set and enforce laws and regulations that govern the way people and firms should behave from laws governing murder and other violent acts, to laws prohibiting the dumping of waste, smoking in public places, misleading advertising and discrimination.

Markets that would otherwise produce outcomes considered socially or economically undesirable will often be regulated by governments, for example, through price controls and regulations governing product quality and safety, health and safety standards in workplaces, the treatment of animals, the disposal of hazardous waste and many other productive activities and practices. ➤ **2.11.2**

The government as a tax setter and collector

All the roles and functions of government have to be paid for. Taxes are generally the main source of finance for government activities. Governments must therefore determine what taxes should be paid and by whom and must then ensure that they collected. However, not all taxes are used to raise public revenue. Some may be used to control what and how much consumers buy of particular products. ➤ **4.3.3**

Local, regional and national government

Government roles, functions and responsibilities are often divided up between different tiers or levels of government.

The **central government** is the national government of a country or nation-state and will be responsible for planning and decision-making on issues that affect the whole country including macroeconomic management, national security and the legal system.

Taxes collected from firms and individuals, from their incomes, spending or wealth, are used to fund government expenditures. Governments must therefore also act as tax setters and tax collectors in their economies.

The central government of a country will also be responsible for:

- managing the nation's currency;

- maintaining diplomatic and trading relationships with other countries;

- negotiating international treaties, for example on trade, defence or fighting climate change;

- if applicable, representing the interests of their country in global organizations such as the United Nations (UN), the World Trade Organization (WTO) and the International Monetary Fund (IMF).

In contrast, local and regional government authorities will usually be responsible for decision-making on issues that affect the towns, cities and administrative areas they govern as well as implementing many national policies, laws and regulations at their local levels.

The split of responsibilities and powers between local and central government authorities varies between different countries. For example, some countries such as the UK, Germany and Canada have very powerful regional governments with many powers to set taxes, make laws and manage public expenditures passed down or 'devolved' to them from their central governments.

▼ Some examples of local and central government roles and responsibilities

Local government	Central government
Refuse collection and waste management	Macroeconomic management
Running local libraries	National law-making and enforcement
Maintaining public parks and baths/swimming pools	Issuing money (notes and coins)
Local road maintenance	Building and maintaining major roads and motorways
Local land-use planning	National security and defence
Enforcing building controls	Police and armed forces
Fire control and public safety	Public education
Enforcement of business trading standards	Public healthcare (i.e. National Health Service)
Provision of social housing	Social benefits such as the State Pension
Street lighting	Accountable for state-owned enterprises
Setting and collecting local taxes	Setting and collecting national taxes

SECTION 4.2.1

The macroeconomic aims of government

What is a macroeconomy?

Macroeconomics is the study of how a national economy works. It involves understanding the interaction between changes in total demand and output and national income, employment and price inflation in an economy. In contrast, **microeconomics** analyses the market behaviour of individual consumers and producers and how different markets work. ➤ **2.1.1**

Macroeconomics and microeconomics are closely related. A **macroeconomy** consists of all the different markets for goods and services, labour, money, foreign exchange and all other traded items. Changes in the behaviour of different producers and consumers in individual markets can therefore affect the distribution of incomes, total output and the overall level of prices, employment and trade in a macroeconomy.

In fact, it is useful to think of a macroeconomy as one big market consisting of the total demand for all goods and services available in the economy and the total supply of all those goods and services. It follows that rising total demand or falling total supply will tend to push up market prices in the economy thereby resulting in a general price inflation. ➤ **4.8.1**

However, a fall in the total supply of goods and services will tend to reduce prices and economic growth as less output is produced. Similarly, falling total demand will help lower price inflation but could result in higher unemployment as firms cut back production in response to lower demand for their goods and services.

The very simple diagram below represents a macroeconomy. The total value of all final goods and services produced in a macroeconomy in a given year is its **gross domestic product (GDP)**. The total output or GDP is paid for by the total expenditure of consumers, firms and government. Workers and owners of land and capital supply their resources to private firms and public sector organizations to produce those goods and services. In return they are paid income, and their total income is therefore the national income. ➤ **4.6.2**

▼ Total demand and supply in a simple macroeconomy

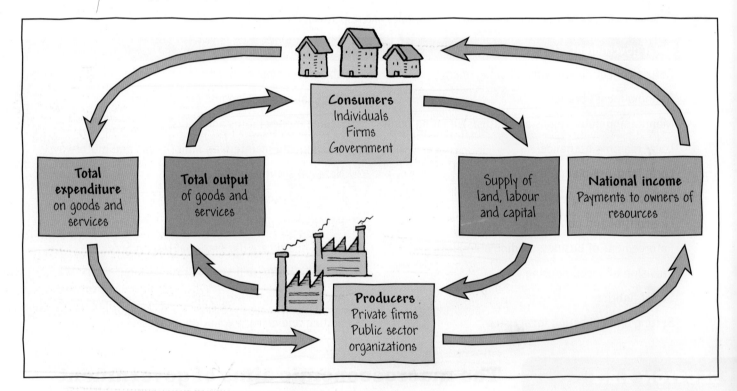

Macroeconomic aims

The total expenditure or **demand** in a macroeconomy is therefore the sum of the following:

- **consumer expenditure** on consumer goods and services;

- **investment expenditure** by firms on machinery and other capital equipment to be used in the production of other goods and services;

- **public sector expenditure** by government organizations on capital and consumer goods and services;

- **exports** of goods and services sold to overseas residents.

Total expenditure in an economy is therefore spent on the total quantity supplied of all goods and services in that economy. This is the sum of all goods and services supplied by private firms and public sector organizations in the economy.

Most national governments have four main economic aims or objectives for their macroeconomies. These are:

1 **economic growth** in the total output and income of the national economy and increased standards of living; ➤ **4.6.2**

2 a high and stable level of **employment**, and therefore a very low level of unemployment (this may be referred to as **full employment**); ➤ **4.7.1**

3 a low and stable rate of **inflation** in the general level of prices; ➤ **4.8.1**

4 a stable **balance of international trade and payments**. ➤ **6.4.1**

A government may also have additional objectives which aim to improve the economic and social welfare of people in the economy, including:

- to reduce poverty and inequalities in income and wealth;

- to reduce pollution and waste, protect the natural environment and therefore encourage more sustainable economic growth.

If a government can achieve these macroeconomic objectives it can help to create a more favourable environment for economic and human development. ➤ **5.4.1**

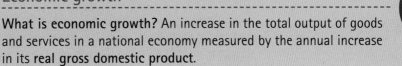

Economic growth

What is economic growth? An increase in the total output of goods and services in a national economy measured by the annual increase in its **real gross domestic product**.

Why is negative growth bad for business and an economy?

Many people are better off today than they were 20 or more years ago because most economies have experienced economic growth over time. However, steady economic growth may not be achieved every year. Sometimes economic growth can turn negative and when this happens:

- There is a sustained reduction in total output or GDP. Fewer people will be employed and so incomes and consumer spending will be falling.

- Firms will lose sales and profits. Many may be forced to close if consumer demand continues to fall.

- There will be fewer business opportunities. Entrepreneurs will not invest in new firms and may move existing production to other countries where economic growth and conditions are better.

- As incomes and profits fall, government revenue from taxes will fall and government spending on roads, schools and healthcare may have to be cut.

Why aim to control economic growth? Sustained economic growth will create new business opportunities and jobs. Output, employment and incomes will rise and living standards will improve.

Possible growth targets: Some governments may set targets for economic growth in their economies. For example, the government of China set an economic growth target for 2018 of 6.5% while the UK government aims to achieve a rate of growth in the UK economy that averages out at around 2.5% each year over the long run.

Full employment/low unemployment

What is unemployment? People who are willing and able to work are unable to find work because of a lack of suitable job opportunities. It is usually measured by the percentage of the adult or working population seeking work or receiving unemployment benefits.

Why is high unemployment bad for business and an economy?

- As unemployment rises, fewer people will be in work and so fewer goods and services will be produced. Total output in the economy will fall.

- Fewer people will be in paid work so total income will be lower. As a result, consumer spending will fall and businesses will lose revenue.

- The government may have to spend more on welfare or social security payments to support the unemployed and their families. Taxes on firms and working people may be increased to pay for the additional government spending. This will reduce their disposable incomes and cause demand to fall. Alternatively, the government may have to cut spending on building roads, on education or supporting new firms.

- People who are unemployed for a long time may deskill (lose their skills).

Why aim to control employment? If a government can reduce unemployment and expand employment opportunities, more people will be in paid work and earning regular incomes. As employment increases, total output will expand, consumer spending will rise, more business opportunities are created and government spending on welfare can be reduced as living standards improve.

Possible employment targets: Different governments will at different times express loose targets for employment or unemployment in their countries. For example, in 2012 the South African government set a target to reduce the unemployment rate from 25% to 6% by 2030. Similarly, in 2010 European Union member countries agreed to target an employment rate of 'at least 75% for persons aged between 20 and 64' across the EU by 2020.

Low and stable price inflation

What is inflation? A sustained increase in the average price of goods and services available for sale in an economy. If inflation is increasing, it means the rate at which prices are rising is accelerating.

Why is high price inflation bad for business and an economy?

- As prices rise, consumers cannot afford to buy as many goods or services as they did before so demand and sales fall. This is because rising prices reduce **real incomes**. Real income is a measure of the purchasing power of money. If a person's income rises by 2% but prices rise by 5%, then that person's real income, and therefore the amount that he or she could have bought with it, will have fallen by 3%.

- Business costs increase as the prices of the goods and services they purchase increase. Workers may also demand higher wages and salaries so they can keep up with rising prices.

- The prices of goods produced in the economy will rise faster than those produced by firms located in countries with lower rates of inflation. As a result, consumers may buy more imported products from overseas firms.

Why aim to control inflation? If a government can reduce price inflation and keep it low, it will make it easier for firms to manage their costs, for exporters to sell their products overseas and for consumers, especially those on low incomes, to continue buying the goods and services they want and need.

Possible inflation targets: Although most governments have little or no direct control over the prices of the vast majority of goods and services in their countries many do however set targets for price inflation. For example, between 2015 and 2017 the government of Indonesia aimed to keep annual price inflation at 3%, plus or minus 1%. Similarly successive UK governments have targeted annual inflation of 2%.

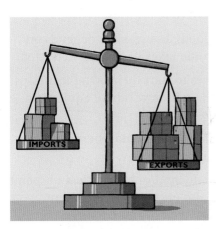

Balance of payments stability

What is the balance of payments? International trade involves the exchange of goods, services and money across national borders. The **balance of payments** of a country provides a record of the value of all its international trade and financial transactions with other countries.

Why is an unfavourable balance of trade and payments bad for business and an economy? No country can produce everything its population needs and wants. Every country must therefore **import** some goods and services from other countries. **Exports** of goods and services to consumers overseas will earn foreign currency that can be used for to pay for imported products.

If a country spends more on imports than it receives from the sale of exports its balance of international trade will be in deficit. This can cause the following problems:

- The country may run out of foreign currency to buy imports and may have to borrow money from overseas.
- The national currency may lose value against other foreign currencies. This means it will be worth less than before and this will make imported goods and services more expensive to buy. In turn this can increase price inflation.
- Firms that need to import materials and parts from overseas to produce their own products will face rising costs.

Why control international trade and payments? A favourable balance of international trade and payments provides opportunities for businesses to export their goods and services overseas. It also provides jobs and incomes and ensures the economy can afford to import a wide variety of goods and services to satisfy consumer needs and wants.

Possible targets: Governments may often announce they want to increase exports, target new markets overseas and/or to reduce their trade deficits with other countries. But few adopt specific targets because international trade is affected by so many global factors beyond the control of any individual country. However, in 2017 the Nigerian government set a target to achieve $100bn in annual revenues from non-oil exports. This included a target to raise $7bn each year from the export of cashew nuts.

Macroeconomic management

All the different markets for factor resources, goods and services in an economy make up the macroeconomy of a country. A macroeconomy therefore has a demand-side and a supply-side just like every individual market. The interaction of total demand and supply will determine the equilibrium level of prices and total level of output and employment in a macroeconomy.

Governments will often therefore intervene in their macroeconomies using 'tools' known as **policy instruments** to change or influence total demand and supply in order to achieve their economic objectives for inflation, employment, output and international trade.

Demand-side policies

Demand-side policies try to influence the level of total demand in an economy using a number of different policy instruments, which are:

- total public expenditure ➤ **4.3.2**
- the overall level of taxation ➤ **4.3.4**
- the rate of interest. ➤ **4.4.2**

These demand-side policy instruments can be effective for these reasons:

- The amount consumers have to spend on goods and services depends on their level of **disposable income** after income taxes have been deducted.

- Taxes on profits will affect people's incentives to start their own businesses and the amount of money firms have to invest in new capital equipment and expanding their scale of production.

- Increasing public expenditure can boost total demand and, therefore, stimulate higher output and employment in an economy.

- As interest rates rise consumers may save more and/or borrow less to spend on consumer goods and services. This may also encourage investments from overseas. As interest rates fall firms may borrow more to invest.

- Public spending and taxes can also be used to redistribute income and wealth from rich people to poorer people.

Supply-side policies

Supply-side policies aim to boost the productive potential of an economy. Boosting the total supply of goods and services in an economy will help to raise its rate of economic growth and reduce inflationary pressures. ➤ **4.5.2**

Supply-side policy instruments are used to reduce or remove barriers to increased employment and higher levels of productivity and to create incentives for firms and workers to increase their output. Supply-side policy instruments will include:

- targeted public expenditures, for example providing government subsidies to firms to encourage them to fund the research and development (R&D) of new and more efficient production processes and products;

- targeted tax changes, for example reducing taxes on wages and profits to increase the reward from work and enterprise;

- new regulations and reforms, for example introducing legislation to outlaw unfair and anti-competitive practices by large, powerful firms. ➤ **3.8.2**

Supply-side policy instruments therefore aim to influence the behaviour of specific groups of consumers and producers in particular markets to help achieve the macroeconomic aims of government.

ECONOMIC GROWTH IS STIMULATED BY COMPETITION — LOWER TAXES, REDUCING THE POWER OF THE UNIONS AND MONOPOLIES, HELPING BUSINESS.

Being instrumental

Read the news articles and headlines below. Use them to identify different objectives governments have for their economies and what they are doing to try to achieve them.

SWEDEN TO CUT TAXES AGAIN

Sweden's government said on Saturday it would cut income tax by a total of 10 billion Swedish crowns ($1.45 billion) from next year, a move it said would boost employment.

Higher taxes on car imports to curb trade deficit

The Vietnam Ministry of Industry and Trade has proposed a rise in import duties on cars and a new luxury tax on mobile phones to narrow its international trade deficit. Payments for imported goods exceeded earnings from exports sold overseas by a record $17.5 billion last year.

Venezuela to increase public spending to boost economy and cut unemployment

The Venezuelan government will increase public spending to boost economic growth and generate employment in response to the global crisis. The government will invest in houses, schools, hospitals, roads and other public works projects, the President told the Venezuelan state newspaper.

Taiwan cuts interest rates to boost exports

Taiwan announced an emergency cut in its interest rate yesterday after data showed exports falling at a record pace.

The central bank said the slump in exports was having a severe impact on the economy. 'Cutting interest rates will help to increase consumer spending,' it said. 'It will also help reduce borrowing costs for companies and help boost new investment.'

'Exports are a key economic driver and if exports are bad, then it will reduce investments, and force companies to cut their workforce' experts warned.

India Raises Interest Rate to 8% to Curb Inflation

India's central bank unexpectedly raised interest rates for the first time in 15 months to combat a surge in inflation sparked by rising food and energy costs.

China launches tax reforms to boost economic growth

China's government announced it would reduce the tax burden on companies by more than 120 billion yuan ($17.6 billion) next year.

The changes will enable companies to get deductions against the taxes they must pay from spending on fixed assets such as new machinery and equipment.

Value added taxes paid by small businesses and the self-employed were reduced to 3% from 6%.

The government said the reforms would help encourage technological upgrading at Chinese companies and boost domestic demand.

Germany sticks to its target for a million electric vehicles by 2020

The German government is sticking to its goal of having 1 million electric vehicles (EVs) on the country's roads by 2020 and has recently announced new incentives to boost demand. German car buyers will now receive a 4,000 euro subsidy towards the cost of each battery electric vehicle and 3,000 euros for plug-in hybrid electric vehicles.

The new proposal does not stop at subsidizing EVs. The German government also plans to invest 300 million euros in roadside charging facilities for EVs between 2017 and 2020.

German car giants including BMW and Volkswagen, have in the past been the major recipients of government subsidies totaling some 350 million to fund the development of EVs and the batteries that power them.

Possible conflicts between macroeconomic aims

Lower unemployment or slower price inflation?

The macroeconomic objectives of a government can prove difficult to achieve individually but especially all at the same time. Macroeconomic policy aims can often conflict.

For example, some policy measures to reduce unemployment and boost economic growth may result in higher rates of price inflation. For example, a government may increase its spending and cut taxes to boost the total demand for goods and services in the economy. This in turn should help to create more jobs and incomes. However, as total demand increases the market prices of many goods and services will also tend to rise.

If price inflation is high and rising, a government may introduce measures to reduce total demand. For example, it may increase taxes on incomes, cut public expenditures and raise interest rates to make borrowing more expensive. Reducing total demand may help to slow down the rate at which prices are rising and many even reduce some product prices, but firms are likely to respond by cutting production and reducing their workforces.

Full employment with low rates of unemployment may therefore be difficult to achieve at the same time as maintaining low and stable price inflation.

More growth, more jobs or more imports?

Demand-side measures to increase total demand in an economy might boost total output, employment and incomes but may also encourage consumers to spend more on imported goods and services. This will affect the stability of the balance of payments. Faster economic growth in the national output may also result in more pollution and waste, possibly conflicting with any environmental objectives. ➤ 4.6.5

Do macroeconomic aims always conflict?

However, not all economists accept there will always be trade-offs or conflicts between government macroeconomic aims. That is, they see no reason why low unemployment, low and stable prices, economic growth and balance of payments stability cannot be achieved together. Government economic policies, they argue, can and should be designed to do so.

If price inflation can be reduced to a low and stable rate then more employment, faster economic growth and a favourable balance of payments can be achieved. Rising national income and employment also means people will become better off, thereby helping to reduce poverty. Rising incomes will also mean tax revenues collected by the government from wages and profits will be increasing and can be used to fund higher welfare payments, investments in new infrastructure such as roads and schools, and other public expenditures that will benefit the economy and growth.

Reducing inflation will help make domestically produced goods and services more competitive. As a result, demand for them will tend to rise at home and in overseas markets. This will help to improve the international trade balance. Firms will respond to rising demand by increasing their output and demand for labour. Firms will also want to invest in new machinery and production facilities as the economy expands. This is because they will be more confident of earning a good profit from their investments. Further, if people expect price inflation to remain low and stable then they are less likely to push for big wage increases to compensate.

Policy conflicts

Look at the macroeconomic data on the US economy between 1990 and 2016 in the graphs below.

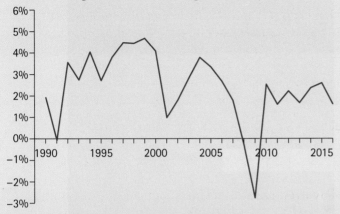

US economic growth (% annual change in real output)

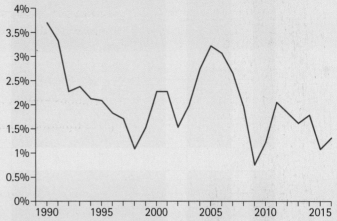

US inflation (% annual change in consumer prices index)

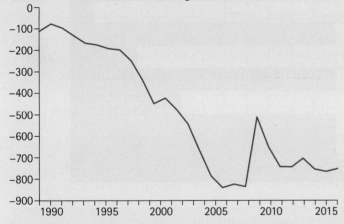

US balance of international trade in goods ($ billion)

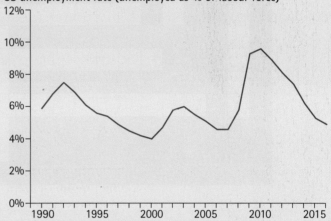

US unemployment rate (unemployed as % of labour force)

1 How successful do you think US governments have been over time in achieving the four main macroeconomic objectives?

2 What evidence is there, if any, from the US economic experience to support the view that economic policy objectives may conflict?

3 Compare and contrast the US economic experience with that of your country over the same period. How successful do you think the national government in your country has been in achieving its macroeconomic aims, and why?

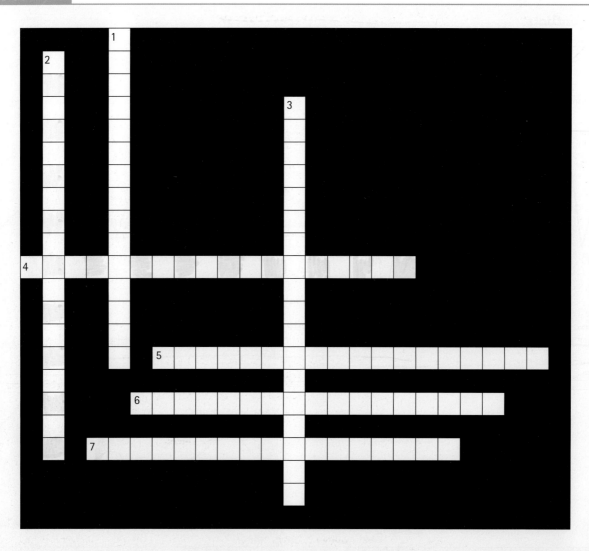

Clues across

4. Government policies that aim to control or influence total demand for goods and services in the economy (6–4, 8)
5. Another term that may be used to describe government objectives for the national economy including low and table prices, full employment and economic growth (13, 3)
6. A collective term for the 'tools' or interventions used by a government including making changes to public spending, taxes and interest rates, that are used to help achieve its macroeconomic aims (6, 11)
7. Another term for general government spending or total public sector spending (6, 11)

Clues down

1. The tier or level of government in a country that is most likely to be responsible for running libraries, maintaining minor roads and enforcing planning and building controls (5, 10)
2. Government policies that aim to boost the productive capacity and output of an economy (6–4, 8)
3. The tier or level of government in a country that is responsible for macroeconomic management, national defence and security and managing international relations (7, 10)

Unit 4.3
Unit 4.4
Unit 4.5

Fiscal policy
Monetary policy
Supply-side policy

IN THIS UNIT

4.3.1	Definition of the budget	▶ Explain the meaning and purpose of a government budget.
4.3.2	Reasons for government spending	▶ Identify the main areas of government spending and the reasons for and effects of spending in these areas.
4.3.3	Reasons for taxation	▶ Understand how taxation is used to finance government spending, influence market outcomes and redistribute incomes.
4.3.4	Principles of taxation	▶ Describe the qualities of a good tax.
4.3.5	Classification of taxes	▶ Identify and contrast the main types of tax (progressive, regressive, proportional, direct and indirect).
4.3.6	Impact of taxation	▶ Analyse the impact of taxation on consumers, producers, government and the macroeconomy.
4.3.7	Definition of fiscal policy	▶ Describe the instruments of fiscal policy (changes in tax and government spending) and their impact on the budget balance or imbalance.
4.3.8	Fiscal policy measures	
4.3.9	Effects of fiscal policy on government macroeconomic aims	▶ Analyse how fiscal policy measures may be used by a government to achieve its macroeconomic aims.
4.4.1	Definition of money supply and monetary policy	▶ Describe the instruments of monetary policy (changes interest rates and the money supply) including how they can influence foreign exchange rates.
4.4.2	Monetary policy measures	
4.4.3	Effects of monetary policy on government macroeconomic aims	▶ Analyse how monetary policy measures may be used by a government to achieve its macroeconomic aims.
4.5.1	Definition of supply-side policy	▶ Describe possible policy measures including improving incentives to work and invest, education and training, labour market reforms, privatization and deregulation.
4.5.2	Supply-side policy measures	
4.5.3	Effects of supply-side policy on government macroeconomic aims	▶ Analyse how supply-side policy measures may be used by a government to achieve its macroeconomic aims.

Definition of the budget

What is the budget?

The Spanish government has approved an austerity budget, including a tax rise for the rich and 8% spending cuts

Australia plans US$3.8 billion budget surplus in two years

Dubai Finance Chief expects budget surplus

Greek crisis worsens as budget deficit grows

Every organization will normally prepare a budget each year so that it can plan and manage its finances.

A budget is simply a forecast of what it will spend and how much it expects to earn from revenue over the next 6 to 12 months. An organization will use its budget forecast to monitor its actual expenditures and revenues as they occur and to look at how similar or how different they are from the forecast and why.

In exactly the same way, a government will prepare a budget each year setting out its plans and forecasts for public spending, taxation and other public revenues. In most countries it is so important it is simply called 'the budget'.

In addition to its forecasts for public expenditure and taxation over the next 12 months, a government will also use its budget to announce changes in tax rates, the introduction of new taxes and, if relevant, the removal of old ones.

Sometimes a government will announce changes in the allocation of public expenditures. Some areas of spending may be cut, for example a reduction in the amount the government plans to spend on defence, while spending on other areas such as healthcare may be increased. New spending initiatives may also be introduced.

- There will be a budget balance if a government plans to spend no more than it will raise in taxes and other public revenues in the same year.

  Balanced budget: public expenditure = public revenues

- If a government plans to spend less in total than it is forecast to receive from total tax and other public revenues there will be a **budget surplus**.

  Budget surplus: public expenditure < public revenue

- In contrast, a government that plans for a **budget deficit** plans to spend more in total than it expects raise in revenue in the same year.

  Budget deficit: public expenditure > public revenue

Budget or bodge it

The figures in the table present the budget forecasts for the government of a small fictitious country for three different years.

Budget plans/forecasts	Year 1	Year 2	Year 3
Total public expenditure ($ million)	250	278	310
Total public revenue ($ million)	270	278	284
Balance on budget ($ million)?			

1   Calculate the budget balance for each year.

2   In which year did the government budget for **a)** a deficit, **b)** a surplus, and **c)** a balanced budget?

Public sector borrowing

In addition to revenues from taxes, a government may also receive other public revenues including:

- interest payments on government loans to private sector firms and overseas governments;

- rents from publicly owned buildings and land rented to the private sector as well any admission charges, for example from public museums and national monuments;

- revenues from government agencies and state-owned enterprises from the sale of goods or services such as postal services and public transport;

- proceeds from the sale (or privatization) of government-owned industries and other publicly owned assets, such as land and public buildings.

However, these other sources of public revenue tend to be relatively small and are unlikely to cover or pay off a budget deficit. If a government spends more than it raises from taxes and any other public revenues then it must borrow the difference.

The amount of money a government needs each year to finance any shortfall of public revenues below total public expenditure is called the **public sector borrowing requirement** or similar.

Governments usually borrow money from the private sector by selling loan stocks or securities, such as government bonds. Short-term debt is generally repaid with interest within one year or less. Long-term debt usually lasts for 10 years or more. Medium-term debt reaches maturity somewhere in between these periods. At maturity the government will repay each bond with interest to the bondholder.

Government debt can be internal debt, owed to private individuals, firms and the banking system within its economy, and external debt owed to overseas banks, residents, governments or international organizations such as the World Bank and International Monetary Fund.

National debt

Each year a government must sell enough debt or secure loans to finance its borrowing requirement. However, every year in which a government borrows more money it will add to its total stock of debt. The total amount of money borrowed by the public sector of a country over time that has yet to be repaid is called the public sector debt or **national debt**.

The national debt is money owed by all levels of government: central, regional, local or municipal government. As the government of a country represents its people and borrows money to finance public spending on their behalf, the national debt is indirectly the debt of taxpayers.

The US national debt was a staggering $19.9 trillion in July 2017, equivalent to around 105% of the US national income. It has risen significantly over time. In 1980 it was less than $1 trillion or around 33% of the US national income.

▼ US national debt...

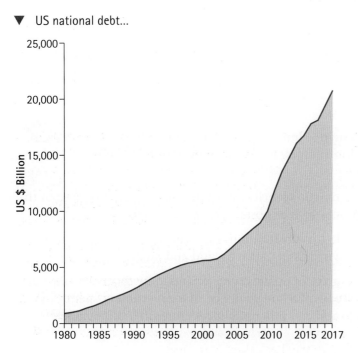

and as a proportion of US GDP

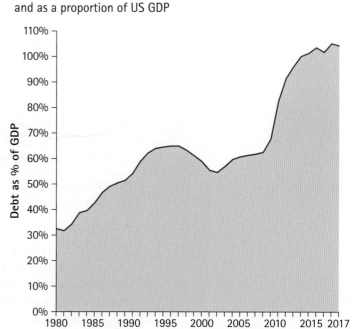

It is useful to compare the national debt of an economy to its national income or GDP because this tells us about the ability of that economy to manage and repay its debts. The table below lists the 10 countries with highest national debt to GDP ratios and the 10 countries with the lowest. You will note that Japan had a national debt in 2016 over twice the size of its national income while countries such as Estonia, Libya and Liberia had relatively little debt compared to the size of their national incomes.

Countries with the highest and lowest ratios of national debt to GDP, 2016

Country	National debt (as % of GDP)	Country	National debt (as % of GDP)
Japan	234.7	Estonia	9.7
Greece	181.6	Libya	10.0
Italy	132.5	Liberia	11.8
Lebanon	132.5	Iran	11.9
Jamaica	130.1	Nigeria	13.2
Portugal	126.2	Russia	13.7
Eritrea	119.8	Algeria	16.8
Cape Verde	116.8	Congo	18.2
Singapore	110.5	Chile	18.5
Grenada	110.0	Oman	18.5

Source: *CIA World Factbook*

As the national debt of a country rises, both in absolute terms and especially as a proportion of its national income, the burden of paying debt interest rises. This burden will increase if the stock of national debt increases at a faster rate than GDP. If economic growth in GDP is slower then debt payments will be rising faster than tax revenues are growing. Taxes will have to increase or public expenditures diverted from other uses to pay the rising interest charges.

However, rising public sector debt and rising interest payments need not be a bad thing as long as the national income or GDP of a country rises faster than the total debt. As income grows, tax revenues will grow by more than enough to meet rising interest charges for the debt. The burden of debt as a proportion of GDP will also be falling. This is just the same for individuals who borrow money from a bank. The burden of their debt and interest payments will fall as their income and ability to pay back their loan rises.

ACTIVITY 4.4

Greece lightning

1 What is a budget deficit?

2 What happened to the budget deficit in Greece over time and why?

3 What has been the impact of successive budget deficits on public sector borrowing and debt in Greece?

4 Why has Greece required financial help from the EU and IMF?

5 Why did the EU and the IMF insist Greece cut its public spending and raises taxes? What impact did this have on the Greek economy?

6 What could be the likely impact on government finances and the economy of Greece if it continues to fail to control its budget deficit?

Greece faces three years of recession – as it tries to slash its budget deficit

Greece has been living well beyond its means in recent years, and its rising level of debt has placed a huge strain on the country's economy as it tries to meet spiralling debt interest charges and loan repayments.

The Greek government borrowed heavily and went on something of a spending spree during the past decade. Public spending soared and public sector wages practically doubled during that time. Despite a legal retirement age of 61 many people in Greece were able to retire on a full state pension as early as age 50. There was also widespread tax evasion.

By 2010 the Greek government had run out of money and was unable to meet its debt repayments. The amount it owed had increased from just over 148bn euros in 2000 to almost 330bn euros in 2010 and because of its high level of debt was unable to borrow any more. As a result the European Union (EU) and International Monetary Fund (IMF) agreed a 110bn euros ($145bn) rescue package on the condition that the Greek government increased taxes and cut public spending, for example on pensions and the wages of public sector workers. This proved very unpopular and resulted in widespread protests and strikes.

Over the next few years the real GDP of Greece fell sharply and unemployment climbed to almost 30%. Fearing the Greek economy was close to collapse, further rescue packages and debt reliefs were agreed with the EU and the IMF.

By 2017 the national debt of Greece was still over 300bn euros and the Greek government was still struggling to meet its loan repayments. In June 2017 the European authorities authorized a further 7.5bn euros in bailout aid to allow the country to continue paying its bills.

Why and how do governments spend public money?

Reasons for government spending

There is wide variation between countries in terms of how much their governments spend each year both in total and as a proportion of total spending in their economies. For example, in 2017 government spending in Cuba accounted for just under 65% of total expenditure in Cuba while in Guatemala, government spending accounted for just 12.5% of the Guatemalan economy.

Despite these wide variations, most countries have seen their public expenditures rising over time as a proportion of total expenditure or GDP. For example, the chart below shows how public expenditure as a percentage of GDP has changed since 1995 in a number of countries including Denmark and the US. Public sector spending as a proportion of GDP fell during the 1990s in many of these economies while they were enjoying healthy economic growth. However, public expenditure increased rapidly in these and other developed economies between 2007 and 2010 as many governments increased their own spending in an attempt to boost total demand, employment and output in their economies during an economic recession that affected many countries. ➤ **4.6.3**

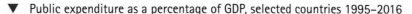

▼ Public expenditure as a percentage of GDP, selected countries 1995–2016

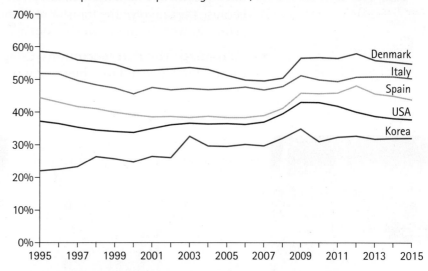

Source: *Organisation for Economic Cooperation and Development, data.oecd.org*

Different governments also spend vastly different amounts on different things. Public spending priorities and needs differ. For example, government spending on public healthcare in the UK is around £145 billion (US$205 billion) each year, accounting for 18% of total public expenditures in the UK in 2017. In contrast, military spending by the government of Saudi Arabia was 190 billion Riyals (US$51 billion) in 2017, some 21% of total public spending in the Kingdom that year.

Despite these wide variations between governments, most government spending has similar objectives:

- **To provide goods and services that are socially and economically desirable** including **public goods**, such as street lighting and national parks, and **merit goods** including education, healthcare and affordable housing for people on low incomes. These goods will be undersupplied in a free market economy. ➤ **1.1.2**

- **To invest in social and economic infrastructure** such as roads and railway networks, reservoirs, schools, hospitals and other public buildings to support growth and human and economic development in their economies. ➤ **5.4.1**

- **To support agriculture and other key industries** by providing financial assistance or **subsidies** to firms to reduce their costs of production and make investments in staff training, new machinery, and the research and development (R&D) of new products, processes and materials.

- **To reduce inequalities in incomes and help vulnerable people**, for example by providing income support and other welfare payments for people and families in need or on low incomes. Financial payments that a government gives to individuals, usually through a social welfare programme such as disability allowances, child support payments, old-age pensions and unemployment compensation, are known as **transfer payments**. This is because they involve the transfer of money collected through taxes from people in work to those who are not able to be economically active.

- **To manage the macroeconomy** using public expenditures and taxes to control total demand to achieve economic growth, reduce unemployment and avoid high and unstable periods of price inflation. ➤ **4.2.1**

▲ Public expenditures will benefit many private sector firms

Many private sector firms therefore benefit directly from different public expenditures or indirectly from their impact on total demand in a macroeconomy. Here are some examples:

- Construction firms benefit from contracts to build roads, schools and other publicly funded infrastructure.

- Office equipment manufacturers benefit from public spending on equipping public offices.

- Farms may benefit from agricultural subsidies to increase their production of food.

- Power companies earn revenue from electricity supplied for street lighting and government buildings.

- The defence industry benefits from orders for defence equipment.

- Public sector workers use their incomes to buy goods and services from firms.

- Some firms receive government grants and subsidies to fund new R&D, to buy equipment and premises, and to train employees.

Cutting or raising public expenditure can therefore have a big impact on consumers, employees and the activities and profitability of many private sector firms, as we will discover in later sections.

Reasons for taxation

Principles of taxation

Taxes are by far the most important source of public sector revenue. Not surprisingly, therefore, as public expenditures around the world have risen over time as the proportion of total expenditure, so too has the tax burden.

▼ Total taxation as a percentage of GDP, selected countries 2017

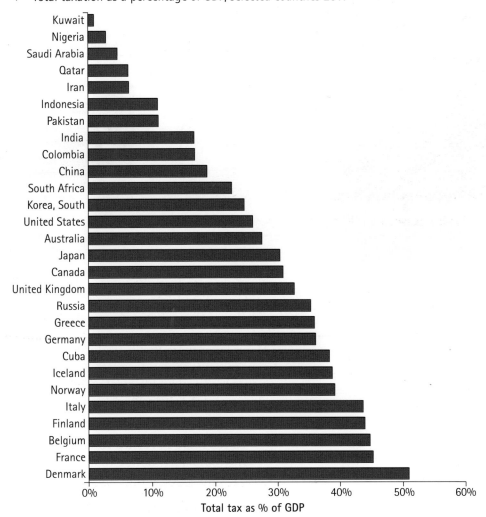

Source: *Heritage Foundation*

The proportion of tax taken from the national income of an economy measures the total **tax burden** in that national economy. Individuals and firms also have personal or corporate tax burdens measured by the amount of tax they each have to pay as a proportion of their incomes. Tax burdens can vary greatly between different individuals, firms and countries depending on the design of their tax systems.

Tax evasion and avoidance

Taxes are compulsory payments backed by laws. Non-payment of tax, or tax evasion, is a punishable offence.

Some taxes can, however, be avoided legally. For example, taxes on cars or petroleum can be avoided by not owning or driving a car. Taxes on cigarettes can be avoided by not smoking. Similarly, wealthy people and multinational companies often avoid taxes in one country by moving their wealth to countries with lower tax rates.

ACTIVITY 4.5

Why have taxes?

For each of the images below suggest reasons why a government might impose taxes. What impacts could such taxes have on economic activity?

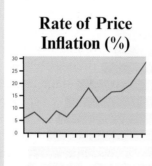

Many taxes were first introduced many hundreds of years ago by kings or governments to pay for wars. For example, the US federal government in 1862 introduced an income tax for the first time to pay for the Civil War. It was 3% of incomes above $600, rising to 5% of incomes above $10,000. Today, the reasons for taxes are far more complex.

- **Taxes raise revenue to fund public expenditures.** Taxes are the main way of raising money to finance public sector spending in most economies.

- **Taxes are used to manage the macroeconomy.** For example, raising taxes can help to reduce the rate of price inflation in an economy by reducing the rate at which total demand is growing. Cutting taxes can therefore increase total demand and help to boost output and employment. ➤ 4.3.8

America's soft drinks industry battles proposals to tax sugary sodas

'Increasing taxes on drinks with high sugar content is the most effective way to reduce consumption' argue researchers at Yale University. They estimate a new tax would reduce the medical costs of treating obesity and dental problems by $50 billion and raise $150 billion in tax revenue in a decade.

However, powerful drinks manufacturers have argued their products should not be singled out over other food products with high sugar content. 'Taxing our industry more will simply harm jobs and people's livelihoods', argued a spokesperson for the industry.

Singapore plans to introduce Southeast Asia's first carbon tax from 2019

A tax of between S$10 and S$20 per ton will be charged on emissions of carbon dioxide and five other greenhouse gases. More than 30 big polluters such as power plants will be required to pay the tax in an attempt to encourage them to invest in cleaner energy sources

A growing number of countries have already introduced or plan to implement taxes on harmful emissions from the burning of fossil fuels such as coal and oil to slow down climate change.

- **Taxes can reduce inequalities in income.** High incomes can be taxed more than lower ones to reduce inequalities between after-tax incomes.

- **Taxes can discourage spending on imported goods.** A tax or tariff on the prices of goods purchased from producers overseas can encourage consumers to buy domestically produced goods instead. This will reduce a balance of payments deficit and boost indigenous output and employment. ➤ **6.2.4**

- **Taxes can discourage the consumption and production of harmful products.** For example, taxes can be used to raise the prices of products such as alcohol and tobacco so that demand for them contracts. ➤ **2.11.2**

- **Taxes can be used to protect the environment.** Increased taxes on productive activities that create pollution or harm the natural environment will reduce the profits associated with these activities. For example, taxes on landfill can encourage firms to recycle more of their waste by making dumping waste in landfill sites more expensive. Similarly, taxes on products that pollute or harm the environment can deter consumption of them. For example, many countries' tax petrol to cut car use and harmful exhaust emissions. ➤ **2.10.3**

ACTIVITY 4.6

When is a tax a good tax?

Look at the imaginary taxes proposed below. For each one consider whether or not it is a good tax or a bad tax from the point of view of:

- ▶ the taxpayer
- ▶ the government
- ▶ the economy.

> **Overtime to be taxed at 95 per cent of earnings.**

> **Pay-as-you-earn income tax to be abolished. Tax-payers will receive bills every two years.**

> **New tax office set up at an annual cost of $15 million to administer tax on pet cats. The government expects its cat tax to raise $7 million in revenue each year.**

> **Tax system to be simplified! All taxes to be abolished and to be replaced by equal tax payment of $2 000 per person per year over the age of 18 years.**

> **Height tax to be introduced on all people under 5 feet and over 6 feet tall, says Minister of Finance, who is 5 feet 6 inches, in his Budget speech.**

What is a good tax?

A good tax should be designed with the following principles in mind.

1 Equity

This means taxes should be fair and tax taxpayers with similar characteristics, such as firms with similar levels of profits in the same industry or people earning the same incomes, in broadly the same way. This could also mean taxing people and firms according to their ability to pay. If most people think that a tax is unfair, they are unlikely to pay it. For example, a tax based on height would be very unfair.

2 Non-distortionary

As far as possible, taxes used to raise revenue should not affect or distort sensible economic behaviour. For example, taxes on incomes and profits should not be set so high as to discourage enterprise or people from working.

3 Certainty

People and firms should know when a tax should be paid and how much they should pay. Tax rates should also be relatively stable from year to year and should not be subject to sudden fluctuations. This allows people and firms to know broadly how much tax they will need to pay in the future and to plan their finances accordingly.

ACTIVITY 4.7

Window tax: Daylight robbery or a smashing idea?

Government proposes new tax

Only a month after the last budget, the Government last night announced plans to once again broaden the existing tax base in the economy. Such plans include imposing a flat rate tax on the number and size of windows in a property.

Speaking at a meeting of industrialists, the Finance Minister told delegates that the issue of reducing the amount of Government borrowing must not be 'glazed over' and that

if the public wished for public sector provision to remain at a high level then they must be prepared to provide the necessary funds.

Raising taxes on income and expenditure would only further reduce demand and output in the economy as work incentives and consumption plans would be damaged.

Business owners speculating that double glazed windows may be sub-

ject to a higher rate of tax have argued that such a move may seriously damage this particular growth area. The Government was, however, quick to reject such fears.

A study of the feasibility of the tax should be ready in time for next year's budget that already promises to provide the economy with a major tax shake up.

(▶)

Divide into groups of three or four. Imagine you have been appointed to research and report on t
proposed window tax. You are to write your report assessing the tax on the following grounds:

a Fairness

b The effect on consumption expenditure, output and employment

c The cost of collection

d The ease with which the tax payable can be calculated.

Your completed reports can form the basis of a class discussion. (You may be surprised to learn that a window tax did exist in the UK many years ago but has long since been abolished.)

4 Convenience

It must be simple and easy for people and firms to pay the taxes they owe on a regular basis. For example, income taxes are often collected by employers every month from the wages and salaries of their employees. People and firms can now also pay their taxes online in many countries using their debit or credit card, or electronic bank account transfers. A government will also need to receive tax revenues on a regular basis to pay for its recurrent expenditures.

5 Simplicity

Taxes should be easy to understand. If they are too complex people and firms may find it difficult to calculate how much tax they owe and could keep getting it wrong.

6 Administrative efficiency

Taxes should be cheap and easy to collect. There is little point introducing a tax if it costs more money to collect than it earns in revenue. For example, a tax costing $10 million to collect but only bringing in $3 million in revenue would be pointless and a waste of public money.

SECTION 4.3.5

Classification of taxes

SECTION 4.3.6

Impact of taxation

Designing a tax system

All of the taxes in a country are together called its tax system. Governments must decide whether they want a progressive, regressive or proportional tax system. Each type of system will affect people and firms differently.

In a **progressive tax** system the proportion of income taken in tax rises as income increases. This means people or firms with higher incomes pay a higher proportion of their income in tax than those on lower incomes. Governments use progressive taxation because they feel those on higher incomes can afford to pay a larger proportion of their incomes in tax and to reduce income inequality after tax.

▼ An example of a progressive tax system

Annual income	% tax rate	Tax paid
$20,000	20%	$4,000
$50,000	40%	$20,000
$80,000	60%	$48,000

In a **regressive tax** system the proportion of income paid in tax falls as income rises. It may be considered unfair to people or firms with low incomes because a much larger fraction of their income is taken as tax although they will in total pay less tax than those on higher incomes.

▼ An example of a regressive tax system

Annual income	% tax rate	Tax paid
$20,000	50%	$10,000
$50,000	40%	$20,000
$80,000	30%	$24,000

A **proportional tax** takes the same proportion of income whatever the level of income. For example, a tax of 20% on all income is an example of a proportional tax. For this reason a proportional tax may also be referred to as a flat tax.

ACTIVITY 4.8

Tax systems

Look at the following graph.

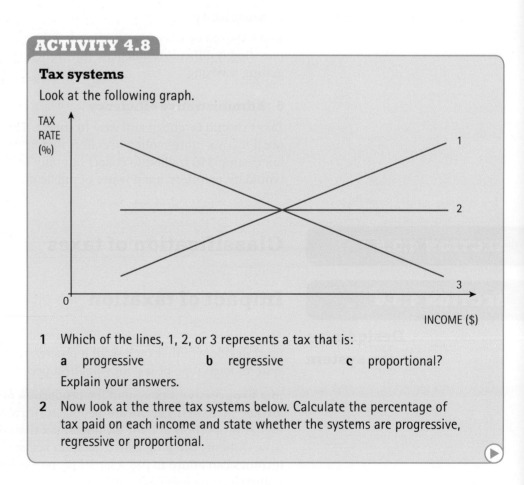

1 Which of the lines, 1, 2, or 3 represents a tax that is:

   a progressive   b regressive   c proportional?

   Explain your answers.

2 Now look at the three tax systems below. Calculate the percentage of tax paid on each income and state whether the systems are progressive, regressive or proportional.

Tax system 1		Tax system 2		Tax system 3	
Annual income	$ tax paid	Annual income	$ tax paid	Annual income	£ tax paid
£5,000	1,500	£10,000	1,000	£8,000	3,200
£15,000	4,500	£16,000	2,400	£12,000	3,600
£25,000	7,500	£30,000	6,600	£20,000	4,000

Direct and indirect taxation

In economics there are two main types of taxes: direct taxes and indirect taxes. Their meaning in law in different countries can differ from how we define these taxes in economics.

Direct taxes are taken directly from individuals or firms and their incomes or wealth. That is, the burden of a direct tax falls on the person or firm responsible for paying it. Direct taxes include income taxes, corporation taxes on company profits, capital gains taxes on property and other valuable assets, and inheritance taxes.

Indirect taxes are taxes taken only indirectly from incomes when they are spent on goods and services. Indirect taxes are therefore sometimes called expenditure or outlay taxes. They include sales taxes, ad valorem taxes, and tariffs and excise duties added to the price of goods and services.

An indirect tax will normally be imposed on producers but they will pass on as much of the burden of the tax as possible to consumers through higher prices.

An indirect tax will increase a firms variable costs of production and therefore cause an upward shift in the firms supply curve. This means less will be supplied at each price and market price will rise. ➤ **2.6.1**

The chart below shows what proportion of total tax revenue was raised from different taxes in South Africa in the 2015–16 financial year. Direct taxes on personal and company incomes raised the most revenue followed by value added tax (VAT) on goods and services. The same pattern can be observed in many developed and developing economies.

▶ Revenue by source and type of tax, South Africa 2015–16

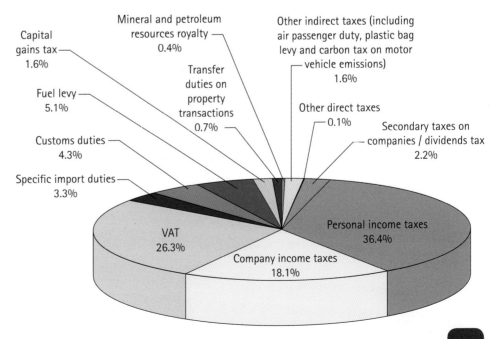

Most taxes are set, or levied, as a percentage (the **tax rate**) of a certain value (the **tax base**). Tax rates can vary significantly from country to country. The table below compares rates of income tax on personal earnings, corporation tax rates on large company profits and value added tax on the prices of many goods and services in a number of different countries.

Notice how similar the corporation tax rates are in many countries. This is because many large companies today are internationally mobile and can relocate their production facilities quite easily anywhere in the world. A country which taxes profits too highly risks losing companies to countries that offer much lower tax rates on profits. Some countries such as Bulgaria and Ireland, among others, offer low corporation taxes on profits in order to attract foreign multinational companies to locate in them. ➤ **6.2.2**

Personal income tax rates vary rather more, and often rise progressively with income, in China and the UK up to 45% of additional income in 2017 and up to 50% in Austria. In contrast, personal incomes, including all forms of salary and capital gains, are not subject to tax in the British Virgin Islands and a number of other Caribbean economies or in any of the United Arab Emirates.

Similarly, corporation taxes on profits are zero rated in the United Arab Emirates except those for foreign banks. In 2017, foreign banks were taxed at 20% of their taxable income in the Emirates of Abu Dhabi, Dubai, Sharjah and Fujairah. The tax is restricted to the taxable income that is earned in each Emirate. Oil companies also pay tax of 55% on their operating profits.

▼ National corporate, income and VAT rates*, selected countries 2017–18

Country	Corporation tax rate %	Personal income tax rate %	VAT (highest rate) %
Austria	25%	21–50%	20%
Bulgaria	10%	10%	20%
British Virgin Islands	0	0	0
China	25%	3–45%	17%
Greece	26%	0–42%	24%
India	30–40%	10–30%	15%
Ireland	12.50%	20–41%	23%
Malta	35%	15–35%	18%
Mexico	30%	0–30%	16%
Sweden	22	0–25%	25%
Turkey	20%	15–35%	18%
United Kingdom	20%	0–45%	20%
United Arab Emirates	0	0	5%

Source: *www.worldwide-tax.com*

National and local taxes

Most taxes are levied by national governments to pay for public expenditures and to help control the macroeconomy. However, regional and local government authorities also spend money to provide local public services. Many receive the bulk of their money in grants from their national governments but some countries also allow local governments to levy their own taxes to raise revenue from local residents and businesses.

There are many examples of local tax systems in the world. For example, in Sweden municipal and county governments can raise money from local income taxes. Tax rates can vary by area and are paid in addition to the national income tax. In 2017–18, the average local income tax rate in Sweden was just over 32%. This meant Swedish residents paid up to 57% of their personal incomes in local and national income taxes.

Similarly, in the USA each state has its own tax system in addition to national taxes. Local taxes usually include taxes on property, income taxes and sales taxes on the prices of goods and services. Some states, including Alaska, Nevada, Florida and Washington, do not levy local income taxes. US cities and counties may also levy additional taxes, for instance to pay directly for the upkeep of parks or schools, or for a police and fire service, local roads and other services. Local taxes on hotel rooms are also common.

Local governments in China can also impose local taxes, including taxes on property, taxes on business turnover and even a slaughter tax on the value of meat from slaughtered animals.

▲ Occupied farmland, the use of rare earth minerals and banquets, among many other items and activities, are taxable in China

EXAM PREPARATION 4.1

a What is the difference between a direct tax and an indirect tax? [2]

b Explain how a reduction in taxation can help to achieve any **two** macroeconomic aims of a government? [4]

c Analyse why a government might wish to increase employment opportunities? [6]

d Discuss the possible consequences of unemployment. [8]

Direct taxes

Income tax

Personal **income tax** is a tax payable from an individual's earnings usually on a pay-as-you-earn basis. Most countries allow people to earn a certain amount of income that is tax-free, usually known as a personal allowance. For example, a person in the UK could earn up to £11,000 in the 2016–17 tax year without having to pay any income tax.

Exactly how much tax a person pays in income tax will depend on how much they earn and in some cases their personal circumstances, for example whether they are single, married, with or without children, old and retired. Income tax in many countries is a progressive tax. That is, higher **marginal tax rates** are applied to progressively higher slices or parts of a person's income. A marginal tax rate is therefore the percentage taken from the next dollar of taxable income above a pre-defined income threshold. The rate may differ for different groups of people. For example, tax-free allowances and marginal rates of tax tend to be more generous for old people and for people with children so that they pay less tax overall than a person who earns the same amount but is single and has no children.

It is useful to distinguish between the average tax rate a person pays and their marginal tax rate. The average tax rate is the total amount of tax paid by a person divided by their total income. The marginal tax rate is the rate of tax paid on each additional dollar of income. A person could therefore pay many different marginal rates of tax on their income, especially if they earn a high income. By adding up the amount of tax paid on each additional slide of income the average tax rate can be calculated.

▼ A simple progressive income tax structure

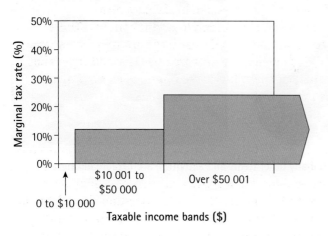

Taxable income bands ($)

For example, the diagram above shows a simple personal income tax with 3 income tax bands, each one with a different and progressively higher marginal rate of tax up to 40%. The first income tax band between $1 and $10,000 is the tax-free personal allowance. No tax is payable by any person on the first $10,000 of their annual taxable incomes.

A person with an annual income of $25,000 will therefore pay a marginal rate of tax of 20% on $15,000 of their income or $3,000 which equates to an average tax rate of 12% on a total income of $25,000. In contrast, a person in the highest marginal tax band with an annual income of $100,000 will pay income tax of $28,000 or an average tax rate of 28% (see the tables below).

▼ How to calculate average tax rates

Person with annual income of $25,000

Taxable income band ($)	Marginal tax rate (A)	Amount of taxable income marginal rate is applied to (B)	Amount of income tax paid (A × B)
$0–10,000	0	$10,000	0
$10,001–50,000	20%	$15,000	$3,000
$50,001 and over	40%	0	0

Total tax paid = $3,000

$$\text{Average rate of tax paid (\%)} = \frac{\text{total tax payable} \times 100}{\text{total income}} = \frac{\$3{,}000 \times 100}{\$25{,}000} = 12\%$$

Person with annual income of $120,000

Taxable income band ($)	Marginal tax rate (A)	Amount of taxable income marginal rate is applied to (B)	Amount of income tax paid (A × B)
$0–10,000	0	$10,000	0
$10,001–50,000	20%	$40,000	$8,000
$50,001 and over	40%	$50,000	$20,000

Total tax paid = $28,000

$$\text{Average rate of tax paid (\%)} = \frac{\text{total tax payable} \times 100}{\text{total income}} = \frac{\$28{,}000 \times 100}{\$100{,}000} = 28\%$$

Income tax is a type of **payroll tax** that employers are required to withhold from the wages of salaries of their employees each week or month. Employees will therefore receive their wages or salaries net of tax deducted. Employers will then pay the income tax they have collected to the government's tax authority. People who are self-employed must provide evidence of their annual earnings and will pay their income tax direct to the government usually in a lump sum once or twice each year.

Other payroll taxes

Other payroll taxes exist in many countries, for example social security contributions to meet the cost of welfare benefits and old-age pensions provided by government, levies to pay for public healthcare and unemployment insurance to pay towards unemployment benefits. These payroll taxes are often based on an individual's earnings but may be payable from an employer's own funds as well as by an employee. Payroll taxes that have to be paid from an employer's own funds are often called employment taxes because they increase the cost of employing workers.

Corporation tax

Corporation tax is levied on the profits of limited companies or corporations and may also be called a profits tax if applied to unincorporated businesses, notably sole traders and partnerships. Sometimes a government may also impose a one-off windfall tax on the profits of a company either thought to be a monopoly and making very significant profits, or benefiting from world events that boosted its profits. For example, the UK has from time to time imposed a windfall tax on the profits of oil companies when they have enjoyed a significant increase in their profits simply as a result of a rise in world oil prices over which they have no direct control.

To encourage new businesses to start up, corporate tax rates on the profits of smaller firms are often set at a low or zero rate in some countries. Corporation tax rates often rise progressively with the scale of profits.

Capital gains tax

It is possible to make a profit from the sale of famous paintings, jewellery, property and other valuable assets that have increased in value over time. Profits made in this way are called capital gains and may be taxed by a government. Sometimes allowances are made, for example for the length of time someone has held an asset – the longer someone has held it the lower the tax the person pays. For example, in Canada, only 50% of a capital gain is classed as taxable income.

Taxes on wealth

Wealth taxes can include taxes on the value of residential and commercial land and property. Wealth taxes can also include inheritance taxes on the transfer of wealth from one person to another upon their death. When an individual dies and leaves his or her house, savings and/or other valuable possessions to someone else, inheritance tax might be payable on the total value inherited.

The impact of direct taxes

Money raised from direct taxes can be used to support many different areas of public expenditure that can benefit people and firms in an economy both directly, for example through the provision of public healthcare, welfare payments and government grants, and indirectly through the impact they can have on economic growth, inflation and job creation.

Advantages of direct taxes

Direct taxes also have a number of other advantages:

✔ High revenue yield

The big advantage of direct taxes like income tax and corporation tax, is that they have a high yield of revenue compared to their cost of collection. The total amount of money collected can be estimated with reasonable accuracy in advance, which is of great help to a government when planning how much it can afford to spend.

✔ They can be used to reduce inequalities in incomes and wealth

The progressive nature of many direct taxes means that wealthier members of society are taxed more heavily than poorer groups, to help reduce inequality.

✔ They are based on ability to pay

A direct tax will usually be based on a person's or firm's ability to pay the tax. Family commitments and dependants can also be taken into consideration and a system of tax allowances can be used to reflect these responsibilities.

Disadvantages of direct taxes

However, direct taxes can also have number of negative impacts in an economy especially if direct tax rates are set too high.

✘ Raising taxes from incomes reduces disposable incomes and consumer demand

Taxes on personal incomes will reduce disposable income: the amount remaining after income and other payroll taxes have been deducted from earnings that people can 'dispose' of how they wish. Therefore, as income taxes rise, consumer spending is likely to fall. Firms producing luxury items are most likely to be affected as consumers continue to buy food and other essential items but reduce their spending on expensive and non-essential goods and services. ➤ 3.2.1

As consumer spending falls the revenues and profits of many firms will decline. In response, firms will reduce their prices to sell off unsold items and will also try to reduce their costs by cutting their workforces and output. Some firms badly affected by falling demand may even be forced to close. In contrast, reducing personal income taxes can help to boost consumer spending and business activity.

✗ Employer payroll taxes may reduce employment

Social contributions paid by employees from their earnings will also reduce their disposable incomes while payroll taxes paid by employers will increase the cost of employing workers. As the cost of employing labour rises firms may reduce their demand for labour and may switch to more capital-intensive methods of production. ➤ **3.6.2**

✗ High income and payroll taxes may reduce labour productivity and economic growth

A high tax take from the earnings of workers will reduce their take-home pay and therefore the reward from employment. As result some workers may choose not to work while others in work may reduce their effort, stop working overtime or developing their skills to seek promotion and higher wages, especially if the tax system is highly progressive. Lower taxes may instead increase employee motivation resulting in higher levels of output. ➤ **3.6.3**

✗ Taxes on profits can reduce enterprise and investment

Taxing profits reduces the reward for enterprise and risk-taking. There may be fewer start-ups and less business growth as a result because firms will have less money after taxes to reinvest in expanding their scale of production. For these reasons many countries have been reducing their corporation tax rates over time to help encourage new enterprise, business investment and job creation in their economies.

✗ High direct tax rates increase tax evasion

As a result tax revenues are lower and a government will spend more on trying to catch those individuals and companies that cheat or lie about their incomes to avoid paying the taxes they are due.

Indirect taxes

Indirect taxes are added to the prices of goods and services and are therefore collected from transactions made by people and organizations. An indirect tax may be a fixed percentage of a price or value or it may be a fixed amount.

The collection and payment of indirect taxes to government is normally the responsibility of producers who will then pass on as much of each tax as they can to consumers through raised prices. This means the incidence of an indirect tax, i.e. who bears the cost of it, will often be shared between a producer of a product and the consumers of that product. For example, in a highly competitive market for a product for which consumer demand is highly price sensitive, producers may be unable to increase their prices to cover the indirect tax. If they do, demand for their product and therefore their revenues may fall significantly. ➤ **2.7.4**

Sales taxes

A **sales tax** is a consumption tax imposed by the government on the sale of finished goods and services. A sales tax can be a fixed amount added to the price of a product or levied as a percentage of its price. Most sales taxes are therefore collected by sellers and then passed on to the government.

Value added tax

Value added tax (VAT) is an **ad valorem tax**. This means it is charged as a percentage of the value of transactions including, for example, payments for electricity, insurance, rent, restaurant bills, tickets for sporting and music events. Unlike a sales tax that is applied only to the final selling price of a finished good or service, VAT is added to the value of unfinished and semi-finished items exchanged between firms at different stages of production. Because VAT is a regressive tax many essential items such as basic foods, nappies, educational books and medicines may be made exempt or zero-rated.

Excise duties

Excise duties are applied to specific goods, such as alcohol, cigarettes, vehicles and petrol. They are normally fixed charges based on the amount sold, such as $1 on a litre of petrol or $2 on a bottle of wine.

Import tariffs

Tariffs are custom duties on the value of imported goods entering a country. Tariffs may be used to raise the prices of certain imported products to protect domestic firms from overseas competition. ➤ **6.2.4**

User charges

User charges are taxes or charges linked to the use of specific goods or activities. For example, they include toll charges to use major bridges or roads and pay for their upkeep. London and other major cities around the world

▲ Indirect taxes include ad valorem taxes, excise duties, user charges and import tariffs

have also introduced congestion charges that charge vehicle drivers a fixed amount to enter these cities during peak periods.

The impacts of indirect taxes

Advantages of indirect taxes

Indirect taxes have a number of desirable qualities and economic impacts:

✔ They can be used to target specific products and activities

Indirect taxes can be used to achieve more socially or economically desirable market outcomes. For example, taxes on cigarettes and alcohol can discourage their consumption to promote healthier lifestyles and to reduce the cost to the government of public health treatment for smoking- and alcohol-related problems. Taxes on oil can help to conserve a valuable non-renewable resource and also help reduce pollution from the burning of oil in energy production and vehicle use. ➤ **2.11.2**

✔ They expand the tax base

Indirect taxes are paid by young, old, employed and unemployed alike when they buy goods and services, not just by people in work with earned incomes. As a result, the effects of indirect taxes are spread more widely across all industrial sectors and groups in a society.

✔ They are cost-effective

Indirect taxes are relatively cheap and easy to collect. The administrative burden of collecting indirect taxes lies mainly with the manufacturers, wholesalers and retailers collecting VAT and with importers paying custom and excise duties.

✔ They are flexible

It is often quicker and easier for a government to alter tax rates for VAT and excise duties than to make changes to income tax and other direct taxes. As such, the effect of these changes on consumption patterns and the macroeconomy is more immediate.

Disadvantages of indirect taxes

However, against these must be weighed a number of disadvantages of indirect taxes:

✗ Their impact is inflationary

The main impact of indirect taxes is to raise the prices of the goods and services to which they are applied. Raising existing taxes or introducing new indirect taxes will therefore add to price inflation and will reduce the real incomes of consumers. As a result, demand for many other goods and services will fall. However, some businesses selling cheaper products may benefit from increasing sales as consumers switch their demand away from more expensive items.

✗ Indirect taxes are regressive and can increase inequalities

Indirect taxes tend to be regressive in nature. That is, their burden as a proportion of income is greater on people with low incomes than it is on people with high incomes.

For example, consider the purchase of a pair shoes for $48 inclusive of VAT at 20% or $8. This amount of tax will take 8% from an income of $100 compared with just 1.6% from an income of $500. Many basic foodstuffs and other essential items, such as medicines, educational books and baby clothes, are exempt from VAT in many countries to reduce the regressiveness of the tax.

✗ Revenues from indirect taxes are less certain and predictable

It is can be difficult for a government to predict accurately how much consumers will spend on goods and services, and therefore revenues from indirect taxes. This makes planning future public expenditure based on likely tax revenues difficult. Employment, earnings and profits tend to be less variable than consumer expenditures over time and so direct tax revenues tend to be more predictable.

✗ They may encourage tax evasion and smuggling

For example, high tariffs on imported goods and excise duties may encourage the illegal smuggling of untaxed or lower taxed items from overseas. As a result governments may have to use up more resources to patrol ports and other entry points to catch smugglers.

ACTIVITY 4.9

A taxing problem

What type of tax is most likely to be applied to the following?

EXAM PREPARATION 4.2

a What measures can a government take to reduce a budget deficit? [2]

b Explain the difference between public expenditure and private expenditure, giving one example of each. [4]

c Analyse the reasons why governments impose taxes. [6]

d Discuss how a government might finance its expenditure. [8]

SECTION 4.3.7 Definition of fiscal policy

SECTION 4.3.8 Fiscal policy measures

SECTION 4.3.9 Effects of fiscal policy measures on government macroeconomic aims

What is fiscal policy? Fiscal policy involves varying the overall level of public expenditure and/or taxation in an economy to manage aggregate demand and influence the level of economic activity.

▼ Fiscal policy instruments can be effective if:

Expansionary fiscal policy

If a government wants to increase aggregate demand in the economy to boost employment and output it can increase its expenditure and/or reduce taxation. This is called a reflationary or **expansionary fiscal policy**.

Cutting taxes on profits may provide firms with an incentive to increase output and investments in new productive capacity. Cutting taxes on personal incomes may encourage more people to participate in the workforce and motivate employees to increase their productivity. It will increase the amount of disposable income people have to spend. However, there is a risk they will simply save this extra money or spend it on imported goods and services.

Governments will often implement an expansionary fiscal policy during an economic downturn or recession, when private sector demand for goods and services is low or falling and unemployment in the economy is high or rising as a result. ➤ **4.6.3**

An expansionary fiscal policy usually means running or increasing a **budget deficit**. The budget refers to the amount a government has to spend each year relative to the amount of revenue it raises from taxation. If public expenditure exceeds total tax revenue the budget will be in deficit and the government will have to borrow money to finance it. ➤ **4.3.1**

➤ **4.3.1**

ACTIVITY 4.10

Can increased public expenditure create jobs?

The diagram below shows how the building of new hospitals by a government could help to increase economic activity. In your own words explain what is happening in the diagram and how an expansionary fiscal policy can boost total demand, output and jobs in an economy. How might the impact of the policy on the economy and your explanation change if the increase in public expenditure is paid for by **a** raising taxes or **b** raising interest rates to encourage people and firms to lend money to the government?

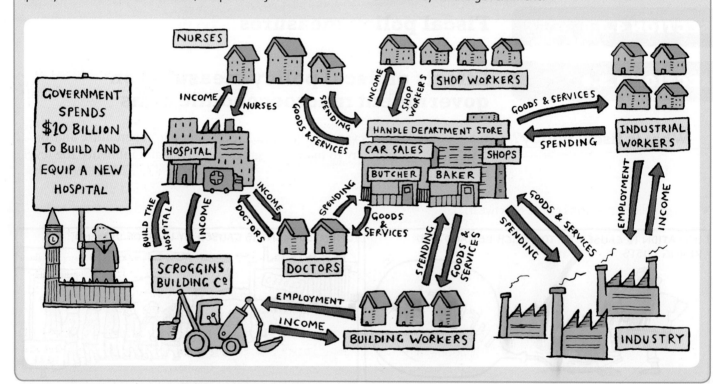

Contractionary fiscal policy

A deflationary or **contractionary fiscal policy** aims to reduce pressure on prices in the economy by cutting aggregate demand through a reduction in public expenditure and/or by raising total taxation. For example, cutting public sector wages and raising personal taxes will reduce total disposable income and consumer expenditure.

The budget deficit will be cut or may even go into surplus if tax revenues exceed public spending. However, a contractionary fiscal policy may reduce employment and growth in output. ➤ **4.6.4**

➤ **4.6.4**

Fiscal policy instruments can also affect the distribution of income

Fiscal policy instruments may also be used to redistribute incomes between rich and poor people in an economy. For example, income taxes may be increased on those with the highest incomes and the money raised used to finance more public services and increased welfare for people on the lowest incomes, or those unable to work because they are old, sick or unemployed.

Taxing people on high incomes to provide income support to people on low incomes can also help to boost overall spending in the economy. This is because people on high incomes tend to save a large proportion of their incomes while people on low incomes tend to spend all or most of their incomes on the goods and services they need. ➤ **3.4**

Problems with fiscal policy

Many economists have criticized the use of fiscal policy to influence the level of total demand and economic activity in an economy. They argue there is not a clear trade-off between higher levels of inflation and lower levels of unemployment. For example, many countries have experienced high inflation and high unemployment at the same time and the overuse of fiscal policy has contributed to these conditions. ➤ **4.8.3**

1 Fiscal policy is cumbersome to use

It is difficult for a government to know precisely when and by how much to expand public spending or cut taxes by during an economic downturn. Boosting total demand by increasing public spending and/or cutting taxes may cause an economy to 'overheat': the general level of prices will rise if aggregate demand expands faster than the aggregate supply of goods and services.

Similarly, if an economy is overheating, deep cuts in public expenditure or increases in taxes that are too severe may result in rising unemployment instead as aggregate demand is reduced.

2 Increases in public expenditure crowds out private spending

To finance an increase in public spending and/or a cut in taxation a government may need to borrow the extra money it needs from the private sector. The more money the private sector lends to a government the less it has available to spend itself. This is called **crowding out**.

To encourage people, firms and the banking system to buy government stocks or bonds, a government will raise interest rates. However, higher interest rates may discourage other people and firms from borrowing money to spend on consumption and investment. If firms invest less in new plant and machinery then their future productive potential, and therefore the rate of economic growth, will be reduced.

As the stock of government borrowing rises, the more a government must spend on interest payments for its debt. This will reduce the amount a government can spend on public sector wages, the construction of new roads, public health care or other public sector projects, or it will require an increase in taxes to cover the cost of additional interest payments.

3 Increasing taxes on incomes and profits can reduce incentives to work and enterprise

If taxes are too high, people and firms may reduce their work effort. This will reduce labour productivity, total output and profits. As productivity falls the cost of production in many firms will increase and they will be less able to compete on product price and quality against more efficient producers overseas. As a result, demand for their goods and services may fall and unemployment may rise.

4 An expansionary fiscal policy creates expectations of inflation

Consumers and producers in an economy may come to expect a future rise in inflation following an expansionary fiscal policy, especially if attempts by their government in the past to boost demand and economic activity have caused the economy to overheat. As a result, if their current government announces it will cut taxes and increase public spending to boost output and growth employees may push for higher wages to protect them from an expected increase in their cost of living. Rising wages will increase production costs and reduce the demand for labour. This in turn may cause a cost-push inflation and rising unemployment. ➤ **4.8.3**

Fiscal rules

Problems with fiscal policy has led a number of countries to develop and follow a number of fiscal rules. These impose targets or constraints on public sector spending, taxation, borrowing and debt. They vary by country and may include:

- A cap on the level of public expenditure as a percentage of the national income or GDP;
- Growth in tax revenues cannot exceed the growth in GDP;
- A debt ceiling expressed as a percentage of GDP;
- Public spending and revenues from taxes must balance over the life of the Parliament or over the economic cycle;
- The public sector should only borrow to pay for capital expenditures which will help to grow the economy.

SECTION 4.4.1

Definition of money supply and monetary policy

SECTION 4.4.2

Monetary policy measures

SECTION 4.4.3

Effects of monetary policy measures on government macroeconomic aims

What is monetary policy?

Monetary policy involves changes in the money supply and/or interest rate in an economy to influence the level of total demand and economic activity. It is also used by a government to influence the exchange rate of its national currency against foreign currencies and, in so doing, to affect the level of international trade and transactions.

The main instrument of monetary policy is the minimum lending rate or rate of interest charged by the central bank to loan money to the banking system

in an economy. Raising or lowering the interest rate will affect
then charge to their business and personal customers to borrow m
the rate of interest savers earn on their savings accounts.

However, a government may also directly increase or decrease the **money
supply** in an economy to help achieve its macroeconomic aims. You will
remember from Unit 3.1.1 that the money supply in a macroeconomy is made
up of notes and coins in circulation plus bank deposits. ➤ **3.1.1**

Expansionary monetary policy

This involves a 'loosening' of monetary policy by cutting interest rates and/or
expanding the money supply to boost total demand. These measures may be
used when unemployment is rising and economic growth is falling or has
turned negative during an economic recession. ➤ **4.6.3**

If interest rates are reduced, people and firms will be able to borrow money
more cheaply than before from banks or by using their credit cards. Lower
interest rates can also make saving money less attractive. Therefore, reducing
interest rates in an economy can help to raise consumer expenditure on goods
and services and increase investment expenditure by private sector firms. This
can help boost output and employment opportunities.

Increasing the money supply in the economy will give people and firms more
money to spend on goods and services. A government may do this by printing
more notes and coins or through **quantitative easing**. This involves the
government using newly created money to buy up financial assets held by
banks, such as government and corporate bonds. Investing in bonds ties up
money for many years but banks are willing to buy bonds issued by the
government and private companies because they pay out an attractive interest
rate when they mature. By buying back these financial assets from banks a
government can increase the quantity of money banks have available to lend
to people and firms. ➤ **3.1.1**

▼ Quantitative easing can boost the money supply and aggregate demand

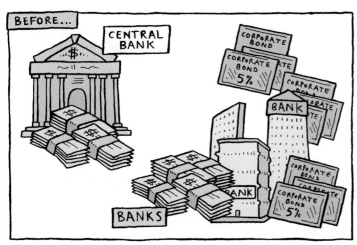
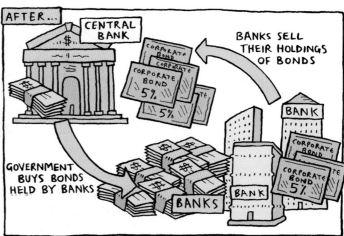

Many governments drastically cut their interest rates and used quantitative easing to boost activity in their economies following the global financial crisis in 2008 and the deep economic recession that followed.

Contractionary monetary policy

This involves raising interest rates and/or cutting the money supply to reduce total demand if the economy is overheating and inflationary pressures are rising. It is also referred to as a tightening of monetary policy. ➤ **4.8.5**

Increasing interest rates will make borrowing more expensive. Reducing the quantity of money in the economy will also restrict the amount consumers and firms have to spend on goods and services. A government can do this by selling government bonds to banks at attractive interest rates. This will reduce the amount of money banks have available to lend to their customers.

However, falling aggregate demand may result in rising unemployment and if firms cut back their investment it can also hurt future economic growth.

Exchange rate policy

Changes in interest rates can be used to influence the exchange rate of a national currency. An exchange rate is the rate at which one currency can be exchanged for another on the foreign exchange market.

For example, on the foreign exchange market residents of India will be able to exchange Indian rupees for US dollars so they can purchase goods and services from the US. Similarly, residents of the USA can use their dollars to buy euros so that they can purchase goods and services from Germany and other European countries in the eurozone. An exchange rate is therefore the price of one currency in terms or another. ➤ **6.3.3**

A fall in the value of the Indian currency against the US dollar means that the price of US dollars has increased and Indian residents will have to use more rupees to buy each dollar. Goods and services purchased from the USA will be more expensive for Indian residents to buy and this will have a negative impact on India's balance of international payments and its inflation rate. The Indian government may therefore increase the interest rate to increase the foreign exchange value of the rupee. As the interest rate in India rises relative to other countries wealthy residents from overseas may buy more rupees so they can save their money in Indian bank accounts. The increase in demand for rupees on the foreign exchange market will push up the price or exchange rate of the currency.

It follows that lowering the interest rate can reduce the exchange rate of a currency. This will reduce the cost to overseas residents of buying goods exported from that country. This can increase export earnings and boost output and employment.

What evidence is there that UK monetary policy notably between 2009 and 2011, but also since, was 'loose'? What was happening to UK fiscal policy at the same time and why? What risks do the articles raise about the policy mix being used by the UK government and why?

In May 2009 the Bank of England in the UK announced it was to introduce a series of measures aimed at increasing the supply of money in the economy.

Technically known as quantitative easing, the aim was to try to increase the amount of funds in the UK banking system. The hope was it would make it easier for the commercial banks to increase their lending levels.

At the same time the Bank also cut the interest rate to just 0.5%, the lowest it had been since the central bank was founded in 1694.

The Bank said increased quantitative easing was necessary as cutting rates would not be enough to help the UK economy out of recession.

In May 2011 the Monetary Policy Committee at the UK Bank of England voted to keep the official bank rate at just 0.5% and agreed it would continue to use quantitative easing to boost bank lending.

A number of economists argued that the UK economic policy mix was unbalanced. Fiscal policy was too tight and monetary policy was too loose. They were worried that the impact of deep cuts in public spending and increased taxes to reduce the budget deficit would harm the supply side of the economy while monetary policy was pumping too much money into the economy and could be inflationary.

The official bank rate in the UK remained on hold at just 0.5% until August 2017 when it was cut further to 0.25% over fears that the UK decision to leave the European Union could harm the economy. A further £60 billion of quantitative easing was also announced bringing the total pumped into the economy since 2009 to £435 billion.

EXAM PREPARATION 4.3

a What is a 'mixed economy'? [2]

b Explain **two** macroeconomic aims a government might have. [4]

c Use the concept of price elasticity of demand to analyse how indirect taxes may be used by a government to (i) increase its revenue, (ii) decrease imports. [6]

d Discuss how some aims of government policy might conflict with each other. [8]

ACTIVITY 4.11

A walk on the supply side

The articles below refer to some different supply-side policies. What are they and how do you think they can help to boost output and employment?

UK plans skills academies to close productivity gap

Workers are to be offered free vocational training as part of a huge government drive to tackle the chronic lack of basic skills among millions of adults, ministers are set to announce today.

The Pakistan Telecommunications Authority today found Mobilink, the country's leading cellular company, guilty of anti-competitive practices by overcharging its 'valued subscribers' for making calls to other cellular operators. The PTA has ordered Mobilink to make revisions to its tariffs.

Romania claims privatization in the energy sector was a step forward towards a healthy economy. New investors entering the energy market will bring substantial benefits to companies and the competition environment.

Milk market deregulation benefits Australian consumer

Six months after the deregulation of Australia's dairy industry, milk prices have fallen by as much as 40 cents a litre with the likelihood of further drops, said the Australian Competition and Consumer Commission (ACCC) this week.

New tax incentives finally approved

After months of back and forth, The European Commission has finally approved the UK's new film industry tax incentives.

The new tax credit is expected to take effect from January 1st, and will benefit film-makers investing at least 25% of their budget in the UK.

Trade unions protest against anti-strike laws

Supply-side policies aim to make markets and industries operate more efficiently in order to expand the productive potential of an economy and increase its total output. Expanding the total output or total supply of goods and services in an economy will help to reduce prices and the rate of price inflation, provide additional employment opportunities and boost the volume of goods available for export. Over the long run, therefore, supply-side policies can help to achieve all the macroeconomic aims of a government at the same time.

Supply-side policy instruments

Supply-side policy instruments may include the following.

Selective tax incentives

Tax cuts can be targeted at different groups of workers, firms or sectors of the economy to encourage them to increase their productivity and expand their productive potential. For example:

- Reducing payroll or income taxes on wages so that workers retain more of their earnings after tax. This can motivate people in employment to work harder and increase their productivity and encourage more unemployed people to seek paid employment;

- Reducing taxes on profits to encourage more entrepreneurs to start their own businesses;

- Reducing taxes on the profits of those companies that increase the amount they invest in new, more advanced capital equipment and in the research and development of new products and more efficient production processes.

Selective subsidies

A **subsidy** is a non-repayable sum of money or 'grant' given to an organization by a government to help it meet its costs and increase its profits. A subsidy is profit-making. In this way subsidies can encourage firms to expand their output and, in so doing, will help to reduce market prices. For example, subsidies be used to support:

- new, small businesses to encourage new business start-ups;

- farms, to encourage them to expand food production;

- capital investments in new technologies, to encourage firms to install new and more productive machinery;

- investments in skills, training, to encourage firms to provide more training for their employees to help them improve their skills and productivity;

- investments in the research and development (R&D) or new, more efficient products and production processes.

Improving education and training

Firms must have access to skilled workers to help them produce goods and services efficiently, undertake R&D and compete successfully in international markets. Skill needs in industry are rising as global competition intensifies and technology advances rapidly. A well-educated and trained workforce will improve productivity and be better able to adapt to new production methods and technologies. A government can assist firms by helping them design and

▲ Tax incentives and subsidies can be used to encourage investments in productive capacity

finance apprenticeship and training programmes, by funding universities and student tuition and providing access for more people to attend colleges and higher education.

Labour market reforms

Labour markets may not function properly for a number of reasons. For example:

- Powerful trade unions may restrict the supply of labour to some occupations. This will force up the market wage making employment more costly and production less profitable. Fewer people will be employed and total output will be lower as a result. Many governments have therefore introduced laws and regulations to restrict the power of trade unions to organize strikes and to restrict labour supply through closed shop arrangements. ➤ **3.4.3**

- If welfare payments received by the unemployed are too generous compared to wages, they may discourage some people from seeking paid employment. In some countries, benefits paid to the unemployed have therefore been reduced, are time-limited and often linked to evidence that a person is actively seeking paid work or is in training. However, cutting payments to support people without paid employment may conflict with government aims to reduce poverty that is often the result of long periods of absence from paid employment. ➤ **5.2.2**

- Some large, powerful firms may pay their low or unskilled workers very low wages causing them to suffer hardship or otherwise forcing them into unemployment and increasing the cost to government of making payments. Minimum wage laws have been introduced in many countries to prevent exploitation of low-paid workers by forcing firms to guarantee them a reasonable or 'living' wage. However, some firms argue that setting a minimum wage at too high a level will increase their employment costs and force them to cut jobs. ➤ **3.3.2**

Competition policy

Competition for customers and sales forces firms to keep their costs and product prices low and improve their products and customer service levels. A lack of competition can therefore be bad for consumers and an economy. For example, some firms are large and powerful enough to control the market supply of a particular product. These firms are monopolies and they may use their market power to restrict competition, charge high prices and earn excessive profits. Laws and regulations are therefore used by many governments to increase competition across markets by imposing fines on firms that are anticompetitive, controlling their prices and even forcing them to break up into smaller firms. ➤ **3.8.2**

Removing trade barriers

Some governments protect domestic firms and jobs in their economies from competition from firms located in other countries, even if those countries are able to produce and sell the same products more cheaply. For example, governments may impose taxes known as tariffs on goods from foreign producers to make them more expensive for consumers to buy or they may restrict the total volume of goods allowed into their countries from overseas. However, because domestic firms are protected from foreign competitors they may put far less effort into reducing their costs and improving their products. Restrictions on international trade can also prevent domestic firms from having access to the best and cheapest sources globally of raw materials, components, skills, services, finance and new technologies. Removing barriers to trade and allowing more international competition can therefore benefit both producers and consumers in an economy. ➤ **6.2.6**

Privatization

Privatization involves the transfer of public sector functions and activities, such as refuse collection, running a prison or public transport services, to private firms who may be able to provide them more efficiently because they want to maximize profits from these activities. If private firms can deliver public services at a lower cost and better quality than the public sector then consumers will benefit and taxes can be lowered. ➤ **2.11.2**

Regulation and deregulation

Regulations are rules and laws that restrict certain activities, such as shop opening hours and limits on noise and pollution levels, or set standards for products and for hygiene and safety in work places. Many are aimed at correcting market failures that would stop markets from delivering outcomes that are socially and economically desirable. ➤ **2.10.2**

For example, regulations are often used to:

- protect consumers from misleading advertising, harmful products, anticompetitive behaviour and dishonest business practices;

- protect key industries and businesses from unfair competition;

- protect employment and the rights of employees to fair treatment and to work in a healthy and safe environment;

- protect the environment and reduce harmful emissions to limit climate change.

For some firms, new or toughened laws and regulations can increase their production costs and reduce their profits. For example, firms may have to employ additional staff and invest in new equipment such as the installation of safety cages or guards around machinery and filters to reduce dust and other pollutants to ensure that they comply with health and safety laws.

Similarly, measures aimed at controlling the anti-competitive behaviour of monopolies will reduce their excessive profits. However, they will benefit new and smaller firms trying to compete with them.

Many firms can therefore gain from regulations. For example, global manufacturers of helmets for motorcyclists such as Arai Helmets of Japan, HJC in the USA and Zhejiang Jixiang Motorcycle Fittings Co. Ltd. in China, enjoyed increased sales following the introduction of laws in many countries making the wearing of crash helmets on motorcycles compulsory. Similarly, the introduction of targets in many countries for reductions in harmful carbon emissions and for energy provided from renewable sources has benefited manufacturers and installers of solar panels and wind turbines.

However, laws and regulations often need to be updated or replaced as economies change and develop due to advances in technology, expanding international trade and the introduction of new products and ways of working. Complying with old and out-of-date regulations will be costly for firms and uses up management and employee time that could otherwise be put to more productive use.

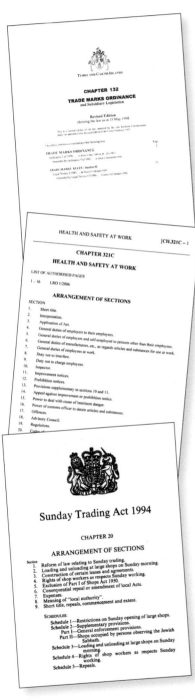

▲ Regulation can be a burden on business. Simplifying or removing obsolete rules and laws is called deregulation

Deregulation therefore helps to remove burdens on business, reduce their production costs and free up resources by simplifying or removing old and unnecessary regulations. For example, reforms in some countries have included removing restrictions on shop opening hours, reducing unnecessary labelling requirements on products and enabling firms to complete their tax returns, applications for patents and other paperwork required by government electronically over the internet.

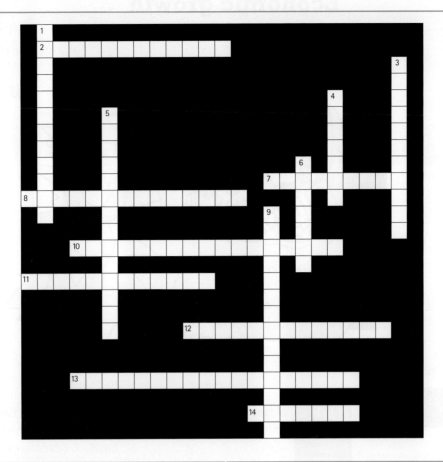

Clues across

2. Term used to describe fiscal policy when it involves increasing public spending and/or cutting taxes in an effort to boost total demand in the economy (12)
7. A government will set out its plans and forecasts for public expenditure and revenues for the year ahead in this each year (3, 6)
8. Term used to describe a 'tightening' of monetary policy when interest rates are raised in an effort reduce borrowing and the rate at which total demand is rising in the economy (14)
10. Term used to describe a collection of policy measures designed to expand the total supply of goods and services in the economy (6-4, 6)
11. The instruments of this government policy are public expenditures and taxes (6, 6)
12. A type of tax that takes proportionally less in tax from a high income than a low income. Indirect taxes have this characteristic (10, 3)
13. A monetary policy action designed to boost the quantity of money held by banks in an economic recession so that they increase their lending. It involves the central bank giving cash to banks in return for their financial assets (12, 6)
14. The assessed value of income, wealth or expenditure on which taxes are levied by a government (3, 4)

Clues down

1. A supply-side policy measure that involves the reform or removal of complex, old or even unnecessary regulations to reduce burdens on businesses (12)
3. A type of tax levied on expenditures on goods or services that is collected by producers but usually passed on to consumers by raising market prices (8, 3)
4. A government plans to spend $37 billion but expects to raise $39 billion in taxes over the coming year. What type of imbalance will there be in its budget? (7)
5. A government demand-side policy that involves changing the interest rate or supply of money in an economy to manage the overall level of economic activity (8, 6)
6. The balance on the budget when a government plans to spend more than it expects to receive from tax revenues over the next year (7)
9. A type of tax designed to take proportionally more in tax from a higher income than a low income (11, 3)

Measurement of economic growth

An important economic relationship

Imagine a very simple and tiny economy with just three people and one $10 note between them. You are one of those people, the baker, and you hold the $10 note. This is the money supply in the economy. ➤ **3.1.1**

You use the $10 note to buy candles from the candlestick maker. This exchange involves the following three transactions:

- The candles are sold for $10 (output; that is, the value of the candles).
- You (the baker) pay $10 for the candles (expenditure).
- The candlestick maker receives $10 in payment for the candles (income).

The candlestick maker now uses her income of $10 to buy meat from the butcher. In turn, the butcher uses his income of $10 from the sale of his meat to buy $10 of bread from your shop. The same $10 has now been circulated three times in the economy.

So, how much was the total value of output in the tiny economy? How much expenditure was there in total in the economy? And how much was the total amount of income earned by the three people in the tiny economy?

The answer to all these questions is $30. The butcher, you (the baker) and the candlestick maker each earned $10 in income from the sale of their output of meat, bread and candles, and they each spent $10 buying up this output from each other. This means there was a circular flow of income, expenditure and output in the tiny economy.

▼ A simple circular flow of income, expenditure and output

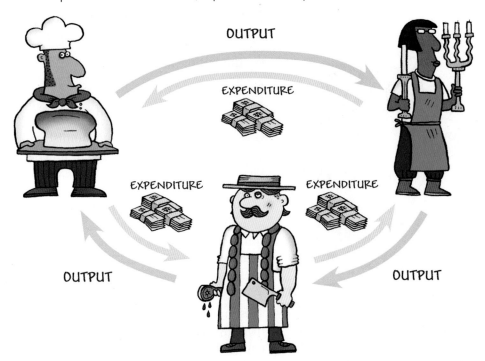

The circular flow of income in this tiny economy demonstrates an important relationship in macroeconomics: the value of output = expenditure = income.

The same relationship is true of all economies, no matter how large or complex they are:

national output = national income = national expenditure

Measuring economic activity

As economists, we would like to measure the total output of goods and services of a country, and monitor how it grows or changes over time. The total value of all goods and services produced by the factors of production of the residents of a country is known as the **national output**.

Factors of production – land, labour and capital – are used to produce the national output. Firms pay workers, and the owners of natural resources and capital, for their use in production. These payments are a cost to firms but an income for labour and owners of factors of production. Similarly, owners of firms will receive income in the form of profits if their businesses are successful. The total amount of income earned by all the factors of production of a country, whether they are employed at home or overseas, is therefore the **national income**.

The value of the total or national output of an economy can be measured by how much people and organizations pay for all the goods and services it comprises. It follows that the total or national output should also be the same as the total or **national expenditure**. What people and organizations spend on goods and services provides income for the people and firms that produce and supply the goods and services.

Gross domestic product (GDP)

The total market value of all final goods and services produced within a macroeconomy in a given period of time is its **gross domestic product** or **GDP**.

There are, therefore, three ways of measuring the GDP or value of economic activity in an economy:

- the output method
- the income method
- the expenditure method.

Government experts and economists collect statistics on all three measures of the GDP of their economy. In practice, however, the values of the three measures do not always add up exactly to the same amount. This is because economic activity is complex. Flows of outputs, incomes and expenditures occur between many millions of different people, firms and governments, all over the world every day. It is also possible that some activities and their transactions are not recorded because people and firms may try to hide their incomes to avoid taxes.

The output method

This involves adding up the value of the output produced each period by every firm in every industry in an economy. However, only final outputs should be counted otherwise the double counting of the value of some outputs can occur. For example, cotton produced by farms is used as an input to the production of clothing and bed linens by the textile manufacturing industry. Similarly, the value of the output of the shipbuilding industry includes output produced by the steel and electronics industries. To avoid the problem of

Value added = $300

double counting, economists will only add up the value added by each firm at each stage of production. ➤ **3.6.3**

Economic activity involves organizing and combining resources to make final outputs that are more desirable to consumers. In this way a business adds value to the resources it uses. The **gross value added (GVA)** by each firm is the market value of its output of goods or services less the value of the inputs used in the production if outputs. GDP is therefore a measure of the total value added to resources in an economy through the production of goods and services.

The income method

This measures the total income earned from the production of goods and services within the economy. The figures provided break down this income into, for example, profits earned by companies and other business organizations and the wages and salaries of employees and the self-employed. However, **transfer payments**, such as welfare payments, unemployment benefits and pensions, from a government to individuals are excluded because they are unearned incomes: there is no corresponding productive activity by the people who receive them. ➤ **4.3.2**

The expenditure method

Most goods and services produced are sold. The value of output can therefore be measured by adding up the total amount spent on all final goods and services produced in an economy. This includes spending by individual households, firms and government organizations. Spending on exports by overseas consumers is also included in this total but spending on imported goods and services must be deducted. This is because imports have been produced in other economies and therefore do not earn profits or other incomes for domestic firms and residents.

▲ Gross domestic expenditure includes consumer expenditure, investment, government expenditure and exports but excludes spending on imports

Real versus nominal GDP

This distinction is very important if we want to determine by how much national output has grown or changed over time. This is because GDP is measured in monetary values. That is, the value of output, income and expenditure in an economy are all measured at their current market values or prices. These measure the **money GDP** or **nominal GDP**. However, these values will rise over time as prices increase due to inflation.

This means that the value of the national output, expenditure and income may increase simply because prices have risen but people may be no better off. Indeed, they may even be worse off if at the same time the total amount of goods and services available in the economy has fallen because real output has decreased.

Nominal GDP can therefore be a misleading indicator of what is happening to the total output of an economy, so economists adjust nominal GDP to exclude the impact of inflation on monetary values. **Real GDP** therefore measures changes in total output assuming prices are unchanged over time. That is, GDP in constant prices provides a measure of the real output of an economy.

For example, in the last year the nominal GDP of a country was $100 billion. In the current year this has increased to $110 billion. However, price inflation was 10% over the same period. This means all of the increase in the nominal GDP is explained by the rise in general level of prices. There was no increase in real GDP.

If price inflation had been, say, 7% over the same 12-month period then $7 billion of the increase in nominal GDP would have been simply due to rising prices. The other $3 billion therefore would have been due to an increase in the real output of firms in the economy. That is, people in the economy enjoyed an increase in the amount of goods and services available to them to satisfy their wants.

Using GDP statistics

Many years ago no one was very interested in collecting national income and output figures. However, during the Second World War many governments realized there was a need to know how much food and ammunition their nations could produce because it was difficult for many to import the essential goods and services they needed during the war. Since then, governments all over the world have collected and published figures on their national output, incomes and expenditures.

GDP statistics can help governments and economists in a number of ways:

1   If a government is better informed about the allocation of resources in its economy and how much they are producing, it can make better decisions on economic policies and how they may affect the resource allocation and production. For example, if a government thinks its economy is producing too many consumer goods and too few capital goods, it may try to encourage the production of capital equipment through higher taxes on consumer goods and lowering taxes on the profits of machinery and equipment manufacturers.

2   It allows comparison to be made of the standard of living in one year compared with the next. If the amount of goods and services produced in an economy has increased over time we might assume many people are better off.

3   The figures allow us to compare the standard of living in different countries or even in different areas of the same country. Dividing GDP by the population gives an indication of the average income of each person (of **GDP per capita**). ➤ **5.1.1**

Definition of economic growth

Causes of economic growth

Economic growth involves increasing the total output produced by resources in an economy. It is therefore measured by an increase in the real GDP of an economy. An increase in output one year compared with previous years can improve the living standards of people by increasing the availability of goods and services, boosting incomes and also creating additional employment opportunities.

If the total supply of goods and services can increase over time in line with rising demand then they can be enjoyed without an increase in their prices. Economic growth can therefore help to keep price inflation low and stable in an economy. ➤ **4.8.5**

In the following diagram, the economy is currently producing at point X below its PPC. Although the economy has the factor resources and capability to produce more goods and services, for example at point Y on its PPC, there is insufficient demand in the economy for more output. So, factor resources are not fully or efficiently employed at point X. ➤ **1.4.2**

If total demand in the economy was to rise, firms would be willing to increase production and would demand more factors of production. As a result the economy will move towards point Y. At this point there is full factor employment and their total output is at its maximum. There has been growth in total output due to the increase in demand but if the economy is to grow further it must permanently increase its productive capacity. This will shift its PPC to the right. At point Z on its new PPC the economy will be able to produce more capital and consumer goods than it was able to previously, at point Y. ➤ **1.4.4**

▼ Long-term economic growth in the productive potential of an economy

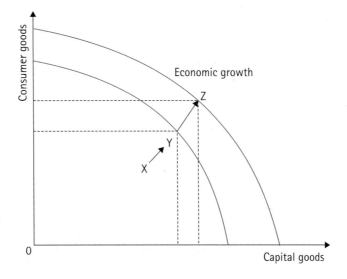

How economies grow

Demand for increased living standards means many governments have a macroeconomic objective to improve their long-term rate of economic growth. Economists measure the rate of economic growth by how much the real GDP has increased each year in an economy.

As economists we want scarce resources to be as fully employed as possible, in the most efficient ways possible, to produce as many goods and services as possible. This will satisfy the most wants.

If resources are unused – that is, if some labour is left unemployed, land disused or capital lying idle – then an increase in the amount of goods and services can be achieved simply by using these available resources more fully. However, it is clearly more difficult for an economy to grow if all its available resources are fully employed. Other changes are therefore required to achieve growth.

1 The discovery of more natural resources

The discovery of gas and oil has given a number of countries the ability to grow rapidly. Indeed, the discovery of more natural resources, including mineral deposits, such as coal and iron ore or even new varieties of fruit or cereals, can help any economy to increase output. Searching for new natural resources, however, costs a lot of money and some countries, particularly those in the developing world, lack the funds to do this.

2 Investment in new capital and infrastructure

Investment by private sector firms involves spending on capital goods such as new machinery, buildings and technology so that they can expand their scale of production, lower their average costs and produce more goods and services in the future. Similarly, investments in modern infrastructure such as road networks, airports and ports by governments can improve access and communications to expand the productive potential of the economy.

By lowering interest rates, a government can make it less costly for private sector firms to borrow money for investment.

3 Technical progress

New inventions and production processes can increase the productivity of existing resources and produce new materials and products. Technical progress is a major driver of economic growth.

Technological advances made in one industrial sector can often 'spill over' into other sectors. For example, fibreglass was originally invented for use as insulation material but is now used in the production of bows and crossbows, roofing panels, automobile and aircraft bodies, surfboards, artificial limbs and many more products. Similarly, the internet is based on a system originally developed by the US Defense Advanced Research Projects Agency to enable communications between military computers to withstand nuclear attack.

Governments can support investments in the research and development (R&D) of new products and processes, either directly through public funding of firms and universities or by providing tax breaks for firms that undertake R&D. They can also encourage R&D by protecting new inventions from copy or theft through the issue of patents.

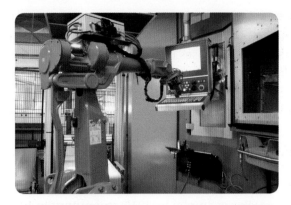

▼ Major advances in technology ha[...]
production processes and the way f[...]

Timeline	Major innovations
1785	Water power Textiles Iron
1845	Steam power Railways Steel Telephones
1900	Refrigeration Plastics Electricity Chemicals Internal combustion engine
1950	Petrochemicals Jet engines and aviation Electronics
1990	Digital cameras Mobile phones Computer software Biotechnology
2000	Wind, wave and solar power Electric cars Social networking
2020 +	?

4 Increasing the quantity and quality of human resources

A larger and more productive work force can boost economic growth. Education and training are often called 'investments in human capital' and will help create a better skilled, knowledgeable and more productive workforce. ➤ **1.2.3**

Improvements in healthcare and medicines can also improve the health and productivity of the workforce and reduce the number of days they are sick and unproductive.

Expanding the work force may require policies to encourage more people into work, for example cutting income taxes and unemployment benefits, and increasing the age at which people can retire and receive a pension from the government. The working population of a country can also be expanded through the inward migration of skilled labour and, in the longer term, through an increase in the birth rate. ➤ **5.3.1**

5 Reallocating resources

An inefficient allocation of resources will constrain economic growth. Moving resources from less productive uses to more productive uses will boost output and growth. Similarly, moving some resources from the production of consumer goods and services into the production of capital goods will help increase the productive potential of an economy.

Causes and consequences of recession

The rate of economic growth is a measure of how quickly or slowly real output rises over time. For example, in 2017 real output in India grew rapidly by 7.3%. In comparison, the US economy grew by only around 2.6% over the same period.

The rate of economic growth in an economy, like any economic variable, can vary over time but while it remains above zero that economy will continue to expand: real output will be increasing each year. A fall in the growth rate, say from 5% to 2% each year, will mean real output is rising more slowly than in the past. In contrast, an increase in the growth rate of an economy, from say 5% to 7% each year means its real output is expanding at a faster rate than in the past.

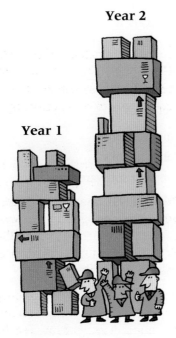

Rapid economic growth

Slow economic growth

Negative economic growth

However, economies can sometime experience periods of negative growth or falling real GDP during:

- an **economic recession** involving a relatively short period of negative growth that may only last for six months or, in some cases, a year or more after which the economy recovers and continues to grow once again;

- an **economic depression** or slump which may last several years during which there is a continuous and substantial fall in real GDP.

During a period of negative economic growth an economy will be producing at a point below its production possibility curve. Factor employment will fall and fewer goods and services will be produced. As a result, incomes will fall and living standards for many people may deteriorate especially if the fall in real GDP is severe and prolonged. ➤ **1.4.2**

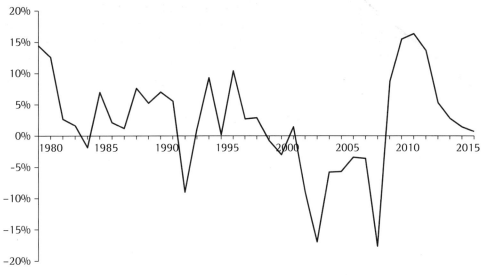

▼ Economic growth in Zimbabwe, % annual growth in real GDP

Source: *data.worldbank.org*

The chart plots the annual rate of economic growth in Zimbabwe since 1980. It shows how the growth rate has bounced up and down over time. Until 1998 annual growth in the real output of the economy was mostly positive: the amount of goods and services it produced was expanding in most years, by as much as 14.4% in 1980 and over 12% in 1981.

However, between 1999 and 2010 the economy of Zimbabwe contracted considerably. There was year-on-year negative economic growth between 1999 and 2018, resulting in widespread unemployment and poverty. By the end of 2008 the economy was producing 50% fewer goods and services than it did in 1998. That is, the size of the economy had more than halved since 1998.

At the same time the economy experienced hyperinflation and the unemployment rate reached 95%. Living standards and life expectancy fell for many Zimbabweans. However, in 2009 the economy of Zimbabwe began to expand once more after a new government of unity was formed and the Zimbabwean currency was abandoned in favour of using the US dollar. This effectively stopped the hyperinflation which had made the Zimbabwean currency worthless and in the four-year period to 2012 output grew rapidly by over 65% before annual growth began to slow down.

ACTIVITY 4.12

Really growing?

The table below shows annual average growth rates in the value of real output or real GDP, in a number of countries from the start of 2010 to the end of 2016.

▼ GDP in constant prices, % annual average growth rate selected countries 2010 and 2016

Country	% annual growth rate	Country	% annual growth rate
Australia	2.62	Mauritius	3.75
Central African Republic	-3.55	Pakistan	3.90
China	8.09	Russian Federation	1.98
Ethiopia	10.16	Slovenia	0.84
Greece	-3.64	Thailand	3.60
India	7.33	United Arab Emirates	4.14

Source: *data.worldbank.org*

1 Which country experienced the fastest rate of economic growth between 2010 and 2016?

2 Which country had the slowest growing economy?

3 Which countries had shrinking economies?

What is the economic cycle?

Most governments want to achieve long-term stable economic growth in the real GDP of their economies. Plotted on a graph over time this should look like a steadily rising line. However, in practice the annual rate of growth in real GDP often varies considerably in the short run and may even turn negative during an economic recession.

The business cycle or **economic cycle** refers to the pattern of recurrent ups and downs (or cyclical fluctuations) observed in real GDP growth over time in many economies. Most economies go through a fairly predictable economic cycle of changes in their rate of economic growth every 5–10 years, some more severe than others.

▼ The economic cycle

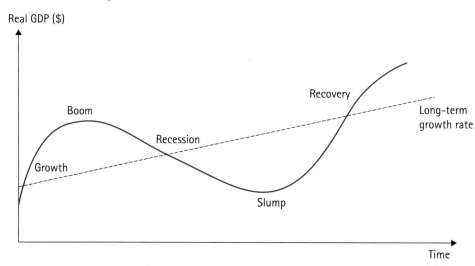

Typically, an economy passes through four distinct phases during one complete economic cycle:

- **Growth**

Economic activity is expanding rapidly. Many firms enjoy increased sales and profits. New business organizations are formed. Output, incomes and employment are all growing.

- **Economic boom**

Aggregate demand, sales and profits peak. There may be rapid inflation as prices rise quickly because demand exceeds the amount of goods and services firms can produce and supply. The economy 'overheats'. Shortages of materials, parts and equipment will increase business costs. There is a shortage of labour. Unemployment is low and wages rise as firms compete to employ skilled workers. The government may raise interest rates to control rising inflation. Consumer confidence and spending may begin to decline as inflation and interest rates rise.

- **Economic recession**

There is a general slowdown in economic activity. Demand for many goods and services begins to fall. Sales and profits decline. Firms cut back their production and workers are made redundant. Unemployment rises and incomes start to fall, causing consumer spending to fall further. As a result, economic growth turns negative. That is, the economy begins to shrink as economic activity falls.

During a recession many firms reduce their investment in new plants and machinery and cut back their demand for materials, parts and equipment. Competition between rival firms increases as they fight to survive. There is disinflation as the rate of inflation declines.

Many countries around the world entered economic recession following a global crash in the financial and property markets in 2008. These sectors had been growing rapidly in the years prior to the crash. Banks and other financial institutions drastically cut back their lending, especially against residential and commercial properties, causing a collapse in the global construction industry and resulting in growing unemployment around the world.

The government may increase public spending, cut taxes and reduce interest rates to encourage consumer borrowing and spending during a recession. ➤ **4.6.6**

A recession that is deep and prolonged may become an economic slump or depression during which economic activity continues to shrink and unemployment remains high for several years. There may be deflation as a result. ➤ **4.8.3**

- **Economic recovery**

Business and consumer confidence starts to recover. Spending on goods and services begins to rise. Sales and profits begin to rise. Firms increase their output and employ more workers. New businesses are formed. Unemployment falls and incomes rise, boosting consumer spending further. The economy starts to expand again.

The 'shape' of economic recessions

Economists often talk about and compare the shape of different economic recessions. This refers to what the plot of real GDP growth during a recession look likes over time on a graph.

A U-shaped recession is a prolonged slump. In contrast, a V-shaped recession refers to a short-lived contraction in the economy followed by rapid and sustained economic recovery.

In official statistics, an economy is normally declared to be in recession if it has experienced negative growth in its GDP for more than two successive three-month periods.

In the USA, the National Bureau of Economic Research (NBER) defines an economic recession as 'a significant decline in economic activity spread across the country, lasting more than a few months, normally visible in falling real GDP growth, real personal income, employment, industrial production, and wholesale-retail sales'.

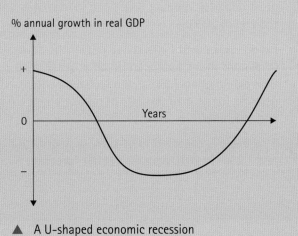

▲ A U-shaped economic recession

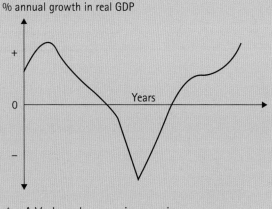

▲ A V-shaped economic recession

Boom or bust?

The charts below show cyclical changes or fluctuations in economic growth in the Maltese and South African economies between 1991 and 2016.

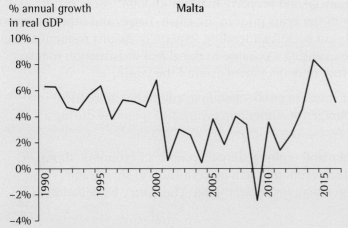

% annual growth in real GDP — Malta

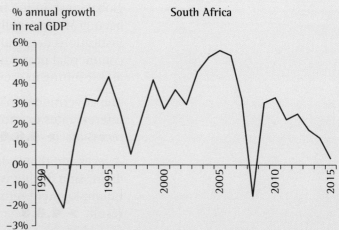

% annual growth in real GDP — South Africa

1 What is the economic cycle?

2 What evidence is there from the charts that Malta and South Africa have economic cycles?

3 In which years did Malta and South Africa experience economic booms?

4 In which years did Malta and South Africa experience economic recessions?

5 Describe what might be happening to consumer expenditure, investment, employment and government revenues during these periods of recession.

ECONOMICS IN ACTION

According to the article, what is a double-dip recession?

Why did this occur in Finland in 2010?

How do you think, or try to find out, how economists might describe a double-dip recession in terms of a letter to represent its 'shape'.

Finland suffers double-dip

Finland has become the first European Union country to suffer a double-dip recession after its economy contracted again in the first quarter of 2010, hit by a port strike in March and a colder than usual winter.

Despite a brief recovery during the last quarter of 2009 data yesterday showed January–March 2010 gross domestic product (GDP) had fallen 0.4% since the end of 2009.

Export-dependent Finland had one of the deepest recessions in the European Union in 2009, with GDP plummeting 7.8% as the global downturn hit demand for its main exports of mobile phones, paper and machines.

A recovery is expected to be slow, with growth of just 1.25% in 2010 and 2% in 2011 forecast.

Consequences of economic growth

The benefits of growth

Sustained economic growth can bring widespread benefits to an economy, its people, firms and government, for example:

- greater availability of goods and services to satisfy consumers' needs and wants

- increased employment opportunities and incomes

- increased sales and profits, and increased business opportunities

- low and stable price inflation, if growth in output matches growth in demand

- increasing tax revenues for a government, that can be invested in more and better roads, schools, healthcare, crime prevention and other merit goods and public services

- improved living standards and economic welfare.

Growth and welfare

▲ Progress at any price?

However, economic growth need not improve the quality of life for everyone. While some people may become rich, many others may remain poor and have a low standard of living. The distribution of income and wealth in many countries is very unequal and may become more so if the benefits of growth are concentrated among relatively few people.

In addition, economic growth can have other negative impacts:

- Technical progress may replace workers with machines so more people become unemployed for long periods of time.

- Growth might only be achieved by producing more capital goods at the expense of consumer goods. However, are people necessarily better off if growth is achieved, for example, by producing more weapons, cigarettes or coal-fired power stations? Equally, are people better off simply because they have more cars, televisions and computer games?

- Economic growth may mean we use up scarce resources at a faster rate. Oil, coal, metals and other natural resources are limited and may soon run out. Forests may be cut down and green space used up at an increasing rate to build more houses, roads, factories, offices and shops.

- Increasing production and energy use may increase noise, air, water and scenic pollution. Marine and wildlife habitats may be destroyed killing many creatures and plants. People may also suffer from more health problems as a result. ➤ 2.10.2

Economic growth can therefore involve a significant opportunity cost in terms of its social and environmental impacts. Because of this, governments around the world are increasingly focused on achieving **sustainable growth**.

Sustainable economic growth involves reducing the rate at which we use up natural resources, reducing waste in production and consumption and reducing harmful emissions by changing the way we produce and consume goods and services.

For governments this means using policies to minimize the costs and harmful effects of economic growth – for example, by encouraging investments in renewable energies, recycling and more efficient production methods, placing restrictions on emissions of harmful pollutants from power stations and vehicle exhausts, raising taxes on petrol to reduce car use, and so on.

ACTIVITY 4.14

Economic boom, environmental bust

China's spectacular economic growth – averaging 8% or more annually over the past two decades – has produced an impressive increase in the standard of living for hundreds of millions of Chinese citizens. However, its economic rise has come at the expense of its environment and public health.

China is now the world's largest source of carbon emissions, having overtaken the USA in 2007, and the air quality of many of its major cities fails to meet international health standards. Studies suggest that poor air quality in Chinese cities causes significant health complications including respiratory and cardiovascular, and contributes to an estimated 1.2 million premature deaths annually. Life expectancy north of the Huai River is now 5.5 years lower than in the south due to air pollution.

In January 2013, Beijing experienced a prolonged bout of smog so severe that citizens dubbed it an "airpocalypse"; the concentration of hazardous particles was forty times the level deemed safe by the World Health Organization (WHO). And again in December 2015, Beijing issued red alerts for severe pollution and municipal authorities closed schools, limited road traffic, halted outdoor construction and paused factory manufacturing.

Coal is largely to blame for the degradation of China's air quality. It is the world's largest coal producer and accounts for about half of global consumption. Mostly burned in the north, coal provides around two-thirds of China's energy although demand for coal now appears to be falling.

There was also a record 17 million new cars on the road in 2014, further contributing to China's high emissions. Car ownership was up to 154 million compared to just 27 million in 2004, according to China's National Bureau of Statistics.

Another trend compounding air problems has been the country's staggering pace of urbanization, a national priority. The government aims to have more than 60 percent of the Chinese population living in cities by 2020, up from 36 percent in 2000. Rapid urbanization increases energy demands to power new manufacturing and industrial centres as well as an increasing number of consumer electronic items purchased by consumers as real wages in the country have risen.

Experts also cite water depletion and pollution as among the country's biggest environmental challenges. China is home to 20 percent of the world's population but only 7 percent of its freshwater sources. Overuse and contamination have produced severe shortages, with nearly 70 percent of the country's water supplies dedicated to agriculture and 20 percent of supplies used in the coal industry, according to Choke Point: China, a non-government organisation.

The rapid growth of industries along China's major rivers has polluted water supplies. In 2014, groundwater supplies in more than 60 percent of major cities were categorized as "bad to very bad," and more than a quarter of China's key rivers as "unfit for human contact." A lack of waste removal and proper processing has exacerbated problems.

Combined with negligent farming practices, overgrazing, and the effects of climate change, the water crisis has turned much of China's arable land into desert. About 1.05 million square miles of China's landmass are undergoing desertification, affecting more than 400 million people, according to the deputy head of China's State Forestry Administration.

Water scarcity, pollution, and desertification are reducing China's ability to sustain its industrial output and produce food and drinkable water for its large population. Environmental degradation therefore poses a serious threat to China's economic growth which could cost the country roughly 3 to 10 percent of its gross national income, according to various estimates.

Recent studies have reported that emissions from China's export industries are also worsening air pollution as far as the western United States. China's neighbours, including Japan and South Korea, have also expressed concern over acid rain and smog affecting their populations. Environmental ministers from the three northeast Asian countries agreed to boost cooperative efforts to curb air pollution and to protect water quality and the maritime environment in 2014.

In response to these growing problems, the Chinese government has mapped out a series of ambitious environmental initiatives. For example, since January 2014, it has required fifteen thousand factories, including large state-owned enterprises, to publicly report real-time figures on air emissions and water discharges. The government also pledged to spend $275 billion over the next five years to clean up the air and $333 billion for water pollution.

China is now also one of the biggest investors in wind, solar and other renewable energy sources. This follows pledges made by China to obtain 15 percent of its energy from clean energy sources including renewables, nuclear and hydropower and to reduce the carbon intensity of its economy by 2020 by 40 to 45 percent from 2005 levels.

1 What is economic growth?

2 According to the article, by how much has the Chinese economy grown each year on average in the recent past?

3 What have been the likely benefits of this growth to Chinese people?

4 According to the article, is the fast pace of economic growth in China sustainable?

5 From the article identify social and environmental costs of economic growth in China.

6 What is the Chinese government doing to try to achieve more sustainable growth?

SECTION 4.6.6

Policy measures and their effectiveness

Policies to promote economic growth

Government policies to promote economic growth will focus on:

- boosting total demand during an economic recession;

- trying to increase total supply by improving long run growth in factor productivity so that factors of production are able to produce more total output.

Demand-side policies

Using fiscal and monetary policy instruments to boost total demand will be important during an economic recession or slump in demand.

- A government may boost total demand by cutting direct taxes and increasing public expenditures. Lower income tax will increase disposable income and encourage consumer spending. Increased spending on welfare payments will also encourage consumer spending while increased spending on capital projects such as new road constructions will help create new jobs by increasing business and household incomes. ➤ 4.3.8

- Monetary policy may also be used to reduce interest rates to encourage higher levels of borrowing and therefore spending in the economy. If lower interest rates fail to boost demand, the government may also instruct the central bank to use measures such as quantitative easing to increase the money supply in the economy. ➤ **4.4.2**

However, boosting total demand during an economic recession will do very little to expand the productive potential of the economy and its rate of long run growth. This requires supply-side policies.

Supply-side policies

Supply-side policies are required to reduce or remove barriers that may prevent improvements in productivity and the productive capacity of the economy. Measures designed to achieve this include:

- Investing in **improvements to education and training**, to increase the skills, knowledge and mobility of the current and future workforce;

- Supporting investments in the **research and development (R&D)** of new, innovative products, technologies, production processes and materials that can be used to produce more and better goods and services;

- Public investments in **modernizing existing and building new economic infrastructure**, such as new power generation and distribution systems, mobile and broadband communications networks, roads, airports and ports, all of which will directly benefit many firms, the process of production and the movement of people, goods and services within an economy;

- Giving **tax cuts and subsidies** to new firms to encourage people to start new businesses;

- **Encouraging multinationals** to locate and invest in the economy thereby boosting output and providing additional jobs;

- Plus other measures aimed at improving resource efficiency including privatization, deregulation, lowering income taxes to improve work incentives and labour market reforms. ➤ **4.5.2**

The main problem with supply-side policies is that they can take a considerable time to work. For example, major infrastructure projects often take many years to build and it may also take several years for investments in education to lead to higher labour productivity.

Such investments also tend to be very expensive. A government may have to increase taxes and/or its borrowing to pay for them. Both actions are likely to reduce or crowd out private sector spending. Unless there is sufficient demand in an economy for their goods and services, firms will be reluctant to increase production and set up new businesses.

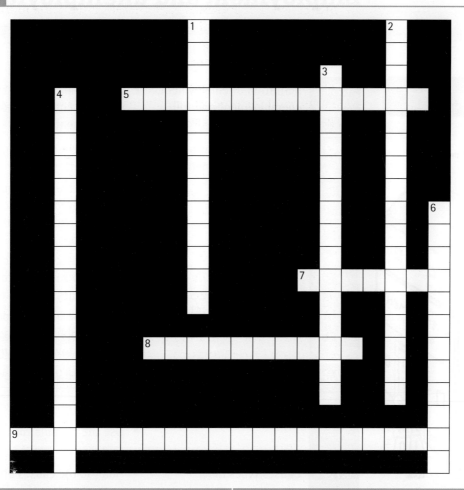

Clues across

5. An increase in the real GDP of an economy (8, 5)
7. The value of the total output of an economy after adjusting for changes in prices over time. It is a measure of GDP at constant prices (4, 1, 1, 1)
8. The money value of the GDP of an economy (7, 1, 1, 1)
9. The total market value of all final goods and services produced within an economy by its factors of production in a given period of time (5, 8, 7)

Clues down

1. The recurrent pattern of fairly predictable fluctuations in the growth rate of real GDP over time that can be observed in many economies (8, 5)
2. Stable growth in real output without depleting natural resources or harming the natural environment (11, 5)
3. The difference between the market value of an output and the cost of inputs used in its production (5, 5, 5)
4. A general slowdown in the rate of economic growth in an economy following an economic boom or peak. Officially, it is usually associated with negative growth in real GDP (8, 9)
6. Average income per head (1-1-1, 3, 6)

IN THIS UNIT:

4.7.1	Definition of employment, unemployment and full employment	▶ Define and distinguish between employment, unemployment and full employment
4.7.2	Changing patterns and levels of employment	▶ Identify the nature and causes of changes in the pattern of employment, including: • an increase in proportion of workers employed in the tertiary sector and formal economy as an economy develops; • a greater proportion of women in the labour force due to changes in social attitudes; • decline in the proportion employed in the public sector as some countries move towards market economies
4.7.3	Measurement of unemployment	▶ Explain how unemployment is measured using claimant counts or labour force surveys ▶ Use the formula for the unemployment rate
4.7.4	Causes/types of unemployment	▶ Analyse the causes of different types of unemployment (frictional, cyclical and structural)
4.7.5	Consequences of unemployment	▶ Discuss the consequences of unemployment for individuals, firms and an economy as a whole
4.7.6	Policies to reduce unemployment	▶ Discuss the range of policies available to a government to reduce unemployment and analyse how effective they might be

Definition of employment, unemployment and full employment

Changing patterns and level of employment

Measurement of unemployment

Most governments share an objective to achieve **full employment** in their economies. This means maintaining a high and stable level of employment in their economies, and keeping unemployment low. Employment provides people with incomes and wealth. In contrast, unemployment is a waste of productive resources.

Because of these objectives, governments and economists will be interested in keeping a close eye on the following employment trends.

▼ Key employment indicators

Labour force	The total number of people of working age in work or actively seeking work
Labour force participation rate	The labour force as a proportion of the total working-age population
Employment by industrial sector	How many people work in agriculture and manufacturing industries, relative to services
Employment status	The number of people employed full-time, part-time or in temporary work
Unemployment	The number of people registered as being without work, and as a proportion of the total labour force (the unemployment rate)

▼ World employment and unemployment, 2000–2016

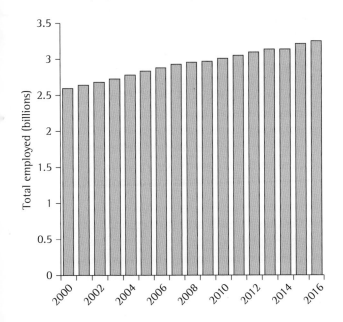

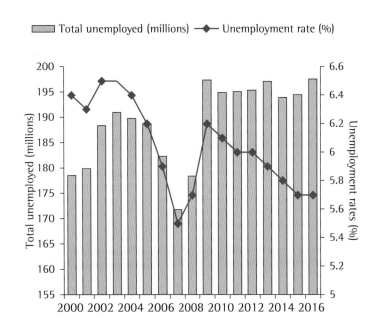

Source: *International Labour Organization (ILO)*

Labour force participation

Between 2000 and 2016 the world labour force grew by around 650 million people, to over 3.4 billion. The **labour force** is the **working population** or **economically active population** of a country. It consists of all those people of working age who are both able and willing to work. That is, it forms the total supply of labour in a country and usually includes people who are employed by private sector firms and public sector organizations, the self-employed, the armed forces, those on work-related government training programmes and even people who are unemployed but looking for work.

People not counted as economically active in the labour force include students in education, retired people, stay-at-home parents, people in prisons or similar institutions, as well as people who simply do not want to work. These form the **dependent population** because they depend on the labour force to produce and supply the goods and services they need and want. ➤ **7.2**

▼ The working and dependent populations

The Young | Housewives | Schoolchildren and Students | The Employed | Self Employed | Armed Forces | The Unemployed | The Old and Severely Disabled

The **labour force participation rate** measures the percentage of the working-age population that is either in work or looking for work and therefore able to produce goods and services. Globally the labour force participation rate has fallen slightly over time, from 65.3% in 1999 to 62.8% in 2017. This means around 63 people in every 100 in the global population of working age is in or seeking paid employment. Much of this decline in participation is explained by the increasing number of younger people in education worldwide and the growing number of old and retired people in many developed countries. ➤ **5.3.3**

However, not all countries have followed the global trend. Participation in the labour force has risen over time in a number of developing countries and especially among females, particularly in Latin America and the Caribbean, Africa, the Arab States and Europe. For example, around just over 48% of females of working age participated in the labour force in Latin American and Caribbean economies in 2000. By 2017 this had increased by 4.6% to almost 53%.

There are a number of reasons for these trends and the regional differences in participation rates. In many developing economies, poverty has forced many people to seek formal paid employment rather than work on the land to grow the food they need and that they hope will yield a surplus they can sell. But many workers in developing economies still earn very low wages. ➤ **5.4.1**

Increasing real wages in many countries have also attracted more females into work. The rising cost of living in many of these countries has also forced many into work to maintain the living standards of their families. This can explain why more mothers are returning to work after raising children, or younger women entering the labour market rather than starting a family even in many developed and relatively high-income economies. Social attitudes have also changed in many countries so that is it now more acceptable for wives and mothers to work. Many more part-time jobs have become available to them so they can balance their family and working commitments.

▼ How labour force participation rates have changed around the world

Source: *International Labour Organization (ILO)*

Employment by industrial sector

However, male participation rates have been falling. Globally, around 79 in every 100 males of working age was in work or seeking work in 2000. By 2017 this had fallen to around 76. This fall has been explained by the changing industrial structure in many developed economies, with traditionally male-dominated sectors such as mining and manufacturing industries shrinking over time as their tertiary sectors have expanded. But falling male participation rates have also been observed in many developing countries as female participation has increased.

In 2017, the agriculture sector employed around 29% of global employees, or just under 1 billion workers. This compared with 21.5% employed in mining, construction and manufacturing industries, and 49.7% in services.

However, there are big regional differences. In high-income economies such as the USA and Europe, agriculture employed just 3.1% of their employees in

2017. The service sector dominates these economies, accounting for just under 75% of their total employment. In stark contrast, agriculture continues to dominate employment in the lowest-income economies in Africa, employing almost 69% of all employees in these economies. ➤ **5.3.3**

Many economies have experienced the same broad trends. The share of employment accounted for by jobs in agriculture has been falling as the share of total employment in services has risen around the world. Globally, services employed almost half of all employees in 2017 compared with just under 41 in every 100 in 1999. However, while employment in manufacturing and construction in many developed economies has declined, these industries have expanded rapidly in newly industrialized economies in regions such as South and East Asia, including China and India.

Changes in the industrial structure of economies have been a cause for some concern. The loss of jobs from agriculture, mining and manufacturing industries in many developed economies has increased unemployment in some cases, especially in economies in which these industries once dominated. Nearly 75 in every 100 employees in developed economies are now employed in services.

▼ Shares of total employment by sector and region (%)

Region	Agriculture		Industry		Services	
	2000	2017	2000	2017	2000	2017
Northern Africa	31.1	24.5	21.7	25.5	47.1	50.0
Sub-Saharan Africa	58.7	55.6	10.3	10.7	31.0	33.7
Latin America and the Caribbean	17.2	15.6	22.4	21.5	60.4	63.0
North America	2.6	1.5	22.5	17.5	74.9	81.0
Arab States	18.0	12.6	21.2	25.1	60.8	62.3
Eastern Asia	45.2	24.8	20.3	24.1	34.6	51.0
South-Eastern Asia and the Pacific	46.9	31.1	16.2	20.7	37.0	48.3
Southern Asia	58.0	43.4	15.9	23.3	26.1	33.3
Northern, Southern and Western Europe	5.5	3.5	28.6	22.3	65.8	74.3
Eastern Europe	19.3	9.8	29.1	28.0	51.7	62.3
Central Asia	40.4	28.3	19.5	22.4	40.1	49.3

Source: *International Labour Organization (ILO)*

The decline of employment in agriculture and the expansion of jobs in industry and services have also meant that many people have moved from rural areas into urban areas in many developing countries. The rapid growth of densely populated urban areas and increasing demand for energy, rising car use and overcrowding are causing many problems. ➤ **5.3.3**

Public sector employment is also declining in some countries as their governments introduce more market reforms in their economies and reduce the size of their public sectors through privatization and efficiency improvements. ➤ **2.11.2**

Employment status

Most workers, especially males, are in **full-time employment** contracts which for many means working Monday to Friday each week, for around seven to eight hours each day. However, hours of work vary greatly in different countries. For example, in 2016 the average worker in France worked around 36 hours each week. This compared with an average of just under 48 hours per worker per week in Columbia and Turkey.

Many countries follow an international standard that defines the working week as 40 hours from Monday to Friday, although clearly many people are employed to work weekends and overtime. For example, the EU Working Time Directive regulates that workers cannot be forced to work for more than 48 hours per week on average.

In many countries, average hours worked per week have fallen over time as working conditions have improved, and as a result of more **part-time employment** opportunities.

There has been rapid growth in part-time employment in the last few decades and in Sunday working in many developed economies. These trends are related to the increase in the female participation rate, but also linked to growth in the services sector, and particularly in retailing. Hiring part-time workers allows firms greater flexibility to remain operational for more hours each day and to use more staff during busy periods.

Unemployment

People without work but who are actively looking for employment are considered to be unemployed. In 2016 around 198 million people were unemployed globally.

Around one in three of the world's unemployed in 2016 were young people. Young workers tend to be the least productive employees until they have developed the skills and experience they need. They are often therefore the first to be laid off when firms cut back staff to reduce their costs or during an economic recession when demand is falling.

Unemployment is usually measured by the number of people officially registered as unemployed and claiming social welfare payments or unemployment benefits. However, in many countries benefits may only be paid for a short period of time, and some people who want to work may not receive any financial help from government. This group might include people who are old or disabled, mothers looking after children at home, students who want to work but instead continue with their education, and people who may only work a few hours each week but would like to work longer.

In practice, therefore, measuring the number of unemployed workers actually seeking work is very difficult and measures can vary by country. Some countries do not pay benefits to unemployed people and may not even count the number of people without paid work, so numbers are estimated where possible from periodic labour force surveys.

▼ Unemployment rate (%) by region

Region	2000	2016
World	6.4	5.7
Northern Africa	15.1	12.1
Sub-Saharan Africa	8.1	7.2
Latin America and the Caribbean	10.9	8.1
North America	4.3	5.1
Arab States	9.7	10.7
Eastern Asia	4.5	4.5
South-Eastern Asia and the Pacific	4.9	3.8
Southern Asia	4.6	4.1
Northern, Southern and Western Europe	8.8	9.3
Eastern Europe	10.9	6.2
Central Asia	10.5	7.9

▼ Countries with the highest unemployment rates (%)

Country	Unemployment rate (%) estimated
Solomon Islands	31.4
Gambia	29.7
Lesotho	27.4
Macedonia	26.7
South Africa	25.9
Bosnia and Herzegovina	25.8
Namibia	25.6
Swaziland	25.3
Occupied Palestinian Territory	24.9
Mozambique	24.4
Greece	23.9
Comoros	20.0

Source: *International Labour Organization (ILO)*

The **unemployment rate** in an economy is the percentage of people in its labour force that are without work and recorded as unemployed. Globally, the unemployment rate fell during the economic boom in the middle of the last decade from 6.4% in 2000 to 5.4% in 2007. However, unemployment rose sharply around the world between 2008 and 2010 as the boom came to end and many economies suffered from falling incomes and demand during a widespread economic downturn that affected many countries. By 2016 the unemployment rate had fallen back to 5.7%. This meant just under 6 in every 100 people of working age in the world labour force was without paid employment in 2016.

The global economic recession from 2008 to 2010 affected some regions far more than others. In some developed economies, including some in the European Union, the unemployment rate climbed from 12.4% in 2007 to over 18% in 2010 with countries such as Spain, Italy and Greece particularly badly hit. In 2016 unemployment remained high in these countries due to their continuing economic difficulties, particularly in Greece where almost one quarter of its workforce remained out of work. However, by 2016 the global unemployment rate had fallen back to 5.7%, as many economies recovered from recession and total unemployment fell by more than the increase in the world labour force over the same period.

Calculating unemployment rates

The table below presents data on the labour force and number of people unemployed in selected countries in 2000 and 2016. From these calculate the unemployment rate in each country for each year using the following formula.

$$\text{Unemployment rate (\%)} = \frac{\text{number unemployed}}{\text{labour force}} \times 100$$

Country	Labour force (000s)		Unemployed (000s)	
	2000	2016	2000	2016
Czech Republic	5,190	5,310	455	215
France	27,379	29,849	2,941	2,971
Japan	67,004	64,811	3,149	2,041
Mexico	40,778	59,388	1,045	2,340
Spain	18,510	22,788	2,552	4,444
Turkey	21,381	30,318	1,389	3,086
USA	147,998	163,905	5,920	7,998

Source: *International Labour Organization (ILO)*

Some of the highest unemployment rates are often observed in many of the least developed economies in the world where low levels of education and skills among the labour force and a lack of paid employment opportunities continue to cause problems for economic development. ➤ **5.4.1**

Causes and types of unemployment

Consequences of unemployment

Casual and seasonal factors

Full employment does not mean zero unemployment. There will always be some **frictional unemployment** as workers leave one job and spend some time looking for a new one. Workers may become unemployed for relatively short periods as they leave jobs they dislike, move to higher paid jobs, move their homes, are made redundant or are sacked. People who are 'in between jobs' do not tend to remain unemployed for long.

Similarly, **seasonal unemployment** occurs because consumer demand for some goods and services is seasonal. For example, the number of jobs in the tourist industry tends to expand during the summer because that is when most people want to take holidays. However, during winter months many workers in hotels and holiday resorts are not required. Agriculture and construction activity also tend to be very seasonal.

Frictional and seasonal unemployment are not a big problem. Most governments, however, are concerned with unemployment that is long-lived and due to more serious problems in their economies.

ACTIVITY 4.16

What causes unemployment?

Look at the extracts below. What do they suggest causes unemployment? In groups, write a report for your government expressing a summary of your thoughts on the possible causes of unemployment and what actions you might take to reduce it.

Firms cut output as consumer spending falls

Government introduces minimum wage law: businesses warn demand for labour will fall

State council votes to increase unemployment tax

Starting January 1, employers will be hit with a 50 percent increase in the taxes they pay to fund unemployment benefits, the Nevada State Employment Security Council decided Tuesday.

Despite business leaders' protests, council members voted to increase the unemployment tax rate to an average of 2 percent on the first $26,600 of each employee's wages, up from the 1.33 percent rate.

The Las Vegas Chamber of Commerce argued that higher taxes will raise the cost of employing people and will force some businesses to lay off more workers.

The Council argued the tax increase is necessary to cover the increasing cost of providing public unemployment insurance.

Unemployed workers in Nevada receive weekly benefit checks that average $325. Some business leaders have argued these benefits are too generous. They suggest a family man on or below average earnings will be better not working and receiving benefits.

700 jobs lost in switch to new technology

At least one quarter of a major newspaper's workforce are to be made redundant this week in a plan to introduce new computerised typesetting and printing machines

Business experts call for help for manufacturing industries

A study by a group of business experts has found that the country's poor export performance and high import penetration is the result of low levels of investment in capital and workforce skills. This has caused a serious decline in the health of the manufacturing industry. The report argues government assistance is required to boost performance and jobs.

Falling aggregate demand

Falling aggregate demand for goods and services can have multiplier effect on output, employment and incomes.

Demand-deficient unemployment or **cyclical unemploy** there is too little demand for goods and services in the eco economic recession. ➤ **4.6.3**

Falling demand during a downturn in an economic cycle will spending on goods and services. Stocks of unsold products w response firms will cut their production and workers may become unemployed.

A change in aggregate demand whatever its source, be it consumption expenditure, investment by firms, government spending and/or spending on exports by overseas consumers, can have widespread effects in an economy. Once under way, a change in expenditure will tend to carry on. Why is this so?

ACTIVITY 4.17

The multiplier effect

A fall in total demand in an economy can have widespread effects. This is known as the multiplier effect.

Here is an example of how unemployment can spread following a fall in demand for automobiles.

Our simple example involves an imaginary car manufacturer called Fast Cars Inc. It has a plant in Malaysia that assembles cars from materials and components made by other companies in the country.

As demand for its cars falls Fast Cars Inc has no need to make so many. As a result, it reduces production and makes 400 of its workers redundant. Now consider how this might spread.

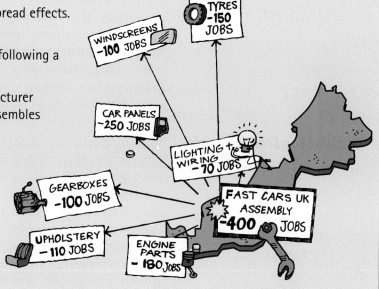

1   How many jobs are lost immediately as a result of the fall in demand for cars?

2   How many jobs are lost in Fast Cars Inc in total?

3   All the factories use electricity. As they now produce fewer cars they do not need to consume much electricity. What may happen to output and employment at power stations?

4   The power stations run on coal and oil. What will happen to the demand for coal and oil? What will happen to coal miners and oil drillers?

5   All the people who have lost their jobs now have less money to spend on clothes, entertainment, food, travel and many other things. What is likely to happen to the level of demand for these goods?

In Activity 4.17, the fall in demand for cars forced Fast Cars to reduce production and cut employment in many of its factories. Fast Cars buys component parts and uses power produced by other firms that also reduce their output as demand for their products falls. The workers who find themselves out of work have less money to spend. Shops suffer and have to reduce their orders from their suppliers. The fall in demand for goods and services becomes more widespread and causes many more firms to reduce their output and employment. As unemployment rises so aggregate demand falls. Firms cut back their demand for labour further. This is known as the **multiplier effect** whereby a relatively small change in total expenditure can cause much larger changes in income, output and employment.

...uctural change

If the fall in demand for some goods and services is permanent because of a change in people's tastes, for example in favour of new goods and services or cheaper sources of supply from overseas firms, the change in demand is called structural.

Structural unemployment arises from long-term changes in the structure of an economy as entire industries in an economy close down because of a lack of demand for the goods or services they produce or because production is moved to countries overseas able to produce at much lower average costs, often because their wages are lower. As a result, many workers are made unemployed and have skills that are no longer wanted. That is, they are occupationally immobile because they lack the skills modern industries want. Retraining them in new skills may help them become more mobile and find new jobs. ➤ **1.2.2**

Structural change can cause prolonged **regional unemployment** if most of the firms in the affected industries are located in one particular area.

Changes in industrial structure is evident in many developed and developing economies. Many years ago far more people were employed in agriculture than in manufacturing industries. Manufacturing has also changed over time in many countries from labour-intensive production in industries such as shipbuilding, coal mining and textiles, to the high-tech capital-intensive production of computers, pharmaceuticals and electronic equipment. Nowadays most workers in developed countries are employed in services.

Technological change

Technological progress has had a major impact on the way many goods and services are produced and sold. Industrial robots and computerized machinery and equipment have been substituted for labour in many modern production processes, giving rise to what has been termed **technological unemployment**. For example, many banks and retailers are reducing the number of staff they employ as more people bank and shop online using the internet. However, as economists we should consider the potential benefits of being able to reallocate these unemployed resources to other uses. For example, there has been a rapid growth in employment in technologically advanced industries such as electronics, biotechnology, renewable energy and mobile communications.

Labour market barriers or failures

Demand and supply conditions will determine the market wage rates for different occupations and how many workers are employed in a free labour market. However, there are often many barriers or failures in labour markets that can result in inefficient market outcomes and a misallocation of resources. ➤ **2.10.2**

1 Powerful trade unions may force up wages

Trade unions may attempt to increase the wages of their members without also improving their labour productivity, for example by restricting the supply of labour to an industry or occupation by insisting all workers belong to the union or by threatening to take industrial action. As wages rise, employers may not be able to afford to employ as many workers and will contract their demand for labour. Reducing the bargaining power of trade unions, it is argued, may allow wages to fall and employment to rise. ➤ **3.4.3**

2 Unemployment benefits may reduce the incentive to work

Some countries provide welfare or unemployment benefits to people who become unemployed. However, some people argue these can reduce people's incentive to seek paid employment, especially if these benefits are too generous.

People who decide not to work (**voluntary unemployment**) could be forced back to work if the benefits they receive are cut. However, this may be unfair to those people who are out of work through no fault of their own, for example because of a fall in the demand for the good or service they produce (**involuntary unemployment**).

3 Other employment costs can reduce the demand for labour

Firms that employ workers may have to pay more than just their wages to do so. As well as wages and salaries, total employment costs may include taxes and contributions to fund publicly provided unemployment and welfare benefits and non-wage costs including sickness, maternity and paternity costs, recruitment and training costs. If any of these additional costs increase, the demand for labour by firms may fall and unemployment will tend to rise. Cutting payroll taxes on employment may therefore increase the demand for labour.

4 A lack of information can prevent people from finding jobs

Unemployment may be higher and people may remain unemployed for longer periods than necessary if they have trouble finding jobs because of a lack of information on employment opportunities or because it costs too much time and money to search for the most suitable ones.

Workers who become unemployed may never be fully aware of all the various jobs that might be suitable for them and the wages, conditions and other factors involved in these jobs. They will spend time and effort looking for the best match for their skills and interests. This of course is beneficial for an economy since it results in a much better allocation of resources. However, if the cost of job search is too high, or if it takes people too long to find suitable jobs and so they make too many compromises by accepting less suitable jobs or by waiting for better jobs to become available, then an economy will suffer: the allocation of resources will not be as good as it could be, productivity will be lower and some work may even not get done.

Governments can help reduce search costs by providing advice and assistance to people looking for employment and by collecting information about job vacancies and providing it at government-funded employment offices and agencies.

5 Minimum wage legislation may reduce labour demand

Many countries have introduced laws that make it an offence for a firm to pay its workers less than a certain hourly, daily or monthly wage. The first national minimum wage laws were introduced by New Zealand in 1896. Minimum wages are designed to raise the market wage rates of the lowest paid workers. However, some employers argue they have been set too high in some countries and this has reduced their demand for labour, especially for low-skilled workers with low levels of productivity. ➤ **3.3.2**

6 Labour immobility prevents workers from finding new jobs

When economists talk of labour immobility they refer to the inability of workers to move easily into other jobs. When unemployed workers are immobile they will tend to remain out of work for longer periods of time.

Occupational immobility refers to the inability of workers to move easily between different occupations because of a lack of transferable skills. For example, an engineer will be unable to get a job as a doctor in a hospital without extensive retraining.

However, in some cases a trade union closed shop may prevent non-union members taking on a particular job. Professional associations of solicitors or architects, for example, may act in the same way and prevent people entering their occupation unless they have taken certain professional examinations.

Some employers may even refuse to employ some people because of their sex or colour, although this is illegal in many countries if it can be proved.

Other workers are immobile if they are unable or unwilling to move to another area to take up a job. In this case a worker is said to be **geographically immobile**. Regional differences in house prices, ties with family and friends, children's schooling and many other factors may prevent people from moving location in search of work. ➤ **1.2.2**

The costs of unemployment

Labour unemployment has been described as a 'drain on a nation' and 'a waste of resources'. In this section we will try to discover the consequences of labour unemployment.

Personal costs

Unemployment can have both economic and emotional costs. People who lose their jobs will lose their income and may have to rely on charity or government benefits. Unemployed people can also lose their working skills if they are unemployed for a long period of time and, without re-training, they may find it even harder to find work. They may become depressed, possibly even ill, and it may also put a strain on other family members and healthcare services.

> The Jamaica Gleaner Youth Link usefully describes some of the personal and social costs of unemployment as follows:
>
> • Persons who are unemployed are unable to earn money to meet their financial obligations.
>
> • In many cases, unemployment results in failure to meet mortgage payments or rent. It may lead to homelessness through foreclosure or eviction.
>
> • Unemployment increases people's susceptibility to malnutrition, illness, mental stress and loss of self-esteem, leading to depression.
>
> • The combination of unemployment, lack of financial resources and social responsibilities may push unemployed workers to take jobs that do not fit their skills or allow them to use their talents.
>
> • Unemployment can cause underemployment, and fear of job loss can cause psychological anxiety.
>
> • During a long period of unemployment, workers can lose their skills, causing a loss of their human capital and future earning potential.
>
> • High levels of unemployment can increase crime and cause civil unrest.

A sorry tale to tell

UNEMPLOYED DROWN THEIR SORROWS

Beneath the national aggregates for disposable income and consumer durables, the country is fostering an underclass of unemployed and unskilled workers, afflicted by family breakdown and also alcoholism, according to recent data.

In recent years a network of advisory and counselling services have grown up, among them Alcoholics Anonymous, reflecting growing alcohol abuse in society and especially among the unemployed. In spite of the fact that the unemployed usually have less to spend on drink and everything else there is a considerably higher proportion of heavy drinkers among unemployed men.

In addition, divorce rates among couples where the man is jobless are noticeably high. There is also a link with chronic illness.

▼ Suicide and unemployment in Japan

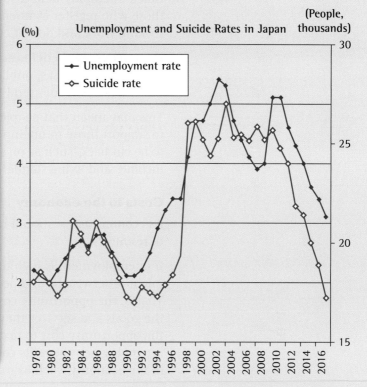

Source: *Statistics Bureau; National Police Agency*

1 What impact can unemployment have on government finances and the economy?

2 How do the articles suggest unemployment can affect families?

3 What other personal costs can an unemployed person face?

4 Ronald Reagan, the 40th president of the USA, once famously described unemployment benefits as 'a pre-paid vacation for freeloaders'. Using information from the articles and drawing on your own experience of people who have been or are unemployed, write a series of short letters of complaint to a national newspaper to express how you might feel about being out of work if you were:

   a a teenager living with parents who are unemployed

   b an unemployed person in their early thirties with children to support

   c a person in their late fifties who until recently has been in work all their life.

For each case, compare your views on how you might feel with the views of others in your class.

Is the REAL cost of unemployment £61 billion per year?

Unemployment costs the taxpayer a massive £61 billion a year, with more than five million who could work claiming benefits, a recent UK study has declared.

The analysis of official data takes into account not just the costs of benefits paid to the unemployed, but also the taxes they and their employers would have paid if they were in work.

Taking into account the potential tax revenue lost, the analysis shows the cost of unemployment in the UK is £61 billion a year. That works out as £2,810 for every household in Britain.

But it in no way measures the true cost in terms of lost opportunities. 'We need more imaginative ways of helping people back into work so that we can reduce the cost of unemployment to families, communities and the taxpayer', said the authors of the study.

Fiscal costs

Governments in many countries pay benefits to people who are unemployed. In many cases the benefits paid may only be enough to pay for food and other necessities and for only a limited period of time. Unemployment benefits, also called unemployment insurance in some countries, are generally given only to those who register as unemployed and on condition that they are actively seeking work and do not currently have a job.

Unemployment benefits are paid from direct and indirect tax revenues. As unemployment rises, public expenditure on unemployment benefits tends to rise but tax revenues tend to fall as incomes and spending fall.

This may mean that people remaining in work may have to pay higher taxes to support those in unemployment. Other public expenditures may also have to be cut back, such as on schools, healthcare and roads. The disposable incomes and living standards of many more people may fall as a result.

Costs to the economy

As economists we should realize that leaving labour unemployed is a waste of resources.

If unemployment is high total output and income will be lower than they might otherwise be and people will have fewer goods and services to enjoy. That is, the opportunity cost of having so many workers unemployed is the goods and services they could have produced instead. In addition, there is the opportunity cost to taxpayers. The tax revenue used to pay for unemployment benefits could have been used to fund other beneficial projects in the economy, such as roads and new hospitals.

SECTION 4.7.6

Policy measures and their effectiveness

Policies to reduce unemployment

As unemployment can be caused by different factors at different times in an economy, reducing it can require different policy approaches.

Demand-side policies

Fiscal and monetary policy instruments can be used to boost total demand during an economic recession.

- A **fiscal policy stimulus** may include tax cuts, for example to increase disposable incomes, and increases in public spending, for example on welfare payments and/or on capital projects such as the building of new roads and other public infrastructure to create new jobs. ➤ **4.3.8**

- A **monetary policy stimulus** involves reducing interest rates to make borrowing money cheaper. In a deep and prolonged recession, a government may also boost the money supply in the economy. ➤ **4.4.2**

Fiscal and monetary policies can therefore provide a short-term boost to total demand in an economy to reduce cyclical unemployment. An economic recovery will always create new jobs as demand rises but it will not reduce unemployment if it has been caused by structural or other factors.

Knowing when to stop boosting demand using fiscal and monetary policies can prove particularly difficult. Inflation is likely to accelerate if total demand is increased by too much and for too long, and exceeds growth in the total supply of goods and services in the economy. To be effective therefore, demand-side policies should be combined with a range of supply-side policies aimed at boosting the long-run productive capacity of the economy so that it is able to expand and create more employment opportunities. However, many new jobs will be in new industries and will require new skills. Many of these new jobs may remain unfilled if workers lack the skills and qualifications they need.

Supply-side policies

Supply-side policy instruments will aim to correct or overcome problems that may reduce people's ability to find new jobs, their incentives to find work and firm's incentives to employ them. Many involve long-term measures that may take several years to have their full effect. They may include:

- **Measures to reduce the occupational mobility of labour** can help to reduce structural and technological unemployment by:

  - providing government training and apprenticeship schemes to teach the unemployed the new skills they need to find new jobs in new, growing industries;

  - raising the school leaving age so young people spend longer in education learning a range of skills and acquiring the qualifications they need to increase their chances of finding paid employment when they leave.

- **Regional subsidies** can be offered to firms to locate themselves in areas where old industries have declined to reduce regional concentrations of structural unemployment. However, these can be expensive and the regeneration of depressed areas will often take a very long time to achieve. Alternatively, subsidies could be offered to unemployed workers to move to areas where there are jobs. This can help to reduce their geographic immobility.

- **Employment subsidies** can be paid to firms to employ people who have been unemployed for a long time while **cuts to payroll taxes** on firms may also encourage them to hire more workers. These again can be expensive and may simply encourage firms to lay off some of their existing workers so they can hire from the pool of unemployed to benefit from the subsidies and tax breaks.

- **Labour market reforms**, including:

  - **restricting the power of trade unions** to prevent firms employing non-unionized workers and to use strikes and other industrial actions to bargain for substantial wage increases that are not matched by improvements in the productivity of union members;

  - **reducing minimum wages**, if they have been set at too high a level and have therefore reduced the demand for low paid workers;

  - **cutting the marginal rate of income tax on low incomes**. Some people may be better off receiving unemployment benefits than accepting a low paid job. Lowering the marginal rate of income tax would therefore increase the financial reward from working relative to unemployment benefits;

  - alternatively or at the same time, **reducing unemployment benefits** both in amount and in the length of time people are able to claim them when they are out of work. These measures may however cause hardship for many unemployed people.

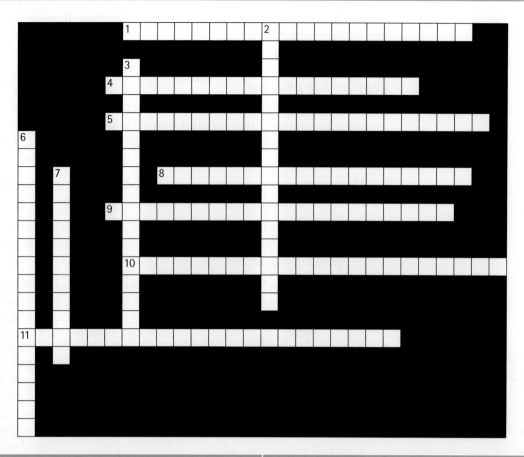

Clues across
1. Periods of joblessness caused by deficient demand during an economic downturn or recession (8, 12)
4. A contract for work that involves the employee working the full number of hours defined by his or her employer as a working week, which is normally around 40 hours each week between Monday to Friday (4-4,11)
5. Joblessness among workers because their skills are out of date and no longer wanted due to changes in demand patterns or technologies that have resulted in the decline of some established industries in an economy (10, 12)
8. A contract for work in which an employee's working time is substantially less than a full working week (4-4, 11)
9. An economic situation in which people on temporary employment contracts lose their jobs during seasonal downturns in activity in particular industries, such as tourism and construction (8, 12)
10. An economic situation in which people find themselves voluntarily out of work usually for short periods of time as they change their jobs (10, 12)
11. The inability of workers to move easily between different occupations because they lack transferable skills. This can prolong structural unemployment (12, 10)

Clues down
2. The proportion of the labour force in an economy that is out of work (12, 4)
3. An effect in economics in which a change in spending produces a much larger change in output and income (10, 6)
6. The percentage of people of working age who choose to be economically active in the labour force (12, 4)
7. The total supply of labour or economically active population in an economy (6, 5)

Unit 4.8   Inflation and deflation

IN THIS UNIT	4.8.1	Definition of inflation and deflation	▶ Define and distinguish between inflation and deflation in the general price level of an economy
	4.8.2	Measurement of inflation and deflation	▶ Describe how a consumer price index (CPI) is used to measure and monitor inflation and deflation
	4.8.3	Causes of inflation and deflation	▶ Explain and distinguish between demand-side and supply-side causes of inflation and deflation
	4.8.4	Consequences of inflation and deflation	▶ Analyse the consequences of inflation and deflation for consumers, workers, savers, lenders, firms and the economy as a whole
	4.8.5	Policies to control inflation and deflation	▶ Discuss the range of policies available to a government to control inflation and deflation and analyse how effective they might be

In the first part of this unit we will look at **price inflation**. It is important to understand what inflation is, how it is measured and the causes and consequences of rising price levels before learning about deflation and the causes and effects of a sustained fall in the general price level in an economy. **Deflation** is therefore covered in the final part of this unit.

Definition of inflation

What is inflation?

Many of the news headlines shown below express concern over how the prices of many goods and services are rising, or inflating, over time. However, not all prices rise at the same rate. The prices of some goods and services may even fall over time, perhaps because consumer demand has dropped or because there has been technical progress that has reduced unit costs. So what exactly is inflation, and why is it a cause for concern for consumers, workers, businesses and governments?

> **13% rise in house prices**

> ROW OVER FARES RISE

> Cheap food era 'over' as prices rise 10pc in supermarkets

> Finance Minister concerned about inflation

> Industry demands inquiry into surging gas bills

> **Price of petrol soars**

> **LCD prices fall; on weak PC sales**

Inflation refers to a general and sustained rise in the level of prices of goods and services. That is, prices of the vast majority of goods and services on sale to consumers just keep on rising and rising. Prices change over time so inflation is always expressed as a rate of change per period of time – per month or per year. For example, in July 2017 the annual inflation rate in the UK was measured at 2.6%. This meant that, on average, the prices of goods and services in the UK had risen by 2.6% since July 2016. However, this general increase in prices was relatively low compared to the inflation rate in 1975. In 1975 the inflation rate in the UK was at 25%: on average, a product that cost £100 at the start of 1975 would have cost £125 by the start of 1976.

But even this inflation rate is low in comparison with the increase in prices some countries have faced at different times in history. For example, the annual inflation rate in Brazil peaked at over 2,000% in the mid-1980s while inflation in Zimbabwe reached a staggering 231,000,000% during 2008. This type of runaway inflation during which prices rise at phenomenal rates and money becomes almost worthless is called **hyperinflation**. ➤ **3.1.1**

Living with 24,000% inflation

Germany in the 1920s is often cited as the best example of so-called 'hyperinflation'. The Berlin government printed huge quantities of worthless paper money to pay off its debts after World War I. People needed a wheelbarrow full of money to buy one loaf of bread; the joke was that thieves would steal the wheelbarrow – and leave the pile of worthless money behind.

Price inflation in the UK

The graph below shows how the annual average rate of price inflation in the UK has varied between 1960 and 2017.

▼ UK price inflation 1960–2017 (% annual change in the Consumer Prices Index: CPI)

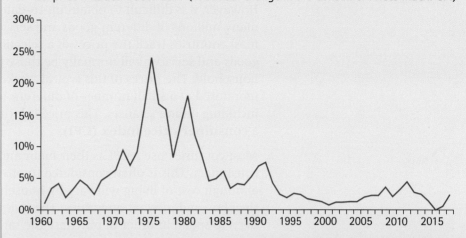

Source: *UK Office for National Statistics*

The UK inflation story is an interesting one but not unlike the experience of many other developed economies.

Between 1960 and 2017, UK price inflation averaged 5.5% each year. This meant that in July 2017 a person in the UK would have had to spend around £21.50 to purchase the same amount of goods and services that £1 did in 1960.

However, while the rate of price inflation in the UK was reasonably low during the 1960s, it accelerated rapidly during the 1970s and became very volatile. Between 1970 and 1990 it averaged 10.2% per year, having peaked at almost 25% in 1975 and at just over 18% in 1980 following a dramatic increase in global oil prices and rising wage costs. As a result unemployment also rose sharply at the same time – an economic situation known as stagflation.

In 1991 inflation peaked again at just over 7.5% but soon after the annual rate in the UK fell and remained relatively low and stable. Between 1992 and 2017 prices increased each year on average by just 2%.

In 2000 and 2015 the annual rate of inflation fell below 1% and reached a record low of –0.1% in the month of April 2015. Negative inflation – a fall in the average level of prices - is called deflation.

However, by mid-2016 inflation in the UK had begun to accelerate again. This followed the decision by the UK to leave the European Union which resulted in a sharp fall in the value of the UK currency pound sterling against the euro and other currencies, making imports to the UK more expensive.

1   From the graph, in which year was UK price inflation at its **a** highest **b** lowest?

2   Over which ten-year period was UK price inflation at its **a** highest **b** lowest?

3   What causes of price inflation can be identified from the passage above?

4   Explain the statement 'Between 1960 and 2017, UK price inflation averaged 5.5% each year. This meant that in July 2017 a person in the UK would have had to spend around £21.50 to purchase the same amount of goods and services that £1 did in 1960'.

Measurement of inflation

Consumer price indices

The rate of price inflation in an economy is measured by calculating the average percentage change in the prices of all goods and services, from one point in time to another, usually each month and year on year.

However, it is difficult to obtain up-to-date price information on all of the many millions of different goods and services exchanged in an economy, so most countries track the prices of a selection of goods and services. These goods and services will normally be those purchased by a 'typical' family or household. The prices of this typical 'basket' of goods and services will then be monitored at a small number of different retail outlets across the economy, including online retailers. This price information will then be used to compile a **consumer price index (CPI)**.

Most countries use a CPI as their main measure of price inflation affecting consumers. This is often considered to provide a cost-of-living index, although cost of living will vary by household according to which products they buy and in what quantities. The index simply indicates what we would need to spend in order to purchase the same things we bought in an earlier period.

A CPI will usually include any sales taxes and excise taxes paid by consumers on their purchases of goods and services, but exclude changes in income taxes and the prices of assets such as stocks and shares, life insurance and housing.

The prices of oil, electricity, gas and food may also be excluded from the calculation of a 'core' CPI used by some governments to set their inflation targets and monetary policies. This is because the prices of these products can be highly volatile, both up and then down again, due to relatively short-lived shortages caused by the weather, such as droughts or severe winters or cutbacks in oil production. These products are therefore excluded from a core CPI on the grounds they can distort measures of more 'usual' or underlying price inflation targeted by government policies.

Calculating a price index

Index number series, or indices, are simply a way of expressing the change in the prices of a number of different products as a movement in just one single number. The average price of the 'basket' of products in the first year of calculation, or **base year**, is given the number 100. Then, if on average the prices of all the goods and services in the same 'basket' rise by 25% over the following year, the price index at the end of the second year will be 125. If in the next year prices rise on average by a further 10%, the price index will rise to 137.5 (that is, 125 × 1.10 = 137.5). This tells us consumer prices have risen on average by 37.5% over a two-year period.

Consider the following simple example to construct a CPI. Imagine there are just 100 households in our simple economy. In the table below, the weekly spending patterns of these households have been observed and recorded over a 12-month period: the base year. The average prices of the goods and services they buy have been calculated for each category of their spending from a sample of different shops.

▼ How to calculate a simple CPI: spending profile of households in base year

Types of goods and services	Proportion of weekly household expenditure spent on each category (%)	Average price ($) of goods and services purchased in each category	Weighted average price ($)
Clothing and footwear	25	$40	0.25 x $40 = $10
Household goods and services	15	$60	0.15 x $60 = $9
Food	40	$5	0.40 x $5 = $2
Travel	20	$20	0.20 x $20 = $4
Total	100%		Price of basket $25

The proportion of total household expenditure spent on each category is used to weight the average prices of each type of good and service to find their weighted average prices. These tell us how big an impact a change in the price of one particular type of good or service will have on the cost of living of our households. For example, from the table it should be clear that a 10% increase in the average price of clothing and footwear, from $40 to $44 per item, will matter more than a 10% increase in the prices of household goods and services, from $60 to $66, because our households spend proportionately more of their weekly expenditures on clothes and shoes. The weighted average price of clothing and footwear purchased is higher than the weighted average price of household products purchased.

Adding up the weighted average prices in the basket of goods and services in the table above sums to $25. We set this overall weighted average price in our base year equal to 100 to begin our CPI.

We now observe how prices and the weekly spending patterns of the same households change over time over the following year in order to recalculate weighted average prices and the CPI.

Notice how both the prices and the proportion of household expenditure spent on each category of goods and services have changed in the table below. The biggest increases in prices have been for food products and household goods and services, up by a significant 60% (from £5 to £8) and 50% (from $60 to $90) respectively. As a result, households are now spending proportionately more on food, up from 40% of total weekly expenditure to 50%, and proportionally less on households products and travel.

▼ How to calculate a simple CPI: spending profile of households in year 1

Types of goods and services	Proportion of weekly household expenditure spent on each category (%)	Average price ($) of goods and services purchased in each category	Weighted average price ($)
Clothing and footwear	25	$44	0.25 x $44 = $11
Household goods and services	10	$90	0.10 x $90 = $9
Food	50	$8	0.50 x $8 = $4
Travel	15	$20	0.15 x $20 = $3
Total	100%		Price of basket $27

The overall weighted average price of the basket of goods and services at the end of year 1 is now $27. This represents an 8% increase in the price of the basket since the base year. That is, consumer price inflation has been 8% over the year since the base year. The consumer price index at the end of year 1 is therefore 108 and it is calculated as follows:

$$\text{CPI in year 1} = \frac{\text{weighted average price year 1}}{\text{weighted average price base year}} = \frac{\$27}{\$25} \times 100 = 108$$

Now imagine we repeat the entire exercise for a further year and calculate a weighted average price for the basket of goods and services of $30. The CPI at the end of year 2 will then be 120.

$$\text{CPI in year 2} = \frac{\text{weighted average price year 2}}{\text{weighted average price base year}} = \frac{\$30}{\$25} \times 100 = 120$$

This tells us that, on average, consumer prices have risen by 20% since the base year.

ACTIVITY 4.19

A calculated problem

1 Continuing the same example above, use the information on average prices and household spending patterns in the table below to calculate the weighted price of the basket of goods and services at the end of years 3 and 4.

Types of goods and services	Proportion of weekly household expenditure spent on each category		Average price ($) of goods and services purchased in each category	
	Year 3	Year 4	Year 3	Year 4
Clothing and footwear	25%	26%	50	55
Household goods and services	15%	14%	100	110
Food	45%	46%	9	10
Travel	15%	14%	22	25

2 Use the weighted average price of the basket at the end of each year to calculate the CPI.

3 Overall, by how much has the weighted average price of the basket of consumer goods and services risen by since the base year?

4 In which year was price inflation at its **a** highest **b** lowest?

5 Suggest why and how you might account for the following changes in the calculation of your consumer price index over time:

▸ changes in the number, structure and composition of households, for example due to inward migration and an ageing population

▸ changes in retailing, for example online retailing over the internet

▸ changes in the quality of goods and services, for example the increased performance and efficiency of cars and household goods such as microwaves and ovens

▸ new goods and services not previously available, such as drones, 3D printers and iPads.

Uses of price indices

There are three main uses of the CPI in most modern economies.

1 As an economic indicator

The CPI is a widely used as a measure of price inflation and therefore as a measure of changes in the cost of living. Governments try to control price inflation using their macroeconomic policies. The CPI in an economy will be used by workers to seek increases in their wages that match or exceed the increase in their cost of living. The CPI will also be used by entrepreneurs in making many business decisions concerning their purchases and the setting of wages and prices.

2 As a price deflator

Rising prices reduce the purchasing power, or real value, of money. Rising prices will therefore reduce the purchasing power of wages, profits, pensions, savings, tax revenues and a host of other economic variables of importance to different groups of people and decision makers. A CPI is therefore used to deflate various economic series to calculate their real or inflation-free values. For example, if annual earnings have risen by 10%, but price inflation increased by 15% over the same period, then the real value of earnings will have fallen by 5% because the purchasing power of those payments will have been reduced by inflation.

3 Indexation

Indexation involves tying certain payments to the rate of increase in price inflation to keep their real value constant. For example, public pensions paid to retired people by a government may be indexed so that they increase by the rate of inflation each year. Similarly, some savings may be index-linked, meaning that the interest rate on those savings is set equal to the official price index, thereby protecting the real value of those savings. Many workers may also be covered by collective bargaining agreements that tie their wage increases to changes in the CPI. A government may also index-link the threshold at which people start to pay tax or higher rates of tax on their incomes, otherwise people would end up paying more income tax simply due to price inflation even if their real incomes were unchanged each year. ➤ **4.3.6**

Is inflation eating into your savings?

...it doesn't have to with our...

Protected Capital Account Inflation linked 9

Early exit fees may apply

Find out more >>

Some problems with price indices

Over time the 'typical' household and the basket of goods and services it buys will tend to change. A CPI will need to take account of these changes but deciding how and when to make them can be difficult. For example, household expenditure patterns will tend to change over time due to:

- changes in tastes and fashion

- the introduction of new goods and services, such as computer game downloads and drones. For example, the personal CD player was added to the UK basket in 1997 but removed in 2006 as its popularity was superseded by MP3 players, notably the iPod which was launched in 2001

- the changing composition of the population and households, due to migration, changes in birth and death rates, and later marriages. ➤ **7.2**

Similarly, a CPI will also need to take account of changes in the quality of goods and services over time, and how and where households buy goods and services, including the introduction of new shops, television shopping channels and the increasing use of online shopping using the internet.

International comparisons of consumer price inflation are difficult to make because household composition and spending patterns can differ significantly by country.

Causes of inflation

Economists today tend to agree that the main cause of inflation is 'too much money chasing too few goods'. This means people are increasing their spending on goods and services at a faster rate than producers can expand the supply the goods and services, because the supply of money in the economy has increased. As a result, there is an excess of aggregate demand, or total demand, for goods and services and market prices are therefore forced to rise. ➤ **2.5.2**

A government can allow the supply of money to rise in an economy by issuing more notes and coins or by allowing the banking system to 'create more credit' that is, by lending more to people and firms to spend. ➤ **3.1.2**

A government may allow the money supply to expand:

- to increase total demand in the economy during an economic recession in an attempt to reduce unemployment

- in response to an increase in demand for goods and services from consumers and firms

- in response to workers' demands for higher wages, or a rise in the other costs of production.

If the money supply expands, people have more money to spend. As they spend this money the increase in demand drives up the prices of the goods and services they buy. To understand why increases in the rate of growth in the money supply cause inflation, let us consider a very simple example.

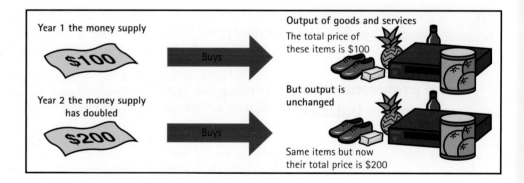

In year 1 the money supply stood at $100 and bought six items with a total price of $100. In the second year output has remained unchanged because there are no more resources available to make any more each year. Now imagine that the money supply doubles to $200. As consumers try to spend this money they find there are no extra goods and services to buy. With a fixed supply prices must rise. Indeed, they double. Inflation is 100%! Clearly, if output could have risen prices need not have gone up by so much, if at all.

A monetary rule

Economists argue that what is true in the simple example above is true for a highly complex economy. Any increase in the supply of money will cause inflation to accelerate if there is no growth in real output. Only if the output of

EXCESSIVE GROWTH IN THE MONEY SUPPLY CAUSES INFLATION.

goods and services rises should the money supply rise, so that people have enough money to buy these extra products.

This means there is a monetary rule a government can follow if it wants to keep inflation low and stable in its economy: it should only allow the supply of money to expand at the same rate as the increase in real output or real GDP over time. Increases in the money supply over and above increases in output are likely to cause prices to rise. However, this may take time. It may take a year or more before inflation increases following an expansion in the money supply. It takes time for consumers' spending to rise, for firms to realize demand has increased and for firms to raise their prices.

Some economists argue that different governments over time only have themselves to blame for the high inflation rates many countries experienced during the 1970s and 1980s. It was because they did not follow the monetary rule. Instead they allowed their money supplies to expand faster than output was growing in their economies in an effort to boost demand and reduce unemployment. For a time the increase in demand would reduce unemployment as firms took on more resources to increase the production of goods and services. However, inflation soon began to rise as aggregate demand grew faster than output. Eventually, the high inflation would reduce the purchasing power of people's incomes and demand for goods and services would begin to fall again. Workers would demand higher wages to keep pace with the rising cost of living, but as wages increased, firms reduced their demand for labour, and unemployment increased once more. As a result, government policy was responsible for **stagflation** – a situation when inflation and unemployment were both high and/or rising together.

Demand-pull inflation

Inflation caused by an increase in total demand is called a **demand-pull inflation**. Aggregate demand in an economy will rise if spending by governments, households and/or firms increases.

An increase in aggregate demand will cause market prices to increase and inflation to rise if firms are unable to increase the supply of goods and services at the same rate as demand.

To finance an increase in aggregate demand consumers and firms may borrow more from the banking system and/or the government can issue more notes and coins. Both these ways of financing an increase in demand involve increasing the supply of money in an economy.

Cost-push inflation

Rising prices can also be the result of changes in the supply-side of an economy. Inflation caused by rising production costs passed on by firms to consumers is a **cost-push inflation**. The cost of producing goods and services can rise because workers demand increases in wages not matched by increased productivity. Firms may raise their prices to cover these higher costs so that their profit margins are unchanged. However, as wages rise the demand for labour will tend to fall and workers could be made unemployed. To prevent a rise in unemployment the government may expand the supply of money to boost aggregate demand.

Continual increases in prices may occur if workers demand further increases in wages to compensate them for rising prices. This will cause a **wage–price** spiral. As prices rise, workers will demand higher wages to keep pace with inflation. However, wage increases will simply add to production costs and so prices will tend to rise even further prompting even higher wage demands, and so on.

Increases in the cost of materials, transport, energy and other costs of production can also place upward pressure in prices. For example, inflation rose rapidly in many economics in the 1970s following significant increases in the world price of oil.

Imported inflation

Rising prices in one country may be 'exported' to other countries through international trade. Rising import prices can cause **imported inflation**. Similarly, a fall in the value of the national currency against the currencies of other countries will mean imports become more expensive in that country. For example, if value of the euro against the Indian rupee falls from €1 = 60 rupees to €1 = 30 rupees, then a product imported to Europe from India priced at 600 rupees will rise from €10 to €20. ➤ **6.3.4**

It has been argued that one of the main reasons why many economies enjoyed relatively low and stable price inflation during the 1990s and in the first decade of this century was because of low wage costs in China and the rapid growth in low cost exports from the Chinese manufacturing industry. However, by 2010 many economists were suggesting that this period would soon end as wages began to rise rapidly in China.

The following article is from mid-2017. Why are there inflationary pressures in China? What impact are these pressures having on the Chinese economy? Why may these pressures be of concern to other countries?

Exit the Dragon

Turns out that "made in China" is not so cheap anymore as labour costs have risen rapidly in the country's vast manufacturing sector. And with China being the world's largest exporter of goods, this could have serious implications for the rest of the world.

Chinese factory workers are now being paid more than ever before. Average hourly wages hit $3.60 in 2016. Although still relatively low compared to many developed economies it's more than five times the hourly manufacturing wage in India and on a par with countries such as Portugal and South Africa.

As China's economy expands at breakneck speed, so has pay for employees. As a result some multinationals are now taking their business elsewhere, which also means China could start losing jobs to other developing countries like Sri Lanka, where hourly factory wages are $0.50.

Clothes manufacturing has been hit "extremely hard," said Ben Cavender, a principal at Shanghai-based China Market Research. "The result has been that factory owners have gone on a massive investment spree outside of China."

Companies with assembly lines in China are also investing in robots in efforts to automate as much as possible to offset labour costs, according to analysts. China's industrial robotics market became the world's largest in 2013, and continues to grow.

And there are signs that wage pressures are now being passed on to consumers. Non-food price inflation is now rising at the fastest pace in years indicating that inflationary pressures are now clearly accelerating throughout the Chinese economy.

Wage-price inflation is the worst kind of inflation because it feeds on itself. As wages rise, companies have to increase the prices of their products. As prices rise further, workers demand still higher wages, and an inflationary spiral which is difficult to stop can get underway, as took place globally in the 1970s.

The benefits of low and stable inflation

Consequences of inflation

Governments often aim to keep inflation in their economies at around 2–3% per year. Low inflation can be beneficial for an economy. It encourages consumers to buy goods and services sooner rather than later as delaying will mean they will have to pay more for the same product.

Low inflation also makes it more appealing to borrow money, since interest rates are also usually low during periods of low inflation. For example, if inflation and interest rates are low and stable, firms will be more optimistic and more confident to borrow money to invest in new plant and machinery, and this will enable higher rates of economic growth in the future. A low and stable demand-pull inflation will also tend to boost profits.

Also, if the government is committed to keeping inflation within a certain target it may result in expectations that inflation will be low, and this will help reduce demands for higher wages by workers and their representatives. In fact, if money wages rise by less than the inflation rate each year, the real cost of employing workers will fall for firms and may encourage them to increase their demand for labour.

ACTIVITY 4.20

How inflation can affect different households

The tables below shows how different income groups in a developed economy might allocate their spending to different goods and services.

1 How does inflation affect the amount of goods and services money can buy?

2 Which income group displayed above will be the most affected by a rise in the price of:

    a   food, heating fuel and housing costs?   **b**   household goods and transport?

3 Are people always worse off if prices rise? Explain your answer.

4 Which income groups above are probably the:

    a   most able to raise their incomes at the same rate as inflation or higher?

    b   least able to raise their incomes at the same rate as inflation?

Exports from a country that has lower price inflation than others will also become more competitive than rival products from overseas producers on international markets. This will help to boost demand for those exports, thereby creating additional incomes and employment opportunities in the low inflation country.

Maintaining low inflation is therefore an important goal for many governments and central banks because of the economic benefits. ➤ **5.1**

However, high and rising rates of inflation can cause significant problems for different groups of people and the economy they live in.

The personal costs of inflation

Inflation erodes the value or **purchasing power** of money. For example, if the price of a good today is $1 but it increases at the rate of 5% each year, its price will rise to $1.05 next year, to $1.28 after 5 years and to $1.63 after

10 years. It follows that a dollar of currency exchanged for the good today will not be enough to purchase that same product in the future.

Looked at another way, $1 of currency today will only be able to purchase the equivalent of 95 cents one year from now, or 78 cents 5 years from now and 61 cents in 10 years' time.

If inflation was 5% per year...

a dollar today will be worth...

78 cents in 5 years from now

61 cents in 10 years from now

If inflation was 10% each year, the purchasing power of the currency would be eroded much faster. After 5 years it would purchase the same as 62 cents will today and just 38 cents after 10 years of annual inflation at 10% per year.

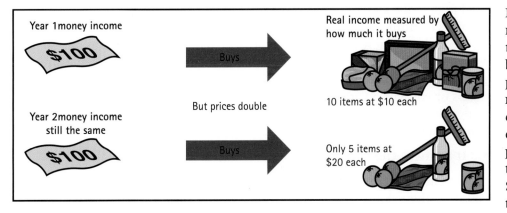

Inflation therefore reduces the **real income** of every person in terms of what their income can buy over time. For example, if a person's **money income** (or **nominal income**) was $100 it could buy 10 products at $10 each. If each one of those products increases in price to $20 that person's money income of $100 will now only buy 5 of those products. That is, his or her real income has fallen. Clearly, if the person could increase his or her money income to $200, that person will be no worse off. However, many people will face hardship if they are unable to increase their money incomes at the same rate as price inflation.

Old-age pensioners, the unemployed and other people who tend to be on fixed incomes and welfare payments are particularly vulnerable to high and rising inflation. If the prices of the goods and services they buy rise they will be unable to afford as much food, heating and other goods and services as they did before. Their real incomes and therefore their living standards will fall. For example, if the general level of prices rises by 10% in one year, real incomes will have fallen by 10%. Increasing pensions and other fixed incomes in line with inflation, known as indexation or index-linking, can help overcome this problem.

In contrast, skilled labour and workers with strong bargaining power will probably be able to secure wage or salary increases that protect their real wages and incomes. Indeed, they may be able to push for an increase in their money incomes that exceeds the rate of inflation. For example, if inflation is 10% in one year and their money incomes increase by 15%, then in real terms they will be 5% better off. However, many workers, especially the low paid and non-unionized workers, may have very little bargaining strength in wage negotiations. As prices rise their real incomes fall and they become worse off. Despite rising food and energy prices during the widespread recession in 2008 and 2009, many workers had their pay frozen or even cut as both governments and firms in many countries cut back their spending. ➤ **5.2**

People who save or lend money may also be badly affected by inflation. If the interest rate received on the money they have saved or loaned is lower than the rate of price inflation the real value of their money will fall. They will be worse off. In contrast, people who have borrowed money will benefit by repaying less in real terms than the amount they were originally loaned.

The costs of inflation to an economy

High and rising inflation can cause many problems in an economy:

- **It imposes additional costs on firms**

In a demand-pull inflation increased consumer spending tends to boost company profits. In contrast, in a cost-push inflation their profits are squeezed. However, all types of inflation can involve 'menu costs'. This is a general term used to describe all types of inconvenience that firms and individuals can face as prices continue to rise. For example, as prices increase firms will have to retype and print new price lists, change price labels, reprint menus and so on. Individual consumers may also face surcharges on products they have already paid for, such as additional charges for holidays to cover higher fuel costs for flights or voyages on cruise ships. Consumers may also have to spend more time searching around for the best bargains as the prices of the products they want continue to rise.

- **It reduces the competitiveness of exports**

If prices in an exporting country are rising at a faster rate than prices in rival countries then exports from that country will become less competitive on international markets. Demand for those exports from overseas consumers may fall. This will have a negative effect on the balance of payments and employment in exporting industries. ➤ **6.4.2**

- **It creates economic uncertainty**

If inflation is high or keeps rising, consumers, firms and governments may find it difficult to plan ahead. They may be uncertain about their costs in the future and the impact inflation may have on their incomes and revenues. Firms may become reluctant to invest in new plant and equipment and individual consumers may be reluctant to spend. Both of these factors could reduce employment and future economic growth.

If inflation is very volatile and becomes a **hyperinflation**, people may lose all confidence in their currency as a medium of exchange and store of value. ➤ **3.1.1**

Shops suffer as pay packets go on food

Sales by retailers of almost everything except food fell in July as households cut back their spending on all but the most essential items, official figures have shown.

Retails sales volumes, a measure of the health of the consumer economy, grew 0.3 per cent in the month, according to the Office for National Statistics. However, only two categories, food and household goods, accounted for the entire increase.

The findings suggest that the squeeze on household finances, which tightened as inflation surged in April, is affecting spending habits. Real wages are shrinking by 0.5 per cent as inflation outpaces pay rises.

Food and drink prices have risen by 2.6 per cent since July last year owing to the collapse in the value of the pound against the euro and other currencies after the UK voted to leave the European Union. The fall in the value of the UK pound has driven up import prices which have started to eat into household incomes.

Statisticians estimate that nearly 40 per cent of every pound is spent in food stores and as food prices rise shoppers are left with less to spend on anything else.

Economists fear that GDP growth will slow this year as a result of weak consumer demand.

1. According to the article, what had caused the rate of price inflation in the UK to increase?

2. Explain the statement 'Real wages are shrinking by 0.5 per cent as inflation outpaces pay rises'.

3. Which groups in the UK were likely to have been most affected by the rise in inflation?

4. What additional economic problems could the increase in inflation cause in the UK?

SECTION 4.8.5

Government policy and inflation

Policies to control inflation

Most governments aim to keep price inflation low and stable in their economies. Some governments even have explicit targets for inflation rates they hope to achieve. For example, the UK government aims to keep the rate of price inflation at around 2% per year. If it rises above or falls below the target the head of the UK central bank must explain why and what the central bank intends to do to get inflation back on target. ➤ **4.2.1**

The rate at which prices are rising in an economy may be reduced by:

- the government announcing it has a long-term inflation target;

- demand-side policies that reduce total demand or slow down the rate at which total demand is growing;

- supply-side policies that boost the rate of growth in output;

- direct controls that cap or limit public sector wages and prices in regulated markets.

Announcing a long term inflation target

If people believe their government will keep the rate of inflation low and stable in the economy then they are less likely to demand big wage increases each year. This in turn will help to reduce the rate at which costs rise and therefore reduce pressures on firms to increase their prices.

Demand-side policies

Controlling total demand in an economy will be important if there is demand-pull inflation caused by rising total demand exceeding growth in total supply. To do so a government can:

- **tighten or contract fiscal policy** by reducing public expenditure and/or raising direct taxes. For example, cutting welfare payments and raising taxes on incomes will reduce real disposable incomes and reduce consumer spending.

- **tighten or contract monetary policy** by increasing interest rates to reduce borrowing. Higher interest rates may also cause the foreign exchange rate to appreciate resulting in a reduction in the imported price of goods and services purchased from producers located overseas. ➤ **6.3.4**

However, policies designed to reduce total demand to control a demand-pull inflation may result in reduced output and employment. Many firms are likely to cut back the quantity of goods or services they produce and supply in response to falling total demand and spending in the economy. ➤ **4.2.2**

Supply-side policies

Expanding the productive capacity and total output of an economy can reduce inflationary pressures caused by rising total demand and production costs.

Market prices will continue to rise if the demand for goods and services grows at a faster rate than their supply can expand. In turn, demand for factors of production by firms will be rising thereby pushing up their market prices. Rising wages, rents and other factor payments will increase production costs and squeeze profits. In response, firms will attempt to cut their costs by cutting production and/or pass on their costs to consumers through raising the prices they charge. ➤ **2.6.1**

However, cost and price inflation need not accelerate if the total supply of goods and services in an economy is able to expand at the same rate as total demand. Supply-side policies designed to achieve this may include:

- increased public sector support for training and retraining workers in new and more advanced skills to boost their mobility and productivity;

- cutting taxes on profits to encourage entrepreneurs to start-up and invest in more firms;

- financial support or tax incentives to encourage firms to invest more in the research and development (R&D) of new, innovative and more efficient products, production processes and materials;

- measures to encourage more competition between firms to lower prices.

Direct controls

Some governments may also introduce direct controls on some prices and wages, notably:

- capping the rate at which public sector wages can increase each year below the rate of inflation or freezing them all together so they remain constant. This will reduce the real disposable incomes and spending power of public sector workers;

- capping the prices firms can charge in markets regulated by the government. These may include the markets for essential goods and services such as electricity and water supplies;

- capping the rate at which regulated firms can increase their prices can help to reduce price inflation. ➤ **2.11.2**

However, the effect of direct controls is relatively limited and can cause significant problems if they are kept in place for too long.

Limits on public sector wages will reduce the attraction of public sector jobs. Hospitals, schools, social services, the police force, armed services and many other public sector organizations will find it increasingly difficult to recruit people to fill job vacancies. The delivery and quality of many public sector services may suffer as a result.

Similarly, capping the prices of private sector firms in regulated markets for too long will squeeze their profits and reduce their incentives to invest in new equipment and service improvements.

Policy choices and their effectiveness

Controlling total demand to reduce inflation is likely to be ineffective if the main causes of rising prices are due to external or global factors, such as rising food and energy prices.

> **Rising food and energy prices driving up inflation across Europe and Central Asia**

> *Global energy prices fuel growth in inflation*

Cutting public spending and raising taxes can also cause hardship for many people and may especially hurt those on low incomes if, for example, they involve reductions in welfare payments and services or cuts to the wages of low paid public sector workers.

Cutting public spending on capital projects, such as investments in new roads, railways and schools, can also damage the long term productive potential of the economy.

While supply-side policies often take longer to work than demand-side policies they will be more effective in the long run if they can permanently raise the rate of growth in the productive capacity and output of the economy. This will allow incomes and demand in the economy to grow over time without creating additional inflationary pressures.

EXAM PREPARATION 4.5

Between 2005 and 2008, global oil prices rose from $40 per barrel to over $140 per barrel. Many economists were concerned about the inflationary impact this could have.

a Define *inflation*. [2]

b Explain how inflation is measured. [4]

c Analyse how high oil prices might cause inflation. [6]

d Discuss the actions that a government might take to control inflation. [8]

Deflation

Imagine you had saved up to buy a new computer, a pair of trainers or bicycle. Imagine also that over time the prices of these products had been falling and economists were predicting their prices would continue to fall over time. Would you buy them now or wait to buy them later? Clearly it would be better to wait until their prices had fallen further unless you really wanted one or more of these products so much that you just had to get them now.

Product prices can fall for a number of reasons, including when:

- their market supply has increased relative to demand
- competition between firms to supply them has increased
- labour productivity rises, increasing output and reducing average costs
- technological advance has reduced their costs of production
- market demand for them has fallen.

Increasing supply, competition, productivity and technological advance are good things for an economy and consumers and have reduced the prices of many products over time, such as mobile phones, televisions, cars, holidays and clothing, in many countries. However, when falling product prices become widespread and prolonged due to a slump in total demand in an economy, the result is **deflation**.

Measuring deflation

Deflation is measured and monitored in the same way as inflation using a consumer price index (CPI). If the prices of goods and service included in the CPI fall over time, the value of the index will also fall. For example, if the CPI is 120 at the end of one year and 108 at the end of the following year it will signify that prices have fallen on average by 10% over the 12-month period. Deflation is therefore the opposite of inflation and should not be confused with **disinflation** during which there is simply a slowdown in the rate at which prices are rising in general.

Deflation involves a continuous decline in the general level of prices in an economy. Many economies have suffered relatively short-lived deflations from time to time during economic downturns when aggregate demand tends to fall, causing many firms to compete more vigorously for available consumer spending.

However, longer periods of deflation do occur and can have very serious consequences. For example, there have been two significant periods of deflation in the world, between 1873 and 1896 following the American Civil War when prices fell in the USA on average by 1.7% a year, and in Britain by 0.8% a year, and during the Great Depression in the early 1930s when the rate of deflation in the USA was around 10% per year and unemployment reached 25% of the workforce. More recently, the worst case of deflation in consumer prices has been experienced by Japan. Price inflation turned negative in 1995 and has remained either very low or negative ever since (at least until 2018 when this book was revised).

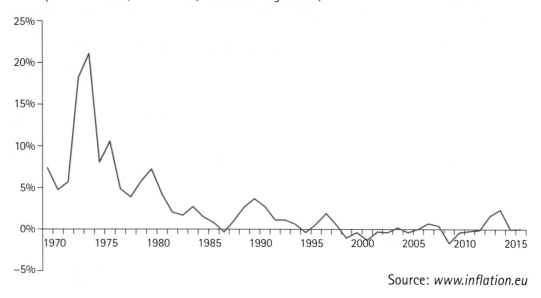

▼ Japanese inflation, 1970–2016 (% annual change in CPI)

Source: *www.inflation.eu*

The consequences of deflation

The following changes will occur during a sustained or **malign deflation**:

- Consumers will delay many spending decisions as they wait for prices to fall further.

- Stocks of unsold goods accumulate so firms cut their prices and this reduces their profits and incentive to invest.

- Firms cut their production and reduce the size of their workforces.

- Household incomes fall as unemployment rises, further reducing demand for goods and services.

- The value of debts held by people and firms rise in real terms as prices fall and this increases the burden of making loan repayments.

- Firms stop investing in new plant and machinery as demand falls and the cost of borrowing rises. This will reduce future growth in the economy.

- The real cost of public spending rises but tax revenues fall as economic activity slumps. This means the government must borrow more money despite the rising real cost of doing so.

- Eventually the economy goes into a deep recession as demand, output, the demand for labour, and incomes continue to fall. Many firms may go out of business because they are unable to make any profit no matter how much they cut their prices by as consumers simply continue to delay their spending further.

Government policy and deflation

It is therefore hard to break out of the downward spiral that can occur in a malign deflation and it will require a major boost to consumer demand and confidence if it is to be achieved.

The first line of defence used by a government is usually to cut interest rates to a low level. However, if prices are falling this means real interest rates will be rising, even if the nominal interest rate is zero.

Imagine interest rates are zero but prices are falling by 5% each year. A woman borrows $1,000 that must be repaid in full after 12 months without interest. However, because of falling prices the real value of her debt has actually increased from $1,000 to $1,050. The real interest rate is effectively 5% even if the actual interest rate charged by a bank is zero.

A government may also print more currency to pump more money into the economy during a malign deflation but people and firms may not increase their own spending as a result if they expect most prices to continue falling. The additional money supply can however be used by the government to fund projects that will draw more people back into employment. An expansionary fiscal policy may also involve tax cuts on incomes and profits to boost demand.

However, all these policies have been tried in Japan yet the economy has continued to struggle with persistent deflation, slow growth and rising unemployment for many years. Japan's problems have been made more difficult by a shrinking and ageing population. This is also reducing demand for many goods and services in the Japanese economy. ➤ **5.3.3**

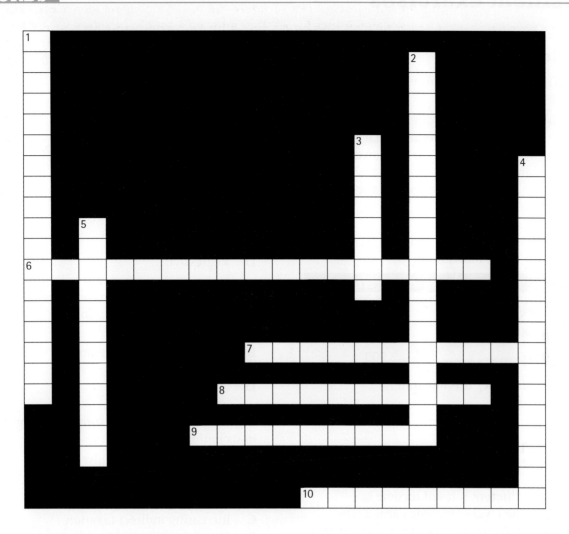

Clues across

6. Rising price levels caused by rising production costs (4, 4, 9)
7. An economic situation in which both price inflation and unemployment are rising (11)
8. The automatic adjustment of a monetary variable, such as wages, taxes or pension benefits, by the change in the consumer or retail price index, so that its value rises at the same rate as inflation (10)
9. A sustained decrease in the general level of prices in an economy (9)
10. A persistent rise in the general level of prices in an economy (9)

Clues down

1. An indicator of inflation that measures changes in the average price of a basket of goods and services purchased by a 'typical' household and expresses these average prices as an index number series (8, 4, 5)
2. A persistent increase in the general level of prices resulting from a continued excess of aggregate demand over supply (6, 4, 9)
3. The year used as the reference point or beginning of a consumer or retail price index in which the average price of the 'typical' basket of products is assigned the number 100 (4, 4)
4. A sustained increase in the prices of products bought from overseas producers either resulting from their rising costs or a fall in the exchange rate against overseas currencies (8, 9)
5. A slowdown in the rate at which the general price level is rising over time (12)

Assessment exercises

Multiple choice

1   When is the budget of a government described as balanced?

    A When direct taxes and indirect taxes are equal

    B When exports and imports are equal

    C When government spending and government revenue are equal

    D When the demand for money and the supply of money are equal

2   The table shows the earnings and total income tax paid each year by an individual.

earnings $	total income tax paid $
5,000	1,000
8,000	2,000
9,000	3,000

Which type of tax does this illustrate?

    A Indirect

    B Progressive

    C Proportional

    D Regressive

3   A country has different rates of income tax depending on the level of income earned. The highest rate of income tax is cut from 35% to 30%. From this statement it can be deduced that taxation will become:

    A Less indirect

    B Less regressive

    C Less progressive

    D More difficult to evade

4   A government collects the following tax revenues in a year.

	$bn
Taxes on goods	40
Taxes on personal incomes	150
Taxes on services	30
Taxes on company profits	60
Customs and excise duties	40
Taxes on property	20

How much did the government raise from indirect taxes?

    A $70bn   **C** $150bn

    B $110bn   **D** $230bn

5   A government fixes the rate of income tax at $0.15 per dollar earned.

Which word describes this type of tax?

    A Indirect

    B Progressive

    C Proportional

    D Regressive

6   Which aim of government policy is most likely to be achieved by an increase in interest rates?

    A Economic growth

    B Greater equality of income

    C Full employment

    D Price stability

7   A government wishes to stimulate economic activity in its national economy.

Which action will assist this?

    A Decreasing government investment

    B Decreasing income tax

    C Increasing indirect taxation

    D Increasing interest rates

8   The government lowers the rate of interest.

Who is most likely to be disadvantaged by this policy?

    A House buyers

    B Manufacturers

    C Retailers

    D Savers

9   The owners of a company discuss the following issue. Which one is least likely to be directly affected by the government's influence on the company?

    A The interest it pays on borrowed money

    B Replacing one of its suppliers

    C Minimum wages it must pay its workers

    D Competition laws

10 A government may adopt a number of supply-side policies to encourage economic growth.

Which of the following is a supply-side policy?

A   Increasing the money supply
B   Lowering interest rates
C   Reducing direct taxation
D   Retraining unemployed workers

11 Economic growth can be defined as:

A   An increase in a country's exports
B   An increase in a country's population
C   An increase in the total output of real GDP
D   A increase in the general price level

12 What is most likely to cause economic growth?

A   A better educated workforce
B   A reduction in savings
C   Decreased wages
D   Higher taxation

13 What is a long-term advantage of economic growth?

A   Lower unemployment
B   Higher incomes
C   Higher prices
D   Lower savings

14 What is typically observed during an economic recession?

A   Falling Gross Domestic Product
B   Falling unemployment
C   Rising living standards
D   Rising consumer price index

15 Which of the following is a supply-side policy that will expand total output in the long-run?

A   An increase in welfare payments
B   An increase in the rate of income tax
C   An increase in spending on higher education
D   An increase in the rate of corporation tax

16 Labour force participation has been rising over time in many countries.

What is the most likely reason for this trend?

A   Unemployment has fallen
B   More females have entered employment
C   The working population has increased
D   More people are retiring earlier

17 Which type of unemployment is most likely to occur when total demand in an economy falls during an economic recession?

A   Seasonal
B   Voluntary
C   Structural
D   Cyclical

18 Many fishermen have become unemployed after new laws to conserve fish stocks in the North Sea were introduced.

What type of unemployment is this?

A   Demand-deficient
B   Frictional
C   Seasonal
D   Structural

19 Look at the labour market data below.

	Millions
Working population	30
People employed	18
People unemployed	6

What are the unemployment rate and the labour force participation rate?

	Unemployment rate %	Participation rate %
A	60	40
B	80	20
C	20	60
D	40	60

20 Government advisers have suggested the following policies to reduce youth unemployment.

Which policy would not increase public expenditure?

A   Cutting the minimum wage paid to young people
B   Raising the school-leaving age
C   Giving a subsidy to employers to recruit young people
D   Introducing national military service for all

21 Which combination of government policies is most likely to be successful at reducing unemployment?

A   Budgeting for a surplus and cutting interest rates
B   Budgeting for a deficit and raising interest rates
C   Budgeting for a surplus and raising interest rates
D   Budgeting for a deficit and cutting interest rates

22 The diagram shows the annual rate of inflation for a country over a five-year period.

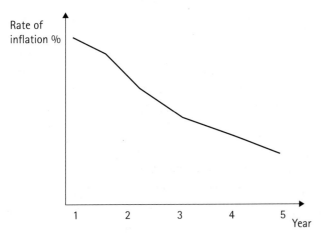

Which statement is true of the period displayed?

A The cost of living was unchanged
B The price level increased
C The retail price index fell
D The value of money increased

23 The table shows some data about an economy.

	Year 1	Year 2
Rate of inflation	4%	6%
Personal incomes	+4%	+5%

What happened between Year 1 and Year 2?

A Both prices and real incomes fell
B Both prices and real incomes rose
C Prices rose but real incomes fell
D Prices fell but real incomes rose

24 The wages of foreign workers living and working in France have been increasing rapidly and, as a result, French firms have been increasing their prices to maintain their profit margins. What type of inflation does this represent?

A Imported inflation
B Cost-push inflation
C Demand-pull inflation
D Hyperinflation

25 What is most likely to cause demand-pull inflation?

A An increase in saving
B An increase in consumer spending
C An increase in interest rates
D An increase in taxes

26 From the following table what is the weighted price index for all items?

Item	Price index	Weight
Food	120	50
Housing	130	40
Services	110	10
All items = 100		

A 360   C 120
B 123   D 100

27 The weight for a product in the consumer price index was increased.

What is most likely to have caused this adjustment?

A The product is new
B The product has improved in quality
C More retailers are selling the product
D Consumers are spending a bigger proportion of their income on the product

28 What is deflation?

A A fall in the general price level
B A fall in the international value of a currency
C A fall in the rate of inflation
D A fall in the real value of money

29 Who will be made worse off during a period of deflation?

A Fixed income earners
B Creditors (lenders)
C Debtors (borrowers)
D People with cash savings

30 Many fishermen have become unemployed after new laws to conserve fish stocks in the North Sea were introduced.

What type of unemployment is this?

A Demand-deficient
B Frictional
C Seasonal
D Structural

Structured questions

1 Venezuela: an economy on the brick of collapse

Venezuela has more oil than any other nation on earth. Revenue from petroleum exports accounts for more than 50% of the country's GDP and roughly 95% of its total exports. As a result, Venezuela was once Latin America's wealthiest nation, but it was plagued by extreme inequality. Successive governments since 1999 promised to fix the country's deep disparity between rich and poor. Government spending on housing and services for millions of poor Venezuelans increased significantly. But critics and economists argued that the spending was irresponsible and unsustainable. Public sector debt ballooned and the country spiralled into a deep economic recession following a plunge in global oil prices in 2014. Government mismanagement, industrial unrest and widespread corruption also caused oil production to plummet. Shortages of food and medical supplies and power blackouts became common.

Unable to fund subsidies and welfare programmes, the government ordered the central bank to print more money. When this drove up inflation, making basic goods unaffordable, it introduced price controls and devalued its foreign exchange rate. This made many imports prohibitively expensive. Businesses shut down and unemployment soared. In response, the government simply printed more money and prices skyrocketed.

▼ Table 1: Annual inflation rate in Venezuela, 2008–2018

Year	Increase in consumer prices index (%)
2008	30.4
2009	27.1
2010	29.8
2011	26.1
2012	21.1
2013	40.6
2014	62.2
2015	121.7
2016	254.9
2017	2,400
2018 (estimate)	13,000

By 2016, inflation had become so rampant that it devoured people's wages. The Venezuelan Government was forced to repeatedly increase the monthly minimum wage but prices continued to rise at a faster rate. People rushed to withdraw their deposits and savings from banks as the economic crisis deepened and banks quickly began to run out of cash. Tight limits were therefore imposed on how much cash people could withdraw from their accounts each day, adding to the already significant levels of hardship and poverty among the population. With prices of basic goods rising so rapidly and out of the reach of many pockets, people were forced to exchange or barter their labour for food and clothing.

According to figures published by the International Monetary Fund in January 2018, Venezuela had lost half of its economy since 2013, unemployment had risen to 30% and by the end of the year annual inflation would be running at over 13,000%. As a result, people had lost all confidence in the national currency, the Bolivar, and it had become virtually worthless.

A   What evidence is there from the extract of overspecialization in Venezuela? [3]

B   Identify **two** causes of inflation in Venezuela from the article. [2]

C   Using information from the table
  (i) describe what happened to inflation in Venezuela between 2008 and 2018 [2]
  (ii) explain in which year the price level was highest in Venezuela. [2]

D   What are the main characteristics of an economic recession? [3]

E   **(i)** What evidence is there from the extract that the Venezuelan economy experienced negative economic growth? [2]
  (ii) Explain how negative economic growth is measured. [2]

F   Using information from the extract, describe **two** functions of a central bank. [4]

G   According to the extract, what functions of commercial banks were affected by the economic crisis in the country? [4]

H   Discuss the impact the high rate of inflation in Venezuela will have had on the ability of its currency, the Bolivar, to function as money. [6]

2   Following the global financial crisis in 2008/9, many countries increased indirect taxes to help close their budget deficits. The International Monetary Fund (IMF), the Organization of Economic Cooperation and Development (OECD) and the European Commission had promoted the shift from direct to indirect taxes to help reduce economic uncertainty, in particular by reducing costs on business to help make them more competitive. For example, reductions in direct taxes such as corporation tax can contribute to the achievement of economic growth and full employment. However, critics argued that indirect taxes are inflationary and regressive.

A   Define *regressive tax*. [2]

B   Explain the difference between a direct tax and an indirect tax. [4]

C   Using a demand and supply diagram, analyse the effect of removing an indirect tax on the market for the product. [6]

D   Discuss whether or not a country would benefit from having full employment. [8]

3 A number of countries, including France, Finland, Hungary, Ireland, Mexico and the UK, have introduced indirect taxes on fizzy drinks with a high sugar content. The World Health Organization has said that taxes are needed to help reverse the rise in obesity across the globe and to reduce the significant external costs associated with excess consumption, including increased public medical expenditures. In contrast, global producers of fizzy drinks argue that taxes do little to reduce consumption and instead risk many thousands of jobs in the drinks industry being moved to other countries.

A Define *an indirect tax*. [2]

B Explain the difference between private costs and external costs. [4]

C Using a demand and supply diagram, analyse the effect of imposing an indirect tax on cans of fizzy drink. [6]

D Discuss what might happen in an economy if a government increased income tax rates. [8]

4 In December 2017 the US Government announced a package of fiscal policy measures designed to boost economic growth in the economy. They included $1.5 trillion of tax cuts and an additional $200 billion of public spending. However, some officials criticized the measures arguing they would increase the US budget deficit and could spark faster inflation.

A What is a *budget deficit*? [2]

B Explain **two** reasons why governments aim for low and stable inflation. [4]

C Analyse how an increase in government spending may create economic growth. [6]

D Discuss whether the use of monetary policy will increase economic growth. [8]

5 Economic development

Economic development involves growth in the productive scale and wealth of an economy. Government policy in many countries generally aims for continuous and sustained economic growth, so that national economies expand, generate more output and incomes, and become more developed.

A developing economy or developed economy has a relatively low level of economic development. Almost 90% of the world's population lives in less-developed economies. Some newly industrializing economies, such as those in South-East Asia, are developing rapidly but have yet to achieve the same high levels of economic and human development characteristics of many modern developed economies.

The level of economic and human development in different economies can be measured and compared using a range of indicators. Gross domestic product per capita, a measure of average income per person, is a commonly used indicator of levels of wealth or poverty but it does not take account of living standards, including the availability of healthcare, education and clean water supplies. Income is also distributed very unequally in many countries. Other development indicators are also used, therefore, such as the adult literacy rate, life expectancy at birth and the number of people earning less than $1 per day.

Many less-developed countries lack the capital required to invest in modern infrastructure, such as road and communication networks, and they also lack the consumer demand required to stimulate investments in an industrial base and services sector. Instead, less-developed countries tend to depend heavily on agriculture for employment and incomes. Rapid population growth is also a feature of many less-developed economies and places further pressure on their scarce resources.

The natural rate of increase in a population is the difference between its birth rate and death rate. Populations in a number of developed countries are shrinking and their average age increasing as birth rates have fallen significantly and below death rates. It is estimated that one in every three people in developed countries will be over 60 by 2050. In contrast, more than a third of the population of less-developed countries is under the age of 15.

Around half the world's population now lives in urban areas, and this is expected to rise as more people move from rural areas to cities in search of work and higher incomes. The number and size of cities is expanding rapidly, especially in many emerging economies. However, increasing urbanization has increased the consumption of scarce natural resources such as trees, open space and water, as more homes, factories, offices, shops and roads are built. Increased energy and car use in cities has also increased pollution, reduced air and water quality, and increased health risks.

Unit 5.1	**Differences in economic development between countries**
Unit 5.2	**Living standards**
Unit 5.3	**Poverty**

Differences in economic development between countries

Economic development involves an increase in the economic welfare or well-being of people through growth in the productive scale and wealth of an economy. Government policies in different countries generally aim for continuous and sustained economic growth, so that their national economies expand from **developing economies** into more **developed economies**. Development objectives therefore tend to include increasing the output and quality of essential goods, including food and shelter and making sure they reach more people in need, improving standards of education and healthcare, investing in better roads and communications, and generally expanding economic and social choice.

However, different countries and even different regions within the same countries in the world today are at very different stages of economic development. Almost every day on the television or in newspapers we learn about the problems many people have living in many less-developed or developing economies.

ACTIVITY 5.1

The characteristics of developed and less-developed economies

These pictures depict typical scenes from less-developed economies and developed economies.
In pairs compare and contrast the pictures and then list what you consider to be key characteristics of a less-developed economy and a developed economy, and how they differ.

Developed economies

A **developed economy** is generally thought of as having large modern efficient farms, a wide range of industries with firms of different sizes producing and selling a wide variety of goods and services, a well-developed road and rail network, modern communication systems, stable government and a relatively healthy, wealthy and educated population. Developed economies are also sometimes called industrialized nations, but this is despite the great majority of their output, income and employment now being created by their service sectors rather than manufacturing industries. ➤ **3.5.1**

Despite these characteristics there is no general rule for designating regions or countries as developed or developing. Nevertheless, it is commonly accepted that countries such as Canada and the USA in North America, Australia and New Zealand in Oceania, Japan in Asia and many countries in Europe are considered to be developed economies.

Developing economies

A **developing economy** or **less-developed economy** has a relatively low level of economic development. Farming methods tend to be poor, sometimes providing scarcely enough food for a rapidly growing population to eat. There are few industries and very few firms producing and selling good-quality goods and services. Road, rail and communication networks are underdeveloped and many people are poor. Many live in poor housing conditions with poor sanitation, receive little or no education, have a low life expectancy and may even lack access to clean water. Many countries in Africa are considered less developed.

Less-developed countries are also called **developing economies**, suggesting that over time they are becoming more prosperous, that their industrial structure is expanding and fewer people suffer the extremes of poverty. However, not all developing countries are developing at the same rate. Some have even experienced prolonged periods of negative growth and falling living standards. For example, between 2002 and 2010 the real GDP of Zimbabwe halved. More recently, the economies of South Sudan and Libya shrank by 10.2% and 9.4% respectively over the 10-year period to April 2017.

In contrast, some countries are developing rapidly, such as India, China and Malaysia in Asia, Poland in Eastern Europe, Brazil and Chile in South America and other countries such as the United Arab Emirates, Turkey and South Africa. These rapidly developing economies or **newly industrialized economies** are undergoing significant growth in their industries and infrastructure but are yet to display the full range of characteristics of modern developed economies.

In recent years new terms have been introduced to describe, for example, the largest and fastest developing economies, Brazil, Russia, India and China, which have been labelled the BRIC countries. Variations on BRIC include BRICK, which recognizes South Korea as a rapidly developing economy, and BRICKS with the addition of South Africa.

Differences in economic development and their causes

Different economies will therefore display different economic characteristics according to their level of economic development. It is useful to compare these characteristics and understand why economies differ. Doing so can help to identify priority areas for improvement and actions that can increase economic growth and welfare in all countries but especially in those with very low and slow economic development.

	Developed economies	Developing economies	Least developed economies
Industrial structure	The largest sector in terms of employment and output is the tertiary sector. Manufacturing output and employment has been declining. The primary sector is relatively small.	The secondary sector (manufacturing and construction) is expanding along with tertiary sector industries. Employment in primary sector industries is shrinking as they become more capital-intensive.	Most workers are employed in agriculture and other primary sector industries. There are very few manufacturing industries. The service or tertiary sector is small.
Educational attainment	Most people spend many years in full-time education and study, from primary schooling through to higher education in colleges and universities.	Investment in the provision of schools and colleges is increasing. Teaching quality and access to full-time education is improving.	Provision is poor and few children attend school regularly or progress to higher education.
Healthcare	Most people have free or subsidized access to high-quality healthcare.	Quality is good and continues to improve and access is widening.	Provision of healthcare is limited and the quality often poor.
Factor productivity	Many industries are capital-intensive. Labour and capital productivity is high.	Labour skills and productivity are increasing. The use of capital to help boost levels of productivity is also increasing.	Most industries are labour-intensive and labour productivity is low.
Saving and investment	Banking systems are well developed. Total savings are relatively high and provide a ready source of capital for investments in firms and infrastructure. Firms and governments are also able to access capital from international sources easily.	Banking systems are developing as average incomes and therefore savings increase. Capital from international sources is also attracted by new investment opportunities. Infrastructure development is often significant and rapid.	Banking systems are underdeveloped. There is a lack of savings because average incomes are low. As a result there is a lack of capital to invest in firms and infrastructure such as road networks and electricity generators and grids.
Population growth	Population growth is slow or even negative because birth rates are low.	Population growth is slowing in many developing economies.	Tends to be high because birth rates are high and exceed death rates.
Incomes	Incomes and living standards are generally high for many people. Consumer spending on services is high.	Incomes and living standards for many people are improving. The amount and variety of affordable goods and services available are growing quickly.	Incomes and living standards for many people are low. Access to many basic goods and services is limited.

From the table above we can identify the main causes and consequences of differences in economic development between countries. These are detailed below.

1 Differences in industrial structure

Although some economies are developing rapidly, many remain overly dependent on agriculture and other primary sector industries to provide jobs, outputs and incomes. Many people produce only enough food for themselves and their families to live on and very little surplus they can sell to earn money. In some areas there has also been overfarming which has reduced the quality and productivity of the land.

For example, the chart on the right shows the distribution of employment in the African country of Liberia, one of the least developed countries in the world. It shows that 70% of the Liberian workforce is currently employed in agriculture. Agriculture is also responsible for producing much Liberia's total output each year. This has changed very little over time. In contrast, the tertiary sector or service industries of many developed economies employ over 70% of their workforces and produce over 70% of their total annual outputs. ➤ **3.5.1**

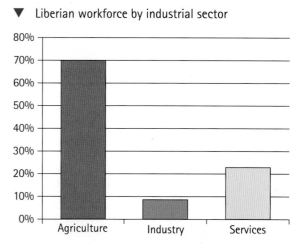

▼ Liberian workforce by industrial sector

2 Differences in education and healthcare (provision, quality and access)

Education and healthcare are merit goods. Widespread consumption of these goods within a country benefits society and the economy. Healthy, educated people are more employable, productive, enterprising and innovative. The quality, level of provision and accessibility of education and healthcare in most developed economies is therefore generally good. Many governments in developed countries provide universal public healthcare and education funded from taxes. High-quality private sector provision is also available to those people able to afford it. In contrast, many people in many of the least developed economies do not have access to good quality education or healthcare.

3 Differences in factor productivity

Factor productivity is high in many developed economies. In contrast, productivity is low in many developing economies because workers are poorly trained or educated, and there is insufficient investment in modern capital equipment. Production methods therefore tend to be old and outdated and many jobs require only manual unskilled labour. Average costs of production will therefore tend to be much higher in many developing countries. ➤ **3.6.3**

4 Differences in savings and investment

As average incomes are so low in many of the least developed economies, there are insufficient funds from savings to provide the capital they need to invest in the development of modern infrastructure and their industries, to grow their economies and to provide more jobs and incomes.

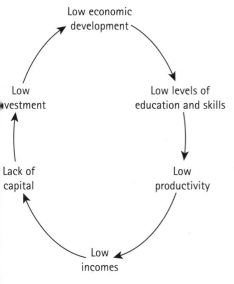

▼ How countries can become trapped in low economic development

5 Differences in population growth

Many less-developed countries have rapidly expanding populations because birth rates remain high while death rates have fallen due to improvements in healthcare. Many developing countries therefore have large and growing juvenile populations that are increasing pressure on their country's scarce resources. In contrast, many developed countries have slow growing or declining populations because birth rates have fallen to very low levels. As a result, the labour supply is decreasing as the number of old and retired people is increasing in these economies. This is also creating a number of problems in these economies. ➤ **5.3.3**

6 Differences in incomes

There are significant differences in average incomes between developed and developing economies. For example, in 2017 the average income per person in the USA was over $59,600. In comparison, average income per person was $1,850 in rapidly developing India and just $322 in Malawi, one of the world's least developed economies. These vast differences in incomes also mean there are vast differences in consumer spending between countries. In countries where consumer spending is low, there will be few profitable business opportunities and few goods and services will be produced. There may be a shortage of many basic goods and services and, as a result, prices will often be high, making them unaffordable for many people.

7 Other factors

Unstable and corrupt governments, and conflicts with neighbouring countries or between different political or religious groups, have often blighted the development of some of the least-developed countries. Money that could have been used to invest in economic development has in some cases been misused by corrupt officials or squandered on buying arms and fighting wars.

ACTIVITY 5.2

Still under development

The charts below show the proportion of total output produced by different sectors in two countries.

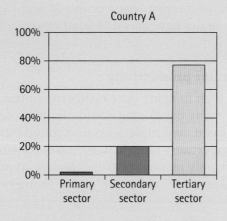

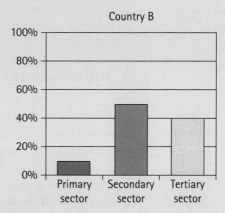

1 Which country do you think has the most developed economy?

2 Which country do you think is a newly industrialized or rapidly developing economy?

3 What do you think the chart for country B could look like in 30 years' time? Give reasons to support your view.

4 Which chart do you think most resembles the industrial structure of the economy of your country?

Do you think the actions described below will help or hinder the development of less-developed and newly industrializing economies in Africa and elsewhere?

The food rush: rising demand in China and West sparks African land grab

A million Chinese farmers have joined the rush to Africa, according to one estimate, underlining concerns that an unchecked 'land grab' not seen since the 19th century is under way.

Some of the world's richest countries are buying or leasing land in some of the world's poorest to satisfy their insatiable appetites for food and fuel. In the new scramble for Africa, nearly 2.5 million hectares (6.2 million acres) of farmland in just five sub-Saharan countries have been bought or rented in the past five years at a total cost of $920 million, research shows.

'Lands that only a short time ago seemed of little outside interest are now being sought by international investors to the tune of hundreds of thousands of hectares,' said a recent report by the International Fund for Agricultural Development (IFAD) and UN Food and Agriculture Organization (FAO).

The report said farmland purchases are being driven by food security concerns, rising demand and changing dietary habits, expanded biofuel production and interest in what is, in theory, an improved investment climate in some African countries.

Beijing's billions buy up resources

China is pouring another $7 billion (£4.4 billion) into Brazil's oil industry, reigniting fears of a global 'land grab' for natural resources.

The agreement follows many similar deals across the world. While much of the developed world is struggling with debts in the aftermath of the financial crisis, China has continued a global spending spree of unprecedented proportions, snapping up everything from oil and gas reserves to mining concessions to agricultural land, with vast reserves of US dollars.

This year alone, Chinese companies have laid out billions of dollars buying up stakes in Canada's oil sands, a Guinean iron ore mine, oil fields in Angola and Uganda, an Argentinian oil company and a major Australian coal-bed methane gas company.

'China is rich in people but short of resources, and it wants to have stable supplies of its own rather than having to buy on the open market,' Jonathan Fenby, China expert and Director of research group Trusted Resources, said.

Indicators of living standards

Comparing living standards and income distribution

Development indicators

The main measure of the level of economic development in a country is the total value of its output or **Gross Domestic Product** (GDP). The higher the GDP of a country, the more developed it is likely to be. In 2017 the world's largest economy was the USA with a GDP of $19.4 trillion.

The pace of economic development in a country is therefore measured by the annual rate of change in its total output, or **real GDP**. In 2017 the world's fastest growing economy was Ethiopia. Its total output grew by 8.3% in 2017 from just under $72 billion at the end of 2016, to almost $78 billion.

Total GDP and the annual rate of growth in real GDP are widely used and internationally comparable measures of economic development, as economic indicators, in different countries. ➤ **4.6.2**

However, measuring and monitoring the total output of different countries and the rate at which output grows over time reveals very little about living standards in those countries and whether economic welfare is improving. Therefore in addition to measures of GDP, a number of other measures or indicators are used to compare economic development and living standards in different countries and to monitor how they are changing over time. These are known as development indicators.

GDP per capita

Dividing the total GDP of a country by its total population will provide a much better indicator of the level of economic development and average living standards in that country because it measures the average income per person or **GDP per capita**.

▼ Countries with highest and lowest GDP per capita, 2017

Country	GDP per capita ($)	Country	GDP per capita ($)
Luxembourg	101,715	Liberia	492
Switzerland	78,245	The Gambia	490
Norway	73,450	Democratic Republic of Congo	474
Macao SAR	68,401	Niger	409
Iceland	67,570	Madagascar	405
Qatar	64,447	Central African Republic	400
Ireland	62,085	Mozambique	378
United States	59,609	South Sudan	366
Australia	55,215	Burundi	343
Denmark	52,871	Malawi	322

Source: *International Monetary Fund World Economic Outlook*

According to the International Monetary Fund, Luxembourg had the highest annual GDP per person in 2017 at $101,715 and Malawi, in south-eastern Africa, had the lowest at just $322.

GDP per capita is high in developed economies suggesting most people have enough money to enjoy a good standard of living. In contrast, average incomes are low in many developing economies. In fact, no more than $500 per person per year in the 10 least developed national economies, all of which are in the African continent. Living standards are therefore generally poor in these countries.

From section 4.6.2 we know that economic growth in a country will increase its total GDP. However, if its population rises at a faster rate, then GDP per capita will fall. That is, people on average will become worse off despite the growth of their economy. For example, in the simple economy described in the table below, GDP per capita has fallen from $10,000 to $9,375 because its population increased at a faster rate than the growth in its total GDP over the same period.

▼ GDP per capita will fall if population growth exceeds GDP growth

Measure	Last year	This year	Annual growth rate (%)
GDP	$500 million	$525 million	5%
Population	50,000	56,000	12%
GDP per capita	$10,000	$9,375	-6.25%

It is therefore important to look at how GDP per capita is changing over time in addition to growth in total GDP. Falling GDP per capita suggests average living standards will be falling, while rising GDP per capita is normally a sign that an economy is developing and average living standards are improving. If prices are rising rapidly at the same time as rising GDP per capita average living standards may actually be falling for many people. ➤ **4.8.4**

Price inflation erodes the real value or purchasing power of people's incomes over time. It is therefore also important to take account of price inflation when calculating changes in GDP per capita over time. This is done by calculating the **real GDP per capita** because real GDP measures the actual increase in goods and services in an economy and excludes the impact of rising prices.

For example, in the simple economy described in the table below, its nominal or money GDP has increased by 10% but only because the general price level has risen by 10% over the same period. That is, there has been no growth in the actual amount of goods and services produced in the economy. Therefore, with the population unchanged, its real GDP per capita has remained constant. That is, people are no better off on average than they were a year earlier.

▼ Real GDP per capita will be unchanged if prices rise at the same rate as GDP

Measure	Last year	This year	Annual growth rate (%)
Nominal GDP	$800 million	$880 million	+10%
Consumer price index	100	110	+10%
Real GDP	$800 million	$880 million	0%
Population	40,000	40,000	0%
Real GDP per capita	$20,000	$20,000	0%

However, real GDP per capita and therefore average living standards would have fallen in the economy if:

1 the general price level had risen faster than the increase in nominal GDP;

2 the population of the country had also expanded over the same period, as in the simple economy described in the table below.

▼ Real GDP per capita will fall if prices rise faster than GDP and population also expands

Measure	Last year	This year	Annual growth rate (%)
Nominal GDP	$800 million	$880 million	+10%
Consumer price index	100	115	+15%
Real GDP	$800 million	$765 million	−5%
Population	40,000	42,000	+5%
Real GDP per capita	$20,000	$18,220	−11%

Real GDP per capita therefore provides the best and most readily available indicator of economic development and average living standards in most countries. However, because it is based on measures of output or income it still has a number of problems.

- It takes no account of what people can buy with their incomes. For example, people in a country with a relatively high average income may be no better off than people in another country with lower average incomes who have more consumer choice and where average prices are much lower.

- It doesn't take account of other important aspects of living standards such as the amount of political and cultural freedom people have in different countries and levels of crime and violence. It also doesn't distinguish between countries where people have access to good quality education and healthcare and those that don't. For example, adult literacy rates (the proportion of people who can read and write) are relatively low in many developing countries.

- It excludes unpaid work people do for charities or voluntary organizations, or which they carry out for themselves, their families or friends. As a result it understates the total output of a country and economic well-being.

- It ignores the impact of economic development and growth on people and the natural environment. For example, polluted air and water supplies can cause health problems and reduce the living standards and well-being of many people.

- It is a measure of the simple average income per person. It takes no account of how the total output or income of a country is divided up between its population. The distribution of income is very unequal in many countries. Some people may be very rich while the majority of the population live in poverty and lack access to good quality healthcare, education, water and housing.

For example, consider China. Rapid economic growth had increased the number of millionaires in the country to almost 1.6 million by 2017, but around 43 million or 3% of the Chinese population had to survive on less than $3.10 per day. Similarly, Saudi Arabia has a reasonably high average income per head of around $21,848 in 2017 but most of the wealth in the country is owned by less than 3% of the population.

Even within developed countries such as the USA there are still big disparities between rich and poor people. For example, in 2017 around 11% of US households had an annual income of $15,000 or less, while 7% of households had annual incomes in excess of $200,000.

Human development index

The **human development index (HDI)** provides a wider measure of living standards and economic welfare than real GDP per capita. It combines three different measures into a single index with a value between 0 and 1. These three measures are:

- living standards, measured by the average gross national income (GNI) per person adjusted for differences in exchange rates and prices in different countries;

- the level of education, measured by how many years on average a person aged 25 will have spent in education and how many years a young child entering school now can be expected to spend in education during his or her life;

- healthcare and the achievement of healthy lifestyles, measured by life expectancy.

Countries can be ranked by their HDI values. In 2015, Norway had the highest HDI of 0.949 and the Central African Republic had the lowest at 0.352. Countries with an HDI equal to or greater than 0.800 are generally thought to have very high human development, while those with an index value less than 0.500 are considered to have low human development.

The main problem with the HDI is the fact that it is a composite index that covers a range of separate indicators. So, for example, it is possible for a country to have relatively high HDI if average income is high and people have good literacy skills but many people are nevertheless poor and have low life expectancy, perhaps due to wars, poor working conditions and lack of access to clean water supplies.

Human Development Index (HDI)

Gross national income per capita measures average income per person	People's incomes are unequal in many countries. For example, economic growth in China increased the number of multi-millionaires in the country to 1.34 million in 2016, but over 100 million people in China still had to survive on less than $3.10 a day.
Education measured by expected years of schooling and average years in schooling	Most adults in countries with the highest HDI values have spent between 7.3 and 13.4 years in education while children entering education for the first time in 2015 can be expected to spend over 16 years in education during their lifetime. In contrast, people in countries with the lowest HDI values have received an average of only 4.3 years of schooling although children starting school for the first time can now be expected to spend up to 9.4 years receiving education during their lifetimes.
Health measured by life expectancy at birth	People in developed countries tend to live longer than people in developing countries because they have better living standards and access to good food and healthcare. Malnutrition, poor sanitation and a lack of healthcare reduce life expectancy in many less-developed countries. On average, a baby born in one of most developed countries in 2016 could expect to live to 76-82 years of age, while a baby born in some of the least developed countries could expect to live to 63-66 years of age. However, in some of the poorest countries in Africa, average life expectancy from birth is less than 55 years.

▼ Human Development Index rankings, 2015

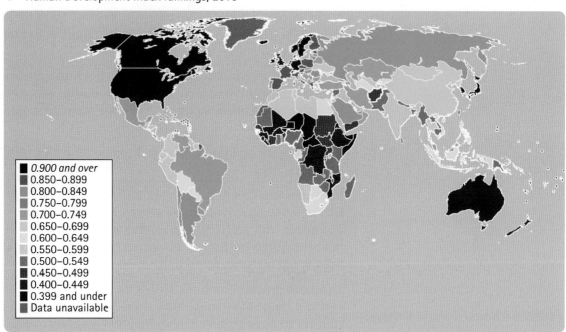

- ■ *0.900 and over*
- ■ 0.850–0.899
- ■ 0.800–0.849
- ■ 0.750–0.799
- ■ 0.700–0.749
- ■ 0.650–0.699
- ■ 0.600–0.649
- ■ 0.550–0.599
- ■ 0.500–0.549
- ■ 0.450–0.499
- ■ 0.400–0.449
- ■ 0.399 and under
- ■ Data unavailable

Source: *Human Development Index values*
(Wikipedia based on 2015 data published by the UNDP 2017)

	Countries with the highest HDI values				Countries with the lowest HDI values	
1	Norway	0.949		179	Eritrea	0.420
2	Australia	0.939		179	Sierra Leone	0.420
3	Switzerland	0.939		181	Mozambique	0.418
4	Germany	0.926		181	South Sudan	0.418
5	Denmark	0.925		183	Guinea	0.414
6	Singapore	0.925		184	Burundi	0.404
7	Netherlands	0.924		185	Burkina Faso	0.402
8	Ireland	0.923		186	Chad	0.396
9	Iceland	0.921		187	Niger	0.353
10	Canada	0.920		188	Central African Republic	0.352

The HDI has also been criticized for failing to take into account other factors that affect living standards including environmental quality, political freedoms and crime rates.

ACTIVITY 5.3

Rich or poor?

Look at the table of different development indicators below for three countries. Which country do you think is developed? Which is a newly industrialized economy? Which is the least developed economy? Is the choice clear-cut in each case? Suggest why the measures and indicator values given may sometimes appear misleading and contradict each other.

Indicator	Country A	Country B	Country C
▸ Life expectancy at birth (years)	68	45	75
▸ Adult literacy rate (%)	71.9	83.2	99.6
▸ GDP per capita (US$)	22,214	5,135	69,841
▸ Population using an improved drinking water source (%)	76	49	100
▸ Prevalence of underweight children under 5 (%)	6	27	less than 5
▸ Share of women in wage employment in non-agricultural sector (%)	44.0	32.4	46.8
▸ Patients successfully treated for tuberculosis (%)	82	46	92
▸ Ratio of land protected to maintain biological diversity to total territorial area (%)	6.4	11.7	13.6
▸ Total carbon dioxide emissions (tons per capita)	7.7	0.9	12.2
▸ Employment to population rate (%)	60	64.9	55.3

Definition of absolute and relative poverty

The causes of poverty

One of the main problems with using real GDP per capita and the HDI to provide measures of average living standards is that they take no account of income inequality and extremes of wealth and poverty in a country.

Poverty is a state of lacking sufficient resources for living and well-being. However, definitions and measures of poverty can vary.

Absolute poverty

Absolute poverty is the inability to afford basic necessities needed to live successfully, such as food, water, education, healthcare and shelter. The extent of absolute poverty in a country is usually measured by the number of people living below a certain level of income.

▲ Poor

Determining the level of income below which people suffer absolute poverty is usually done by finding the total cost of all the essential resources that an average human adult needs to consume to survive.

For example, in 2017 the World Bank defined 'extreme poverty' as the condition in which a person is trying to survive on less than $1.90 per day and 'moderate poverty' as living on less than $3.10 per day. In 2016, an estimated 11% of the world's population lived in extreme poverty, half of which lived in sub-Saharan Africa.

However, absolute poverty is not just about income. According to the United Nations, absolute poverty is 'a condition characterized by severe deprivation of basic human needs, including food, safe drinking water, sanitation facilities, health, shelter, education and information. It depends not only on income but also on access to services.'

Other indicators of absolute poverty may therefore include levels of malnutrition, the number of underweight children, access to safe drinking water, levels of unemployment and the number of people living in slums.

Relative poverty

Relative poverty is a condition of having fewer resources than others in the same society. It is usually measured by the extent to which a person's or a household's financial resources fall below the average income level in the economy.

▲ Relatively poor

Despite incomes and standards of living rising in many countries, gains in income and welfare are often not shared equally across the population. This means despite everyone becoming better off over time, some people remain relatively poor compared with many others. For example, 43 million were estimated to be living in relative poverty in the USA in 2015 out of total population of 321 million people.

Relative poverty is therefore a comparative measure and similar to measuring income inequality, but it also takes account of access to essential and other services such as education, healthcare and travel, and ownership of consumer

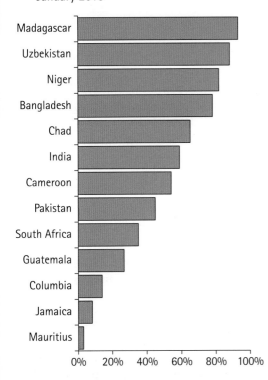

durables such as washing machines, freezers and even television. People without all or some of these goods may be considered relatively poor in many developed economies although they are considerably better off than many people in many developing countries who survive on less than $3.10 per day, have no shelter and lack access to clean water and sanitation.

While cases of absolute poverty are rare in developed economies, relative poverty can be significant if there are a large number people enjoying much higher incomes than others, and may even increase even if these economies are growing and incomes and living standards are generally rising.

Perversely, relative poverty will be cut in developed economies if the incomes and living standards of the vast majority of people fall because it will reduce the gap between low and high incomes.

The **global multidimensional poverty index (MPI)** combines a range of indicators to monitor economic hardship in over 100 developing countries. Like the HDI it looks at living standards, education and health but uses a larger number of indicators of household deprivation. The MPI therefore tells us a lot more about the causes and consequences of poverty than income-based measures of poverty.

▼ Multidimensional poverty index (MPI)

MPI dimensions	Indicators	A household is deprived if...
Living standards	Electricity	It has no electricity
	Sanitation	Its sanitation facility is not improved or it is improved but shared with other households.
	Drinking water	It does not have access to improved drinking water or safe drinking water is at least a 30-minute walk from home.
	Flooring	It has a dirt, sand, dung, or 'other' type of floor
	Cooking fuel	If it cooks with dung, wood, or charcoal
	Ownership of assets	If it does not own more than one of these assets: radio, TV, telephone, bicycle, motorbike, or refrigerator, and does not own a car or truck
Education	Years of schooling	If no household member aged 10 years or older has completed five years of schooling
	Child school attendance	If any school-aged child is not attending school up to the age at which he/she would complete class 8 (usually at age 13-14)
Health	Nutrition	If any adult under 70 years of age or any child is undernourished
	Child mortality	If any child has died in the family in the last five years

According to the MPI a total of 1.45 billion people from 103 developing countries were multidimensionally poor in 2017. Half of the multidimensionally poor were children under the age of 17 years.

What causes poverty?

The descent into poverty

According to a UN backed report, the war in Syria has forced 80% of its population into poverty, reduced their average life expectancy by 20 years and caused substantial economic losses of over $200 billion since the conflict began in 2010.

The report identifies the "systematic collapse and destruction" of Syria's economic wealth, infrastructure, institutions and workforce. Unemployment rose sharply from 15% in 2011 to 58% by the end of 2014.

The Joseph Rowntree Foundation estimates 3.7 million people in the UK in employment do not earn enough to meet their minimum needs, and that low wage growth and rising prices will make it harder for them to escape poverty.

Transparency International finds that corruption hits poor people hardest. Findings from Mexico, for example, show that the typical poor family must spend one-third of their income on bribes to public officials.

The UN Investigates Poverty in the US and Finds Extreme Inequality

UN officials visited a number of US states last year to examine the incidence and causes of poverty. In Alabama they were shocked to find diseases like E. Coli and parasites like hookworm were widespread despite being more typically associated with underdeveloped countries.

The main culprits were poor sanitation and sewage management services. Many Alabama residents lacked these services. In some states — like Mississippi, New Mexico and Louisiana — one-in-three children were found to be living in poverty and more than one-fifth of all American children were homeless.

In addition, many adults also faced poverty due to uncontrollable circumstances, like medical issues, disabilities, old age or discrimination.

Poor climate, poorer people?

Environmental degradation, over-dependence on agriculture and rapid population growth are creating a vicious circle in many developing countries.

Environmental changes are having a dramatic impact on many countries in Africa because:
- they are highly dependent on natural resources and agriculture, which are the most vulnerable to changes in climate conditions;
- they have poor infrastructure, such as roads, telecommunications and flood defences;
- their high poverty rate undermines the ability of local populations to prepare for and adapt to climate shocks such as floods, hurricanes and droughts.

For example, Lake Chad, which borders Chad, Niger, Nigeria and Cameroon, has shrunk by 90% since the 1960s. Some 25 million people depend on the lake for food and their livelihoods from farming, fisheries and livestock. Thousands of fishermen and farmers have become unemployed in recent years, losing their main source of income.

From the articles above, try to identify and list as many of the causes of poverty as you can.

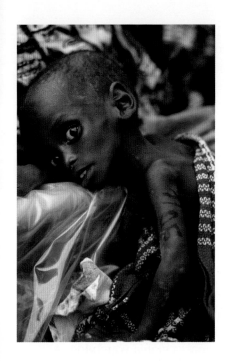

There are many factors that cause people to live in poverty: a lack of resources to ensure sustainable lives, lack of income, limited or lack of access to education and other public services and loss of livelihood as a result of unemployment, natural disaster or war. These factors often work together and reinforce each other such that that the people who live in poverty find it difficult to escape from it.

1 Lack of resources

Any individual in any country, developed or developing, that lacks access to sufficient resources to provide an income, food and a place to live, will very likely live in poverty. However, because many developing countries lack productive resources, such as skilled labour, capital and modern technologies which in turn results in low economic development, many more people in developing countries live in extreme poverty than in developed countries.

2 Lack of education

An educated workforce is a more productive workforce. A good education can therefore increase prosperity and living standards. People who lack a good basic education are therefore less employable than those who are well educated. They will find it difficult to find well-paid jobs and will often suffer long periods of unemployment between jobs. While some people in developed countries may fail through choice to regularly attend school, to read books or achieve good exam results, many more people in developing countries simply lack access to a good basic education because provision is so poor.

3 Low wages

Some jobs are low paid but even in countries with minimum wages they may be insufficient to prevent workers from being poor and unable to buy sufficient goods and services to enjoy a reasonable standard of living. ➤ **2.11.12**

4 Unemployment

The loss of income associated with unemployment is one the main causes of relative poverty in developed economies and absolute poverty in many developing economies. Unemployment is high in many developing countries notably those where employment opportunities are limited due to a lack of modern industries, where education is poor and where diseases and illnesses that prevent people from working may be widespread due to poor nutrition and insufficient healthcare.

5 Old age, disability and ill health

All these factors can prevent people from working and earning an income. Although government support through state pensions and welfare payments may be available in many developed economies to people with little or no income who are old, disabled or long-term sick, the support provided is often not enough to lift these people out of poverty. Many less-developed economies lack the resources and institutions necessary to provide similar support.

6 Vulnerability to climate change and natural disasters

Droughts, floods, hurricanes and other unexpected climatic and natural events destroy property and cause deaths, illness and loss of income. Poor countries lack the resources to prepare for and deal with such events and, therefore, will often take far longer to recover from them. For example, in 2017 Ethiopia suffered its worst drought for 50 years leaving 18 million people in need of food aid.

7 Wars and internal conflicts

Output, trade and GDP will often fall during prolonged wars or conflicts as scarce resources are diverted from more productive uses into funding arms, weapons and armies. Many homes, shops, schools, hospitals, factories and government buildings are often destroyed along with roads and telecommunications and may take many years to rebuild. The main income earners in many families may be killed or injured so they are unable to continue working.

8 Corruption

Corruption is widespread in many of the least developed countries. For example, in 2016 seven out of 10 people in Liberia reported they have had to pay bribes to local officials to access basic services like healthcare and schooling, according to Transparency International, a global watchdog. A statement released by the organization states, 'Corruption creates and increases poverty and exclusion. While corrupt individuals with political power enjoy a lavish life, millions of people are deprived of their basic needs like food, health, education, housing, access to clean water and sanitation.'

SECTION 5.3.3

Measures to alleviate poverty

Policies to alleviate poverty and redistribute income

Poverty is not only socially divisive but can also hold back economic development in a country. Governments will therefore often intervene in their economies in an attempt to reduce poverty in a number of ways.

- **Promoting economic growth.** The benefits of growth can include increased jobs, incomes and living standards. It can increase tax revenues that a government can use to invest in modern infrastructure, industrial development and improved education and healthcare. ➤ **4.6.6**

- **Improving the quantity and quality of education** and also access to education. A well-educated and skilled workforce can help to lift people out of poverty by improving their job prospects and earning potential once they leave school or college.

- **Measures to reduce unemployment,** which is a major cause of poverty in many countries. These may include expansionary fiscal and monetary policies to increase total demand in an economy, but also government training programmes to teach unemployed workers new skills. ➤ **4.7.4**

- **Progressive taxes** can be applied to personal incomes to reduce income inequality and relative poverty because people on higher incomes will pay a greater overall percentage of their incomes in tax. ➤ **4.3.4**

- **Reducing indirect taxes** such as VAT and excise duties on essential items would make them more affordable but richer people would also benefit from this policy.

- Money raised from taxes can fund **welfare services** and provide **income support** to people on very low incomes. For example, elderly people, single parents and disabled people may be unable to work and may have insufficient incomes or savings to afford essential goods and services.

- Tax revenues can also be used to subsidize the building of free or **low-cost** homes for poor families to live in, and to provide them with free healthcare and travel.

- Introducing **minimum wage laws** to raise the wages of the lowest paid employees. ➤ **2.11.2**

International measures to reduce poverty

However, governments in some of the least developed economies often lack the resources to reduce poverty in their countries. Some may also lack the skills or will to do so. As a result, governments and aid agencies from more developed economies often provide help to less developed economies in an attempt to improve the living standards and economic welfare of people living in extreme poverty. This overseas aid can take a number of forms.

- **Food aid** is intended for starving and malnourished people but sometimes may be stolen by other people and sold for profit.

- **Technological aid,** for example, in the form of advanced machinery and other capital equipment or training in modern production techniques to help developing countries to develop new industries and improve their productivity.

- **Financial aid and low-cost loans,** for example, to support investments in modern infrastructure projects such as the construction of airports, power stations and reservoirs.

- **Debt relief** involves the full or partial cancellation of loans from overseas governments and institutions. It relieves the burden on some of the poorest countries of paying interest charges and meeting debt repayments. For example, the **highly indebted poor countries (HIPC) programme** was initiated by the IMF and the World Bank in 1996. It provides debt relief and low-interest loans to cancel or reduce the external debt repayments of 40 of the world's least developed countries with the highest levels of poverty and external debts.

However, some economists argue that overseas aid has not worked and that much of it has been wasted or diverted away from those people who need it the most. This is believed by some economists because of the following reasons.

1. Overseas aid often has too many strings or conditions attached. Governments of developing countries providing aid often require those countries receiving it to employ their firms and experts to design and build their infrastructure projects or to install, operate and maintain the advanced equipment they provide.

Tens of millions in foreign aid wasted on salaries and commissions

Overseas aid failing to reach the poor

2. Many less-developed countries are poorly managed or do not have the skills they need to invest financial aid wisely in projects that will help their economies grow. Aid providers also find it difficult to monitor how well the money is being used.

Corruption epidemic is wasting billions in aid

3 Some governments of developing countries are corrupt and overseas aid can be misused to fund lavish lifestyles for government officials.

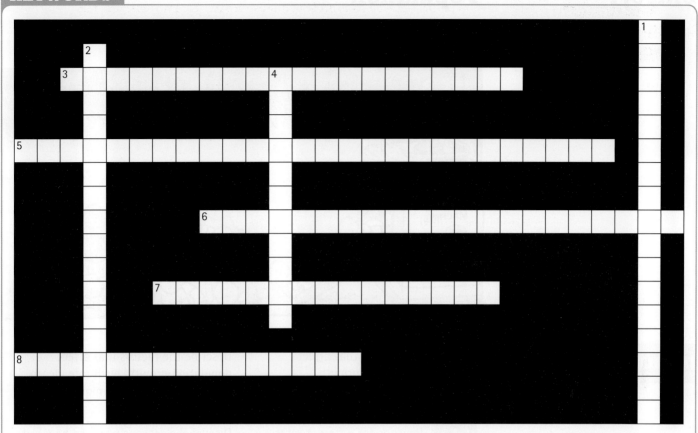

Clues across

3. A country with a relatively low level of economic development (4, 9, 7)

5. A term used to describe a country that is undergoing significant growth in its industries and infrastructure but is yet to display the full range of characteristics of a modern developed economy (5, 14, 7)

6. A statistical measure complied from different development indicators by the United Nations to measure and contrast economic development in different countries (5, 11, 5)

7. An economic condition of having fewer resources than others in the same society, usually measured by the extent to which a person's or household's financial resources fall below the average income level of others in their economy (8, 7)

8. An economic condition of lacking both money and basic necessities needed to live successfully, such as food, water, education, healthcare, and shelter (8, 7)

Clues down

1. A measure of the number of people of working age as a proportion of the total population in a country who can read and write (5, 8, 4)

2. A country with a high level of economic development, including high average incomes; good-quality housing, legal and education systems; modern infrastructure and a wide range of industries (9, 7)

4. The voluntary transfer of resources from one country to the benefit of another, for example to help it reduce poverty and improve its level of economic development. This help may be in the form of financial or technological assistance, food supplies and debt relief (8, 3)

5.4.1	The factors that affect population growth	▸ Describe the factors that affect population growth: birth rate, death rate, net migration, immigration and emigration
5.4.2	Reasons for different rates of population growth in different countries	▸ Discuss the reasons why and how birth rates, death rate and net migration vary between countries
5.4.3	The effects of changes in the size and structure of population on different countries	▸ Understand the concept of an optimum population ▸ Analyse the effects of increases and decreases in population size and changes in the age and gender distribution of population

SECTION 5.4.1

The factors that affect population growth

SECTION 5.4.2

Reasons for different rates of population growth in different countries

Global population growth

Since the 18th century the world has experienced a population explosion, and it is still increasing faster than ever before. While there is potential for the production of more goods and services, natural resources are limited, and, as fast as goods and services are produced, so the needs and wants of an ever-increasing world population grow. The population of the world is increasing by over 70 million people each year, or 200,000 a day. Imagine a city the size of Madrid in Spain being added every month, and the people in those new cities being on average only four to five weeks old!

The population explosion started in Europe after the Industrial Revolution in the 18th century. Improvements in housing, sanitation and medicine reduced the number of deaths and helped increase the number of births. The population of Europe rose by over 300% in a 160-year period after 1750. Many of these Europeans moved overseas.

▼ World population, annual average growth rates by major region, 1800–2050

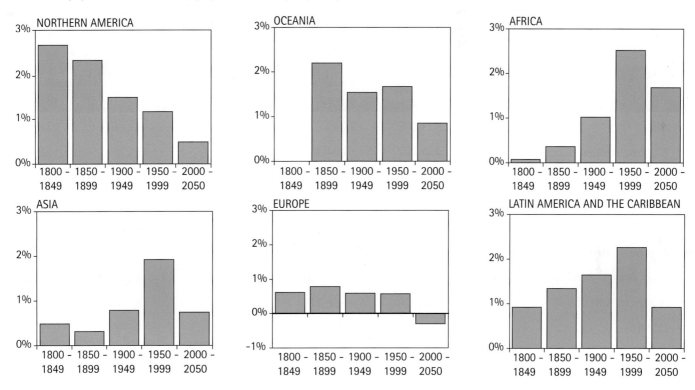

Source: 'World Population Prospects, 2017' (United Nations Population Division)

In the 20th century population growth in Europe and many developed countries has slowed down. In some European countries recently there has even been negative population growth as people have been moving overseas and birth rates have fallen to low levels.

The new population explosion is in developing countries, particularly in Asia and Africa. Around 4.5 billion people, almost 60% of the world's population, currently live in Asia. The two largest countries by population, China and India, together account for around 37% of the world's population. Africa follows with 1.25 billion people, almost 18% of the world's population while Europe has 742 million inhabitants, around 10% of the world's population.

The populations of Asia and Africa are forecast to continue growing rapidly, from around 5.7 billion people in 2018 to 7.8 billion by 2050 – an increase of over 35%. In contrast, the population of Europe is expected to shrink from 733 million to around 712 million people.

The world population is expected to reach 9.8 billion by 2050. Just under 90% of all these people will live in countries currently considered as developing.

The causes of population change

There are three ways in which a country's population can increase.

1. The number of babies being born increases.
2. The number of people dying falls.
3. More people arrive from overseas to become residents of a country (**immigration**) than there are people leaving the same country to live overseas (**emigration**).

▼ Population size and components of growth, by major area 2000–2015

Region	Population 2015 (thousands)	Births	Deaths	Net migration	Total growth
		(change over period 2000–2015, thousands)			
World	7,383,009	2,049,635	811,634	0	1,238,002
More developed regions	1,253,207	204,382	184,916	43,236	62,702
Less developed regions	6,129,802	1,845,254	626,718	-43,236	1,175,300
Africa	1,194,370	548,607	163,079	-8,724	376,804
Asia	4,419,898	1,141,908	428,972	-23,409	689,527
Europe	740,814	116,408	124,202	21,407	13,613
Latin America and the Caribbean	632,381	167,193	50,657	-9,950	106,586
Northern America	356,004	66,176	41,148	18,131	43,159
Oceania	39,543	9,342	3,574	2,546	8,314

Source: *United Nations Population Division*

The **natural rate of increase in a population** is the difference between the birth rate and death rate. In most countries birth rates exceed death rates so populations are growing. For example, over the period 2000 to 2015 births exceeded deaths globally by almost 1.24 billion. Most of these births occurred in less-developed countries. This means that an average of 234 babies were born in less-developed countries every minute over the period 2000 to 2015. Compare this to an average of 79 deaths per minute over the same period – a net increase in populations of these countries of 155 people each minute. In contrast, there were only 26 babies born every minute and just 23 deaths per minute in developed countries over the same period. This means the natural rate of population growth in developed countries averaged just three people per minute between 2000 and 2015.

In contrast, the natural rate of change in population in many European countries has recently been negative because birth rates have fallen below death rates. From 2000 to 2015 deaths in European countries exceeded births by over 7.7 million. The population of Europe only expanded by just over 13.6 million people over the 15-year period due to **net inward migration** of over 21 million people, notably from countries in Africa and Asia. However, within Europe itself many Eastern European countries were losing population to Western European countries such as the UK and France. Birth rates fell below death rates as many younger people from countries such as Bulgaria, Belarus and the Czech Republic have migrated overseas. This is called **net outward migration**.

Births

In some countries more babies are born than in others. The average number of children born in a country each year compared to the total population is known as the **birth rate**, which is normally expressed as the number of births for every 1,000 people in the population. The birth rate in Japan in 2017 was 7.7 births for every 1,000 Japanese citizens but it used to be much higher. In the early 1970s the birth rate in Japan was over 19 per 1,000. Falling birth rates have been observed in many developed countries.

▼ Countries with highest and lowest birth rates, 2017

Country/area	Highest birth rates (births per 1,000 of population)	Country/area	Lowest birth rates (births per 1,000 of population)
Angola	44.2	San Marino	8.6
Niger	44.2	Greece	8.4
Mali	43.9	Taiwan	8.3
Uganda	42.9	South Korea	8.3
Zambia	41.5	Slovenia	8.2
Burundi	41.3	Puerto Rico	8.1
Burkina Faso	41.2	Japan	7.7
Malawi	41	Andorra	7.5
Somalia	39.6	Saint Pierre and Miquelon	7.1
Liberia	38.3	Monaco	6.6

Source: *CIA World Factbook*

All the countries with the highest birth rates in 2017 were in Africa. In many of these countries there are on average six or more children for every adult female in the population. In contrast, many countries with low birth rates are in the Far East and Eastern Europe. In all these countries there is on average fewer than two children born per adult female. The overall world birth rate in 2017 was 18.5 births per 1,000 people.

There are a number of reasons for differences in birth rates between countries, and changing birth rates over time.

1 Living standards

Improvements in the quality and availability of food, housing, clean water, sanitation and medical care result in fewer babies dying. Many years ago many children would die before they could go to work and earn money to help their families. As a result, people often had large families in case some of their children died. As living standards improved in many developed countries, fewer babies died and so people did not have as many children.

In less-developed countries birth rates remain high because many children still die, and people want large families so that the children can work to produce food and earn incomes.

Average number of children per adult female, 2017

Countries with 5 or more children born per female

Niger* Angola* Mali*

Burundi Somalia Burkino Faso

Uganda Zambia Malawi

Afghanistan Mozambique

South Sudan Nigeria Liberia

(* 6 or more)

Countries with less than 1.25 children born per female

Puerto Rico Hong Kong

Taiwan Macau

Singapore

Source: *CIA World Factbook*

2 Contraception

The increased use of contraception and abortion has dramatically reduced birth rates in developed countries. The contraceptive pill for women was first introduced in the 1960s and has a 99% success rate in preventing pregnancy. However, because of a lack of sex education in some less-developed countries, many people are unaware of birth control. Perhaps they should learn from Japan's success in reducing its birth rate from 36 births per 1,000 people to 17 per 1,000 people in just 15 years after the introduction of birth control in 1966.

3 Custom and religion

Many people, notably in many of the least developed countries, hold religious beliefs that will not allow them to use contraception. But customs are changing. In developed countries it has become less fashionable and less socially acceptable to have large families so birth rates have fallen.

4 Changes in female employment

In developed countries, many women are in full-time or part-time employment. Working women may not wish to break their careers to bring up children. Children are also expensive to raise. Not only will the mother have to give up work for a while, but she may also have to pay a childminder to look after her children if she returns to work. Female participation in the workforce is also rising in many developing countries. ➤ **6.2**

5 Marriage

Most people have children when they are married. In many developed countries people are tending to marry later in life and this has reduced birth rates. For example, in the UK the average age of a new mother at all births increased from 26 years of age in 1971 to almost 29 years of age in 2016.

Deaths

If people start to live longer it increases the size of the population. The number of people who die each year compared to every 1,000 people measures the **death rate**. The global death rate in 2016 was just under eight deaths for every 1,000 people. The countries with the highest death rates in 2016, of over 13 deaths per 1,000, included many in Africa as well as Russia and a number of developing countries in Eastern Europe. These death rates are similar to the death rate in the UK and many other developed countries over 100 years ago. The UK death rate is now just over nine per 1,000 of population. In contrast, many of the countries with the very lowest death rates in 2017, of less than three deaths per 1,000, were in the Middle East.

▼ Countries with highest and lowest death rates, 2017

Country/area	Highest death rates (deaths per 1,000 of population)	Country/area	Lowest death rates (deaths per 1,000 of population)
Lesotho	14.9	Jordan	3.8
Lithuania	14.5	Libya	3.6
Bulgaria	14.5	Brunei	3.6
Latvia	14.4	West Bank	3.5
Ukraine	14.4	Singapore	3.5
Guinea-Bissau	14.1	Saudi Arabia	3.3
Chad	14.0	Oman	3.3
Afghanistan	13.7	Turks and Caicos Islands	3.2
Russia	13.6	Gaza Strip	3.2
Serbia	13.6	Bahrain	2.7

Source: *CIA World Factbook*

A number of factors affect death rates and help to explain differences between countries.

1 Age distribution

Countries with a relatively young population might be expected to have lower death rates than countries in which the average age of their population is much higher. For example, the average age of the population of Qatar in 2016 was just over 31 years and less than 1% of its population was over 65 years of age. In contrast, in Bulgaria where the death rate is much higher, the average age was over 43 years and almost 20% of its population were over 65 years of age.

2 Living standards

Better-quality food, clothing, sanitation and shelter, and an increased emphasis on cleanliness, have all helped improve health and life expectancy in developed countries. In the less-developed world a lack of the right types of food to provide vitamins and proteins has meant some people in these areas continue to die of malnutrition. However, in developed countries many people smoke and eat fatty foods, causing cancers and heart disease. These health problems occur far less in developing countries.

3 Medical advances and healthcare

Advances in medicine and healthcare in many countries have reduced the number of deaths from diseases. For example, killer diseases such as smallpox, cholera and tuberculosis can be prevented or even cured by modern medicines.

However, life expectancy at birth still remains low in many of the world's least developed countries. Over half of all deaths in these countries occur during pregnancy or are due to malnutrition and communicable diseases such as HIV/aids and malaria, compared to just 7% of deaths in developed countries. In contrast, heart disease, strokes, Alzheimer's disease and respiratory diseases were the biggest killers in developed countries. These conditions are more often associated with older people.

▼ Average life expectancy at birth, 2016

Country/area	Years	Country/area	Years
Monaco	89.5	Mozambique	53.3
Japan	85	Lesotho	53
Singapore	85	Zambia	52.5
Macau	84.5	Somalia	52.4
San Marino	83.3	Central African Republic	52.3
Iceland	83	Gabon	52.1
Hong Kong	82.9	Swaziland	51.6
Andorra	82.8	Afghanistan	51.3
Switzerland	82.6	Guinea-Bissau	50.6
Guernsey	82.5	Chad	50.2

Source: *CIA World Factbook*

4 Natural disasters and wars

Natural disasters such as hurricanes, floods and earthquakes, famines due to lack of rain and poor harvests, and wars and criminal violence can also have a significant effect on death rates and life expectancy over time in some countries.

▲ The Japanese tsunami on 10 March 2011 claimed over 70,000 lives due to devastating flooding

▲ An estimated 465,000 people were killed during the conflict in Syria between March 2011 and March 2017, according to the Syrian Observatory for Human Rights

Migration Net migration measures the difference between immigration and emigration to and from a country. Between 2000 and 2015 over 43 million more people each year emigrated from less-developed countries to more-developed countries than migrated in the opposite direction. Net migration from Asian countries accounted for much of this. On average, net outward migration from Asia was 23 million over the same period. In contrast, net inward migration to Europe was 21 million, more than offsetting a natural population decline of almost 8 million over the 15-year period as birth rates fell below death rates.

Such international migration has economic, social and political implications. Increasing numbers of migrants from developing countries moving to developed countries have helped to boost their working populations, but has also increased the demand for housing, education and welfare. This has placed pressure on government finances. In some cases, tensions can occur between different ethnic groups as a result. But countries that lose people through emigration can also face problems caused by a loss of skilled workers leaving to find higher-paid work overseas, such as nurses and doctors, engineers and entrepreneurs.

EXAM PREPARATION 5.2

a   Define *birth rate*.   [2]

b   Explain **two** possible causes of a fall in a country's birth rate.   [4]

c   Analyse the reasons for differences between the expected age structure
    of the population of a developing country and a developed country.   [6]

c   Life expectancy at birth can be as low as just 50 years in some developing
    countries due to disease, high infant mortality and other health-related
    problems. As a result governments have allocated large amounts of
    expenditure to developing new hospitals and to providing health education
    programmes.

    Discuss in what ways this policy might affect other major government
    economic policies.   [8]

The effects of changes in the size and structure of population on different countries

ACTIVITY 5.5

Explosion!

The world population reached 1 billion around 1804. The second billion was added 123 years later in 1927, the third billion just 33 years later in 1960. It then took just 14 years for the world population to grow by another 1 billion people to reach 4 billion.

The graph below illustrates this population explosion. By 2017 the world population had reached 7.6 billion and is expected to grow to 9.6 billion by 2050.

▼ The world population explosion

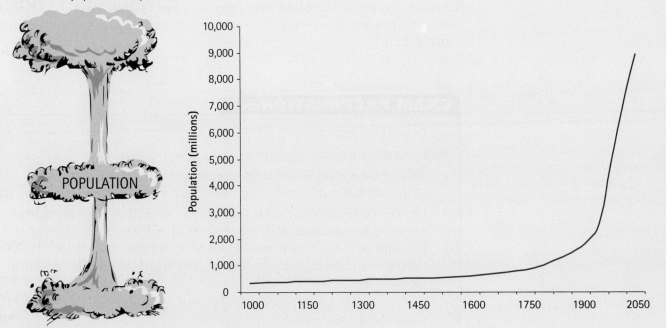

1 As the world population increases, what will happen to the total of needs and wants in the world?

2 If resources are scarce, such as oil, coal, metals, fertile soils and clean air, what will happen to the rate at which we use them up?

3 The population of the world rises as fewer people die and live to an old age, and as more babies are born. What is likely to happen to the demand for the following?

- Food
- Consumer goods
- Education
- Healthcare
- Housing
- Transport

4 If one country is unable to produce enough goods and services for the needs and wants of its population, how should it try to obtain more of these products?

- What is likely to happen to the country's balance of international trade?
- If it is unable to obtain more goods and services what is likely to happen to prices in the country?

Is population growth a cause for concern?

In 1798 the Reverend Thomas Malthus wrote about population growth in the UK. At the time of writing, the UK population was growing fast and this seemed to support his view that increasing numbers of people would only bring misery. There would be too many people and too few resources. That is, there would be **overpopulation**. As a result, people would start to starve and there would be famines and plagues as people lacked the strength to fight off disease. Wars would start as countries tried to take over each other's resources to support their own populations. Population growth would eventually be stopped.

However, Malthus was proved wrong in the UK. Although the population increased four times over during the 19th century, technology and productivity increased sufficiently to meet the needs of a growing population. Output of food increased and new methods of transport allowed food to be brought to Britain from the vast agricultural lands of the USA. More houses were needed and the building of these provided work and incomes for people. Increasing numbers of people meant more consumers. This increase in demand expanded the markets for goods and services, stimulating investment in new capital equipment to produce them and creating employment for many more people. Economic growth occurred, and, despite the costs of increased congestion in growing cities and increasing pollution from factories, living standards rose.

Nevertheless, many people still believe Malthus will eventually be proved right. Rapid population growth in many developing countries is increasing pressure on scarce resources, particularly natural resources, as more and more people, farms and factories compete for land and access to safe drinking water. Cutting down trees to make way for intensively farmed land can cause it to become depleted of soil and nutrients, increasing the risk of famine.

Among many experts expressing concerns over continued population growth, the UK chief scientist, Professor John Beddington, warned changing conditions could create a 'perfect storm' by 2030. Rising populations, food shortages, insufficient water and energy resources may unleash public unrest, cross-border conflicts and mass migration from the worst-affected regions.

Beddington said food reserves are at a 50-year low but the world will need 50% more energy, food, and water by 2030. Similarly, the United Nations' Food and Agriculture Organization (FAO) has warned that the world will have to produce 70% more food by 2050 to feed a projected extra 2 billion people.

Do you agree with the predictions made? How does the article illustrate the concept of opportunity cost? Should countries allocate more scarce resources to developing new technologies and equipment and less to the production of consumer goods? Do you think governments should introduce population controls?

World faces 'perfect storm' of problems by 2030

In a major speech to environmental groups and politicians, Professor John Beddington, who took up the position of UK chief scientific adviser in 2008, will say that the world is heading for major upheavals which are due to come to a head in 2030.

He will tell the government's Sustainable Development UK conference that growing populations and success in alleviating poverty in developing countries will trigger a surge in demand for food, water and energy over the next two decades, at a time when governments must also make major progress in combating climate change.

'We head into a perfect storm in 2030, because all of these things are operating on the same time frame,'

he said. 'If we don't address this, we can expect major destabilisation, an increase in rioting and potentially significant problems with international migration, as people move out to avoid food and water shortages,' he added.

Beddington said a major technological push is needed to develop renewable energy supplies, boost crop yields and better utilise existing water supplies.

Looming water shortages in China have already prompted officials to build 59 new reservoirs to catch meltwater from mountain glaciers, which will be circulated into the water supply.

The dependent population

Imagine there are five people living in your home: your mother and father, your sister and a grandparent. Your mother is the only person at work. She earns $150 per week, which is used to provide food, clothing and shelter as well as the other goods and services for five people including herself. That is, your father, you and your sister and a grandparent all depend on your mother going to work. Clearly, if there was just your mother and father their standard of living would be much higher. They would have more money to spend on themselves. If, on the other hand, they had more children, all the family would have a lower standard of living as the mother's income and the goods and services it buys would have to be shared out between more people. As the number of dependants rise, everybody will be worse off unless the productivity of scarce resources also rises. The same applies to the population as a whole.

People in work produce goods and services not only for themselves but also for people not in work. For example, in South Africa there are approximately 56 million people, of which 18 million people make up the working population or labour force. The rest of the population of about 38 million people rely on the labour force to produce the goods and services they need and want. These 38 million people are therefore the **dependent population**: that part of a population that does not work and relies on others for the goods and services they consume.

From these figures we can calculate the **dependency ratio** in South Africa. This ratio compares the number of people in the dependent population of a country with the working population in the same country. ➤ **4.7.1**

$$\text{Dependency ratio} = \frac{\text{dependent population}}{\text{working population}}$$

Using the figures for South Africa the dependency ratio is 2.1 (38 million/ 18 million). That is, every person in the labour force not only supports himself or herself but also 2.1 people who are not in work.

The dependent population of a country includes the very young, schoolchildren, students, housewives and old-age pensioners. Any increase in these groups of people will increase the dependency ratio in a country. The higher the ratio the greater the burden on the working population, and therefore the entire economy, of supporting people not in work or unable to work.

▼ The dependent population includes both young and old

More resources, and expenditure on them, will have to be devoted to education for the young, and medical and welfare services for young and old alike. In a country such as Sweden, where many essential services and merit goods are provided by the government using tax-payers' money, this means working people will have to pay more tax to support dependants. In addition, if people in work cannot produce enough goods and services to satisfy the needs and wants of a growing dependent population, the country will have to use some of its income to purchase more and more imported goods from abroad. Its balance of international trade may become unfavourable. ➤ **6.4.2**

The dependency ratio has increased in many countries for a number of reasons; the school leaving age has been increased over time; more young people are encouraged to stay on in full-time education after leaving school; people are living longer and the number of elderly people has increased; and an increasing number of people have taken early retirement. To offset this in part, many governments have increased the age at which people can officially retire from their jobs and receive a basic pension from the government. Some governments have also introduced compulsory pension savings schemes and have transferred many care services for the elderly to the private sector to encourage greater and more efficient provision.

However, many developing countries face some of the biggest problems. Improvements in healthcare have reduced child mortality rates and increased life expectancies. As a result, their already large dependent populations are increasing further, placing more strain on their scarce resources.

What impact will the changes below have on dependent populations? What are the economic costs and benefits of countries such as France, Australia and many others in raising state retirement ages and school leaving ages?

France raises its retirement age from 60 to 62

France has increased its minimum retirement age from 60 to 62 but many people will soon have to wait until they are 67 before they can receive their full state pension. They will also have to pay contributions for a further 2 years before they can claim their full pension entitlement. The full pension contribution period is currently 41 years but will rise to 43 years by 2020.

The reforms are designed to bring France's public finances under tighter control. The French government's budget deficit was 5 per cent of gross domestic product in 2012 when the first wave of pension reforms were announced. The current government aims to reduce it to 2.6 per cent by the end of 2018.

The new pension reforms brings France closer into line with other European countries, including the UK, Germany and Greece, which have all raised retirement ages and taken other measures to cut their budget deficits.

Minimum school leaving age jumps to 17 in Australia

Students will be forced to spend an additional two years in school or go into a vocational training programme under a government plan to raise the minimum leaving age to 17.

The 60-year-old laws allowing students to finish school at 15 will be changed to ensure that all students complete their year 10 School Certificate. After that, students will not be able to leave unless they are enrolled in a vocational training programme.

'It will mean over the course of your lifetime, you're much less likely to be unemployed, over the course of your working life, you're much more likely to earn a better income, and there are also are additional health benefits and so on,' said the Australian premier in support of the changes.

What is an optimum population?

A country will be considered underpopulated if it does not have enough human resources to make the best use of its other natural and man-made resources. That is, there is not enough labour to maximize the amount of output of goods and services that can be produced for people to enjoy. In this case a government may provide help to families to have more children, for example by providing income support, free childcare and employment policies that allow parents more time off work to look after children. A government may also encourage the immigration of skilled labour.

Someone to depend on

Below is a table of figures showing the total population and working population in a number of countries in 2016.

Country	Population (millions)	Working population (millions)
China	1,378.7	995.1
India	1,324.2	873.9
USA	323.1	213.1
Indonesia	261.1	175.3
Brazil	207.7	144.6
Pakistan	193.2	117.1
Nigeria	186.0	98.9
Bangladesh	163.0	107.6
Russia	144.3	99.5
Japan	127.0	76.8

Source: *World Bank*

1   For each country calculate:

   a   the size of the dependent population

   b   the dependency ratio

2   Which countries have:

   a   the highest dependency ratio?

   b   the lowest dependency ratio?

3   What effect would the following have on the dependency ratio of a country?

   a   A fall in the number of people in employment.

   b   An increase in the number of old people.

   c   An increase in the number of births.

   d   An increase in employment.

   e   A decrease in the number of births.

   f   Net inward migration by people of working age

4   Of the above factors in question 3, which are characteristic of:

   •   developing economies?   •   both types of economies?

   •   developed economies?

5   **a**   What is meant by overpopulation?

   b   Can Japan be considered overpopulated? Explain.

In contrast, a country will be overpopulated, as Malthus envisaged, if there are too many people and too few resources to support them. Unless a government can increase the productivity of resources through new technologies or working practices it may have to seek ways to limit further population growth and even encourage people to move overseas to reduce the overall population.

The optimum size of a population will therefore be that which will allow a country to maximize output per head of the population from its existing resources. However, because technologies and the quality and quantity of labour skills and other resources can change over time it is difficult to identify what an optimum population should be at any point. The concept also fails to take account of any social costs or issues different populations and levels of production may create. ➤ **2.10.2**

Population structure

Demography involves studying the characteristics of and changes in population. This includes examining and comparing the structure of populations in different countries and considering how changes in structure can affect economies. The following characteristics of populations are relevant:

- age distribution: how many people there are in different age groups
- sex distribution: the balance of males and females
- geographic distribution: where people live
- occupational distribution: where people work.

Young or old?

The **age distribution** of a population refers to the number of people, or percentage of the population, in each age group. With falling birth and death rates in many developed countries, the average age of their populations is rising: there are a growing number of middle-aged and elderly people. For example, in 2016 over one quarter of the population of Japan and over 20% of the populations of Bulgaria, Germany, Greece, Finland, Portugal and Italy were over 65 years of age. In contrast, 15% or less of their populations and those of many other developed countries were under 15 years of age.

In contrast, in many developing countries more than one-third of their population is under the age of 15, with some countries having almost half their populations made up of children. For example, just over 50% of the population of Niger is under 15 years of age with just 2.5% over 65 years of age. Niger if one of the least developed countries in the world but has the fastest growing population.

Similarly, children made up 47% or more of the populations of Angola, D.R. Congo, Chad, Mali, Somalia and Uganda in 2016. This means that a large proportion of these countries' populations is too young to work and will have to depend on those who can, at least until they too are old enough to work.

'Youngest' countries	% of population		'Oldest' countries	% of population	
	Under 15 years	Over 65 years		Under 15 years	Over 65 years
Niger	50.2	2.5	Japan	12.9	26.6
Uganda	48.0	2.2	Italy	13.6	22.7
Mali	47.8	2.5	Germany	13.1	21.3
Chad	47.4	2.5	Portugal	13.9	21.1
Angola	47.0	2.4	Finland	16.4	20.8
Somalia	46.5	2.7	Bulgaria	14.1	20.5
D.R. Congo	46.3	3.4	Greece	14.3	20.2
Gambia	45.5	2.3	Sweden	17.4	19.8
Burkina Faso	45.4	2.4	Latvia	15.4	19.5
Zambia	45.1	2.5	Denmark	16.6	19.4

Source: *World Bank*

In 1960, just under 5% of the world's population was aged 65 years or over. By 2018, that proportion had risen to 8.4% and it is expected to reach 17%, or 1.6 billion people, in 2050. One in every three people in developed countries will be over 65 by this time.

As the number of elderly people grows in many countries it will increase pressure on their working populations to support more non-working people. In 1960, there were just over 11 people of working age for every person aged 65 or older. By 2016, that number had fallen to 8. By 2050, the ratio of people of working age to people aged over 65 years is expected to fall to 4:1. These changes will also affect the allocation of resources in these economies. More resources will be needed to produce the goods and services older people want and need, such as more healthcare, pensions and leisure facilities. However, falling birth rates may mean less resources will be needed for maternity clinics, nurseries and schools.

Males and females

The ratio of males to females in a population reflects its **sex distribution**. Like most other species the human sex ratio is around 1:1. The sex ratio of the entire world population is estimated to be around 101 males for every 100 females.

The sex ratio tends to vary naturally by age but can also be affected by such factors as war and also influenced or even controlled by governments. Slightly more male babies tend to be born than females but the ratio of females to males tends to even out by adulthood. However, because females tend to live longer than males in many countries there are more females to males on average in older age groups. For example, in India there were 1.1 females for every male in the age group 65 and over in 2016. In the 85 years or over age group the ratio of females to males was 1.5. The same pattern can be observed in most countries.

Gender imbalance, an excess of males or females, has been observed in a number of countries and can occur for a number of reasons:

- Wars result in many deaths among young adult male populations.

- Violence towards females observed in some developing countries is creating an excess of males. For example, honour killings of females by their family members take place in some societies in the Middle East and Asia if, for example, a female member is thought to have shamed her family by going out with a male from another religious group, refusing to enter into an arranged marriage or having an affair with another man outside of her marriage.

- Gender imbalance can result from sex selection through abortion or even gender-based infanticide (selective killing of children of the same sex). In some less-developed countries, male children are often considered more productive and capable of work than females. Government policies and religious beliefs may also reinforce these views. For example, the extremist group Taliban which ruled large parts of Afghanistan from 1996 until 2001 banned females from receiving education during this period.

- Sex-specific inward migration to a country, often by male guest workers brought in by companies to work in construction and other industries, can cause gender imbalance. For example, a large number of male expatriates in the population of Qatar working in its petrochemical industry has resulted in a highly skewed sex ratio in the country of almost two males to every female.

High sex ratios at birth in some Asian countries are now attributed to sex-selective abortion and infanticide due to a strong preference for sons. This will affect future marriage patterns and fertility patterns resulting in fewer births in future and an ageing population. Eventually, it could cause unrest among young adult males who are unable to find female partners.

China admits its gender imbalance is "the most serious" in the world

Chinese health authorities have described the gender imbalance among newborns as "the most serious and prolonged" in the world and the direct impact of the country's one-child policy.

China imposed strict population controls in the 1970s in an attempt to slow growth of its huge population, but one side effect was a jump in gender selection of babies.

Like many other Asian nations, China has a traditional bias for sons. Although sex-selective abortion is prohibited, the practice remains widespread, especially in rural areas, while many other families abandon their female babies to die soon after birth or transfer them for adoption to overseas families to ensure their one child is a son.

About 118 boys are born for every 100 girls compared to the global average of 103 boys to 107 girls. In some regions such as the southern provinces of Guangdong and Hainan, the ratio is even worse with 130 male newborns to 100 girls

The authorities have warned that large sex ratio imbalances could lead to instability as more men remain unmarried or unable to find a female partner, resulting in a rise in anti-social and violent behaviour. The ability of the population to reproduce will also be harmed. Many a nalysts say the one-child policy has already shrunk China's labóur force and reduced economic growth.

Although China relaxed its family planning restrictions in 2013 to allow families to raise two children, critics have argued the change is too little and came too late to reverse the significant negative effects the policy had already had on the economy and society.

It has been reported that acute gender imbalance in countries such as China and also India, which has an estimated 44 million more males than females, is contributing to social and economic problems such as increasing prostitution, alcoholism, HIV/AIDS, and violence and the kidnapping and sale of women for forced marriage or into the sex trade.

Population pyramids

The age and sex distribution of a population can be displayed on a **population pyramid**. The pyramids in Activity 5.7 compare the age and sex distribution of the population of a developed country with the population of a developing country. Along the bottom axis is the number or percentage of males to the left of the vertical axis, and to the right the number or percentage of females. The vertical axis shows age in ascending ranges. The pyramid for the developed country bulges in the middle due to their ageing populations as birth and death rates remain low.

In contrast, many of the least-developed countries have pyramids with wide bases and narrow tops because birth rates are high and life expectancy is low.

Where do people live?

The **geographic distribution** or regional distribution of a population refers to where people live. Most people, almost 90% of the world's population, live in developing countries. This places significant pressure on scarce resources in these countries.

ACTIVITY 5.7

Population pyramids

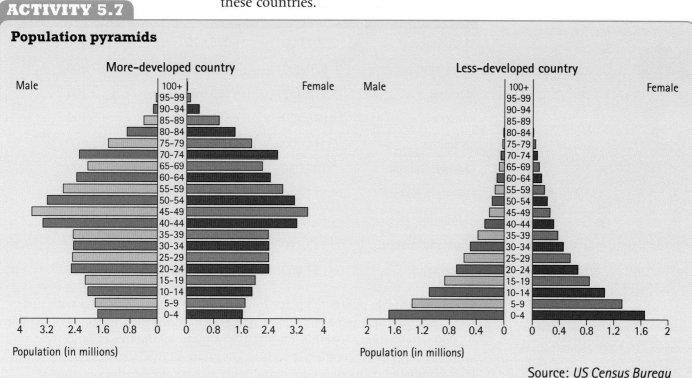

Source: *US Census Bureau*

1 Looking at the pyramids, which group of countries have the highest dependency ratios for:

   a those under 15 years of age?   **b** those over 60 years of age?

2 Which group of countries has the highest birth rate?

3 Which group of countries has the highest life expectancy?

4 List 10 countries that individually are likely to have similar population structures to those shown by the pyramids.

5 What is an 'ageing population'? Which group of countries has an ageing population? Describe likely impacts this will have on their economies.

▼ Most densely populated countries and areas, latest available data as at January 2018

Country/area	Population	Area (km²)	Density (people per km²)
Macau	541,200	29.2	18,534
Monaco	33,000	1.95	16,923
Singapore	5,076,700	710.2	7,148
Hong Kong	7,264,100	1,104	6,349
Gibraltar	31,000	6.8	4,559
Vatican City	826	0.44	1,877
Bahrain	1,234,596	750	1,646
Malta	417,617	316	1,322
Bermuda	65,000	53	1,226
Sint Maarten	37,429	34	1,101

▼ Least densely populated countries and areas, latest available data as at January 2018

Country/Area	Population	Area (km²)	Density (people per km²)
Mauritania	3,291,000	1,025,520	3.200
Suriname	520,000	163,820	3.200
Iceland	318,452	103,000	3.100
Australia	22,648,720	7,682,300	3.100
Namibia	2,171,000	824,292	2.600
French Guiana	187,056	90,000	2.100
Western Sahara	513,000	266,000	1.900
Mongolia	2,671,000	1,564,116	1.700
Falkland Islands	3,140	12,173	0.260
Greenland	57,000	2,175,600	0.026

The most densely populated place in the world is Macau in China with just over 18,500 people per km². The principality of Monaco in Europe is next with 33,000 people living together on just 1.95 square kilometres of land. The world average is 51 people per square kilometre of the Earth's surface. The least populated country is Greenland with an average density of just one person for every 38.1 km², or 0.026 people per km² , largely because much of Greenland is frozen over all year round.

Within countries the geographic distribution of population can also vary widely and has changed significantly over time. Around half the world's population today lives in urban areas, and this is expected to rise to around 60%, or 5 billion people, by 2030. The movement of people from rural areas to urban areas has helped increase production of goods and services, and raised living standards.

However, increasing urbanization has also resulted in the increased consumption of scarce natural resources such as trees, open space and water as more homes, factories, offices, shops and roads have been built. Increased energy and car use in cities has increased pollution, reduced air and water quality, and increased health risks. The rapid growth of cities in many countries, but particularly in newly industrialized countries, is therefore some cause for concern.

According to the United Nations, Dhaka in Bangladesh was the world's most populated city in 2015 with an average of 44,500 people living on each square kilometre of land space. Mumbai in India was the next most densely populated city with 31,700 people per km².

The number of mega-cities or agglomerations in the world with over 10 million residents has also increased from just five in the late 1960s to 18 in 2000 and numbered 47 by 2017. Tokyo in Japan was the largest with over 38.1 million residents. Guangzhou and Shanghai in China, Seoul in South Korea, Jakarta in Indonesia, Karachi in Pakistan and Delhi in India, all had 25 million residents in 2017.

▼ World population density, population per km² in 2015

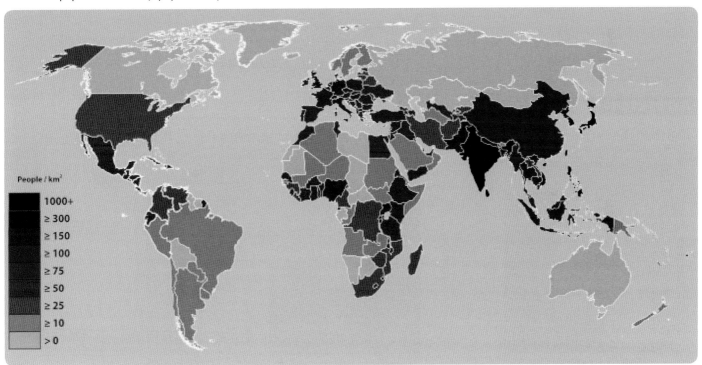

People / km²

1000+
≥ 300
≥ 150
≥ 100
≥ 75
≥ 50
≥ 25
≥ 10
> 0

Where do people work?

The **occupational distribution** of a population refers to the types of jobs people do. In 2017 the total population of working age in the world was about 4.9 billion people. Of these around 29% worked in agriculture (down from 42% in 1991), 22% in industry (up slightly from just under 21% in 1991), and almost 50% in services (up from 38% in 1991). Most employed people in developed countries work in services while most employees in the least-developed countries work in agriculture.

By 2050 the global population of working age people is expected to be around 6.1 billion. Some 5.3 billion of these will be in developing countries, of which some 1.9 billion (or 31% of the global forecast) will live in India and China. The trend in fast-developing economies, such as India and China, is for more and more people to move out of agriculture and other primary industries into employment in their rapidly expanding manufacturing and service industries.

▼ Employment by industry, 2017

Countries/areas with highest proportion of employees in agricultural sector	Percentage of workforce in agriculture	Countries/areas with highest proportion of employees in tertiary sector	Percentage of workforce in services
Burundi	91.1%	Luxembourg	88.5%
Burkina Faso	80.0%	Guam	85.7%
Lao	78.3%	Hong Kong	84.9%
Chad	76.6%	Singapore	82.6%
Mozambique	75.0%	Macao	82.1%
Rwanda	75.0%	Bahamas	81.9%
Madagascar	74.2%	Netherlands	81.9%
Nepal	72.6%	USA	81.3%
Central African Republic	72.2%	Israel	81.0%
Somalia	72.0%	Puerto Rico	80.5%

Source: *World Bank*

ACTIVITY 5.8

The charts below represent the proportion of people employed in different sectors in three different countries.

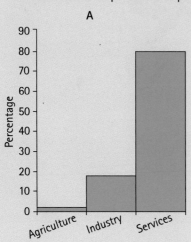

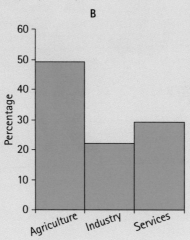

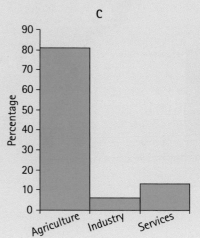

1 Which chart do you think represents:
   i   a country that is developing rapidly?
   ii a less-developed or low-income country?
   iii a developed or high-income country?
2 Suggest how living standards might differ between the three different countries.
3 Increasing numbers of females are entering employment in developed countries. How might this affect the birth rate in these countries?
4 Suggest three other factors that have caused birth rates to fall in developed countries over the last 50 years or so.

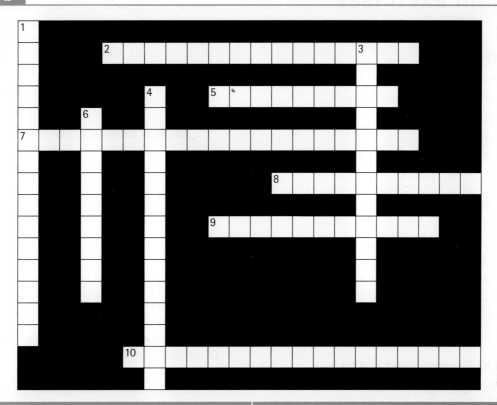

Clues across

2. An excess of males or females in a population, usually caused by factors other than nature, such as sex-selection bias, wars and male-dominated inward economic migration (6, 9)

5. A measure of the number of babies born per period per 1,000 people in a population (5, 4)

7. That part of a population that does not work and relies on others for the goods and services they consume (9, 10)

8. The act of leaving one's country to live overseas (10)

9. Inward migration: the introduction of people from overseas into the population of a country (11)

10. A graph that shows the distribution of males and females in various age groups in a human population (10, 7)

Clues down

1. A measure that contrasts the number of people in the dependent population of a country with the working population in the same country (10, 5)

3. The difference between immigrants and emigrants of a country per period of time (3, 9)

4. An economic condition in which there are too many people and too few resources (14)

6. A measure of the number of people who die per period per 1,000 people in a population (5, 4)

Assessment exercises

Multiple choice

1   Which one of the following characteristics is most likely to be found in a developed economy?

A   Low infant mortality rate
B   Low investment rate
C   Low life expectancy
D   Low literacy rate

2   What is most likely to happen as a country develops?

A   A greater proportion of the workforce will be employed in the service sector
B   The average age will decrease
C   The birth rate will increase
D   There will be reduced occupational mobility of labour

3   What is most likely to be found in a typical developing country?

A   A good education sector
B   A small average family size
C   A small percentage of very old people
D   High spending on entertainment

4   What is likely to happen as a developing country becomes more developed?

A   A higher percentage of children will attend school
B   Infant mortality will rise
C   Life expectancy will fall
D   The agricultural sector will increase in importance

5   Changes in the average standard of living of a country is best measured by changes in

A   GDP
B   GDP per head
C   Real GDP
D   Real GDP per head

6   Botswana has achieved high rates of economic growth.

What is most likely to have fallen as a result of this economic growth?

A   Employment
B   Income per head
C   Infant mortality rate
D   Adult literacy rates

7   The table gives information on four countries. Which country is likely to be most developed?

	Population (m)	Gross domestic product (GDP) ($ billion)	Life expectancy (years)
A	100	800	51
B	1,000	1,600	63
C	60	600	48
D	150	6,000	63

8   Why is the human development index (HDI) a better indicator of comparative living standards than real GDP per head?

A   It is adjusted for differences in exchange rates
B   It includes price inflation
C   It uses more measures of living standards
D   It includes taxes

9   What combination will usually be observed in a developed country?

A   A high rate of population growth with a low level of labour productivity
B   A high GDP per head with a low level of employment
C   A high rate of adult literacy with a low level of absolute poverty
D   A high birth rate with a low death rate

10 The table gives information about four countries.

Which country is likely to have the highest standard of living?

	GDP per head ($)	Life expectancy at birth	% of workforce in services
A	500	55	48
B	900	55	62
C	900	67	62
D	800	67	44

11 What is most likely to be found in a developed country?

A   A small proportion of income spent on leisure
B   A small average family size
C   A small number of people over 65 years of age
D   A small number of university graduates

12 What will help to increase the level of economic development in a country?

    A A higher infant mortality rate

    B A higher inflation rate

    C A higher interest rate

    D A higher literacy rate

13 The Government of Belarus wishes to help its very poorest people.

Which policy could most likely to achieve this?

    A Reducing capital gains tax

    B Reducing housing subsidies

    C Reducing indirect taxation

    D Reducing inheritance tax

14 The global population increased from 5.26 billion in 1990 to just over 7.6 billion in 2017. It is predicted to rise to 9.6 billion by 2050.

What is most likely to explain this?

    A An increase in the death rate in developing countries

    B An increase in migration from developing to developed countries

    C An increase in the birth rate in developing countries

    D An increase in the death rate in developed countries

15 When must there be a rise in the population of a country?

    A When the birth rate is greater than death rate and there is net emigration

    B When the birth rate is greater than death rate and there is no migration

    C When the death rate is greater than birth rate and there is net immigration

    D When the death rate is greater than birth rate and there is no migration

16 The death rate of a country is most likely to fall if:

    A Housing conditions deteriorate

    B More people smoke

    C Health care deteriorates

    D People's diets improve

17 What might explain high population growth in some developing countries?

    A High birth rates and falling death rates

    B High immigration and low emigration

    C Falling birth rates and rising death rates

    D Falling life expectancy

18 What is overpopulation?

    A Too many people to an area of land

    B High population density

    C Too many people and too few resources

    D Rapid population growth

19 A country is predicted to have 5 million fewer children by 2050, 10 fewer people of working age and 21 million more people aged over 65.

What will be the likely effect on the country of these changes?

    A Birth rates will fall

    B The average age of the population will fall

    C The dependency ratio will rise

    D Real GDP per head will rise

20 The Chinese Government is concerned about two population problems – overpopulation and a gender imbalance, with males outnumbering females.

In 2007 it reduced the number of babies that foreigners are allowed to adopt; almost all of the babies are girls.

What short-term effect is this likely to have had on the size of China's population and gender imbalance?

	size of population	gender imbalance
A	Increase	Increase
B	Increase	Reduce
C	Reduce	Increase
D	Reduce	Reduce

21 Which factor is most likely to reduce the average age of a population in a developed country?

    A A lower birth rate

    B A lower death rate

    C Emigration

    D Immigration

22 Other things being equal, what will cause a population both to increase and to age?

    A A fall in the birth rate

    B A rise in both the birth rate and the death rate

    C A rise in the death rate and a fall in the birth rate

    D A fall in the death rate

Structured questions

1 Ethiopia's 'economic miracle'

Ethiopia has one of the fastest-growing economies in the world and is Africa's second most populous country. It is a mixed economy with a large public sector. The banking, telecommunication and transportation sectors of the economy are dominated by government-owned companies. However, the Ethiopian Government is in the process of privatizing many state-owned enterprises and moving toward a market economy.

In 2000, Ethiopia was the third poorest country in the world. Its annual GDP per capita was only about $120. More than 50% of the population lived below the global poverty line, the highest poverty rate in the world.

However, since 2003 the country has experienced average economic growth of around 10.4% each year and in 2017 it overtook Kenya as East Africa's largest economy. This growth helped to lift over 5 million people out of poverty, although it remains one of the poorest countries in the world. Around 30% of the current population of 108 million people still live on less than a few dollars each day and almost 6 million people depend on food aid.

▼ Figure 1: Economic growth in Ethiopia 2000–2017

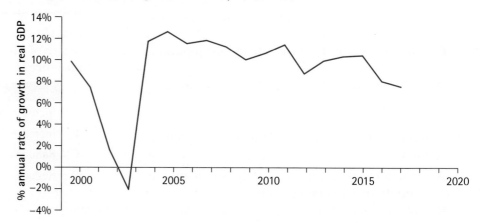

The government has introduced a number of policies to reduce poverty. One of these is to increase government spending on education and healthcare. The percentage of children attending primary school has doubled over the last decade to 90% and the percentage of children attending secondary school has also been increasing, although many still fail to complete their education. Infant and child mortality have also fallen and the population's general health has improved but average life expectancy from birth remains relatively low at just under 65 years.

Almost 50% of Ethiopia's population is under the age of 18, and even though enrolment in education has increased significantly, job creation has not caught up with the increased output from schools and colleges. By 2050, the UN expects the country to grow to 190 million people, from around 100 million today, making it among the fastest-growing large countries in terms of population, too. The country must create hundreds of thousands of new jobs every year just to keep up with population growth.

Ethiopia's economy is concentrated in the services and agriculture sectors. The World Bank estimates that half the growth in the economy since 2004 has come from services, like hospitality and transportation, which was mostly a result of country's urbanization. Agriculture, meanwhile, accounted for just 3.6% of the growth during the period. The Ethiopian Government is therefore seeking to raise productivity in agriculture, which accounts for 85% of employment in the country and some 40–50% percent of its GDP. There has been little investment in this sector. Many farms lack capital equipment such as tractors and ploughs. The country also has to import much of its food, as domestic agricultural output falls well short of domestic demand. The government is therefore encouraging farmers to expand in a sustainable way and to focus their resources on producing for export high value agricultural products with a price-inelastic demand.

Ethiopia still has many problems despite its recent economic performance, from excessive bureaucracy and high taxes and levies to a shortage of foreign currency due to a large trade deficit that restricts its ability to purchase important technologies. The economy also remains vulnerable to drought and unpredictable flooding because of its dependence on agriculture. Inflation is also beginning to rise once again in the economy, most notably the prices of many basic foods which increased by over 13% in 2017. The price of non-food items was also accelerating primarily due increases in the prices of clothing, footwear, household goods and furnishings.

A The extract reports that the Ethiopian Government 'is in the process of privatizing many state-owned enterprises and moving toward a market economy'. Explain the meaning of this statement. [4]

B Using information from the extract, identify **two** reasons why Ethiopia has a low Human Development Index (HDI) value. [2]

C Using information from the extract, calculate the number of people estimated to be living in poverty in Ethiopia in 2017. [2]

D From figure 1, in which year did the Ethiopian economy (i) expand at its faster rate, and (ii) shrink due to negative growth? [2]

E Explain how an increase in government spending on education and healthcare could reduce poverty in a country such as Ethiopia. [5]

F Explain why the rate of population growth in many developing countries differs from the rate of growth in developed countries. [6]

G Using information from the extract, explain whether agriculture in Ethiopia is capital-intensive or labour-intensive. [2]

H Discuss whether focusing resources in the agricultural sector on the production of products with inelastic demand will benefit Ethiopian farmers. [5]

I From the extract, identify **two** possible causes of the rise in inflation in Ethiopia in 2017. [2]

2   Due to strong economic growth, Albania grew from the poorest nation in Europe in the early 1990s to middle-income status in 2008, with poverty declining by half during that period. The unemployment rate in the country has fallen sharply since a peak of over 22% in 1995, but remains relatively high at 13.6% (January 2018). Over the same period real GDP per head increased from US $1,500 to over $4,600.

    A Define *real GDP per head*.   [2]

    B Explain **two** reasons why a country may experience a decline in living standards at the same time as an increase in its real GDP per head.   [4]

    C Analyse the reasons why a government might be concerned to maintain a low rate of unemployment.   [6]

    D Discuss the changes you might expect to observe over time in the structure and occupational distribution of the population of a developing country as it becomes more developed.   [8]

3   Estonia is a small country in Northern Europe on the Baltic Sea. The country has experienced some significant changes to its economy and population. It was once a planned economy but has been moving closer to a market economy since reforms were first introduced in 1991. It is now considered to have the best performing labour markets in the European Union. Its death rate has also decreased considerably over the last 30 years. To expand its working population, the country adopted an 'open' immigration policy and this has encouraged an increasing number of people to migrate to the country despite its relatively high youth unemployment rate.

    A Define *death rate*.   [2]

    B Explain **two** causes of a fall in a country's death rate.   [4]

    C Analyse the reasons why some people may migrate to a country with a high unemployment rate.   [6]

    D Discuss whether a government should encourage population growth in an attempt to expand the supply of labour in its economy.   [8]

4   Around 1 in 10 adults have not been educated to read or write. Over 75% of the world's 780 million illiterate adults live in developing countries and women represent almost two-thirds of all illiterate adults globally.

    A Distinguish between *relative poverty* and *absolute poverty*.   [2]

    B Explain **two** reasons why education in a developing country is often provided by the public sector.   [4]

    C Another indicator of living standards, apart from education, is GDP. Analyse how useful this is in comparing the living standards between two countries.   [6]

    D Discuss what effect investment in the education system might have in a developing country.   [8]

International trade and globalization

Most countries specialize in the production of a relatively limited variety of goods and services in order to maximize output from their scarce resources. Any surplus output they produce can be traded internationally with other countries that may be more efficient at producing other goods and services. Through international trade, countries can obtain a wider variety of goods and services at a lower cost than they could otherwise produce themselves. Global trade also allows firms and consumers to benefit from the biggest and cheapest sources of labour, raw materials and technologies from anywhere in the world.

However, growing international trade is increasing the rate at which natural resources are being depleted and the transportation of ever more people and goods across international borders has increased greenhouse gas emissions. Increasing trade with rapidly expanding economies is also threatening jobs in many developed economies and reducing opportunities for growth in some developing economies. Established businesses may lose market share and may even be forced to close if they cannot compete with firms located in low-cost economies. Small businesses in developing economies may also be unable to grow if consumers in their countries are able to buy imported products far more cheaply than locally made products.

Some governments may try to protect firms in their economies from the impact overseas competition can have on production, employment and incomes using trade barriers. This can involve imposing taxes or 'tariffs' on the prices of goods imported from low-cost producers overseas or simply restricting the amount that can be imported. But trade barriers restrict free trade, consumer choice and economic growth.

International transactions between one country and the rest of the world are recorded in its balance of payments. Exports of goods and services to overseas consumers earn revenues. Imports require payments to overseas producers. International trade therefore also involves the exchange of national currencies. Currencies are exchanged on the global foreign exchange market. Changes in market demand and supply conditions for different foreign currencies can therefore affect their market value and, in turn, the prices of exports and imports.

An appreciation in the value of a national currency against other currencies will make exports from firms located in that country more expensive to buy in overseas markets. Demand for exports may fall as a result, reducing the sales and profits of exporting firms. However, import prices will rise causing imported inflation and increasing production costs for those firms that rely on imports of materials and components from overseas suppliers to produce their own finished products.

In contrast, a depreciation in the value of a national currency will make exports from firms located in that country cheaper to buy overseas. Demand for exports may rise, boosting revenues and employment opportunities. Import prices will increase and demand for them from domestic consumers is likely to contract. A depreciation in the value of a national currency on the foreign exchange market can therefore help to reduce a trade deficit by boosting demand for exports and reducing the demand for imports.

Unit 6.1   International specialization
Unit 6.2   Globalization, free trade and protection

Definition of globalization

When people joke about the world getting smaller they are referring to the increasing ease with which people can travel around the world and the fact that our shops are full of a great variety of products from many different countries. But in fact, this means the world is getting bigger. That is, the size of the global economy is growing as global travel and communications are becoming easier and cheaper and more goods and services are exchanged internationally between producers and consumers in different countries.

Tens of thousands protest at Summit in Seoul

Tens of thousands of anti-globalization activists have rallied in Seoul to protest a summit of the Group of 20 major economies.

The activists accuse the world's biggest economies of violating workers' rights and threatening social welfare programs by cutting public spending. South Korean police estimated the size of the rally at 20,000, while organizers said it drew 40,000 people.

The activists also oppose a proposed free trade agreement between the United States and South Korea.

Politicians, business and trade union leaders, environmental groups, consumers and the media frequently talk about the impact this 'globalization' is having on our economies and daily lives. For example, they may welcome inward investment from overseas companies, access to a greater variety of goods from other countries and the growing ease of overseas travel. But they also raise concerns about increasing numbers of firms moving production to low-wage economies and the effect this is having on jobs, and the dangers of global climate change caused by increasing pollution. Sometimes these concerns have caused many thousands of people to protest against increasing globalization.

Globalization can mean different things to different people. This is because it is a wide term used to describe economic, social, technological, cultural and political changes that are increasing interactions and interdependencies between people, firms and entire economies all across the globe.

Despite this ambiguity over what the term means, what is clear is that the spread and pace of globalization has been increasing over time as:

- the global population is increasing, expanding the number of potential consumers in many countries;

- the global economy expands as industrial output, employment, incomes and consumer spending continue to rise in many economies, especially in rapidly developing economies such as India and China;

- improvements in the speed of international communications and transport and the lowering of costs make it easier and cheaper to discuss business, transport goods and to travel all over the world;

- it is becoming easier for workers to move from one country to another for employment especially within **multinational companies** with operations in more than one country; ➤ **6.2.2**

- economies are becoming more open. This means they are exchanging more goods, services, technologies, ideas and capital internationally than ever before. An **open economy** is a national economy that engages in trade with other economies. ➤ **6.2.3**

More Filipino workers moving to Europe as demand for manpower continues to rise

Vietnam spends billions of dollars to import farm produce

Free trade agreements between South East Asian countries have made import products cheaper and more favourable for consumers.

Surging exports spur Thailand's economic growth

Dubai hit hard by global financial crisis

Turkish exporters creating new jobs

Turkish companies have successfully penetrated new markets across the Middle East. Iran, Syria and Iraq are becoming key markets for Turkish exports.

China loans Angola US $15 billion

Many of these changes have been happening for a long time so globalization is not really new but the reason why we are so much more interested in it and using the term more and more today is because the pace of these changes has increased.

Rapid globalization is the result of increasing wealth, the development of new technologies and faster and cheaper communications, allowing people to order goods and services and make payments via the internet or over a telephone from anywhere in the world. Also, the transition of many former planned economies to free market economies has reduced barriers to international trade and allowed people and finance to move more freely between countries. As a result, many of these economies are now growing rapidly. But their rapid growth has also meant that scarce resources are being used up even faster and external costs, in terms of pollution and destruction of the environment, are rising.

Globalization is also affecting how and where production takes place in the world, and therefore where jobs and incomes are created. Global competition is rising and threatening the market shares of many established businesses in developed economies. For many years, the USA has been the largest economy in the world. In recent years, however, the US share of the global economy has shrunk to approximately 25% from a peak of 33% in 1985. This trend is likely to continue as the economies of many newly industrialized countries, such as China and India, continue to grow rapidly. China became the world's second largest economy in 2010 after overtaking Japan.

Anglesey Sea Salt goes Global

From its origins in a family kitchen, Anglesey Sea Salt has built a loyal UK customer base. It is now also on the market in over 20 countries.

Over 40% of company turnover came from exports. Exports are extremely important for future growth, including expansion into new and existing markets as demand for different sea salt products increases in many different countries.

Pure salt is the key export, followed by flavoured salts, oak-smoked water and bespoke gifts. Europe is the most successful export market, followed by North America.

Anglesey sea salt is also exported to Japan for use in manufacturing premium quality soy sauce and miso. Company visits to Tokyo and Hong Kong have been well received with new orders and great potential for future growth.

However, going global has not been without its challenges – the cost of carriage for premium products can price Anglesey Sea Salt out of overseas markets while competition from lower cost producers in China and India is also increasing. There are also complicated labelling requirements and regulations to comply with in different overseas markets that increase costs.

1 How has globalization affected Anglesey Sea Salt?

2 Identify two benefits and two problems globalization has created for the company.

SECTION 6.1.2

Specialization at a national level

SECTION 6.1.3

Advantages and disadvantages of specialization at a national level

What is international specialization?

Globalization has increased the possibilities for national specialization because it has opened up opportunities for countries to trade their goods and services with each other. Recall from Unit 3 how people have specialized in particular skills and occupations. This has allowed them to become more productive over time and therefore to produce more goods and services using their limited resources.

For the same reasons, countries will usually specialize in the production of those goods and services that make best use of the natural or other factor resources with which they are most abundantly endowed. For example, Saudi Arabia specializes in the production of oil because it is located over vast natural oil reserves. Similarly, an abundance of rich, low-cost land in the USA has enabled it to become the world's largest producer of corn. Similarly, an abundance of land, low-cost labour and suitable climatic conditions have made India and China the largest producers of rice in the world.

China has also been able to take advantage of its huge labour force to become a major producer of low-cost manufactured goods and is also now the world's largest manufacturer of wind turbines for renewable energy generation, recently overtaking Denmark and Germany.

Depending on the factor resources they have, certain countries therefore have advantages over others in producing certain goods or services. Specialization at a national level enables those countries to use their resources in the most efficient way possible. In turn this will allow them to produce far more of those goods or services their resources are best able to produce and to produce them more cheaply than producers could in other countries with different factor resources.

For example, imagine if Iceland tried to produce oranges. It would need to build vast greenhouses and use up a lot of power heating them and creating artificial sunlight. Growing oranges in Iceland would therefore be very expensive. Much better therefore to buy them from Spain or another country that is able to grow them easily and cheaply because it has a warm and sunny climate.

Because countries will often produce far more of the goods or services they specialize in than consumers in their own economies are willing or able to consume, they have a surplus they are able to trade internationally. International specialization therefore enables or requires international trade to take place so that each country can exchange its surplus products for the other goods and services it needs or wants that are produced in other countries.

Through international trade some countries have therefore become famous for the goods and services they produce, even if in some cases other countries make the same or very similar products. This is because their industries have developed a reputation among consumers worldwide for making these products cheaper and/or better than anywhere else.

There are many examples, including Italian shoes and clothes, Belgian chocolates, German beers, Swiss watches, Scotch whisky, Cuban cigars, Spanish olive oil, US aircraft and military equipment, and many more.

US aircraft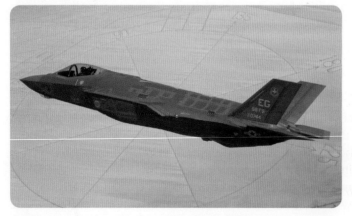

Spanish olive oil

Italian shoes

▲ Some examples of international specialization

Something special

1   Try to identify and list five or more goods or services that are not produced in your country and have to be purchased from producers located overseas.

2   Try to identify and list at least 10 goods and services that are produced by firms in your country but are also imported from overseas.

3   Look at the countries and products listed below. Which product do you think each country is best known for?

Saudi Arabia	France	Fish	Beef
Iceland	India	Tea	Lamb
Norway	Jamaica	Timber	Wine
Germany	New Zealand	Oil	Coffee
Argentina	Kenya	Manufactured goods	Tourism

4   Suggest ways in which you and your family benefit from international specialization and trade.

The advantages of international specialization

Specialization, at a national level, in the production of relatively limited range of products can therefore benefit a country in a number of ways.

1   Higher levels of output

Just like specialization by individuals, countries can specialize in what they do best. It allows a country to use its resources in the best or most efficient way possible and to produce its chosen goods or services at scale. This allows more of those goods and services to be produced and at a lower average cost per unit because of economies of scale in production. Therefore, when more and more countries specialize, it increases world output and the global economy expands.

2   Increased employment and incomes

Specialization leads to increased output, increased business opportunities and the creation of more jobs.

3   Economic growth and improved living standards

Using resources more efficiently, increasing output and creating more opportunities for business and employment will contribute to increased economic growth and higher living standards.

4   Opportunities for increased international trade

International trade takes place because certain countries have a cost or quality advantage over others in the production of certain goods or services. Through international trade a country can therefore sell the goods or services in which it specializes to many more consumers all over the world and, in turn, it can obtain the best or cheapest goods and services available from other countries.

Many of the benefits of national specialization are therefore the result of international trade:

- Firms located in one country are able to sell more because they have access to much larger international markets. This allows them to expand their scale of production and enjoy economies of scale.

- Consumers in a country will be able to choose from a much wider variety of goods and services and from many more producers or suppliers located in different countries.

- There is more competition because firms must also now compete against firms located in other countries producing the same or similar products. Increased competition is good for consumers because it forces firms to reduce their costs and prices, and to improve their products.

These advantages or gains from trade are considered in more detail later. ➤ **6.2.3**

The disadvantages of international specialization

However, despite the clear benefits to individual countries and to the global economy from specialization in production at a national level, it can also create some problems.

1 Structural unemployment may occur as a country becomes more specialized

Prior to specialization, a country may produce many different goods and services in a variety of different industries. Moving towards specialization will involve concentrating its resources on a smaller number of products and therefore industries. This may be more efficient and increase total output and jobs in the long run but in the short run there may be structural unemployment as other industries decline.

2 The risk of over-specialization

A country that is dependent on just one or a very small number of industries to provide the vast majority of its output, employment and income could suffer a catastrophic economic shock if there is prolonged decline in global demand for its products.

3 Consumer choice may be limited

Unless a country trades internationally, consumers in that country are likely to have far fewer goods and services to choose from if it specializes in the production of a narrow range of products.

4 The risk of over-exploitation of resources

Resources in which a country have a natural advantage, such as oil reserves or mineral deposits, may be used up or depleted at a faster rate to satisfy the demands of overseas consumers. This may result in economic collapse if a country is economically dependent on the extraction and international sale of these natural resources and has few other industries.

5 An over-reliance on other countries to supply essential goods and services

A country that specializes in the production of a narrow range of products must trade with other countries to obtain the other goods and services it needs. Strikes in other countries, weather or transportation problems may hold up supplies or they may be put at risk if relations between the trading countries break down.

In fact, many of the disadvantages associated with specialization at a national level are really those that may result from unfavourable and uncontrolled international trading. We will consider these in more detail later. ➤ **6.2.3**

From the articles below, identify how each of the countries involved may benefit or be disadvantaged by international specialization and trade?

Trade boost for Singapore's economy

Singapore has been ranked one of the most open economies in the world. The economy is therefore heavily reliant on international trade with the bulk of its revenues coming from exports of integrated circuits, computers and other electronic items as well as chemicals and services, particularly financial services. These have recently received a boost as global demand recovers. As result the economy expanded by 3.5 percent in 2017, its fastest pace since 2014.

Australian company enjoys sweet dreams in Asia

Ferndale Confectionery makes sugar-free and fat-free confectionery suitable for diabetics. It started as a small family business in 1995, selling its products to local retailers but by 2004 was exporting to eight international markets. It has now added Japan, Korea and China to that list and to meet increasing local and international demand it is investing in a new state-of-the-art facility that will see at least 20 new jobs screated in the next year.

2,500 jobs in UK tyre industry threatened by flood of cheap imports of tyres from China, warns the UK Retread Manufacturers Association (RMA)

Sun, sea and specialization in the Caribbean

Like many of Caribbean islands, the main industry and source of revenue for the Turks and Caicos Islands is tourism which is primarily focused on the island of Providenciales at the north of the island chain.

However, this hasn't always been the case. As recently as 1964, Providenciales did not have a single wheeled vehicle and the main industries on the islands were fishing and salt production. These industries were concentrated on some of the more southerly islands and have since declined, decimating the local economies of these islands.

Over the last 40 years tourism has become the biggest industry and employer in the economy especially since the development of an international airport on Providenciales in 1968 and a cruise terminal on Grand Turk in 2006.

With very few other industries, the Turks and Caicos Islands must import most of the capital and consumer goods its population needs, including food. It also means that the Islands are vulnerable to changing global economic conditions and particularly in the US and Canadian economies. Most tourist arrivals are from the USA and Canada and between 2008 and 2010 tourism numbers declined sharply during a global economic recession. As a result, many local businesses and new developments in the Islands collapsed and unemployment soared. The GDP of the small economy was estimated to have fallen by almost 20%. However, by 2016 tourism had rebounded and numbers had increased materially providing a welcome boost for the economy and for government revenues from indirect taxes.

The role of multinational companies (MNCs)

What is a multinational?

A key feature of globalization has been the development and growth of **multinationals**.

A multinational is a truly 'global business' with premises and productive operations in more than one country. That is, a multinational will own a number of **subsidiary** companies located in other countries which will produce goods and services in those countries. These goods and services can then be sold to consumers in these countries or exported around the world. The headquarters of a multinational will normally be based in its country of origin.

Multinationals are some of the largest business organizations in the world, often selling many billions of dollars' worth of goods and services, and employing many thousands of workers globally. Many of the biggest multinationals are US-based and Chinese state-owned enterprises with interests in oil and gas exploration and petroleum.

In 2015 the largest multinational company was was just over $482 billion. The company has its headquarters in the USA and, as of 31 January 2017, operated 11,695 retail stores and clubs in 28 countries. Second largest with revenues of $246 billion was US global oil and gas producer Exxon-Mobil. It has business operations in over 200 countries. However, the most profitable multinational in 2015 was US company Apple Inc. with profits of over $53 billion from over 495 retail stores in 18 countries and from online sales in many more.

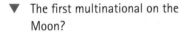
▼ The first multinational on the Moon?

▼ World's 10 largest multinationals by revenue, 2016

Company name	Main sectors	Total revenue (US$ billion)	Employees	County of origin
Walmart	Retail	$482.1	2,300,000	US
State Grid	Electric utility	$329.6	927,839	China
China National Petroleum	Oil and gas	$299.3	1,589,508	China
Sinopec Group	Oil and gas	$294.3	810,538	China
Royal Dutch Shell	Oil and gas	$272.2	90,000	Netherlands/UK
Exxon–Mobil	Oil and gas	$246.2	75,600	US
Volkswagen	Automotive	$236.6	610,076	Germany
Toyota	Automotive	$236.6	348,877	Japan
Apple	Consumer electronics	$233.7	110,000	US
BP	Oil and gas	$226.0	79,800	UK

▼ Royal Dutch Shell and Walmart – two of the largest publicly traded companies in the world

ACTIVITY 6.4

Global giants

The following table lists a number of multinational companies. Try to find out their country of origin and their main activities to complete the table. The first one has been completed for you.

Company	Country of origin	Main business activities
Volkswagen	Germany	Automotive
Carrefour		
General Electric		
Siemens		
Sinopec		
Samsung		
Nestlé		
HSBC Holdings		
ArcelorMittal		

Of the world's largest 100 economic entities in 2015 in terms of total income, 69 were corporations and just 31 were national economies. For example, Walmart, Exxon-Mobil, Royal Dutch Shell, Volkswagen, Toyota Motors and Apple were individually larger than countries including Switzerland, Norway, Russia, Saudi Arabia and Austria measured by their total annual incomes. Multinational companies are also responsible for two-thirds of total world trade and global industries can be dominated by a handful of these global giants.

Advantages of being a multinational

The global presence and size of many multinational companies gives these organizations a number of key advantages. A multinational can:

- reach many more consumers globally and sell far more than other types of business
- avoid trade barriers by locating operations in countries that apply tariffs and quotas to imports from businesses located overseas ➤ **6.2.4**
- minimize transport costs by locating plants in different countries to be near to sources of materials or key overseas consumer markets
- minimize its wage costs by locating operations in countries where wages and other employment costs are low
- raise significant amounts of new capital for business expansion, research and development (R&D), and to employ workers and managers with the highest skills
- reduce the average cost of producing each unit of output below the average costs of smaller firms because of its large scale of production. ➤ **3.5.5**

What's the big attraction?

Calls from Vietnam animal feed industry for government to protect businesses

Foreign livestock firms now hold over 70% of the animal feed market in Vietnam, pushing out local businesses and making it difficult for them to compete fairly, according to local industry representatives who are calling for the government to step in 'while local firms are suffering losses, and reducing production, foreign ones are growing in Vietnam, dominating the market and increasing prices unreasonably to earn huge profits,' said the Vietnam Animal Feed Association.

Toyota to create 800 new jobs in South Africa

Japanese car manufacturer, Toyota, has announced it is to invest R363 million (US$51million) in a parts distribution ware-house in Ekurhuleni, east of Johannesburg, creating about 800 jobs.

Foreign companies boost tax revenues in Xiamen

37 subsidiaries of 17 of the top 500 global companies in Xiamen in China, including Dell Inc, Boeing and Toyota, contributed RMB 674 million in taxes in the first seven months of 2011, an 88.27% increase from the previous year.

Reports claim Walmart's Chinese Plants Plants Exploit Workers

US retailer, Walmart Stores Inc., uses Chinese factories that deny overtime pay and maternity leave to workers and pay less than the local minimum wage, according to three reports from labour monitoring group released today.

Ecuador's President has called for an international boycott of major US oil corporation Chevron, blaming it for polluting the Amazon.

Amazon in New UK Tax Avoidance Row

The internet retail giant Amazon is facing fresh claims of tax avoidance after its latest accounts showed it generated sales of £4.3bn in the UK last year yet paid only £4m in corporation tax.

When customers order goods from Amazon.co.uk their payments are transferred to its Luxembourg subsidiary, Amazon EU SARL, where corporate taxes on profits are much lower than in the UK.

Amazon has faced fierce criticism from rival retailers, politicians and consumers over the amount of tax it pays in the UK.

UK benefits from inward investment

Last year the UK attracted over 1,430 foreign companies and investment projects, many in high technology areas such as software development, advanced engineering, IT and life sciences. More than 94,500 jobs were associated with these investments totalling over £43 billion.

▶ Using the articles identify as many possible benefits and drawbacks to a country of attracting multinationals to locate and operate within their national economies.

How multinationals can benefit their host countries

National governments will often compete with each other to attract multinationals to their countries, because:

- They provide jobs and incomes for local workers. This helps to reduce unemployment.

- They invest capital in new or expanded business premises, new machinery and modern equipment. Capital received from overseas that is invested directly into productive assets in a country is called **foreign direct investment (FDI)**. This 'inward investment' helps to boost the productive capacity of the economy and, therefore, economic growth. ▶ **4.6.3**

- They increase the amount and variety of goods and services available to domestic consumers and will compete with domestic firms thereby offering consumers more choice. The increase in competition will force other businesses to improve their efficiency in order to cut their prices and increase product quality to attract and retrain customers.

- They bring new ideas, technologies and skills into a country which domestic firms and employees can learn and benefit from, helping to increase their productivity.

- They pay taxes on their profits and purchases from domestic firms which increases the revenue available to government to finance its public expenditures.

- Some of the additional output produced by multinationals may be sold overseas which will increase the export earnings of the host country. ➤ **6.4.2**

How multinationals may create problems for host countries

Many multinationals provide significant benefits to national economies, employees and consumers. However, some multinational corporations have been criticized for using their size and power to exploit their host countries.

For example, in the late 1990s, Coca-Cola was accused of bringing in armed groups to intimidate, kidnap and torture trade union leaders who were trying to improve working conditions for employees at their bottling plant in Columbia. Many other US multinational companies with factories in Columbia, including Occidental Petroleum and the food producer Del Monte, were accused of similar offences by the Permanent People's Tribunal in Columbia which included professors, human rights commissioners, doctors, judges and social workers from a number of other countries.

Elsewhere, in India, Coca-Cola was accused by the India Resource Centre of polluting groundwater and soil, causing water shortages and having high levels of pesticide in its soft drinks.

While these and other multinational companies deny these and similar claims, it is clear that some global corporations may be able to use their power in many developing countries to ignore local laws and regulations and to exploit local workers and natural resources in order to minimize their costs and maximize their profits.

- **They may force local competitors out of business.** Multinationals will often compete with local businesses. Their cost advantages allow them to sell their products at much lower prices causing local businesses producing and selling the same or similar items to lose sales. As a result, many smaller, local firms may be forced out of business by multinationals. As local competition and consumer choice is reduced, multinationals can begin to raise their prices.

- **They can move their profits between countries to avoid paying corporate taxes.** A multinational may move the profits it has earned in one country to another to reduce the tax it will have to pay in that country on its profits. This involves the transfer or **repatriation of profits** to its headquarters or subsidiary companies overseas. A multinational may even be able to avoid taxes altogether by moving its profits to a country that has no corporation or profits tax, or to some developing economies which may have poor legal and tax collection systems.

- **They may use their power to get generous subsidies and tax advantages from host countries.** Multinationals can move their production to the most profitable and advantageous locations anywhere in the world. Many governments provide generous incentives to multinationals to encourage them to stay in their national economies because of the investments, jobs and incomes that would be lost if one or more multinational leave a country.

- **Some multinationals may exploit workers in low-wage economies.** Many of the jobs created by multinationals in other countries, particularly in developing economies, involve low-skilled and low-paid work on mass production lines. Workers in less-developed economies may be paid far less to do the same or even more work than employees in more developed economies by their multinational employers. Health and safety standards may also be lower in some developing economies and employment laws weaker.

- **They may exploit natural resources and damage the environment.** Some multinationals may use up scarce natural resources, create pollution and cause significant damage in their host countries. This is because laws and regulations to protect the natural environment may be weak or not enforced in some developing and less-developed countries.

ECONOMICS IN ACTION

Should developing countries encourage multinationals to locate in their economies?

Toyota boosts car production in Indonesia

Toyota Motor Corp and subsidiary Daihatsu are to build a new small, low-cost car in Indonesia aimed at consumers there and in neighbouring countries.

Mini-vehicle specialist Daihatsu, 51 per cent owned by Toyota, will invest around $250 million in a new high-tech factory able to build 100,000 cars annually in Indonesia, 70 per cent of which it will supply to its parent company.

A spokesperson for Toyota and Daihatsu said the project will contribute to Indonesian society in the area of motorization. At the same time, it will help develop local parts and supply businesses and create jobs.

Toyota aims to make Indonesia its second big production base in Southeast Asia after Thailand.

SECTION 6.2.2

What is international trade?

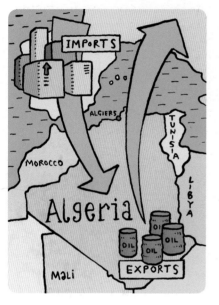

The benefits of free trade

International specialization requires international trade. This is because no country is self-sufficient and able to produce all the goods and services it needs and wants with its limited resources. All countries therefore need to trade internationally in order to survive. For example, oil and gas production is the largest industry in Algeria in Northern Africa and accounts for around one-third of its total national output each year. International trade therefore allows Algeria to benefit from specialization.

Because Algeria produces more natural oil and gas and petroleum products than the country needs it sells the surplus to consumers in other countries. It also supplies some fruit and vegetables, animal products, iron ore and zinc to international markets. ➤ **6.4.1**

The sale of exports earns the country revenues of around $75 billion each year that can be used to buy other goods and services from overseas that firms in Algeria are less able to produce using their resources. Products purchased from overseas include farm machinery, many food and drink products and a wide range of clothes and other consumer goods.

National economies such as Algeria, in which industries specialize in the production of a relatively narrow range of goods or services, are therefore able to enjoy a much wider variety of products through international trade.

However, Algeria has also attracted inward investment from overseas companies, including in its oil and gas and financial services sector. For example, 12 of Algeria's banking groups are foreign-owned.

International trade therefore involves the movement and exchange of physical goods such as materials, component parts, equipment and finished products as well as services and money across international borders:

- Goods and services sold by firms located in one country to consumers in other countries are called **exports**. Revenues received from the sale of exports will increase the total income of a country;

- Goods and services purchased by consumers in one country from producers located in other countries are called **imports**. The purchase of imports involves making payments overseas which therefore reduces the total income available in a country to spend on goods and services produced locally.

In order to make payments to each other for the goods and services they trade, countries must also exchange their national currencies on the foreign exchange market. ➤ **6.3.2**

How trade patterns are changing

For many years international trade flows between countries were dominated by raw materials such as iron ore, oil and wheat. Much of this trade was from less-developed countries in the southern hemisphere to the more-developed, industrialized economies in the northern hemisphere. However, global trade patterns have since changed significantly.

▼ Value of global trade in physical goods, 1960–2016

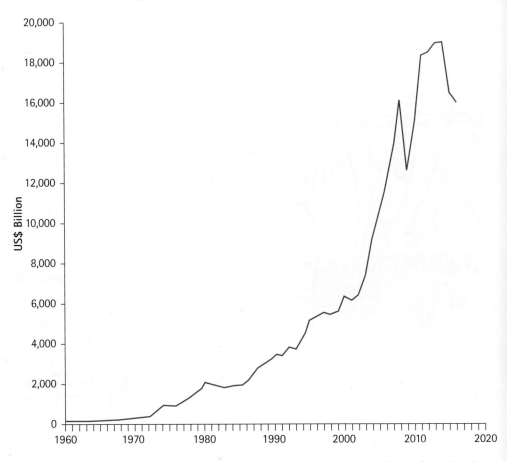

Source: *World Trade Organization*

In 1960 the total global value of goods traded internationally was just $130 billion with the USA, Germany and the United Kingdom accounting for 32% of total exports. By 2014 this had risen to $19 trillion before falling back to just under $16 billion in 2016. Then the largest exporter of goods in the world was China, followed by the USA and Germany. Together they accounted for almost 31% of physical exports globally in 2016.

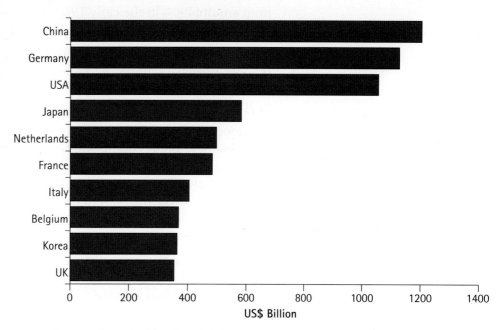

▼ Top 10 exporters of physical goods, 2016

US$ Billion

Source: *World Trade Statistical Review 2017, World Trade Organization*

Trade in manufactured goods has grown significantly. They accounted for over 50% of the global value of exports of physical goods in the early 1960s. This share had risen to almost 74% by the mid-1990s and has remained between 65% and 74% since. The globalization of production has increased trade in manufactured goods while technological advances in transport, particularly containerization, have meant faster and more efficient handling of goods in bulk at ports.

▼ Global trade in physical goods, % share by major category

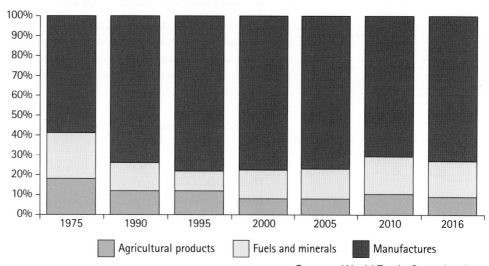

☐ Agricultural products　☐ Fuels and minerals　■ Manufactures

Source: *World Trade Organization*

In contrast, the share of agricultural products in world trade has fallen, from around 28% in the early 1960s to below 10% in 2016. Processed food products have increased and now account for nearly half of agricultural trade.

International trade in commercial services, including computer and information services, financial services, telecommunications, transportation and travel, has also increased rapidly, from just under $1.5 trillion in 2000 to $4.8 trillion in 2016. Services account for around 23% of world trade values.

Developed countries still accounted for three-quarters of the global trade in 2000, but developing countries saw their share climb to over 40% by 2016 and it continues to rise. Many industrial processes which initially took place in developed countries have relocated to countries offering lower production costs, namely from lower wages. As a result, global trade flows are now characterized by significant flows of goods from developing economies to developed ones.

The gains from international trade

An **open economy** is a national economy that engages freely in international trade with other economies. Doing so has a number of advantages. These advantages are often referred to as the **gains from trade**.

1 International trade allows countries to benefit from specialization

If there was no international trade, countries would be forced to become self-sufficient by producing as many of the goods and services their citizens need and want themselves. Resources would be allocated to the production of a wide variety of goods and services rather than to their most efficient uses. This would mean total output was lower and costs higher than could otherwise be the case.

Instead, international trade enables economies to specialize in the production of those goods and services their natural, human and man-made resources are best able to produce, and then trade their surplus outputs with other countries to obtain the other goods and services they need and want. Through specialization and trade therefore, output, incomes and living standards will be much higher.

2 International trade increases consumer choice

Consumers can enjoy a greater variety of goods and services from different countries all over the world. For example, they can choose to buy clothes from France, or clothes from Italy, Spain, China or the USA. Take a quick look around your own home to see how many goods were produced by business organizations overseas.

3 International trade increases competition and efficiency

Through international trade, firms will have to compete with goods and services imported from overseas. This helps them to become more efficient and increase their sales. Consumers will also benefit from lower prices. For example, Algerian farms producing cereals and animal products such as wool will have to produce these products for a similar price and quality as imported cereals and wool otherwise Algerian consumers will simply buy them from producers overseas.

4 International trade creates additional business opportunities

A firm may be unable to expand in its home country because the size of the consumer market is relatively small. However, growing consumer markets overseas create additional opportunities for sales and business growth. Through international trade, a firm can expand its sales and scale of production because it is able to sell its products to a much larger number of consumers globally. This will allow a firm to reduce its production costs, due to economies of scale increase revenues and earn more profit. ➤ **3.5.5**

5 Free trade enables firms to benefit from the best workforces, resources and technologies from anywhere in the world

Having access to international markets allows a business to find the best and lowest cost sources of materials and components from different producers in other countries. For example, the Airbus 380, the largest passenger aircraft in the world, is assembled in Toulouse in France by the European company Airbus using components from over 500 suppliers in Spain, Germany, Japan, the UK, the USA, China, India, Romania, the United Arab Emirates and many other countries. Wages and material costs are lower in countries such as China and India than in Europe. As a result, Airbus is buying an increasing number of components for the Airbus 380 and other aircraft it manufactures from businesses overseas for it factories in Europe. Airbus also has a joint venture in China to manufacture its Airbus 320 aircraft. Employment and incomes are consequently rising in many overseas firms.

A firm can also import the latest equipment and ideas developed in other countries, borrow money from banks overseas offering the lowest interest rates and advertise for foreign workers with the skills it needs if these are lacking in its own country.

6 International trade increases economic interdependency and reduces the potential for conflict

A further argument used for free trade is that it helps to promote more international cooperation and peace. If economies are more dependent upon one another for goods and services then armed conflicts may be less likely.

The disadvantages of uncontrolled trade

Despite the many gains from trade, increasing international trade may also cause a number of problems.

1 International trade with low-cost economies is threatening jobs in many developed economies and reducing opportunities for growth in some developing economies

Increasing global trade and competition, especially from rapidly growing economies, is threatening many established businesses in developed economies and new, small businesses trying to grow in many less-developed economies. Established businesses may lose market share and may even be forced to close if they cannot compete with larger overseas businesses or new businesses in low-cost economies. Small businesses in less-developed economies may also be unable to grow if consumers in their countries are able to buy imported products far more cheaply than locally made products.

2 International trade is contributing to rapid resource depletion and climate change

The rate at which we are using up the Earth's natural resources is increasing because international trade has increased access to a greater number and variety of products for us to consume. In addition, increasing travel and the increased transportation of ever more goods across international borders by road, rail, ship or airfreight is polluting the atmosphere with more and more greenhouse gases. This is contributing to global climate change that may have a disastrous, long-term and irreversible effect on the planet.

3 International trade may increase the exploitation of workers and the environment

The free movement of capital internationally has made it easy for multinational firms to shift their production from countries where wages and other costs are high, to less-developed countries where wages, land prices and taxes on profits are lower. This shift, some people argue, has not only increased the unemployment rate in many developed economies, but in some cases it has also led to the exploitation of workers in less-developed economies where health and safety laws may be more relaxed or easier to ignore. In some cases it has also resulted in environmental damage in less-developed countries where environmental protection laws are weak or their governments choose not to enforce them.

4 International trade may be increasing the gap between rich and poor countries

Some economists argue it will be free trade and not overseas aid that will help to lift the poorest countries out of poverty. By selling their goods and services overseas, less-developed countries can expand their industries, earn additional income and create jobs for their populations.

However, in direct contrast, some people argue that international trade has instead increased the gap between rich and poor countries. This is said to happen because multinational firms and consumers from many developed and rapidly developing economies dominate the global demand for many natural resources, including foodstuffs, timber, zinc, tin, copper and other ores, and use their purchasing power to force down global prices. This has reduced revenues for producers of natural resources in less-developed economies. For example, China, the USA, Japan and India consume over 50% of all the natural rubber produced in the world each year.

Increasing international trade can therefore create economic conflict. As a result, some countries have introduced policies to restrict international trade and protect production, employment and incomes in their economies from increasing competition from overseas producers.

SECTION 6.2.3

Methods of protection

SECTION 6.2.4

Reasons for protection

SECTION 6.2.5

Consequences of protection

Barriers to trade

Trade protection involves the use of **trade barriers** by governments to restrict international market access and competition. The article below in Activity 6.6 describes a number of trade protection methods.

1 Tariffs

These are indirect taxes on the prices of imported goods to make them more expensive to discourage domestic consumers from buying them. For example, the article in Activity 6.6 below reports that Russia has introduced tariffs on the price of imported poultry to protect its meat farmers from US farms who are able to supply these products at lower prices. The use of tariffs, however, can encourage retaliation from other countries.

Many neighbouring countries in different regions of the world have agreed to form **customs unions** to trade freely with each other but to impose a common tariff on all goods and services imported from non-member countries. Examples of customs unions include the European Union, the South African Customs Unions and MERCOSUR between a number of countries in Latin America.

ACTIVITY 6.6

Barricading the borders

From the article below identify:

▸ different barriers used by governments to restrict international trade and competition

▸ reasons why governments use trade barriers

▸ the impact trade barriers could have on consumers, workers and businesses in different countries

▸ arguments against the use of trade barriers.

More Trade Restrictions as Global Slump Deepens

Just over a month ago world leaders agreed to reject trade protectionism and stick to free trade principles to fight the global economic slowdown. Yet an increasing number of countries are already breaking that promise.

For example, in a move designed to protect its battered manufacturers from foreign imports, Indonesia is slapping restrictions and quotas on another 500 products this month and demanding special licenses and new fees on imports. Russia is also increasing tariffs on imported poultry – a move that has angered US farmers: Russia is the single largest market for US poultry producers, which this year exported $740 million worth to Russian consumers.

France is launching a government fund to protect French companies from foreign takeovers while Argentina and Brazil are seeking to raise tariffs on products from leather goods and peaches to imported wine and textiles.

The list of countries making access to their markets harder also includes the United States. The US government's $17.4 billion bailout of the US auto industry has been branded an unfair subsidy by many because it places foreign competitors at a disadvantage. At the same time Russia, the largest car market in Europe, increased taxes on imported foreign cars by 35 per cent.

In hard times, analysts say, nations are more inclined to take steps that inhibit trade, often with dire consequences for consumers, businesses and entire economies.

'Because exporting firms face overseas competition they tend to be innovative, dynamic and capable of generating good job growth,' said a US professor of trade policy. 'If trade barriers shut these firms down, their suppliers shut down, job losses get worse, and you can quickly have an entire economy spiraling downward.'

2 Subsidies

These are grants paid to domestic producers to help reduce their production costs and sell their products at lower prices than imported products. For example, the USA is among a number of countries that have been accused by others of giving producers in their farming, steel and automotive industries unfair subsidies to lower their costs and prices.

A disadvantage of subsidies is that to pay for them consumers and firms may have to pay higher taxes instead.

3 Quotas

A quota is a limit on the number of imports allowed into a country each month or year. Restricting the supply of imported products will push up their market prices relative to locally produced substitutes.

4 Embargo

An embargo is a ban on the importation of a particular product, or on all imports from a particular country. For example, embargoes are often used to control trade in weapons and other products with countries involved in conflicts or abuses of human rights. An embargo may be also used to stop the import of dangerous drugs or to exert political pressure on other countries.

However, embargoes may also be introduced on health grounds. For example, between 1996 and 2005 beef exports from the UK were banned in the European Union and many countries outside it because of fears about the spread of BSE ('mad cow disease') from UK herds to overseas cattle and possibly even to humans. Similarly, in 2011 a number of countries restricted imports of Japanese food produced on farms contaminated by radiation leaked from Japan's nuclear power stations at Fukushima. The nuclear plants were badly damaged following a huge tsunami in March 2011.

5 Excessive quality standards and bureaucracy

Countries can increase costs on exporters and slow down the flow of imports by introducing complex and unreasonable quality controls, standards and licensing requirements.

A government may set arbitrary and excessive quality standards on imported goods so many fail and can be rejected. Or it may keep changing product labelling and other regulations so that exporters are unable to keep up with new requirements.

An **import licence** is a document issued by a government customs authority approving the importation of certain goods into its territory. They can be used as a barrier to trade if they are issued selectively against another country's goods in order to protect a domestic industry from foreign competition. Application forms can also be made time-consuming and difficult to complete causing delays and uncertainty about whether or not goods will be allowed in to a country

Subsidies, quotas, embargoes, licensing regulations and arbitrary standards are all examples of **non-tariff barriers**.

Arguments for trade barriers

1 To protect infant industries

Barriers to trade can be used to protect **infant industries**, also known as **sunrise industries**, such as those involving new technologies. This gives new firms the chance to develop, grow and become globally competitive.

EU trade ban will cause fruit shortage

British supermarkets face severe shortages of oranges, grapefruits and other citrus fruits this summer because of a highly contentious import ban on fruit from South Africa and South America. The ban will 'protect' European citrus plants from pests.

New, small businesses in newly developing industries with the potential to provide many more jobs and incomes in the future, may not get the chance to develop and grow if they are quickly eliminated by competition from lower-cost economies overseas. Providing them with protection from overseas competition may allow them to grow to take advantage of economies of scale and become internationally competitive. The danger is that infant industries may continue to require protection from cheaper imports even when they have become established.

2 To protect sunset industries

Sunset industries are declining industries. They still employ many people in an economy and the closure of firms in these industries could result in high regional employment, especially if they are located together to benefit from external economies of scale. ➤ **3.5.5**

Many manufacturing industries in developed countries have been in decline for many years because of competition for newly industrialized economies.

To slow down the rate of their decline in these industries trade barriers may be used to protect them from cheaper overseas imports to allow employees to retrain or relocate for other jobs.

3 To protect strategic industries

Many governments seek to protect their agricultural, energy and defence industries so they are not entirely dependent on supplies from overseas. For example, in 2017 India introduced 30% tariffs on imports of chickpeas and lentils in an effort to protect Indian farmers from cheaper overseas imports. If Indian farmers were forced out of business because they could not compete with cheap imports it would leave the country vulnerable to future food shortages and much higher food prices if, for example, natural disasters or even wars overseas affected vital food imports. Overseas suppliers might also use their market power to restrict supplies and to force up prices. ➤ **3.8.2**

4 To protect domestic firms from dumping

Dumping is a type of predatory pricing and unfair competition. It involves one country 'flooding' another with a product at a price significantly below its global market price to increase sales and force producers in the importing country out of business. Once this has happened and the overseas market has been 'captured', exporting firms can raise their prices.

Exporting firms are usually only able to price below average production costs if they are receiving generous subsidies from their own government. For example, Australia recently accused Indonesia and China of dumping glass on the Australian market to boost Indonesian and Chinese glass sales at the expense of Australian producers.

5 To limit over-specialization

Free trade encourages countries to specialize in the goods in which they have a comparative advantage. However, a country that specializes in the production of too narrow a range of products is at greater economic risk from a fall in global demand for one or more of them. Trade barriers can therefore help a country to maintain a wider range of different industries that would otherwise be threatened by overseas competition and thereby prevent over-specialization in production.

6 To correct a trade imbalance

A country that spends more on imports than it earns from the sale of its export will have a significant trade imbalance. Cutting spending on imports using tariff and non-tariff barriers can help to reduce a trade deficit. ➤ **6.4.2**

7 Because other countries use trade barriers

Before any country removes its barriers to trade on foreign goods it will want to be sure that other countries will remove barriers to trade in its exports. With so many countries engaged in international trade it is very difficult to get agreement on removal of barriers to trade.

What is dumping in international trade? How can it benefit the USA? What is the likely impact on Chinese industry? If it was minded to, what possible non-tariff barriers could China impose on US imports?

US automakers accused of dumping vehicles

China has accused automakers in the United States of dumping sedans and sports utility vehicles with engines larger than 2.5 litres into the country.

The Ministry of Commerce said in a statement on its website that US subsidies for its automotive industry and dumping have caused substantial harm to the Chinese industry. However, the ministry said it will not levy temporary anti-dumping taxes or adopt other retaliatory measures.

The statement also said the ministry has given the relevant companies 10 days to submit written comments and evidence, and promises to examine further based on any new material.

The ministry began the anti-dumping investigation in November 2009. Five manufacturers, including General Motors, Chrysler and BMW, were listed in the ministry's statement. Dumping margins (the difference between the usual product price and the export price) range from 2 per cent to 21.5 per cent, and subsidy rates enjoyed by US automakers were up to 12.9 per cent of costs.

General Motors, which had the highest dumping margins and subsidy rates, said it was unaware of the statement, and declined to comment further.

Experts said the ministry's move is in accordance with World Trade Organization (WTO) rules, and the action will cause limited harm to the US automotive industry.

Arguments against trade barriers

The main argument against the use of trade barriers is that they reduce the gains from trade, notably the following.

1 They restrict consumer choice

Less international trade means consumers will have fewer goods and services to choose from and producers to purchase them from.

2 They restrict new revenue and employment opportunities

Trade barriers restrict the ability of firms to seek out new markets for their products overseas that will allow them to expand their scale of production and increase their demand for labour. Increasing the cost of imported materials and restricting their supply may harm domestic firms that use the materials in their production processes. Production costs will rise and production may also be disrupted due to supply shortages.

3 They protect inefficient domestic firms

If domestic firms are protected from overseas competition there is less pressure on them to improve their productivity and efficiency. Lack of competition can cause x-inefficiency. Production costs and consumer prices will be higher than they might otherwise be and product quality could also be lower as a result. ➤ **3.8.2**

4 Other countries may retaliate

If one country introduces trade barriers to restrict imports from other countries, those affected may introduce similar restrictions on trade with that country in retaliation. A trade war may develop. Fewer goods and services will be traded and prices will rise. This is clearly bad for consumers but if it continues it can also mean higher unemployment and slower economic growth as firms are forced out of business.

Breaking down barriers

Trade liberalization involves reducing or removing barriers to trade between countries. The World Trade Organization (WTO) helps to negotiate reductions in trade barriers and to resolve trade disputes between member countries.

Trade integration between countries involves their agreement to promote free trade with each other, with the aim of securing benefits from increased international specialization and trade.

Trade integration usually results in the formation of **regional trading blocs** whereby countries in a specific region eliminate trade barriers between each other while continuing to protect themselves from imports from non-members. The North American Free Trade Area (NAFTA), the Caribbean Community (CARICOM) and the European Union (EU) are examples of Trading Blocs.

In a **free trade area** such as NAFTA (between the USA and Canada), member countries agree to eliminate trade barriers between themselves but each country continues to operate its own particular barriers against imports of non-members.

In contrast, in a **customs union**, such as CARICOM and the EU, member countries will eliminate trade barriers between themselves but will all apply a common external tariff to imports from non-members.

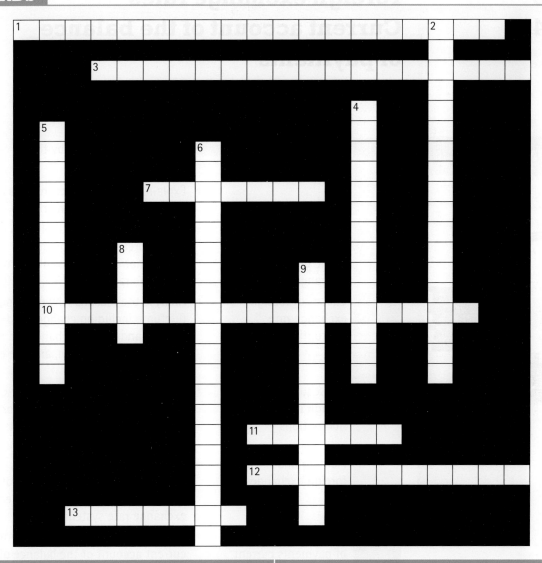

Clues across

1. The removal of or reduction in trade barriers between countries (4, 14)
3. The term used to describe the ability of a country or region to produce a good or service at a lower average cost per unit than any other country or region is able to (8, 9)
7. A form of international predatory pricing and unfair competition used by overseas producers to flood another country with cheap products to force its firms out of business (7)
10. A term used to describe subsidies, quotas, and embargoes, licensing regulations, arbitrary standards and all other non-tax trade restrictions (3-5, 8)
11. A tax levied on the price of an imported product to contract domestic demand for it (6)
12. A national economy that engages in free international trade (4, 7)
13. A ban introduced by one or more countries on the importation of a specific product or all products from another country (7)

Clues down

2. The movement and exchange of physical goods such as materials, component parts, equipment and finished products as well as services, ideas, currencies and labour across international borders (13, 5)
4. Another term used to describe the economic benefits of international trade (5, 4, 5)
5. The use of trade barriers by governments to protect their domestic industries and employment from global competition (13)
6. The term used to describe the ability of a region or country to produce a good or service at a lower opportunity cost than another (11, 9)
8. A restriction on the volume of an imported good allowed into a country (5)
9. Government measures designed to restrict international trade and competition from overseas producers (5, 7)

Unit 6.3
Unit 6.4

Foreign exchange rates
Current account of the balance of payments

Definition of a foreign exchange rate

Determination of foreign exchange rates in the global foreign exchange market

The foreign exchange market

If you travel overseas on holiday you will need to have some notes and coins of the national currency of each country you visit in order to buy things. To obtain these notes and coins you will need to swap them for the money you use in your country. Every country has its own national currency and the amount you get in return for your own currency is called its **exchange rate**.

Similarly, firms involved in international trade must exchange different national currencies. This is true for any organization that:

IMPORTS	▸ buys materials, components or finished goods from firms overseas ▸ buys services from overseas suppliers
EXPORTS	▸ sells and ships materials, components or finished goods to business, government or individual consumers overseas ▸ sells services to business, government or individual consumers overseas
INVESTS	▸ buys shares in the ownership of overseas companies ▸ invests in premises and equipment to start and run business operations in other countries.

Payments for imports, exports and to make other payments overseas therefore require the exchange of different national currencies. This takes place on the global **foreign exchange market**.

Foreign currencies can be bought and sold just like any other product. The foreign exchange market consists of all those people, organizations and governments willing and able to buy or sell national currencies. It is the world's largest financial market and is sometimes simply referred to as the Forex or FX market.

For example, listed in the table on the next page are just some of the many reasons why there is an international demand for a currency such as the US dollar and why US dollars are supplied to satisfy that demand.

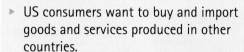

- Consumers in other countries want to buy and import goods and services produced in the USA.
- US-owned multinational firms with locations in other countries will want to send their profits back to their US headquarters.
- Overseas firms located in the USA want to pay their US workers in dollars.
- Residents in other countries want to save money with US banks because they offer good interest rates.
- Currency speculators hold US dollars because they believe the dollar will rise in value against other currencies.
- People and firms overseas want to buy shares in US companies.
- A US resident working overseas sends a gift of money back to his or her family in the USA.
- Foreign-owned banks provide loans to US firms.
- Overseas governments want to hold reserves of US dollars to settle international payments deficits.
- Overseas companies buy dollars to invest in business properties, equipment and other assets in the USA.
- Overseas governments lend money to the US government.

- US consumers want to buy and import goods and services produced in other countries.
- Foreign-owned multinational firms with locations in the USA will exchange dollars for their own national currencies to repatriate their profits.
- US firms located in other countries will pay their overseas workers in their local currencies.
- US residents want to save money with banks located overseas because they offer better interest rates.
- Currency speculators sell their US dollars because they believe the dollar will fall in value against other currencies.
- US firms and individuals buy shares in foreign companies.
- A resident of another country working temporarily in the USA sends a gift of money back to his or her family overseas.
- US-owned banks provide loans to firm overseas.
- The US government draws on its reserves of US dollars to settle an international payments deficit.
- US companies exchange dollars for other currencies to invest in business properties, equipment and other assets in other countries.
- The US government lends money to overseas governments.

What determines the exchange rate of a currency?

The equilibrium market price of one national currency in terms of another is its exchange rate. For example, an **exchange rate** of US$1 = 100 Kenyan shillings means that it will cost 100 Kenyan shillings to buy a US dollar, or one US dollar to buy 100 Kenyan shillings. Similarly, if US $1 = 3 Malaysian ringgits it means 3 ringgits can be exchanged for 1 US dollar. Every currency has an exchange rate in terms of every other national currency in the world.

For example, in the table and reading down each column, the price of 1 US dollar at midday on 24 January 2018 was 0.81 euros, or 63.69 Indian rupees, or 3.67 UAE dirham and so on. Similarly, one rupee exchanged for 0.058 UAE dirham that same day.

	US dollar US$	Indian rupee Rs	UAE dirham Dh	Argentine peso $	Egyptian pound £	Euro €
US dollar US$	US$1.00	Rs0.016	Dh0.27	$0.052	£0.056	€1.23
Indian rupee Rs	Rs63.69	Rs1.00	Dh17.34	$3.29	£3.59	€78.63
UAE dirham Dh	Dh3.67	Dh0.058	Dh1.00	$0.19	£0.21	€4.53
Argentine peso $	$19.33	$0.30	$5.26	$1.00	£1.09	€23.86
Egyptian pound £	£17.70	£0.28	£4.82	£0.92	£1.00	€21.85
Euro €	€0.81	€0.013	€0.22	€0.042	€0.046	€1.00

The exchange rate of each currency in terms of another will be determined by the market demand and supply conditions for each of those currencies. Just as for any other product demand for a particular currency will tend to contract as the price or exchange rate of that currency rises. In contrast, the market supply of the currency will tend to expand as its exchange rate rises. ➤ **2.6.1**

The diagram below shows the demand for US dollars (DD) and the supply of US dollars (SS) on the foreign exchange market. The price of a dollar is given in Brazilian reals but it could be expressed in terms of any other foreign currency. US residents will supply dollars to buy reals in order to buy goods and services from Brazil. Brazilian residents will demand US dollars to make payments to US residents. They will sell reals in exchange for US dollars. Equilibrium in the market for US dollars is determined where the market demand for dollars is equal to their supply. In the diagram below this occurs at US $1 = 2 reals. So, for example, if a Brazilian consumer imports a car from a US manufacturer priced at $20,000, the equivalent price in Brazil will be 40,000 reals.

▼ Equilibrium in the foreign exchange market

▼ Market demand and supply for US dollars

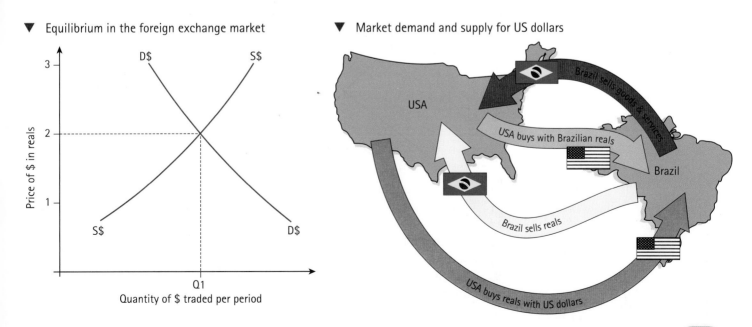

Causes of foreign exchange rate fluctuations

Why do exchange rates fluctuate?

The governments of some countries control or fix the exchange rate of their national currency, but most countries have **floating exchange rates**. This means they are determined by the global demand for their currencies and their global supply.

Changes in the demand for and supply of a national currency will therefore cause its exchange rate to change or 'fluctuate' over time.

An increase in the demand for a currency, for example because consumers are buying more goods and services from that country, will increase its exchange rate against other currencies. A rise in the value of one currency against others is referred to as an **appreciation** in the exchange rate.

▼ An appreciation in the $ following an increase in demand for the currency

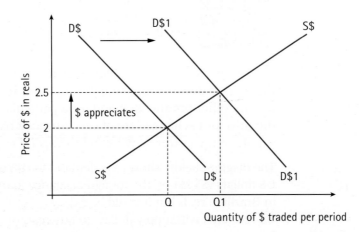

In contrast, if the global market supply of a currency rises, for example because firms are investing more overseas and therefore selling their national currency to buy foreign currencies, the exchange rate of that currency will fall. This is referred to as a **depreciation** in the exchange rate.

▼ A depreciation in the $ following an increase in supply of the currency

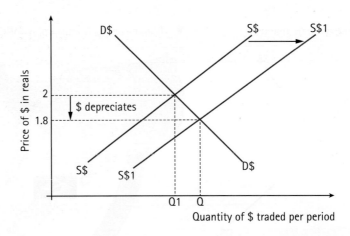

It follows that a fall in the market supply of dollars (from S$1S$1 to SS above) will therefore cause the $ exchange rate to appreciate (from $1 = 1.8 reals to $1 = 2 reals), while a fall in demand for $ (from D$1D$1 to DD in the first diagram) will cause a fall in its exchange rate (from $1 = 2.5 reals to $1 = 2 reals).

Floating around the world

The articles below describe changing economic conditions that could affect the exchange rate between the US dollar ($) and the euro (€), the currency used in eurozone countries, including France, Germany and Spain, within the European Union. For each article, complete the following tasks.

1 Identify how economic conditions are changing.

2 Suggest how the changed economic conditions might have affected **a** the demand for dollars, and/or **b** the supply of dollars.

3 Identify what has happened or could happen to the value of the US dollar on the foreign exchange market. Has or will the $ depreciate or appreciate against the €?

4 Copy the diagram of the foreign exchange market for the US dollar against the euro. Use your diagram to show how the demand for dollars or supply of dollars is likely to change based on your answers to question 2 and the impact this will have on the $ to € exchange rate.

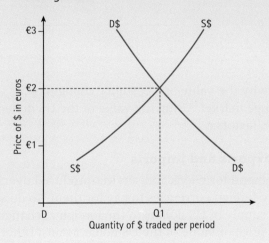

USD falls as tensions with North Korea rise

The US dollar fell sharply today amid escalating concerns about the rising tensions between the US and North Korea.

Intense speculation that North Korea is planning to launch another nuclear missile led to a substantial drop in demand for the dollar.

The markets are worried about the potential for conflict on the Korean peninsula and the impact this could have on future growth prospects for the US economy.

Euro falls on inflation news

The euro weakened yesterday against a basket of currencies after a report showed that Eurozone consumer prices rose last month.

The Consumer Prices Index rose 0.4 per cent last month as food and energy costs increased. Economists expect consumer prices, outside of food and energy, to increase this year as more companies pass on their rising costs to consumers. The jump in price inflation could make European goods less competitive on international markets.

USD exchange rate falters as imports surge

The value of the US dollar fell sharply against other currencies on world markets at the weekend as data from the US Commerce Department revealed a widening trade deficit with the rest of the world.

US imports of physical goods exceeded exports in November by $50 billion, up from $49 billion in the previous month.

A widening deficit, with a rising number of imports, is a sign that US consumers and businesses are spending more. However, it also means that more of their money is going overseas.

US dollar strengthens on talk of interest rate rise

The value of the US dollar is strengthening on the foreign exchange market this morning following recent comments from policymakers suggesting that the US central bank is preparing to tighten monetary policy by raising interest rates.

Historically the value of the US Dollar has been highly sensitive to interest rates because rising interest rates attract greater inflows of foreign capital due to their promise of higher yields on savings and investments.

There are a number of reasons why the value of a currency changes or fluctuates on the foreign exchange market. Using the value of the US dollar as our example, these are the main factors.

1 Changes in demand for exports and imports

If US residents increase their demand for goods and services produced overseas then they will need to buy more foreign currencies to pay for them. To do so, they will have to increase their supply of US dollars to the foreign exchange market. As a result, the market price or value of the US dollar against other currencies will fall or depreciate.

If, on the other hand, residents of other countries want to buy more goods and services produced in the US then they will need to buy more US dollars to pay for them. There will be an increase in the demand for US dollars on the foreign exchange market. As a result, the market price or value of the US dollar against other currencies will rise or appreciate.

Changes in the demand for exports from or imports to a country will therefore cause its exchange rate to fluctuate in the following ways, using trade between the USA and France as an example.

Changes in product market conditions		Impact on foreign exchange market conditions		
In the USA	In France	Market for US dollars	Value of US dollar against the euro	Value of euro against the US dollar
US demand for imports from France increases	France exports more goods and services to the US	US supplies more US dollars to buy euros	US dollar depreciates	Euro appreciates
US demand for imports from France decreases	France exports fewer goods and services to the US	US reduces its supply of US dollars to buy euros	US dollar appreciates	Euro depreciates
French demand for US exports increases	France increases it demand for goods and services from the US	France increases its demand for US dollars	US dollar appreciates	Euro depreciates
French demand for US imports falls	France reduces its demand for goods and services from the US	France reduces its demand for US dollars	US dollar depreciates	Euro appreciates

2 Inflation

If the US inflation rate is higher than that of other countries, the price of US goods and services will be rising faster than the prices of overseas products. As a result, US goods will become less attractive. Demand for US exports, and therefore for US dollars, will fall. On the other hand, as the prices of imports become more competitive, US residents will spend more on imported goods and will therefore supply more US dollars in exchange for overseas currencies. High US inflation will therefore tend to reduce the value of the dollar.

3 Changes in interest rates

When US interest rates are high or rising, overseas residents may be keen to save or invest money in US banks and other financial institutions. The demand for the US dollar will rise, increasing its value. The US government can use interest rates to influence the US dollar exchange rate and therefore the price of exports and imports. A rise in interest rates in other countries relative to the USA may lead to the withdrawal of overseas capital from the USA with a depressing effect on the value of the dollar.

4 Speculation

A foreign currency speculator is a person or a firm such as a bank that tries to make a profit from the buying and selling of foreign currencies.

For example, if speculators think the value of the US dollar is likely to fall, perhaps because the US current account deficit is increasing or because of international instability that may negatively affect the US economy, they may sell their holdings of US dollars and buy other currencies. This increase in the supply of US dollars on the foreign exchange market will reduce their value. The speculators can then buy back US dollars at a lower exchange rate. The difference between the price they sold US dollars for and the price they later pay to buy back US dollars will be their profit.

The following diagram illustrates how speculators can gain from exchange rate fluctuations.

If instead speculators speculate that the value of the US dollar will rise on the foreign exchange market, for example because they believe the US central bank is about to increase interest rates, they may buy US dollars now and sell them again later when they have risen in value. Of course the increase in demand for US dollars as a result will help to push up its exchange rate anyway while the increased sale of foreign currencies in exchange for dollars will tend to reduce the value of these currencies on the market.

5 The entry or departure of multinational companies

The loss of a major multinational company from a country could have a significant negative impact on the foreign exchange rate of the national currency. The loss of the multinational could result in big job losses and falling incomes as well reduced exports. All of these factors could reduce demand for the currency on the foreign exchange market. ➤ **6.2.2**

However, the entry of a major multinational into a country could have the opposite effect especially if it boosts exports from the country. This will have the effect of increasing demand for the currency of the host country on the foreign exchange market.

▼ Causes of exchange rate fluctuations – a summary

The currency of a country may depreciate in value if...	The currency of a country may appreciate in value if...
▶ It buys more imports. To do so it must sell more of its currency to buy other currencies.	▶ It sells more exports. As a result there is an increase in demand for its currency from consumers overseas.
▶ Its interest rates fall relative to those in other countries so people move their savings to banks overseas.	▶ Its interest rates rise relative to those in other countries. This attracts an inflow of savings from overseas residents.
▶ Its inflation rate rises relative to inflation in other countries. This makes its exports more expensive. Overseas demand for its exports and currency will fall.	▶ Its inflation rate is lower than inflation in other countries. This improves the price competitiveness of its exports. Overseas demand for its exports and currency will rise.
▶ People and businesses speculate that its currency will soon fall in value and therefore sell their holdings of the currency.	▶ People and businesses speculate that its currency will soon rise in value and therefore increase their holdings of the currency.
▶ Major companies cease trading in the country or relocate overseas resulting in a reduction in output, employment and incomes and damaging its future growth prospects.	▶ Multinationals locate operations in the country boosting output, employment, incomes and its future economic prospects.

Consequences of foreign exchange rate fluctuations

How changes in exchange rates affect the prices of imports and exports

Imagine you are about to go on holiday to the USA. You have booked a hotel over the internet for $60 per night for eight nights and will therefore be expected to pay the sum of $480 in US dollars at the end of your stay. Each unit of your national currency currently exchanges for 2 US dollars so you have calculated your eight-night stay will cost you just 240 units of your currency. However, imagine your horror when you come to pay your hotel bill at finding out the US dollar has appreciated considerably on the foreign exchange market since you booked your trip. A unit of your national currency can now only be exchanged for $1.50. This means you will now need to exchange 320 units of your currency to obtain $480 to pay your hotel bill – an increase in your cost by a further 80 units of your currency.

Before

After

The same will be true for all other consumers in the world who buy goods or services from the USA if the US dollar has appreciated in value against their national currencies. They will have to pay more for US imports. For example, every year Egypt imports around $60 billion worth of goods from other countries, of which around $5 billion are imported from the USA. To pay for the US imports Egyptian importers must sell Egyptian pounds to buy US dollars. If the value of the Egyptian pound fell by 10% against the US dollar, the cost of the same imports from the US will therefore rise by 10% to $5.5 billion.

Even relatively small changes in exchange rates between different national currencies may therefore have a significant impact on the competitiveness of firms engaged in international trade and therefore on their costs, revenues and profitability.

For example, Activity 6.8 asks you to consider the impact changes in the exchange rate between the US dollar and Egyptian pound could have on firms and consumers in these two economies.

ACTIVITY 6.8

Receiving a pounding

The cartoons below tell a story about two Egyptian businesses engaged in overseas trade. One exports components to US business consumers. The other imports parts from US businesses.

Develop a story to go with the cartoons to describe what is happening to exchange rates and how they are affecting each business.

The consequences of an appreciation in the exchange rate of a currency

In Activity 6.8 above there has been an **appreciation** in the value of the Egyptian pound against the US dollar. This means its value has increased against the US dollar. Egyptian pounds will now cost US residents more to buy on the foreign exchange market making imports from Egypt more expensive.

The appreciation in the value of the Egyptian pound therefore had the following impacts on the Egyptian firms in the activity.

▼ Impact on Egyptian firms exporting goods to the US

At £1 = $0.20	At £1 = $0.40
Egyptian goods priced at £100 each will sell for $20 in the US.	The same items priced at £100 each will now cost $40 to buy in the US: ▸ the international competitiveness of Egyptian goods is reduced; ▸ if US demand for Egyptian goods is price elastic there is likely to be a significant fall in US demand for them; ▸ exports to the US will fall and exporters in Egypt will lose revenue.

The rise in the value of the Egyptian pound therefore increased the price of Egyptian goods for sale in the US relative to the prices of the same or similar items produced by firms in the US or other countries.

This is because twice as many US dollars than before must be exchanged for the same amount of Egyptian pounds in order to import the same amount of goods from Egypt. As a result US consumers are likely to reduce their demand for Egyptian goods. If their demand is price elastic then the total amount they spend on imports from Egypt will fall. This will reduce the sales revenue, market share and profitability of the Egyptian firms exporting their products to the US.

However, the appreciation in the value of the Egyptian pound against the US dollar is beneficial for consumers of US goods in Egypt. This is because it reduces the prices of US imports. Egyptian firms purchasing parts and materials from US suppliers will therefore enjoy a reduction in their costs of production and, other things unchanged, an increase in their profitability.

US suppliers should in turn benefit from increased revenues from higher export sales to Egypt if Egyptian demand for US goods is price elastic.

▼ Impact on Egyptian firms importing goods from the US

At £1 = $0.20	At £1 = $0.40
US goods priced at $4 each will cost £20 in Egypt.	The same items priced at $4 each will now cost £10 to buy in Egypt: ▸ the international competitiveness of US goods is increased; ▸ Egyptian firms importing goods from the US will benefit from a reduction in their costs; ▸ if Egyptian demand for US goods is price elastic there is likely to be a significant increase in Egyptian demand for them (i.e. US suppliers will enjoy an increase in sales and revenues).

ACTIVITY 6.9

Appreciating the price impact

A clothing manufacturer located in Thailand makes and exports winter coats for the European market.

Each coat is priced for sale to shops in Europe at 4,000 Thai baht (THB).

Today's exchange rate is 1 THB = 0.025 euros, or 40 THB = 1 euro. The price of each coat in euros is therefore 100 euros.

1 What would be the price of each coat if the euro depreciated against the baht to 1 euro = 32 THB?

2 What would be the price of each coat if the euro appreciated against the baht to 1 euro = 50 THB?

3 If the demand for winter coats in Europe is price elastic what is likely to happen to consumer demand for the coats and the sales revenue of the manufacturer in Thailand following each change in the exchange rate?

The consequences of a depreciation in the exchange rate of a currency

Consider now how changes in exchange rates can affect the world's largest producer of hazelnuts and each year exports around 230,000 tonnes, mostly to European countries and in particular to Germany.

The Hassas Export Co., based in Tehran, is one of Iran's leading exporters of pistachio nuts and each month sends around 4000 tonnes to Germany. Its exports compete internationally with pistachio nuts exported from the US and Turkey.

Atrimex Gmbh in Hamburg Germany is a major importer of pistachios to sell to food processing companies and retail outlets all over Europe. To pay for the nuts it imports from the Hassas Export Co. it needs to exchange the European currency, the euro (€), for Iranian rials.

Iran sells pistachio nuts to Germany

Germany pays for nuts with Iranian rials

Iran sells Iranian rials on foreign exchange market

Germany buys rials with euros

IRAN

GERMANY

Imagine that Nutfields in Germany places regular order with Prodiga in Turkey to supply 10 tonnes of hazelnuts per month at a price of 20,000 Turkish lira per tonne.

	Last month the exchange rate was €1 = 4 lira	This month the lira has depreciated against the euro to €1 = 5 lira
1 euro = 4 lira 1 euro = 5 lira Turkish lira depreciates against the euro	▶ Nutfields had to exchange €5,000 for 20,000 lira to buy each tonne of hazelnuts it imported that month from Prodiga. ▶ The total cost of 10 tonnes of imported nuts in euros that month was therefore €50,000 (i.e. €5,000 × 10 tonnes).	▶ Now, Nutfields will only have to exchange €4,000 for 20,000 lira to buy each tonne of hazelnuts it imports from Prodiga. ▶ The purchase of 100 tonnes this month will therefore cost Nutfields €40,000 (i.e. €4,000 × 10 tonnes) – a cost saving of €20,000 over last month.

In the table above there has been a **depreciation** in the foreign exchange rate of the Turkish lira against the euro. German residents will now be able to buy more lira with their euros making their imports from Turkey cheaper.

As a result of the deprecation in the Turkish lira, Nutfields may decide to buy more nuts from Prodiga because the imported price of its nuts has fallen. If so, Prodiga will be able to increase its sales of nuts to Nutfields and other importers in Germany and benefit from increased export revenues.

Potty about exchange rates

A chain of craft shops in the USA imports ornate garden pots from Malaysia. The business imports 100 pots each month. The currency of Malaysia is the ringgit (MYR).

Each pot costs 30 MYR to import.

Today's exchange rate is US$1 = 3 MYR. The cost of each pot in US dollars is therefore $10. The business sells each pot for US $16 which earns a profit margin of US $6 per pot.

1   What would be the total cost of importing 100 pots each month if the US dollar depreciated against the Malaysian ringgit to US $1 = 2 MYR?

2   What would be the total cost of importing 100 pots each month if the US dollar appreciated against the Malaysian ringgit to US $1 = 4 MYR?

3   If the US importer decides not to change the selling price of the pots, what will happen to its profits following each change in the exchange rate?

Changes in exchange rates can therefore greatly affect the prices we pay for many goods and services because they are imported from producers located overseas or have imported components that will affect their costs of production. A fall in the value of a national currency relative to other currencies will make imports to that country more expensive to buy. If a country relies heavily on imported goods this will cause imported inflation. ➤ **4.8.3**

However, a depreciation in the value of a national currency against other currencies can be beneficial for a country that relies heavily on sales of exports to provide jobs and incomes. Because the currency is cheaper to buy in terms of foreign currencies it will reduce the prices of exports from that country in international markets and make them more competitive. As a result, demand for its exports may expand.

In contrast, an appreciation in the value of a national currency will make imports to that country cheaper but increase the prices of its exports on international markets. This in turn could have an unfavourable impact on its balance of trade and international transactions with the rest of the world. ➤ **6.4.2**

SECTION 6.3.5

Managing floating exchange rates

Floating and fixed exchange rates

Rapid and significant fluctuations in exchange rates can create a lot of uncertainty for countries engaged in international trade. Prices of exports and imports will change rapidly affecting the costs, revenues and profits of many firms. This in turn can badly affect price inflation and employment in open economies. Governments may therefore intervene in the foreign exchange market to manage their floating exchange rates to stop them from fluctuating too wildly and causing economic uncertainty.

Typically, a government will do this by either buying or selling its own currency. This is called **managed floating** or dirty floating and is the main reason why central banks hold reserves of gold and different currencies. ➤ **3.1.2**

A steep rise in the value of a national currency against other currencies will make its exports more expensive to buy overseas. As a result, export producers may experience a fall in sales and cut back their output and employment. In order to stop its currency value from rising too much and making exports uncompetitive a government may increase the supply of its currency to the foreign exchange market. It can do this by selling its reserves of the national currency. The increase in the supply of the currency should lower its market exchange rate. Alternatively, a government may cut interest rates to reduce overseas demand for its currency by reducing the incentive for overseas residents to save or invest in its country.

In contrast, a sharp fall in the value of a currency will make imports more expensive to buy because currency values overseas will have risen. To prevent imported inflation a government may use its gold and foreign currency reserves to buy up its own national currency on the foreign exchange market. This increase in the demand for its currency on the global foreign exchange market will help push up its market exchange rate. By selling reserves of foreign currencies this will also increase their market supply and thereby help to reduce their exchange rate. Alternatively, interest rates could be raised to curb domestic spending on imports and to stimulate demand for the currency from overseas investors looking for a high return on their money.

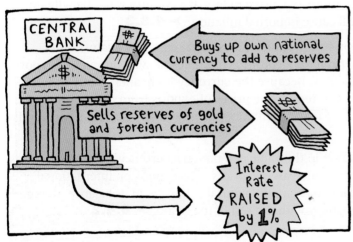

▲ To reduce imported inflation a government may aim to increase the value of its currency by buying up its national currency using its gold and foreign currency reserves and/or by raising interest rates to attract savings from overseas residents

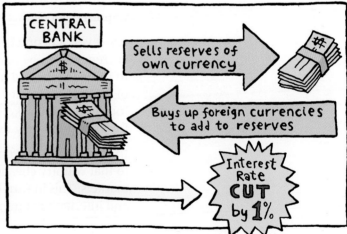

▲ To boost demand for exports a government may seek to reduce the value of its currency by selling reserves of its national currency and/or cutting interest rates

Fixed exchange rates

In the same way as managed flexibility, a government can use its reserves of gold and foreign currency to buy or sell its currency on the foreign exchange market to stabilize or maintain a fixed value for its exchange rate against another currency or basket of foreign currencies.

This will mean buying up its national currency on the foreign exchange market when its value is low or falling below its desired value, and increasing its supply by selling off its reserves when its value is high or rising above its desired value.

In a **fixed exchange rate system**, a government or the central bank acting on the government's behalf will intervene in the above ways in the foreign exchange market so that the value of its currency remains the same or close to a desired exchange rate target.

Although very few countries now have fixed exchange rate systems many more countries have in the past fixed or 'pegged' their exchange rates often against the US dollar, given the scale and importance of the US economy and the US dollar in world trade for many years. Even the Chinese government, which had fixed its exchange rate for many years, announced in 2010 it would return to a managed floating system.

Many governments have fixed their exchange rates in the past to control the prices of exports and imports and thereby reduce uncertainty for exporters and importers that would otherwise be created by fluctuations in exchange rates.

In a fixed exchange rate system firms must also keep their costs under control so they can price their exports competitively in international markets. This is because their government will not allow the exchange rate of their currency to depreciate to help make exports cheaper overseas to boost demand for them. A fixed exchange rate will also keep imported inflation under control.

▼ How a fixed exchange rate system works

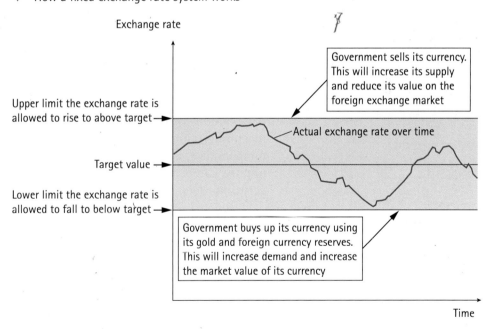

However, as economic conditions change it can become more difficult to maintain a fixed exchange rate. For example, it becomes expensive for a country to keep on buying up supplies of its currency on the foreign exchange market to hold up its value. A country could soon run out of foreign currency reserves doing this.

Similarly, maintaining an exchange rate at a very low level in order to make exports cheap on international markets may cause trade disputes with other countries. Their own firms may find it difficult to compete with such cheap imports at home and in overseas markets thereby placing jobs and incomes at risk. ➤ **6.2.5**

SECTION 6.4.1

Accounting for international transactions

Structure of the current account of the balance of payments

Each year countries such as the USA, China, Germany, Egypt and India produce and sell many billions of dollars' worth of goods and services to each other and to many other countries. Goods and services made by producers in one country and supplied to consumers in other countries are exports. In return, exporting firms receive payments from the sale of exports from overseas. The sale of exports therefore results in an inflow of currency to a country.

At the same time, these same countries buy many billions of dollars' worth of goods and services from each other and many other countries. Goods and services purchased by consumers in one country from suppliers located in others are **imports** to that country. The purchase of imports therefore results in an outflow of foreign currency from a country to make payments to overseas suppliers.

Inflows and outflows of money to and from a country resulting from its international transactions with other countries will be recorded in the national income and expenditure accounts of that country.

Trade in goods

Trade in goods involves the exchange of physical products between countries, including natural resources such as crude oil and timber, parts and components for use in the production of goods, and finished products such as machinery, clothes, cars and processed foodstuffs. Trade in goods, or merchandize, is also called **visible trade** simply because visible exports and imports can be seen, touched and weighed as they pass through ports and across borders.

When a country such as Japan sells exports of physical goods including machinery and other manufactured goods to other countries, it earns income. The income received from exports will therefore be recorded as credits in its national accounts.

However, when Japan buys imported goods from other countries it must make payments to overseas suppliers. Imports of goods therefore involve a loss or leakage of income from an economy. These losses will be recorded as debits in its national accounts.

▼ Visible exports and imports

Oil

Machinery

Trade in services

Trade in services is also called **invisible trade**. Exports and imports of services, such as insurance, banking and tourism, cannot be seen or touched like physical goods, hence the name invisible.

If a Japanese resident goes on holiday to Europe, he or she will pay for overseas services such as hotel accommodation, tickets for public transport and eating in European restaurants. The money spent by the Japanese tourist in Europe will be an invisible import to Japan because it involves a debit of income from the Japanese economy to pay for services produced overseas. Imports of services by Japanese residents will therefore be recorded as debits in the national accounts of Japan.

If, on the other hand, a Kenyan resident buys insurance over the internet from a Japanese insurance company, he or she will pay insurance to the Japanese company. The income received will be an invisible export of Japan and will be recorded as a credit in the national accounts of the country.

Other incomes

In addition to trade in goods and services it is also important for a country to keep a record of all other flows of income between its residents and residents of other countries.

For example, Japan may receive incomes from investments made by Japanese residents overseas. This will include profits received by a Japanese company from an overseas company that it owns. Similarly, Japanese residents working in other countries will receive wages from their overseas employers. Both forms of income will credit the Japanese economy.

In contrast, any income leaving Japan to make payments to overseas residents will be recorded as debits in its national accounts. For example, when a resident of the UK with a savings account in a Japanese bank receives interest payments or when a Japanese resident donates of money to an overseas charity.

Debit or credit?

The following cartoons and descriptions describe international transactions between the UK and other countries. Which of the transactions would you record as a credit to the national accounts of the UK and which would you record as a debit?

A Wine bought from France

C Italian insures his ship in the UK

B UK tourist takes holiday in the USA

BANQUE

D UK resident uses foreign bank

F UK car dealer buys Japanese cars

E Foreign company uses UK advertising agency

NEW BIZZO

G German worker receives wages from his UK-based employer

H UK resident receives pension from Japanese-based company

The current account of the balance of payments

A country will record all its monetary transactions with the rest of the world each period in an account called its **balance of payments**.

The **current account** is a key account in the balance of payments of a country. The government of a country will use the current account to record all cross-border flows of incomes between its residents and residents of other countries.

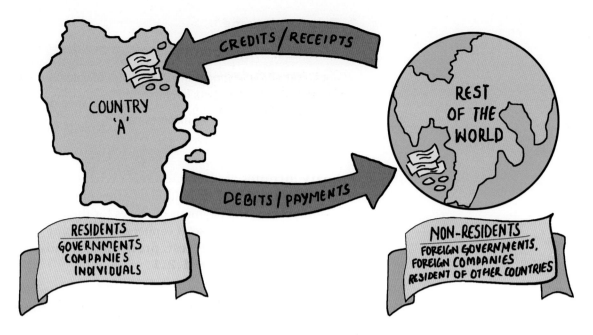

The current account on the balance of payments is therefore split into four component parts or sections as follows:

1 Trade in goods

What's included?	How is it used?
Exports of goods (credits)	To calculate the
Imports of goods (debits)	balance of trade in goods (credits – debits)

2 Trade in services

What's included?	How is it used?
Exports of services (credits)	To calculate the
Imports of services (debits)	balance of trade in services (credits – debits)

The first two sections of the current account are therefore used to record incomes received from the sale of exports to overseas residents and payments made to overseas residents to buy imports which represent a leakage of income from the country.

If the total value of credits from trade in goods and services exceeds the total value of debits in the same period the country will record a **balance of trade surplus**.

If, however, the total value of credits from trade in goods and services is less than the total value of debits in the same period the country will record a **balance of trade deficit**.

Balance of trade = balance of trade in goods + balance of trade in services

3 Primary income

What's included?	How is it used?
Wages, rent and investment incomes received from non-residents (credits) Wages, rent and investment incomes paid to non-residents (debits)	To calculate the **balance of primary income** (credits – debits)

Primary incomes are factor rewards exchanged between residents and non-residents for the use of each other's factors of production. Primary incomes therefore include the payment of wages for the use of labour, rent for the use of land, interest for the use of capital and profits or dividend payments to owners of companies. **Interest, profits and dividends** are also known as **investment incomes**. ➤ **1.2.1**

For example, the US current account will be credited with primary income when a US resident earns interest on his savings account in a bank in Belize or if a US company receives profits from a company it owns in Ireland.

Debits from the US current account will therefore include rent paid by a US agricultural company to an Indian landowner to farm his land and the payment of wages by a US company to its Chinese employees.

4 Secondary income

What's included?	How is it used?
Current transfers received from non-residents (credits) Current transfers to non-residents (debits)	To calculate the **balance of secondary income** or **net current transfers** (credits – debits)

Unlike incomes received from the sale of exports or from the use of factors of production overseas, **secondary incomes** are simply transfers of money or benefits between residents and non-residents. They are not payments for goods or services or for the use of factor resources.

Secondary incomes are also known as **current transfers**. They include pensions, social contributions, welfare payments, taxes collected from wages and other primary incomes, gifts of money and payments or receipts of foreign aid.

Credits for current transfers received by residents will therefore include any pensions they receive from overseas pension companies and any welfare payments they receive from a foreign government while living in another country. The government of the country may also collect taxes from primary incomes payable to non-residents.

Debits for current transfers leaving a country will therefore include any pensions or welfare payments paid to overseas residents and any taxes collected by foreign governments from primary incomes earned by residents from their employment or investments in other countries. A country may also provide financial aid in the form of grants to support people and projects in low-income countries. ➤ **5.2.3**

Calculating the current account balance

Each period government statisticians will add up all the credits on the current account and all the debits. Deducting the sum of debits from the sum of credits will give the final balance on the current account.

- If total credits exceed total debits there will is a **current account surplus**. This means the country has earned more from trade, primary incomes and transfers than it has lost in payments for imports, primary incomes and transfers to residents of other countries. A current account surplus therefore increases the gross national income of a country.

- If total credits are less than total debits there is a **current account deficit**. This means the country has paid out more for imports, primary incomes and transfers to residents of other countries than it has received from them in the same period. A current account deficit therefore reduces the gross national income of a country. ➤ **4.6.2**

The balance of the current account can also be calculated each period by adding together the balance on each section on the account:

- **balance of trade in goods**
- **balance of trade in services**
- **balance of primary income**
- **balance of secondary income (or net current transfers).**

The table below summarizes the current account on the balance of payments of Germany and the USA in 2016.

▼ Current accounts of Germany and the USA, 2016

Section	Entries		Germany euros (billions)	United States US$ (billions)
1	Exports of goods (credits)	X	259	+1,455
	Imports of goods (debits)	M	278	-2,208
	Balance of trade in goods (G)	(X – M)	-19	-753
2	Exports of services (credits)	X'	259	+752
	Imports of services (debits)	M'	278	-505
	Balance of trade in services (S)	(X' – M')	-19	+247
3	Primary income receipts (credits)	Pc	195	+813
	Primary income payments (debits)	Pd	135	-640
	Balance on primary income (PI)	(Pc – Pd)	+60	+173
4	Secondary income receipts (credits)	Tc	72	+131
	Secondary income payments (debits)	Td	112	-255
	Balance on secondary income (CT)	(Tc – Td)	-40	-120
	Balance on current account	(G + S + PI + CT)	+268	-453

Sources: *Deutsche Bundesbank* and *US Bureau of Economic Analysis*

The table shows that the balance of trade in goods and services generally has the largest impact on the current account balance. Flows of primary incomes and current transfers between most countries are usually small in comparison to their payments for exports and imports.

Countries with large and regular current account surpluses tend to specialize in the production and export of high quality or mass-produced manufactured goods or natural resources such as oil and minerals. In 2016, according to the World Bank, the ten countries with the largest current account surpluses were Germany, China, Japan, South Korea, the Netherlands, Switzerland, Singapore, Italy, Thailand and Russia.

In contrast, the US had the largest current account deficit globally in 2016 and it has been in deficit for many years. Developed countries, such as the United States, often run current account deficits, while rapidly developing economies often run current account surpluses.

ACTIVITY 6.12

A balancing act

The table below contains data from the current account on the balance of payments of Australia in 2016 while the chart shows what has happened to its current account position since 1960.

Calculate the end of year balance on each component or section and the overall balance on the current account.

▼ Current account components, 2016

CREDITS	Australian dollars (AUS$ billions)
Goods	257.5
Services	71.5
Primary income	62.7
Secondary income	8.6
DEBITS	
Goods	266.7
Services	76.5
Primary income	91.1
Secondary income	10.3
Balance on current account?	

▼ Balance on current account, 1960–2016

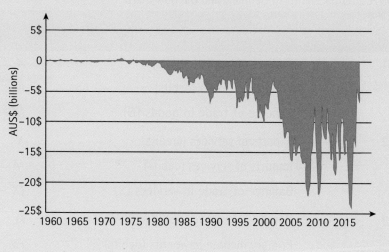

2 What does the balance on the current account reveal about Australia's external trade with the rest of the world in 2016? Use the chart to analyse how this has changed over time.

Causes and consequences of current account deficit and surplus

Policies to achieve balance of payments stability

Trade imbalances

From the previous section we know that the balance of payments on current account of a country will be in deficit if more money is flowing out of its economy to make overseas payments than it receives from the sale of its exports or other credits from overseas. A country will have a current account surplus if the reverse is true.

By far the largest transactions recorded in a current account are revenues from the sale of exports and payments made overseas for the purchase of imports. That is, the current account position of most countries will be dependent on their balance of trade.

Large trade imbalances, whether a big trade deficit or a big trade surplus, can cause problems for a national economy. Consider a very simple example where there are just two countries in the world engaged in international trade with each other. Let's call these countries Surpland and Dearth. Surpland exports far more to Dearth than it buys from Dearth and therefore has a trade surplus. Dearth buys more imports from Surpland than she sells in exports and therefore has a trade deficit. Clearly, because Surpland has a trade surplus, it follows that Dearth must have a trade deficit. In fact, this will also be true in the real world. If one or more countries have a trade surplus, then one or more other countries must have a trade deficit equal in value to the total surplus of other countries.

Problems with a trade deficit

A growing trade deficit may be a sign of economic expansion or recovery in an economy as people and firms increase their spending on all goods and services. Imports of capital goods can also help an economy to expand production in the long run.

However, a large and growing trade deficit may be a symptom of slow or negative economic growth and a declining industrial base, with fewer firms in the economy over time able to produce goods and services for export or to compete at home with imported products. This will reduce employment and incomes in the economy.

Governments therefore often worry that continuous and significant trade deficits could create difficult economic problems:

- If more money is paid out for imports than is earned from the sale of exports then this loss of money from the economy means less is available for residents to spend on domestic goods and services. Domestic firms that experience a fall in demand for their products may cut back production and reduce their demand for labour, resulting in higher unemployment.

- Because more currency is being supplied to pay for imports than overseas countries demand to buy exports, the value of the exchange rate will fall. As a result, imports will become more expensive for domestic consumers to buy. There will be imported inflation. If demand for imports is generally price inelastic then demand will not fall by very much and spending on imported products will rise at the expense of spending on domestically produced goods and services.

- To pay for annual deficits a country may need to borrow money from overseas. Total debt will rise and more income will have to be used each year to pay interest charges. This will increase the amount of money flowing out of the economy and reduce over time the amount of money it has to invest in new productive activities or spend on domestically produced products. This will harm economic growth. ➤ **6.3**

A government may therefore try to correct a persistent and large trade deficit because of the economic problems it may cause. It can do so in the following ways.

1 Do nothing, because a floating exchange rate should correct it

Trade deficits should be self-correcting if the exchange rate is allowed to adjust freely. A country with a trade deficit spends more on imports than other countries spend buying its exports. This implies that its demand for foreign currency to buy imports will exceed foreign demand for its national currency to buy its exports. The value of its currency against other currencies will therefore tend to fall because it has trade deficit. This will make imports more expensive to buy while reducing the prices of exports sold overseas. As a result, domestic demand for imports should fall and overseas demand for exports should rise until trade balance is restored at a new lower equilibrium exchange rate.

For example, Argentina has a large trade deficit with neighbouring Brazil in Latin America. Argentina's main export is soybeans. Because Argentina has a trade deficit with Brazil it means that Argentina will have to supply more pesos to buy reals to pay for imports from Brazil than Brazil spends buying pesos. As a result there will be downward pressure on the peso exchange rate against the real. As the peso falls in value soybean exports to Brazil will become cheaper to buy. For example, if the price of a ton of soybeans is 100 pesos and the exchange rate is 1 peso = 0.5 reals, then the imported price of Argentinean soybeans will be 50 reals in Brazil. If the peso falls in value to 1 peso = 0.4 reals then each ton of soybeans can now be imported at a price of 40 reals. If demand for soybeans by Brazilian consumers is price elastic then Argentinean producers of soybeans should enjoy an increase in demand and revenue for their exports thereby helping to close Argentina's trade deficit with Brazil. This is illustrated in the diagram below.

▼ How a depreciation in the value of a currency can reduce a trade deficit

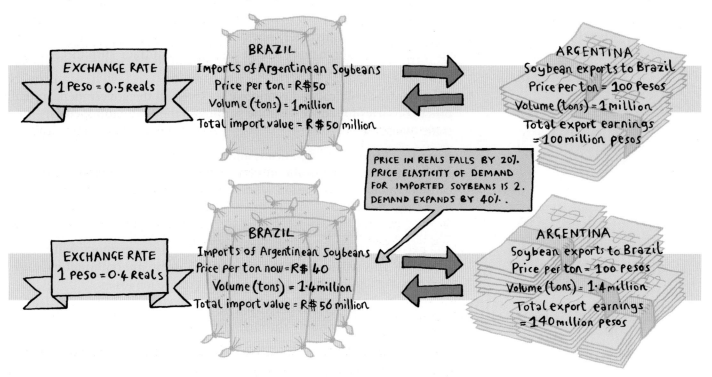

This adjustment mechanism is not present if the exchange rate is fixed and not allowed to fall in value. The government of a country with a large trade deficit and a fixed exchange rate will have to use up more of its reserves of gold and foreign currencies buying up its own national currency to maintain its fixed value. ➤ **6.3.5**

Alternatively the government could devalue its currency against the currencies of its major trading partners. **Devaluation** involves setting and maintaining a lower fixed exchange rate against one or more country.

2 Use contractionary fiscal policy

A government may cut public expenditure and raise taxes to reduce total demand in their economy so people have less to spend on imports. This will help to reduce a trade deficit. However, the fall in demand may also affect domestic firms who may cut output and employment in response. ➤ **4.3.8**

3 Raise interest rates

A government may attempt to attract more inward investment to help offset a trade deficit by raising interest rates. Higher interest rates will also make borrowing more expensive and reduce spending on imports. ➤ **4.4.2**

4 Introduce trade barriers

Trade barriers can make overseas products more expensive and difficult to import, for example by placing a tariff or excise duty on their imported price or by restricting the amount that can enter the country through a quota or embargo. If demand for the imports is price elastic, the increase in their prices will cause demand for them to fall significantly. ➤ **6.2.4**

A country may also subsidize the production of exports so they can be sold more cheaply overseas and provide employment opportunities at home. However, trade barriers restrict free trade and consumer choice, and often lead to other countries retaliating with trade barriers of their own.

Problems with a trade surplus

In contrast, it is not immediately obvious why having a trade surplus should be a problem. However, having a large and persistent trade surplus can also cause problems for an economy:

- There may be political and economic pressure on the government from other countries to reduce its trade surplus so they can reduce their trade deficits.

- Exporting firms enjoy significant and rising overseas revenues from the sale of their exports, but the increase in income from exports may cause demand-push inflation when it is spent in the domestic economy. ➤ **4.8.3**

- Because the trade balance is in surplus, demand for the national currency will exceed its supply and therefore the value of the currency will rise and stay high. This will increase the price of exports in international markets and could result in falling demand and therefore job losses.

- A persistent trade surplus may itself be a symptom of rapid industrial expansion of the economy through growth in exports and/or a government policy of maintaining an artificially low exchange rate to keep export prices low and import prices high. This will help create demand for domestically produced goods at home and overseas, thereby boosting output and employment.

To correct a damaging trade surplus a government may take the following actions to increase spending on imports and/or reduce demand for exports:

1 Do nothing, because a floating exchange rate should correct it

If there is trade surplus, demand for the national currency overseas to pay for exports will exceed its supply in payment for imports. The value of the exchange rate will therefore rise. This will make imports cheaper to buy while increasing the prices of exports sold overseas. As a result, domestic demand for imports should rise and overseas demand for exports should fall until trade balance is restored at a new, higher equilibrium exchange rate.

Again, this adjustment mechanism will not take place if the surplus country has a fixed exchange rate. Because there will be market pressure on the exchange rate to rise, the government will have to sell more of its currency to maintain its fixed value. Alternatively, it could set a new higher fixed value for its currency against the currencies of its major trading partners in order to make its exports to them more expensive and its imports from them cheaper.

2 Use expansionary fiscal policy

Increasing public spending and lowering taxes can boost total demand in an economy, including for imported goods and services.

3 Lower interest rates

Lowering interest rates can help to correct a trade surplus by lowering the cost of borrowing and thereby encouraging increased spending on imports. It will also lower the return overseas investors can expect from their inward investments in the economy. This may persuade some to invest elsewhere. In turn this will reduce demand for the currency and reduce upward pressure on the exchange rate.

4 Remove trade barriers

Removing trade barriers can increase the flow of imports into an economy and reduce their prices, thereby encouraging increased spending on them.

EXAM PREPARATION 6.3

In September 2017 it was forecast that the Japanese Yen would strengthen against the US dollar and that fluctuations in the Japanese exchange rate against other currencies would reduce.

a   Define *currency exchange rate*. [2]

b   Explain **two** reasons why exchange rates fluctuate. [4]

c   Analyse the possible consequences for an economy if its currency 'was gaining strength.' [6]

d   A country has a deficit on its balance of payments on current account. Discuss **two** policies, other than exchange rate changes, that a government might use to try to achieve a surplus rather than a deficit. [8]

Is a trade deficit always bad news for an economy? Based on the article below, should the growing trade deficit worry the government of Bangladesh? What actions could it consider taking to correct it?

Bangladesh trade deficit widens

Bangladesh's trade deficit grew by $1.07 billion to $4.95 billion in the first half of the 2010/11 financial year compared to a year ago, due to a rising import bill as global food and oil prices hit record highs.

The jump reflected increased imports of food grains, industrial supplies and materials and capital goods as trade began to bounce back from the sharp fall caused by the global financial crisis.

Although imports to the country rose 36 per cent to $15.2 billion in the July–December period from a year earlier, exports grew strongly by 41 percent to $10.26 billion.

'Bangladesh typically runs a trade deficit but soaring global commodity prices and increased volumes are pushing the gap wider', said Mustafa K. Mujeri, Director General of the Bangladesh Institute of Development Studies.

'But it is also good for the economy as imports of capital goods and other industrial raw materials are rising on the back of economic recovery. This will help to boost economic growth.'

Is the US trade deficit really bad news?

One reason for a trade deficit can be that the deficit country is growing faster than its trading partners. Faster growth attracts new investment, which, along with rising incomes, allows the deficit country to buy more imports.

When Americans buy imports, foreigners must do something with the dollars they earn. They can either use the dollars to buy American exports or to invest in American assets, such as government bonds, company shares, real estate and factories, which offer the prospect of a better return than investments in their own countries. In the global economy, some countries, such as the United States, are therefore net importers of investment capital and thus always tend run a trade deficit. Inward investment in new capital goods can expand the productive capacity of the economy, creating more employment opportunities and wealth.

This also helps to explain why trade deficits have tended to expand in times of relative prosperity, and to contract in times of recession. During a recession people stop buying many imported goods and going on holidays overseas. When an economy is growing rapidly, people tend to spend more on all goods and services, including imports.

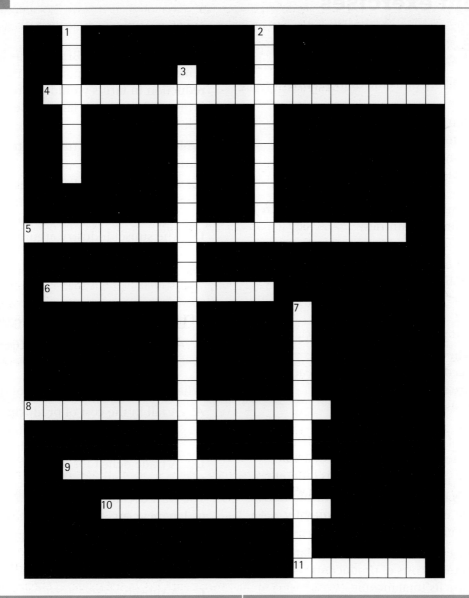

Clues across

4. This will be recorded if a country pays more for its imports of goods and services than it earns from exports in the same period (7, 2, 5, 7)
5. The market price or external value of currency in terms of another currency (7, 8, 4)
6. A fall in the foreign exchange rate of a currency (12)
8. Another term used to describe receipts and payments of secondary incomes recorded in the current account (7, 9)
9. The section in the balance of payments of a country is used to record credits and debits from trade and flows of incomes between its residents and non-residents (8, 7)
10. A rise in the external value of a currency against one of more foreign currencies (12)
11. This will be recorded on the current account of a country if the total value of credits to the account exceeds the total value of debits from the account in the same period (7)

Clues down

1. Term used to describe an exchange rate that is determined freely by foreign exchange market conditions without government intervention (8)
2. A deliberate reduction in the value of a fixed exchange rate, usually to improve the price competitiveness of exports from that country (11)
3. The global market for the exchange of national currencies (7, 8, 6)
7. Term used to describe factor payments exchanged between the residents and non-residents of a country and recorded in the current account on its balance of payments (7, 7)

Assessment exercises

Multiple choice

1 What is the least likely outcome of increasing globalization?

A An increase in multinational companies
B Increasing international capital flows
C Unrestricted international migration
D More trade integration

2 What might encourage increased specialization in production in different countries?

A Free trade
B Inefficiencies in production
C Labour immobility
D Tariffs

3 What is an advantage of international specialization?

A Consumer choice is limited
B Countries become too dependent on each other
C Resources are used more efficiently
D Transport costs are reduced

4 The central area of a country produces coffee for which it has an ideal climate. The coastal area produces coconuts because its climate is different.

Assuming there is no change in market conditions, what will happen if this country subsequently produces coffee in both areas?

A It will increase the productivity of its land
B It will increase its costs of production
C It will increase its total income
D It will make the best use of its resources

5 Which policy would best enable a government to encourage greater specialization in the use of its country's resources?

A Encouraging diversification in industry
B Protecting small businesses
C Reducing tariffs on imports
D Subsidizing job creation in rural areas

6 What must be involved in free international trade?

A Unrestricted exchange of goods and services
B Zero transportation costs
C Unrestricted cross-border movement of labour
D International specialization

7 Drinks producers in Brazil are resisting plans to remove tariffs on imported drinks. They claim that a reduction in tariffs would destroy the emerging drinks industry with large-scale imports of cheap drinks.

Which argument for trade protection are they putting forward?

A The declining industry argument
B The infant industry argument
C The strategic industry argument
D The sunset industry argument

8 The following is a headline from a newspaper.

> ### USA to impose tariffs of 40% on imported steel

What is the most likely result of these tariffs?

A A fall in the cost of producing cars in the USA
B A fall in exports of steel from the USA
C A rise in employment in the USA's steel industry
D A trade deficit for the USA

9 The USA decides to introduce a limit on the import of Japanese cars to 15 % of the total market volume.

What method of trade protection will be used?

A An embargo
B A quota
C A subsidy
D A tariff

10 Which government policy is most likely to increase the volume of exports from a country?

A Currency devaluation
B Embargoes
C Quotas
D Tariffs

11 The introduction of a tariff on imported goods is likely to:

   A Ensure that the domestic industry becomes more efficient

   B Increase the demand for domestically produced goods

   C Reduce the price of domestically produced goods

   D Reduce the price of imported goods into the country

12 What would contribute to a fall in the value of the Egyptian pound on the foreign exchange market?

   A A fall in interest rates in other countries

   B A rise in the number of foreign tourists visiting Egypt

   C The removal of import tariffs by the USA

   D The value of Egyptian imports increasing more than the value of Egyptian exports

13 What is a depreciation in the value of a currency?

   A A fall in its external value

   B A fall in its internal value

   C A rise in its external value

   D A rise in its internal value

14 Ethiopia has operated a managed floating exchange rate system since 1992 and is the largest exporter of coffee in Africa. In 2017 it devalued its currency by 15%.

What would have been the most likely consequence of this action?

   A Ethiopia paid less in foreign currencies for imports

   B Ethiopia increased its demand for imports

   C Ethiopia's exports became more competitive

   D Ethiopia increased its trade deficit

15 A fall in the exchange rate of the Canadian dollar will:

   A Reduce a Canadian trade surplus

   B Reduce the foreign price of Canadian exports

   C Reduce the price of imports to Canada

   D Reduce Canadian price inflation

16 Which of the following changes will increase demand for imports?

   A Income taxes are increased

   B Interest rates rise

   C The exchange rate appreciates

   D The government introduces tariffs

17 Which of the following transactions will be recorded as a debit to trade in services in the current account of Pakistan?

   A A resident of Pakistan buys a car manufactured in Germany

   B A Chinese bank loans money to the government of Pakistan

   C A resident of Pakistan buys insurance from a UK company

   D A Japanese tourist spends money while on holiday in Pakistan

18 Which two items, in addition to trade in goods and services, are included in the current account of the balance of payments?

   A Foreign reserves and international investment

   B Government spending and international borrowing

   C Primary incomes and current transfers

   D Taxes and subsidies

19 The UK has a deficit on its current account of the balance of payments. It has increased in recent years. Which of the following would have contributed to the increase in the size of the deficit?

   A Increased sales of goods to non-residents

   B Increased earnings from UK investments in foreign companies

   C Increased numbers of foreign tourists visiting the UK

   D Increased UK foreign aid to less developed countries

20 Worldwide campaigns to reduce smoking will affect Tanzania, which has relied on tobacco for its main export earnings.

What is likely to happen if Tanzania is successful in replacing its earnings from tobacco by developing its tourist trade?

   A The number of jobs required in the service sector will decrease

   B The primary sector will become more significant in the economy

   C There will be greater expenditure on new roads and infrastructure

   D Its balance of trade in goods will deteriorate as its balance of trade in services improves

21 A country increases its demand for oil to be used in the production and distribution of goods. The country has also experienced a rise in incomes which has resulted in a big increase in demand for goods, some of which it imports.

What is likely to happen to the country's balance of trade in goods and to the price of oil?

	Balance of trade in goods	Price of oil
A	worsens	falls
B	improves	falls
C	worsens	rises
D	improves	rises

22 A newspaper reported that exports from Sweden remained low for five months as changes in exchange rate meant that Swedish goods became more expensive to buy overseas.

What else most likely happened?

A Imported goods became cheaper in Sweden
B Swedish consumers switched their demand to goods produced in Sweden
C The Swedish current account improved
D The Swedish balance of trade improved

23 Japan is a major trading partner of Indonesia. What is likely to happen to the prices of Indonesian exports and imports if its currency, the Rupiah, appreciates against the Japanese yen?

	Prices of exports to Japan	Prices of imports from Japan
A	increase	increase
B	decrease	decrease
C	decrease	increase
D	increase	decrease

24 What would increase the deficit on a country's balance of trade?

A A domestic firm invests in a foreign country
B Foreign tourists visiting the country spend less money
C People buy imported cars instead of home-produced cars
D Teams of doctors are sent to a country that has experienced an earthquake

25 The table shows the trade in goods balance and the current account balance of the balance of payments for four countries during a year.

Which country had the largest surplus on its trade in services, assuming net flows of primary income and current transfers were zero in all countries?

Country	Balance of trade in goods ($ billion)	Balance on current account ($ billion)
A	12.4	12.2
B	8.8	8.6
C	15.6	15.2
D	10.3	10.8

26 A government may use trade barriers to restrict free trade.

What is an economic reason for doing this?
A To encourage overspecialization
B To improve the balance of trade
C To increase a current account deficit
D To make imports cheaper

27 In 2018 the US trade deficit with China reached a record high. What could have caused this?

A Increased competitiveness of goods made in the US
B Increased earnings by US investors in Chinese companies
C Increased numbers of Chinese visitors to the US
D Increased spending by US residents on Chinese imports

28 Which of the following policy measures could help to reduce a deficit on the current account of the balance of payments?

A Reducing income taxes
B Allowing the exchange rate to depreciate
C Removing restrictions on consumer credit
D Removing trade barriers

Structured questions

1   The challenges facing South Africa

South Africa is one of the world's leading mining and mineral-processing countries. It is the second largest producer of gold and the world's largest producer of chrome, manganese, platinum, vanadium and vermiculite. It is also the world's third largest coal exporter. Although mining's contribution to the national GDP has fallen from 21% in 1970 to 7.3% in 2016, the sector still accounts for almost 28% of physical exports.

South Africa also has a large agricultural sector and is a net exporter of farming products, while machinery and transportation equipment make up more than one-third of the value of the country's imports.

▼   Figure 1: South Africa balance of trade in goods, 1995–2016

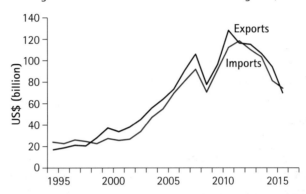

Source: *The Observatory for Economic Complexity, atlas.media.mit.edu/en/*

Tariffs are applied to many imports to the country, although many rates have been lowered to improve international trade. However, in a recent statement the ogvernment said it would continue to use trade restrictions to defend domestic industries and support industrial development if other countries become more protectionist. For example, in 2015 it introduced measures to protect its cement industry from cheap imports of cement from Pakistan. Subsequently, cement imports to South African from Pakistan fell by 30% year-on-year.

As a largely open and free-market economy, South Africa encourages foreign investment in both the public and private sectors. The potential attractiveness of South Africa is high, but its performance so far has been relatively weak as the country faces a number of serious social and economic challenges.

Compared to other emerging economies, economic growth in South Africa has been low. Between 2011 and 2016, the South African economy expanded at an average annual rate of just 1.8%. In 2016, its GDP had reached US$294bn but GDP per capita had fallen from a peak of US$8,050 in 2011 to US$5,273 and roughly half the country lives in poverty, with over one in four people of working age unemployed. While educational attainment has expanded significantly among young people in recent years, a large share of the population still does not reach upper secondary or tertiary education according to OECD indicators.

The country also suffers from a high crime rate, high levels of corruption and a high level of public debt. However, key economic reforms have been introduced with the aim of reducing the debt burden and creating greater macroeconomic stability. The government's fiscal strategy combines containing public spending increases and raising tax revenues.

Interest rates are also now being lowered to help boost economic growth, after monetary policy was tightened during 2016 in an effort to control rising inflation. At 6.59% the annual inflation rate was well above the government's target band of between 3 to 6%. One factor driving this was a large depreciation in the value of the South African currency, the rand. Demand for the currency fell sharply in March 2015 following the release of weaker growth forecasts for the economy.

A Using data from the extract, calculate the value of the total output of the mining sector in South Africa in 2016. [2]

B Using figure 1, explain what happened to South Africa's balance of trade in goods between 2000 and 2016. [2]

C Explain **two** types of trade protection the South African Government might use. [4]

D Explain **two** ways in which multinational companies could help developing countries such as South Africa. [4]

E Analyse the relationship between educational attainment and economic growth. [5]

F Explain why GDP per capita fell between 2011 and 2016. [2]

G What effect will the government's fiscal strategy have on the budget deficit? [2]

H Using information from the extract, draw a demand and supply diagram to show what happened to the foreign exchange rate of the South African currency in 2015. [4]

I Discuss whether an increase in interest rates will control rising inflation. [5]

2 Germany recorded the world's largest surplus on the current account of its balance of payments in 2017. Capital goods accounted for over 40% of its total exports and international demand for them has been growing. However, the German Government has been criticized for not doing more to encourage imports.

A Where are exports of capital goods recorded in the balance of payments of a country? [2]

B Explain any **two** of the four sections of the current account. [4]

C Analyse how a government could reduce the surplus on the country's current account of the balance of payments. [6]

D Discuss whether an increase in exports from a country will increase its foreign exchange rate. [8]

3 Fluctuations in a country's foreign exchange rate can have a significant impact on its economy and balance of payments.

A Identify **two** causes of a fall in a country's foreign exchange rate. [2]

B Explain **two** reasons why a country's export revenue might increase when export prices rise. [4]

C Analyse the effects a fall in a country's foreign exchange rate could have on its total output. [6]

D Discuss whether total employment is likely to increase in a country following an improvement in its balance of payments on current account. [8]

Index